PJ 161

B 3093 . H413
SCHLEIERMACHER

W9-BXD-834

TRUTH
and
METHOD

88.50

TRUTH
AND
METHOD

Hans-Georg Gadamer

A Continuum Book
THE SEABURY PRESS • NEW YORK

BD
241
.G313

The Seabury Press
815 Second Avenue
New York, N.Y. 10017

English translation copyright © 1975 by Sheed and Ward Ltd. First published 1975. All rights reserved. Originally published as *Wahrheit und Methode*, by J. C. B. Mohr (Paul Siebeck) Tübingen 1960. The translation was edited by Garrett Barden and John Cumming from the second (1965) edition.

Printed in the United States of America.

LIBRARY OF CONGRESS CATALOGING IN PUBLICATION DATA

Gadamer, Hans-Georg, 1900-
  Truth and method.

  (A Continuum book)
  Translation of Wahrheit und Methode.
Includes bibliographical references and index.
  1. Humanities—Methodology. 2. Hermeneutics.
3. Aesthetics. I. Title.
BD241.G313   111.8'3   75-2053
ISBN 0-8164-9220-4

CANISIUS COLLEGE LIBRARY
BUFFALO, N. Y.

Catch only what you've thrown yourself, all is
mere skill and little gain;
but when you're suddenly the catcher of a ball
thrown by an eternal partner
with accurate and measured swing
towards you, to your centre, in an arch
from the great bridgebuilding of God:
why catching then becomes a power—
not yours, a world's.

Rainer Maria Rilke

Contents

Introduction

These studies are concerned with the problem of hermeneutics. ✓
The phenomenon of understanding and of the correct interpretation of what has been understood is not just a problem proper to
the methodology of the human sciences. For a long time, there
has been a theological and a legal hermeneutics, which were not
so much theoretical as related to, and an aid to, the practical activity of the judge or clergyman who had completed his
theoretical training. From its historical origin, the problem of
hermeneutics goes beyond the limits that the concept of method
sets to modern science. The understanding and the interpretation of texts is not merely a concern of science, but is obviously
part of the total human experience of the world. The hermeneutic phenomenon is basically not a problem of method at all. It is
not concerned with a method of understanding, by means of
which texts are subjected to scientific investigation like all other
objects of experience. It is not concerned primarily with the
amassing of ratified knowledge which satisfies the methodological ideal of science—yet it is concerned, here too, with knowledge and with truth. In understanding tradition not only are
texts understood, but insights are gained and truths acknowledged. But what kind of insight and what kind of truth?

In the face of the dominant position of modern science in the
philosophical clarification and justification of the concept of
knowledge and the concept of truth, this question does not appear legitimate. Yet it is unavoidable, even within the sciences.
The phenomenon of understanding not only pervades all human
relations to the world. It also has an independent validity within

science and resists any attempt to change it into a method of science. The following investigation starts with the resistance within modern science against the universal claim of scientific method. It is concerned to seek that experience of truth that transcends the sphere of the control of scientific method wherever it is to be found, and to inquire into its legitimacy. Hence the human sciences are joined with modes of experience which lie outside science: with the experiences of philosophy, of art, and of history itself. These are all modes of experience in which a truth is communicated that cannot be verified by the methodological means proper to science.

Contemporary philosophy is well aware of this. But it is quite a different question how far the claim to truth of these modes of experience outside science can be philosophically legitimated. The current interest in the hermeneutic phenomenon rests, I think, on the fact that only a more profound investigation of the phenomenon of understanding can provide this legitimation. This conviction is strongly supported by the importance attached in contemporary philosophical work to the history of philosophy. In regard to the historical tradition of philosophy, we encounter understanding as a superior experience enabling us easily to see through the appearance of historical method characteristic of philosophico-historical research. It is part of the elementary experience of philosophy that when we try to understand the classics of philosophical thought, they posit, of themselves, a claim to truth that the contemporary consciousness can neither reject nor transcend. The naïve self-respect of the present moment may rebel against the idea that the philosophical awareness admits the possibility that one's own philosophical insight may be inferior to that of Plato or Aristotle, Leibniz, Kant or Hegel. One might think it a weakness in contemporary philosophy that it seeks to interpret and assimilate its classical heritage with this acknowledgment of its own weakness. But it is undoubtedly a far greater weakness of philosophical thinking not to face this kind of investigation into oneself, but foolishly to play at being Faustus. It is clear that in the understanding of the texts of these great thinkers, a truth is recognised that could not be attained in any other way, even if this contradicts the yardstick of research and progress by which science measures itself.

The same thing is true of the experience of art. Here the scientific research pursued by the 'science of art' is aware from the start that it can neither replace nor surpass the experience of art. That truth is experienced through a work of art that we cannot attain in any other way constitutes the philosophic importance of art, which asserts itself against all reasoning. Hence together with the experience of philosophy, the experience of art issues the most pressing challenge to the scientific consciousness to acknowledge its own limits.

Hence the following investigation starts with a critique of aesthetic consciousness, in order to defend that experience of truth that comes to us through the work of art against the aesthetic theory that lets itself be restricted to a scientific concept of truth. But the book does not stop at the justification of the truth of art; instead it tries to develop from this starting-point a concept of knowledge and of truth which corresponds to the whole of our hermeneutic experience. Just as in the experience of art we are concerned with truths that go essentially beyond the range of methodical knowledge, so the same thing is true of the whole of the human sciences, in which our historical tradition in all its forms is certainly made the object of investigation, but at the same time in it truth comes to speech. The experience of historical tradition goes quite beyond that in it which can be investigated. It is true or untrue not only in the sense concerning which historical criticism decides, but always mediates truth, in which one must try to share.

Hence these studies on hermeneutics, which start from the experience of art and of historical tradition, seek to present the hermeneutic phenomenon in its full extent. It is a question of recognising in it an experience of truth that must not only be justified philosophically, but which is itself a mode of philosophising. The hermeneutics developed here is not, therefore, a methodology of the human sciences, but an attempt to understand what the human sciences truly are, beyond their methodological self-consciousness, and what connects them with the totality of our experience of world. If we make understanding the object of our reflection, the aim is not an art or technique of understanding, as traditional literary and theological hermeneutics sought to be. Such an art or technique would fail to recognise that, in view of the truth that speaks to us out of tradition, the formalism of artistic ability would arrogate to itself a false superiority. Even though in the following I shall demonstrate how much there is of event in all understanding, and how little the traditions in which we stand are weakened by modern historical consciousness, it is not my intention to make prescriptions for the sciences or the conduct of life, but to try to correct false thinking about what they are.

I hope in this way to reinforce an insight that is threatened with oblivion in our swiftly changing age. What changes forces itself far more on the attention than what remains the same. That is a general law of our intellectual life. Hence the perspectives which come from the experience of historical change are always in danger of distortion because they forget the hidden constants. I feel that we are living in a state of constant overstimulation of our historical consciousness. It is a consequence of this over-stimulation and, as I hope to show, a bad short-circuit if one reacts to this over-estimation of historical change by invoking the eternal orders of nature and summoning the naturalness of man to legitimate the idea of natural law. It is not only that historical tradition and the natural order of life constitute the unity of the world in which we live as men; the way that we experience one another, the way that we experience historical traditions, the way that we experience the natural givenness of our existence and of our world, constitutes a truly hermeneutic universe, in which we are not imprisoned, as if behind insurmountable barriers, but to which we are opened.

A reflection on what truth is in the human sciences must not seek to derive itself from the tradition, the validity of which it has recognised. Hence it must, for its own method of working, endeavour to acquire as much historical self-transparency as possible. In its concern to understand the universe of understanding better than seems possible under the modern scientific notion of cognition, it has to try to establish a new relation to the concepts which it uses. It must be aware of the fact that its own understanding and interpretation is not a construction out of principles, but the development of an event which goes back a long way. Hence it will not be able to use its concepts unquestioningly, but will have to take over whatever features of the original meaning of its concepts have come down to it.

The philosophical endeavour of our day differs from the classical tradition of philosophy in that it is not a direct and unbroken continuation of it. In spite of all its connections with its historical origin, philosophy today is well aware of the historical distance between it and its classical models. This is found, above all, in its changed attitude to the concept. However important and fundamental were the transformations which took place with the Latinisation of the Greek concepts and with the translation of Latin conceptual language into the modern languages, the emergence of historical consciousness over the last few centuries is a much more radical development. Since then, the continuity of the Western philosophical tradition has been effective only in a fragmentary way. We have lost that naïve innocence with which traditional concepts were made to support one's own thinking. Since that time, the attitude of science towards these concepts has become strangely detached, whether its concern with them is a scholarly, not to say self-consciously archaic, recording process, or a technical handling which makes its own use of concepts as tools. Neither of these truly satisfies the hermeneutic experience. The conceptual world in which philosophising develops has already influenced us in the same way that the language in which we live conditions us. If thought is to be conscientious, it must become aware of these anterior influences. It is a new critical consciousness that now has to accompany all responsible philosophising and which takes the linguistic and thinking habits built up in the individual in his communication with his environment and places them before the forum of the historical tradition to which we all belong.

The following investigation tries to satisfy this demand by combining as closely as possible an inquiry into the history of concepts with a factual exposition of its theme. That conscientiousness of phenomenological description which Husserl has made a duty for us all; the breadth of the historical horizon in which Dilthey has placed all philosophising; and, not least, the penetration of both these influences by the impulse received from Heidegger, indicate the yardstick by which the writer desires to be measured, and which, despite all imperfection in the execution, he would like to see applied without reservation.

Foreword to the Second Edition

The second edition of *Truth and Method* is virtually unaltered. Its readers include its critics, and the attention that it has received undoubtedly obliges the author to improve the whole by drawing on all the really valuable suggestions they have offered.[1] And yet a line of thought that has matured over many years has its own stability. However much one tries to see through the critic's eyes, one's own generally pervasive viewpoint prevails.

The three years that have passed since the publication of the first edition have proved too short a time for the author to put the whole again in question, and to use effectively all that he has learned from criticism and from his own more recent work.[2]

Perhaps I may briefly outline the intention and claim of the work. My revival of the expression 'hermeneutics', with its long tradition, has apparently led to some misunderstandings.[3] I did not intend to produce an art or technique of understanding, in the manner of the earlier hermeneutics. I did not wish to elaborate a system of rules to describe, let alone direct, the methodical procedure of the human sciences. Nor was it my aim to investigate the theoretical foundation of work in these fields in order to put my findings to practical ends. If there is any practical consequence of the present investigation, it certainly has nothing to do with an unscientific 'commitment'; instead, it is concerned with the 'scientific' integrity of acknowledging the commitment involved in all understanding. My real concern was and is philosophic: not what we do or what we ought to do, but what happens to us over and above our wanting and doing.

xvi

Hence the methods of the human sciences are not at issue here. My starting point is that the historic human sciences, as they emerged from German romanticism and became imbued with the spirit of modern science, maintained a humanistic heritage which distinguishes them from all other kinds of modern research and brings them close to other, quite different, extra-scientific experiences, and especially those proper to art. In Germany (which has always been pre-revolutionary) the tradition of aesthetic humanism remained vitally influential in the development of the modern conception of science. In other countries more political consciousness may have entered into 'the humanities', lettres: in short, everything formerly known as the humaniora.

This does not prevent the methods of modern natural science from having an application to the social world. Possibly the growing rationalisation of society and the scientific techniques of its administration are more characteristic of our age than the vast progress of modern science. The methodical spirit of science permeates everywhere. Therefore I did not remotely intend to deny the necessity of methodical work within the human sciences (Geisteswissenschaften). Nor did I propose to revive the ancient dispute on method between the natural and the human sciences. It is hardly a question of a contrast of methods. To this extent, Windelband and Rickert's question concerning the limits of concept-formation in the natural sciences seems to me misconceived. The difference that confronts us is not in the method, but in the objectives of knowledge. The question I have asked seeks to discover and bring into consciousness something that methodological dispute serves only to conceal and neglect, something that does not so much confine or limit modern science as precede it and make it possible. This does not make its own immanent law of advance any less decisive. It would be vain to appeal to the human desire for knowledge and the human capacity for achievement to be more considerate in their treatment of the natural and social orders of our world. Moral preaching in the guise of science seems rather absurd, as does the presumption of a philosopher who deduces from principles the way in which 'science' must change in order to become philosophically legitimate.

Therefore it seems quite erroneous in this connection to invoke the famous Kantian distinction between quaestio juris and quaestio facti. Kant certainly did not wish to lay down for modern science what it must do in order to stand honourably before the judgment-seat of reason. He asked a philosophic question:

What are the conditions of our knowledge, by virtue of which modern science is possible, and how far does it extend? Thus the following investigation also asks a philosophic question. But it does not ask it only of the so-called human sciences (among which precedence would then be accorded to certain traditional disciplines). It does not ask it only of science and its modes of experience, but of all human experience of the world and human living. It asks (to put it in Kantian terms): How is understanding possible? This is a question which precedes any action of understanding on the part of subjectivity, including the methodical activity of the 'understanding sciences' (verstehende Geisteswissenschaften) and their norms and rules. Heidegger's temporal analytics of human existence (Dasein) has, I think, shown convincingly that understanding is not just one of the various possible behaviours of the subject, but the mode of being of There-being itself. This is the sense in which the term 'hermeneutics' has been used here. It denotes the basic being-in-motion of There-being which constitutes its finiteness and historicity, and hence includes the whole of its experience of the world. Not caprice, or even an elaboration of a single aspect, but the nature of the thing itself makes the movement of understanding comprehensive and universal.

I cannot agree with those who maintain that the limits of the hermeneutical aspect are revealed in confrontation with extra-historical modes of being, such as the mathematical or aesthetic.[4] Admittedly it is true that, say, the aesthetic quality of a work of art depends on structural laws and a level of embodied form and shape which ultimately transcend all the limitations of its historical origin or cultural context. I shall not discuss how far, in relation to a work of art, the 'sense of quality' represents an independent possibility of knowledge, or whether, like all taste, it is not only formally developed, but also shaped and fashioned.[5] At any rate, taste is necessarily formed by something that does not indicate for what that taste is formed. To that extent, it may always include particular, preferred types of content and exclude others. But in any case it is true that everyone who experiences a work of art gathers this experience wholly within himself: namely, into the totality of his self-understanding, within which it means something to him. I go so far as to assert that the achievement of understanding, which in this way embraces the experience of the work of art, surpasses all historicism in the sphere of aesthetic experience. Of course there appears to be an obvious distinction between the original world structure established by a work of art, and its continued existence in the changed circumstances of the world thereafter.[6] But where exactly does the dividing line lie between the present world and the world that comes to be? How is the original life-significance transformed into the reflected experience that is cultural significance? It seems to me that the concept of aesthetic non-differentiation, which I have coined in this connection, is wholly valid; that here there are no clear divisions, and the movement of understanding cannot be restricted to the reflective pleasure prescribed by aesthetic differentiation. It should be admitted that, say, an ancient image of the gods that was not displayed in a temple as a work of art in order to give aesthetic, reflective pleasure, and is now on show in a museum, contains, in the way it stands before us today, the world of religious experience from which it came; the important consequence is that its world is still part of ours. It is the hermeneutic universe that embraces both.[7]

There are other respects in which the universality of the hermeneutical aspect cannot be arbitrarily restricted or curtailed. No mere artifice of composition persuaded me to begin with the experience of art in order to assure the phenomenon of understanding that breadth which is proper to it. Here the aesthetics of genius has done important preparatory work in showing that the experience of the work of art always fundamentally surpasses any subjective horizon of interpretation, whether that of the artist or that of the recipient. The mens auctoris is not admissible as a yardstick for the meaning of a work of art. Even the idea of a work-in-itself, divorced from its constantly renewed reality of being experienced, always has something abstract about it. I think I have already shown why this idea only describes an intention, but does not permit a dogmatic solution. At any rate, the purpose of my investigation is not to offer a general theory of interpretation and a differential account of its methods (which E. Betti has done so well) but to discover what is common to all modes of understanding and to show that understanding is never subjective behaviour toward a given 'object', but towards its effective history—the history of its influence; in other words, understanding belongs to the being of that which is understood.

Therefore I do not find convincing the objection that the reproduction of a musical work of art is interpretation in a different sense from, say, the process of understanding when reading a poem or looking at a painting. All reproduction is primarily interpretation and seeks, as such, to be correct. In this sense it, too, is 'understanding'.[8]

I believe that the universality of the hermeneutical viewpoint

cannot be restricted even where it is a question of the multitude
of historical concerns and interests subsumed under the science
of history. Certainly there are many modes of historical writing
and research. There is no question of every historical observation being based on a conscious act of reflection on effective-
history. The history of the North American Eskimo tribes is
certainly quite independent of whether and when these tribes
influenced the 'universal history of Europe'. Yet one cannot
seriously deny that reflection on effective-history will prove to
be important even in relation to this historical task. Whoever
reads, in fifty or a hundred years, the history of these tribes as it
is written today will not only find it old-fashioned (for in the
meantime he will know more or interpret the sources more correctly) he will also be able to see that in the 1960s people read the
sources differently because they were moved by different questions, prejudices and interests. Ultimately historical writing and
research would be reduced to nullity if withdrawn from the
sphere of the study of effective-history. The very universality of
the hermeneutical problem precedes every kind of interest in
history, because it is concerned with what is always fundamental
to the historical question.[9] And what is historical research without the historical question? In the language that I use, justified
by investigation into semantic history, this means: application is
an element of understanding itself. If, in this connection, I put
the legal historian and the practising lawyer on the same level, I
do not deny that the former has exclusively a 'contemplative',
and the other a practical, task. Yet application is involved in the
activities of both. How could the legal meaning of a law be
different for either? It is true that, for example, the judge has the
practical task of passing judgment, and many considerations of
legal politics may enter in, which the legal historian (with the
same law before him) does not consider. But does that make
their legal understanding of the law any different? The judge's
decision, which has a practical effect on life, aims at being a
correct and never an arbitrary application of the law; hence it
must rely on a 'correct' interpretation, which necessarily includes the mediation between history and the present in the act
of understanding itself.

The legal historian, of course, will also have to evaluate 'historically' a law correctly understood in this way, and this always
means that he must assess its historical importance; since he will
always be guided by his own historical fore-understanding and
prejudices, he may do this 'wrongly'. That means that again
there is mediation between the past and the present: that is,

application. The course of history, to which the history of research belongs, generally teaches us this. But it obviously does
not mean that the historian has done something which he should
not have done, and which he should or could have been prevented from doing by some hermeneutical canon. I am not
speaking of the errors of legal history, but of accurate findings.
The legal historian—like the judge—has his 'methods' of avoiding mistakes, in which I agree entirely with the legal historian.[10]
But the hermeneutical interest of the philosopher begins only
when error has been successfully avoided. Then both historians
and dogmaticians testify to a truth that extends beyond what
they know, insofar as their own transient present is discernible
in what they do.

From the viewpoint of philosophical hermeneutics, the contrast between historical and dogmatic method has no absolute
validity. This raises the question of the extent to which the
hermeneutical viewpoint itself enjoys historical or dogmatic
validity.[11] If the principle of effective-history is made into a
general structural element in understanding, then this thesis undoubtedly includes no historical relativity, but seeks absolute
validity—and yet a hermeneutical consciousness exists only
under specific historical conditions. Tradition, part of whose
nature is the handing-on of traditional material, must have become questionable for an explicit consciousness of the hermeneutic task of appropriating tradition to have been formed.
Hence we find in Augustine such a consciousness in regard
to the old testament; and, during the reformation, Protestant
hermeneutics developed from an insistence on understanding
scripture solely on its own basis (sola scriptura) as against the
principle of tradition held by the Roman church. But certainly
since the birth of historical consciousness, which involves a
fundamental distance between the present and all historical
transmission, understanding has been a task requiring methodical direction. My thesis is that the element of effective-history
is operative in all understanding of tradition, even where the
methodology of the modern historical sciences has been largely
adopted, which makes what has grown historically and has been
transmitted historically an object to be established like an experimental finding—as if tradition were as alien and, from the
human point of view, as unintelligible, as an object of physics.

Hence there is a certain legitimate ambiguity in the concept of
the consciousness of history, as I have used it. This ambiguity is
that it is used to mean at once the consciousness obtained in the
course of history and determined by history, and the very con-

sciousness of this gaining and determining. Obviously the burden of my argument is that this quality of being determined by
effective-history still dominates the modern, historical and scientific consciousness and that beyond any possible knowledge
of this domination. The effective-historical consciousness is so
radically finite that our whole being, achieved in the totality of
our destiny, inevitably transcends its knowledge of itself. But
that is a fundamental insight which ought not to be limited to any
specific historical situation; an insight which, however, in the
face of modern historical research and of the methodological
ideal of the objectivity of science, meets with particular resistance in the self-understanding of science.

We are certainly entitled to ask the reflective historical question: Why, just now, at this precise moment in history, has this
fundamental insight into the element of effective-history in all
understanding become possible? My investigations offer an indirect answer to this question. Only after the failure of the naïve
historicism of the very century of historicism does it become
clear that the contrast between unhistorical-dogmatic and historical, between tradition and historical science, between ancient
and modern, is not absolute. The famous querelle des anciens et
des modernes ceases to be a real alternative.

Hence what is here asserted, the universality of the hermeneutic aspect and especially what is elicited about language as
the form in which understanding is achieved, embraces the
'pre-hermeneutic' consciousness as well as all modes of hermeneutic consciousness. Even the naïve appropriation of tradition is a 'retelling', although it ought not to be described as a
'fusion of horizon' (see p 486 below).

And now to the basic question: How far does the aspect of
understanding itself and its linguisticity reach? Can it support
the general philosophical inference in the proposition, 'Being
that can be understood is language'? Surely the universality of
language requires the untenable metaphysical conclusion that
'everything' is only language and language event? True, the obvious reference to the ineffable does not necessarily affect the
universality of language. The infinity of the dialogue in which
understanding is achieved makes any reference to the ineffable
itself relative. But is understanding the sole and sufficient access
to the reality of history? Obviously there is a danger that the
actual reality of the event, especially its absurdity and contingency, will be weakened and seen falsely in terms of sense-
experience.

Hence it was my purpose to show that the historicism of

Droysen and Dilthey, despite all the opposition of the historical school to Hegel's spiritualism, was seduced by its hermeneutic starting-point into reading history as a book: as one, moreover, intelligible from the first letter to the last. Despite all its protest against a philosophy of history in which the necessity of the idea is the nucleus of all events, the historical hermeneutics of Dilthey could not avoid letting history culminate in intellectual history. That was my criticism. Yet surely this danger recurs in regard to the present work? However, the traditional formation of ideas, especially the hermeneutic circle of whole and part, which is the starting-point of my attempt to lay the foundations of hermeneutics, does not necessarily require this conclusion. The idea of the whole is itself to be understood only relatively. The totality of meaning that has to be understood in history or tradition is never the meaning of the totality of history. The danger of docetism seems banished when historical tradition is not conceived as an object of historical knowledge or of philosophical conception, but as an effective moment of one's own being. The finite nature of one's own understanding is the manner in which reality, resistance, the absurd, and the unintelligible assert themselves. If one takes this finiteness seriously, then one must also take the reality of history seriously.

The same problem makes the experience of the 'Thou' so decisive for all self-understanding. The section on experience has a systematic and a key position in my investigations. There the experience of the 'Thou' also throws light on the idea of the effective-historical experience. The experience of the 'Thou' also manifests the paradoxical element that something standing over against me asserts its own rights and requires absolute recognition; and in that very process is 'understood'. But I believe that I have shown correctly that this understanding does not at all understand the 'Thou', but what the 'Thou' truly says to us. One truth I refer to is the truth that becomes visible to me only through the 'Thou', and only by my letting myself be told something by it. It is the same with historical tradition. It would not deserve the interest we take in it if it did not have something to teach us that we could not know by ourselves. It is in this sense that the statement 'being that can be understood is language' is to be read. It does not intend an absolute mastery over being by the one who understands but, on the contrary, that being is not experienced where something can be constructed by us and is to that extent conceived, but that it is experienced where what is happening can merely be understood.

This involves a question of philosophical procedure, which

was raised in a number of critical comments on my book. I should like to call it the 'problem of phenomenological immanence'. It is true that my book is phenomenological in its method. This may seem paradoxical inasmuch as Heidegger's criticism of the transcendental question and his thinking of 'reversal' form the basis of my treatment of the universal hermeneutic problem. I consider, however, that the principle of phenomenological demonstration can be applied to this usage of Heidegger's, which at last reveals the hermeneutic problem. I have therefore preserved the term 'hermeneutics', which the early Heidegger used, not in the sense of a methodical art, but as a theory of the real experience that thinking is. Hence I must emphasise that my analyses of play or of language are intended in a purely phenomenological sense.[12] Play is more than the consciousness of the player; and so it is more than a subjective attitude. Language is more than the consciousness of the speaker; so it, too, is more than a subjective attitude. This is what may be described as an experience of the subject and has nothing to do with 'mythology' or 'mystification'.[13]

This fundamental methodical approach has nothing to do with any metaphysical conclusions. In writings published subsequently, especially in my research reports 'Hermeneutik und Historismus' (cf pp 460–491 below) and 'Die phänomenologische Bewegung' (in the *Philosophische Rundschau*) I have recorded my acceptance of the conclusions of Kant's *Critique of Pure Reason,* and regard statements that proceed by wholly dialectical means from the finite to the infinite, from human experience to what exists in itself, from the temporal to the eternal, as doing no more than set limits, and consider that philosophy can derive no actual knowledge from them. Nevertheless, the tradition of metaphysics and especially of its last great creation, Hegel's speculative dialectic, remains close to us. The task, the 'infinite relation', remains. But the mode of demonstrating it seeks to free itself from the embrace of the synthetic power of the Hegelian dialectic, and even from the 'logic' which developed from the dialectic of Plato, and to take its stand in the movement of that discourse in which word and idea first become what they are.[14]

Hence the demand for a reflexive self-grounding, as made from the viewpoint of the speculatively conducted transcendental philosophy of Fichte, Hegel and Husserl, is unfulfilled. But is the discourse with the whole of our philosophical tradition, in which we stand, and which, as philosophers, we are, purposeless? Do we need to justify what has always supported us?

This raises a final question which concerns less the method than the contents of the hermeneutic universalism that I have outlined. Does not the universality of understanding involve a onesidedness in its contents, inasmuch as it lacks a critical principle in relation to tradition and, as it were, espouses a universal optimism? However much it is the nature of tradition to exist only through being appropriated, it still is part of the nature of man to be able to break with tradition, to criticise and dissolve it, and is not what takes place in the work of remaking the real into an instrument of human purpose something far more basic in our relationship to being? To this extent, does not the ontological universality of understanding result in a certain one-sidedness? Understanding certainly does not mean merely the assimilation of traditional opinion or the acknowledgment of what tradition has made sacred. Heidegger, who first described the idea of understanding as the universal determinateness of There-being, means the very projective character of understanding, ie the futural character of There-being. I shall not deny, however, that within the universal context of the elements of understanding I have emphasised the element of the assimilation of what is past and handed down. Heidegger also, like many of my critics, would probably feel the lack of an ultimate radicality in the drawing of conclusions. What does the end of metaphysics as a science mean? What does its ending in science mean? When science expands into a total technocracy and thus brings on the 'cosmic night' of the 'forgetfulness of being', the nihilism that Nietzsche prophesied, then may one look at the last fading light of the sun that is set in the evening sky, instead of turning around to look for the first shimmer of its return?

It seems to me, however, that the onesidedness of hermeneutic universalism has the truth of a corrective. It enlightens the modern attitude of making, producing and constructing about the necessary conditions to which it is subject. In particular, it limits the position of the philosopher in the modern world. However much he may be called to make radical inferences from everything, the role of prophet, of Cassandra, of preacher or even of know-all does not suit him.

What man needs is not only a persistent asking of ultimate questions, but the sense of what is feasible, what is possible, what is correct, here and now. The philosopher, of all people, must, I think, be aware of the tension between what he claims to achieve and the reality in which he finds himself.

The hermeneutic consciousness, which must be awakened and kept awake, recognises that in the age of science the claim of superiority made by philosophic thought has something vague and unreal about it. But it seeks to confront the will of man, which is more than ever intensifying its criticism of what has gone before to the point of becoming a utopian or eschatological consciousness, with something from the truth of remembrance: with what is still and ever again real.

* * *

The essay 'Hermeneutics and Historicism', which was published only when I had finished this book, and which was intended as a means of dealing with the relevant literature, now appears, with some additions, as a supplement (pp 460–491 below).

In the English edition, there is included as a second supplement a translation of 'Jusqu'à quel point la langue préforme-t-elle la pensée?' which appeared in *Demitizzazione e Ideologia* edited by E. Castelli, Rome, 1973.

FIRST PART
THE QUESTION OF TRUTH AS IT EMERGES IN THE EXPERIENCE OF ART

I

The Transcending of the Aesthetic Dimension

1 THE SIGNIFICANCE OF THE HUMANIST TRADITION FOR THE HUMAN SCIENCES

(A) THE PROBLEM OF METHOD

The logical self-reflection which accompanied the development of the human sciences in the nineteenth century is wholly dominated by the model of the natural sciences. Just a glance at the history of the word Geisteswissenschaft shows this, although this word acquires the meaning that is familiar to us only in its plural form. The human sciences (Geisteswissenschaften) so obviously understand themselves from the analogy with the natural sciences that the idealistic echo that lies in the idea of Geist ('spirit') and of a science of Geist fades into the background. The word Geisteswissenschaften was made popular chiefly by the translator of John Stuart Mill's *Logic*. In the supplement to his work Mill seeks to outline the possibilities of applying inductive logic to the human sciences. The translator calls these Geisteswissenschaften.[1] From this very context of Mill's *Logic* it is apparent that it is not a question of recognising that the human sciences have their own logic but, on the contrary, to show that it is the inductive method, basic to all experiential science, which alone is valid in this field too. In this Mill stands in an English tradition of which Hume has given most effective formulation in the introduction to his *Treatise*.[2] Human science also is concerned with establishing similarities, regularities and conformities to a law which would make it possible to predict the individual phenomena and processes. In the field of natural phenomena this goal cannot always be reached everywhere to the same extent, but the reason for this is only that the data on which the similarities are to be established cannot always be obtained in sufficient quantity. Thus the method

5

of meteorology is just the same as that of physics, but its data are not so full and therefore its predictions are more uncertain. The same is true in the field of moral and social phenomena. The use of the inductive method there is also free from all metaphysical assumptions and remains quite independent of how one considers the realisation of the phenomena that one is observing. One does not discover causes for particular effects, but simply establishes regularities. Thus it is quite unimportant whether one believes, say, in the freedom of the will or not—one can still make predictions in the sphere of social life. To make deductions from regularities concerning the phenomena to be expected does not include any assumption about the character of the context whose regularity makes prediction possible. The involvement of free decisions—if they exist—does not interfere with the regular process, but itself belongs to the general and regular quality which is discovered through induction. It is the ideal of a science of society that is programmatically developed here, and which has been followed by research with success in many fields. One only has to think of social psychology.

But now the real problem that the human sciences present to thought is that one has not properly grasped the nature of the human sciences if one measures them by the yardstick of an increasing knowledge of regularity. The experience of the socio-historical world cannot be raised to a science by the inductive procedure of the natural sciences. Whatever 'science' may mean here and even if all historical knowledge includes the application of general experience to the particular object of investigation, historical research does not endeavour to grasp the concrete phenomenon as an instance of a general rule. The individual case does not serve only to corroborate a regularity from which predictions can in turn be made. Its ideal is rather to understand the phenomenon itself in its unique and historical concreteness. However much general experience is involved, the aim is not to confirm and expand these general experiences in order to attain knowledge of a law, eg how men, peoples and states evolve, but to understand how this man, this people or this state is what it has become—more generally, how has it happened that it is so.

What kind of knowledge is it that understands that something is so because it understands that it has so come about? What does 'science' mean here? Even if one recognises that the ideal of this knowledge is fundamentally different in character and intention from the natural sciences, one will still be tempted to describe them in a merely negative way as the 'inexact sciences'. Although the important and just comparison that Hermann Helmholtz made in his famous speech of 1862 between the natural and the human sciences laid great emphasis on the superior and humane significance of the human sciences, their logical description was still a negative one which was based on the methodological ideal of the natural sciences.[3] Helmholtz distinguished between two kinds of induction: logical and artistic-instinctive induction. That means, however, that his distinction was basically not logical but psychological. Both make use of the inductive conclusion, but the conclusions of the human sciences are unconsciously arrived at. Hence the practice of induction in the human sciences is tied to particular psychological conditions. It requires a kind of tact and other intellectual qualities as well, eg a well-stocked memory and the acceptance of authorities, whereas the self-conscious inferences of the natural scientist depend entirely on the use of his own reason. Even if one recognises that this great natural scientist has resisted the temptation of making his own scientific way of working into a generally binding norm, he obviously did not have any other logical way of characterising the procedure of the human sciences than by the concept of induction which was familiar to him from Mill's *Logic*. The fact that the new mechanics and their triumph in the astronomy of Newton were a model for the sciences of the eighteenth century was still so strong in Helmholtz's mind that the question of what the philosophical conditions were that made possible the birth of this new science in the seventeenth century was utterly remote from him. Today we know what an influence the Paris Occamist school had.[4] For Helmholtz the methodological ideal of the natural sciences needed neither historical derivation nor epistemological restriction, and that is why he could not logically comprehend the method of the human sciences any differently.

At the same time there was the pressing task of raising a branch of knowledge such as that of the 'historical school', which was in fact in full flower, to logical self-consciousness. As early as 1843 J. G. Droysen, the author and discoverer of the history of hellenism, wrote, 'there is, I suppose, no field of knowledge that is so far from being theoretically justified, defined and ordered than history'. Droysen called for a Kant who, in a categorical imperative of history 'would show the living source from which the historical life of mankind flowed'. He expressed the hope 'that the more profoundly grasped idea of history will be the centre of gravity in which the chaotic movement of the human sciences will gain discipline and the possibility of further progress.'[5]

The image of the natural sciences involved here by Droysen is

not intended in terms of content, in the sense of a theoretical
scientific model that has to be matched but, on the contrary, in
the sense that the human sciences must be firmly established as
a group of sciences just as independent as their counterparts.
Droysen's *Historik* is the attempt to carry this out.

Even Dilthey, on whom the scientific method and the empiricism of Mill's *Logic* had a much stronger effect, retained the
romantic, idealistic heritage in the concept of spirit (Geist). He
always thought himself superior to English empiricism, because
he directly apprehended what distinguished the historical school
from all thinking in terms of the natural sciences and of natural
law. 'The properly empirical procedure to replace prejudiced
dogmatic empiricism can come only from Germany. Mill is
dogmatic because of his lack of historical formation'—this was
the note Dilthey made in his copy of Mill's *Logic.* [6] In fact all the
arduous work of decades that Dilthey devoted to laying the
foundations of the human sciences was a constant debate with
the logical demand that Mill's famous last chapter made on the
human sciences.

Nevertheless, Dilthey let himself be profoundly influenced by
the model of the natural sciences, even when he was endeavouring to justify the very methodological independence of the
human ones. Two pieces of evidence will make this clear and
will, as it were, point the way for our own investigation. In his
obituary for Wilhelm Scherer, Dilthey emphasises that the spirit
of the natural sciences guided Scherer's procedure, and he attempts to give the reason why Scherer let himself be so influenced by English empiricism: 'He was a modern man, and the
world of our forebears was no longer the home of his spirit and
his heart, but his historical object'.[7] Hence Dilthey saw scientific knowledge as involving the dissolution of the connection
with life: the establishing of a distance from its own history,
which alone makes it possible for that history to become an
object. We may indeed acknowledge that the handling of the
inductive and comparative methods by Scherer and by Dilthey
was governed by genuine individual tact and that this tact presupposes a spiritual culture which indicates in fact the survival
in them of the world of classical culture and of the romantic
belief in individuality. Nevertheless it is the model of the natural
sciences that guides their scientific self-understanding.

A second reference makes this particularly clear, where
Dilthey refers to the independence of the methods of the human
sciences and explains this in view of its object.[8] At first acquaintance this seems soundly Aristotelian and could indicate a

genuine detachment from the scientific model. But in his account of this independence of the methods of the human sciences Dilthey falls back on the old Baconian natura parendo
vincitur,[9] a principle which practically flies in the face of the
classical and romantic heritage which Dilthey seeks to retain.
Thus it must be said that even Dilthey, whose historical culture
gives him a superiority over his contemporary neo-Kantians, did
not, in his logic, actually progress very far beyond the simple
statements made by Helmholtz. However much Dilthey might
have defended the epistemological independence of the human
sciences, what is called 'method' in modern science, remains
everywhere the same and is seen only in an especially exemplary
form in the natural sciences. The human sciences have no special method. But one might well ask, with Helmholtz, to what
extent method is significant in this case and whether the other
conditions under which the human sciences are pursued are not
perhaps far more important than inductive logic. Helmholtz had
indicated this correctly when, in order to do justice to the human
sciences, he emphasised memory and authority and spoke of the
psychological tact that here replaced the conscious drawing of
inferences. What is the basis of this tact? How is it acquired?
Does what is scientific about the human sciences not lie rather
here than in its methodology?

Because the human sciences prompt this question and thus
cannot be fitted into the modern concept of science, they are,
and remain, a problem for philosophy itself. The answer that
Helmholtz and his century gave to this question cannot suffice.
They follow Kant, in that they model the idea of science and
knowledge on the natural sciences and seek the distinguishing
feature of the human sciences in the artistic element (artistic
feeling, artistic induction). But the picture that Helmholtz gives
of work in the natural sciences is rather one-sided, seeing that he
does not believe in 'sudden flashes of intuition' (or in so-called
'inspirations') and sees scientific work only as the 'iron procedure of self-conscious reasoning'. He refers to John Stewart
Mill's view that 'the inductive sciences have done more in modern times for the progress of the methods of logic than all the
professional philosophers'.[10] They are, for him, the model of
scientific method as such.

Now Helmholtz knows that historical knowledge is determined by a quite different kind of experience from the one that
serves in the investigation of the laws of nature. Thus he seeks
to establish why the inductive method in historical research proceeds under conditions different from those obtaining in the

study of nature. To this end he uses the distinction between nature and freedom, which is the basis of Kantian philosophy. Historical study is different because there are no natural laws but, rather, the voluntary acceptance of practical laws, ie commandments. The world of human freedom does not manifest the same absence of exceptions as natural laws.

This line of thought, however, is not very convincing. It is not true to Kant's intentions to base the inductive investigation of the world of human freedom on his distinction between nature and freedom, nor is it true to the logic of induction itself. Here Mill was more consistent, in that he methodically excluded the problem of freedom. Moreover, the inconsistency with which Helmholtz invokes Kant in order to do justice to the human sciences is of no real value, for even according to Helmholtz the empiricism of the human sciences is to be regarded in the same way as that of meteorology, namely as renunciation and resignation.

But in fact the human sciences are a long way from regarding themselves as simply inferior to the natural sciences. Possessed of the intellectual heritage of German classicism they developed the proud awareness of being the true heirs of humanism. The period of German classicism had not only brought a renewal of literature and of aesthetic criticism which moved beyond the outmoded ideal of taste of the baroque and the rationalism of the enlightenment, it had also given to the idea of humanity, and to the ideal of enlightened reason, a fundamentally new content. Herder, more than anyone, transcended the perfectionism of the enlightenment with his new ideal of 'reaching up to humanity', and thus prepared the ground for the growth of the historical sciences in the nineteenth century. The idea of self-formation or cultivation (Begriff der Bildung), which became supremely important at the time, was perhaps the greatest idea of the eighteenth century, and it is this idea which is the atmosphere breathed by the human sciences of the nineteenth century, even if they are unable to offer any epistemological justification for it.

(B) LEADING HUMANISTIC CONCEPTS

(i) Bildung (culture)

The concept of Bildung most clearly indicates the profound intellectual change that still causes us to experience the century of Goethe as contemporary, whereas the baroque era already appears like a primaeval age of history. Key concepts and words

with which we customarily operate acquired their definition
then, and if we are not to accept language automatically, but to
strive for a reasoned historical self-understanding, we must face
a whole host of questions of verbal and conceptual history. In
what follows it is possible to do no more than begin the great
task that faces investigators, as an aid to our philosophical inquiry. Concepts such as 'art', 'history', 'the creative',
'Weltanschauung', 'experience', 'genius', 'external world', 'interiority', 'expression', 'style', 'symbol', which we use automatically, contain a wealth of history.

If we consider the concept of Bildung, the importance of
which we have emphasised for the human sciences, we are in a
fortunate situation. Here a previous investigation[11] gives us a
fine view of the history of the word: its origin in mediaeval
mysticism, its continuance in the mysticism of the baroque, its
religious spiritualisation in Klopstock's *Messiah,* which dominates the whole period, and finally Herder's basic definition as
'reaching up to humanity'. The cult of Bildung in the nineteenth
century preserved the profounder dimension of the word, and
our notion of Bildung is determined by this.

The first important observation about the familiar content of
the word Bildung is that the earlier idea of a 'natural shape'
which refers to external appearance (the shape of the limbs, the
well-formed figure) and in general to the shapes created by nature, eg a mountain formation—Gebirgsbildung) was at that
time detached almost entirely from the new idea. Now Bildung
is intimately associated with the idea of culture and designates
primarily the properly human way of developing one's natural
talents and capacities. Between Kant and Hegel the form that
Herder had given to the concept was perfected. Kant still does
not use the word Bildung in this connection. He speaks of the
'culture' of a capacity (or of a 'natural talent') which as such is
an act of freedom by the acting subject. Thus among the duties
to oneself he mentions not letting one's talents rust, without
using the word Bildung.[12] Hegel, however, already speaks of
Sichbilden ('educating or cultivating oneself') and Bildung,
when he takes up the same Kantian idea of duties towards
oneself,[13] and Wilhelm von Humboldt, with his sensitive ear,
already detects a difference in meaning between Kultur and Bildung: 'but if in our language we say Bildung, we mean something
both higher and more inward, namely the attitude of mind
which, from the knowledge and the feeling of the total intellectual and moral endeavour, flows harmoniously into sensibility
and character'.[14] Bildung here no longer means 'culture', ie the

Truth and Method

development of capacities or talents. The rise of the word
Bildung calls rather on the ancient mystical tradition, according
to which man carries in his soul the image of God after whom he
is fashioned and must cultivate it in himself. The Latin equivalent for Bildung is formatio, and accordingly in other languages,
eg in English (in Shaftesbury), 'form' and 'formation'. In German also the corresponding derivations of the idea of forma, eg
Formierung and Formation, have long vied with the word
Bildung. Since the Aristotelianism of the renaissance the word
forma has been completely separated from its technical meaning
and interpreted in a purely dynamic and natural way. Yet the
victory of the word Bildung over 'form' does not seem to be
fortuitous. For in Bildung there is Bild. The idea of 'form' lacks
the mysterious ambiguity of Bild, which can mean both
Nachbild ('image', 'copy') and Vorbild ('model').

In accordance with the frequent carry-over from becoming to
being, Bildung (as also the contemporary use of 'formation')
describes more the result of this process of becoming than the
process itself. The carry-over is especially clear here because
the result of Bildung is not achieved in the manner of a technical
construction, but grows out of the inner process of formation and
cultivation and therefore remains in a constant state of further
continued Bildung. It is not accidental that in this the word
Bildung resembles the Greek physis. Like nature, Bildung has
no goals outside itself. (The word Bildungsziel—the goal of
cultivation—is to be regarded with the suspicion appropriate to
such a secondary kind of Bildung. Bildung as such cannot be a
goal, it cannot as such be sought, except in the reflective thematic of the educator). In this the concept of Bildung transcends
that of the mere cultivation of given talents, from which concept
it is derived. The cultivation of a talent is the development of
something that is given, so that the practice and cultivation of it
is a mere means to an end. Thus the educational content of a
grammar-book is simply a means and not itself an end. Its assimilation simply improves one's linguistic ability. In Bildung,
contrariwise, that by which and through which one is formed
becomes completely one's own. To some extent everything that
is received is absorbed, but in Bildung what is absorbed is not
like a means that has lost its function. Rather in acquired
Bildung nothing disappears, but everything is preserved. Bildung is a genuine historical idea, and because of this historical character of 'preservation' is important for understanding in
the human sciences.

Thus even a preliminary glance at the linguistic history of

Bildung introduces us to the range of historical ideas that Hegel first introduced within the sphere of the 'first philosophy'. In fact Hegel has worked out very acutely what Bildung is. We follow him, initially.[15] He saw also that philosophy (and, we may add, the human sciences, Geisteswissenschaften) 'has, in Bildung, the condition of its existence'. For the being of Geist (spirit) has an essential connection with the idea of Bildung.

Man is characterised by the break with the immediate and the natural that the intellectual, rational side of his nature demands of him. 'In this sphere he is not, by nature, what he should be'— and hence he needs Bildung. What Hegel calls the formal nature of Bildung depends on its universality. Through the concept of promotion to the universal Hegel conceives, in a unified way, what his age understood by Bildung. Promotion to the universal is not something that is limited to theoretical Bildung and does not mean only a theoretical attitude in contrast to a practical one, but covers the essential determination of human rationality as a whole. It is the universal nature of human Bildung to constitute itself as a universal intellectual being. Whoever abandons himself to his particularity is ungebildet ('unformed'), eg if someone gives way to blind anger without measure or sense of proportion. Hegel shows that basically such a man is lacking in the power of abstraction. He cannot turn his gaze from himself towards something universal from which his own particular being is determined in measure and proportion.

Hence Bildung, as being raised to the universal, is a task for man. It requires the sacrifice of particularity for the sake of the universal. But sacrifice of particularity means, in negative terms, the restraint of desire and hence freedom from the object of desire and freedom for its objectivity. Here the deductions of the Phenomenological Dialectic complement what is stated in the *Propädeutik.* In his *Phenomenology of Spirit* Hegel works out the genesis of a truly free self-consciousness 'in-and-for-itself' and shows that it is the essence of work to form rather than to consume a thing.[16] In the independent existence that work gives to the thing, working consciousness finds itself again as an independent consciousness. Work is restrained desire. In forming the object, that is, being selflessly active and concerned with a universal, working consciousness raises itself above the immediacy of its existence to universality—or, as Hegel puts it, by forming the thing it forms itself. What he means is that in acquiring a capacity, a skill, man gains the sense of himself. What seemed denied him in the selflessness of serving, inasmuch as he subjected himself to something that was foreign to him, is given to him in as much as he is working consciousness. As such he finds in himself his own significance, and it is quite right to say of work that it forms. The self-awareness of working consciousness contains all the elements that make up practical Bildung: the distancing from the immediacy of desire, of personal need and private interest and the unreasonable demand of a universal.

In his *Propädeutik* Hegel demonstrates the nature of practical Bildung, of taking the universal upon oneself by means of a number of examples. It is found in the moderation which limits the excessive satisfaction of needs and of the use of one's strength by a general consideration—that of health. It is found in the circumspection that, while concerned with the individual situation or business, remains open to the observation of what else might be necessary. But every choice of profession has something of this. For every profession has something about it of fate, of external necessity, and asks of one to give oneself to tasks that one would not seek out as a private aim. Practical Bildung is seen in one's filling one's profession wholly, in all its aspects. But this includes overcoming the element in it that is alien to the particularity which is oneself, and making it wholly one's own. Thus to give oneself to the universality of a profession is at the same time 'to know how to limit oneself, ie to make one's profession wholly one's concern. Then it is no longer a limitation'.

Even in this description by Hegel of practical Bildung, one can recognise the basic tendency of the historical spirit: to reconcile itself with itself, to recognise oneself in other being. It becomes completely clear in the idea of theoretical Bildung, for to have a theoretical attitude is, as such, already alienation, namely the necessity of 'dealing with something that is not immediate, something that is alien, with something that belongs to memory and to thought'. Theoretical Bildung goes beyond what man knows and experiences immediately. It consists in learning to allow what is different from oneself and to find universal viewpoints from which one can grasp the thing, 'the objective thing in its freedom', without selfish interest.[17] That is why any acquisition of Bildung involves the development of theoretical interests, and Hegel declares the world and language of antiquity to be especially suitable for this, in that this world is remote and alien enough to be able to bring about the necessary separation of ourselves from ourselves, 'but it contains at the same time all the exit points and threads of the return to oneself, for becoming acquainted with it and for finding oneself again, but oneself according to the truly universal essence of spirit'.[18]

In these words of Hegel, The Gymnasium director, we recognise the classicist's prejudice that it is particularly the world of classical antiquity in which the universal nature of the spirit can be most easily found. But the basic idea is correct. To seek one's own in the alien, to become at home in it, is the basic movement of spirit, whose being is only return to itself from what is other. Hence all theoretical Bildung, even the acquisition of foreign languages and conceptual worlds, is merely the continuation of a process of Bildung which begins much earlier. Every single individual that raises himself out of his natural being to the spiritual finds in the language, customs and institutions of his people a pre-given body of material which, as in learning to speak, he has to make his own. Thus every individual is always engaged in the process of Bildung and in getting beyond his naturalness, inasmuch as the world into which he is growing is one that is humanly constituted through language and custom. Hegel emphasises that a people gives itself its existence in its world. It works out from itself and thus exteriorises what it is in itself.

Thus it is clear that it is not alienation as such, but the return to oneself, which presumes a prior alienation, that constitutes the essence of Bildung. Bildung is not only, however, the process which produces the historical raising of the mind to the universal, but it is at the same time the element within which the educated man (Gebildete) moves. What kind of element is this? The questions that we would put to Helmholtz arise here. Hegel's answer cannot satisfy us, for Hegel sees Bildung as perfected in the movement of alienation and appropriation in a complete mastery of substance, in the dissolution of all concrete being, reached only in the absolute knowledge of philosophy.

But we may recognise that Bildung is an element of spirit without being tied to Hegel's philosophy of absolute spirit, just as the insight into the historicity of consciousness is not tied to his philosophy of world history. We must realise that the idea of perfect Bildung remains a necessary ideal even for the historical sciences that depart from Hegel. For Bildung is the element in which they move. Even what earlier usage, with reference to physical appearance, called 'perfection of form' is not so much the last state of a development as the mature state that has left all development behind and makes possible the harmonious movement of all the limbs. It is precisely in this sense that the human sciences presuppose that the scientific consciousness is already formed and for that very reason possesses the right, unlearnable and inimitable tact that bears the judgment and the mode of knowledge of the human sciences.

The way that Helmholtz describes the human sciences' mode

of working, especially what he calls craftsmanlike feeling and
tact, in fact presupposes this element of Bildung, within which
the mind has a particular free mobility. Thus Helmholtz speaks
of the 'readiness with which the most varied experiences must
flow into the memory of the historian or literary critic'.[19] That
may seem to be written rather superficially, from the viewpoint
of that ideal of the 'iron procedure of self-conscious reasons',
from which the natural scientist considers himself. The idea of
memory, as he uses it, is not sufficient to explain the process
that is involved here. In fact this tact or feeling is not properly
understood if one thinks of it as a supervening mental compe-
tence which uses a powerful memory and so arrives at knowledge not strictly available for examination. What makes this
function of tact possible, what leads to its acquisition and possession, is not merely a piece of psychological equipment that is
favorable to knowledge in the human sciences.

   Moreover, the nature of memory is not properly understood if
it is regarded as merely a general capacity or aptitude. Remembering, forgetting, and recalling belong to the historical constitution of man and are themselves part of his history and his
Bildung. Whoever uses his memory as a mere faculty—and all
the technical side of memory is such a use—does not yet possess
it as something that is absolutely his own. Memory must be
formed; for memory is not memory for anything and everything.
One has a memory for many things, and not for others; one
wants to preserve one thing in memory and banish another. It is
time to rescue the phenomenon of memory from being regarded
merely as a psychological faculty and to see it as an essential
element of the finite historical being of man. Forgetting belongs
within the context of remembering and recalling in a way that
has long been ignored; forgetting is not merely an absence and a
lack but, as Nietzsche pointed out, a condition of the life of
mind.[20] Only by forgetting does the mind have the chance of
total renewal, the capacity to see everything with fresh eyes, so
that what is long familiar combines with the new into a many
levelled unity. 'Retention' is ambiguous. As memory (mneme) it
contains the connection with remembering (anamnesis).[21] But
the same thing is also true of the concept of tact that Helmholtz
uses. By 'tact' we understand a particular sensitivity and sensi-
tiveness to situations, and how to behave in them, for which we
cannot find any knowledge from general principles. Hence an
essential part of tact is inexplicitness and inexpressibility. One
can say something tactfully; but that will always mean that one
passes over something tactfully and leaves it unsaid, and it is

tactless to express what one can only pass over. But to pass over something does not mean to avert the gaze from something, but to watch it in such a way that rather than knock against it, one slips by it. Thus tact helps one to preserve distance, it avoids the offensive, the intrusive, the violation of the intimate sphere of the person.

The tact of which Helmholtz speaks is not simply identical with this phenomenon of manners and customs, but there is an essential community between them. For the tact which functions in the human sciences is not simply a feeling and unconscious, but is at the same time a mode of knowing and a mode of being. This can be seen more clearly from the above analysis of the idea of Bildung. What Helmholtz calls 'tact' includes Bildung and is a function both of aesthetic and of historical Bildung. One must have a sense of the aesthetic and the historical or have this sense formed, if one is to be able to rely on one's tact in work in the human sciences. Because this sense is not simply part of one's natural equipment we rightly speak of the aesthetic or historical consciousness, and not properly of sense. Still, this consciousness accords well with the immediacy of the senses, ie it is able to make sure distinctions and evaluations in the individual case, without being able to give its reasons. Thus someone who has a sense of the aesthetic is able to distinguish between beautiful and ugly, good or bad qualities, and whoever has a sense of the historical knows what is possible for an age and what not, and has a sense of the difference of the past in relation to the present.

If all that presupposes Bildung, that means that it is not a question of the procedure or attitude, but of what has come into being. It is worthless to observe more closely, to study a tradition more thoroughly, if there is not already a trained receptivity towards the 'otherness' of the work of art or of the past. That is what, following Hegel, we emphasised as the general characteristic of Bildung, to keep oneself open to what is other, to other, more universal points of view. It embraces a general sense of proportion and distance in relation to itself, and hence is capable of being raised above itself to universality. To distance oneself from oneself and from one's private purposes means to look at these in the way that others see them. This universality is by no means a universality of concept or of the understanding. A particular is not determined by a universal, nothing is proved conclusively. The universal viewpoints to which the cultivated man (gebildet) keeps himself open are not a fixed applicable yardstick, but are present to him only as the viewpoints of possible others. Thus the cultivated consciousness (gebildet) has in fact more the character of a sense. For every sense, eg vision (the sense of sight), is already universal in that it embraces its sphere, remains open to a particular field, and grasps the distinctions within what is opened to it in this way. Cultivated consciousness goes beyond each of the natural senses in that the latter are limited to one particular sphere at a time, whereas it is active in all directions. It is a universal sense.

A universal and common sense is, in fact, a formulation of the nature, of Bildung suggestive of an extensive historical context. Helmholtz's reflection on the idea of Bildung, which lies at the basis of his thinking, leads us far back into the history of this idea. We must pursue this context a little if we want to release the problem that the human sciences present for philosophy from the artificial narrowness in which nineteenth-century methodology was caught. The modern concept of science and the associated concept of method are insufficient. What makes the human sciences into sciences can be understood more easily from the tradition of the concept of Bildung than from the concept of method in modern science. It is on the humanistic tradition that we must rely. In its resistance to the claims of modern science it gains a new significance.

It would be worth making a separate investigation into the way in which, since the days of humanism, criticism of 'scholastic' science has made itself heard and how this criticism has changed with the changes of its opponent. Originally it was classical influences which reasserted themselves. The enthusiasm with which the humanists proclaimed the Greek language and the path of eruditio was more than an antiquarian passion. The revival of the classical languages brought with it a new valuation of rhetoric. It was fighting the 'school', ie scholastic science, and supported an ideal of human wisdom that was not reached in the 'school'—an antithesis which in fact is found at the very beginning of philosophy. Plato's critique of sophism and, still more, his peculiarly ambivalent attitude towards Isocrates, indicate the philosophical problem that emerges here. With the new methodological awareness of seventeenth-century science this old problem inevitably became more acute. In view of the claims this new science made to exclusivity the question was raised with increased urgency of whether in the humanistic concept of Bildung there was not a special source of truth. In fact we shall see that it is from the survival of the humanistic idea of Bildung that the human sciences of the nineteenth century draw, without admitting it, their own life.

At the same time it is obvious that it is not mathematics, but humanistic studies that are important here. For what could the new methodology of the seventeenth century mean for the human sciences? One has only to read the appropriate chapters of the *Logique de Port-Royal* concerning the rules of reason applied to historical truths to see how little can be achieved in the human sciences by this idea of method.[22] What comes out is pretty trivial, when eg it says that in order to judge an event in its truth one must take account of the accompanying circumstances (circonstances). With this kind of argument the Jansenists sought to provide a methodical way of showing to what extent miracles deserved belief. They countered an uncontrolled belief in miracles with the spirit of the new method and sought to legitimate in this way the true miracles of biblical and of church tradition. The new science in the service of the old church—that this situation could not last is only too clear, and one can imagine what inevitably happened when the christian presuppositions themselves were questioned. When the methodological ideal of the natural sciences was applied to the credibility of the historical testimonies of sciptural tradition it inevitably led to results that were catastrophic for christianity. The distance between the criticism of miracles in the style of the Jansenists to historical criticism of the bible is not far. Spinoza is a good example of this. I shall show later that a logical application of this method as the only norm for the truth of the human sciences would amount to their self-annihilation.

(ii) Sensus communis

In this situation it is important to remember the humanistic tradition, and to ask what is to be learned from it in regard to the mode of knowledge of the human sciences. Vico's *De nostri temporis studiorum ratione* makes a good starting-point.[23]

Vico's defence of humanism derives, as the very title shows, from the Jesuit pedagogical system and is directed as much against Jansenism as against Descartes. Like his outline of a 'new science', Vico's pedagogical manifesto is based on old truths. He appeals to the sensus communis, common sense, and to the humanistic ideal of eloquentia—elements already present in the classical concept of wisdom. 'Talking well' (eu legein) has always had two meanings; it is not merely a rhetorical ideal. It also means saying the right thing, ie the truth, and is not just the art of speaking—of saying whatsoever well.

This ideal was proclaimed in the ancient world just as much by teachers of philosophy as by those of rhetoric. Rhetoric was always in conflict with philosophy and, as against the idle speculations of the sophists, claimed to teach true wisdom. Here Vico, himself a teacher of rhetoric, is in a humanistic tradition that stems from antiquity. This tradition is obviously important for the self-understanding of the human sciences; especially so is the positive ambiguity of the rhetorical ideal, which is condemned not only by Plato, but by the anti-rhetorical methodology of modern times. In Vico, we already find much of what will concern us. But apart from the rhetorical element, his appeal to common sense contains another element from classical tradition. This is the contrast between the scholar and the wise man on whom the scholar depends, a contrast that is drawn for the first time in the cynics' conception of Socrates, and has its intellectual basis in the distinction between the ideas of sophia and phronesis which was first elaborated by Aristotle, developed by the peripatetics as a critique of the theoretical ideal of life,[24] and contributed in the Hellenistic period to the image of the wise man, especially after the Greek ideal of Bildung had been fused with the self-consciousness of the leading political class of Rome. Late Roman legal science also developed against the background of an art and practice of law that is closer to the practical ideal of phronesis than to the theoretical ideal of sophia.[25]

With the renaissance of classical philosophy and rhetoric, the image of Socrates became the counter-cry against science, as is shown, in particular, in the figure of the idiota, the layman, who assumes a totally new role between the scholar and the wise man.[26] Likewise the rhetorical tradition of humanism quoted Socrates and the sceptical critique of the dogmatists. We find that Vico criticises the stoics because they believe in reason as the regula veri and, contrariwise, praises the old academicians who assert only the knowledge of not knowing anything; and the new ones, because they excel in the art of arguing (which is part of rhetoric).

Vico's appeal to the sensus communis undoubtedly has a special flavour within this humanistic tradition. In this sphere of knowledge also there is a querelle des anciens et des modernes. It is no longer the contrast with the 'school', but the particular contrast with modern science that Vico has in mind. He does not dispute the positive aspects of modern critical science, but shows their limitation. Even with this new science and its mathematical methodology we still cannot do without the wisdom of the ancients and their cultivation of prudentia and eloquentia. The most important thing in education is still something else, the training in the sensus communis, which is not nourished on the true, but on the probable. The main thing for our purposes is that sensus communis here obviously does not mean only that general faculty in all men, but the sense that founds community. According to Vico, what gives the human will its direction is not the abstract generality of reason, but the concrete generality that represents the community of a group, a people, a nation, or the whole human race. Hence the development of this sense of the community is of prime importance for living.

On this general sense of the true and the right, which is not a knowledge based on argumentation, but enables one to discover what is obvious (verisimile), Vico bases the significance and the independent rights of rhetoric. Education cannot, he says, tread the path of critical research. Youth demands images for its imagination and for the forming of its memory. But the study of the sciences in the spirit of modern criticism does not achieve this. Thus Vico supplements the critica of Cartesianism with the old topica. This is the art of finding arguments and serves to develop the sense of what is convincing, which works instinctively and ex-tempore and for this very reason cannot be replaced by science.

These prescriptions of Vico have an apologetical air. They indirectly recognise science's new concept of truth in the very fact that they defend the rights of the probable. As we have seen, he follows here the ancient rhetorical tradition that goes back to Plato. But what Vico means goes far beyond the defence of rhetorical persuasion. The old Aristotelian distinction between practical and theoretical knowledge is operative here—a distinction which cannot be reduced to that between the true and the probable. Practical knowledge, phronesis, is another kind of knowledge.[27] Primarily, it means that it is directed towards the concrete situation. Thus it must grasp the 'circumstances' in their infinite variety. This is what Vico expressly emphasises about it. It is true that his main concern is to show that this kind of knowledge is outside the rational concept of knowledge, but this is not in fact mere resignation. The Aristotelian distinction refers to something else apart from the distinction between knowledge from general principles and knowledge of the concrete. Nor does he mean only the capacity to subsume the individual case under a general category that we call 'judgment'. Rather, there is a positive ethical element involved that passes into the Roman Stoic teaching about the sensus communis. The

grasp and moral control of the concrete situation require this
subsumption of what is given under the universal; ie the goal that
one is pursuing so that the right thing may result. Hence it assumes a direction of the will, ie moral being (hexis). That is why
Aristotle considers phronesis as an 'intellectual virtue'. He sees
it not only as a capacity (dunamis), but as a determination of
moral being which cannot exist without the totality of the 'ethical virtues', which in turn cannot exist without it. Although the
practice of this virtue means that one distinguishes what should
be done from what should not, it is not simply practical shrewd-
ness and general cleverness. The distinction between what
should and should not be done includes the distinction between
the proper and the improper and thus presumes a moral attitude,
which it continues to develop.

It is this idea propounded by Aristotle against Plato's 'idea of
the good' to which Vico's point about the sensus communis in
fact goes back. In scholasticism, say for St. Thomas in his commentary on the *De Anima*,[28] the sensus communis is the common root of the outer senses, ie the faculty that combines them,
that make judgments about what is given, a faculty that is given
to all men.[29] For Vico, however, the sensus communis is the
sense of the right and the general good that is to be found in all
men, moreover, a sense that is acquired through living in the
community and is determined by its structures and aims. This
idea sounds related to the natural law, like the koinai ennoiai of
the stoics. But the sensus communis is not, in this sense, a
Greek idea and definitely does not mean the koine dunamis of
which Aristotle speaks in the *De Anima,* when he seeks to reconcile the doctrine of the specific senses (aisthesis idia) with
the phenomenological finding that shows all perception to be a
differentiation and an intention of the universal. Rather Vico
goes back to the old Roman idea of the sensus communis, as
found especially in the Roman classics which, when faced with
Greek cultivation, held firmly to the value and significance of
their own traditions of public and social life. A critical note,
directed against the theoretical speculations of the philosophers
can be heard in the Roman concept of the sensus communis; and
that note Vico sounds again from his different position of opposition to modern science (the critica).

There is something immediately obvious about grounding
literary and historical studies and the methods of the human
sciences in this idea of the sensus communis. For their object,
the moral and historical existence of man, as they take shape in
his activities, is itself largely determined by the sensus com-

munis. Thus an argument based on universals, a reasoned proof, is not sufficient, because what is important is the circumstances. But this is only a negative formulation. The sense of the community mediates a unique positive knowledge. The procedure of historical research does not work simply by admitting 'belief in other people's testimony' (Tetens[30]) in the place of a 'self-conscious process of logic' (Helmholtz). Nor is it at all true that such knowledge has only a lesser claim to truth. D'Alembert is correct when he writes: 'Probability operates principally in the case of historical facts, and in general for all past, present and future events, which we attribute to a kind of chance because we do not unravel the causes. That part of this knowledge whose object is the present and the past, although it may be founded on testimony alone, often produces in us a conviction that is as strong as that which gives birth to axioms'.[31]

Historia is a totally different source of truth from theoretical reason. This is what Cicero meant when he called it the vita memoriae.[32] It exists in its own right because human passions cannot be governed by the universal prescriptions of reason. In this sphere one needs, rather, convincing examples as only history can offer them. That is why Bacon describes historia, which gives these examples, almost as another way of philosophising (alia ratio philosophandi).[33]

This, too, is negative enough in its formulation. But we shall see that in all these versions the category of moral knowledge, as recognised by Aristotle, is operative. It will be important to recall this for the adequate self-understanding of the human sciences.

Vico's return to the Roman idea of the sensus communis, and his defence of humanist rhetoric against modern science is of special interest to us, for it gives us an element in human scientific knowledge that was no longer available in the nineteenth-century self-understanding of the human sciences. Vico lived in an unbroken tradition of rhetorical and humanist culture and had only to reassert anew its ageless claim. Finally, it was always known that the possibilities of rational proof and instruction did not fully exhaust the sphere of knowledge. Hence Vico's appeal to the sensus communis belongs, as we have seen, in a wider context that goes right back to antiquity and the continued effect of which into the present day is the subject of our book.[34]

We, on the contrary, must feel our way back into this tradition by first showing the difficulties that result from the application of the modern concept of method to the human sciences. Let us therefore consider how this tradition became so impoverished and the claim to truth of the knowledge of the modern sciences came to be measured by a standard foreign to it, namely, the methodical thinking of modern science.

Vico and the general unbroken rhetorical tradition of Italy do not directly influence this development, which was determined chiefly by the German 'historical school'. One can discern hardly any influence of Vico on the eighteenth century. But he was not alone in his appeal to the sensus communis. He has an important parallel in Shaftesbury, who had a powerful influence on the eighteenth century. Shaftesbury places the evaluation of the social significance of wit and humour under sensus communis and explicitly cites the Roman classics and their humanist interpreters.[35] As we have noted, the concept of the sensus communis undoubtedly reminds us of the Stoics and of the natural law. Nevertheless, it is impossible to deny the validity of the humanistic interpretation, based on the Roman classics, which Shaftesbury follows. According to Shaftesbury, the humanists understood by sensus communis the sense of the general good, but also 'love of the community or society, natural affection, humanity, obligingness'. They adopt a term from Marcus Aurelius, koinonoemosune[36]—a most unusual and artificial word, confirming that the concept of sensus communis does not originate with the Greek philosophers, but has the stoical conception sounding in it like a harmonic. The humanist Salmasius describes the content of this word as moderatam, usitatam et ordinariam hominis mentem, que in commune quodam modo consulit nec omnia ad commodum suum refert, respectumque etiam habet eorum, cum quibus versatur, modeste, modiceque de se sentiens. It is not so much a feature given to all men, part of the natural law, as a social virtue, a virtue of the heart more than of the head, that Shaftesbury is thinking of. And if he understands wit and humour in terms of it, then in this also he is following ancient Roman concepts that include in humanitas a refined savoir vivre, the attitude of the man who understands a joke and makes one because he is aware of a deeper union with his interlocutor. (Shaftesbury explicitly limits wit and humour to social intercourse among friends). If the sensus communis appears here almost as a virtue of social intercourse, there is nevertheless a moral, even a metaphysical basis implied.

It is the intellectual and social virtue of sympathy of which Shaftesbury is thinking and on which he based, as we know, not only morality, but an entire aesthetic metaphysics. His successors, above all Hutcheson[37] and Hume, elaborated his suggestions into the doctrine of the moral sense, which was later to serve as a foil to Kantian ethics.

The idea of 'common sense' acquired a quite central systematic function in Scottish philosophy, which was directed polemically against metaphysics and against its dissolution in scepticism, and built up its new system on the basis of original and natural judgments of common sense (Thomas Reid)[38]. Doubtless this was influenced by the Aristotelian-scholastic tradition of the concept of sensus communis. The enquiry into the senses and their capacity to provide knowledge comes from this tradition and is intended ultimately to correct the exaggerations of philosophical speculation. At the same time, however, the connection between common sense and society is preserved: 'They serve to direct us in the common affairs of life, where our reasoning faculty would leave us in the dark'. In their eyes, the philosophy of sound understanding, of 'good sense', is not only a cure for the 'moon-sickness' of metaphysics, but also contains the basis of a moral philosophy that really does justice to the life of society.

The moral element in the concept of 'common sense' or of le bon sens has remained up to the present day and distinguishes these from the German concept of der gesunde Menschenverstand ('sound understanding'). Take as an example the fine speech on le bon sens which Henri Bergson made in 1895 at the prize-giving in the Sorbonne.[39] His criticism of the abstractions of natural science, of language and of legal thinking, his passionate appeal to the énergie intérieure d'une intelligence qui se reconquiert à tout moment sur elle-meme, éliminant les idées faites pour laisser la place libre aux idées qui se font (p 88—inner energy of an intelligence which at each moment wins itself back to itself, eliminating those already formed ideas to give place to those in process), was called, in France, le bon sens. The definition of this concept certainly contained, as is natural, a reference to the senses, but it obviously goes without saying that for Bergson, unlike the senses, le bon sens refers to the milieu social: Tandis que les autres sens nous mettent en rapport avec des choses, le bon sens préside à nos relations avec des personnes (p 85—while the other senses relate us to things, 'good sense' governs our relations with persons). It is a kind of genius for practical life, but less a gift than the constant task of adjustement toujours renouvelé des situations toujours nouvelles (constantly renewed adaptation to new situations), a work of adapting general principles to reality, through which justice is realised, a tact de la vérité pratique (tactfulness in practical truth), a rectitude du jugement, qui vient de la droiture de l'ame (p 88—rightness of judgment, that stems from correctness of soul). Le bon sens, for Bergson, is, as the common source of thought and will, a sens social, which avoids equally the mistakes of the scientific dogmatists who are looking for social laws as those of the metaphysical utopians, Peut-être n'a-t-il pas de méthode à proprement parler, mais plutôt une certaine manière de faire (Perhaps there is not, properly speaking, method, but rather a certain way of acting). It is true that he speaks of the importance of classical studies for the development of this bon sens—he sees them as an attempt to break through the 'ice of words' and to discover the free flow of thought below (p 91)—but he does not ask the contrary question, namely how helpful le bon sens is for classical studies, ie he does not speak of its hermeneutic function. His question has nothing to do with the sciences, but with the independent significance of le bon sens for life. We are only emphasising the unquestioned dominance of the moral and political meaning of this concept in his mind and that of his hearers.

It is very characteristic that the self-reflection of the human sciences in the nineteenth century did not proceed under the influence of the moralistic tradition of philosophy, to which both Vico and Shaftesbury belong and which is represented primarily by France, the classical land of le bon sens, but under that of the German philosophy of the age of Kant and Goethe. Whereas in England and the Romance countries the idea of the sensus communis is not even today just a critical slogan, but is a general civic quality, in Germany the followers of Shaftesbury and Hutcheson did not, even in the eighteenth century, take over the political and social element contained in sensus communis. The metaphysics of the schools and popular philosophy of the eighteenth century, however much they were orientated towards the leading countries of the enlightenment, England and France, learning from them and imitating them, could not absorb into themselves that for which the social and political conditions were utterly lacking. The concept of sensus communis was taken over, but in the removal of all political content it lost its real critical significance. Sensus communis was understood as a purely theoretical faculty, theoretical judgment, on a level with moral consciousness (conscience) and taste. Thus it was fitted into a scholasticism of the basic faculties, of which Herder provided the critique (in the fourth kritischen Wäldchen, directed against Ridel), and which made him the forerunner of historicism in the field of aesthetics also.

And yet there is one important exception: Pietism. It was

important not only for a man of the world like Shaftesbury against the 'school' to delimit the claims of science, i e of demonstratio, and to appeal to the sensus communis, but also for the preacher, who seeks to reach the hearts of his congregation. Thus the Swabian Pietist Oetinger explicitly relied on Shaftesbury's defence of the sensus communis. We find sensus communis translated simply as 'heart' and the following description: 'The sensus communis is concerned only with things that all men see daily before them, things that hold an entire society together, things that are concerned both with truths and statements, ways and forms of expressing the statements . . .'[40]. Oetinger is concerned to show that it is not just a question of the clarity of the concepts—it is 'not enough for living knowledge'. Rather, there must be 'certain anticipations and predilections present'. 'Fathers are moved without proof to care for their children; love does not demonstrate, but often rends the heart against reason at the beloved's reproach'. Oetinger's appeal to the sensus communis against the rationalism of the 'school' is especially interesting for us because we find it with him in an expressly hermeneutical application. For Oetinger, as a churchman, the important thing is the understanding of Scripture. Because the mathematical, demonstrative method fails here, he demands another, the 'generative method', ie the 'organic presentation of Scripture, so that justice may be planted like a shoot'.

Oetinger also made the concept of sensus communis the object of an extended and learned investigation, which is likewise directed against rationalism[41]. He sees in it the source of all truths, the very ars inveniendi, in contrast to Leibniz, who bases everything on a mere calculus metaphysicus (excluso omni gusto interno). According to Oetinger the true basis of the sensus communis is the idea of vita, life (sensus communis vitae gaudens). As against the violent anatomisation of nature through experiment and calculation he sees the natural development of the simple to the complex as the universal law of growth of the divine creation and, likewise, of the human spirit. For the idea of all knowledge originating in the sensus communis he quotes Wolff, Bernoulli and Pascal, Maupertuis' investigation into the origin of language, Bacon, Fénélon etc and defines the sensus communis as viva et penetrans perceptio objectorum toti humanitati obviorum, ex immediato tactu et intuitu eorum, quae sunt simplicissima.

From this second sentence it is apparent that Oetinger combines throughout the humanistic, political meaning of the word with the peripatetic concept of sensus communis. The above definition reminds one here and there (immediato tactu et intuitu) of Aristotle's doctrine of nous. The Aristotelian question of the common dunamis, which combines seeing, hearing etc, is accepted by him and serves to confirm the actual divine mystery of life. The divine mystery of life is its simplicity—even if man has lost it through the fall, he can still find his way back, through the grace of God, to unity and simplicity: operatio logous, praesentia Dei simplificat diversa in unum (p 162). The presence of God consists in life itself, in this 'communal sense' that distinguishes all living things from dead—it is no accident that he mentions the polyp and the star-fish which, however much they are dissected, regenerate themselves and form new individuals. In man the same divine power operates in the form of the instinct and inner stimulation to discover the traces of God and to recognise what has the greatest connection with human happiness and life. Oetinger expressly distinguishes receptivity to the common truths that are useful to all men at all times and places, 'sensible' truths, as opposed to rational truths. The communal sense is a complex of instincts, ie a natural drive towards that on which the true happiness of life depends, and to that extent an effect of the presence of God. Instincts are not to be understood, with Leibniz, as affects, ie as confusae repraesentationes, for they are not transient, but permanent tendencies and have a dictatorial, divine, irresistible force.[42] Sensus communis, based on these, is of special importance[43] for our knowledge, precisely because they are a gift of God. Oetinger writes that the ratio often governs itself by rules even without God, but this sense always operates with God. Just as nature is different from art, so sense and ratio are different. God works through nature in a simultaneous increase in growth that spreads regularly throughout the whole. Art, however, begins with some particular part. The senses imitate nature, the ratio art (p 247).

Interestingly enough, this statement comes from a hermeneutical context, as indeed in this learned work the 'Sapientia Salomonis' represents the ultimate object and highest example of knowledge. It is the chapter on the use (usus) of the sensus communis. Here Oetinger attacks the hermeneutical theory of the Wolffian school. More important than all hermeneutical rules is to be sensu plenus. This thesis is naturally a spiritualistic extreme, but it still has its logical foundation in the idea of vita or the sensus communis. Its hermeneutical significance can be illustrated by the sentence: 'the ideas that can be found in scripture and in the works of God are the more fruitful and purified the more that each can be seen in the whole and all can be seen in each'.[44] Here that which people like to call 'intuition' in the nineteenth and twentieth centuries is brought back to its metaphysical foundation: that is to the structure of living, organic being, of being the whole in each individual: cyclus vitae centrum suum in corde habet, quod infinita simul percipit per sensum communem (Praef).

More profound than all hermeneutical knowledge of rules is the application to oneself: applicentur regulae ad se ipsum ante omnia et tum habebitur clavis ad intelligentiam proverbiorum Salomonis (p 207).[45] From this point Oetinger is able to bring his ideas into harmony with those of Shaftesbury who, as he says, is the only one to have written about sensus communis under this name. But he also quotes others who have noted the one-sidedness of the rational method, eg Pascal's distinction between esprit géométrique and esprit de finesse. Nevertheless, the Swabian Pietist is more interested in theology than in politics or society, and this interest crystallises around the concept of sensus communis.

Of course other Pietist theologians have emphasised application against the dominant rationalism in the same way as Oetinger, as we can see from the example of Rambach, whose very influential hermeneutics also included application. But the supplanting of pietistic tendencies in the later eighteenth century caused the hermeneutic function of sensus communis to decline to a mere corrective: that which contradicts the consensus of feelings, judgments and conclusions, ie the sensus communis, cannot be correct.[46] In contrast to the importance that Shaftesbury assigned to the sensus communis for society and state, this negative function shows the emptying and intellectualising of the idea that took place during the German enlightenment.

(iii) Judgment

It may be because of this development of the concept in the eighteenth century in Germany that the concept of sensus communis is so closely connected with the concept of judgment. Gesunder Menschenverstand ('good sense'), sometimes called gemeiner Verstand, is in fact largely characterised by judgment. The difference between a fool and a sensible man is that the former lacks judgment, ie he is not able to subsume correctly and hence cannot apply correctly what he has learned and knows. The introduction of the word 'judgment' in the eighteenth century was intended to convey the idea of judicium,

which was considered to be a basic intellectual virtue. In the
same way the English moral philosophers emphasise that moral
and aesthetic judgments do not obey reason, but have the
character of sentiment (or taste), and Tetens, one of the representatives of the German enlightenment, similarly sees the
sensus communis as a judicium without reflection.[47] In fact the
work of judgment, subsuming a particular under a universal,
recognising something as an example of a rule, cannot be logically demonstrated. Thus judgment requires a principle to guide
its application. In order to follow this principle it would need
another faculty of judgment, as Kant shrewdly noted.[48] So it
cannot be taught in general, but only practised from case to case,
and is therefore more a faculty like the senses. It is something
that cannot be learned, because no demonstration from concepts
is able to guide the application of rules.

Consequently the philosophy of the German enlightenment
did not consider judgment among the higher but among the lower
powers of the mind. In this, it took a direction greatly divergent
from the original Roman sense of sensus communis, and continued the scholastic tradition. This was to be especially important for aesthetics. Baumgarten, for example, is quite certain
that what judgment recognises is the sensible individual, the
unique thing, and what it judges in the individual thing is its
perfection or imperfection.[49] It must be noted that this definition
of judgment does not simply apply a pre-given concept of the
thing, but that the sensible individual is grasped in as much as
the agreement of the many with the one is observed. This is not
the application of the universal but the internal agreement between distinct things. As we can see, this is already what Kant
later calls 'reflective judgment' and understands as judgment
according to real and formal appropriateness. A concept is not
given, but the individual object is judged 'immanently'. Kant
calls this an aesthetic judgment, and just as Baumgarten described the iudicium sensitivum as gustus, so Kant repeats: 'A
sensible judgment of perfection is called taste'.[50]

We shall see later that this aesthetic development of the concept of iudicium, for which Gottsched was primarily responsible
in the eighteenth century, acquired a systematic significance for
Kant, although it will also emerge that the Kantian distinction
between a determinant and a reflective judgment is not without
its problems.[51] Nor can the meaning of sensus communis be
limited merely to aesthetic judgment. From the use that Vico
and Shaftesbury make of this idea, it appears that sensus communis is not primarily a formal capacity, an intellectual faculty

that has to be used but already embraces a sum of judgments and judgmental criteria that determine its contents.

Common sense is seen primarily in the judgments about right and wrong, proper and improper, that it makes. Whosoever has a sound judgment is not thereby enabled to judge particulars under universal viewpoints, but he knows what is important, i e he sees things from right and sound points of view. A swindler who correctly judges the weakness of men and always does the right thing in his trickeries nevertheless does not posses 'sound judgment' in the highest sense of the term. Thus the universality (Allgemeinheit) that is ascribed to the faculty of judgment is something by no means as common (gemein) as Kant sees it. Judgment is not so much a faculty as a demand that has to be made of all. Everyone has enough "sense of the common' (gemeinen Sinn), ie judgment, that he can be expected to show a 'sense of the community' (Gemeinsinn), genuine moral and civic solidarity, but that means judgment of right and wrong, and a concern for the 'common good'. This is what makes Vico's reliance on the humanistic tradition so impressive for against the intellectualisation of the idea of the sense of the community, he holds firmly on to all the wealth of meaning that lived in the Roman tradition of this word (and to this day is characteristic of the Latin race). Similarly, when Shaftesbury took up the idea it was, as we have seen, also a link with the political and social tradition of humanism. The sensus communis is an element of social and moral being. Even when, as in pietism or in Scottish philosophy, this concept was associated with a polemical attack on metaphysics, it still retained its original critical function.

By contrast, Kant's version of this idea in his Kritik der Urteilskraft has quite a different emphasis.[52] There is no longer any systematic place for the basic moral sense of the concept. As we know, he developed his moral philosophy in downright opposition to the doctrine of 'moral feeling' that had been worked out in English philosophy. Thus he totally excluded the idea of the sensus communis from moral philosophy.

What appears with the unconditionality of a moral law cannot be based on a feeling, not even if one does not mean an individual feeling, but the commonness of moral experience. For the character of a moral law totally excludes any comparative reflection about others. The unconditionality of a moral law certainly does not mean that the moral consciousness must remain rigid in judging others. Rather it is a moral command to detach oneself from the subjective private conditions of one's own judgment and to shift one's ground to the standpoint of the other person.

But this unconditionality also means that the moral consciousness cannot avoid reference to the judgment of others. The obli-
gatoriness of the precept is universal in a stricter sense than
that to which the universality of a feeling can ever attain. The
application of the moral law to the determining of the will is a
matter for judgment. But since it is a question of judgment
operating under the laws of pure practical reason, its task consists precisely in preserving one from the 'empiricism of practical reason, which places the practical concepts of good and bad
merely in experiential succession'.[53] This is done by pure practical reason.

There is also the other question for Kant of how one is able to
plant in the human mind the stern law of pure practical reason.
He deals with this in the Methodenlehre der reinen, praktischen
Vernunft, which 'endeavours to provide a brief outline of the
method of engendering and cultivating genuine moral attitudes'.
For this he in fact relies on ordinary human reason and desires to
cultivate and form practical judgment, and certainly aesthetic
elements play their part also.[54] But that there can be this kind of
cultivation of moral feeling is not really part of moral philosophy
and certainly is not concerned with its foundations. For Kant
asks that the direction of our will be determined only by the
motives that rest on the self-legislation of the pure practical
reason. This cannot be based on a mere commonness of feeling,
but only on 'an obscure but still surely guiding practical act of
will', to clarify and strengthen which is the task of the *Critique of
Practical Reason.*

The sensus communis plays no part in Kant — not even in the
logical sense. What Kant treats in the transcendental doctrine of
judgment, ie the doctrine of schematism and the principles,[55] no
longer has anything to do with the sensus communis. For here
we have ideas which are supposed to refer to their objects a
priori, and not the subsumption of the particular under the universal. When, however, we are really concerned with the faculty
of grasping the particular as an instance of the universal and we
speak of sound understanding, then this is, according to Kant,
something that is 'common', ie 'something that one finds everywhere, but to possess which is by no means any merit or advantage'.[56] The only significance of this sound understanding
is that it is a preliminary stage of the cultivated and enlightened
reason. It is active in an obscure differentiation of judgment
which one calls feeling, but it still judges according to concepts
'as commonly only according to obscurely imagined principles'[57] and certainly cannot be considered as a special sense

of community. The general logical use of judgment, which goes back to the sensus communis, contains no principle.[58]

Thus of the whole range of what could be called a sense faculty of judgment there remains for Kant only the judgment of aesthetic taste. Here one may speak of a true sense of community. Doubtful though it may be whether one may speak of knowledge in connection with aesthetic taste, and certain though it is that aesthetic judgments are not made according to concepts, it is still the case that aesthetic taste contains the idea of univeral agreement, even if it is sensuous and not conceptual. Thus the true sense of community, says Kant, is 'taste'.

That is a paradoxical formulation when we consider how the eighteenth century enjoyed discussing precisely diversities of human taste. But even if one draws no sceptical, relativistic conclusions from differences of taste, but holds on to the idea of good taste, it sounds paradoxical to call good taste, this strange gift which distinguishes the members of a cultivated society from all other men, a sense of community. In the sense of an empirical statement that would, in fact, be absurd, and we shall see how far this description has meaning for Kant for a transcendental purpose, ie, as an a priori justification for undertaking a criticism of taste. But we shall also have to ask how the claim to truth of the sense of community is affected by limiting the concept of the sense of the community to a judgment of taste about what is-beautiful, and in what way the Kantian subjective a priori of taste has affected the self-understanding of science.

(iv) Taste

Again we must go back further in time. It is not only a question of limiting the concept of the sense of community to taste, but of limiting the concept of taste itself. The long history of this idea, before Kant made it the basis of his *Critique of Judgment,* shows that the idea of taste was originally more a moral than an aesthetic idea. It describes an ideal of genuine humanity and its character is due to the effort to take a critical stand against the dogmatism of the 'school'. It was only later that the use of the idea was limited to the aesthetic.

Balthasar Gracian[59] stands at the beginning of this history. Gracian starts from the view that the sense of taste, this most animal and most inward of our senses, still contains the beginnings of the differentiation that we make in the judgment of things. Thus the sensuous differentiation of taste, that is in the most immediate way an acceptance or rejection, is in fact not merely an instinct, but strikes the balance between sensory instinct and intellectual freedom. The sense of taste is able to gain the distance of choice and of judgment in relation to that which is the most urgent necessity of life. Thus Gracian already sees in taste a 'spiritualisation of animality' and rightly points out that there is cultivation (cultura), not only of the mind (ingenio), but also of taste (gusto). This is true also, of course, of the sense of taste. There are men who have 'a good tongue', gourmets who cultivate these delights. This idea of gusto is the starting point for Gracian's ideal of social education. His ideal of the educated man (of the discreto) is that, as an hombre en su punto, he achieves the proper freedom of distance from all the things of life and society, so that he is able to make distinctions and choices consciously and from a superior position.

This ideal of Bildung (cultivation) established by Gracian was supposed to be a completely new departure. It replaced that of the christian courtier (Castiglione). It is remarkable within the history of Western ideals of Bildung for being independent of class. It is the ideal of a society based on Bildung.[60]

This ideal of social Bildung seems to emerge everywhere in the wake of absolutism and its suppression of the hereditary aristocracy. Thus the history of the idea of taste follows the history of absolutism from Spain to France and England and is closely bound up with the antecedents of the third estate. Taste is not only the ideal created by a new society, but we see this ideal of 'good taste' producing what was subsequently called 'good society'. Its criteria are no longer birth and rank but simply the shared nature of its judgments or, rather, its capacity to rise above the narrowness of interests and private predilections to the title of judgment.

The concept of taste undoubtedly includes a mode of knowing. It is through good taste that we are capable of standing back from ourselves and our private preferences. Thus taste, in its essential nature, is not private, but a social phenomenon of the first order. It can even counter the private inclinations of the individual like a court of law, in the name of a universality that it represents. One can like something that one's own taste rejects. The verdict of taste is curiously decisive. As we say, de gustibus non disputandum (Kant rightly says that in matters of taste there can be a disagreement, but not a disputation),[61] not just because there are no general conceptual criteria that must be accepted by everyone, but because one does not look for them and would not even think it right if they existed. One must have taste—one cannot learn through demonstration, nor can one replace it by mere imitation. Nevertheless, taste is not a mere private quality, for it always desires to be good taste. The decisiveness of the judgment of taste includes its claim to validity. Good taste is always sure of its judgment, ie it is essentially sure taste, an acceptance and rejection that includes no hesitation, no surreptitious glances at others, no searching for reasons.

Taste is something like a sense. In its operation it has no knowledge of reasons. If taste registers a negative reaction to something, it is not able to say why. But it knows it with the greatest certainty. Sureness of taste is therefore safety from the tasteless. It is a remarkable thing that we are more sensitive to the negative in the operation of taste. Taste really seeks, not what is tasteful, but what does not offend it. That, above all, is what taste judges. Taste is practically defined by the fact that it is offended by what is tasteless and thus avoids it, like anything else that threatens injury. Thus the idea of 'bad taste' is not an original counter-phenomenon to 'good taste'. The opposite of the latter is to have 'no taste'. Good taste is a sensitivity which so naturally avoids anything obvious that its reaction is quite incomprehensible to someone who has no taste.

A phenomenon closely connected with taste is fashion. Here the element of social generalisation that the idea of taste contains becomes a determining reality. But the very distinction from fashion shows that the universality of taste has quite a different basis and is not the same as empirical generalness. (This is the essential point for Kant). The very word 'fashion' (Mode) implies that it is concerned with a changeable law (modus) within a constant whole of a social attitude. What is merely a matter of mode has no other norm than that given by the activity of all. Fashion regulates as it likes only those things that can equally well be one way as another. It is indeed constituted by empirical generalness, consideration for others, comparison and seeing things from the general point of view. Thus fashion creates a social dependence which it is difficult to shake off. Kant is quite right when he considers it better to be a fool in fashion than to be against fashion[62]—even if it is still folly to take fashion too seriously.

As against this, the phenomenon of taste is an intellectual faculty of differentiation. Taste operates in community, but it is not subservient to it. On the contrary, good taste is distinguished by the fact that it is able to adapt itself to the direction of taste represented by fashion or, contrariwise, is able to adapt what is demanded by fashion to its own good taste. Part of the idea of taste, then, is that one observes measure even in fashion, not following blindly its changing demands, but using one's own judgment. One holds to one's own 'style', ie one relates the demands of fashion to a whole that one's own taste keeps in view and accepts only what harmonises with this whole and fits together as it does.

Thus it is primarily a question of taste not only to recognise this or that as beautiful, but to have an eye to the whole, with which everything that is beautiful must harmonise.[63] Thus taste is not a community sense, in that it is dependent on an empirical universality, the complete unanimity of the judgments of others. It does not say that everyone will agree with our judgment, but that they should agree with it (as Kant says[64]). Against the tyranny exercised by fashion, sure taste preserves a specific freedom and superiority. This is its real normative power, which is peculiar to it alone, the knowledge that it is certain of the agreement of an ideal community. In contrast to the ruling of taste by fashion, we see here the ideality of good taste. It follows that taste makes an act of knowledge—in a manner, it is true, which cannot be separated from the concrete situation on which it operates and cannot be reduced to rules and concepts.

Just this is obviously what gives the idea of taste its original breadth, that it constitutes a special way of knowing. It belongs in the area of that which grasps in the individual object, in the manner of reflective judgment, the general category under which it is to be subsumed. Both taste and judgment are evaluations of the object in relation to a whole in order to see if it fits in with everything else, whether, then, it is 'fitting'.[65] One must have a 'sense' for it—it cannot be demonstrated.

This kind of sense is obviously needed wherever a whole is intended, but not given as a whole, that is conceived in purposive concepts. Thus taste is in no way limited to what is beautiful in nature and art, judging it in respect of its decorative quality, but embraces the whole area of morality and manners. Even the ideas of morality are never given as a whole or determined in a normative, unambiguous way. Rather the ordering of life by the rules of law and morality is incomplete and needs productive supplementation. Judgment is necessary in order to make a correct evaluation of the concrete instance. We are familiar with this function of judgment especially from jurisprudence, where the supplementary function of 'hermeneutics' consists in producing a concretisation of law.

It is always a question of something more than the correct application of general principles. Moreover, our knowledge of law and morality is always supplemented from the individual case, even productively determined by it. The judge does not only apply the law in concreto, but contributes through his very judgment to the development of the law ('judges' law'). Like law, morality is constantly developed through the fecundity of the individual case. Thus it is by no means the case that judgment is productive only in the area of nature and art as the evaluation of the beautiful and sublime. One cannot even say, with Kant,[66] that a productivity of judgment is what is 'chiefly' seen in this area. Rather, the beautiful in nature and art is to be supplemented by the whole 'ocean' of the beautiful spread throughout the moral reality of man.

It is only with the exercise of pure theoretical and practical reason that one can speak of the subsumption of the individual under a given universal (Kant's determinant judgment). But in fact even here there is an aesthetic judgment involved. This is indirectly acknowledged by Kant, inasmuch as he acknowledges the value of examples for sharpening the judgment. Admittedly he adds the limitation: "Correctness and precision of intellectual insight, on the other hand, they more usually somewhat impair. For only very seldom do they adequately fulfil the requirements of the rule (as casus in terminis)'.[67] But the other side of this qualification is obviously that the case which functions as an example is in fact something different from just a case of the rule. Hence to do real justice to it—be this merely in technical or practical judgment—always includes an aesthetic element. To this extent, the distinction between the determinant and the reflective judgment, on which Kant bases his critique of judgment, is not absolute.[68]

It is clearly not only a matter of logical, but of aesthetic judgment. The individual case on which judgment works is never simply a case; it is not exhausted by being a particular example of a general law or concept. Rather, it is always an 'individual case', and it is significant that we call it a special case, because the rule does not comprehend it. Every judgment about something that is intended to be understood in its concrete individuality, as the situations in which we have to act demand of us, is—strictly speaking—a judgment about a special case. That means simply that the evaluation of the case does not merely apply the measure of the universal principle according to which it is judged, but itself co-determines it, supplements and corrects it. From this it follows ultimately that all moral decisions require taste—not as if this most individual balancing of decision is the only thing that governs them, but it is an indispensable element. It is truly an act of undemonstrable tact to hit the target and give to the application of the universal, the moral law (Kant), a discipline, which reason itself cannot. Thus taste is not the ground, but the supreme perfection of the moral judgment. The man who finds that what is bad goes against his taste has the greatest assurance in the acceptance of the good and the rejection of the bad—as great as the assurance of the most vital of our senses which chooses or rejects food.

Thus the emergence of the concept of taste in the seventeenth century, the social and socially cohesive function of which we have indicated above, has connections with moral philosophy that go back to antiquity.

This is a humanistic and thus ultimately a Greek component at work within a moral philosophy that is determined by Christianity. Greek ethics—the ethics of measure of the Pythagoreans and Plato, the ethics of the mean (mesotes) that Aristotle developed—is in a profound and comprehensive sense an ethics of good taste.[69]

It is true that such a thesis sounds strange to our ears. For one reason, because we generally fail to recognise the ideal normative element in the concept of taste and are still affected by the relativistic-sceptical argument about differences of taste. But, above all, we are influenced by Kant's achievement in moral philosophy, which purified ethics from all aesthetics and feeling. If we now examine the importance of Kant's *Critique of Judgment* for the history of the human sciences, we must say that his giving to aesthetics a transcendental philosophical basis had major consequences and constituted a turning point. It was the end of a tradition, but also the beginning of a new development. It limited the idea of taste to an area in which, as a special principle of judgment, it could claim independent validity—and, by so doing, limited the concept of knowledge to the theoretical and practical use of reason. His transcendental purpose was fulfilled by the limited phenomenon of judgment of the beautiful (and sublime) and removed the more general experimental concept of taste and the activity of aesthetic judgment in the area of law and morality from the centre of philosophy.[70]

The importance of this cannot be easily overestimated, for what was here surrendered was that element in which literary and historical studies lived, and when they sought to set themselves up systematically under the name of 'human sciences' beside the natural sciences, it was the only possible source of their full self-understanding. Now Kant's transcendental analysis made it impossible to acknowledge the claim to truth of the tradition, to the cultivation and study of which they devoted themselves. But this meant that the unique method of the human sciences lost its justification.

What Kant sought to justify by his critique of aesthetic judgment was the subjective universality of aesthetic taste in which there is no longer any knowledge of the object, and in the area of the 'fine arts' the superiority of the genius above all rules of aesthetics. Thus romantic hermeneutics and history found a point of contact for their self-understanding only in the concept of genius stressed by Kant's aesthetics. That was the other role of Kant's influence. The transcendental justification of aesthetic judgment was the basis of the autonomy of aesthetic consciousness; in the same way historical consciousness also was to be justified. The radical subjectivisation involved in Kant's new basis for aesthetics was a completely new departure. In discrediting any kind of theoretical knowledge apart from that of natural science, it compelled the human sciences to rely on the methodology of the natural sciences in self-analysis. But it made this reliance easier by offering as a subsidiary contribution the 'artistic element', 'feeling', and 'empathy'. Helmholtz's description of the human sciences, which I considered above[71] is, in both its aspects, a good example of the Kantian influence.

If we want to show the inadequacies of this kind of self-interpretation on the part of the human sciences and open up more appropriate possibilities, we shall have to proceed with the problems of aesthetics. The transcendental function that Kant ascribes to the aesthetic judgment is sufficient to distinguish it from conceptual knowledge and hence to determine the phenomena of the beautiful and of art. But is it right to reserve the concept of truth for conceptual knowledge? Must we not also admit that the work of art possesses truth? We shall see that to acknowledge this places not only the phenomenon of art but also that of history in a new light.[72]

2 THE SUBJECTIVISATION OF AESTHETICS IN THE KANTIAN CRITIQUE

(A) KANT'S DOCTRINE OF TASTE AND GENIUS

(i) The transcendental quality of taste

Kant himself was surprised to find, in the process of investigating the foundations of taste, an a priori element which went

beyond empirical universality.[73] This insight gave birth to the
Critique of Judgment. It is no longer a mere critique of taste in
the sense in which taste is the object of critical judgment by an
observer. It is a critique of critique; that is, it is concerned with
the status of this kind of critical attitude in matters of taste. It is
no longer a mere question of empirical principles which are supposed to justify a widespread and dominant taste such as, for
example, the favourite problem of the origins of differences in
taste, but it is concerned with a genuine a priori that, in itself,
would be a total justification of the possibility of criticism.

Clearly the value of the beautiful cannot be derived and
proved from a universal principle. No one supposes that questions of taste can be decided by argument and proof. Still, it is
equally clear that good taste will never be a truly empirical universal, so that the appeal to the prevailing taste misses the real
nature of taste. We saw that it lies in its nature not to submit
blindly to popular values and to chosen models and simply imitate them. In the area of aesthetic taste the model and pattern
certainly has its proper function but, as Kant rightly says, not for
imitation, but for following.[74] The model and example encourages taste to go its own way, but it does not do the latter's job for
it. 'For taste must be an original faculty'.[75]

On the other hand our outline of the history of the concept has
shown clearly enough that in taste it is not particular preference
that decides, in the case of an aesthetic judgment, but a supra-
empirical norm is operative. We shall be able to see that Kant's
grounding of aesthetics on the judgment of taste does justice to
both aspects of the phenomenon, its empirical non-universality
and its a priori claim to universality. But the price that he pays
for this legitimation of criticism in the area of taste is that he
denies that taste has any significance as knowledge. It is a subjective principle to which he reduces sensus communis. In it
nothing is known of the objects which are judged as beautiful,
but it is stated only that a priori there is a feeling of pleasure
connected with them in the subjective consciousness. As we
know, Kant sees this feeling as based on the finality that the
representation of the object possesses for our faculty of knowledge. It is a free play of imagination and understanding, a subjective relationship that is altogether appropriate to knowledge
and that exhibits the reason for the pleasure in the object. This
appropriate, subjective relationship in fact, is in its idea the
same for all, ie it is universally communicable and thus grounds
the claim that the judgment of taste possesses universality.

This is the principle that Kant discovers in aesthetic judgment. It is its own law. Inasmuch, it is an a priori effect of the beautiful which stands halfway between a mere sensuous and empirical agreement in matters of taste and a rationalistic universal observance of a rule. Admittedly, if one takes its relationship to Lebensgefühl (lit. 'feeling of life') as its only basis, one can no longer call taste a cognitio sensitive. In it no knowledge of the object is imparted, but nor is it simply a question of a subjective reaction, as produced by what is pleasant to the senses. Taste is 'reflective'.

When Kant thus calls taste the true sensus communis,[76] he is no longer considering the great moral and political tradition of the concept of sensus communis that we outlined above. Rather, he sees this idea as comprising two elements: first, the universality of taste inasmuch as it is the result of the free play of all our cognitive powers and is not limited to a specific area like an external sense, secondly the communal quality of taste, inasmuch as, according to Kant, it abstracts from all such subjective, private conditions as attractiveness and emotion. Thus the universality of this 'sense' is negatively determined in both its aspects by that from which something is abstracted, and not positively by what grounds communicability and creates community.

Yet it is true that for Kant the old connection between taste and society remains valid. But the 'culture of taste' is treated only as an appendage in 'The Methodology of Taste'.[77] There the humaniora, as represented by the Greek model, is the sociability appropriate to humanity, and the cultivation of moral feeling is the way in which genuine taste is able to assume a definite unchangeable form.[78] Thus the definiteness of the contents of taste is not part of its transcendental function. Kant is interested only insofar as there is a special principle of aesthetic judgment, and that is why he is interested only in the pure judgment of taste.

It accords with his transcendental design that in analysing taste one can take examples of aesthetic pleasure as well from natural beauty, as from the decorative and from artistic representation. The type of object, the idea of which pleases, does not affect the essence of the aesthetic judgment. The critique of aesthetic judgment does not seek to be a philosophy of art —however much art is an object of this judgment. The concept of the 'pure aesthetic judgment of taste' is a methodological abstraction which bears no relation to the difference between nature and art. Thus it is necessary to make a more exact examination of Kant's aesthetics and relate them to the interpretations made of them in the philosophy of art, especially in relation to

the idea of genius. To this end we shall consider Kant's remarkable and much discussed doctrine of free and dependent
beauty.[79]

(ii) The doctrine of free and dependent beauty

Kant here discusses the difference between the 'pure' and the
'intellectualised' judgment of taste, which corresponds to the
contrast between 'free' beauty and that which is 'dependent' (on
an idea). This is a particularly dangerous doctrine for the understanding of art, since free natural beauty and—in the sphere of
art—the ornament appear as the beauty proper to the pure judgment of taste, since these are beauiful 'in themselves'. Wherever a concept is brought in—and that is the case not only in the
area of poetry, but in all representational art—the situation
seems the same as in the examples of 'dependent' beauty quoted
by Kant. His examples—man, animal, building—are natural
things as they occur in the world dominated by human ends, or
things that have been manufactured for human ends. With all
these things the fact that they are ordered to an end is a limitation of aesthetic pleasure. Thus Kant considers that tattooing,
decorating the human form, is objectionable, although it could
'directly' arouse pleasure. Certainly, Kant is not speaking here
of art as such (not merely of the 'beautiful representation of a
thing'), but equally much of beautiful things (of nature or architecture).

The distinction between natural and artistic beauty, which he
himself later discusses (§ 48), is not important here, but when
among the examples of free beauty apart from flowers he also
mentions a carpet with arabesque designs and music ('without a
theme' or even 'without a text'), then that is an indirect indication of all the things included as 'objects which come under a
particular concept' and hence must be included under conditional, unfree beauty: the whole realm of poetry, of the plastic
arts and of architecture, as well as all the objects of nature that
we do not look at simply in terms of their beauty like decorative
flowers. In all these cases the judgment of taste is obscured and
limited. It seems impossible to do justice to art if aesthetics is
founded in the 'pure judgment of taste'—unless the criterion of
taste is made merely a pre-condition. The introduction of the
concept of genius in the latter parts of the *Critique of Judgment*
may be thus understood. But that would mean a subsequent
shifting of emphasis. For this is not the issue to begin with. Here
(in § 16) the standpoint of taste is so far from being a mere

precondition that, rather, it claims to exhaust the nature of aesthetic judgment and protect it against any limitation by 'intellectual' criteria. And even though Kant sees that it can be the same object that is judged from the two different points of view of free and of dependent beauty, the ideal arbiter of taste nevertheless seems to be he who judges according to 'what he has present to his senses' and not according to 'what he has present to his thoughts'. True beauty is that of flowers and of ornament, which in our world, dominated by ends, present themselves immediately and of themselves as beauties and hence do not require any conscious disregarding of any concept or purpose.

If one looks a little closer, however, this conception fits neither Kant's words nor the object that he sees. The presumed shift in Kant's standpoint from taste to genius does not occur; one has only to learn to recognise the hidden preparation of the later development in the beginning. There is no doubt that those limitations that forbid a man to be tattooed or a church to be decorated with a particular ornament are not deplored by Kant, but demanded by him; Kant regards such detraction from the aesthetic pleasure as, from the moral point of view, a gain. The examples of free beauty are obviously not intended to exhibit beauty proper, but only to ensure that pleasure as such is not a judgment on the perfection of the object. And if, at the end of the section (§ 16), Kant believes that the distinction between the two kinds of beauty—or rather between two relationships to the beautiful—enables him to settle many disputes about beauty on the part of critics, still this possibility of settling disputes of taste is merely, as it were, an after-thought which requires the co-operation of the two approaches. Indeed, most commonly the two approaches will be united in accord.

This unity will always be given where 'looking to a concept' does not destroy freedom of imagination. Without contradicting himself, Kant can describe it as a legitimate condition of aesthetic pleasure that there is no conflict with purposive elements. And as the isolation of beauties which exist freely in themselves was artificial ('taste', in any case, seems to prove itself most where not only the right thing is chosen, but the right thing for the right place), one can and must go beyond the standpoint of that pure judgment of taste by saying that it is assuredly not a question of beauty when a particular concept of the understanding is illustrated schematically through the imagination, but only when imagination is in free harmony with the understanding, ie where it can be productive. But this productive construction by

imagination is not richest where it is merely free, as in the con-
volutions of the arabesque, but where it has free play in which
the understanding's desire for unity does not so much confine it
as sketch suggestions for its activity.

(iii) *The doctrine of the ideal of beauty*

The last remarks have stated more than is actually to be found in
Kant's text, but the development of his thought (§ 17) justifies
this interpretation. The balance of this section becomes apparent only after careful examination. The normative idea of beauty
which is discussed there at length is not the main thing and does
not represent the ideal of beauty towards which taste of its nature strives. There is an ideal of beauty of the human form, in the
'expression of the moral', 'without which the object could not be
universally pleasing'. Judgment according to an ideal of beauty
is then, as Kant says, not a mere judgment of taste. The important consequence of this doctrine will prove to be that something
must be more than merely tastefully pleasant in order to please
as a work of art.

Surprisingly, although we have just seen that real beauty
seemed to preclude being tied down by ideas of purpose, here
the reverse is stated of a beautiful house, a beautiful tree, a
beautiful garden etc, ie that we can imagine no ideal of these
things, 'because these ends are *not sufficiently* (my italics) determined and fixed by their concept, and consequently their finality, is almost as free as in the case of beauty that is quite at
large'. There is an ideal of beauty only of the human form,
because it alone is capable of a beauty fixed by a concept of end.
This doctrine, propounded by Winckelmann and Lessing,[80]
takes up a key position in Kant's foundation of aesthetics. And
this thesis shows clearly how little a formal aesthetic of taste
(arabesque aesthetic) corresponds to the Kantian idea.

The doctrine of the ideal of beauty is based on the difference
between the normative idea and the rational idea or ideal of
beauty. The aesthetic normative idea is found in all natural genera. The way that a beautiful animal (eg a cow: Myron) should
look is the standard by which to judge the individual example.
Thus this normative idea is a single intuition of the imagination
as 'between all singular intuitions of individuals—a floating
image for the whole genus'. But the representation of such a
normative idea does not arouse pleasure because of its beauty,
but merely 'because it does not contradict any condition under
which alone a thing belonging to this genus can be beautiful'. It
is not the ideal of beauty, but merely of correctness.

This is also true of the normative idea of the human form. But there is a true ideal of the beauty of the human form in the 'expression of the moral'. Expression of the moral: if we combine that with the later doctrine of aesthetic ideas and of beauty as the symbol of morality, then we can see that the doctrine of the ideal of beauty also prepares the way for treating the nature of art.[81] The application to art theory in the spirit of Winckelmann's classicism is obvious.[82] What Kant means is obviously that in the representation of the human form the object represented and what speaks to us in this representation as artistic meaning are one. There can be no other meaning in this representation than is already expressed in the form and appearance of what is represented. In Kantian terms, the intellectualised and interested pleasure in this represented ideal of beauty does not distract us from the aesthetic pleasure, but is rather one with it. Only in the representation of the human form does the whole meaning of the work speak to us simultaneously as the expression of its object.[83]

The nature of all art, as Hegel formulated it, is that it 'presents man with himself',[84] other natural objects—not only the human form—can express moral ideas in artistic presentation. All artistic representation, whether it is landscape, still life, even any inspired view of nature, achieves this. Here, however, Kant is right: the expression of moral value is then borrowed. Man, though, expresses these ideas in his own being, and because he is what he is. A tree that is stunted because of unfavourable conditions of growth may seem wretched to us, but this wretchedness is not an expression of the tree which feels wretched and from the point of view of the ideal of the tree to be stunted is not 'wretchedness'. The wretched man, however, measured by the human-moral ideal itself, is wretched (and not only because we demand of him an ideal of the human that is simply not valid for him, measured by which he would express wretchedness for us without being wretched). Hegel understood that perfectly in his lectures on aesthetics when he described the expression of the moral as the 'radiance of the spiritual'.[85]

Thus the formalism of 'dry pleasure' leads to the decisive break-up not only of rationalism in aesthetics, but of every universal (cosmological) doctrine of beauty. Precisely with that classicist distinction between normative idea and the ideal of beauty Kant destroys the grounds on which the aesthetics of perfection finds its unique, incomparable beauty in the complete presence to the senses of every existing thing. Only now can 'art' become an autonomous phenomenon. Its task is no longer the representation of the ideals of nature, but the self-encounter of man in

nature and in the human, historical world. Kant's demonstration
that the beautiful pleases without a concept does not gainsay the
fact that only the beautiful thing that seems significant to us
evokes our total interest. The very recognition of the non-con-
ceptuality of taste leads beyond an aesthetics of mere taste.

(iv) The concern for the beautiful in nature and in art

When Kant raises the question of the interest that is taken in the
beautiful not empirically, but a priori, this question of the interest in the beautiful as opposed to the fundamental statement
of the absence of interest in aesthetic pleasure raises a new
problem and completes the transition from the standpoint of
taste to the standpoint of genius. It is the same doctrine that is
developed in connection with both phenomena. It is important,
in establishing foundations, to free the 'critique of taste' from
sensualistic and rationalistic prejudices. It is quite in order that
here the question of the type of object being aesthetically judged
(and thus the whole question of the relation between the beauty
of nature and that of art) is not asked by Kant. But this dimension of the question is necessarily opened up if one thinks the
standpoint of taste through—which involves going beyond it.[86]
The interesting significance of the beautiful is the really operative problem in the Kantian aesthetic. It is different for nature
and art, and the comparison between the naturally and the artistically beautiful brings the problem to a head.

Here we find Kant himself.[87] As we would expect, it is not for
the sake of art that Kant goes beyond 'disinterested pleasure'
and enquires into the interest in the beautiful. From the doctrine
of the ideal of beauty we had derived one advantage of art as
against natural beauty: the advantage of being a more direct
expression of the moral. Kant, on the contrary, emphasises
primarily (§ 42) the advantage of natural over artistic beauty. It
is not only for the pure aesthetic judgment that natural beauty
has an advantage, namely to make it clear that the beautiful
depends on the consonance of the thing represented with our
cognitive faculty. This is so clearly the case with natural beauty
because it possesses no significance of content, and thus manifests the judgment of taste in its unintellectualised purity.

But it does not have only this methodological advantage; according to Kant it also has one of content, and he obviously
thinks a great deal of this point of his doctrine. Beautiful nature
is able to arouse an immediate interest, namely a moral one.
Finding the beautiful forms of nature beautiful points beyond

itself to the thought 'that nature has produced that beauty'. Where this thought arouses interest we have cultivation of the moral sensibility. While Kant, instructed by Rousseau, refuses to argue back from the refinement of taste for the beautiful in general to moral sensibility, the sense of the beauty of nature is for Kant a special case. That nature is beautiful arouses interest only in someone who 'has already developed his interest in the morally good.' Hence the interest in natural beauty is 'related to the moral sphere'. By observing the unintentional consonance of nature with our pleasure, which is independent of any interest, ie the wonderful finality of nature for us, it points to us as to the ultimate goal of creation, to our 'moral destiny'.

Here the rejection of perfection-aesthetics fits beautifully with the moral significance of natural beauty. Precisely because in nature we find no ends in themselves and yet find beauty, ie a conformity with the goal of our pleasures, nature gives us a 'sign' that we are in fact the ultimate end, the final goal of creation. The dissolution of ancient cosmological thought, which assigned man his place in the total structure of being and to each existant its goal of perfection, gives the world, which ceases to be beautiful as a structure of absolute ends, the new beauty of finality for us. It becomes 'nature', whose innocence consists in the fact that it knows nothing of man and of his social vices. Nevertheless it has something to say to us. In the light of the idea of an intelligible destiny for mankind, nature, as beautiful, finds a language that brings it to us.

Naturally the significance of art also depends on the fact that it speaks to us, that it confronts man with himself in his morally determined existence. But the products of art exist only in order to address us in this way—natural objects, however, do not exist to address us in this way. This is the significant interest of the naturally beautiful, that it is still able to make us conscious of our moral purpose. Art cannot communicate to us this self-discovery of man in unintentional reality. That man can encounter himself in art is not the confirmation of himself by another.

That is right, as far as it goes. The conclusiveness of Kant's argument is impressive, but he does not employ the appropriate criteria for the phenomenon of art. One can make a counter-argument. The advantage that natural beauty has over artistic beauty is only the other side of natural beauty's lack of specific expressive power. Thus, contrariwise, one can see the advantage of art over natural beauty in the fact that the language of art is a demanding language which does not offer itself freely and vaguely for interpretation according to one's mood, but speaks to us in a significant and definite way. And the wonderful and mysterious thing about art is that this definiteness is by no means a fetter for our mind, but in fact opens up the area in which freedom operates in the play of our mental faculties. Kant is right when he says[88] that art must be able 'to be looked at as nature', ie please without betraying the constraint of rules. We do not consider the intentional agreement of what is represented with reality we know, we do not look to see what it resembles, we do not measure its claim to significance by a criterion that we already know well, but on the contrary this criterion, the 'idea' becomes, in an unlimited way, 'aesthetically expanded'.[89]

Kant's definition of art as the 'beautiful representation of a thing'[90] takes account of this inasmuch as even the ugly is beautiful in its representation through art. Nevertheless, the actual nature of art emerges badly from the contrast with natural beauty. If the idea of a thing were presented only in a beautiful way, that would be a representation according to the rules, and would fulfil only the minimum requirement of all beauty. But for Kant art is more than the 'beautiful representation of an object': it is the presentation of aesthetic ideas, ie of something that lies beyond all concepts. The concept of the genius seeks to formulate this insight of Kant's.

It cannot be denied that the doctrine of aesthetic ideas, through whose representation the artist infinitely expands the given concept and encourages the free play of the mental faculties, has something unsatisfactory about it for a modern reader. It looks as if these ideas were being connected to the already dominant concept like the attributes of a deity to its form. The traditional superiority of the rational concept over the inexponible aesthetic representation is so strong that even with Kant there arises the false appearance of the concept preceding the aesthetic idea, where it is not at all the understanding, but the imagination that is chief among the faculties involved.[91] The aesthetician will find enough other statements in the light of which it is difficult for Kant to hold on to his leading insight into the incomprehensibility of the beautiful while at the same time preserving its compelling quality, without involuntarily claiming the superiority of the idea.

But the basic lines of his thinking are free from these faults and are of an impressive logicality, which reaches its climax in the function of the concept of genius in the account of the basis of art. Even without going into a more detailed interpretation of this 'capacity to represent aesthetic ideas', it may be indicated that Kant here is not deflected from his concern with transcendental philosophy and pushed into the cul-de-sac of a psychology of artistic creation. Rather, the irrationality of genius brings out an element of productive creation, shown both in creator and recipient, namely that there is no other way of laying hold of the meaning of a work of art than in the unique form of the work and in the mystery of its impression which can never be fully expressed by any language. Hence the concept of the genius corresponds to what Kant sees as the crucial thing about aesthetic taste, namely the playful facility of one's mental powers, the expansion of vitality which comes from the harmony between imagination and understanding, and invites one to linger before the beautiful. Genius is a manifestation of this vivifying spirit for, as opposed to the pedant's rigid adherence to rules, genius shows the free sweep of invention and thus an originality which creates new models.

(v) The relation between taste and genius

In this situation the question arises of how Kant sees the mutual relation between taste and genius. Kant preserves for taste its privileged position, inasmuch as the works of art that are the art of genius stand under the guiding aspect of beauty. One may find the subsequent improvements to the invention of genius that are required by taste regrettable, but taste is the necessary discipline that genius needs. Thus, in cases of conflict, Kant considers that taste should prevail. But this is not an important question for, basically, taste has common ground with genius. The art of genius is to make the free play of the mental faculties communicable. This is achieved by the aesthetic ideas that it invents. But communicability of a state of mind, of pleasure, was characteristic of the aesthetic pleasure of taste. It is a faculty of judgment, ie a reflective taste, but what it reflects about is that state of mind which is the stimulation of the cognitive powers, which is given by both natural and artistic beauty. Thus the systematic significance of the concept of genius is limited to the particular case of the artistically beautiful, whereas the concept of taste is universal.

That Kant makes the concept of genius serve his transcendental concern completely and does not slip into empirical psychology is clearly shown by his limiting the concept of genius to artistic creation. If he withholds this name from the great inventors and investigators in the spheres of science and technology,[92] this is, seen in terms of empirical psychology, quite unfair. Wherever one must 'come upon something' that cannot be found through learning and methodical work alone, ie wherever there is inventio, where something is due to inspiration and not to methodical calculation, the important thing is ingenium, genius. And yet Kant's intention is correct: only the work of art is naturally so determined that it can be created only by genius. It is only with the artist that the 'invention'—the work—remains, according to its very nature, related to the spirit—the spirit that creates as well as the one that judges and enjoys. Only there can inventions not be imitated, and hence it is right when Kant speaks (only here) of genius—from a transcendental point of view—and defines art as the art of genius. All other achievements and inventions of genius, however much genius there may be in the invention, are not determined in their essence by it.

I maintain that for Kant the concept of genius was really only a complement to what was of interest to him 'for transcendental reasons' in aesthetic judgment. We should not forget that the second part of the *Critique of Judgment* is concerned only with nature (and with its being judged by concepts of finality) and not at all with art. Thus for the systematic intention of the whole, the application of aesthetic judgment to the beautiful and sublime in nature is more important than the transcendental foundation of art. The 'finality of nature for our cognitive faculties' which, as we have seen, is possible only in the case of natural beauty (and not of art) has, as the transcendental principle of aesthetic judgment, at the same time the function of preparing the understanding for applying the concept of finality to nature.[93] Thus the critique of taste, ie aesthetics, is a preparation for teleology. It is Kant's philosophical intention to legitimate teleology, whose constitutive claim in the knowledge of nature had been destroyed by the *Critique of Pure Reason,* as a principle of judgment—an intention which brings the whole of his philosophy to a systematic conclusion. Judgment provides the bridge between understanding and reason. The intelligible towards which taste points, the supersensible substrate in man, contains at the same time the mediation between concepts of nature and concepts of freedom.[94] This is the systematic significance that the problem of natural beauty has for Kant: it grounds the central position of teleology. It alone, not art, can assist the legitimation of the concept of finality for the judgment of nature. For this systematic reason alone the 'pure' judgment of taste provides the essential basis of the third *Critique.*

But even within the critique of aesthetic judgment there is no question of the position of genius ousting that of taste. One has only to look at how Kant describes the genius; the genius is a favourite of nature—just as natural beauty is looked on as a favour of nature. We must be able to look at art as if it were nature. Through genius, nature gives art its rules. In all these phrases[95] the concept of nature is the uncontested criterion.

Thus what the concept of genius achieves is only to place the products of art aesthetically on the same level as natural beauty. Art also is looked at aesthetically, ie it also is a case for reflective judgment. What is intentionally produced, and hence purposive, is not to be related to an idea, but seeks to please in being simply judged—just like natural beauty. 'Art is art created by genius' means that for artistic beauty also there is no other principle of judgment, no criterion of concept and knowledge than that of its finality for the feeling of freedom in the play of our cognitive faculties. Beauty in nature or art [96] has the same a priori principle, which lies entirely within subjectivity. The autonomy of aesthetic judgment does not mean that there is an autonomous sphere of validity for beautiful objects. Kant's transcendental reflection on the a priori of judgment justifies the claim of the aesthetic judgment, but basically it does not permit a philosophical aesthetics in the sense of a philosophy of art (Kant himself says that no doctrine or metaphysics here corresponded to the critique).[97]

(B) THE AESTHETICS OF GENIUS AND THE CONCEPT OF EXPERIENCE

(i) The dominance of the idea of genius

The basing of aesthetic judgment on an a priori of subjectivity was to acquire a quite new significance when the significance of transcendental philosophical reflection changed with Kant's successors. If the metaphysical background which is the basis of the superiority of natural beauty in Kant, and, which ties the concept of genius back to nature, no longer exists, the problem of art is raised in a new way. Even the way in which Schiller took up Kant's *Critique of Judgment* and put the whole weight of his moral and pedagogic temperament behind the idea of an 'aesthetic education', gave art—rather than taste and judgment, as with Kant—pride of place.

From the standpoint of art the relationship of the Kantian ideas of taste and genius is basically changed. It was genius which had to become the more comprehensive idea and, contrariwise, the phenomenon of taste had to be devalued.

Now, even in Kant himself, there is some justification for this

CANISIUS COLLEGE LIBRARY
BUFFALO, N. Y.

reversal of values. According to Kant also it is of some significance for the judging faculty of taste that art is the creation of
genius. One of the things that taste judges is whether a work of
art has soul or whether it is soulless. Kant says of artistic beauty
that 'in the judgment of such an object the possibility of this
—and hence of genius in it—must be considered',[98] and in
another place makes the obvious point that without genius not
only art, but also a correct, independent taste to judge it, is not
possible.[99] Therefore the standpoint of taste, inasmuch as this is
practised on its most important object, art, passes inevitably into
that of genius. Genius in understanding corresponds to genius in
creation. Kant does not express it in this way, but the concept of
soul that he uses here[100] is equally valid for both aspects. That is
the basis on which more must be built later.

It is in fact clear that the concept of taste loses its significance
if the phenomenon of art steps into the foreground. The standpoint of taste is secondary to the work of art. The sensitivity in
selection that is its nature often has a levelling function when
compared with the originality of the artistic work of genius.
Taste avoids the unusual and the monstrous. It is concerned
with the surface of things, it does not involve itself with what is
original about an artistic production. Even in the rise of the idea
of genius in the eighteenth century we find a polemical edge
against the idea of taste. It was directed against classicist aesthetics with the demand that the ideal of taste of French classicism
should find room for Shakespeare (Lessing). Kant is to this extent old-fashioned and adopts an intermediate position inasmuch
as he held, for his transcendental purposes, to the concept of
taste which the Sturm und Drang not only violently dismissed,
but also violently demolished.

But when Kant passes from this general laying of the foundations to the specific problems of the philosophy of art, he himself
points beyond the standpoint of taste, and speaks of the idea of a
perfection of taste.[101] But what is that? The normative character
of taste includes the possibility of its formation and perfecting.
Perfect taste, which it is important to achieve, will assume, according to Kant, a definite unchangeable form. That is quite
logical, however absurd it may sound to our ears. For if taste is
to be good taste, this puts paid to the whole relativism of taste
presumed by aesthetic scepticism. It would embrace all works of
art that have 'quality', so certainly all those that are created by
genius.

Thus we see that the idea of perfect taste which Kant discusses would be more appropriately defined by the idea of genius.
Obviously it would be impossible to apply the idea of perfect

taste within the sphere of natural beauty. It might be acceptable in the case of horticulture, but Kant has logically assigned horticulture to the sphere of the artistically beautiful.[102] But confronted with natural beauty, say, the beauty of a landscape, the idea of a perfect taste is quite out of place. Would it consist in giving a proper value to everything that is beautiful in nature? Can there be a selection in this sphere? Is there an order of merit? Is a sunny landscape more beautiful than one shrouded in rain? Is there anything ugly in nature? Or only variously attractive in various moods, differently pleasing for different tastes? Kant may be right when he considers it an important moral consideration whether or not nature can be pleasing to a person. But has it any meaning to distinguish between good and bad taste in relation to it? Where, however, this distinction is beyond question, namely in relation to art and what has been created by man, taste is, as we have seen, only a limiting condition of the beautiful and does not contain its principle. Thus the idea of a perfect taste in relation to nature as well as to art is dubious. One does violence to the concept of taste if one does not include in it its variability. If it is anything, taste is a testimony to the changeableness of all human things and the relativity of all human values.

Kant's grounding of his aesthetics on the concept of taste is not wholly satisfactory. It seems much more appropriate to use the concept of genius, that Kant develops as a transcendental principle for artistic beauty, as a universal aesthetic principle. For it fulfils much better than does the concept of taste the requirement of being changeless in the stream of time. The miracle of art—that mysterious perfection possessed by successful artistic creations—is visible throughout all ages. It seems possible to subordinate the idea of taste to the transcendental account of the basis of art and to understand by taste the sure sense for artistic genius. The Kantian statement 'Fine art is the art of genius' then becomes a transcendental principle for aesthetics. Aesthetics is ultimately possible only as the philosophy of art.

German idealism drew this conclusion. Fichte and Schelling, who followed Kant's doctrine of transcendental imagination in other respects also, made new use of this idea in their aesthetics. Unlike Kant they considered the standpoint of art, as that of the unconscious production of genius, all-embracing, embracing even nature, which is understood as a product of the spirit.[103]

But now the basis of aesthetics has shifted. Like the concept of taste the concept of natural beauty is also devalued, or differently understood. The moral interest in natural beauty that Kant had so enthusiastically described now retreats behind the self-encounter of man in works of art. In Hegel's magnificent aesthetics natural beauty exists only as a 'reflection of the spirit'. There is in fact no longer any independent element in the systematic whole of aesthetics.[104]

Obviously the indefiniteness with which beautiful nature presents itself to the interpreting and understanding spirit allows us to agree with Hegel that 'its substance (is) contained in the spirit'.[105] Hegel draws here, aesthetically speaking, an absolutely correct inference to which I came close in the foregoing when I spoke of the inappropriateness of the application of the idea of taste to nature. For a verdict on the beauty of a landscape undoubtedly depends on the artistic taste of the time. One has only to think of the description of the ugliness of Alpine landscape which we still find in the eighteenth century—the effect, as we know, of the spirit of artificial symmetry that dominates the century of absolutism. Thus Hegel's aesthetics is based squarely on the standpoint of art. In art man encounters himself, spirit meets spirit.

For the development of modern aesthetics it is important to bear in mind that here also, as in the whole sphere of systematic philosophy, speculative idealism has had an effect which greatly exceeds its recognised importance. The violent rejection of the dogmatic schematism of the Hegelian school in the middle of the nineteenth century led to the demand for a renewal of criticism under the banner of 'back to Kant'. That was equally true of aesthetics. However brilliantly art was used for history of world-views like that given by Hegel in his aesthetics, this method of a priori history writing which was used a lot in the Hegelian school (Rosenkranz, Schosler etc) was quickly discredited. The demand for a return to Kant, which arose in opposition to this could not now, however, be a real return and a recovery of the horizon of Kant's critiques. Rather, the phenomenon of art and the concept of the genius remained at the centre of aesthetics; the problem of natural beauty and the concept of taste were more peripheral.

This is seen in linguistic usage as well. Kant's limitation of the concept of genius to the artist (which I have examined above), did not prevail; on the contrary, in the nineteenth century the concept of genius was elevated to become a universal concept of value and—together with the idea of the creative—achieved a true apotheosis. It was the romantic and idealistic concept of unconscious production which lay behind this development and acquired, through Schopenhauer and the philosophy of the unconscious, enormous popular influence. I have shown that this kind of systematic predominance of the concept of genius over the concept of taste is not Kantian. Kant's main concern, however, which was to give aesthetics an autonomous basis freed from the criterion of the concept, and not to raise the question of truth in the sphere of art, but to base aesthetic judgment on the subjective a priori of our feeling of life, the harmony of our capacity for 'knowledge in general', which is the essence of both taste and genius, was in accord with the irrationalism and the cult of genius in the nineteenth century. Kant's theory of the 'heightening of the feeling of life' in aesthetic pleasure helped the idea of 'genius' to develop into a comprehensive concept of life, especially after Fichte had elevated the position of genius, and of what genius created, to a universal transcendental position. Hence, by trying to derive all objective validity from transcendental subjectivity, neo-Kantianism declared the concept of experience to be the very stuff of consciousness.[106]

(ii) On the history of the word Erlebnis (experience)

It is surprising to find that, unlike Erleben, the word Erlebnis became common only in the 1870s. In the eighteenth century it is not found at all, and even Schiller and Goethe do not know it.[107] Its first appearance, seemingly, is in one of Hegel's letters.[108] But even in the thirties and forties I know of only occasional instances (in Tieck, Alexis and Gutzkow). The word appears equally seldom in the fifties and sixties and appears suddenly with some frequency in the seventies. The word comes into general use at the same time as it begins to be used in biographical writing.[109]

Since it is a secondary formation from the word erleben, which is older and appears often in the age of Goethe, we must find the reason for the new word by analysing the meaning of (to experience) erleben. Erleben means primarily 'to be still alive when something happens'. From this the word has a note of the immediacy with which something real is grasped—unlike something of which one presumes to know, but the confirmation of which through one's own experience is lacking, whether it is taken over from others or comes from hearsay, or whether it is worked out, surmised or imagined. What is experienced is always what one has experienced oneself.

But at the same time the form das Erlebte is used to mean the permanent content of what is experienced. This content is like a yield or a residue that acquires permanence, weight and significance from out of the transience of experiencing. Both meanings obviously lie behind the form Erlebnis; both the immediacy, which precedes all interpretation, treatment, or communication, and merely offers a starting point for interpretation and material for working, as well as its discovered yield, its lasting residue.

It is in accord with this double meaning of the word erleben that it is biographical literature through which the word Erlebnis takes root. The essence of biography, especially the nine-teenth-century biographies of artists and poets, is to understand the works from the life. Their achievement consists precisely in communicating the two meanings that we have distinguished in 'experience' and in seeing these meanings as a productive union: something became an 'experience' inasmuch as it is not only experienced, but inasmuch as its being experienced has a particular emphasis that gives it lasting importance. An 'ex-perience' of this kind gains a wholly new quality of being in artistic expression. Dilthey's famous title *Das Erlebnis und die Dichtung (Experience and Poetry)* succinctly formulates the as-sociation. In fact, Dilthey was the first to give a conceptual function to the word that was soon to become so popular and so closely connected with such an obvious value that many Euro-pean languages took it over as a loan word. But it is reasonable to assume that what actually happened in the life of the language was simply underlined in Dilthey's use of the term.

With Dilthey we are able to isolate with some ease the diverse elements operative in the linguistically and conceptually new form of the word Erlebnis. The title *Das Erlebnis und die Dich-tung* is late enough (1905). The first version of the essay on Goethe it contains, which Dilthey first published in 1877, cer-tainly has some examples of the word Erlebnis, but nothing of the later terminological definiteness of the concept. It is worth investigating more exactly the earlier forms of the later, concep-tually established meaning of Erlebnis. It seems more than mere chance that it is in a biography of Goethe (and in an essay on this) that the word suddenly appears with any frequency. Goethe more than anyone else tempts one to invent this word, since his poetry acquires a new kind of intelligibility from what he experienced. He said himself that all his poetry had the character of a great confession.[110] Hermann Grimm's biography of Goethe follows this *und die Dichtung.* In this essay Dilthey compares Goethe with Rousseau, and in order to describe the new kind of writing which Rousseau based on the world of his inner experiences, he employs the expression das Erleben. In the paraphrase of Rousseau we also find the expression die Erlebnisse früher Tage[112] ('the experiences of early days').

However, even in the early Dilthey the meaning of the word Erlebnis is still rather uncertain. That is shown clearly by a pas-

sage from which Dilthey cut the word Erlebnis in later editions.
'According to what he experienced and in accordance with
his ignorance of the world, put together as experience (Erlebnis)
our of his imagination'.[113] Again he is speaking of Rousseau.
But an imaginary experience does not fit the original meaning
of erleben, not even Dilthey's own later technical usage, in
which Erlebnis means what is directly given, the ultimate material for all imaginative forming.[114] The coined word Erlebnis, of
course, expresses the criticism of the rationalism of the enlightenment which, following Rousseau, emphasised the concept of
life (Leben). It was probably Rousseau's influence on German
classicism which introduced the criterion of Erlebtsein (being
experienced) and hence made possible the formation of the word
Erlebnis.[115] But the concept of life is also the metaphysical
background for the speculative thought of German idealism, and
plays a fundamental role in Fichte, Hegel and even Schleiermacher. As against the abstraction of the understanding and the
particularity of perception or representation, this concept implies the connection with totality, with infinity. This is clearly
audible in the tone which the word Erlebnis has even today.

Schleiermacher's appeal to living feeling against the cold
rationalism of the enlightenment, Schiller's call for aesthetic
freedom against mechanistic society, Hegel's contrasting of life
(later, of spirit) with 'positivity', were the forerunners of the
protest against modern industrial society which at the beginning
of our century caused the words Erlebnis and Erleben to become
almost sacred clarion calls. The rebellion of the Jugend Bewegung (Youth Movement) against bourgeois culture and its
forms was inspired by these ideas, the influence of Friedrich
Nietzche and Henry Bergson played its part, but also a 'spiritual
movement' like that around Stefan George and, not least, the
seismographical accuracy with which the philosophy of Georg
Simmel reacted to these events are all part of the same thing.
The life philosophy of our own day follows on its romantic predecessors. The rejection of the mechanisation of life in contemporary society puts such an obvious emphasis on the word that
its conceptual implications remain totally hidden.[116]

Thus we must understand Dilthey's coining of the concept in
the light of the previous history of the word among the romantics
and remember that Dilthey was Schleiermacher's biographer. It
is true that we do not yet find the word Erlebnis in Schleiermacher, not even, apparently, the word Erleben. But there is no
lack of synonyms that cover the range of meaning of Erlebnis,[117]
and the pantheistic background is always clearly in evidence.

Every act, as an element of life, remains connected with the infinity of life that manifests itself in it. Everything finite is an expression, a representation of the infinite.

In fact we find in Dilthey's biography of Schleiermacher, in the description of religious contemplation, a particularly pregnant use of the word Erlebnis, which supports the conception: 'Each one of his experiences (Erlebnisse) existing by itself is a separate picture of the universe taken out of the explanatory context'.[118]

(iii) The concept of Erlebnis

Having considered the history of the word let us now examine the history of the concept Erlebnis. We know from the foregoing that Dilthey's concept of Erlebnis clearly contains two elements, the pantheistic and the positivist, the experience (Erlebnis) and still more its result (Ergebnis). This is not an accident, but a result of his own intermediate position between speculation and empiricism, which we shall have to consider later. Since he is concerned to give an epistemological justification to the work of the human sciences, he is dominated throughout by the question of what is truly given. Thus his concepts are motivated by this epistomological purpose or rather by the requirements of epistemology itself—a purpose which is reflected in the linguistic process which was analysed above. Just as the remoteness from experience and the hunger for experience, which come from the distress caused by the complicated workings of civilisation transformed by the industrial revolution, brought the word Erlebnis into general usage, so the new distanced attitude that historical consciousness takes to tradition, gives to the concept of Erlebnis its epistemological function. This characterises the development of the human sciences in the nineteenth century that they not only acknowledge the natural sciences as a model in an external way, but that, coming from the same background as modern science, they develop the same feeling for experiment and research. If the alienation which the age of mechanics felt from nature as the natural world was expressed epistemologically in the concept of self-consciousness and in the rule of certainty, developed into a method of 'clear and distinct perception', the human sciences of the nineteenth century felt a similar alienation from the world of history. The intellectual creations of the past, art and history, are no longer automatically part of the present, but are objects of research, data from which a past can be made present. Thus the concept of the given is important also for Dilthey's construction of the concept of experience.

The given in the sphere of the human sciences is of a special kind, and Dilthey seeks to formulate this with his concept of 'experience'. Following Descartes' formulation of the res cogitans he defines the idea of experience by reflexivity, by interiority, and from this particular mode of being given he seeks to give an epistemological justification of the knowledge of the world of history. The primary data, to which the interpretation of historical objects goes back, are not data of experiment and measurement, but units of meaning. That is what the concept of experience states: the structures of meaning which we meet in the human sciences, however strange and incomprehensible they may seem to us, can be reduced to ultimate units of what is given in consciousness, unities which themselves no longer contain anything, alien, objective, in need of interpretation. These are units of experience that are themselves units of significance.

We shall see how crucial it is for Dilthey's thought that the ultimate unit of consciousness is not named 'sensation', as was automatic in Kantianism and in the positivist epistemology of the nineteenth century up to Ernst Mach, but 'experience'. Thus he limits the constructive ideal of a building up of knowledge from atoms of sensation and offers instead a more sharply defined version of the concept of the given. The unit of experience (and not the psychic elements into which it can be analysed) represents the true unit of what is given. Thus in the epistemology of the human sciences we see an idea of life which restricts the mechanistic model.

This concept of life is conceived teleologically; life, for Dilthey, is productivity. As life objectifies itself in structures of meaning, all understanding of meaning is 'a translating back of the objectivations of life into the spiritual livingness from which they emerged'. Thus the concept of experience is the epistemological basis for all knowledge of the objective.

The epistemological function that the concept of experience has in Husserl's phenomenology is equally universal. In the fifth logical investigation (chapter 2) the phenomenological concept of experience is expressly distinguished from the popular one. The unit of experience is not understood as a piece of the actual flow of experience of an 'I', but as our intentional relation. The sense unit 'experience' is teleological here too. Experiences exist only insofar as something is experienced and meant in them. It is true that Husserl also recognises non-intentional experiences, but these pass, as material elements, into the sense unit of intentional experiences. Thus for Husserl the idea of experience becomes the comprehensive name for all acts of consciousness whose essence is intentionality.[119]

Thus both in Dilthey and in Husserl, both in life-philosophy and in phenomenology, the idea of experience is primarily a purely epistemological one. It is used by them in its teleological meaning, but is not conceptually determined. That it is life that manifests itself in experience means only that it is the ultimate to which we come back. The history of the word provided a certain justification for this conceptual construction of performance. For we have seen that the word 'experience' has a condensing, intensifying meaning. If something is called or considered an experience its meaning rounds it into the unity of a significant whole. An experience is as much distinguished from other experiences—in which other things are experienced—as from the rest of life in which 'nothing' is experienced. An experience is no longer just something that flows past quickly in the stream of the life of consciousness—it is meant as a unity and thus attains a new mode of being one. Thus it is quite understandable that the word emerges in biographical literature and ultimately stems from its use in autobiography. What can be called an experience establishes itself in memory. We mean the lasting meaning that an experience has for someone who has had it. This is the reason for talking about an intentional experience and the teleological structure of consciousness. On the other hand, however, in the notion of experience there is also a contrast of life with mere concept. The experience has a definite immediacy which eludes every opinion about its meaning. Everything that is experienced is experienced by oneself, and it is part of its meaning that it belongs to the unity of this self and thus contains an inalienable and irreplaceable relation to the whole of this one life. Thus its being is not exhausted in what can be said of it and in what can be grasped as its meaning. The autobiographical or biographical reflection, in which its meaning is determined, remains fused with the whole movement of life and constantly, accompanies it. It is practically the mode of being of experience to be so determinative that one is never finished with it. Nietzsche says 'all experiences last a long time in profound men'.[120] He means that they are not soon forgotten, it takes a long time to assimilate them, and this is their real being and significance, rather than the original content as such. What we emphatically call an experience thus means something unforgettable and irreplaceable that is inexhaustible in terms of the understanding and determination of its meaning.[121]

Seen philosophically, the ambiguity that we have noted in the concept of experience means that this concept is not wholly exhausted by its role of being the ultimate giveness and basis of all knowledge. There is something else quite different in the idea of 'experience' that needs to be recognised and reveals a set of problems that have still to be dealt with: its inner relation to life.[122]

There were two starting points for this more widely ramified theme concerning the relationship between life and experience, and we shall see subsequently how Dilthey, and more especially Husserl, became caught up in the problems. Here we see the crucial importance of Kant's critique of any substantial doctrine of the soul and, different from it, of the transcendental unity of self-consciousness, the synthetic unity of apperception. This critique of rationalist psychology gave rise to the idea of a psychology according to critical method, such as Paul Natorp undertook in 1888[123] and on which Richard Hönigswald later based the concept of Denkpsychologie.[124] Natorp saw the object of critical psychology as the awareness which the immediacy of experience reveals and developed the method of a universal subjectivisation as the mode of research of reconstructive psychology. Natorp later supported and further elaborated his basic idea by a thorough criticism of the terminology of contemporary psychological research, but as early as 1888 the basic idea was there that the concreteness of the original experience, ie the totality of consciousness, represents an undifferentiated unity that is differentiated and determined by the objectivising method of knowledge. 'But consciousness means life, ie a thoroughgoing reciprocal relationship'. This is seen particularly in the relationships between consciousness and time: 'Consciousness is not given as an event in time, but time as the form of consciousness'.[125]

In the same year, 1888, in which Natorp thus opposed the dominant trend of psychology, Henri Bergson's first book appeared, *Les données immédiates de la conscience,* a critical attack on the contemporary psychophysics, which, just as firmly as Natorp, used the idea of life against the objectivising and spatialising tendency of psychological terminology. Here we find totally similar statements about 'consciousness' and its undivided concretion as in Natorp. Bergson coined for it the now famous name durée, which expresses the absolute continuity of the psychic. Bergson understands this as 'organisation', ie he defines it from the mode of being of life (etre vivant), in which every element is representative of the whole (représentatif du tout). He compares the inner penetration of all elements in the consciousness with the way in which in listening to the melody all the notes intermingle. For Bergson it is also the anti-Cartesian element of the concept of life that he defends against objectivising science.[126]

If one examines more precisely what is here called 'life' and what part of it is active in the concept of experience we see that the relationship of life to experience is not that of a universal to a particular. Rather, the unity of experience determined by its intentional content stands in an immediate relationship to the whole, to the totality of life. Bergson speaks of the representation of the whole, and similarly Natorp's concept of reciprocal relationship is an expression of the 'organic' relationship of part and whole that takes place here. It was primarily Georg Simmel who analysed the idea of life in this aspect as the 'reaching out of life beyond itself'.[127]

The representation of the whole in the experience of the moment obviously goes far beyond the fact of its being determined by its object. Every experience is, in Schleiermacher's words, 'an element of eternal life'.[128] Georg Simmel, who was largely responsible for the word Erlebnis becoming so fashionable, sees the important thing about the concept of experience as being 'that the objective does not only become, as in knowing, an image and idea, but an element in the life process itself'.[129] He even says that every experience has something about it of adventure.[130] But what is an adventure? An adventure is by no means just an episode. Episodes are a succession of details which have no inner coherence and for that very reason have no permanent significance. An adventure, however, interrupts the customary course of events, but is positively and significantly related to the context which it interrupts. Thus an adventure lets life become felt as a whole, in its breadth and in its strength. Here lies the fascination of an adventure. It removes the conditions and obligations of everyday life. It ventures out into the uncertain.

But at the same time it knows that, as an adventure, it has an exceptional character and thus remains related to the return of the everyday, into which the adventure cannot be taken. Thus the adventure is 'passed through', like a test, from which one emerges enriched and more mature.

There is an element of this, in fact, in every experience. Every experience is taken out of the continuity of life and at the same time related to the whole of one's life. It is not simply that it remains a living experience only until it is fully integrated into the context of one's life-consciousness, but the very way in which it is 'preserved' through its being worked into the whole of life-consciousness, goes far beyond any 'significance' it might be thought to have. Because it is itself within the whole of life, in it too the whole of life is present.

Thus at the end of our conceptual analysis of experience we can see what affinity there exists between the structure of experience as such and the mode of being of the aesthetic. The aesthetic experience is not just one kind of experience among others, but represents the essence of experience itself. As the work of art as such is a world for itself, what is experienced aesthetically is, as an experience, removed from all connections with actuality. The work of art would seem almost by definition to become an aesthetic experience: that means, however, that it suddenly takes the person experiencing it out of the context of his life, by the power of the work of art, and yet relates him back to the whole of his existence. In the experience of art there is present a fullness of meaning which belongs not only to this particular content or object but rather stands for the meaningful whole of life. An aesthetic experience always contains the experience of an infinite whole. Precisely because it does not combine with others to make one open experiential flow, but immediately represents the whole, its significance is infinite.

Inasmuch as the aesthetic experience, as was said above, is an exemplary instance of the meaning of the concept experience, it is clear that the concept of experience is a determining feature of the foundations of art. The work of art is understood as the perfecting of the symbolic representation of life, towards which every experience tends. Hence it is itself marked out as the object of aesthetic experience. For aesthetics the conclusion follows that so called Erlebniskunst (the art of experience) appears as the true art.

(iv) The limits of the art of experience and the rehabilitation of allegory

The concept of Erlebniskunst contains an important ambiguity. Erlebniskunst obviously meant originally that art comes from experience and is an expression of experience. But in a derived sense the concept of Erlebniskunst is then used for art that is intended for the aesthetic experience. Both are obviously connected. The significance of that, the being of which is to be the expression of an experience, cannot be grasped except through an experience.

The concept of Erlebniskunst is, as always in such a case, conditioned by the experience of the limits set to it. Only when it is no longer self-evident that a work of art is the transformation of experiences, and when it is no longer self-evident that this transformation is due to the experience of an inspiration of genius which, with the assuredness of a somnambulist, creates the work of art, which then becomes an experience for the man exposed to it, does the concept of Erlebniskunst become clear in its outline. The period of Goethe seems remarkable to us for the self-evidence of these assumptions, a period that is a whole age, an epoch. Only because it is, for us, self-contained, and because we can see beyond it are we able to see it within its own limits and have a concept of it.

Slowly we realise that this period is only an episode in the total history of art and literature. Curtius's excellent work on mediaeval literary aesthetics gives us a good idea of this.[131] If we start to look beyond the limits of Erlebniskunst and have recourse to other criteria, new areas open up within European art which from the classical period up to the age of the baroque was dominated by quite other standards of value than that of having been experienced. Strange artistic worlds are revealed to our gaze.

Undoubtedly, all this can become an 'experience' for us. This aesthetic self-understanding is always available. But it cannot be denied that the work of art itself, which becomes an experience for us in this way, was not meant to be understood thus. Genius and being experienced, our criteria of value, are not adequate here. We may also remember quite different criteria and say, for example, that it is not the genuineness of the experience or of the intensity of its expression, but the ingenious manipulation of fixed forms and modes of statement which makes the work of art a work of art. This difference in criteria is true of all kinds of art, but is particularly notable in the literary arts.[132] As late as the eighteenth century we find poetry and rhetoric side by side in a way that is surprising to modern consciousness. Kant sees in both 'a free play of the imagination and a serious business of the understanding'.[133] Both poetry and rhetoric are for him fine arts and are 'free', insofar as the harmony of both kinds of knowledge, that of the senses and that of the understanding, undesignedly succeeds in both. Against this tradition the criterion of being experienced and of the inspiration of genius inevitably introduced a quite different idea of 'free' art, to which poetry belongs only inasmuch as everything transient is removed from it, and from which rhetoric is totally removed.

Thus the decline in the value of rhetoric in the nineteenth century is the inevitable consequence of the application of the doctrine of the unconscious creation of genius. We shall pursue one particular example of this: the history of the concepts of symbol and allegory, the relation between which changes in the modern period.

Even scholars who are interested in linguistic history often fail to take sufficient account of the fact that the aesthetic contrast between allegory and symbol—which seems self-evident to us—is only the result of the philosophical development of the last two centuries, and can be so little expected before then that the question to be asked is rather how the need for this distinction and opposition arose. It is clear that Winckelmann, whose influence on the aesthetics and philosophy of history of the time was very great, used both concepts synonymously and the same is true of the whole of the aesthetic literature of the eighteenth century. The meanings of the two words have in fact something in common. Both words refer to something whose meaning does not consist in its external appearance or sound, but in a significance that lies beyond it. Their common quality is that, in both, one thing stands for another. This meaningful relatedness through which the non-sensuous is made apparent to the senses is found as well in the field of poetry and the plastic arts as in that of the religious and sacramental.

It would need a more exact investigation to discover to what extent the classical use of the words 'symbol' and 'allegory' prepared the later contrast between the two with which we are familiar. Here only a few basic lines can be laid down. Of course the two ideas originally had nothing to do with each other. Allegory originally belonged to the sphere of talk, of the logos, and is therefore a rhetorical or hermeneutical figure. Instead of what is actually meant, something else, more tangible, is said, but in such a way as to suggest the other.[134] Symbol, however, is not limited to the sphere of the logos, for a symbol is not related by its meaning to another meaning, but its own sensuous nature has 'meaning'. It is something which is shown and enables one to recognise something else. Obviously a symbol is something which has validity not only because of its content, but because it can be 'produced', ie because it is a document,[135] by means of which the members of a community recognise one another: whether it is a religious symbol or appears in a secular context, as a badge or a pass or a pass-word—in every case the meaning of the symbolon depends on its physical presence and acquires its representative function only through the fact of its being shown or spoken.

Although the two concepts allegory and symbol belong to different spheres they are close to one another, not only because of their common structure of representation of one thing by another, but also because they both find their chief application in the religious sphere. Allegory arises from the theological need to eliminate undesirable material from a religious tradition —originally from Homer—and to recognise valid truths behind it. It acquires an equivalent function in rhetoric wherever circumlocution and indirect statement appear more appropriate. The concept of symbol now approaches this rhetorical-hermeneutical concept of allegory (symbol, in the sense of allegory, seems to appear for the first time in Chrysippus[136]), especially through the christian transformation of neoplatonism. Pseudo-Denys, at the very beginning of his magnum opus defends the necessity to proceed symbolically (symbolikos) by referring to the incommensurability of the suprasensual being of God with our minds, accustomed to the world of the senses. Thus symbolon here acquires an anagogic function;[137] it leads up to the knowledge of the divine—just as allegorical speech leads to a 'higher' meaning. The allegorical procedure of interpretation and the symbolical procedure of knowledge have the same justification: it is not possible to know the divine in any other way than by starting from the world of the senses.

But there is a metaphysical background to the concept of symbol which is entirely lacking in the rhetorical use of allegory. It is possible to be led up from the sensible to the divine. For the world of the senses is not mere nothingness and darkness but the outflowing and reflection of truth. The modern concept of symbol cannot be understood without this gnostic function and its metaphysical background. The only reason that the word 'symbol' can be raised from its original application as a document, sign or pass, to the philosophical idea of a mysterious sign, and thus become similar to a hieroglyph which can be interpreted only by an initiate, is that the symbol is not a random choice or creation of a sign, but presupposes a metaphysical connection of visible and invisible. The inseparability of visible appearance and invisible significance, this 'coincidence' of two spheres, lies at the basis of all forms of religious cult. The development into the aesthetic sphere is also easy to understand. According to Solger[138] the symbolic refers to an 'existence in which the idea is recognised in some way or another', ie the inward unity of ideal and appearance that is typical of the work of art. Whereas allegory creates this meaningful unity only by pointing to something else.

But the concept of allegory also has been considerably widened, inasmuch as allegory does not mean only the figure of speech and the interpreted sense (sensus allegoricus), but also corresponding images representing abstract concepts in art. Obviously here the concepts of rhetoric and poetics were the model for the aesthetic concept in the sphere of the plastic arts.[139] The rhetorical element in the concept of allegory remains important for this development in meaning insofar as allegory does not assume an original metaphysical relationship, such as a symbol claims but, rather, a connection created by convention and dogmatic agreement, which enables one to use a presentation in images for something that is imageless.

Thus one might sum up the linguistic trends of meaning which led at the end of the eighteenth century to the symbol and the symbolic, as what is inwardly and essentially significant being contrasted with the external and artificial significance of allegory. The symbol is the coincidence of the sensible and the non-sensible, allegory the meaningful relation of the sensible to the non-sensible.

Now, under the influence of the concept of genius and of the subjectivisation of 'expression', this difference of meanings became a contrast of values. The symbol, as what can be interpreted inexhaustibly, because it is indefinite, is opposed to allegory, understood as standing in a more exact relation to meaning and exhausted by it, as art is opposed to non-art. The very indefiniteness of its meaning is what gave the victory to the word and concept of the symbolic when the rationalist aesthetic of the age of enlightenment succumbed to critical philosophy and the aesthetics of genius. It is worthwhile reviewing this connection in detail.

Kant's logical analysis of the concept of symbol in §59 of the *Critique of Judgment* threw the clearest light on this point and was decisive: he contrasts symbolic and schematic representation. It is representation (and not just description as in so-called logical 'symbolism'); but symbolic representation does not present a concept directly (as does transcendental schematism in Kant's philosophy), but only indirectly 'through which the expression does not contain the proper schema for the concept, but merely a symbol for reflection'. This concept of symbolic representation is one of the most brilliant results of Kantian thought. He thus does justice to the theological truth that had found its scholastic form in the analogia entis and keeps human concepts separate from God. Beyond this he discovers—referring specifically to the fact that this 'business requires a more profound investigation'—the symbolic way that language works (its constant use of metaphor) and finally applies the concept of the analogy, in particular, in order to describe the relationship of the beautiful to the morally good, which can be neither subordination nor equality. 'The beautiful is the symbol of the morally good'. In this formula, as cautious as it is pregnant, Kant combines the demand of full freedom of reflection for aesthetic judgment with its humane significance—an idea which was to be of the greatest historical consequence. Schiller was in this his successor.[140] When he based the idea of an aesthetic education of man on the analogy of beauty and morality, formulated by Kant, he was able to pursue a line explicitly laid down by Kant: 'Taste makes, as it were, the transition from the charm of sense to habitual moral interest possible without too violent a leap'.[141]

The question is, how did this concept of symbol become, in the way we are familiar with, the counter-concept to allegory? Of this we can, at first, find nothing in Schiller, even though he shares the criticism of the cold and artificial allegory which Klopstock, Lessing, the young Goethe, Karl-Philipp Moritz and others directed at the time against Winckelmann.[142] It is only in the correspondence between Schiller and Goethe that we have the beginnings of the new form of the concept of symbol. In his well-known letter of August 17, 1797, Goethe describes the sentimental mood which his impressions of Frankfurt arouse in him, and says of the objects that induce this 'that they are properly symbolic, ie, as I hardly need to say, they are eminent examples which stand, in a characteristic multiplicity, as representatives for many others, and embrace a certain totality . . .'. He attaches importance to this experience, because it is intended to help him to escape the 'million-headed hydra of empiricism'. Schiller supports him in this and finds this sentimental mode of feeling wholly in accord with 'what we have agreed on in this sphere'. But with Goethe it is, as we know, not so much an aesthetic experience as an experience of reality, for which he apparently draws from early Protestant usage the concept of the symbolic.

Schiller values his idealist objections to such a conception of the symbols of reality and thus pushes the meaning of 'symbol' towards the aesthetic. Goethe's art-loving friend Meyer also follows this aesthetic application of the concept of the symbol, in order to distinguish the true work of art from allegory. But for Goethe himself the contrast between symbol and allegory in art theory is only a special phenomenon in the general tendency towards the significant, which he seeks in all appearances. Thus he applies the concept of the symbol to colours, because there also 'the true relationship expresses at the same time the meaning'. Here the influence of the traditional hermeneutical schema of *allegorice, symbolice mystice* is clear,[143] to the point of his finally writing the sentence, so typical of him: 'Everything that takes place is a symbol, and, in fully representing itself, it points towards everything else'.[144]

In philosophical aesthetics this use of language must have established itself via the Greek 'religion of art'. This is shown clearly by Schelling's development of the philosophy of art out of mythology. Karl-Philipp Moritz, to whom Schelling refers, had, for mythological poetry, already in his *Götterlehre* (doctrine of the gods) rejected 'dissolution into mere allegory', but still he did not use for this 'language of fantasy' the expression 'symbol'. Schelling, however, writes: 'Mythology in general and any piece of mythological literature in particular is not to be understood schematically or allegorically, but symbolically. For the demand of absolute artistic representation is: representation with complete indifference, so that the universal is wholly the particular, and the particular at the same time wholly the universal, and does not simply mean it'.[145] When Schelling thus (in his criticism of Heine's view of Homer) establishes the true relationship between mythology and allegory, he is at the same time giving to the concept of symbol its central position within the philosophy of art. Similarly, we find in Solger the statement that all art is symbolic.[146] Solger means that the work of art is the existence of the 'idea' itself—and not that an 'idea sought apart from the actual work of art' is what its meaning is. For this is what is characteristic of the work of art, the creation of genius: that its importance lies in the phenomenon itself and is not arbitrarily transported into it. Schelling refers to the translation of the word 'symbol' into German as Sinnbild ('meaning image'), 'as concrete, resembling only itself, like an image, and yet as universal and full of meaning as a concept'.[147] In fact, even in Goethe's concept of symbol the main emphasis is on the fact that it is the idea itself that gives itself existence in it. Only because in the concept of symbol the inner unity of symbol and what is symbolised is implied, was it possible for this concept to become the basic universal concept of aesthetics. A symbol is the coincidence of sensible appearance and supra-sensible meaning, and this coincidence is, like the original significance of the Greek *symbolon* and its continuance in terminological usage of the various religious denominations, not a subsequent coordination, as in the use of signs, but the union of two things that belong to each other: all symbolism, through which 'the priesthood reflects higher knowledge', rests, rather, on that 'original connection' between gods and men, writes Friedrich Creuzer,[148] whose *Symbolik* set about the vexed question of interpreting the enigmatic symbolism of earlier times.

The extension of the concept of symbol to a universal aesthetic principle did not take place without difficulty. For the inner unity of image and significance which the symbol demands is not simple. The symbol does not simply remove the tension between the world of ideas and the world of the senses: there can be a disproportion between form and essence, expression and contents. In particular the religious function of the symbol lives from this tension. The possibility of the instantaneous and total coincidence of the appearance with the infinite in a religious ceremony on the basis of this tension assumes that it is an inner harmony between the finite and the infinite that fills the symbol with meaning. Thus the religious form of the symbol corresponds exactly to its original nature, the dividing of what is one and reuniting it again.

The disproportion of form and essence is essential to the symbol inasmuch as the latter points by its meaning beyond its physical appearance. It is the origin of that indeterminate quality, that undecidedness between form and essence that is peculiar to the symbol. This disproportion is obviously greater, the more obscure and more meaningful the symbol is—and lesser, the more the meaning penetrates the form: that was Creuzer's idea.[149] Hegel's limitation of the use of the symbol to the symbolic art of the East is based ultimately on this disproportion of image and meaning. Excess of meaning is characteristic of a particular art form,[150] which differs from classical art in that this disproportion is not found in the latter. But to say this is obviously to give, quite consciously, a rigidity and an artificial narrowness to the concept which, as we saw, does not so much seek to express the disproportion, as also the coincidence of image and meaning. It must also be admitted that Hegelian limitation of the concept of the symbolic (despite its many followers) ran counter to the tendency of modern aesthetics which since Schelling sought to emphasise precisely the unity of appearance and meaning in this concept, in order thereby to justify aesthetic autonomy against the claims of the concept.[151]

Let us now pursue the corresponding devaluation of allegory. The abandonment of French classicism in German aesthetics from the time of Lessing and Herder may have played a part.[152] Still, Solger retains the expression of the allegorical in a very real sense for the whole of christian art, and Friedrich Schlegel goes even further. He says: all beauty is allegory (Gespräch über Poesie). Hegel's use of the concept 'symbolic' (like Creuzer's) is still very close to this concept of the allegorical. But this usage of the philosophers, based on the romantic ideas on the relation of the ineffable to language and the discovery of the allegorical poetry of the East, was no longer retained by the cultivated humanism of the nineteenth century. An appeal was made to Weimar classicism, and in fact the demotion of allegory was the dominant concern of German classicism, which inevitably followed the liberation of art from the fetters of rationalism and the emphasis on the concept of genius. Allegory is certainly not merely a concern of genius. It rests on firm traditions and has always a fixed, stateable meaning which does not resist rational comprehension through the concept—on the contrary, the concept and concern of allegory is closely bound up with dogmatics: with the rationalisation of the mythical (as in the Greek age of enlightenment) or with the christian interpretation of scripture in terms of the unity of a doctrine (as in patristics) and finally with the reconciliation of the christian tradition and classical culture, which is the basis of the culture and literature of modern Europe and the last universal form of which was the baroque. With the rupture of this tradition allegory too was finished. For the moment art freed itself from all dogmatic bonds and could be defined by the unconscious production of genius, allegory inevitably became aesthetically questionable.

Thus we see Goethe's work in aesthetics having a strong influence in the direction of making the symbolic a positive, and the allegorical a negative, artistic concept. His own poetry, especially, had the same effect, in that it was seen as the confession of his life; a poetic formation of experience. The criterion of experience, which he himself set up, became in the nineteenth century the chief yardstick of value. Whatever in Goethe's work did not confirm to this criterion—such as the poetry of his old age—was, in accordance with the realistic spirit of the century, dismissed as allegorically 'overladen'.

This ultimately has an affect also on the development of philosophical aesthetics, which accepts the concept of the symbol in the universal Goethean sense, but works entirely on the basis of the opposition between reality and art, ie from the 'standpoint of art' and the nineteenth century aesthetic religion of culture. F. T. Vischer is typical of this view; the further he grows away from Hegel the more he extends Hegel's concept of symbol and sees in the symbol one of the basic accomplishments of subjectivity. The 'dark symbolism of the mind' gives to what in itself lacks a soul (nature or phenomenal appearances) soul and significance. Since the aesthetic consciousness—as opposed to the mythical-religious—knows that it is free, the symbolism that it imparts to everything is also 'free'. However vague the symbol still remains, admitting various interpretations, it can no longer be characterised by its privative relation to the concept. Rather, it has its own positivity as a creation of the human mind. It is the perfect agreement of appearance and idea which is now—with Schelling—emphasised in the concept of symbol, whereas non-agreement is for allegory or mythical consciousness.[153] As late as Cassirer we find similarly aesthetic symbolism distinguished from mythical symbolism by the fact that in the aesthetic symbol the tension between image and meaning has been equilibrated—a last echo of the classicist concept of the 'religion of art'.[154]

From this survey of the linguistic history of 'symbol' and 'allegory' I draw a factual inference. The fixed quality of the contrast between the two concepts of the symbol that has emerged 'organically', and the cold, rational allegory, becomes less certain when we see its connection with the aesthetics of genius and of experience. If the rediscovery of the art of the baroque (something that can be clearly seen in the antique market) and, especially in recent decades of baroque poetry, together with modern aesthetic research, has led to a certain reinstatement of allegory, we can now see the theoretical reason for this. The foundation of nineteenth century aesthetics was the freedom of the symbol-making activity of the mind. But is that a sufficient foundation? Is this symbol-making activity not also in fact limited by the continued existence of a mythical, allegorical tradition? If this is recognised, however, the contrast between symbol and allegory again becomes relative, whereas the prejudice of the aesthetics of experience made it appear absolute. Equally, the difference of the aesthetic consciousness from the mythical can hardly be considered as absolute.

The raising of such questions involves a thorough revision of fundamental concepts of aesthetics. Obviously we are concerned here with more than a change in taste and in aesthetic evaluation. Rather, the idea of aesthetic consciousness itself becomes doubtful and thus the standpoint of art to which it belongs. Is the aesthetic attitude to a work of art the appropriate one? Or is what we call 'aesthetic consciousness' an abstraction? The new estimation of allegory of which we have spoken indicates that there is, in aesthetic consciousness too, a dogmatic element. And if the difference between the mythical and the aesthetic consciousness is not absolute does not the concept of art itself become questionable; for it is, as we have seen, a product of aesthetic consciousness? At any rate, it cannot be doubted that the great ages in the history of art were those in which people without any aesthetic consciousness and without our concept of 'art' surrounded themselves with creations whose religious or secular life-function could be understood by everyone and which to no-one gave solely aesthetic pleasure. Can the idea of the aesthetic experience be applied to these without reducing their true being?

3 THE RETRIEVAL OF THE QUESTION OF ARTISTIC TRUTH

(A) THAT AESTHETIC CULTIVATION IS OPEN TO QUESTION

In order to estimate correctly the extent of this question, we shall first undertake an historical inquiry to discover the specific, historically developed meaning of the concept of 'aesthetic consciousness'. Obviously today we no longer mean by 'aesthetic' what Kant still connected with the word when he called the doctrine of space and time 'transcendental aesthetics' and called the doctrine of the beautiful and sublime in nature and art a 'criticism of aesthetic judgment'. The turning-point seems to have been Schiller, who transformed the transcendental idea of taste into a moral demand and formulated it as an imperative: adopt an aesthetic attitude to things.[155] In his aesthetic writings Schiller turned the radical subjectivisation, through which Kant had justified transcendentally the judgment of taste and its claim to universality, from a methodical condition to one of content.

It is true that he was able to follow Kant himself, inasmuch as Kant had already accorded to taste the significance of a transition from an enjoyment of the senses to a moral feeling.[156] But when Schiller proclaimed art as a practising of freedom, he was referring more to Fichte than to Kant. The free play of the faculties of knowledge, on which Kant had based the a priori of taste and of genius, he understood anthropologically on the basis of Fichte's theory of instinct, in that the play impulse was to bring about the harmony between the form impulse and the matter impulse. The cultivation of this instinct is the goal of aesthetic education.

This had far-reaching consequences. For now art, as the art of beautiful appearance, was contrasted with practical reality and understood in terms of this contrast. Instead of art and nature complementing each other, as had always seemed to be the case, they were contrasted as appearance and reality. Traditionally it is the purpose of 'art', which also embraces all the conscious transformation of nature for use by humans, to complete its supplementing and fulfilling activity within the areas given and left free by nature.[157] And 'les beaux arts', as long as they are seen in this framework, are a perfecting of reality and not an external masking, veiling or transfiguration of it. But if the contrast between reality and appearance determines the concept of art, this breaks up the inclusive framework of nature. Art becomes a standpoint of its own and establishes its own autonomous claim to supremacy.

Where art rules, it is the laws of beauty that are in force and the frontiers of reality are transcended. It is the 'ideal kingdom', which is to be defended against all limitation, even against the moralistic guardianship of state and society. It is probably part of the inner shift in the ontological basis of Schiller's aesthetics that his great plan in the *Briefe über die ästhetische Erziehung* changes in its working out. As we know, an education to art comes through an education by art. In place of the true moral and political freedom, for which art should prepare us, we have the culture of an 'aesthetic state', an educated society which is interested in art.[158] But this places the overcoming of the Kantian dualism of the world of the senses and the world of morality, which is represented by the freedom of aesthetic play and the harmony of the work of art within a new conflict. The reconciliation of ideal and life through art is merely a particular reconciliation. Beauty and art give to reality only a fleeting and transfiguring radiance. The freedom of spirit to which they raise one up is freedom merely in an aesthetic state and not in reality. Thus at the basis of the aesthetic reconciliation of the Kantian dualism of being and moral obligation there is a more profound, unresolved dualism. It is the prose of alienated reality against which the poetry of aesthetic reconciliation must seek its own self-consciousness.

The concept of reality to which Schiller opposes poetry is undoubtedly no longer Kantian. For Kant always starts, as we have seen, from natural beauty. But inasmuch as Kant limited his concept of knowledge wholly to the possibility of 'pure natural science', for the sake of his criticism of dogmatic metaphysics, and thus gave to the nominalist concept of reality an unquestioned validity, the ontological difficulty in which nineteenth-century aesthetics found itself goes back ultimately to Kant himself. Under the domination of nominalist prejudice, aesthetic being can be only inadequately and imperfectly understood.

Basically it is to the phenomenological criticism of the psychology and epistemology of the nineteenth century that we owe the liberation from the concepts that prevented an appropriate understanding of aesthetic being. It has shown the error in all attempts to conceive the mode of aesthetic being in terms of the experience of reality and as a modification of it.[159] All such ideas as imitation, appearance, irreality, illusion, magic, dream, assume a relationship to something from which the aesthetic is different. But the phenomenological return to the aesthetic experience teaches us that the latter does not think in terms of this relationship but sees, rather, actual truth in what it experiences. It is in accordance with this that the aesthetic experience cannot, by its nature, be disappointed by a more genuine experience of reality. It is, however, characteristic of all the above-mentioned modifications of the experience of reality that to them an experience of disappointment necessarily corresponds. What was only appearance has now revealed itself, what lacked reality acquires it, what was magical loses its magic, what was illusion is seen through, and from what was a dream we awaken. If the aesthetic is mere appearance in this sense,. then its power—like the terror of dreams—could last only so long as there was no doubt of the reality of the appearance, and would lose its truth on waking.

The shift of the ontological definition of the aesthetic to the sphere of aesthetic appearance has its theoretical basis in the fact that the domination of the scientific epistemological model leads to the discrediting of all the possibilities of knowing that lie outside this new method.

Let us recall that, in the well-known quotation from which we started, Helmholtz was not able to characterise the different quality that the work of the human sciences had from that of the natural sciences in any better way than by describing it as 'artistic'. To this theoretical relationship there corresponds positively what we may call the 'aesthetic consciousness'. It is given with the 'standpoint of art', which Schiller was the first to found. For as the art of the 'beautiful appearance' is opposed to reality, so the aesthetic consciousness includes an alienation from reality—it is a form of the 'alienated spirit', which is how Hegel understood culture. To be able to adopt an aesthetic attitude is

part of the educated consciousness.[160] For in the aesthetic consciousness we find the features that distinguish the educated
consciousness: being raised to the universal, distancing from the
particularity of immediate acceptance or rejection, the acceptance of what does not correspond to one's own expectancy or
preference.

We have discussed above the meaning of the concept of taste
in this context. However, the unity of an ideal of taste that
distinguishes and binds together a society is different in character from that which constitutes the figure of aesthetic cultivation. Taste still obeys a criterion of content. What is valid in a
society, what taste dominates in it, characterises the community
of social life. Such a society chooses and knows what belongs to
it and what does not. Even the possession of artistic interests is
not random and universal in its ideas, but what artists create and
what the society values belong together in the unity of a style of
life and ideal of taste.

The idea of aesthetic cultivation, however—as we derived it
from Schiller—consists precisely in no longer permitting any
criterion of content and dissolving the connection of the work of
art with its world. An expression of this is the universal expansion of possessions that the aesthetically-formed consciousness
lays claim to. Everything that it acknowledges as having 'quality' belongs to it. It no longer chooses among it, because itself it
is nothing, nor seeks to be anything, against which choice could
measure itself. As aesthetic consciousness it has been derived
from defining and definite taste, but has gone beyond it and itself
represents a total lack of definiteness. The connection of the
work of art with its world is no longer of any importance to it
but, on the contrary, the aesthetic consciousness is the experiencing centre from which everything considered to be art is
measured.

What we call a work of art and experience aesthetically depends on a process of abstraction. By disregarding everything in
which a work is rooted (its original context of life, and the religious or secular function which gave it its significance), it becomes visible as the 'pure work of art'. This abstraction of the
aesthetic consciousness performs a task that is positive in itself.
It shows what a pure work of art is, and allows it to exist in its
own right. I call this 'aesthetic differentiation'.

Unlike the differentiation that a definite taste, with its own
content, undertakes in selection and rejection, this is an abstraction that selects only in relation to the aesthetic quality as such.

It is performed in the self-consciousness of the 'aesthetic experience'. The aesthetic experience is supposed to be directed towards the work proper—what it ignores are its extra-aesthetic elements, such as purpose, function, the meaning of its content. These elements may be significant enough inasmuch as they place the work in its world and thus determine the whole meaningfulness that it originally possessed. But the artistic nature of the work must be able to be distinguished from all that. It practically defines aesthetic consciousness to say that it performs this differentiation of what is aesthetically intended from everything that is outside the aesthetic sphere. It abstracts from all the conditions of a work's accessibility. Thus this kind of differentiation is itself a specifically aesthetic one. It distinguishes the aesthetic quality of a work from all elements of content which induce us to take up an attitude towards it, moral or religious, and presents it solely by itself in its aesthetic being. Similarly, in the reproductive arts it differentiates between the original (drama or composition) and its performance, and in such a way that both the original, as against the reproduction, and the reproduction in itself, as against the original or other possible interpretation, can be the object of aesthetic consciousness. It is the capacity of aesthetic consciousness to be able to make this aesthetic differentiation everywhere and to see everything 'aesthetically'.

Thus aesthetic consciousness has the character of simultaneity, because it claims that it contains everything of artistic value. The form of reflection in which it moves, as aesthetic, is therefore not only contemporaneous. For inasmuch as aesthetic consciousness raises everything that it admits to simultaneity in itself, it constitutes itself as historical at the same time. Not only that it includes historical knowledge and uses it as a distinguishing mark:[161] the dissolution of all taste determined by content, which is proper to its aesthetic nature, is seen also explicitly in the creation of artists who turn to the historical. The historical picture, which does not owe its origin to a contemporary need to depict, but is a representation in historical retrospection, the historical novel, but above all the historicising forms in which the architecture of the nineteenth century indulged in continual stylistic reminiscence, show the close relationship between the aesthetic and the historical elements in the cultural consciousness.

It might be objected that simultaneity does not arise first with aesthetic differentiation, but has always been an integral product

of historical living. At least the great works of architecture continue to exist in the life of the present as living witnesses of the
past and all preservation of tradition in manners and behaviour,
images and decoration does the same thing, inasmuch as it too
mediates an older life to that of the present day. But aesthetic
cultural consciousness is different from this. It does not see
itself as this kind of integration of the ages, but the simultaneity
peculiar to it is based on the historical relativity of taste which it
is aware of. Only through being ready not simply to dismiss taste
that differs from one's own 'good' taste, does mere contemporaneity become a fundamental simultaneity. In place of the
unity of a taste we now have a mobile feeling for quality.[162]

The 'aesthetic differentiation' which, as aesthetic awareness,
it performs creates also an external existence of its own. It
proves its productivity by giving to simultaneity its shades: the
'universal library' in the sphere of literature, the museum, the
theatre, the concert hall etc. It is important to see the difference
between what has happened here and what existed before. The
museum, for example, is not simply a collection that has been
made public. Rather the older collections (of the courts and of
the towns) reflected the choice of a particular taste and contained primarily the works of the same 'school', which was considered to be a model. A museum, however, is the collection of
such collections and characteristically finds its perfection in
concealing the fact of its own growth from out of such collections, either by historically re-arranging the whole or by extending it and making it as comprehensive as possible. Similarly one
could show in the case of the theatre or the concerts over the last
century how the programmes have moved further and further
away from contemporary work and have adapted themselves to
the need for self-confirmation which is characteristic of the cultured society that supports these institutions. Even art forms
which seem to be opposed to the simultaneity of the aesthetic
experience, such as architecture, are drawn into it, either
through the modern technique of reproduction which turns
buildings into pictures, or else through modern tourism, which
turns travelling into an armchair browsing through picture
books.[163]

Thus through 'aesthetic differentiation' the work loses its
place and the world to which it belongs insofar as it belongs to
aesthetic consciousness. On the other hand, this is paralleled by
the artist also losing his place in the world. This is seen in the
discrediting of what is called commissioned art. It is necessary
for a public awareness that is dominated by the age of the art of

experience to be explicitly reminded that creation out of a free inspiration without a commission, a given theme and a given occasion, was formerly the exception rather than the rule in artistic work, whereas today we feel that an architect is someone sui generis because, unlike the poet, painter or musician, he is not independent of commission and occasion. The free artist creates without a commission. He seems marked out by the complete independence of his creativity and thus acquires the characteristic social features of an outsider, whose style of life cannot be measured by the yardstick of general morality. The idea of the bohemian which arose in the nineteenth century reflects this process. The home of the gypsies became the generic word for the artist's way of life.

But at the same time the artist, who is as 'free as a bird or a fish', bears the burden of a vocation which makes him an ambiguous figure. For a social culture that has fallen away from its religious traditions expects more from art than is in accordance with aesthetic consciousness which takes the 'standpoint of art'. The romantic support for a new mythology, as expressed by F. Schlegel, Schelling, Hölderlin and the young Hegel,[164] but as found also in the paintings and reflections of Runge, gives the artist and his task in the world the consciousness of a new consecration. He is something like a 'secular saviour' (Immermann), whose creations are expected to achieve in a small way the propitiation of disaster, for which an unsaved world hopes. This claim has since determined the tragedy of the artist in the world, for any fulfilment of it is always only a particular one, and that means in fact its refutation. The experimental search for new symbols or a new myth which will unite everyone may certainly create a public and create a community, but since every artist finds his own community, the particularity of this community-creating merely testifies to the disintegration that is taking place. It is only the universal form of aesthetic culture that unites everyone.

The actual process of culture, ie the elevaton to the universal, is here disintegrated, as it were, in itself. 'The readiness of intellectual reflection to move in generalities, to consider anything at all from whatever point of view it adopts, and thus to clothe it with ideas' is, according to Hegel, the way not to get involved with the real content of ideas. Immermann calls this free self-pouring of the spirit within itself something 'extravagantly self-indulgent'.[165] He thus describes the situation produced by the classical literature and philosophy of the age of Goethe, when the epigones found all forms of the spirit already existing

and hence exchanged the true task of culture, the refining away
of the alien and the crude, for its enjoyment. It had become easy
to write a good poem, and, for that very reason, hard to be a
poet.

(B) CRITIQUE OF THE ABSTRACTION OF AESTHETIC CONSCIOUSNESS

Let us now consider the concept of aesthetic differentiation,
whose cultural role we have described, and discuss the theoretical difficulties contained in the concept of the aesthetic. Abstraction until only the 'purely aesthetic' is left is obviously a
self-contradictory process. This seems to me to emerge clearly
from the most logical attempt to develop a systematic aesthetics
on the basis of the Kantian distinctions which was undertaken
by Richard Hamann.[166] Hamann's work is notable for the fact
that he really does go back to Kant's transcendental intention
and thus demolishes the onesided criterion of Erlebniskunst. In
concentrating on the aesthetic element wherever it is to be
found, he does justice to the aesthetics of such particular applied
forms as monumental and advertising design. But even here
Hamann holds to the task of aesthetic differentiation. For he
distinguishes in these the aesthetic from the non-aesthetic relationships in which it stands, just as we can say outside the experience of art that someone behaves aesthetically. Thus the
problem of aesthetics is once more accorded its full breadth and
the transcendental question reinstated that had been abandoned
through the standpoint of art and its distinction between beautiful appearance and harsh reality. The aesthetic experience is
indifferent to whether its object is real or not, whether the scene
is the stage or whether it is real life. The aesthetic consciousness
has an unlimited sovereignty over everything.

But Hamann's attempt fails at the opposite end, namely, in
the concept of art that he logically pushes so far out of the sphere
of the aesthetic that it coincides with virtuosity.[167] Here aesthetic differentiation is pushed to its furthest extreme. It even
abstracts from art.

The basic aesthetic idea which is Hamann's starting-point is
'the significance of perception in its own right'. This concept
obviously means the same as Kant's theory of its congruity with
the state of our cognitive faculty. As for Kant, so for Hamann
the criterion of the concept or of meaning which is essential for
knowledge, is thus suspended. Linguistically the word Bedeut-

samkeit, (the quality of possessing significance) is a secondary formation from Bedeutung and transposes the connection with a particular meaning into the sphere of the uncertain. A thing is beudeutsam, if its meaning (Bedeutung) is unstated or unknown. Eigenbedeutsamkeit, however, goes even beyond that. If a thing is eigenbedeutsam (significant in its own right) rather than fremdbedeutsam (significant in relation to something else), it seeks to break off any connection with everything that could determine its meaning. Can such an idea be a solid ground for aesthetics? Can one use the concept 'significant in its own right' for a perception at all? Must we not also allow of aesthetic experience what we say of perception, namely that it perceives truth, ie remains related to knowledge?

In fact, it is well here to recall Aristotle. He has shown aesthesis that all tends to a universal, even if every sense has its own specific field and thus what is immediately given in it is not universal. But the specific perception of something given by the senses as such is an abstraction. In fact we see what is given to us individually by the senses in relation to something universal. We recognise, for example, a white phenomenon as a man.[168]

Now 'aesthetic' vision is certainly characterised by its not hurrying to relate what one sees to a universal, the known significance, the intended purpose etc, but by dwelling on it as something aesthetic. But that still does not stop us from seeing relationships, eg recognising that this white phenomenon which we admire aesthetically is in fact a man. Thus our perception is never a simple reflection of what is presented to the senses.

On the contrary, we have learned from modern psychology, especially from the trenchant criticism that Scheler, following W. Koehler, E. Strauss, M. Wertheimer and others, made of the idea of pure perception as a response to a stimulus,[169] that this idea owes its origin to an epistemological dogmatism. Its true sense is merely a normative one, in that the idea of response to a stimulus is the ideal end result of the destruction of all instinct fantasies, the consequence of a great sobering-up process that finally enabled one to see what was there, instead of what the instinct fantasy imagined. But that means that the pure perception defined by the idea of response to stimulus is merely an ideal limiting case.

There is a second point, however. Even perception conceived as an adequate response to a stimulus would never be a mere mirroring of what is there. For it would always remain an understanding of something as something. All understanding as . . . . is an articulation of what is there, in that it looks away from . . .

looks at . . . . sees together as. . . . All of this can take place in
the centre of an observation or can be merely taken in at the side
or in the background. Thus there is no doubt that vision, as an
articulating reading of what is there, removes, as it were, a lot of
what is there from sight, so that for sight, it is simply not there
any more. Equally, it is led by its expectations to read in what is
not there at all. Let us also remember the tendency to invariance
operative within vision itself, so that one always sees things, as
far as possible, in the same way.

This criticism of the theory of pure perception, undertaken on
the basis of pragmatic experience, was then made a matter of
principle by Heidegger. This means, however, that it is also
valid for aesthetic consciousness, although here one does not
simply look beyond what one sees, eg to its general use for some
end, but dwells on it. Lingering vision and assimilation is not a
simple perception of what is there, but is itself understanding as
. . . the mode of being of what is observed 'aesthetically' is not
presence-at-hand. In the case of significant representation, in
works of plastic art, providing that they are not non-represen-
tational and abstract, the fact of their significance obviously
directs the way that what is seen is understood. Only if we
recognise what is represented are we able to 'read' a picture, in
fact that is what makes it, fundamentally, a picture. Seeing
means differentiation. While we are still trying various ways of
dividing up what we see or hesitate between versions, as with
certain trick pictures, we don't yet see what is there. The trick
picture is, as it were, the artificial perpetuation of this hesitation,
the 'agony' of seeing. The same is true of the literary work. Only
when we understand a text—that is, at least be in command of its
language—can it be for us a work of literary art. Even if we hear
absolute music we must 'understand' it. And only when we
understand it, when it is 'clear' to us, does it exist for us as an
artistic creation. Thus, although absolute music is a pure movement of form as such, a kind of auditory mathematics where there
is no content with an objective meaning that we can discern, to
understand it nevertheless involves entering into a relation with
what is meaningful. It is the indefiniteness of this relation that
is the specific relation to meaning of this kind of music.[170]

Pure seeing and pure hearing are dogmatic abstractions which
artificially reduce phenomena. Perception always includes
meaning. Thus it is a mistaken formalism, which cannot
moreover invoke the name of Kant, to seek the unity of the
aesthetic object solely in its form as opposed to its content.
Kant, with his concept of form, intended something quite differ-

ent. For him the concept of form refers to the structure of the aesthetic object,[171] not as opposed to the meaningful content of a work of art, but to the purely sensuous attractiveness of the material. The so-called objective content is not material waiting for subsequent formation, but is already bound up with the unity of form and meaning in the work of art.

The word 'motif', common in the language of painters, illustrates this. It can be as well objective as abstract—anyway as a motif it is, seen ontologically, non-material (aneu hules). That does not mean that it is in any way without content. Rather, what makes a motif is that it has unity in a convincing way and that the artist has carried through this unity as the unity of a meaning, just as the viewer sees it as a unity. In this connection Kant speaks of 'aesthetic ideas', to which 'much that is unnameable' is added.[172] That is his way of going beyond the transcendental purity of the aesthetic and recognising the mode of being of art. As we have shown above, he was far from seeking to avoid the 'intellectualisation' of pure aesthetic pleasure. The arabesque is by no means his aesthetic ideal, but merely a favourite methodological example. In order to do justice to art, aesthetics must go beyond itself and surrender the 'purity' of the aesthetic.[173] But does this give it a really firm position? In Kant the concept of genius possessed the transcendental function through which the concept of art was grounded. We saw how this concept of genius became extended in his successors to become the universal basis of aesthetics. But is the concept of genius really suited to this?

Modern artistic consciousness seems to contradict this. A kind of 'twilight of genius' seems to have set in. The idea of the somnabulatory unconsciousness with which genius creates—an idea that can, however, be legitimated by Goethe's description of his own manner of writing poetry—appears to us today as false romanticism. A poet like Paul Valéry has opposed to it the criterion of an artist and engineer such as Leonardo da Vinci, in whose total genius craftsmanship, mechanical invention, and artistic genius were still indistinguishably one.[174] The general awareness, however, is still influenced by the effects of the eighteenth-century cult of genius and the sacralisation of art that we have found to be characteristic of the bourgeois society of the nineteenth century. This is confirmed inasmuch as the concept of genius is now conceived, fundamentally, from the point of view of the observer. This classical idea seems cogent, not to the creative, but to the critical spirit. What to the observer seems to be a miracle, something that it is inconceivable that anyone could create, is mirrored in the miraculous nature of creation through the inspiration of genius. Those who create are then able, in contemplating themselves, to use the same categories, and thus the genius cult of the eighteenth century was certainly nourished also by artists.[175] But they have never gone as far in self-apotheosis as bourgeois society would have allowed them to. The self-knowledge of the artist remains far more down-to-earth. He sees possibilities of making and succeeding and questions of 'technique', where the observer seeks inspiration, mystery and deeper meaning.[176]

If one wants to take account of this criticism of the theory of the unconscious productivity of genius, one is again faced with the problem that Kant had solved by the transcendental function that he allotted to the idea of genius. What is a work of art and how is it different from the product of a craftsman or even from some mechanical creation, ie something of aesthetically inferior value? For Kant and idealism the work of art was, by definition, the work of genius. Its characteristic, of being completely successful and exemplary, was proved by the fact that it offered to pleasure and contemplation an inexhaustible object of lingering attention and interpretation. That the genius of creation is matched by genius in appreciating was already part of Kant's theory of taste and genius, K. P. Moritz and Goethe taught even more explicitly.

How can the nature of artistic pleasure and the difference between what a craftsman has made and an artist has created be understood without the concept of genius?

How can even the perfecton of a work of art, its being finished, be conceived? Whatever else is made or produced takes the criterion of its perfection from its purpose, ie is determined by the use that is to be made of it. The work is finished if it answers to the purpose for which it is intended.[177] How is one, then, to understand the criterion for the perfection of a work of art? However rationally and soberly one may consider artistic 'production', much that we call works of art is not intended to be used, and none derives the measure of its completion from such a purpose. Does not, then, the work's existence appear to be the breaking-off of a formative process which actually points beyond it? Perhaps it is not at all completable in itself?

Paul Valéry, in fact, thought this was the case. But he did not work out the consequence that followed for someone who encounters a work of art and endeavours to understand it. If it is true that a work of art is not, in itself, completable, what is the criterion for correct reception and understanding? A chance and random breaking-off of a formative process cannot contain anything binding.[178] From this, then, it follows that what he makes of what he finds must be left to the recipient. One way of understanding a work of art is then no less legitimate than another. There is no criterion of an appropriate reaction. Not only that the artist himself does not possess one—the aesthetics of genius would agree here. Rather, every encounter with the work has the rank and the justification of a new production. This seems to me an untenable hermeneutic nihilism. If Valéry sometimes drew these conclusions for his work[179] in order to avoid the myth of the unconscious production of genius, he has, in my view, become entangled in it, for now he transfers to reader and interpreter the authority of absolute creation which he himself no longer desires to exert. But genius in understanding is, in fact, of no more help than genius in creation.

The same difficulty arises if one starts from the idea of the aesthetic experience instead of from the idea of the genius. On this subject the fundamental essay by George von Lukács, 'Die Subjekt-Objekt Beziehung in der Ästhetik'[180] revealed the problem. He ascribes to the aesthetic sphere a Heraclitean structure, by which he means that the unity of the aesthetic object is not something that is actually given. The work of art is only a form, a mere modal point in the possible variety of aesthetic experiences in which only the aesthetic object is present. As is evident, absolute discontinuity, ie the disintegration of the unity of the aesthetic object into the multiplicity of experiences, is the necessary consequence of an aesthetics of experience. Following Lukács' ideas, Oskar Becker has stated outright that 'in terms of time the work exists only in a moment [ie now]; it is "now" this work and now it is this work no longer'![181] Actually, that is logical. Basing aesthetics on experience leads to an absolute series of points, which annihilates both the unity of the work of art and the identity of the artist with himself, and the identity of the man understanding or enjoying the work of art.[182]

Kierkegaard seems to me to have shown the untenability of this position, in that he recognised the destructive consequence of subjectivism and was the first to describe the self-destruction of aesthetic immediacy. His theory of the aesthetic stage of existence is developed from the standpoint of the moralist who has seen how desperate and untenable is existence in pure immediacy and discontinuity. Hence his criticism of the aesthetic consciousness is of fundamental importance because he shows the inner contradictions of aesthetic existence, so that it is forced to go beyond itself. In that the aesthetic stage of exist-

ence proves itself untenable, it is recognised that even the
phenomenon of art imposes a task on existence; namely, despite
the demands of the absorbing presence of the particular aesthetic impression, of achieving that continuity of self-understanding
which alone can support human existence.[183] If one still wanted
to attempt a definition of aesthetic existence which constituted it outside the hermeneutic continuity of human existence, the point of Kierkegaard's criticism would, in my view,
have been missed. Even if it may be admitted that in the aesthetic phenomenon there appear limits to the historical self-
understanding of existence that correspond to the limit set up by
that part of nature that, posited in the mind as its condition, is
projected into the mental sphere in many different forms—myth,
dream—as the unconscious preformation of conscious life, we
still have no point of view which would allow us to see, from
outside, what limits and conditions us from itself and ourselves,
as beings that are limited and conditioned in this way. Even
that which is closed to our understanding is experienced by ourselves as something limiting and thus belongs to the continuity
of self-understanding in which human existence moves. The
recognition of the 'impermanence of the beautiful and the ad-
venturousness of the artist' (Hinfälligkeit des Schönen und der
Abenteuerlichkeit des Künstlers) is thus, in fact, not the description of a mode of being outside the 'hermeneutic phenomenology of existence', but is rather the formulation of the need of
preserving, in spite of this discontinuity of aesthetic being and
aesthetic experience, the hermeneutic continuity which constitutes our being.[184]

The pantheon of art is not a timeless presence which offers
itself to pure aesthetic consciousness but the assembled
achievements of the human mind as it has realised itself historically. Aesthetic experience also is a mode of self-understanding.
But all self-understanding takes place in relation to something
else that is understood and includes the unity and sameness of
this other. Inasmuch as we encounter the work of art in the
world and a world in the individual work of art, this does not
remain a strange universe into which we are magically transported for a time. Rather, we learn to understand ourselves in it,
and that means that we preserve the discontinuity of the experience in the continuity of our existence. Therefore it is necessary
to adopt an attitude to the beautiful and to art that does not lay
claim to immediacy, but corresponds to the historical reality of
man. The appeal to immediacy, to the genius of the moment, to
the significance of the 'experience', cannot withstand the claim

of human existence to continuity and unity of self-under-standing. The experience of art must not be side-tracked into the uncommittedness of the aesthetic awareness.

This negative insight, expressed positively, means that art is knowledge and the experience of the work of art is a sharing of this knowledge.

This raises the question of how one can do justice to the truth of aesthetic experience and overcome the radical subjectivisa-tion of the aesthetic that began with Kant's *Critique of Aesthetic Judgment*. We have shown that it was a methodological ab-straction corresponding to a quite particular transcendental task of laying foundations which led Kant to relate aesthetic judg-ment entirely to the condition of the subject. If, however, this aesthetic abstraction was subsequently understood as a content and was changed into the demand to understand art purely aes-thetically, we can now see how this demand for abstraction ends in an indissoluble contradiction with the true experience of art.

Is there to be no knowledge in art? Does not the experience of art contain a claim to truth which is certainly different from that of science, but equally certainly is not inferior to it? And is not the task of aesthetics precisely to provide a basis for the fact that artistic experience is a mode of knowledge of a unique kind, certainly different from that sensory knowledge which provides science with the data from which it constructs the knowledge of nature, and certainly different from all moral rational knowledge and indeed from all conceptual knowledge, but still knowledge, ie the transmission of truth?

This can hardly be recognised if, with Kant, one measures the truth of knowledge by the scientific concept of knowledge and the scientific concept of reality. It is necessary to take the idea of experience more broadly then Kant did, so that the experi-ence of the work of art can be understood as experience. For this we can appeal to Hegel's fine lectures on aesthetics. Here the truth that lies in every artistic experience is recognised and at the same time mediated with historical consciousness. Hence aesthetics becomes a history of world-views, ie a history of truth, as it is seen in the mirror of art. It is also a fundamental recognition of the task that I formulated of justifying the knowl-edge of truth in the experience of art itself.

The concept of world-view, which first appears in Hegel in the *Phänomenologie des Geistes*[185] as a term for Kant's and Fichte's postulatory amplification of the basic moral experience to a moral world order, acquires only in aesthetics its proper significance. It is the multiplicity and the possible change of world-views that has given to the concept of world-view its familiar ring.[186] But the history of art is the chief example of this, because this historical multiplicity cannot be resolved into the unity of a progress towards true art. It is true that Hegel was able to recognise the truth of art only by letting the inclusive knowledge of philosophy surpass it and by constructing the history of world-views, like world history and the history of philosophy, from the developed self-consciousness of the present. But this cannot be seen simply as mistaken, in that the sphere of the subjective mind is far exceeded. This move beyond it remains a lasting element of truth in Hegelian thought. Certainly, inasmuch as it makes the truth of the concept all powerful, which resolves all experience within itself, Hegel's philosophy at the same time disavows the way of truth that it has recognised in the experience of art. If we want to justify this in its own right, then we must realise fully what 'truth' here means. It is in the human sciences as a whole that an answer to this question must be found. For they do not seek to surpass, but to understand the variety of experiences—aesthetic, historical, religious or political consciousness—but that means that they anticipate truth in them. We shall have to go into the relationship between Hegel and the self-understanding of the human sciences represented by the 'historical school' and the way in which they differ as to what makes it possible to understand properly what truth means in the human sciences. At any rate, we shall not be able to do justice to the problem of art from the point of view of aesthetic consciousness, but only within this wider framework.

We made only one step in this direction in seeking to correct the self-interpretation of the aesthetic consciousness and in retrieving the question of the truth of art, of which the aesthetic experience is a testimony. Thus our concern is to see the experience of art in such a way that it is understood as experience. The experience of art is not to be falsified by being turned into a possession of aesthetic culture and hence neutralised in its proper claim. We shall see that this involves a far-reaching hermeneutical consequence, inasmuch as all encounter with the language of art is an encounter with a still unfinished process and is itself part of this process. This is what must be emphasised against the aesthetic consciousness and its neutralisation of the truth question.

If speculative idealism sought to overcome the aesthetic subjectivism and agnosticism, based on Kant, by elevating itself to the standpoint of infinite knowledge, then, as we have seen, this gnostic self-redemption of finitude involved making art a part of philosophy. Instead of this we shall have to hold firmly to the standpoint of finiteness. The productive thing about Heidegger's criticism of modern subjectivism seems to me that his temporal interpretation of being has opened up new possibilities. Interpretation of being from the horizon of time does not mean, as it is constantly misunderstood to mean, that There-being is radically temporal, so that it can no longer be considered as everlasting or eternal, but that it can be understood only in relation to its own time and future. If this were the meaning it would not be a critique and an overcoming of subjectivism, but an 'existentialist' radicalisation of it, which one could easily foresee would have a collectivist future. The philosophical question, however, which is involved here, is directed precisely at this subjectivism itself. The latter is driven to its final point only in order to question it. The philosophical question asks what is the being of self-understanding? With this question it totally transcends the horizon of this self-understanding. In removing time as its hidden ground, it does not preach blind commitment out of nihilistic despair, but opens itself to a hitherto concealed experience, transcending thinking from the position of subjectivity, an experience that Heidegger calls 'being'.

In order to do justice to the experience of art we began with the criticism of the aesthetic consciousness. The experience of art acknowledges that it cannot present the perfect truth of what it experiences in terms of final knowledge. Here there is no absolute progress and no final exhaustion of what lies in a work of art. The experience of art knows this of itself. At the same time it is necessary not simply to accept what the aesthetic consciousness considers to be its experience. For it considers it, as we say, in the final analysis as the discontinuity of experiences. But we have found this to be unacceptable.

We do not, then, ask the experience of art to tell us how it thinks of itself, but what it is in truth and what its truth is, even if it does not know what it is and cannot say what it knows—just so Heidegger has asked what metaphysics is, in contrast to what it thinks itself to be. In the experience of art we see a genuine experience induced by the work, which does not leave him who has it unchanged, and we enquire into the mode of being of that which is experienced in this way. So we hope to understand better what kind of truth it is that encounters us there.

We shall see that this opens up the dimension in which, in the 'understanding' with which the human sciences are concerned, the question of truth is raised in a new way.

If we want to know what truth in the field of the human sciences is, we shall have to ask the philosophical question of the whole procedure of the human sciences in the same way that Heidegger asked it of metaphysics, and that we have asked it of aesthetic consciousness. But we shall not be able simply to accept the human sciences' own account of themselves, but must ask what their mode of understanding in truth is. The question of the truth of art in particular can serve to prepare the way for this wider-ranging question, because the experience of the work of art includes understanding, and thus itself represents a hermeneutical phenomenon—but not at all in the sense of a scientific method. Rather, the understanding belongs to the encounter with the work of art itself, so that this connection can be illuminated only on the basis of the mode of being of the work of art itself.

II

The Ontology of the Work of Art and Its Hermeneutical Significance

1 PLAY AS THE CLUE TO ONTOLOGICAL EXPLANATION

(A) THE CONCEPT OF PLAY

I select as my starting-point a notion that has played a major role in aesthetics: the concept of play. I wish to free this concept from the subjective meaning which it has in Kant and Schiller and which dominates the whole of modern aesthetics and philosophy of man. If, in connection with the experience of art, we speak of play, this refers neither to the attitude nor even to the state of mind of the creator or of those enjoying the work of art, nor to the freedom of a subjectivity expressed in play, but to the mode of being of the work of art itself. In analysing aesthetic consciousness we recognised that the concept of aesthetic consciousness confronted with an object does not correspond to the real situation. This is why the concept of play is important in my exposition.

We can certainly distinguish between play and the attitude of the player, which, as such, belongs with the other attitudes of subjectivity. Thus it can be said that for the player play is not serious: that is why he plays. We can try to define the concept of play from this point of view. What is merely play is not serious. Play has its own relation to what is serious. It is not only that the latter gives it its 'purpose': we play 'for the sake of recreation', as Aristotle says.[1] It is more important that play itself contains its own, even sacred, seriousness. Yet, in the attitude of play, all those purposive relations which determine active and caring existence have not simply disappeared, but in a curious way acquire a different quality. The player himself knows that play is only play and exists in a world which is determined by the seriousness of purposes. But he does not know this in such a way that, as a player, he actually intends this relation to seriousness. Play fulfils its purpose only if the player loses himself in his play. It is not that relation to seriousness which directs us away from play, but only seriousness in playing makes the play wholly play. One who doesn't take the game seriously is a spoilsport. The mode of being of play does not allow the player to behave towards play as if it were an object. The player knows very well what play is, and that what he is doing is 'only a game'; but he does not know what exactly he 'knows' in knowing that.

Our question concerning the nature of play itself cannot, therefore, find an answer if we look to the subjective reflection of the player to provide it.[2] Instead, we are enquiring into the mode of being of play as such. We have seen that it is not the aesthetic consciousness, but the experience of art and thus the question of the mode of being of the work of art that must form the object of our examination. But this was precisely the experience of the work of art which I maintained in opposition to the levelling process of the aesthetic consciousness: namely, that the work of art is not an object that stands over against a subject for itself. Instead the work of art has its true being in the fact that it becomes an experience changing the person experiencing it. The 'subject' of the experience of art, that which remains and endures, is not the subjectivity of the person who experiences it, but the work itself. This is the point at which the mode of being of play becomes significant. For play has its own essence, independent of the consciousness of those who play. Play also exists—indeed, exists properly—when the thematic horizon is not limited by any being-for-itself of subjectivity, and where there are no subjects who are behaving 'playfully'.

The players are not the subjects of play; instead play merely reaches presentation through the players. We can see this first from the use of the word, especially from its multiple metaphorical applications, which Buytendijk in particular has noted.[3]

The metaphorical usage has here, as always, a methodological priority. If a word is applied to a sphere to which it did not originally belong, the actual 'original' meaning emerges quite clearly. Language has performed in advance a work of abstraction which is, as such, the task of conceptual analysis. Now thinking needs only to make use of this advance achievement.

The same is also true of etymologies. They are far less reliable because they are abstractions which are not performed by language, but by linguistic science, which can never be wholly verified by language itself: that is, by their actual usage. Hence even when they are right, they are not proofs, but advance achievements of conceptual analysis, and only in this obtain a firm foundation.[4]

If we examine how the word 'play' is used and concentrate on its so-called transferred meanings we find talk of the play of light, the play of the waves, the play of a component in a bearing-case, the inter-play of limbs, the play of forces, the play of gnats, even a play on words. In each case what is intended is the to-and-fro movement which is not tied to any goal which would bring it to an end. This accords with the original meaning of the word spiel as 'dance', which is still found in many word forms (eg in Spielmann, jongleur).[5] The movement which is play has no goal which brings it to an end; rather it renews itself in constant repetition. The movement backwards and forwards is obviously so central for the definition of a game that it is not important who or what performs this movement. The movement of play as such has, as it were, no substrate. It is the game that is played—it is irrelevant whether or not there is a subject who plays. The play is the performance of the movement as such. Thus we speak of the play of colours and do not mean only that there is one colour, that plays against another, but that there is one process or sight, in which one can see a changing variety of colours.

Hence the mode of being of play is not such that there must be a subject who takes up a playing attitude in order that the game may be played. Rather, the most original sense of playing is the medial one. Thus we say that something is 'playing' somewhere or at some time, that something is going on (sich abspielt, im Spiele ist).[6]

This linguistic observation seems to me to be an indirect indication that play is not to be understood as a kind of activity. As far as language is concerned, the actual subject of play is obviously not the subjectivity of an individual who among other activities also plays, but instead the play itself. Only we are so used to relating a phenomenon such as playing to the sphere of subjectivity and its attitudes that we remain closed to these indications from the spirit of language.

However, modern research has conceived the nature of play so widely that it is led more or less to the verge of that attitude to it that is based on subjectivity. Huizinga has investigated the element of play in all cultures and above all worked out the connection of children's and animal play with the 'sacred plays of the religious cult'. That led him to recognise the curious lack of decisiveness in the playing consciousness, which makes it absolutely impossible to decide between belief and non-belief.

'The savage himself knows no conceptional distinction between being and playing; he knows of no identity, image or symbol. And that is why it may be asked whether one does not get closest to the mental condition of the savage in his sacred actions by holding on to the primary idea of play. In our idea of play the difference between faith and pretence is dissolved'.[7]

Here the primacy of play over the consciousness of the player is fundamentally acknowledged and, in fact, even the experiences of play that the psychologist and anthropologist have to describe are illuminated afresh if one starts from the medial sense of the word spielen. Play obviously represents an order in which the to-and-fro motion of play follows of itself. It is part of play that the movement is not only without goal or purpose but also without effort. It happens, as it were, by itself. The ease of play, which naturally does not mean that there is any real absence of effort, but phenomenologically refers only to the absence of strain,[8] is experienced subjectively as relaxation. The structure of play absorbs the player into itself, and thus takes from him the burden of the initiative, which constitutes the actual strain of existence. This is seen also in the spontaneous tendency to repetition that emerges in the player and in the constant self-renewal of play, which influences its form (eg the refrain).

The fact that the mode of being of play is so close to the mobile form of nature permits us to make an important methodological conclusion. It is obviously not correct to say that animals too play and that we can even say metaphorically that water and light play. Rather, on the contrary, we can say that man too plays. His playing is a natural process. The meaning of his play, precisely because—and insofar as—he is part of nature, is a pure self-presentation. Thus it becomes finally meaningless to distinguish in this sphere between literal and metaphorical usage.

But above all there comes from this medial sense of play the connection with the being of the work of art. Nature, inasmuch as it is without purpose or intention, as it is, without exertion, a constantly self-renewing play, can appear as a model for art. Thus Friedrich Schlegel writes: 'All the sacred games of art are only remote imitations of the infinite play of the world, the eternally self-creating work of art'.[9]

Another question that Huizinga discusses is also clarified as a result of the fundamental role of the to-and-fro movement of play namely the playful character of the contest. It is true that it does not appear to the contestant that he is playing. But there arises through the contest the tense movement to-and-fro from which the victor emerges, thus showing the whole to be a game. The movement to-and-fro obviously belongs so essentially to the game that there is an ultimate sense in which you cannot have a game by yourself. In order for there to be a game, there always has to be, not necessarily literally another player, but something else with which the player plays and which automatically responds to his move with a counter-move. Thus the cat at play chooses the ball of wool because it responds to play, and ball games will be with us forever because the ball is freely mobile in every direction, appearing to do surprising things of its own accord.

The primacy of the game over the players engaged in it is experienced by the players themselves in a special way, where it is a question of human subjectivity that adopts an attitude of play. Once more it is the improper uses of the word that offer the most information about its proper essence. Thus we say of someone that he plays with possibilities or with plans. What we mean is clear. He still has not committed himself to the possibilities as to serious aims. He still has the freedom to decide one way or the other, for one or the other possibility. On the other hand this freedom is not without danger. Rather the game itself is a risk for the player. One can only play with serious possibilities. This means obviously that one may become so engrossed in them that they, as it were, outplay one and prevail over one. The attraction of the game, which it exercises on the player, lies in this risk. One enjoys a freedom of decision, which at the same time is endangered and irrevocably limited. One has only to think of jig-saw puzzles, games of patience etc. But the same is true in serious matters. If someone, for the sake of enjoying his own freedom of decision, avoids making pressing decisions or plays with possibilities that he is not seriously envisaging and which, therefore, offer no risk that he will choose them and thereby limit himself, we say he is only 'playing with life' (verspielt).

This suggests a general characteristic of the way in which the nature of play is reflected in an attitude of play: all playing is a being-played. The attraction of a game, the fascination it exerts, consists precisely in the fact that the game tends to master the players. Even when it is a case of games in which one seeks to accomplish tasks that one has set oneself, there is a risk whether or not it will 'work', 'succeed', and 'succeed again', which is the attraction of the game. Whoever 'tries' is in fact the one who is tried. The real subject of the game (this is shown in precisely those experiences in which there is only a single player) is not the player, but instead the game itself. The game is what holds the player in its spell, draws him into play, and keeps him there.

This is shown also by the fact that games have their own proper spirit.[10] But even this does not refer to the mood or the mental state of those who play the game. Rather, this difference of mental attitude in the playing of different games and in the desire to play them is a result and not the cause of the difference of the games themselves. Games themselves differ from one another by their spirit. The reason for this is that the to-and-fro movement, which is what constitutes the game, is differently arranged. The particular nature of a game lies in the rules and structures which prescribe the way that the area of the game is filled. This is true universally, whenever there is a game. It is true, for example, of the play of fountains and of playing animals. The area in which the game is played is, as it were, set by the nature of the game itself and is defined far more by the structure that determines the movement of the game than by what it comes up against, ie the boundaries of the free area, which limits movement from outside.

Apart from these general determining factors, it seems to me characteristic of human play that it plays something. That means that the structure of movement to which it submits has a definite quality which the player 'chooses'. He first of all expressly separates off his playing behavior from his other behaviour by wanting to play. But even within his readiness to play he makes a choice. He chooses this game and not that. It accords with this that the movement of the game is not simply the free area in which one 'plays oneself out', but is one that is specially marked out and reserved for the movement of the game. The human game requires its playing field. The setting apart of the playing field—just like that of sacred precincts, as Huizinga rightly points out[11]—sets the sphere of play as a closed world without transition and mediation over against the world of aims. That all play is a playing of something is true here, where the ordered to-and-fro movement of the game is determined as an attitude and marks itself off from other attitudes. The playing man is, even in his play, still someone who takes up an attitude, even if the proper essence of the game consists in his getting rid of the tension which he feels in his attitude to his aims. This determines more exactly why playing is always a playing of something. Every game presents the man who plays it with a task. He cannot enjoy the freedom of playing himself out except by transforming the aims of his behaviour into mere tasks of the game. Thus the child gives itself a task in playing with the ball, and such tasks are playful ones, because the purpose of the game is not really the solution of the task, but the ordering and shaping of the movement of the game itself.

Obviously the characteristic lightness and sense of relief which we find in the attitude of play depends on the particular character of the task set by the game, and comes from solving it.

One can say that to perform a task successfully 'represents it'. One can say this all the more when it is a question of a game, for here the fulfilment of the task does not point to any purposive context. Play is really limited to representing itself. Thus its mode of being is self-representation. But self-representation is a universal aspect of the being of nature. We know today how inadequate biological conceptions of purpose are when it comes to understanding the form of living things.[12] It is likewise true of play that to ask what its life-function is and its biological purpose is is an inadequate approach. It is, pre-eminently, self-representation.

The self-representation of human play depends, as we have seen, on behaviour which is tied to the make-believe goals of the game, but the 'meaning' of the latter does not in fact depend on achieving these goals. Rather, in spending oneself on the task of the game, one is, in fact, playing oneself out. The self-representation of the game involves the player's achieving, as it were, his own self-representation by playing, ie representing something. Only because play is always representation is human play able to find the task of the game in representation itself. Thus there are games which must be called representation games, either in that, by the use of meaningful allusion, they have something about them of representation (say 'Tinker, Tailor, Soldier, Sailor') or in that the game itself consists in representing something (eg when children play motor-cars).

All representation is potentially representative for someone. That this possibility is intended is the characteristic feature of the playful nature of art. The closed world of play lets down as it were, one of its walls.[13] A religious rite and a play in a theatre obviously do not represent in the same sense as the playing child. Their being is not exhausted by the fact that they represent; at the same time they point beyond themselves to the audience which is sharing in them. Play here is no longer the mere self-representation of an ordered movement, nor mere representation, in which the playing child is totally absorbed, but it is 'representing for someone'. This assignment in all representation comes to the fore here and is constitutive of the being of art.

In general, games, however much they are in essence rep-

resentations and however much the players represent themselves in them, are not represented for anyone, ie they are not
aimed at an audience. Children play for themselves, even when
they represent. And not even those games, eg sports, which are
played before spectators are aimed at them. Indeed, they
threaten to lose their real play character as a contest precisely by
becoming a show. A procession as part of a religious rite is more
than a demonstration, since its real meaning is to embrace the
whole religious community. And yet the religious act is a
genuine representation for the community, and equally a theatrical drama is a playful act that, of its nature, calls for an audience.
The representation of a god in a religious rite, the representation
of a myth in a play, are play not only in the sense that the
participating players are wholly absorbed in the representative
play and find in it their heightened self-representation, but also
in that the players represent a meaningful whole for an audience.
Thus it is not really the absence of a fourth wall that turned the
play into a show. Rather, openness towards the spectator is part
of the closedness of the play. The audience only completes what
the play as such is.[14]

This is the point which shows the importance of the medial
nature of the play process. We have seen that play does not have
its being in the consciousness or the attitude of the player, but on
the contrary draws the latter into its area and fills him with its
spirit. The player experiences the game as a reality that surpasses him. This is more than ever the case where it itself is 'intended' as such a reality—for instance the play which appears as
representation for an audience.

Even a theatrical drama remains a game, ie it has the structure
of a game, which is that of a closed world. But the religious or
profane drama, however much it represents a world that is
wholly closed within itself, is as if open toward the side of the
spectator, in whom it achieves its whole significance. The
players play their roles as in any game, and thus the play is
represented, but the play itself is the whole, comprising players
and spectators. In fact, it is experienced properly by, and presents itself as what is 'meant' to, one who is not acting in the play,
but is watching. In him the game is raised, as it were, to its
perfection.

For the players this means that they do not simply fulfil their
roles as in any game—rather, they play their roles, they represent them for the audience. Their mode of participation in the
game is no longer determined by the fact that they are completely absorbed in it, but by their playing their role in relation

and regard to the whole of the play, in which not they, but the audience is to become absorbed. When a play activity becomes a play in the theatre a total switch takes place. It puts the spectator in the place of the player. He—and not the player—is the person for and in whom the play takes place. Of course this does not mean that the player is not able to experience the significance of the whole, in which he plays his representing role. The spectator has only methodological precedence. In that the play is presented for him, it becomes apparent that it bears within itself a meaning that must be understood and that can therefore be detached from the behaviour of the player. Basically the difference between the player and the spectator is removed here. The requirement that the play itself be intended in its meaningfulness is the same for both.

This is still the case even when the play community is sealed off against all spectators, either because it opposes the social institutionalisation of artistic life, as in so-called chamber music, which seeks to be music-making in a fuller sense, because it is performed for the players themselves and not for an audience. If someone performs music in this way, he is also in fact trying to make the music 'sound well', but that means that it would be properly there for any listener. Artistic presentation, by its nature, exists for someone, even if there is no one there who listens or watches only.

(B) TRANSFORMATION INTO STRUCTURE AND TOTAL MEDIATION

I call this development, in which human play finds its true perfection in being art, 'the transformation into structure'. Only through this development does play acquire its ideality, so that it can be intended and understood as play. Only now does it emerge as detached from the representing activity of the players and consist in the pure appearance of what they are playing. As such the play—even the unforeseen elements of improvisation—is fundamentally repeatable and hence permanent. It has the character of a work, of an ergon and not only of energeia.[15] In this sense I call it a structure.

What can be separated in this way from the representing activity of the player still remains dependent on representation. This dependence does not mean that it is only through the particular persons representing it that the play acquires its definite meaning, not even through him who as the originator of the work is its real creator, the artist. Rather, the play has, in relation to them all, an absolute autonomy, and that is what is suggested by the idea of transformation.

The implications for the definition of the nature of art emerge when one takes the sense of transformation seriously. Transformation is not change, even a change that is especially far-reaching. A change always means that what is changed also remains the same and is held on to. However totally it may change, something changes in it. In terms of categories, all change (alloiosis) belongs in the sphere of quality, ie of an accident of substance. But transformation means that something is suddenly and as a whole something else, that this other transformed thing that it has become is its true being, in comparison with which its earlier being is nothing. When we find someone transformed we mean precisely this, that he has become, as it were, another person. There cannot here be any transition of gradual change leading from one to the other, since the one is the denial of the other. Thus the transformation into a structure means that what existed previously no longer exists. But also that what now exists, what represents itself in the play of art, is what is lasting and true.

It is clear here that to start from subjectivity is to miss the point. What no longer exists is the players—with the poet or the composer being considered as one of the players. None of them has his own existence for himself, which he retains so that his acting would mean that he 'only acts'. If we describe from the point of view of the actor what his acting is, then obviously it is not transformation, but disguise. A man who is disguised does not want to be recognised, but instead to appear as someone else and be taken for him. In the eyes of others he no longer wants to be himself, but to be taken for someone else. Thus he does not want to be discovered or recognised. He plays another person, but in the way that we play something in our daily intercourse with other people, ie that we merely pretend, act a part and create an impression. A person who plays such a game denies, to all appearances, continuity with himself. But in truth that means that he holds on to this continuity with himself for himself and only keeps it from those before whom he is acting.

According to all that we have observed concerning the nature of play, this subjective distinction between oneself and the play, which is what acting a part is, is not the true nature of play. Play itself is, rather, transformation of such a kind that the identity of the player does not continue to exist for anybody. Everybody asks instead what it is supposed to be, what is 'meant'. The players (or poets) no longer exist, but only what of theirs is played.

But, above all, what no longer exists is the world, in which we live as our own. Transformation into a structure is not simply transposition into another world. Certainly it is another, closed world in which play takes place. But inasmuch as it is a structure, it has, so to speak, found its measure in itself and measures itself by nothing outside it. Thus the action of a drama—in this it still entirely resembles the religious act—exists absolutely as something that rests within itself. It no longer permits of any comparison with reality as the secret measure of all copied similarity. It is raised above all such comparisons—and hence also above the question whether it is all real—because a superior truth speaks from it. Even Plato, the most radical critic of the high estimation of art in the history of philosophy, speaks sometimes, without differentiating between them, of the comedy and tragedy of life and of the stage.[16] For this difference disappears if one knows how to see the meaning of the game that unfolds before one. The pleasure offered in the spectacle is the same in both cases: it is the joy of knowledge.

This gives the full meaning to what we called transformation into a structure. The transformation is a transformation into the true. It is not enchantment in the sense of a bewitchment that waits for the redeeming word that will transform things to what they were, but it is itself redemption and transformation back into true being. In the representation of play, what is emerges. In it is produced and brought to the light what otherwise is constantly hidden and withdrawn. If someone knows how to perceive the comedy and tragedy of life, he is able to resist the suggestiveness of purposes which conceal the game that is played with us.

'Reality' always stands in a horizon of the future of observed and feared or, at any rate, still undecided possibilities. Hence it is always the case that mutually exclusive expectations are aroused, not all of which can be fulfilled. The undecidedness of the future is what permits such a superfluity of expectations that reality necessarily falls behind them. If, now, in a particular case, a meaningful whole completes and fulfils itself in reality, such that no lines of meaning scatter in the void, then this reality is itself like a drama. Equally, someone who is able to see the whole of reality as a closed circle of meaning, in which everything is fulfilled, will speak of the comedy and tragedy of life. In these cases, in which reality is understood as a play, there emerges what the reality of play is, which we call the play of art. The being of all play is always realisation, sheer fulfilment, energeia which has its telos within itself. The world of the work of art, in which play expresses itself fully in the unity of its course, is in fact a wholly transformed world. By means of it everyone recognises that that is how things are.

Thus the concept of transformation characterises the independent and superior mode of being of what we called structures. From this viewpoint 'reality' is defined as what is untransformed, and art as the raising up of this reality into its truth. Also the classical theory of art, which bases all art on the idea of mimesis, imitation, has obviously started from play which, in the form of dancing, is the representation of the divine.[17]

But the concept of imitation can only describe the play of art if one retains the element of knowledge contained in imitation. What is represented is there—this is the original imitative situation. If a person imitates something, he produces what he knows and in the way that he knows it. A child begins to play by imitation, doing what he knows and affirming his own being in the process. Also, children's delight in dressing-up, to which Aristotle refers, does not seek to be a hiding of themselves, a pretence, in order to be discovered and recognised behind it but, on the contrary, a representation of such a kind that only what is represented exists. The child does not want at any cost to be discovered behind his disguise. He intends that what he represents should exist, and if something is to be guessed, then this is it. What it "is" should be recognised.[18]

We have established that the element of knowledge in imitation is recognition. But what is recognition? A more exact analysis of the phenomenon will make quite clear to us the nature of representation, which is what we are concerned with. As we know, Aristotle emphasises that artistic representation even makes the unpleasant appear as pleasant,[19] and Kant for this reason defined art as the beautiful representation of something, because it is even able to make the ugly appear beautiful.[20] But this obviously does not refer to artificiality and artistic technique. One does not, as with a circus performer, admire the art with which something is done. This has only secondary interest. What one experiences in a work of art and what one is directed towards is rather how true it is, ie to what extent one knows and recognises something and oneself.

But we do not understand what recognition is in its profoundest nature, if we only see that something that we know already is known again, ie that what is familiar is recognised again. The joy of recognition is rather that more becomes known than is already known. In recognition what we know emerges, as if through an illumination, from all the chance and variable circumstances that condition it and is grasped in its essence. It is known as something.

This is the central motif of Platonism. In his theory of anamnesis Plato combined the mythical idea of remembrance with his dialectic, which sought in the logo, ie the ideality of language, the truth of being.[21] In fact this kind of idealism of being is already suggested in the phenomenon of recognition. The 'known' enters into its true being and manifests itself as what it is only when it is recognised. As recognised it is grasped in its essence, detached from its accidental aspects. This is wholly true of the kind of recognition that takes place in relation to what is represented in a play. This kind of representation leaves behind it everything that is accidental and unessential, eg the private particular being of the actor. He disappears entirely in the recognition of what he is representing. But even that which is represented, a well-known event of mythological tradition, is raised by its representation, as it were, to its own validity and truth. With regard to the recognition of the true, the being of representation is superior to the being of the material represented, the Achilles of Homer more than the original Achilles.

Thus the basic mimic situation that we are discussing not only involves what is represented being there, but also that it has in this way come to exist more fully. Imitation and representation are not merely a second version, a copy, but a recognition of the essence. Because they are not merely repetition, but a 'bringing forth', the spectator is also involved in them. They contain the essential relation to everyone for whom the representation exists.

Indeed, one can say even more: the presentation of the essence, far from being a mere imitation, is necessarily revelatory. When someone makes an imitation, he has to leave out and to heighten. Because he is pointing to something, he has to exaggerate, whether he likes it or not. Hence there exists an unbridgeable gulf between the one thing, that is a likeness, and the other that it seeks to resemble. As we know, Plato insisted on this ontological gulf, on the greater or lesser distance between the copy and the original and for this reason considered imitation and representation in the play of art, as an imitation of an imitation, in the third rank.[22] Nevertheless, in the representation of art, recognition is operative, which has the character of genuine knowledge of essence, and since Plato considers all knowledge of being to be recognition, this is the ground of Aristotle's remark that poetry is more philosophical than history.[23]

Thus imitation, as representation, has a clear cognitive function. Therefore the idea of imitation was able to continue in the theory of art for as long as the significance of art as knowledge was unquestioned. But that is valid only while it is held that knowledge of the true is knowledge of the essence,[24] for art supports this kind of knowledge in a convincing way. For the nominalism of modern science, however, and its idea of reality, from which Kant drew the conclusion that aesthetics has nothing to do with knowledge, the concept of mimesis has lost its aesthetic force.

Having seen the difficulties of this subjective development in aesthetics, we are forced to return to the older tradition. If art is not the variety of changing experiences whose object is each time filled subjectively with meaning like an empty mould, representation must be recognised as the mode of being of the work of art. This was prepared for by the idea of representation being derived from the idea of play, in that self-representation is the true nature of play—and hence of the work of art also. The playing of the play is what speaks to the spectator, through its representation, and this in such a way that the spectator, despite the distance between it and himself, still belongs to it.

This is seen most clearly in the type of representation that is a religious rite. Here the relation to the community is obvious. An aesthetic consciousness, however reflective, can no longer consider that only the aesthetic differentiation, which sees the aesthetic object in its own right, discovers the true meaning of the religious picture or the religious rite. No one will be able to hold that the performance of the ritual act is unessential to religious truth.

This is equally true for drama, and what it is as a piece of literature. The performance of a play, likewise, cannot be simply detached from the play itself, as if it were something that is not part of its essential being, but is as subjective and fluid as the aesthetic experiences in which it is experienced. Rather, in the performance, and only in it—as we see most clearly in the case of music—do we encounter the work itself, as the divine is encountered in the religious rite. Here the methodological advantage of starting from the idea of play becomes clear. The work of art cannot be simply isolated from the 'contingency' of the chance conditions in which it appears, and where there is this kind of isolation, the result is an abstraction which reduces the actual being of the work. It itself belongs to the world to which it represents itself. A drama exists really only when it is played, and certainly music must resound.

My thesis, then, is that the being of art cannot be determined as an object of an aesthetic awareness because, on the contrary, the aesthetic attitude is more than it knows of itself. It is a part of the essential process of representation and is an essential part of play as play.

What are the ontological consequences of this? If we start in this way from the play character of play, what emerges for the closer definition of the nature of aesthetic being? This much is clear: drama and the work of art understood in its own terms is not a mere schema of rules or prescriptions of attitudes, within which play can freely realise itself. The playing of the drama does not ask to be understood as the satisfying of a need to play, but as the coming into existence of the work of literature itself. And so there arises the question of the being proper to a poetic work that comes to be only in performance and in theatrical representation, although it is still its own proper being that is there represented.

Let us recall the phrase used above of the 'transformation into a structure'. Play is structure—this means that despite its dependence on being played it is a meaningful whole which can be repeatedly represented as such and the significance of which can be understood. But the structure is also play, because—despite this theoretical unity—it achieves its full being only each time it is played. It is the complementary nature of the two sides of the one thing that we seek to underline, as against the abstraction of aesthetic differentiation.

We may now formulate this by opposing to aesthetic differentiation, the properly constitutive element of aesthetic consciousness, 'aesthetic non-differentiation'. It has become clear that what is imitated in imitation, what is formed by the poet, represented by the actor, recognised by the spectator is to such an extent what is meant—that in which the significance of the representation lies—that the poetic formation or the achievement involved in the representation are not distinguished from it. When a distinction is made, it is between the material and the forming, between the poem and the 'conception'. But these distinctions are of a secondary nature. What the actor plays and the spectator recognises are the forms and the action itself, as they are intended by the poet. Thus we have here a double mimesis: the writer represents and the actor represents. But even this double mimesis is one: it is the same thing that comes to existence in each case.

More exactly, one can say that the mimic representation of the performance brings into being-there what the written play actually requires. The double distinction between a drama and its subject matter and a drama and performance corresponds to a double non-distinction as the unity of the truth which one recognises in the play of art. It is to move out of the actual experience of a piece of literature if one investigates the origin of the plot on which it is based, and equally it is to move out of the actual

experience of the drama if the spectator reflects about the conception behind a performance or about the proficiency of the
actors. This kind of reflection already contains the aesthetic
differentiation of the work itself from its representation. But for
the meaningfulness of the experience as such it is, as we have
seen, not even important whether the tragic or comic scene
which is played before one takes place on the stage or in life—if
one is only a spectator. What we have called a structure is one
insofar as it presents itself as a meaningful whole. It does not
exist in itself, nor is it experienced in a communication accidental to it, but it gains, through being communicated, its proper
being.

No matter how much the variety of the performances or reali-
sations of such a structure goes back to the conception of the
players—it also does not remain enclosed in the subjectivity of
what they think, but it is embodied there. Thus it is not at all a
question of a mere subjective variety of conceptions, but of the
possibilities of being that the work itself possesses, which lays
itself out in the variety of its aspects.

This is not to deny that here there is a possible starting-point
for aesthetic reflection. In different performances of the same
play, say, one can distinguish between one kind of mediation
and another, just as one can conceive the conditions of access to
works of art of a different kind in various ways, eg when one
looks at a building from the point of view of how it would look on
its own or how its surroundings ought to look. Or when one
is faced with the question of the restoration of a painting. In
all these cases the work itself is distinguished from its
'representation'.[25] But one fails to appreciate the compelling
quality of the work of art if one regards the variations possible in
the representation as free and optional. In fact they are all subject to the supreme criterion of the 'right' representation.[26]

We know this in the modern theatre as the tradition that stems
from a production, the creation of a role, or the practice of a
musical performance. Here there is no random succession, a
mere variety of conceptions, but rather from the constant following of models and from a productive and changing development
there is cultivated a tradition with which every new attempt
must come to terms. The interpretative artist too has a sure
consciousness of this. The way that he approaches a work or a
role is always related in some way to models which did the same.
But it has nothing to do with blind imitation. Although the tradition that is created by a great actor, producer or musician remains effective as a model, it is not a brake on free creation, but

has become so one with the work that the concern with this model stimulates the creative interpretative powers of an artist no less than the concern with the work itself. The reproductive arts have this special quality that the works with which they are concerned are explicitly left open to this kind of re-creation and thus have visibly opened the identity and continuity of the work of art towards its future.[27]

Perhaps the criterion that determines here whether something is 'a correct representation' is a highly mobile and relative one. But the compelling quality of the representation is not lessened by the fact that it cannot have any fixed criterion. Thus we do not allow the interpretation of a piece of music or a drama the freedom to take the fixed 'text' as a basis for a lot of ad-lib effects, and yet we would regard the canonisation of a particular interpretation, eg in a gramophone recording conducted by the composer, or the detailed notes on performance which come from the canonised first performance, as a failure to understand the actual task of interpretation. A 'correctness', striven for in this way, would not do justice to the true binding nature of the work, which imposes itself on every interpreter in a special and immediate way and does not allow him to make things easy for himself by simply imitating a model.

It is also, as we know, wrong to limit the 'freedom' of interpretative choice to externals or marginal phenomena and not rather to think of the whole of an interpretation in a way that is both bound and free. Interpretation is probably, in a certain sense, re-creation, but this re-creation does not follow the process of the creative act, but the lines of the created work which has to be brought to representation in accord with the meaning the interpreter finds in it. Thus, for example, performances of music played on old instruments are not as faithful as they seem. Rather, they are an imitation of an imitation and in danger 'of standing at a third remove from the truth' (Plato).

In view of the finite nature of our historical existence there is, it would seem, something absurd about the whole idea of a uniquely correct interpretation. We shall come back to this in another context. Here the obvious fact, that every interpretation seeks to be correct, serves only to confirm that the non-differentiation of the interpretation from the work itself is the actual experience of the work. This accords with the fact that the aesthetic consciousness is generally able to make the aesthetic distinction between the work and its interpretation only in a critical way, ie where the interpretation breaks down. The communication of the work is, in principle, a total one.

Total communication means that the communicating element cancels itself out. In other words, reproduction (in the case of drama and music, but also with the recitation of stories or poetry) does not become, as such, thematic, but the work presents itself through it and in it. We shall see that the same is true of the character of approach and encounter in which buildings and statues present themselves. Here also the approach is not, as such, thematic, but neither is it true that one would have to abstract from life-references in order to grasp the work itself. Rather, it exists within them. The fact that works come out of a past from which they stretch into the present as permanent monuments, still does not make their being into an object of aesthetic or historical consciousness. As long as they still fulfil their function, they are contemporaneous with every age. Even if their place is only in museums as works of art, they are not entirely alienated from themselves. Not only does a work of art never completely lose the trace of its original function which enables an expert to reconstruct it, but the work of art that has its place next to others in a gallery is still its own origin. It affirms itself, and the way in which it does that—by 'killing' other things or using them profitably to complement itself—is still part of itself.

We ask what this identity is that presents itself so differently in the changing course of ages and circumstances. It does not disintegrate into the changing aspects of itself so that it would lose all identity, but it is there in them all. They all belong to it. They are all contemporaneous with it. Thus we have the task of giving an interpretation of the work of art in terms of time.

(C) THE TEMPORALITY OF THE AESTHETIC

What kind of contemporaneity is this? What kind of temporality belongs to aesthetic being? This contemporaneity and presentness of aesthetic being is called, in general, its timelessness. But this timelessness has to be thought of together with the temporality to which it essentially belongs. Timelessness is primarily only a dialectical feature which arises out of temporality and in contrast with it. Even if one speaks of two kinds of temporality, a historical and a supra-historical one, as does Sedlmayr, for example, following Baader and with reference to Bollnow, in an effort to determine the temporality of the work of art,[28] one cannot move beyond a dialectical tension between the two. The supra-historical 'sacred' time, in which the 'present' is not the fleeting movement but the fullness of time, is described from the point of view of existential temporality. The inadequacy of this kind of antithesis emerges when one inevitably discovers that 'true time' projects into historical-existential 'appearance time'. This kind of projection would obviously have the character of an epiphany, but this means that for the experiencing consciousness it is without continuity.

This involves again all the difficulties of the aesthetic awareness, which we pointed out above. For it is precisely continuity that every understanding of time has to achieve, even when it is a question of the temporality of a work of art. Here the misunderstanding of Heidegger's ontological exposition of the time horizon avenges itself. Instead of holding on to the methodological significance of the existential analytic of There-being, people treat this existential, historical temporality of There-being, determined by care and the movement towards death, ie radical finiteness, as one among many possible ways of understanding existence, and it is forgotten that it is the mode of being of understanding itself which is here revealed as temporality. The withdrawal of the proper temporality of the work of art as 'sacred time' from transient historical time remains, in fact, a mere mirroring of the human and finite experience of art. Only a biblical theology of time, starting not from the standpoint of human self-understanding, but from divine revelation, would be able to speak of a 'sacred time' and theologically justify the analogy between the timelessness of the work of art and this 'sacred time'. Without this kind of theological justification, to speak of 'sacred time' obscures the real problem, which does not lie in the atemporality of the work of art but in its temporality. Thus we take up our question again: what kind of temporality is this?[29]

We started from the position that the work of art is play, ie that its actual being cannot be detached from its representation and that in the representation the unity and identity of a structure emerge. To be dependent on self-representation is part of its nature. This means that however much it may be changed and distorted in the representation, it still remains itself. This constitutes the validity of every representation, that it contains a relation to the structure itself and submits itself to the criterion of its correctness. Even the extreme of a wholly distorting representation confirms this. It becomes known as a distortion inasmuch as the representation is intended and appreciated as the representation of the structure. The representation has, in an indissoluble, indelible way the character of the repetition. Re-

petition does not mean here that something is repeated in the
literal sense, ie can be reduced to something original. Rather,
every repetition is equally an original of the work.

We know this kind of highly puzzling time structure from
festivals.[30] It is in the nature, at least of periodic festivals, to be
repeated. We call that the return of the festival. But the return-
ing festival is neither another, nor the mere remembrance of the
one that was originally celebrated. The originally sacral character of all festivals obviously excludes the kind of distinction that
we know in the time-experience of the present; memory and
expectation. The time-experience of the festival is rather its
celebration, a present time sui generis.

The temporal character of celebration is difficult to grasp on
the basis of the customary chronological experience of succession. If the return of the festival is related to the usual experience of time and its dimensions, it appears as historical
temporality. The festival changes from one time to the next.
For there are always other things going on at the same time.
Nevertheless it would still remain, under this historical aspect,
one and the same festival that undergoes this kind of change. It
was originally of a certain nature and was celebrated in this way,
then different, and then different again.

However, this aspect does not cover the time character of the
festival that comes from its being celebrated. For the essence of
the festival its historical connections are secondary. As a festival it is not an identity, in the manner of an historical event, but
neither is it determined by its origin so that there was once the
'real' festival—as distinct from the way in which it came later to
be celebrated. From the start it belonged to it that it should be
regularly celebrated. Thus it is its own original essence always
to be something different (even when celebrated in exactly the
same way). An entity that exists only by always being something
different is temporal in a more radical sense than everything that
belongs to history. It has its being only in becoming and in
return.[31]

A festival exists only in being celebrated. This is not to say
that it is of a subjective character and has its being only in the
subjectivity of those celebrating it. Rather the festival is celebrated because it is there. The same is true of drama—it must be
represented for the spectator, and yet its being is by no means
just the point of intersection of the experiences that the spectators have. Rather the contrary is true, that the being of the
spectator is determined by his being there present. To be present
does not mean simply to be in the presence of something else

that is there at the same time. To be present means to share. If someone was present at something, he knows all about how it really was. It is only in a derived sense that presence at something means also a kind of subjective attitude, that of attention to something. Thus to watch something is a genuine mode of sharing. Perhaps we may remind the reader of the idea of sacral communion which lies behind the original Greek idea of theoria. Theoros means someone who takes part in a mission to a festival. Such a person has no other qualification and function than to be there. Thus the theoros is a spectator in the literal sense of the word, who shares in the solemn act through his presence at it and in this way acquires his sacred quality: for example, of inviolability.

In the same way, Greek metaphysics still conceives the nature of theoria and of nous as pure presence to what is truly real,[32] and also the capacity to be able to act theoretically is defined for us by the fact that in attending to something it is possible to forget one's own purposes.[33] But theoria is not to be conceived primarily as an attitude of subjectivity, as a self-determination of the subjective consciousness, but in terms of what it is contemplating. Theoria is a true sharing, not something active, but something passive (pathos), namely being totally involved in and carried away by what one sees. It is from this point that people have tried recently to explain the religious background of the Greek idea of reason.[34]

We started by saying that the true being of the spectator, who is part of the play of art, cannot be adequately understood in terms of subjectivity, as an attitude of the aesthetic consciousness. But this does not mean that the nature of the spectator cannot be described in terms of being present at something, in the way that we pointed out. To be present, as a subjective act of a human attitude, has the character of being outside oneself. Even Plato, in his *Phaedrus,* makes the mistake of judging the ecstasy of being outside oneself from the point of view of rational reasonableness and of seeing it as the mere negation of being within oneself, ie as a kind of madness. In fact, being outside oneself is the positive possibility of being wholly with something else. This kind of being present is a self-forgetfulness, and it is the nature of the spectator to give himself in self-forgetfulness to what he is watching. Self-forgetfulness here is anything but a primitive condition, for it arises from the attention to the object, which is the positive act of the spectator.[35]

Obviously there is an important difference between a spectator who gives himself entirely to the play of art, and someone who merely gapes at something out of curiosity. It is also characteristic of curiosity that it is as if drawn away by what it looks at, that it forgets itself entirely in it, and cannot tear itself away from it. But the important thing about an object of curiosity is that it is basically of no concern to the spectator, it has no meaning for him. There is nothing in it which he would really be able to come back to and which would focus his attention. For it is the formal quality of novelty, ie abstract difference, which makes up the charm of what one looks at. This is seen in the fact that its dialectical complement is becoming bored and jaded. Whereas that which presents itself to the spectator as the play of art does not simply exhaust itself in the ecstatic emotion of the moment, but has a claim to permanence and the permanence of a claim.

The word 'claim' does not occur here by accident. In the type of theological reflection which started with Kierkegaard and which we call 'dialectical theology' this idea has made possible a theological explanation of what is meant by Kierkegaard's notion of simultaneity. A claim is something lasting. Its justification (or pretended justification) is the first thing. Because a claim continues, it can be affirmed at any time. A claim exists against someone and must therefore be asserted against him; but the concept of a claim also contains the idea that it is not itself a fixed demand, the fulfilment of which is agreed by both sides, but is, rather, the ground for such. A claim is the legal basis for an unspecified demand. If it is to be answered in such a way as to be settled, then it must first take the form of a demand when it is made. It belongs to the permanence of a claim that it is concretised into a demand.

The application to lutheran theology is that the claim of the call to faith persists since the proclamation of the gospel and is made afresh in preaching. The words of the sermon perform this total mediation which otherwise is the work of the religious rite, say, of the mass. We shall see that the word is called also in other ways to mediate contemporaneity, and that therefore in the problem of hermeneutics it has the chief place.

At any rate 'contemporaneity' forms part of the being of the work of art. It constitutes the nature of 'being present'. It is not the simultaneity of the aesthetic consciousness, for that simultaneity refers to the coexistence and the equal validity of different aesthetic objects of experience in the one consciousness. Contemporaneity, however, here means that a single thing that presents itself to us achieves in its presentation full presentness, however remote its origin may be. Thus contemporaneity is not a mode of givenness in consciousness, but a task for consciousness and an achievement that is required of it. It consists in holding on to the object in such a way that it becomes contemporaneous, but this means that all mediation is dissolved in total presentness.

This idea of contemporaneity comes, as we know, from Kierkegaard, who gave to it a particular theological emphasis.[36] Contemporaneity, for Kierkegaard, does not mean existing at the same time, but is a formulation of the believer's task of so totally combining one's own presence and the redeeming act of Christ, that the latter is experienced as something present (not as something in the past) and is taken seriously as such. Against this the simultaneity of the aesthetic consciousness depends on the concealment of the task that contemporaneity sets.

Hence contemporaneity is something that is found especially in the religious act, and in the sermon. The sense of being present is here the genuine sharing in the redemptive action itself. No one can doubt that the aesthetic differentiation, eg of a 'beautiful' ceremony or of a 'good' sermon is, in view of the appeal that is made to us, misplaced. Now I maintain that the same thing is basically true for the experience of art. Here also mediation must be conceived as total. Neither the separate life of the creating artist—his biography—nor that of the performer who acts a work, nor that of the spectator who is watching the play, has any separate legitimacy in the face of the being of the work of art.

What unfolds before one is for every one so lifted out of the continuing progression of the world and so self-enclosed as to make an independent circle of meaning that no one is motivated to go beyond it to another future and reality. The spectator is set at an absolute distance which makes any practical, purposive share in it impossible. But the distance is, in the literal sense, aesthetic distance, for it is the distance from seeing that makes possible the proper and comprehensive sharing in what is represented before one. Thus to the ecstatic self-forgetfulness of the spectator there corresponds his continuity with himself. Precisely that in which he loses himself as a spectator requires his own continuity. It is the truth of his own world, the religious and moral world in which he lives, which presents itself to him and in which he recognises himself. Just as the parousia, absolute presence, describes the ontological mode of aesthetic being, and a work of art is the same wherever it becomes such a presence, so the absolute moment in which a spectator stands is at once self-forgetfulness and reconciliation with self. That which detaches him from everything also gives him back the whole of his being.

The dependence of aesthetic being on representation does not mean any deficiency, any lack of autonomous determination of meaning. It belongs to its essence. The spectator is an essential element of the kind of play that we call aesthetic. Let us remember here the famous definition of tragedy which we find in Aristotle's *Poetics*. There the attitude of the spectator is expressly included in the definition.

(D) THE EXAMPLE OF THE TRAGIC

The Aristotelian theory of tragedy may serve as an example for the structure of aesthetic being as a whole. It exists in the content of a poetics and seems to be valid only for dramatic poetry. However, the tragic is a basic phenomenon, a meaningful structure which does not exist only in tragedy, the tragic work of art in the narrower sense, but can have its place also in other artistic genres, especially epic. Indeed, it is not even a specifically artistic phenomenon, inasmuch as it is found also in life. For this reason, the tragic is seen by modern scholars (Richard Hamann, Max Scheler[37]) as something extra-aesthetic. It is an ethical and metaphysical phenomenon that enters into the sphere of aesthetic problems only from outside. But after we have seen how questionable the idea of the aesthetic is, we must now raise the contrary issue, namely, whether the tragic is not, rather, a basic aesthetic phenomenon. The nature of the aesthetic has emerged for us as play and representation. Thus we may also consult the theory of the tragic play, the poetics of tragedy, as to the essence of the tragic.

What we find reflected in thought about the tragic, from Aristotle down to the present, is by no means of an unchangeable nature. There is no doubt that the essence of tragedy is presented in Attic tragedy in a unique way; and differently for Aristotle, for whom Euripides was the 'most tragic',[38] differently again for someone to whom Aeschylus reveals the truth of the tragic phenomenon, and very differently for someone who thinks of Shakespeare. But this change does not simply mean that the question of the unified nature of the tragic would be without an object, but rather, on the contrary, that the phenomenon presents itself in an outline given by a historical unity. The reflection of classical tragedy in modern tragedy of which Kierkegaard speaks is constantly present in all modern thinking on the tragic. If we start with Aristotle, we shall see the whole scope of the tragic phenomenon. In his famous definition of tragedy Aristotle made a point that had a great influence on the problem of the aesthetic: he included in the definition of tragedy the effect on the spectator.

I cannot hope to treat his famous and much discussed definition fully here. But the mere fact that the spectator is taken into the definition makes clear what was said above concerning the essential part that the spectator plays in a drama. The way in which the spectator is part of it makes apparent the meaningfulness of the figure of play. Thus the distance that the spectator retains from the drama is not an optional attitude, but the essential relation whose ground lies in the meaningful unity of the play. Tragedy is the unity of a tragic succession of events that is experienced as such. But what is experienced as a tragic succession of events, even if it is not a play that is shown on the stage, but a tragedy in 'life', is a closed circle of meaning that resists, of itself, all penetration and influence. What is understood as tragic must simply be accepted. Hence it is, in fact, a basic 'aesthetic' phenomenon.

We learn from Aristotle that the representation of the tragic action has a specific effect on the spectator. The representation works through eleos and phobos. The traditional translation of these emotions by 'pity' and 'terror' gives them a far too subjective tinge. Aristotle is not at all concerned with pity or with the evaluation of pity as it has changed through the centuries,[39] and fear is similarly not to be understood as an inner emotion. Rather both are events that overwhelm man and sweep him away. Eleos is the distress that comes over us in the face of what we call distressing. Thus the fate of Oedipus is distressing (the example that Aristotle always returns to). The English word 'distress' is a good equivalent because it too refers not merely to an inner state, but likewise to its manifestation. Accordingly, phobos is not just a state of mind but, as Aristotle says, a cold shudder[40] that makes one's blood run cold, that makes one shiver. In the particular sense in which, in this definition of tragedy, phobos is combined with eleos, phobos means the shivers of apprehension which come over us for someone whom we see rushing to his destruction and for whom we fear. Distress and apprehension are modes of ecstasis, being outside oneself, which testify to the power of what is taking place before us.

Now Aristotle says of these emotions that they are what the play uses in order to purify us of them. As is well-known, this translation is doubtful, especially the sense of the genitive.[41] But what Aristotle means seems to me to be quite independent of this, and this must ultimately show why two conceptions so different grammatically can continue to be held so firmly. It seems clear to me that Aristotle is thinking of the tragic pensiveness that comes over the spectator at a tragedy. But pensiveness is a kind of relief and resolution, in which pain and pleasure are variously mixed. How can Aristotle call this condition a purification? What is the impure element in feeling, and how is this removed in the tragic emotion? The answer seems to me the following: being overcome by distress and horror involves a painful division. There is a disjunction with what is happening, a refusal to accept, that rebels against the agonising events. But it is precisely the effect of the tragic catastrophe that this disjunction with what exists is removed. The heart is freed from constraint. We are freed not only from the spell in which the painful and horrifying nature of the tragic destiny had held us, but at the same time we are free from everything that divides us from what is.

Thus tragic pensiveness reflects a kind of affirmation, a return to ourselves, and if, as is often the case in modern tragedy, the hero is affected in his own consciousness by the emotion, he himself shares a little in this affirmation, in that he accepts his fate.

But what is the real object of this affirmation? What is affirmed? Certainly not the justice of a moral world order. The notorious tragic theory of guilt that scarcely retains any importance for Aristotle is not a suitable explanation for modern tragedy. For tragedy does not exist where guilt and expiation correspond to each other in the right measure, where a moral bill of guilt is paid in full. Nor in modern tragedy can and must there be a full subjectivisation of guilt and of fate. Rather the excess of tragic consequences is typical of the nature of the tragic. Despite all the subjectivisation of guilt in modern tragedy it still retains an element of that classical sense of the power of destiny that, in the very disproportion between guilt and fate, reveals itself as the same for all. Hebbel seems to stand on the borderline of what can still be called tragedy, so exactly is subjective guilt fitted into the course of the tragic action. For the same reason the idea of christian tragedy presents a special problem, since in the light of divine salvation history the values of happiness and misfourtune that are constitutive of the tragic action no longer determine human destiny. Even Kierkegaard's[42] brilliant contrast of the classical suffering that followed from a curse laid on a family, with the suffering that rends the consciousness that is not at one with itself, but involved in conflict, only reaches the bounds of the tragic. His rewritten *Antigone*[43] would no longer be a tragedy.

So we must repeat the question: what is affirmed here of the spectator? Obviously it is the disproportionate, terrible immensity of the consequences that flow from a guilty deed which is the real claim made on the spectator. The tragic affirmation is the fulfilment of this claim. It has the character of a genuine communion. It is something truly common which is experienced in such an excess of tragic suffering. The spectator recognises himself and his own finiteness in the face of the power of fate. What happens to the great ones of the earth has an exemplary significance. The tragic emotion is not a response to the tragic course of events as such or to the justice of the fate that overtakes the hero, but to the metaphysical order of being that is true for all. To see that 'this is how it is' is a kind of self-knowledge for the spectator, who emerges with new insight from the illusions in which he lives. The tragic affirmation is an insight which the spectator has by virtue of the continuity of significance in which he places himself.

It follows from this analysis of the tragic not only that it is a basic aesthetic idea, inasmuch as the distance of the spectator is part of the essence of the tragic but, more importantly, that the distance of the spectator, which determines the nature of the aesthetic, does not include the 'aesthetic differentiation' which we recognised as a feature of 'aesthetic consciousness'. The spectator does not hold himself aloof at a distance of aesthetic consciousness enjoying the art of representation,[44] but in the communion of being present. The real emphasis of the tragic phenomenon lies ultimately on what is represented and recognised and to share in it is not a question of choice. However much the tragic play that is performed solemnly in the theatre represents an exceptional situation in the life of everyone, it is not an experience of an adventure producing a temporary intoxication from which one re-awakens to one's true being, but the emotion that seizes the spectator deepens in fact his continuity with himself. The tragic emotion flows from the self-knowledge that the spectator acquires. He finds himself in the tragic action, because it is his own world, familiar to him from religious or historical tradition, that he encounters, and even if this tradition is no longer binding for a later consciousness—as was already the case with Aristotle, and was certainly true of Seneca or Corneille—there is more in the continuing effect of such tragic works and themes than merely the continuing validity of a literary model. It is not only assumed that the spectator is still familiar with the legend, but it is also necessary that its language still really reaches him. Only then can the encounter with the tragic theme and tragic work become an encounter with self.

What is true here of the tragic, however, is true in a far wider context. For the writer, free invention is always only one side of a communication which is conditioned by what is pre-given as valid. He does not freely invent his plot, however much he imagines that he does. Rather there remains up to the present-day some of the old basis of the mimesis theory. The free invention of the writer is the presentation of a common truth that is binding on the writer also.

It is the same with the other arts, especially the plastic arts. The aesthetic myth of freely creative imagination that trans-forms experience into literature proves only that in the nine-teenth century the store of mythical and historical tradition was no longer a self-evident possession. But even then the aesthetic myth of imagination and of the invention of genius is an exaggeration that does not stand up to reality. The choice of material and the formation of it still does not proceed from the free discretion of the artist and is not the mere expression of his inner life. Rather does the artist address people whose minds are prepared and chooses what he expects will have an effect on them. He himself stands in the same tradition as the public that he is aiming at and which he gathers around him. In this sense it is true that he does not need to know explicitly as an individual, a thinking consciousness, what he is doing and what his work says. It is never simply a strange world of magic, of intoxication, of dream to which the play, sculptor or viewer is swept away, but it is always his own world to which he comes to belong more fully by recognising himself more profoundly in it. There re-mains a continuity of meaning which links the work of art with the world of real existence and from which even the alienated consciousness of a cultured society never quite detaches itself.

Let us sum up. What is aesthetic being? We have sought to show something general in the idea of play and of the transfor-mation into a structure, which is characteristic of the play of art: namely, that the presentation or performance of a work of litera-ture or of music is something essential, and not incidental, for in this is merely completed what the works of art already are: the being there of what is represented in them. The specific tempo-rality of aesthetic being, of having its being in the process of being represented, becomes existent in reproduction as a separate, independent phenomenon.

Now we may ask whether this has effectively general validity, so that the character of aesthetic being can be determined from it. Can this also be applied to works of sculptural and architectural art? Let us ask this question first of the plastic arts. We shall find that the most plastic of the arts, architecture, is especially instructive.

2. AESTHETIC AND HERMENEUTICAL CONSEQUENCES

(A) THE ONTOLOGICAL VALUE OF THE PICTURE

It appears at first as if, in the plastic arts, the work is of such a clear identity that there is no variability of representation. What varies does not seem to belong to the side of the work itself and thus has a subjective character. Thus from the subjective side there might be limitations that affect adversely the full experiencing of the work, but these subjective limitations can basically be overcome. We can experience every work of plastic art 'immediately' as itself, ie without its needing further mediation to us. In the case of reproductions of statues, these certainly do not belong to the work of art itself. But inasmuch as there are always subjective conditions under which a work of sculpture is accessible, we must obviously disregard these if we want to experience it itself. Thus aesthetic differentiation seems to have its full legitimacy here.

It can appeal, in particular, to what general usage calls a 'picture'. By this we understand, above all, the modern framed picture that is not tied to a particular place and offers itself entirely by itself in virtue of the frame which encloses it, hence making it possible for such pictures to be put side by side in any order, as we see in the modern gallery. This kind of picture apparently has nothing of the objective dependence on mediation which we emphasised in the case of drama and music. And the picture that is painted for an exhibition or a gallery, which is becoming the rule as the commissioning of art declines, conforms visibly to the abstraction required of aesthetic awareness and to the theory of inspiration that is formulated in the aesthetics of genius. The picture thus appears to confirm the immediacy of aesthetic consciousness. It is a powerful witness to its claim to universality, and it is obviously not a coincidence that aesthetic consciousness, that develops the concept of art and the artistic as a way of understanding traditional structures and so performs aesthetic differentiation, is simultaneous with the creation of collections that gather together everything that we look at in this way in a museum. Thus we make every work of art, as it were, into a picture. By detaching it from all its connections with life and the particular conditions of our approach to it, we frame it like a picture and hang it up.

Thus it is necessary to investigate more closely the mode of being of a picture and to ask whether the nature of the aesthetic which I described in terms of play is valid also for a picture.

The question of the mode of being of a picture, which I pose here, is an enquiry into what is common to all the different forms of picture. This involves a task of abstraction, but this abstraction is not something arbitrary undertaken by philosophical reflection, but something that it finds performed by the aesthetic consciousness, for which everything is a picture that can be treated by the painting techniques of the time. There is certainly no historical truth in this use of the idea of the picture. Contemporary research into the history of art gives us ample evidence that what we call a picture has a varied history.[45] The full 'sovereignty of a picture' (Theodor Hetzer) was not reached until the stage of western painting that we call high renaissance. Here for the first time we have pictures that stand entirely by themselves and, even without a frame and a setting, are in themselves unified and closed structures. In, for example, the concinnitas that L. B. Alberti requires of a 'picture', we can see a good theoretical expression of the new artistic ideal that determines the painting of the renaissance.

The interesting thing here, however, is that it is the classical definitions of the beautiful that the theoretician of the "picture" presents here. That the beautiful is of such a nature that nothing can be taken from it and nothing added without destroying it, was familiar to Aristotle, for whom there was certainly no such thing as a picture in Alberti's sense.[46] This points to the fact that the concept of the 'picture' can still have a general sense which cannot be limited simply to a particular phase of the history of painting. Even the Ottonian miniature or the Byzantine ikon is a picture in a further sense, though the painting in the case follows quite different principles and is to be thought of rather as a 'picture sign'.[47] In the same way the aesthetic concept of a picture will always inevitably include sculpture, which is one of the plastic arts. This is no arbitrary generalisation, but corresponds to an historical problem of philosophical aesthetics, which ultimately goes back to the role of the image in Platonism and is expressed in the usage of the word.[48]

The idea of the picture in recent centuries cannot automatically be taken as a starting point. Our present investigation seeks to rid itself of that assumption. It seeks to find a way of understanding the mode of being of a picture that detaches it both from the relation to aesthetic consciousness and from the concept of the picture to which the modern gallery has accustomed us, and to take up the concept of the decorative, discredited by the aesthetics of experience. It is no mere accident if it agrees in this with modern research into the history of art, which has done away with the naive ideas of picture and sculpture that, in the age of experience art, dominated not only aesthetic awareness, but also the thinking of art history. Rather, underlying aesthetic research and philosophical reflection is the same crisis of the picture that the existence of the modern industrial and administrative state and its functionalised society has produced. Only since we no longer have any room for pictures do we know that pictures are not just pictures, but also demand room.[49]

The intention of the present conceptual analysis, however, is not aesthetic, but ontological. Its first task, the criticism of traditional aesthetics, is only a stage on the way to acquiring a viewpoint which covers both art and history. In our analysis of the idea of a picture we are concerned with two questions only. We are asking in what respect the picture is different from a copy (that is, we are raising the problem of an original picture) and, further, in what way the relation of the picture to its world follows from this.

Thus the concept of the picture goes beyond the concept of representation used hitherto, because a picture has an essential relation to its original.

To take the first question, here the concept of representation becomes involved with the concept of the picture that is related to its original. In the interpretative arts from which we started, we spoke of representation, but not of a picture. Representation appeared there, as it were, twice. Both the piece of writing and its reproduction, say on the stage, is representation. And it was of key importance for us that the actual experience of art passes through this double representation without differentiating them. The world which appears in the play of representation does not stand like a copy next to the real world, but is the latter in the heightened truth of its being. And certainly reproduction, eg performance on the stage, is not a copy beside which the original performance of the drama itself retains its separate existence. The concept of mimesis, applied to both kinds of representation, did not mean a copy so much as the appearance of what is represented. Without the mimesis of the work the world is not there as it is there in the work, and without reproduction the work is not there. Hence, in representation, the presence of what is represented is completed. We shall see the justification of the basic meaning of this ontological interwovenness of original and reproductive being and the methodological priority which we have accorded the interpretative arts, if the insight that we have gained from them proves itself also in the case of plastic arts. It is true that one cannot speak, with the latter, of reproduction as the real being of the work. On the contrary, as an original the picture resists reproduction. It seems equally clear that what is depicted in a copy has a being that is independent of the picture, so much so that as against what is represented the picture seems to have diminished being. Thus we are involved in the ontological problems of original and copy.

We start from the position that the mode of being of the work of art is representation and ask ourselves how the meaning of representation can be verified by what we call a picture. Representation cannot here mean copying. We shall have to define the mode of being of the picture more exactly by distinguishing the way in which the representation is related to something that is original, from the relation of the copy to the original.

For this we need to make a more exact analysis in which the old priority of what is living, the zoon, and especially of the person, will be considered.[50] It is of the nature of the copy that it has no other task but to resemble the original. The measure of its success is that one recognises the original in the copy. This means that it is its nature to lose its own independent existence and to serve entirely the communication of what is copied. Thus the ideal copy would be the mirror image, for its being can effectively disappear; it exists only for someone who looks into the mirror, and is nothing beyond its mere appearance. But in fact it is not a picture or a reflection at all, for it has no separate existence. The mirror reflects the picture, ie a mirror makes what it reflects visible to someone only for as long as he looks in it and sees his own reflection or whatever else is reflected in it. It is not, however, accidental that we still speak here of an image, and not of a copy or illustration. For in the mirror image what exists appears in the image so that we have the thing itself in the mirror image. But a copy always requires to be seen in relation to what is meant by it. It is a copy that does not seek to be anything but the reproduction of something and has its only function in its identification (eg as a passport photo or a picture in a sales catalogue). A copy cancels itself out in the sense that it functions as a means and, like all means, loses its function when it reaches its goal. It exists by itself in order to cancel itself out. This self-cancelling of the copy is a purposive element in the being of the copy itself. If there is a change in purpose, eg if the copy is compared with the original and judgment passed on the resemblance, ie the copy distinguished from the original, it presents its own appearance, like any other means or tool that is not being used, but examined. But it does not have its real function in the reflective activity of comparison and distinction, but in pointing, through the similarity, to what is copied. Thus it fulfils itself in its self-cancelling.

A picture, however, is not destined to be cancelled out, for it is not a means to an end. Here the picture itself is what is meant, in that the important thing is how what is represented in it is represented. This means first of all that one is not simply directed away from it to what is represented. Rather, the representation remains essentially connected with what is represented, indeed, is part of it. This is the reason why the mirror throws back an image and not a copy: it is the image of what is represented in the mirror and is inseparable from its presence. The mirror can give a distorted image, certainly, but that is merely an imperfection: it does not properly fulfil its function. Thus the mirror confirms the basic point that, unlike a picture, the intention is the original unity and non-differentiation of representation and what is represented. It is the image of what is represented—it is 'its' image, and not that of the mirror, that is seen in the mirror.

If it is only at the beginning of the history of the picture, in its prehistory, as it were, that we find picture magic, which depends on the identity and non-differentiation of picture and what is pictured, still this does not mean that an increasingly differentiated consciousness of the picture that grows further and further away from magical identity can ever detach itself entirely from it.[51] Rather, non-differentiation remains an essential feature of all experience of pictures. The irreplaceability of the picture, its fragility, its 'sacredness' are all explained in the ontology of the picture here presented. Even the sacralisation of 'art' in the nineteenth century, described earlier, is accounted for.

The aesthetic idea of the picture, however, is not fully covered by the model of the mirror image. It only shows the ontological inseparability of the picture from what is represented. But this is important enough, in that it makes clear that the primary intention, unlike the case of a picture, does not distinguish between what is represented and the representation. That special intention of differentiation that we called aesthetic differentiation is only a secondary structure based on this. It sees the representation as such in distinction from what is represented. It does not do it by viewing the copy of what is represented in the representation, as one looks at other copies. It does not desire the picture to cancel itself in order to let what is depicted exist by itself. On the contrary, the picture affirms its own being in order to let what is depicted exist.

Here the guiding function of the mirror image also loses its validity. The mirror image is a mere appearance, ie it has no real being and is understood in its fleeting existence as something that depends on being reflected. But the picture has its own being. This being as representation, as precisely that in which it is not the same as what is represented, gives to it, as opposed to the mere reflected image, the positive distinction of being a picture. Even the mechanical techniques of today can be used in an artistic way, in that they bring out of what is imaged something that is not to be found in simply looking at the image. This kind of picture is not a copy, for it represents something which without it would not represent itself in this way. It says something about the original.

Hence representation remains limited in an essential sense to the original that is represented in it. But it is more than a copy. That the representation is a picture—and not the original itself—does not mean anything negative, any mere diminution of being, but rather an autonomous reality. So the relation of the picture to the original is basically quite different from what it is to a copy. It is no longer a one-sided relationship. That the picture has its own reality means now that the original is represented it experiences, as it were, an increase in being. The not necessarily mean that it is dependent on this particular representation in order to appear. It can also present itself as what it is in another way. But if it represents itself in this way, this is no longer any casual event, but is part of its own being. Every such representation is an ontological event and belongs to the ontological level of what is represented. Through being represented it experiences, as it were, an increase in being. The particular import of the picture is determined ontologically as an emanation of the original.

It is of the nature of an emanation that what emanates is an overflow. That from which it proceeds does not thereby become less. The development of this idea by neoplatonic philosophy, which uses it to break the bonds of Greek substance ontology, is the basis of the positive ontological level of the picture. For if what originally is one, does not grow less through the outflow of the many from it, this means that being becomes more.

It seems that the Greek fathers used this kind of neoplatonist thinking in overcoming the old testament's hatred of images when it came to christology. In the incarnation of God they saw the fundamental recognition of the visible appearance and thus legitimated works of art. In this overcoming of the ban on images we can see the event through which the development of the plastic arts became possible in the christian West.[52]

Thus the ontological relationship between original and copy is the basis of the ontological reality of the picture. But it is important to see that the Platonic conceptual relationship between copy and original does not exhaust the ontological value of what we call a picture. It seems to me that this mode of being cannot be better characterised than by an idea of canon law: representation.[53]

Obviously the concept of representation does not appear by accident when we want to determine the ontological level of the picture as against the copy. There must be an essential modification, almost a reversal of the ontological relationship of original and copy if the picture is an element of "representation" and thus has its own ontological status. The picture then has an independence that also affects the original. For strictly speaking it is only through the picture that the original becomes the original picture, ie it is the picture that makes what is represented into a picture.

This can be shown simply in the special case of the representational picture. The way the ruler, the statesman, the hero shows and presents himself is represented in the picture. What does this mean? Not that the man represented acquires a new, more real mode of appearance through the picture. Rather it is the other way round: it is because the ruler, the statesman and the hero must show and present himself to his followers, because he must represent, that the picture gains its own reality. Nevertheless there is here a turning-point. When he shows himself he must fulfil the expectations that his picture arouses. Only because he has part of his being in showing himself is he represented in the picture. First, then, there is undoubtedly self-representation, and secondly the representation in the picture of this self-representation. Pictorial representation is a special case of public representation. But the second has an effect on the first. If someone's being includes as such an essential part the showing of himself, he no longer belongs to himself.[54] For example, he can no longer avoid being represented by the picture and, because these representations determine the picture that people have of him, he must ultimately show himself as his picture prescribes. Paradoxical as it may sound, the original becomes a picture only through the picture, and yet the picture is nothing but the appearance of the original.[55]

We have verified this 'ontology' of the picture so far by secular examples. But, as we know, only the religious picture shows the full ontological power of the picture.[56] For it is really true of the appearance of the divine that it acquires its pictorial quality only through the word and the picture. Thus the meaning of the religious picture is an exemplary one. In it we can see without any doubt that a picture is not a copy of a copied being, but is in ontological communion with what is copied. It is clear from this example that art as a whole and in a universal sense brings an increase in 'pictorialness' to being. Word and picture are not mere imitative illustrations, but allow what they represent to be for the first time what it is.

In aesthetics we see the ontological aspect of the picture in the special problem of the formation and the change of types. The special interest here seems to derive from the fact that here there is a dual creation of pictures, inasmuch as plastic art does in relation to the poetic and religious tradition what the latter already does itself. Herodotus' statement that Homer and Hesiod created the Greek gods means that they introduced into the varied religious tradition of the Greeks the theological systematism of a family of gods, and thus created distinct forms, both in form (eidos) and function (time).[57] Here poetry did the work of theology. By starting the relations of the gods to one another it set up a systematic whole.

It made possible the creation of fixed types, inasmuch as it gave to plastic art the task of forming and elaborating them. As the poetic word goes beyond local cults and unifies religious consciousness, it presents plastic art with a new task. For the poetic always retains a curious indeterminate quality, in that in the intellectual universality of language it presents something that is still open to all kinds of imaginative elaboration. It is plastic art that fixes and thus creates the types. This is true even when one does not confuse the creating of an 'image' of the divine with the invention of gods and refuses Feuerbach's reversal of the imago dei thesis of Genesis.[58] This anthropological reversal and reinterpretation of religious experience which became current in the nineteenth century, arises from that same subjectivism which lies at the basis of modern aesthetic thought.

As a counter to this subjectivist attitude of modern aesthetics I developed the concept of play as the artistic event proper. This approach has now proved its value, in that the picture—and with it the whole of art that is not dependent on reproduction—is an ontological event and hence cannot be properly understood as the object of aesthetic consciousness, but rather is to be grasped in its ontological structure when one starts from such phenomena as that of representation. The picture is an ontological event—in it being becomes meaningfully visible. The quality of being an original is thus not limited to the 'copying' function of the picture, and thus not to the particular area of 'objective' painting and plastic art, from which architecture would remain excluded. The quality of being an original, rather, is an element that is founded in the representative character of art. The 'ideality' of the work of art is not to be defined by its relation to an idea which is to be imitated and reproduced but, with Hegel, as the "appearance" of the idea itself. From the basis of such an ontology of the image the superior position of the framed picture that belongs in a collection of paintings and answers to aesthetic consciousness can be shown to fail. The picture contains an indissoluble connection with its world.

(B) THE ONTOLOGICAL FOUNDATION OF THE OCCASIONAL AND THE DECORATIVE

If we proceed from the point of view that the work of art cannot be understood in terms of 'aesthetic consciousness', then many phenomena, which have a marginal importance for modern aesthetics, lose what is problematical about them and, indeed, even move into the centre of an 'aesthetic' questioning which is not artificially abbreviated.

I refer to things such as portraits, poems dedicated to someone, or even contemporary references in comedy. The aesthetic concepts of the portrait, the dedicated poem, the contemporary allusion are, of course, themselves cultivated by aesthetic consciousness. What is common to all of these is presented to aesthetic consciousness in the character of occasionality which such art forms possess. Occasionality means that their meaning is partly determined by the occasion for which they are intended, so that it contains more than it would without this occasion.[59] Hence the portrait contains a relation to the man represented, a relation that it does not need to be placed in, but which is expressly intended in the representation itself and is characteristic of it as portrait.

The important thing is that this occasionality is part of what the work is saying and is not something forced on it by its in-

terpreter. This is why such art forms as the portrait, in which so
much is obvious, have no real place in an aesthetics based on the
concept of experience. A portrait contains, in its own pictorial
content, its relation to the original. This does not mean simply
that the picture is in fact painted after this original, but that it
intends this.

This becomes clear from the way in which it differs from the
model which the painter uses for a genre picture or for a figure
composition. In the portrait the individuality of the man portrayed is represented. If, however, a picture shows the model as
an individuality, as an interesting type whom the painter has got
to sit for him, then this is an objection to the picture; for one then
no longer sees in the picture what the painter presents, but
something of the untransformed material. Hence it destroys the
meaning of the picture of a figure if we recognise in it the well-
known model of a painter. For a model is a disappearing
schema. The relation to the original that served the painter must
be extinguished in the picture.

We also call a 'model' that by means of which something else
that cannot be seen becomes visible: eg the model of a planned
house or the model of an atom. The painter's model is not meant
as herself. She serves only to wear a costume or to make gestures clear—like a dressed-up doll. Contrariwise, someone represented in the portrait is so much himself that he does not
appear to be dressed up, even if the splendid costume he is
wearing attracts attention: for splendour of appearance is part of
him. He is the person who he is for others.[60] To interpret a work
of literature in terms of its biographical or historical sources is
sometimes to do no more than the art historian who would look
at the works of a painter in terms of his models.

The difference between the model and the portrait shows us
what 'occasionality' means here. Occasionality in the sense intended clearly lies in a work's claim to significance, in contradis-
tinction from whatever is observed in it or can be deduced from
it that goes against this claim. A portrait desires to be understood as a portrait, even when the relation to the original is
practically crushed by the actual pictorial content of the picture.
This is particularly clear in the case of pictures which are not
portraits, but which contain, as one says, elements of portrai-
ture. They too cause one to ask after the original that can be
seen behind the picture, and therefore they are more than a mere
model which is simply a schema that disappears. It is the same
with works of literature in which literary protraits may be contained, without their therefore necessarily falling a victim to the
pseudo-artistic indiscretion of being a roman à clef.[61]

However fluid and controversial the borderline between the allusion to something specific and the other documentary contents of a work, there is still the basic question whether one accepts the claim to meaning that the work makes, or simply regards it as an historical document that one merely consults. The historian will seek out all the elements that can communicate to him something of the past, even if it counters the work's claim to meaning. He will examine works of art in order to discover the models: that is, the connections with their own age that are woven into them, even if they were not recognised by the contemporary observer, and are not important for the meaning of the whole. This is not occasionality in the present sense, which is that it is part of a work's own claim to meaning to point to a particular original. It is not, then, left to the observer's whim to decide whether a work has such occasional elements or not. A portrait really is a portrait, and does not just become it through and for those who see in it the person portrayed. Although the relation to the original resides in the work itself, it is still right to call it 'occasional'. For the portrait does not say who the man portrayed is, but only that it is a particular individual (and not a type). We can only 'recognise' who it is if the man portrayed is known to us, and only be sure if there is a title or some other information to go on. At any rate there resides in the picture an unredeemed but fundamentally redeemable pledge of its meaning. This occasionality is part of the essential import of the 'picture', quite apart from whether or not it is known to the observer.

We can see this in the fact that a portrait also appears as a portrait (and the representation of a particular person in a picture appears portrait-like) even if one does not know the sitter. There is then something in the picture that is not fully realised by the viewer, namely that which is occasional about it. But what is not fully realised is not therefore not there; it is there in a quite unambiguous way. The same thing is true of many poetic phenomena. Pindar's poems of victory, a comedy that is critical of its age, but also such literary phenomena as the odes and satires of Horace are entirely occasional in nature. The occasional in such works has acquired so permanent a form that, even without being realised or understood, it is still part of the total meaning. Someone might explain to us the particular historical context, but this would be only secondary for the poem as a whole. He would be only filling out the meaning that exists in the poem itself.

It is important to recognise that what I call occasionality here is in no way a diminution of the artistic claim and meaning

of such works. For that which presents itself to aesthetic subjectivity as 'the irruption of time into play',[62] and appeared in the
age of experiential art as a lessening of the aesthetic meaning of a
work, is in fact only the subjective aspect of that ontological
relationship that has been developed above. A work of art belongs so closely to that to which it is related that it enriches its
being as if through a new event of being. To be fixed in a picture,
addressed in a poem, to be the object of an allusion from the
stage, are not incidental things remote from the essential nature,
but they are presentations of this nature itself. What was said in
general about the ontological status of the picture includes these
occasional elements. The element of occasionality which we
find in those things presents itself as the particular case of a
general relationship appropriate to the being of the work of art:
namely, to experience from the 'occasion' of its coming-to-
presentation a continued determination of its significance.

This is seen most clearly in the interpretative arts, especially
in drama and music, which wait for the occasion in order to exist
and find their form only through that occasion. Hence the stage
is a political institution because only the performance brings out
everything that is in the play, its allusions and its echoes. No one
knows beforehand what will come across and what will have no
resonance. Every performance is an event, but not one that
would in any way be separate from the work—the work itself is
what 'takes place' in the performative event. It is its nature to be
occasional in such a way that the occasion of the performance
makes it speak and brings out what is in it. The producer who
stages the play shows his ability in being able to make use of the
occasion. But he acts according to the directions of the writer,
whose whole work is a stage direction. This is quite clearly the
case with a musical work—the score is really only a direction.
Aesthetic differentiation may judge what the music would be
like in performance by the inner structure of sound read in the
score, but no one doubts that listening to music is not reading.

It is thus of the nature of dramatic or musical works that their
performance at different times and on different occasions is, and
must be, different. Now it is important to see that, mutatis
mutandis, this is also true of the plastic arts. But in the latter it is
not the case either that the work exists *an sich* and only the
effect varies: it is the work of art itself that displays itself under
different conditions. The viewer of today not only sees in a different way, but he sees different things. We only have to think of
the way that the idea of the pale marble of antiquity has ruled our
taste, of our attitude to preservation, since the renaissance, or of

the reflection of classicist feeling in the romantic north as found in the purist spirituality of gothic cathedrals.

But specifically occasional art forms, such as the parabasis in classical comedy or the caricature in politics, which are intended for a quite specific occasion, and finally the portrait itself, are forms of the universal occasionality characteristic of the work of art inasmuch as it determines itself anew from occasion to occasion. Likewise, the unique determinateness through which an element, occasional in this narrower sense, is fulfilled in the work of art, gains, in the being of the work, a universality that renders it capable of yet further fulfilment. The uniqueness of its relation to the occasion can never be fully realised and it is this now unrealisable relation that remains present and effective in the work itself. In this sense the portrait too is independent of the uniqueness of its relation to the original, and contains the latter even in transcending it.

The portrait is only an intensified form of the general nature of a picture. Every picture is an increase of being and is essentially determined as representation, as coming-to-presentation. In the special case of the portrait this representation acquires a personal significance, in that here an individual is presented in a representative way. For this means that the man represented represents himself in his portrait and is represented by his portrait. The picture is not only a picture and certainly not only a copy, it belongs to the present or to the present memory of the man represented. This is its real nature. To this extent the portrait is a special case of the general ontological value assigned to the picture as such. What comes into being in it is not already contained in what his acquaintances see in the sitter. The best judges of a portrait are never the nearest relatives nor even the sitter himself. For a portrait never tries to reproduce the individual it represents as he appears in the eyes of the people near him. Of necessity, what it shows is an idealisation, which can run through an infinite number of stages from the representative to the most intimate. This kind of idealisation does not alter the fact that in a portrait an individual is represented, and not a type, however much the portrayed individual may be transformed in the portrait from the incidental and the private into the essential quality of his true appearance.

Religions or secular monuments display the universal ontological value of a picture more clearly than the intimate portrait does. For it is on this that their public function depends. A monument holds what is represented in it in a specific state of presentness which is obviously something quite different from

that of the aesthetic consciousness.[63] It does not live only from
the autonomous expressive power of a picture. This is clear
from the fact that things other than works of art: eg symbols or
inscriptions, can have the same function. The familiarity of that
of which the monument should remind us, is always assumed: its
potential presence, as it were. The figure of a god, the picture of
a king, the memorial put up to someone, assume that the god, the
king, the hero, the event, the victory, or the peace treaty already
possess a presence affecting everyone. The statue that represents them thus adds nothing other than, say, an inscription: it
holds it present in this general meaning. Nevertheless, if it is a
work of art, this means not only that it adds something to this
given meaning, but also that it can say something of its own, and
thus becomes independent of the anterior knowledge of which it
is the bearer.

What a picture is remains, despite all aesthetic differentiation,
a manifestation of what it represents, even if it makes it manifest
through its autonomous expressive power. This is obvious in the
case of the religious picture; but the difference between the sacred and the secular is relative in a work of art. Even an individual portrait, if it is a work of art, shares in the mysterious
radiation of being that flows from the level of being of that which
is represented.

We may illustrate this by an example: Justi[64] once described
Velasquez's *The Surrender of Breda* as a 'military sacrament'.
He meant that the picture was not a group portrait, nor simply
an historical picture. What is caught in this picture is not just a
solemn event as such. The solemnity of this ceremony is present
in the picture in this way because the ceremony itself has a
pictorial quality and is performed like a sacrament. There are
things that need to be, and are suitable for being, depicted; they
are, as it were, perfected in their being only when represented in
a picture. It is not accidental that religious terms seem appropriate when one is defending the particular level of being of works
of fine art against an aesthetic levelling out.

It is consistent with the present viewpoint that the difference
between profane (secular) and sacred should be only relative.
We need only recall the meaning and the history of the word
'profane': the 'profane' is the place in the front of the sanctuary.
The concept of the profane and of its derivative, profanation,
always presuppose the sacred. Actually, the difference between
profane and sacred could only be relative in classical antiquity
from which it stems, since the whole sphere of life was sacrally
ordered and determined. Only christianity enables us to under-

stand profaneness in a stricter sense. The new testament de-demonised the world to such an extent that room was made for an absolute contrast between the profane and the religious. The church's promise of salvation means that the world is still only 'this world'. The special nature of this claim of the church also creates the tension between it and the state, which comes with the end of the classical world, and thus the concept of the profane acquires its own topicality. The entire history of the middle ages is dominated by the tension between church and state. It is the spiritualistic deepening of the idea of the christian church that ultimately makes the secular state possible. The historical significance of the high middle ages is that it created the secular world, and gave its wide modern meaning to the notion of the 'profane'.[65] But that does not alter the fact that the profane has remained a concept related to the area of the sacred and determined by it alone. There is no such thing as profaneness by itself.[66]

The relativity of profane and sacred is not only part of the dialectic of concepts, but can be seen as a reality in the phenomenon of the picture. A work of art always has something sacred about it. True, a religious work of art or a monument on show in a museum can no longer be desecrated in the same sense as one that has remained in its original place. But this means only that it has in fact already suffered an injury, in that it has become an object in a museum. Obviously this is true not only of religious works of art. We sometimes have the same feeling in an antique shop when the old pieces on sale still have some trace of intimate life about them; it seems somehow scandalous to us, a kind of offence to piety, a profanation. Ultimately every work of art has something about it that protests against profanation.

This seems decisively proved by the fact that even pure aesthetic consciousness is familiar with the idea of profanation. It always experiences the destruction of works of art as a sacrilege. (The German word Frevel is to-day rarely used except in the phrase Kunst-Frevel. Frevel=sacrilege, outrage; kunst =art).

This is a characteristic feature of the modern aesthetic religion of culture, for which there is plenty of evidence. For example, the word 'vandalism', which goes back to mediaeval times, only became popular in the reaction against the destructiveness of the Jacobins in the French Revolution. To destroy works of art is to break into a world protected by its holiness. Even an 'autonomous' aesthetic consciousness cannot deny that art is more than it would admit to.

All these considerations justify a characterisation of the mode of being of art in general in terms of presentation; this includes play and picture, communion and representation. The work of art is conceived as an ontological event and the abstraction to which aesthetic differentiation commits it is dissolved. A picture is an event of presentation. Its relation to the original is so far from being a reduction of the autonomy of its being that, on the contrary, I had to speak, in regard to the picture, of an 'increase of being'. The use of concepts from the sphere of the holy seemed appropriate.

Now it is important not to confuse the special sense of representation proper to the work of art with the sacred representation performed by, say, the symbol. Not all forms of representation have the character of 'art'. Symbols and badges are also forms of representation. They too indicate something, and this makes them representations.

In the logical analysis of the nature of expression and meaning carried out in this century, the structure of indicating, common to all these forms of representation, has been investigated in great detail.[67] I mention this work here for another purpose. We are not concerned primarily with the problem of meaning, but with the nature of a picture. We want to grasp its nature without being confused by the abstraction performed by aesthetic consciousness. It behooves us to examine the nature of indicating, in order to discover both similarities and differences.

The essence of the picture stands, as it were, midway between two extremes: these extremes of representation are pure indication (the essence of the sign), and pure representation (the essence of the symbol). There is something of both in a picture. Its representing includes the element of indicating what is represented in it. We saw that this emerges most clearly in specific forms such as the portrait, for which the relation to the original is essential. At the same time a picture is not a sign. For a sign is nothing but what its function demands; and that is, to point away from itself. In order to be able to fulfil this function, of course, it must first draw attention to itself. It must be striking: that is, it must be clearly defined and present itself as an indicator, like a poster. But neither a sign nor a poster is a picture. It should not attract attention to itself in a way that would cause one to linger over it, for it is there only to make present something that is not present, and in such a way that the thing that is not present is the only thing that is expressed.[68] It should not captivate by its own intrinsic pictorial interest. The same is true of all signs: for instance, traffic signs, book-markers, and the like. There is something schematic and abstract about them, because they point not to themselves, but to what is not present, eg to the curve ahead or to one's page. (Even natural signs, eg indications of the weather, have their indicative function only through abstraction. If we look at the sky and are filled with the beauty of what we see there and linger over it, we experience a shift in the direction of our attention that causes its sign character to retreat into the background.)

Of all signs, the memento seems to have most reality of its own. It refers to the past and so is effectively a sign, but it is also precious in itself since, being an element of the past that has not disappeared, it keeps the past present for us. But it is clear that this characteristic is not grounded in the specific being of the object. A memento only has value as a memento for someone who already—ie still—recalls the past. Mementos lose their value when the past of which they remind one no longer has any meaning. Furthermore, someone who not only uses mementos to remind him, but makes a cult of them and lives in the past as if it were the present, has a disturbed relation to reality.

Hence a picture is certainly not a sign. Even a memento does not cause us to linger over it, but over the past that it represents for us. But a picture fulfils its function of pointing to what it represents only through its own import. By concentrating on it, we also put ourselves in contact with what is represented. The picture points by causing us to linger over it. For its being is, as I pointed out, that it is not absolutely different from what it represents, but shares in the being of that. We say that what is represented comes to itself in the picture. It experiences an increase in being. But that means that it is there in the picture itself. It is merely an aesthetic reflection—I called it 'aesthetic differentiation'—that abstracts from this presence of the original in the picture.

The difference between a picture and a sign has an ontological basis. The picture does not disappear behind its pointing function but, in its own being, shares in what it represents.

This ontological sharing is part of the nature, not only of a picture, but of what we call a 'symbol'. Neither symbol nor picture indicate anything that is not at the same time present in themselves. Hence the problem arises of differentiating between the mode of being of a picture and the mode of being of a symbol.[69]

There is an obvious distinction between a symbol and a sign, in that the former is more like a picture. The representational function of a symbol is not merely to point to something that is not present. Instead, a symbol manifests as present something that really is present. This is seen in the original meaning of 'symbol'. When a symbol is used for a sign of recognition between separated friends or the scattered members of a religious community to show that they belong together, such a symbol undoubtedly functions as a sign. But it is more than a sign. It not only points to the fact that people belong together, but proves and visibly presents that fact. The tessera hospitalis is a relic of past living and proves through its existence what it indicates: it makes the past itself present again and causes it to be recognised as valid. It is especially true of religious symbols not only that they function as distinguishing marks, but that it is the meaning of these symbols that is understood by everyone, unites everyone and can therefore assume a sign function. Hence what is to be symbolised is undoubtedly in need of representation, inasmuch as it is itself non-sensible, infinite and unrepresentable, but it is also capable of it. It is only because it is present itself that it can be present in the symbol.

A symbol not only points to something, but it represents, in that it takes the place of something. But to take the place of something means to make something present that is not present. Thus the symbol takes the place of something in representing: that is, it makes something immediately present. Only because the symbol presents in this way the presence of what it represents, is it treated with the reverence due to that which it symbolises. Such symbols as a crucifix, a flag, a uniform are so representative of what is revered that the latter is present in them.

That the concept of representation that was used above in describing the picture essentially belongs here is shown by the closeness between representation in the picture and the representative function of the symbol. In both cases, what they represent is itself present. At the same time a picture as such is not a symbol; symbols do not need to be pictorial. They perform their representative function through their mere existence and manifesting of themselves, but of themselves they say nothing about what they symbolise. They must be known, in the way that one must know a sign, if one is to understand what they indicate. Hence they do not mean an increase of being for what is represented. It is true that it is part of the being of what is represented to make itself present in symbols in this way. But its own being is not determined in its nature by the fact that the symbols are there and are shown. It is not there any more fully when they are there. They are merely representatives. Hence their own significance is of no importance, even if they have any. They are representatives and receive their representative function of being from what they are supposed to represent. The picture also represents, but through itself, through the extra significance that it brings. But that means that in it what is represented—the 'original'—is more fully there, more properly just as it truly is.

Hence a picture is equipoised halfway between a sign and a symbol. Its representative function is neither a pure pointing-to-something, nor a pure taking-the-place-of-something. It is this intermediate position which raises it to its own unique level of being. Artificial signs and symbols alike do not—like the picture—acquire their functional significance from their own content, but must be taken as signs or as symbols. We call this origin of their functional significance their 'institution'. It is decisive in determining the ontological quality of a picture (which is what we are concerned with), that in regard to a picture there is no such thing as an 'institution' in the same sense.

By 'institution' is meant the origin of the sign or of the symbolic function. The so-called 'natural' signs also, eg all the indications and presages of an event in nature are, in this fundamental sense, instituted. That means that they only have a sign function when they are taken as a sign. But they are only taken as a sign on the basis of a previous relationship between the sign and what is signified. This is true also of all artificial signs. Here the establishment of the sign is agreed by convention, and the originating act by which it is arrived at called 'institution'. On the institution of the sign depends primarily its indicative significance; for example, that of the traffic sign on the decision of the Ministry of Transport, that of the souvenir on the meaning given to its preservation etc. Equally the symbol has to be instituted, for only this gives it its representative character. For it is not its own ontological content which gives it its significance, but an institution, a constitution, a consecration that gives significance to what is, in itself, without significance: for example, the sign of sovereignty, the flag, the crucifix.

It is important to see that a work of art, on the other hand, does not owe its real meaning to an institution of this kind, even if it is a religious picture or a secular memorial. The public act of consecration or unveiling which assigns to it its purpose does not give it its significance. Rather, it is already a structure with a signifying-function of its own, as a pictorial or non-pictorial representation, before it is assigned its function as a memorial. The setting-up and consecration of a memorial—and it is not by accident that we talk of religious and secular works of architecture as of architectural monuments, when historical distance has consecrated them—therefore only realises a function that is already implied in the proper import of the work itself.

This is the reason why works of art can assume definite real functions and resist others: for instance, religious or secular, public or private ones. They are instituted and set up as memorials of reverence, honour or piety, only because they themselves prescribe and help to fashion this kind of functional context. They themselves lay claim to their place, and even if they are displaced, eg are housed in a modern collection, the trace of their original purpose cannot be destroyed. It is part of their being because their being is representation.

If one considers the exemplary significance of these particular forms, one sees that forms of art which, from the point of view of the art of experience (Erlebniskunst), are peripheral, become central: namely, all those whose proper import points beyond them into the totality of a context determined by them and for them. The greatest and most distinguished of these forms is architecture.

A work of architecture extends beyond itself in two ways. It is as much determined by the aim which it is to serve as by the place that it is to take up in a total spatial context. Every architect has to consider both these things. His plan is influenced by the fact that the building has to serve a particular living purpose and must be adapted to particular architectural circumstances. Hence we call a successful building a 'happy solution', and mean by this both that it perfectly fulfills its purpose and that its construction has added something new to the spatial dimensions of a town or a landscape. Through this dual ordering the building presents a true increase of being: it is a work of art.

It is not a work of art if it simply stands anywhere, as a building that is a blot on the landscape, but only if it represents the solution of a building problem. Aesthetics acknowledges only those works of art which are in some way memorable and calls these 'architectural monuments'. If a building is a work of art, then it is not only the artistic solution of a building problem posed by the contexts of purpose and of life to which it originally belongs, but somehow preserves these, so that it is visibly present even though the present manifestation of the original purposes is strange. Something in it points back to the original. Where the original intention has become completely unrecognisable or its unity destroyed by too many subsequent alterations, then the building itself will become incomprehensible. Thus architecture, this most 'statuary' of all art forms, shows how secondary 'aesthetic differentiation' is. A building is never primarily a work of art. Its purpose, through which it belongs in the context of life, cannot be separated from itself without its losing some of its reality. If it has become merely an object of the aesthetic consciousness, then it has merely a shadowy reality and lives a distorted life only in the degenerate form of an object of interest to tourists, or a subject for photography. The 'work of art in itself' proves to be a pure abstraction.

In fact the presence of the great architectural monuments of the past in the modern world and its buildings pose the task of the integration of past and present. Works of architecture do not stand motionless on the shore of the stream of history, but are borne along by it. Even if historically-minded ages seek to reconstruct the architecture of an earlier age, they cannot try to turn back the wheel of history, but must mediate in a new and better way between the past and the present. Even the restorer or the preserver of ancient monuments remains an artist of his time.

The especial importance that architecture has for our enquiry is that in it too that element of mediation can be seen without which a work of art has no real 'presentness'. Thus even where representation does not take place through reproduction (which everyone knows belongs to its own present time) past and present are brought together in a work of art. That every work of art has its own world does not mean that when its original world is altered it has its reality in an alienated aesthetic consciousness. Architecture is an example of this, for its connections with the world are irredeemably part of it.

But this involves a further point. Architecture gives shape to space. Space is what surrounds everything that exists in space. That is why architecture embraces all the other forms of representation: all works of plastic art, all ornament. Moreover, to the representational arts of poetry, music, acting and dancing it gives their place. By embracing all the arts, it everywhere asserts its own perspective. That perspective is: decoration. Architecture preserves it even against those forms of art whose works are not decorative, but are gathered within themselves through the closedness of their circle of meaning. Modern research has begun to recall that this is true of all works of plastic art whose place was assigned them when they were commissioned. Even the free-standing statue on a pedestal is not really removed from the decorative context, but serves the representative heightening of a context of life in which it finds an ornamental place.[70] Even poetry and music, which have the freest mobility and can be read or performed anywhere, are not suited to any space whatever, but to one that is appropriate, a theatre, a concert-hall or a church. Here also it is not a question of subsequently finding an external setting for a work that is complete in itself, but the space-creating potentiality of the work itself has to be obeyed, which itself has to adapt as much to what is given as make its own conditions. (Think only of the problem of acoustics, which is not only technical, but architectural.)

Hence the comprehensive situation of architecture in relation to all the arts involves a twofold mediation. As the art which creates space it both shapes it and leaves it free. It not only embraces all the decorative aspects of the shaping of space, including ornament, but is itself decorative in nature. The nature of decoration consists in performing that two-sided mediation; namely to draw the attention of the viewer to itself, to satisfy his taste, and then to redirect it away from itself to the greater whole of the context of life which it accompanies.

This is true of the whole span of the decorative, from municipal architecture to the individual ornament. A building should certainly be the solution of an artistic problem and thus draw to itself the wonder and admiration of the viewer. At the same time it should fit into a living unity and not be an end in itself. It seeks to fit into this unity by providing ornament, a background of mood, or a framework. The same is true for each individual piece of work that the architect carries out, including ornament which should not draw attention to itself, but fulfill its accompanying decorative function. But even the extreme case of ornament still has something of the duality of decorative mediation about it. Certainly, it should not invite the attention to linger and be itself noticed as a decorative motif, but have merely an accompanying effect. Thus in general it will not have any objective content or will so iron it out through stylisation or repetition that one's eye glides across it. It is not intended that the forms of nature used in an ornament should be recognised. If a repetitive pattern is seen as what it actually is, then its repetition becomes unbearably monotonous. But on the other hand it should not have a dead or monotonous effect, for as an accompaniment it should have an enlivening effect and in this way must, to some extent, draw attention to itself.

On looking at the full extent of decorative tasks given to the architect, it is clear that it is the downfall of that prejudice of the aesthetic consciousness according to which the actual work of art is what is, outside all space and all time, the object of an aesthetic experience. One also sees that the usual distinction between a proper work of art and mere decoration demands revision.

The concept of the decorative is here obviously conceived as an antithesis to a 'real work of art' from its origin in 'the inspiration of genius'. The argument was more or less that what is only decorative is not the art of genius, but mere craftsmanship. It is only a means, subordinated to what it is supposed to decorate, and can therefore be replaced, like any other means subordinated to an end, by another appropriate means. It has no share in the uniqueness of the work of art.

In fact the concept of decoration must be freed from this antithetical relationship to the concept of the art of experience and be grounded in the ontological structure of representation, which we have seen as the mode of being of the work of art. We have only to remember that, in their original meaning, the ornamental and the decorative were the beautiful as such. It is necessary to recover this ancient insight. Ornament or decoration is determined by its relation to what it decorates, by what carries it. It does not possess an aesthetic import of its own which only afterwards acquires a limiting condition by its relation to what it is decorating. Even Kant, who endorsed this opinion, admits in his famous judgment on tattooing that ornament is ornament only when it suits the wearer.[71] It is part of taste not only to find something beautiful in itself, but also to know where it belongs and where not. Ornament is not primarily something by itself that is then applied to something else but belongs to the self-presentation of its wearer. Ornament is part of the presentation. But presentation is an ontological event; it is representation. An ornament, a decoration, a piece of sculpture set up in a chosen place are representative in the same sense that, say, the church in which they are to be found is itself representative.

Hence the concept of the decorative serves to complete our enquiry into the mode of being of the aesthetic. We shall see later other reasons for reinstating the old, transcendental meaning of the beautiful. What we mean by representation is, at any rate, a universal ontological structural element of the aesthetic, an ontological event and not an experiential event which occurs at the moment of artistic creation and is only repeated each time in the mind of the viewer. Starting from the universal significance of play, we saw the ontological significance of representation in the fact that 'reproduction' is the original mode of being of the original art. Now we have confirmed that painting and the plastic arts generally are, ontologically speaking, of the same mode of being. The specific mode of the work of art's presence is the coming into representation of being.

(C) THE BORDERLINE POSITION OF LITERATURE

We now have the test case of whether the ontological aspect I have developed applies to the mode of being of literature. Here apparently there is no representation that could claim an ontological value of its own. Reading is a wholly internal event. In it there seems to be a complete detachment from all occasion and contingency, as in, for example, public reading or performance. The only condition of literature is its linguistic tradition and its being understood in reading. Is not the aesthetic differentiation, with which aesthetic consciousness operates independently in relation to the work, legitimated by the autonomy of the reading consciousness? Literature seems to be poetry alienated from its ontological value. It could be said of every book —not only of that one famous one[72]—that it is for everyone and no one.

But is this an appropriate conception of literature? Does it not ultimately stem from a romantic projection from the alienated consciousness of culture? For literature as the object of reading is a late development, but certainly not the written word as such. That is part of the original givenness of all great poetry. Modern research has abandoned the romantic notions of the oral nature of epic poetry: that, say, of Homer. The written word is much older than we previously thought, and seems to have been part of the intellectual element of poetry from the beginning. Poetry already exists as 'literature' before being consumed as reading matter. Hence the ascendancy of private reading over public that we find later (we need only think of Aristotle's turning away from the theatre) brings nothing fundamentally new.

This is immediately obvious so long as the reading is reading aloud. But there is obviously no sharp differentiation from silent reading. All reading that is understanding is always a kind of reproduction and interpretation. Emphasis, rhythmic ordering and the like are also part of wholly silent reading. The significant and its understanding are so closely connected with the actual physical quality of language that understanding always contains an inner speaking as well.

If this is the case, then the consequence is unavoidable that literature—say in its proper art form, the novel— has just as original an existence in being read, as the epic has in being declaimed by the rhapsodist or the picture in being looked at by the spectator. According to this, the reading of a book would still remain an event in which the content presented itself. True, literature and the reading of it have the maximum degree of freedom and mobility.[73] This is seen simply in the fact that one does not need to read a book at one sitting, so that, if one wants to go on with it, one has to take it up again; this has no analogy in listening to music or looking at a picture, yet shows that reading is related to the unity of the text.

Literature as an art-form can be understood only from the ontology of the work of art, and not from the aesthetic experiences that occur in the course of the reading. To be read is an essential part of the literary work of art, like a public reading or performance. They are stages of what is called in general 'reproduction', but which in fact is the original mode of being of all interpretative arts, and has proved eminently suitable for the definition of the mode of being of all art.

But this has a further consequence. The concept of literature is not unrelated to the reader. Literature is not the dead continuance of an estranged being made available to the experience of a later period. Literature is a function of intellectual preservation and tradition, and therefore brings its hidden history into every age. From the establishment of the canon of classical literature, by the Alexandrian philologists, the entire tradition of the copying and preservation of the 'classics' is a living cultural tradition which does not simply preserve what exists, but acknowledges it as a model and passes it on as an example to be followed. Through all changes of taste, that entity that we call 'classical literature' remains as a model for all later writers, up to the time of the dubious conflict between the anciens and the modernes, and beyond.

Only the development of historical consciousness changes this living unity of world literature from the immediacy of its normative claim as a unity into a question of literary history. But this is a process that is unfinished and perhaps never can be finished. It was Goethe who first formulated the idea of 'world literature' in the German language,[74] but for Goethe it was still quite automatic to use such an idea in a normative sense. It has not died out even today, for we still say that a work of lasting importance belongs to world literature.

What belongs to world literature has its place in the consciousness of all. It belongs to the 'world'. Now the world which considers a work to belong to world literature may be far removed from the original world in which this work was born. It is at any rate no longer the same 'world'. But even then the normative sense contained in the idea of world literature means that works that belong to world literature remain eloquent although the world to which they speak is quite different. Similarly, the existence of literature in translation shows that something is presented in such works that is true and valid for all time. Thus it is by no means the case that world literature is an alienated form of that which constitutes the mode of being of a work according to its original purpose. It is rather the historical mode of being of literature that makes it possible for something to belong to world literature.

The normative quality accorded by the fact that a work belongs to world literature places the phenomenon of literature under a new aspect. For if a work, with its own value as a literary work of art, is declared to belong to world literature, then the concept of literature is far wider than that of the literary work of art. An entire written tradition partakes of the mode of being of literature—not only religious, legal, economic, public and private texts of all kinds, but those writings in which these texts are scientifically treated and interpreted: namely, the human sciences as a whole. Moreover, all scientific research has the form of literature, insofar as it is essentially bound to language. If words can be written down, then they are literature, in the widest sense.

We may ask ourselves, then, whether what we have discovered concerning the mode of being of art still applies to this wide significance of literature. Must we keep the normative sense of literature which we elaborated above for those literary works that can be considered as works of art, and must we say of these alone that they share in the quality of being of art? Do the other forms of literature have no share in it?

Or is there no such sharp division here? There are works of scholarship whose literary merit has caused them to be considered as works of art and part of world literature. This is clear from the point of view of aesthetic consciousness, inasmuch as the latter does not consider the significance of its contents, but only the quality of its form as important. But since our criticism of the aesthetic consciousness has limited the validity of that point of view, this principle of division between literary art and literature will be a dubious one for us. We have seen that aesthetic consciousness is not able to grasp the essential truth even of a literary work of art. Instead, it has in common with all other literary texts that it speaks to us in terms of the significance of its contents. Our understanding is not specifically concerned with the achievement of form that belongs to it as a work of art, but with what it says to us.

The difference between a literary work of art and any other literary text is not so fundamental. It is true that there is a difference between the language of poetry and the language of prose, and again between the language of poetic prose and of 'scientific' prose. These differences can certainly also be considered from the point of view of literary form. But the essential difference of these various 'languages' obviously lies elsewhere: namely, in the distinction between the claims to truth that each makes. All literary works have a profound community in that the linguistic form makes effective the significance of the contents to be expressed. In this light, the understanding of texts by, say, a historian is not so very different from the experience of art. And it is not mere chance that the concept of literature embraces not only works of literary art, but everything that has been transmitted in writing.

At any rate it is not by chance that literature is the place where art and science merge. The mode of being of literature has something unique and incomparable about it. It presents a specific problem of translation to the understanding. There is nothing so strange and at the same time so demanding as the written word. Not even the encounter with speakers of a foreign language can be compared with this strangeness, since the language of gesture and of sound always contains an element of immediate understanding. The written word and what partakes of it—literature—is the intelligibility of mind transferred to the most alien medium. Nothing is so purely the trace of the mind as writing, but also nothing is so dependent on the understanding mind. In its deciphering and interpretation a miracle takes place: the transformation of something strange and dead into a total simultaneity and familiarity. This is like nothing else that has come down to us from the past. The remnants of the life of the past, what is left of buildings, tools, the contents of graves, are weather-beaten by the storms of time that have swept over them, whereas a written tradition, when deciphered and read, is to such an extent pure mind that it speaks to us as if in the present. That is why the capacity to read, to understand what is written, is like a secret art, even a magic that looses and binds us. In it time and space seem to be suspended. The man who is able to read what has been handed down in writing testifies to and achieves the sheer presence of the past.

Hence we can see that in our context, despite all aesthetic

divisions, the concept of literature is as broad as possible. As we were able to show that the being of the work of art is play which needs to be perceived by the spectator in order to be completed, so it is universally true of texts that only in the process of understanding is the dead trace of meaning transformed back into living meaning. We must ask whether what was seen to be true of the experience of art is also true of texts as a whole, including those that are not works of art. We saw that the work of art is fully realised only when it is 'presented', and were forced to the conclusion that all literary works of art can achieve completion only when they are read. Is this true also of the understanding of any text? Is the meaning of all texts realised only when they are understood? In other words, does understanding belong to the meaning of a text just as being heard belongs to the meaning of music? Can we still talk of understanding if we adopt as free an attitude to the meaning of the text as the player does to his score?

(D) RECONSTRUCTION AND INTEGRATION AS HERMENEUTICAL TASKS

The classical discipline concerned with the art of understanding texts is hermeneutics. If my argument is correct, however, then the real problem of hermeneutics is quite different from its common acceptance. It points in the same direction in which my criticism of the aesthetic consciousness has moved the problem of aesthetics. In fact, hermeneutics would then have to be understood in so comprehensive a sense as to embrace the whole sphere of art and its complex of questions. Every work of art, not only literature, must be understood like any other text that requires understanding, and this kind of understanding has to be acquired. This gives to the hermeneutical consciousness a comprehensive breadth that surpasses even that of the aesthetic consciousness. Aesthetics has to be absorbed into hermeneutics. This statement not only reveals the extent of the problem, but is substantially accurate. Conversely, hermeneutics must be so determined as a whole that it does justice to the experience of art. Understanding must be conceived as a part of the process of the coming into being of meaning, in which the significance of all statements—those of art and those of everything else that has been transmitted—is formed and made complete.

In the nineteenth century, the old theological and literary ancillary discipline of hermeneutics was developed into a system which made it the basis of all the human sciences. It wholly transcended its original pragmatic purpose of making it possible, or easier, to understand literary texts. It is not only the literary tradition that is estranged and in need of new and more appropriate assimilation, but all that no longer expresses itself in and through its own world—that is, everything that is handed down, whether art or the other spiritual creations of the past, law, religion, philosophy and so forth—is estranged from its original meaning and depends, for its unlocking and communicating, on that spirit that we, like the Greeks, name Hermes: the messenger of the gods. It is to the development of historical consciousness that hermeneutics owes its central function within the human sciences. But we may ask whether the whole range of the problem that it poses can be properly grasped on the basis of the premises of historical consciousness.

Work in this field hitherto, defined primarily by Wilhelm Dilthey's hermeneutical grounding of the human sciences[75] and by his research into the origins of hermeneutics,[76] determined in its way the dimensions of the hermeneutical problem. Today's task could be to free ourselves from the dominant influence of Dilthey's approach to the question, and the prejudices of the discipline that he founded: namely Geistesgeschichte (cultural history).

To give a preliminary indication of what is involved and to combine the systematic result of my argument so far with the new extension of the problem, let us consider first the hermeneutical task set by the phenomenon of art. However clearly I showed that aesthetic differentiation was an abstraction that could not cancel and transcend the attachment of the work of art to its world, it remains irrefutable that art is never simply past, but is able to cross the gulf of time by virtue of its own meaningful presence. Hence art offers, in both ways, an excellent example of understanding. Even though it is no mere object of historical consciousness, understanding it always includes historical mediation. What, then, is the task of hermeneutics in relation to it?

Schleiermacher and Hegel suggest two very different ways of answering this question. They might be described as reconstruction and integration. The primary point for Schleiermacher as for Hegel is the consciousness of loss and estrangement in relation to tradition, which rouses them to hermeneutical reflection. Nevertheless, they define the task of hermeneutics very differently.

Schleiermacher (whose theory of hermeneutics will be considered later) is wholly concerned to reproduce in the understanding the original purpose of a work. For art and literature which are transmitted to us from the past are wrenched from the context of their original world. As my analysis revealed, this is true of all art, including literature, but it is seen with particular clarity in the case of plastic art. Schleiermacher says that it is no longer the natural and primary thing 'when works of art come into general commerce. Part of the intelligibility of each one derives from its original purpose. Hence the work of art loses something of its significance if it is torn from its original context, unless this happens to be historically preserved.' He even says: 'Hence a work of art, too, is really rooted in its own soil. It loses its meaning when it is wrenched from this environment and enters into general commerce; it is like something that has been saved from the fire but still bears the marks of the burning upon it'.[77]

Surely, then, the work of art enjoys its true significance only where it originally belongs? Is to grasp its significance, then, to re-establish, in a sense, this original world? If it is acknowledged that the work of art is not a timeless object of aesthetic experience, but belongs to a world that endorses it with its significance, it would follow that the true significance of the work of art can be understood only in terms of its origin and genesis within that world. Hence all the various means of historical reconstruction, the re-establishment of the 'world' to which it belongs, the re-establishment of the original situation about which the creative artist was writing, performance in the original style, and so on, can claim to reveal the true meaning of a work of art and guard against misunderstanding and false reproduction. This is, in fact, Schleiermacher's conception and the tacit premise of his entire hermeneutics. According to Schleiermacher, historical knowledge opens the way towards replacing what is lost and re-establishing tradition, inasmuch as it brings back the circumstances of the situation and restores it 'as it was'. The work of hermeneutics seeks to rediscover the point of contact in the mind of the artist which will open up fully the significance of a work of art, just as in the case of texts it seeks to reproduce the writer's original words.

The reconstruction of the conditions in which a work that has come down to us from the past fulfilled its original purpose is undoubtedly an important aid to its understanding. But it may be asked whether what is then obtained is really what we look for as the meaning of the work of art, and whether it is correct to see understanding as a second creation, the reproduction of the original production. Ultimately, this view of hermeneutics is as foolish as all restitution and restoration of past life. The reconstruction of the original circumstances, like all restoration, is a pointless undertaking in view of the historicity of our being. What is reconstructed, a life brought back from the lost past, is not the original. In its continuance in an estranged state it acquires only a secondary, cultural, existence. The recent tendency to take works of art out of a museum and put them back in the place for which they were originally intended, or to restore architectural monuments to their original form, merely confirms this judgment. Even the painting taken from the museum and replaced in the church, or the building restored to its original condition are not what they once were—they become simply tourist attractions. Similarly, a hermeneutics that regarded understanding as the reconstruction of the original would be no more than the recovery of a dead meaning.

Hegel, in contrast, indicates another possibility of balancing out the profit and loss of the hermeneutical enterprise. He shows his clear grasp of the futility of restoration when he writes of the decline of the classical world and its religion of art that the works of the Muses 'are now what they are for us—beautiful fruits torn from the tree. A friendly fate presents them to us as a girl might offer those fruits. We have not the real life of their being—the tree that bore them, the earth and elements, the climate that determined their substance, the seasonal changes that governed their growth. Nor does fate give us, with those works of art, their world, the spring and summer of the ethical life in which they bloomed and ripened, but only the veiled memory of this reality'.[78] And he calls the relationship of posterity to those works of art that have been handed down an 'external activity' that 'wipes spots of rain or dust from this fruit and instead of the internal elements of the surrounding, productive and lifegiving reality of the ethical world substitutes the elaborate structure of the dead elements of its external existence, of language, of its historical features and so forth. And this not in order to live within that reality but merely to represent it within oneself'.[79]

What Hegel is describing here is precisely what is involved in Schleiermacher's demand for historical preservation except that with Hegel there is a negative emphasis. The search for those circumstances which would add to the significance of works of art cannot succeed in reproducing them. They remain fruit torn from the tree. To place them in their historical context does not give one a living relationship with them but rather one of mere imaginative representation. Hegel does not deny the legitimacy of taking up an historical attitude towards the art of the past. On the contrary, he affirms the principle of art-historical research—but this, like any 'historical' relation, is, in Hegel's eyes, an external activity.

The authentic task of the thinking mind in relation to history, including the history of art, is not, according to Hegel, an external one inasmuch as the mind would see itself represented in history in a higher way. Developing his image of the girl who offers the fruit torn from the tree, he writes: 'But as the girl who presents the plucked fruit is more than Nature that presented it in the first place with all its conditions and elements—trees, air, light and so on—in so far as she combines all these in a higher way in the light of self-consciousness in her eyes and in her gestures, so also is the spirit of destiny which gives us these works of art, greater than the ethical life and reality of a particular people, for it is the interior recollection of the still external spirit manifest in them. It is the spirit of tragic fate that gathers all these individual gods and attributes of substance within one Pantheon, into its spirit conscious of itself as spirit'.

Here Hegel goes beyond the entire dimension in which Schleiermacher conceived the problem of understanding. Hegel raises it to the level at which he has established philosophy as the highest form of absolute Mind. That self-consciousness of spirit that, as the text has it, comprehends the truth of art within itself in a higher way, culminates in the absolute knowledge of philosophy. For Hegel, then, it is philosophy, the historical self-penetration of spirit, that carries out the hermeneutical task. It is the most extreme counter-position to the self-forgetfulness of historical consciousness. For it, the historical attitude of imaginative representation is changed into a thinking attitude towards the past. Here Hegel states a definite truth, inasmuch as the essential nature of the historical spirit does not consist in the restoration of the past, but in thoughtful mediation with contemporary life. Hegel is right when he does not conceive of such thoughtful mediation as an external and supplementary relationship, but places it on the same level as the truth of art itself. In this way he wholly transcends Schleiermacher's idea of hermeneutics. The question of the truth of art forces us, too, to undertake a critique of both aesthetic and historical consciousness, inasmuch as we are enquiring into the truth that manifests itself in art and history.

SECOND PART

THE EXTENSION OF THE QUESTION OF TRUTH TO UNDERSTANDING IN THE HUMAN SCIENCES

*Qui non intelligit res, non potest
ex verbis sensum elicere*
M. Luther

I

Historical preparation

1 THE QUESTIONABLENESS OF ROMANTIC HERMENEUTICS AND OF ITS APPLICATION TO THE STUDY OF HISTORY

(A) THE CHANGE IN HERMENEUTICS BETWEEN THE ENLIGHTENMENT AND ROMANTICISM

If we are to follow Hegel rather than Schleiermacher, the history of hermeneutics must place its emphases quite differently. Its culmination will no longer consist in the liberation of historical understanding from every dogmatic bias, and we shall no longer be able to see the rise of hermeneutics as Dilthey, following Schleiermacher, presented it. We must, rather, retrace Dilthey's steps and look out for goals other than those of Dilthey's historical self-consciousness. We shall entirely disregard the dogmatic interest in the hermeneutical problem that the old testament presented even to the early church[1] and shall be content to pursue the development of the hermeneutical method in the modern period, which results in the development of historical consciousness.

(i) The pre-history of romantic hermeneutics

The art or technique of understanding and interpretation developed along two paths, theological and literary critical, from one analogous impulse. Theological hermeneutics, as Dilthey showed,[2] from the reformers' defence of their own understanding of scripture against the attack of the Tridentine theologians and their appeal to the essential place of tradition; literary critical hermeneutics as a tool of the humanist claim to revive classical literature. Both involve a revival of something that was not absolutely unknown, but whose meaning had become alien and unavailable. Classical literature, though constantly present as cultural material, had been completely absorbed within the christian world. Similarly, the bible was the church's sacred book and as such was constantly read, but the understanding of it was determined and—as the reformers insisted—obscured, by the dogmatic tradition of the church. Both traditions are dealing with a foreign language and not with the universal scholar's language of the Latin middle ages, so that the study of the tradition in its original source made it necessary to learn Greek and Hebrew as well to purify Latin. Hermeneutics claims to reveal, by specialised techniques, the original meaning of the texts in both traditions, humanistic literature and the bible. It is significant that the humanistic tradition became united, through Luther and Melanchthon, with the reform.

Insofar as scriptural hermeneutics is regarded as the pre-history of the hermeneutics of the modern human sciences, it is based on the scriptural principle of the reformation. Luther's position is more or less the following:[3] scripture is sui ipsius interpres. We do not need tradition to reach the proper understanding of it, nor do we need an art of interpretation in the style of the ancient teaching of the fourfold meaning of scripture, but the text of the scripture has a clear sense that can be derived from itself, the sensus literalis. The allegorical method in particular, which had formerly seemed indispensable for the dogmatic unity of the teachings of scripture, is now legitimate only where the allegorical intention is given in scripture itself. Thus it is appropriate when dealing with the parables. The old testament, however, should not acquire its specifically christian relevance through an allegorical interpretation. We must take it literally, and precisely by being understood literally, and seen as the expression of the law which Christ's saving deed removes, does it acquire a christian significance.

The literal meaning of scripture, however, is not clearly available in every place and at every moment. For it is the whole of scripture that guides the understanding of the individual passage: and again this whole can be reached only through the cumulative understanding of individual passages. This circular relationship between the whole and the parts is not new. It was already known to classical rhetoric, which compares perfect speech with the organic body, with the relationship between head and limbs. Luther and his successors[4] applied this image, familiar from classical rhetoric, to the process of understanding and developed the universal principle of textual interpretation that all the details of a text were to be understood from the contextus (context) and from the scopus, the unified sense at which the whole aims.[5]

Insofar as the theology of the reformers relies on this principle in the interpretation of scripture it remains bound to a postulate that is itself dogmatically founded. It postulates that the bible is itself a unity. Judged from the historical point of view of the eighteenth century, reformed theology is also dogmatic and excludes any sound individual interpretation of scripture that takes account of the relative context of a text, its purpose and its composition.

Indeed, reformed theology does not even seem to be consistent. By ultimately asserting the protestant credal formulae as guides to the understanding of the unity of the bible, it too does away with the scriptural principle, in favour of a rather brief reformation theology, but of Dilthey.[6] He discusses these contradictions of protestant hermeneutics from within the full self-awareness of the historical sciences. We shall still have to consider whether this self-consciousness, precisely in regard to the theological meaning of scriptural exegesis, is really justified and whether the literary and hermeneutical principle of understanding texts in their own terms is not itself unsatisfactory and always in need of support from a generally unacknowledged dogmatic guideline.

We can ask this question today, however, after the historical enlightenment realised the full extent of its possibilities: Dilthey's studies on the origin of hermeneutics manifest a logical continuity that is convincing, given the modern concept of science. Hermeneutics had to rid itself one day of all its dogmatic limitations and become free to be itself, so that it could rise to the universal significance of an historical organon. This took place in the eighteenth century, when men like Semler and Ernesti realised that to understand scripture properly it was necessary to recognise the differences between the authors of it, ie to abandon the idea of the dogmatic unity of the canon. With this 'liberation of interpretation from dogma' (Dilthey), the collection of the christian sacred writings came to be seen as a collection of historical sources that, as works of literature, had to submit not only to grammatical but also to historical interpretation.[7] Understanding them in terms of their total context now necessarily also required the historical restitution of the living context to which the documents belong. The old interpretative principle of understanding the part in terms of the whole was no longer related and limited to the dogmatic unity of the canon, but was concerned with the totality of the historical reality to which the individual historical document belonged.

And as there is no longer any difference between the interpretation of sacred or secular writings, and hence only one hermeneutics, this hermeneutics has ultimately not only the propaedeutic function of all historical research—as the art of the correct interpretation of literary sources—but involves the whole business of historical research itself. For what is true of the written sources, that every sentence in them can be understood only from its context, is also true of their content. Its meaning is not fixed. The historical context in which the individual objects, large or small, of historical research appear in their true relative meaning is itself a whole, in terms of which every individual thing is to be understood in its full significance, and which in turn is to be fully understood in terms of these individual things. History is, as it were, the great dark book, the collected work of the human spirit, written in the languages of the past, the text of which we have to try to understand. Historical research sees itself according to the model of literary interpretation of which it makes use. We shall see that this is, in fact, the model according to which Dilthey founded the historical view of the world.

In Dilthey's eyes, then, hermeneutics acquires its own real nature only when it changes from serving a dogmatic task —which, for the christian theologian, is the right proclamation of the gospel—into functioning as a historical organon. If, however, the ideal of the historical enlightenment, which Dilthey pursued, should prove to be an illusion, then the pre-history of hermeneutics that he outlined will also acquire a quite different significance. The evolution to historical consciousness is not, then, its liberation from the chains of dogma but a transformation of its nature. Precisely the same thing is true of literary critical hermeneutics. For the ars critica was based primarily on the uncritically accepted exemplariness of classical antiquity, the literary tradition of which was its province. It, too, must change its nature if there is no longer any clear relation of model to copy between classical antiquity and the present. That this is the case is shown by the querelle des anciens et des modernes, which sounds the general theme for the whole period from French classicism to the German classical period. This problem resulted in the development of historical reflection, which finally demolished the claim of classical antiquity to be normative. In the case, then, of both literary criticism and theology, it is the same process that led ultimately to the conception of a universal hermeneutics, for which the particular exemplary nature of tradition is no longer a presupposition of the hermeneutical task.

The development of a science of hermeneutics, as performed by Schleiermacher in his debate with the critics F. A. Wolf and F. Ast, and in the further elaboration of the theological hermeneutics of Ernesti is not, then, just another state in the history of the art of understanding. Actually, the history of understanding has been accompanied, since the days of classical literary criticism, by theoretical reflection. But these reflections have the character of a 'technique', ie they seek to serve the art of understanding, just as rhetoric seeks to serve the art of speaking, 'poetics' the art and appreciation of poetry. In this sense the theological hermeneutics of the fathers and that of the reformation were techniques. But now understanding as such becomes a problem. The universality of this problem shows that understanding has become a task in a new sense, and hence theoretical reflection acquires a new significance. It is no longer a technique guiding the practice of critic or theologian. Schleiermacher, it is true, calls his hermeneutics a technique, but in a quite different, systematic sense. He seeks the theoretical foundation for the procedure common to theologians and literary critics, by reaching back beyond the concerns of each to the more fundamental relation of the understanding of meanings.

The critics who were his immediate predecessors had had a different attitude. For them, hermeneutics was determined by the content of what was to be understood—and this was the obvious unity of classical and christian literature. Ast's goal of a universal hermeneutics, 'the demonstration of the unity of Greek and christian life' expresses what, basically, all 'christian humanists' think.[8] Schleiermacher, on the other hand, no longer seeks the unity of hermeneutics in the unity of the content of tradition, to which understanding has to be applied, but apart from any particular content, in the unity of a procedure that is not divided even by the way in which the ideas are transmitted—whether in writing or orally, in a foreign language or in one's own. The effort of understanding is found wherever there is no immediate understanding, ie whenever the possibility of misunderstanding has to be reckoned with.

Schleiermacher's idea of a universal hermeneutics starts from this: that the experience of the alien and the possibility of misunderstanding is a universal one. It is true that this alien quality is greater and more open to misunderstanding in artistic than in non-artistic uttcrance, greater with written than with oral utterance, which is, as it were, continually interpreted by the living voice. But precisely the extension of the hermeneutical task to the 'significant conversation', which is especially charac-

teristic of Schleiermacher, shows how fundamentally the meaning of alienness, which hermeneutics is supposed to overcome,
has changed when compared with the task of hermeneutics
hitherto. In a new and universal sense, alienness is inextricably
given with the individuality of the 'Thou'.

We should not, however, take the lively, even brilliant sense
of human individuality that characterises Schleiermacher as an
individual idiosyncrasy that influenced his theory. It is, rather,
the critical rejection of everything that was regarded in the
enlightenment, under the rubric of 'rational ideas' (Vernünftige
Gedanken), as the common nature of humanity, which forced
him to undertake a wholly new approach to the problem of the
relation to tradition.[9] The art of understanding is subjected to a
fundamental theoretical examination and universal cultivation,
because neither scripturally nor rationally founded agreement
can any longer constitute the dogmatic guideline of all textual
understanding. Thus it was necessary for Schleiermacher to
provide a fundamental motivation for hermeneutical reflection
and thus place the problem of hermeneutics in a hitherto unknown framework.

To provide the right background for the particular turn that
Schleiermacher gives to the history of hermeneutics, let us
consider a point which Schleiermacher himself does not treat at
all and which, since Schleiermacher, has totally disappeared
from the sphere of hermeneutics (this curiously narrows
Dilthey's historical interest in the history of hermeneutics), but
which in fact dominates the problem of hermeneutics and must
be taken into account if we are to understand Schleiermacher's
place in its history. Our starting-point is the proposition that to
understand means primarily for two people to understand one
another. Understanding is primarily agreement or harmony with
another person. Men generally understand each other directly,
ie they are in dialogue until they reach agreement. Understanding, then, is always understanding about something. Understanding each other means understanding each other on a topic
or the like. From language we learn that the topic is not some
random self-contained object of discussion, independently of
which the process of mutual understanding proceeds, but rather
is the path and goal of mutual understanding itself. And if two
men understand each other independently of any topic, then this
means that they understand each other not only in this or that
respect, but in all the essential things that unite human beings.
Understanding becomes a special task only when this natural life
in which each means and understands the same thing, is dis-

turbed. Only when misunderstandings have arisen or an opinion is unintelligible to us, is natural life in the meant context so impeded that the meaning becomes something fixed, something given as the meaning of the other or of the text. And even here agreement, and not merely understanding, is generally sought and this in such a way that again one proceeds via the object. Only if all these movements which make up the art of conversation—argument, question and answer, objection and refutation, which are undertaken in regard to a text as an inner dialogue of the soul seeking understanding—are in vain, will the question recur; only then does the effort of understanding become aware of the individuality of the 'Thou' and take account of his uniqueness. If we are dealing with a foreign language, the text will already be the object of a grammatical, linguistic interpretation, but that is only a preliminary condition. The real problem of understanding obviously arises when, in the endeavour to understand the content of what is said, the reflective question arises how such an opinion has been reached. For it is clear that this kind of question reveals an alienness of a quite different kind and is ultimately a waiver of shared meaning.

Spinoza's critique of the bible is a good example of this (and at the same time one of the earliest). In chapter 7 of the *Tractatus theologico-politicus,* Spinoza elaborates his method of interpreting scripture on the basis of the interpretation of nature: we have to derive the meaning (mens) of the authors from this historical data, inasmuch as things are related in these books (stories of miracles and revelations) which cannot be derived from the principles known to us by natural reason. Independently of the fact that scripture undoubtedly on the whole has a moral significance, in these things which are, in themselves, incomprehensible (imperceptibiles), all the important issues can be understood, if only we understand the mind of the author 'historically', ie overcome our prejudices and think of nothing other than what the author could have had in mind.

The necessity of the historical interpretation 'in the spirit of the writer' follows, then, from the hieroglyphic and incomprehensible nature of the contents. No one so interprets Euclid, says Spinoza, that he pays any heed to the life, studies and habits (vita, studium et mores) of that author,[10] and this is true also for the spirit of the bible in moral matters (circa documenta moralia). Only because there are incomprehensible things (res imperceptibiles) in the stories of the bible, does our understanding of them depend on our being able to derive the author's meaning from the whole of his work (ut mentem auctoris per-

cipiamus). And here, in fact, it does not matter whether what is
meant corresponds to our insight (the sensus orationum), since
we want to know only the meaning of the statements, but not
their truth (veritas). For this we need to exclude all preconceived opinions, even those of reason.

Thus the 'naturalness' of the understanding of scripture depends on the fact that what is obvious can be apprehended
clearly, and what is not so can be understood 'historically'. The
overthrow of the immediate understanding of things in their
truth is the motive for proceeding via history. What this statement of the interpretative principle means for Spinoza's own
relationship to the tradition of scripture is a separate question.
In any case, for Spinoza, the extent of what can be understood
only in this historical way is very great, even if the spirit of the
whole (quod ipsa veram virtutem doceat) is obvious and what is
obvious is of overwhelming significance.

If we go back to the pre-history of historical hermeneutics in
this way, the first thing to be noted is that between literary
criticism and natural science in their early visions of themselves
there is a close correspondence. That has a dual meaning. On
the one hand, the 'naturalness' of the scientific procedure is
supposed to apply also to the attitude to scriptural tradition, and
is supported by the historical method. But on the other, naturalness, which in the art of criticism, practised in scriptural exegesis, is the art of understanding from a context, assigns to the
investigation of nature the task of deciphering the 'book of
nature'.[11] To this extent scientific method is based on the model
of literary criticism.

This is seen in the fact that it is the knowledge gained from the
scriptures and authorities that is the enemy against which the
new science of nature has to assert itself. As against this, the
new science has its own methodology, that leads through
mathematics and reason to an insight into what is intelligible in
itself.

The historical critique of scripture that emerges fully in the
eighteenth century has its dogmatic basis, as our nod to Spinoza
has shown, in the enlightenment's belief in reason. In a similar
way other forerunners of historical thinking, among whom there
were, in the eighteenth century, many now long forgotten
names, have tried to give guidelines for the understanding and
the interpretation of historical books. Among them Chladenius[12]
has been especially signalled out as a precursor of romantic
hermeneutics,[13] and in fact we find in him the interesting concept of the 'point of view' which grounds why we see a thing in

one way and not in another, a concept from optics, which the author explicitly borrows from Leibniz.

However, as we learn from the title of his work, Chladenius is basically put in a false light if we see his hermeneutics as an early form of historical methodology. It is not just that the case of 'the interpretation of historical books' is not at all the most important point—in every case it is a question of the actual content of the writings—but the whole problem of interpretation appears to him basically as pedagogical and occasional. Interpretation is concerned explicitly with 'rational discourses and writings'. For him, interpretation means 'adducing those ideas that are necessary for the perfect understanding of a passage'. Thus interpretation does not serve 'to indicate the true understanding of a passage', but it is expressly intended to remove obscurities in texts that hinder the student in his 'full understanding' (preface). In interpretation one must accommodate oneself to the insight of the student (§ 102).

Thus, for Chladenius, understanding and interpretation are not the same thing (§ 648). It is clear that it is quite an exceptional thing for a passage to require interpretation, and that, in general, a passage is understood when what the passage deals with is understood, whether it be that one is reminded by the passage of that object or that it is only through the passage that one gains knowledge of that object (§ 682). Undoubtedly the important thing here for understanding is still the understanding of the object, the objective insight. It is not a historical, nor a psychological, genetic procedure.

Nevertheless, the author is quite certain that the art of interpretation has acquired a new and special urgency, inasmuch as the art of interpretation at the same time justifies the interpretation. It is obviously not necessary as long as 'the student has the same knowledge as the interpreter' (so that what is to be understood is clear without needing to be demonstrated) or 'because of the trust placed in the interpreter'. Neither condition seems to him to be fulfilled in his own time; the latter insofar as (in the spirit of the enlightenment) 'the students want to see with their own eyes', the former insofar as with the growth of knowledge—ie with the advance of science—the obscurity of the things to be understood grows ever greater (§ 668f). Thus the need for a hermeneutics is given precisely with the decline of self-evident understanding.

In this way the occasional motivation of interpretation finally exhibits its fundamental significance. Chladenius reaches a highly interesting conclusion. He sees that to understand an author perfectly is not the same thing as to understand speech or writing perfectly (§ 86). The norm for the understanding of a book is not the author's meaning. For, 'since men cannot be aware of everything, their words, speech and writing can mean something that they themselves did not intend to say or write', and consequently 'when trying to understand their writings, one can rightly think of things that had not occurred to the writers'.

Even if the reverse is the case, 'that an author meant more than one has been able to understand', the real task of hermeneutics is not, for him, to understand these extra things, but the books themselves in their true, ie objective meaning. Because 'all men's books and speech have something incomprehensible about them'—namely, obscurities because of a lack of objective knowledge—it is necessary to have correct interpretation: 'unfruitful passages can become fruitful for us', as they 'encourage many thoughts'.

It should be noted that in all this Chladenius is not considering edifying scriptural exegesis, but explicitly disregards the 'sacred writings', for which the 'philosophical art of interpretation' is only a preliminary. Nor is he attempting to argue that everything that can be thought (every 'application') is part of the meaning of a book, but only what corresponds to the intentions of the writer. But this is clearly not meant in the sense of an historic-psychological limitation, but refers to an objective correspondence which, as he states explicitly, exegetically takes account of theology.[14]

(ii) Schleiermacher's project of a universal hermeneutics

Accordingly the pre-history of nineteenth-century hermeneutics looks very different if we no longer look at it with Dilthey's preconceptions. What a gulf lies between Spinoza and Chladenius on the one hand and Schleiermacher on the other! Unintelligibility, which for Spinoza motivates the detour via the historical and for Chladenius involves the art of interpretation in a sense entirely directed towards the object, has for Schleiermacher a quite different and universal significance.

The first interesting difference, as I see it, is that Schleiermacher speaks not so much of lack of understanding as of misunderstanding. What he has in mind is no longer the pedagogical function of interpretation, which assists the understanding of the other, the student; for him interpretation and understanding are closely interwoven, like the outer and the inner word, and every problem of interpretation is, in fact, a problem of understanding. He is concerned solely with the subtilitas intelligendi, not with the subtilitas explicandi[15] (let alone applicatio).[16] But, above all, Schleiermacher explicitly distinguishes between a looser hermeneutical praxis, in which understanding follows automatically, and a stricter one, which starts from the view that what follows automatically is misunderstanding.[17] His particular achievement, which was to develop a real art of understanding instead of an 'aggregate of observations', is based on this distinction. This is something fundamentally new. For from now on we are no longer concerned with the difficulties and failures of understanding as occasional, but as integral elements, which have to be excluded. Thus Schleiermacher even defines hermeneutics as 'the art of avoiding misunderstandings'. It rises above the pedagogical occasionality of interpretation and acquires the independence of a method, inasmuch as 'misunderstanding follows automatically and understanding must be desired and sought at every point'.[18] The avoidance of misunderstanding: 'all tasks are contained in this negative expression'. Schleiermacher sees its positive resolution in a canon of grammatical and psychological rules of interpretation, which even in the mind of the interpreter are quite distinct from commitment to a dogmatic content.

Now Schleiermacher was undoubtedly not the first to limit the scope of hermeneutics to making intelligible what others have said in speech and text. The art of hermeneutics has never been the organon of the study of things. This distinguishes it from the start from what Schleiermacher calls dialectic. But indirectly, wherever an attempt is made to understand (eg scripture or the classics), there is reference to the truth that lies hidden in the text and must be brought to light. What is to be understood is, in fact, not thought as part of another's life, but as a truth. Precisely for this reason hermeneutics has an ancillary function and remains part of the study of things. Schleiermacher takes account of this, insofar as he relates hermeneutics, within the system of sciences, to dialectics.

Nevertheless, the task that he sets himself is precisely that of isolating the process of understanding. He seeks to make it an independent method of its own. For Schleiermacher this also involves freeing himself from the limited aims that constitute the nature of hermeneutics for his predecessors, Wolf and Ast. He does not accept that it should be restricted to foreign languages, or to the written word, 'as if the same thing could not take place in conversation and in listening to a speech'.[19]

This is more than an extension of the hermeneutical problem

from the understanding of what is written down to the understanding of discourse in general; it suggests a fundamental shift. What is to be understood is now not only the exact words and their objective meaning, but also the individuality of the speaker, that is, the author. Schleiermacher holds that the author can really be understood only by going back to the origin of the thought. What is for Spinoza a limiting case of intelligibility and hence requires a detour via the historical, is for Schleiermacher the norm and the preliminary condition for the development of his views on understanding. What he finds 'most neglected, and even largely ignored' is 'the understanding of a succession of thoughts as an emerging element of life, as an act that is connected with many others, even of another kind'.

Thus beside grammatical interpretation he places psychological (technical) interpretation. This is his original contribution. We shall pass over Schleiermacher's brilliant comments on grammatical interpretation. They contain remarks on the role that the pre-given totality of language plays for the writer—and hence also for his interpreter—as well as on the significance of the whole of a literature for an individual work. It may be, as from a recent investigation of Schleiermacher's unpublished texts seems probable,[20] that the psychological interpretation only gradually came to dominate the development of Schleiermacher's thought. At any rate, this psychological interpretation became the main influence on the theorists of the nineteenth century, Savigny, Boeckh, Steinthal and, above all, Dilthey.

Even in the case of the bible, where the interpretation of each writer in terms of his individual psychology is of less moment than the significance of what is dogmatically uniform and common to them,[21] Schleiermacher still regards the methodological distinction between literary criticism and dogmatics as essential.[22] Hermeneutics includes grammatical and psychological interpretation. But Schleiermacher's particular contribution is psychological interpretation. It is ultimately a divinatory process, a placing of oneself within the mind of the author, an apprehension of the 'inner origin' of the composition of a work,[23] a recreation of the creative act. Thus understanding is a reproduction related to an original production, a knowing of what has been known (Boeckh),[24] a reconstruction that starts from the vital moment of conception, the 'germinal decision' as the composition's point of organisation.[25]

This kind of isolating description of understanding means, however, that the structure of thought that we seek to understand as an utterance or as a text is not to be understood in terms of its objective contents, but as an aesthetic construct, as a work of art or 'artistic thought'. If we hold on to this, we shall understand why it cannot be a question of the relation to the object (Schleiermacher's 'being'). Schleiermacher is following the aesthetic definitions of Kant when he says that 'artistic thought can be distinguished only by the greater or lesser pleasure' and is 'properly only the momentaneous act of the subject'.[26] Now the pre-condition of there being an understanding at all is that this 'artistic thought' is not a mere momentaneous act, but expresses itself. Schleiermacher sees in 'artistic thoughts' life-moments which contain so much pleasure that they burst into utterance, but they remain even then—however much pleasure they evoke in the 'originals of artistic works'—individual thought, a free construction unbounded by the being (object). This is precisely what distinguishes poetic from scientific texts.[27] By this, Schleiermacher undoubtedly means that poetic utterance is not subject to the already described criterion of agreement concerning the object, because what is said in it cannot be separated from the way in which it is said. The Trojan War, for example, exists in Homer's poem—a person who is concerned with the objective reality of history is no longer reading Homer as poetic discourse. No one would maintain that Homer's poem had gained in artistic reality as a result of the archeologists' excavations. What has to be understood here is not a common thought about an object, but individual thought that by its very nature is a free construction and the free expression of an individual being.

But it is characteristic of Schleiermacher that he seeks this element of free production everywhere. Even the dialogue, of which we have just spoken, is differentiated by Schleiermacher in the same way when, as well as 'dialogue proper' that is concerned with the common search for meaning and is the original form of dialectics, he speaks of 'free dialogue', which he considers as part of artistic thought. In the latter the content of the thoughts 'plays almost no part'. Dialogue is nothing but the mutual stimulation of thought ('and has no other natural end than the gradual exhaustion of the process described'),[28] a kind of artistic construction in the reciprocity of communication.

Insofar as utterance is not merely an inner product of thought, but is also communication and has, as such, an external form, it is not simply the immediate manifestation of the thought, but presupposes reflection. This is true, of course, of what is written down, and hence of all texts. They are always presentation through art.[29] But where utterance is an art, so is understanding. Thus all utterances and all texts are basically related to the art of understanding, hermeneutics, and this explains the connection between rhetoric (which is a part of aesthetics) and hermeneutics; every act of understanding is for Schleiermacher the inverse of an act of speech, the reconstruction of a construction. Thus hermeneutics is a kind of inversion of rhetoric and poetics.

We may be somewhat surprised to find poetry linked in this way with the art of speaking,[30] for it seems to us precisely the distinction and dignity of poetry that in it language is not speech, ie that it possesses a unity of meaning and form that is independent of any connection with speech, with being addressed or persuaded. Schleiermacher's conception of 'artistic thought', however, in which he includes poetry and rhetoric, is not concerned with the product, but with the attitude of the subject. Thus speech here is regarded purely as art, ie disregarding any reference to purpose or fact, as an expression of a creative productivity. Of course the borderline between the artistic and the non-artistic is not a clearly defined one, as is that between non-artistic (immediate) understanding and the understanding reached through particular techniques. Insofar as this production takes place mechanically according to laws and rules and not in an unconscious, 'inspired' way, the process of composition will be consciously re-performed by the interpreter; but if it is the individual, truly creative product of genius, then there can be no such re-creation according to rules. Genius creates models and rules. It creates new ways of using language, new literary forms. Schleiermacher takes full acccount of this difference. Corresponding, in hermeneutics, to the production of genius, is divination, the immediate solution, which ultimately presupposes a kind of corresponding genius. But if the frontier is fluid between non-artistic and artistic, mechanical and genial production, insofar as an individuality is always expressed and hence an element of rule-free genius always at work—as with children, who grow into a language—so it follows that the ultimate ground of all understanding must always be a divinatory act of corresponding genius, the possibility of which depends on a pre-existing connection between all individualities.

This is, in fact, Schleiermacher's presupposition, namely that all individuality is a manifestation of universal life and hence 'everyone carries a tiny bit of everyone else within himself, so that divination is stimulated by comparison with oneself'. Thus he is able to say that the individuality of the author can be directly grasped 'by, as it were, transforming oneself into the other'. Since Schleiermacher represents understanding as related in this way to the problem of individuality, the task of hermeneutics presents itself to him as a universal one. For both extremes of alienness and familiarity are given with the relative difference of all individuality. The 'method' of understanding will be concerned equally with what is common, by comparison, and with what is individual, by divination; it will be both comparative and divinatory. But it remains in both respects 'art', because it cannot be turned into a mechanical application of rules. The divinatory remains as essential ingredient.[31]

On the basis of this aesthetic metaphysics of individuality the hermeneutical principles used by the literary critic and the theologian undergo an important change. Schleiermacher follows Friedrich Ast and the whole hermeneutical and rhetorical tradition when he regards as an essential ingredient of understanding that the meaning of the part is always discovered only from the context, ie ultimately from the whole. This is, of course, true of the grammatical understanding of any sentence as well as its setting within the context of the whole work, even of the whole of that literature or of the literary form concerned; but Schleiermacher applies it to the psychological understanding that sees every thought construct as an element in the total context of a man's life.

It was always clear that this was logically a circular argument, in as far as the whole, in terms of which the individual element is to be understood, is not given before the individual element, unless in the manner of a dogmatic canon (as governs the catholic and, as we saw, to some degree the protestant understanding of scripture) or of some analogous preconception of the spirit of an age (as, for example, when Ast presumes that retribution characterises the spirit of the ancient world).

But Schleiermacher says that these dogmatic guide-lines cannot claim any prior validity and hence are only relative limitations of the circular argument. Fundamentally, understanding is always a movement in this kind of circle, which is why the repeated return from the whole to the parts, and vice versa, is essential. Moreover, this cycle is constantly expanding, in that the concept of the whole is relative, and when it is placed in ever larger contexts the understanding of the individual element is always affected. Schleiermacher applies to hermeneutics his recurrent procedure of a polar dialectical description and thus takes account of the inner provisional and infinite nature of understanding, by developing it on the basis of the old hermeneutical principle of the whole and the parts. But this characteristic speculative relativisation is intended more as as descriptive schema for the process of process of understanding than as a fundamental principle. This is seen in the fact that he assumes something like complete understanding when this divinatory transcription takes place, 'when all the individual elements at last suddenly seem to receive full illumination'.

We might ask if such phrases (which we also find in Boeckh with the same meaning) are to be taken strictly or only as a description of a relative completeness of understanding. It is true that Schleiermacher saw—as did, even more definitely, Wilhelm von Humboldt—individuality as a mystery that could never be quite grasped; but even this statement requires to be taken only in a relative way: the barrier that remains here for reason and understanding is not in every sense insuperable. It is to be overcome by feeling, an immediate, sympathetic and conatural understanding. Hermeneutics is an art and not a mechanical process. Thus it brings its work, understanding, to completion like a work of art.

The limitation of this hermeneutics based on the concept of individuality is now seen in the fact that Schleiermacher does not find the task of literary and of scriptural exegesis, ie of understanding a text written in a foreign language and coming from a past age, fundamentally more problematical than any other kind of understanding. It is true that, even according to Schleiermacher, there is a special task when a gulf of time has to be bridged. Schleiermacher calls it 'placing oneself on the same level as the original reader'. But the linguistic and historic establishing of this similarity is for him only an ideal precondition for the actual act of understanding, which is not for him placing oneself on the same level as the original reader, but on the same level as the author, through which this text is revealed as a unique manifestation of the life of its author. Schleiermacher's problem is not historical obscurity, but the obscurity of the 'Thou'.

It may be asked, however, whether it is possible to distinguish in this way between the establishing of a similarity with the original reader and the process of understanding. In fact the ideal pre-condition of placing oneself on the same level as the original reader cannot be realised before the actual attempt of understanding, but is wholly bound up with it. The meaning of a contemporary text, with whose language or content we are unfamiliar, is revealed only in the manner described, in the oscillating movement between whole and part. Schleiermacher recognises this. It is always in this movement that we learn to understand an alien meaning, a foreign language or a strange past. The circular movement is necessary because 'nothing that needs interpretation can be understood at once'.[32] For even within one's own language it is still true that the reader must completely assimilate both the vocabulary of the writer from his writings and, even more, the uniqueness of what he says. From these statements, which are found in Schleiermacher himself, it follows that the process of placing oneself on the same level as the original reader is not a preliminary operation that can be detached from the actual effort of understanding, which Schleiermacher sees as placing oneself on the same level as the writer.

Let us consider in more detail what Schleiermacher means by this relationship of similarity, for it cannot of course mean simple identification. Production and reproduction remain essentially distinct operations. Thus Schleiermacher asserts that the object is to understand a writer better than he understood himself, a formula that has been respected ever since and in the changing interpretation of which the whole history of modern hermeneutics can be read. Indeed, this statement contains the whole problem of hermeneutics. It would be valuable, therefore, to go further into its meaning.

What it means for Schleiermacher is clear. He sees the act of understanding as the reconstructive completion of the production. This inevitably makes conscious many things of which the writer may be unconscious. It is obvious that here Schleiermacher is applying the aesthetics of genius to his universal hermeneutics. The mode of creation of the artistic genius is the model on which this theory of unconscious production and necessarily conscious reproduction is based.[33]

In fact the formula, understood in this way, can be regarded as a principle of all criticism, insofar as the latter is seen as the understanding of artistic utterance. The better understanding that distinguishes the interpreter from the writer does not refer to the understanding of the objects of which the text speaks, but simply to the understanding of the text, ie of what the author meant and expressed. This understanding can be called 'better' insofar as the explicit—and hence worked out—understanding of a statement involves a greater degree of knowledge of its actual contents. Thus the sentence says something almost self-evident. A person who learns to understand a text in a foreign language will bring into explicit consciousness its grammatical rules and literary forms which the author followed without noticing, because he lived in the language and in its means of artistic expression. The same thing is true of all production by artistic genius and its reception by others. We must remember this especially in regard to the interpretation of poetry. There too it is necessary to understand a poet better than he understood himself, for he did not 'understand himself' at all when he formed the construct that is his text.

From this there follows also the point—which hermeneutics ought never to forget—that the artist who creates something is not the ideal interpreter of it. As an interpreter he has no automatic priority as an authority over the man who is simply receiving his work. He is, insofar as he reflects on his own work, his own reader. The meaning that he, as reader, gives to his own work is not authoritative. The only criterion of interpretation is the significance of his creation, what it 'means'. Thus the idea of production by genius performs an important theoretical task, in that it does away with the distinction between interpreter and author. It makes it possible for both to be placed on the same level, insofar as it is not reflective self-interpretation, but the unconscious meaning of the author that is to be understood. This is what Schleiermacher means by his paradoxical formula.

Since Schleiermacher others, including August Boeckh, Steinthal and Dilthey, have repeated his formula in the same sense: 'The literary critic understands the speaker and poet better than he understands himself and better than his contemporaries understood him, for he brings clearly into consciousness what was actually but only unconsciously, present in the other'.[35] Through the 'knowledge of psychological laws' the critic, according to Steinthal, can deepen his understanding by grasping the causality, the genesis of the work of literature, and the mechanics of the literary mind.

Steinthal's repetition of Schleiermacher's statement already shows the effect of the investigation of psychological laws, which takes as its model the investigation of nature. Dilthey is freer here, because he preserves more firmly the connexion with the aesthetics of genius. He applies the formula, in particular, to the interpretation of poetry. To understand the 'idea' of a poem from its 'inner form' can of course be called 'understanding it better'. Dilthey regards this as the 'highest triumph of hermeneutics',[36] for the philosophical import of great poetry is revealed when the latter is understood as free creation. Free creation is not bound by external conditions or those of subject matter and can therefore be grasped only as 'inner form'.

But we might ask whether this ideal case of 'free creation' can really function as a criterion for the problem of hermeneutics;

indeed, whether even the understanding of works of art can be sufficiently grasped according to this measure. We must also ask whether the statement that the aim is to understand an author better than he understood himself still retains its original meaning when taken in conjunction with the presupposition of the aesthetics of genius, or whether it has not changed into something completely new.

In fact, Schleiermacher's formula has a history. Bollnow, who has investigated the subject,[37] quotes two places where this statement can be found before Schleiermacher, namely in Fichte[38] and in Kant.[39] He has not been able to find any earlier evidence. For this reason, Bollnow assumes that it was an oral tradition, a kind of critical rule of the trade that people passed on and Schleiermacher took up.

For both external and internal reasons this seems to me highly unlikely. This sophisticated methodological formula, which is still often used today as a licence for arbitrary interpretations and is accordingly attacked, does not seem consistent with the philological mind. As 'humanists', they take pride in recognising the absolute exemplary nature of classical texts. For the true humanist his author is certainly not such that the interpreter would claim to understand the work better than did the author himself. We must not forget that the highest aim of the humanist was not originally to 'understand' his models, but to imitate or even surpass them. Hence he was originally bound to his models, not only as an expositor, but also as an imitator—if not a rival. Like the dogmatic commitment to the bible, the humanist's commitment to the classics had to give way to a looser attachment, if the work of the interpreter was to reach the extreme degree of self-confidence expressed in the statement we are considering.

Hence it is likely that not until Schleiermacher, with whom hermeneutics became an independent method, irrespective of content, could such a statement be used that claimed so fundamentally the superiority of the interpreter over his object. On closer examination, this fits in with the use of the idea by Fichte and Kant, for the context in which this statement—presumed to be a 'critical rule of the trade'—is used shows that Fichte and Kant meant something quite different by it. It is not, with them, a principle of criticism, but a philosophical claim to move, through greater conceptual clarity, beyond the contradictions of a given theory. Thus it is a principle that, entirely in the spirit of rationalism, claims, solely through thought, through the development of the implications of an author's ideas, to achieve insights that correspond to the real intention of the author —insights that he would have to share if his thinking had been clear enough. Even the hermeneutically impossible thesis in which Fichte involves himself in the polemic against the dominant interpretation of Kant, that 'the inventor of a system is one thing, its expositors and followers another',[40] as well as his claim to 'interpret Kant according to the spirit'[41] are satisfied by the claim to increasing knowledge of the object of thought. Thus the disputed formula makes no claim beyond that of philosophic critique of the object. Someone who is able to think his way better through what an author is talking about will be able to see what the author says in the light of a truth that is still hidden from the author. In this sense the principle that one must understand an author better than he understands himself is a very old one, as old as scientific criticism itself,[42] but it acquires its stamp as a formula for objective philosophical criticism in the spirit of rationalism. As such it has a sense completely different from Schleiermacher's rule. It is likely that Schleiermacher reinterpreted this principle of philosophical criticism and made it a principle of the literary art of interpretation.[43] This would clearly indicate the position of Schleiermacher and the romantics. In creating a universal hermeneutics they oust the critique based on the understanding of the object from the sphere of scientific interpretation.

Schleiermacher's formula, as he understands it, no longer includes the object itself under discussion, but sees the statement that a text presents as a free production, independent of its knowledge content. Accordingly he organises hermeneutics, which for him is concerned with the understanding of everything that is cast in language, according to the standard example of language. The speech of the individual is in fact a free creative activity, however limited its possibilities are by the fixed forms that language has taken. Language is an expressive field, and its pre-eminence in the field of hermeneutics means, for Schleiermacher, that as an interpreter he sees the texts, independently of their claim to truth, as pure expressive phenomena.

Even history is for him simply the display of this free creation, that of a divine productivity, and he sees the historical attitude as the observation and enjoyment of this mighty spectacle. The diary entry by Schleiermacher that Dilthey quotes[44] describes beautifully this romantic reflective enjoyment of history: 'True historical significance rises above history. Phenomena exist, like miracles, only to direct our attention towards the Spirit that playfully generates them'.

When we read this, we can see how tremendous the step had to be that was to lead from Schleiermacher's hermeneutics to a universal understanding of the historical sciences. However universal the hermeneutics that Schleiermacher evolved, it was a universality with very perceptible limits to it. His hermeneutics, in fact, had in mind texts whose authority was undisputed. Undoubtedly it is an important step in the development of historical consciousness that understanding and interpretation—both of the bible and of the literature of classical antiquity—was now completely detached from all dogmatic interest. Neither the saving truth of scripture nor the canonical exemplariness of the classics was to influence a procedure that was able to grasp every text as an expression of life and ignore the truth of what was said.

The interest, however, that was the reason for this methodological abstraction of Schleiermacher's was not that of the historian, but of the theologian. He sought to teach how speech and a written tradition were to be understood, because theology was concerned with one particular tradition, the biblical. For this reason his hermeneutical theory was still a long way from a historiography that could serve as a methodological organon for the human sciences. Its goal was the exact understanding of particular texts, which was to be aided by the universal character of historical contexts. This is Schleiermacher's limitation, and the historical view of the world had to move beyond it.

(B) THE CONNECTION BETWEEN THE HISTORICAL SCHOOL AND ROMANTIC HERMENEUTICS

(i) Rejection of the ideal of universal history

We must ask how historians were able to understand their own work in terms of their own hermeneutical theory. Their subject is not the individual text, but universal history. It falls to the historian to understand the history of mankind as a whole. The individual text has no value in itself, but serves only as a source, ie only as material to mediate knowledge of the historical context, just like the other silent relics of the past. Hence the historical school could not really build on Schleiermacher's hermeneutics.

But the historical view of the world, which pursues the great goal of understanding universal history, had been based on the romantic theory of individuality and the corresponding hermeneutics. This can be put negatively by saying that the a priori nature of the historical relation to life which tradition represents for the present, had not yet been made the subject of methodological reflection. Rather, historians saw their task as that of investigating what has been transmitted, and thus making the past available to the present. The basic scheme, according to which the historical school conceives the methodology of universal history is therefore really none other than that which applies to every text: the schema of whole and part. It certainly makes a difference whether one is trying to understand a text as a literary structure in terms of its intention and composition, or whether one seeks to use it as a document in the investigation of a larger historical context, concerning which it gives information that is to be examined critically. Nevertheless both literary and historical enquiry stress now the one and now the other approach. Historical interpretation, for example, can serve as a means to understand the context of a text even when, from another perspective, it sees in the text simply a source which is part of the totality of the historical tradition.

We find this expressed in clear methodological terms neither in Ranke, nor in the acute methodologist Droysen, but for the first time in Dilthey, who consciously takes up romantic hermeneutics and expands it into a historical method, indeed, into an epistemology of the human sciences. Dilthey's logical analysis of the concept of continuity in history is, in fact, the application to history of the hermeneutical principle that we can understand a detail only in terms of the whole text, and the whole only in terms of the detail. We find that our texts are not only the sources, but historical reality itself is a text that has to be understood. But in thus applying hermeneutics to the study of history Dilthey is only the interpreter of the historical school. He is formulating what Ranke and Droysen really think.

So we see that romantic hermeneutics and the background to it, the pantheistic metaphysics of individuality, was a decisive influence on the theory of historical research in the nineteenth century. This had an adverse influence on the moral sciences and the world-view of the historical school. We shall see that Hegel's philosophy of world history, against which the historical school rebelled, recognised far more profoundly the importance of history for the being of spirit and the knowledge of truth than did the great historians, who would not admit their dependence on him. Schleiermacher's concept of individuality, which accorded so well with the concerns of theology, aesthetics and literary criticism, was not only a critical category to be used against the aprioristic construction of the philosophy of history, but also provided for the historical sciences a methodological orientation that directed them, no less than the natural sciences, towards research, ie to the only basis for progressive experience. Thus resistance to the philosophy of world history drove history into the paths of literary interpretation. It was its pride that it conceived the continuity of the world not teleologically, nor in the style of pre- or post-romantic enlightenment, in terms of a final state, which would be, as it were, the end of history, a day of judgment for world history. Rather there does not exist for it any end of history or anything outside it. Hence the whole course of universal history can be won only from historical tradition itself. But this is precisely the claim of literary hermeneutics, namely the meaning of a text can be understood from itself. Thus the foundation for the study of history is hermeneutics.

Now, however, the ideal of universal history must become a special problem for the historical world-view, inasmuch as the book of history is a fragment that, so far as any particular present time is concerned, breaks off in the dark. The universal framework of history lacks the self-containedness that a text has for the critic and which, for the historian, makes a biography, or the history of a nation that has departed from the world-historical stage, or even the history of a period that is over and now lies behind us, into a complete unit of meaning, a text intelligible within itself.

We shall see that Dilthey also thought in terms of these relative units and hence built wholly on this basis of romantic hermeneutics. What has to be understood in both cases is a totality of meaning which, in both cases, has the same detachment from the person understanding it. It is always another individuality that must be judged according to its own concepts and criteria of value, 'moments', and can nevertheless be understood because 'I' and 'Thou' are of the same life.

The hermeneutical basis can support us thus far. But neither this detachment of the object from its interpreter nor the self-containedness of content in a totality of meaning can possibly support the central task of the historian, universal history. For history is not only not completed, but we stand within it as those understanding, as a conditioned and finite link in a continuing chain. It would be reasonable, on the basis of this problematical situation in regard to universal history, to doubt whether hermeneutics can really be the foundation for the study of history. Universal history is not a mere marginal and residual problem of historical investigation, but its very heart. Even the 'historical school' knew that fundamentally there can be no other history than universal history, because the unique significance of the detail can be determined only from the whole. How can the empirical researcher, to whom the whole can never be given, manage without losing his rights to the philosopher and his a priori arbitrariness?

Let us consider first how the 'historical school' tries to deal with this problem of universal history. For this we have to start further afield, although within the theoretical context presented by the historical school we are pursuing only the problem of universal history and hence are restricting ourselves to Ranke and Droysen.

We remember how the historical school distinguished itself from Hegel. Its chief characteristic is its turning away from the aprioristic construction of world history. It is its new claim that not speculative philosophy, but only historical research can lead to a universal view of history.

It was Herder's critique of the enlightenment's schema of the philosophy of history that made this development possible. Herder's attack against the enlightenment's pride in reason had its most effective weapon in the exemplary character of classical antiquity, which Winckelmann, in particular, had proclaimed. The 'history of the art of antiquity' was obviously more than an historical account. It was a critique of the present and a programme. But because of the ambiguity of any critique of the present, the proclamation of the exemplary character of Greek art, which was supposed to erect a new ideal for one's own present, was still a genuine step towards historical knowledge. The past, which is here offered as a model for the present, proves to be something that is unique and unrepeatable precisely because the reasons for its being of a particular character are investigated.

Herder needed to go only a little beyond the basis laid down by Winckelmann, and see the dialectical relationship in all the past between what is exemplary and what is unrepeatable, in order to set a universal historical world view against the enlightenment's teleological view of history. To think historically now means to acknowledge that each period has its own right to exist, and its own perfection. Herder took this step. The historical world view could not yet be fully realised as long as classicist prejudices accorded a special, paradigmatic place to classical antiquity. For not only a teleology in the style of the enlightenment's belief in reason, but also a converse teleology that assigns perfection to the past or to the beginning of history still recognises a criterion that is beyond history.

There are many ways of conceiving history in terms of a criterion that lies beyond it. Wilhelm von Humboldt's classicism sees history as the loss and decline of the perfection of Greek life. The gnostic theology of history of Goethe's time, the influence of which on the young Ranke has been recently demonstrated,[45] conceives the future as the re-establishment of a lost perfection of some primal time. Hegel reconciled the aesthetic exemplariness of classical antiquity with the self-confidence of the present, by describing the art religion of the Greeks as a form of the spirit that had been superseded and proclaiming, in the philosophical self-consciousness of freedom, the perfect fulfillment of history in the present. All these are ways of conceiving history that invoke a criterion that remains outside history.

However, the denial of this kind of a priori, unhistorical criterion, which comes at the beginning of the historical enquiry of the nineteenth century, is not as free from metaphysical assumptions as it believes itself to be when it sees itself as scientific research. This can be seen from the analysis of the leading ideas of this historical world view. It is true that the purpose of these ideas is to avoid the straitjacket of an a priori historical construction; but although they are directed polemically against the idealistic concept of the spirit they remain related to it. This will come out very clearly in Dilthey's philosophical analysis of this world view.

Its starting point is entirely determined by its antithesis to the 'philosophy of history'. The common basic assumption of all these representatives of this historical world view, Ranke, Droysen and Dilthey, is that idea, being and freedom do not find any full or even sufficient expression in historical reality. This must not be seen as a mere lack or shortcoming. Rather, they see the constitutive principle of history in the fact that the idea always has only an imperfect representation in history. Only because of this does philosophy have to be replaced by historical research to inform man about himself and his place in this world. The idea of a history that would be the pure representation of the idea would involve its rejection as an independent way to truth.

But on the other hand historical reality is not merely a heavy, opaque medium, mindless matter, rigid necessity against which the spirit beats in vain and in whose bonds it suffocates. Moreover, this kind of gnostic, neoplatonic view of process as emergence into the external world of appearance does not do justice to the metaphysical value of history and hence to the status of historical science as knowledge. The unfolding of human life in time has its own productivity. It is the plenitude and variety of the human that realises itself progressively in the unending vicissitudes of human destinies: this is a reasonable formulation of the basic assumption of the historical school. Its connection with the classicism of the age of Goethe is obvious.

The guiding thought here is, basically, a humanist ideal. Wilhelm von Humboldt saw the specific perfection of Greece in the rich variety of great individual forms that it manifests. Of course the great historians were not to be limited to this kind of classicist ideal; rather they followed Herder. But what can the historical world view that starts with Herder do, now that it no longer recognises the pre-eminences of a classical age, other than see the whole of world history in terms of the same criterion that Wilhelm von Humboldt used in order to justify the special position of classical antiquity? A rich variety of individual phenomena is not only the distinguishing work of Greek life, it is the mark of historical life in general, and that is what constitutes the value and meaning of history. This is intended to provide an answer to the anxious question concerning the meaning of the spectacle of brilliant victories and terrible defeats that troubles the human heart.

The advantage of this answer is that its humanistic ideal does not contain any particular content, but is based on the formal idea of the greatest variety. This kind of ideal is truly universal, for it cannot be shaken by any historical experience, any disturbing evidence of the transience of human things. History has a meaning in itself. What seems to speak against this—the transience of all that is earthly—is in fact its real basis. In its very impermanence lies the mystery of an inexhaustible productivity of historical life.

The question is only how the unity of world history can be conceived in terms of this criterion and formal ideal of history and the knowledge of it be justified. First, Ranke: 'Every event that is truly part of world history, that never consists solely of sheer destruction, but rather is able to engender in the fleeting present moment something for the future, includes within itself a full and immediate sense of its own indestructible value'.[46]

Neither the pre-eminent position of classical antiquity nor that of the present or of the future to which it leads, neither decline nor progress—those traditional basic categories of universal history—can be reconciled with genuine historical thought. On the other hand, the celebrated immediate relationship between all periods and God can very easily be combined with this idea of the continuity of world history. For continuity—Herder calls it 'order in the succession of events'—is the manifestation of historical reality itself. What is historically real emerges 'according to strict laws: subsequent events place the nature and the effect of what has just preceded in a bright, common light'.[47] The first statement, then, concerning the formal structure of history—that of coming into being in its very passing away—is that, persisting throughout the changing destinies of men, there is an unbroken continuity of life.

It is possible, however, to see from this what Ranke considers an "event that is truly part of world history" and what the continuity of world history is really based on. It has no fixed goal that can be discovered outside itself. To this extent there is no necessity, knowable a priori, at work in history. But the structure of historical continuity is still a teleological one, and its criterion is the successful outcome. We saw that subsequent events indicate the importance of those preceding them. Ranke may have meant this as a mere condition of historical knowledge. In fact it is also the basis of the peculiar importance of history. Whether something is successful or not not only determines the significance of a single event and is responsible for its producing a lasting effect or passing unnoticed, but success or failure causes a whole series of actions and events to be meaningful or meaningless. The ontological structure of history itself, then, is teleological, although without a telos.[48] The concept of the event that is truly part of world history, which Ranke uses, is defined by this. It is such if it 'makes history', ie if it has an effect that lends it a continuing historical importance. Hence the elements of historical continuity, in fact, are determined by an unconscious teleology that unites them and excludes the insignificant from this continuity.

(ii) Ranke's historical world-view

This kind of teleology cannot, of course, be demonstrated in terms of philosophical conception. It does not make world-history into an a priori system in which the actors are placed, as within a mechanism that is unconsciously directing them. It is, rather, compatible with the freedom of action. Ranke is able to say that the constructive links of the historical whole are 'scenes of freedom'.[49] This expression means that in the infinite web of events there are particularly significant incidents in which historical decisions are, as it were, concentrated. Decisions are made

wherever actions are performed in freedom, but that this decision really decides something, ie that a decision makes history
and reveals in its effect its full and lasting significance is the
mark of truly historical moments. They give to the historical
whole its articulation. We call such moments, in which a freely
chosen action has a decisive effect on history, epoch-making
moments or crises, and the individuals whose actions have this
effect can be called, to use Hegel's phrase, 'historic individuals'.
Ranke calls them 'original minds which intervene independently
in the battle of ideas and world forces and gather together the
most powerful ones, on which the future depends'. This is
absolutely Hegelian thinking.

We have a highly informative reflection of Ranke's on the
question of how the historical whole follows from such free
decisions: 'Let us admit that history can never have the unity of
a philosophical system; but it is not without an inner continuity.
Before us we see a range of successive events that condition one
another. When I say "condition", I do not mean with absolute
necessity. The great thing is, rather, that human freedom is
involved everywhere. The writing of history follows the scenes
of freedom. This is its greatest attraction. But freedom is combined with power, germinal power. Without the latter the former
disappears, both in the events of the world and in the sphere of
ideas. At every moment something new can begin, something
whose sole origin is the primary and common source of all
human activity. Nothing exists entirely for the sake of something else, nothing is entirely identical with the reality of something else. But there is still a deep inner unity present
everywhere, of which no one is entirely independent. Beside
freedom stands necessity. It consists in what has already been
formed and cannot be destroyed, which is the basis of all new
activity. What has already come into being constitutes the
continuity with what is coming into being. But even this continuity itself is not a thing to be arbitrarily accepted, but it has
come into existence in one particular way, and not another. It is,
likewise, an object of knowledge. A long series of events—
succeeding, simultaneous to, one another—linked together in
this way constitute a century, an epoch. . . .'[50]

The significant thing about this account is the way in which
the concept of freedom is linked to the concept of power. Power
is obviously the central category of the historical view of the
world. Herder had already used it to get away from the
enlightenment's schema of progress and especially from the
concept of reason that underlay it.[51] The concept of power has a

central place within the historical world view because in it interiority and exteriority are held in a peculiar unity in tension. All power exists only in its expression. The expression is not only the manifestation of the power, but its reality. Hegel was quite right when he developed dialectically the inner correspondence between power and expression. But this dialectic also shows that power is more than its expression. It possesses potentiality also, ie it is not only the cause of a particular effect, but the capacity, wherever it is used, to have that effect. Thus its mode of being is different from that of the effect. It has the mode of 'suspension'—a word that suggests itself because it expresses precisely the independent existence of power as against the indefiniteness of that in which it may express itself. It follows from this that power cannot be known or measured in terms of its expression, but only experienced as an indwelling. The observation of an effect always shows only the cause, and not the power, if the power is an inner surplus over the cause that belongs to the effect. This surplus, of which we are aware in the cause, can certainly be understood also in terms of the effect, in the resistance it offers, in that the offering of resistance is itself an expression of power. But even then it is an awareness in which power is experienced. Interiority is the mode of experiencing power, because power, of its nature, is related to itself alone. In his *Phänomenologie des Geistes*, Hegel has convincingly demonstrated the dialectical cancelling out of the concept of power in the infinity of life, which is related to itself alone and dwells in itself.[52]

Thus Ranke's formulation acquires a world-historical character within the history of thought and philosophy. Plato was first to remark, in this connection, the reflexive structure of Dunamis,[53] and this made it possible for it to be applied to the nature of the soul; this Aristotle did in his doctrine of the dunameis, the powers of the soul. Power is, in its ontological nature, 'inwardness'. Thus it is quite correct for Ranke to write: 'Freedom is combined with power'. For power that is more than its expression is always freedom. This is of decisive importance for the historian. He knows that everything could have been different, and every acting human being could also have acted differently. The power that makes history is not mechanical power. Ranke excludes this specifically by saying 'germinal power' and speaking of 'the primary and common source of all human activity'—this is, for Ranke, freedom.

It is not a contradiction of freedom for it to be limited. We can see this from the nature of power when it expresses itself. That is why Ranke can say: 'Beside freedom stands necessity'. For necessity does not mean here a cause that excludes freedom, but the resistance that the free power encounters. Here the truth of the dialectic of power that Hegel revealed is made manifest.[54] The resistance that free power encounters is itself freedom. The necessity we are concerned with here is the power of what has been transmitted and of those who are acting against one, which is pre-given before any operation of free activity. By excluding many things as impossible, it limits action to the possible. Necessity itself comes from freedom and is itself qualified by the freedom that reckons with it. Logically it is a question of hypothetical necessity (the ex hupotheseos anagkaion) and, in terms of content, we are not concerned with nature, but with historical being: what has come into being cannot simply be destroyed. Hence it is 'the basis of all new activity', as Ranke says, and yet it is something that has come about through actions. In that what has come into existence persists as a foundation for the new, it sets the new action within the unity of a context. Ranke says: 'What has already come into being constitutes the continuity with what is coming into being'. This very obscure sentence obviously seeks to express the nature of historical reality: that what comes into being is free, but that the freedom from which it comes is always limited by what has come into being, ie by the situation into which it comes. Ideas used by historians, such as power, force, determining tendency, all seek to reveal the essence of historical being, in that they imply that the idea is always represented in history in an incomplete way only. It is not the plans and views of those who act which constitutes the meaning of the process, but it is historical effects which reveal the historical powers. The historical powers, which are the carriers of historical development, are not the monadic subjectivity of the individual. Rather, all individuation is itself already partly characterised by the reality that stands over against it, and that is why individuality is not subjectivity, but living power. Even states are such living powers for Ranke. He said of them explicitly that they were not 'divisions of the universal', but individualities, "real spiritual beings"'.[55] Ranke calls them 'thoughts of God', in order to indicate that it is their own living power that causes them to exist and not some human creation or desire or some plan that men can grasp.

The use of the category of power now makes it possible to think of continuity in history as a primary given. Power is real always only as an interplay of powers, and history is this interplay of power that produces a continuity. Both Ranke and

Droysen say in this connection that history is a 'growing aggregate', in order to reject all claim to an a priori construction of world history, and they consider this view based wholly on experience.[56] The question is, however, whether there is not more assumed here than they know. That universal history is a growing aggregate means that it is a whole—though an unfinished one. But this is by no means obvious. Items that are qualitatively different cannot be added up. Adding up, rather, presupposes that the unity, in terms of which they are grouped together, is already the criterion of that grouping. But this presupposition is an assertion. The idea of unity in history is, in fact, not as formal and as independent of the understanding of the contents of history as it appears.[57]

The world of history has not always been conceived from the aspect of the unity of world history. It can also, for example, as with Herodotus, be considered as a moral phenomenon. As such it offers a large number of instances, but no unity. What justifies talk of the unity of world history? This question used to be answered easily when the assumption was made of a unity of goal, and hence of a plan, in history. But what is the common denominator that allows an aggregate to be made of historical events, if this kind of goal and this kind of plan in history is not accepted?

If the reality of history is conceived as an inter-play of forces, this concept is obviously not enough to make its unity necessary. What guided Herder and Humboldt, the ideal of the rich variety of the manifestations of human life, does not ground, as such, any true unity. There must be the something that emerges in the continuity of events as a goal giving an orientation to the whole. In fact, the place that is occupied in the eschatologies of the philosophy of history, both of religious origin and in their secularised versions, is here empty.[58] No preconceived idea concerning the significance of history should prejudice historical research. However, the self-evident assumption of historical research is that history constitutes a unity. Thus Droysen can explicitly acknowledge the idea of the unity of world history as a regulative idea, even if it is not a concept of the plan of providence.

However, there lies in this postulate a further assumption that determines it. The idea of the unity of world history includes the uninterrupted continuity of the development of world history. This idea of continuity is primarily formal in nature and does not imply any actual contents. It also is like an a priori of research that invites one to penetrate ever more deeply into the complex-

ities of historical continuity. To this extent it is only methodological naiveté on Ranke's part when he speaks of the 'admirable
constancy' of historical development.[59] What he actually means
by this is not the structure of continuity, but the contents that
emerge in this constant development. That something unique
finally emerges from the vast and multifarious whole of historical development, namely the unity of Western civilisation
which, produced by the Germanic and Romance peoples,
spreads over the whole earth, is what arouses his admiration.

Admittedly, even if we acknowledge this concrete significance of Ranke's admiration of continuity, Ranke's naiveté is
still there. That world history has produced Western culture in a
continuous development is again not a mere fact of experience of
which historical consciousness takes cognisance, but a condition
of historical consciousness itself, ie something that need not
have happened or could be cancelled out by new experience.
Rather, only because history has taken this course can the
question of the significance of history be raised by a world-
historical consciousness and the unity of its continuity be meant.

For this we can quote Ranke himself. He regards it as the
main difference between the Eastern and the Western system
that in the West historical continuity constitutes the form of
cultural existence.[60] Thus it is not by chance that the unity of
history depends on the unity of Western civilisation, to which
Western science in general and history as science, in particular,
belong. And it is also not by chance that this Western civilisation
is characterised by christianity, which has its absolute temporal
moment in the unique redemptive event. Ranke recognised
something of this when he saw in the christian religion the
restoration of man to the 'immediacy of God', which he set, in
romantic fashion, at the primaeval beginning of all history.[61] But
we shall still see that the fundamental significance of this situation has not been fully realised in the philosophical reflection of
the representatives of the world view.

Thus the empirical attitude of the historical school has its
philosophical assumptions. It was Droysen, the perceptive
methodologist, who freed it from its empirical disguise and
recognised its fundamental significance. His basic viewpoint is
that continuity is the essence of history, because history, unlike
nature, includes the element of time. Here Droysen constantly
quotes Aristotle's statement about the soul, that it increases
within itself (epidosis eis hauto). Unlike the mere repetitiveness
of nature, history is characterised by this constancy within itself.
But this involves preservation and at the same time going

beyond what is preserved. Both embrace self-knowledge. Thus history itself is not only an object of knowledge but it is determined in its being through its self-knowledge. 'Knowledge of it is itself' (*Historik* § 15). The admirable constancy of the historical development of which Ranke spoke is based on the consciousness of continuity, a consciousness that makes history history (*Historik* § 48).

It would be quite wrong to see this only as an idealist prejudice. Rather, this a priori of historical thought is itself an historical reality. Jakob Burckhardt is quite right when he sees in the continuity of the Western cultural tradition the very condition of the existence of Western culture.[62] The collapse of this tradition, the rise of a new barbarism, which Burckhardt prophesied, would not, for the historical world view, be a catastrophe within history, but the end of world history itself, at least inasmuch as it seeks to understand itself as a world-historical unity. It is important to recognise this presupposition in the enquiry of the historical school concerning universal history, precisely because fundamentally its existence is denied.

Thus the hermeneutical self-understanding of the historical school, as we saw in Ranke and Droysen, has its ultimate foundation in the idea of universal history. The historical school, however, was not able to accept Hegel's explanation of the unity of world history by the concept of Spirit. That the goal of Spirit is achieved in the perfect self-consciousness of the historical present which constitutes the significance of history is an eschatological self-interpretation which basically destroys history by turning it into a speculative concept. The historical school was, instead, forced into a theological understanding of itself. If it was not to do away with its own nature of thinking of itself as continuous research, it had to relate its own finite and limited knowledge to a divine spirit, to which things are known in their perfection. It is the old ideal of infinite understanding applied to the knowledge of history. Ranke writes: 'I imagine the Deity—if I may allow myself this observation—as seeing the whole of historical humanity in its totality (since no time lies before the Deity), and finding it all equally valuable'.[63]

Here the idea of infinite understanding (intellectus infinitus) for which everything exists simultaneously (omnia simul) is transformed into the original image of historical impartiality. It is approached by the historian, who knows that all epochs and all historical phenomena are equally justified before God. Thus the consciousness of the historian represents the perfect culmination of human self-consciousness. The more he is able to recognise the unique indestructible value of every phenomenon, that is, to think historically, the more his thought is God-like.[64] That is why Ranke has compared the office of historian with that of priest. Closeness to God is for the lutheran Ranke the real content of the christian gospel. The re-establishment of this closeness, which existed before the fall, does not take place through the church's means of grace alone. The historian has a share in it also, in that he makes mankind, which has 'fallen into' history, the object of this study, and knows mankind in the closeness to God which it has never entirely lost.

Universal history, world history, are not, in fact, aggregates of a formal kind, which refer to the totality of process; rather, in historical thinking, the universe, as the divine creation, is raised to a consciousness of itself. True, this is not a conceptual consciousness; the ultimate result of the study of history is 'sympathy, co-knowledge of the universe'.[65] It is against this pantheistic background that Ranke's famous remark that he would like to extinguish himself is to be understood. Of course this self-extinction is, in fact, as Dilthey objected,[66] the expansion of the self to make a universe within. But it is not by chance that Ranke does not take this further mental step, which leads Dilthey to his psychological grounding of the human sciences. For Ranke, self-extinction is still a form of real sharing. We must not understand this concept of sharing in a psychological and subjective way, but must conceive it in terms of the underlying concept of life. Because all historical manifestations are manifestations of universal life, a share in them is a share in life.

This gives the word 'understanding' its almost religious tone. To understand is to have a direct share in life, without there being the mental intermediary of the concept. Just this is what the historian is concerned with: not relating reality to ideas, but everywhere reaching the point where 'life thinks and thought lives'. In being understood, the phenomena of historical life are seen as the manifestations of universal life, of the divinity. This understanding and penetration mean, indeed, more than an achievement of human knowledge and more than the mere creation of an inner universe, in the way that Dilthey, against Ranke, reformulated the ideal of the historian. It is a metaphysical statement, that brings Ranke very close to Fichte and Hegel, when he says: 'The clear, full, lived insight is the very pith of Being made visible and transparent to itself'.[67] It is quite obvious from such a remark how close, fundamentally, Ranke has remained to German idealism. The full self-transparency of Being, which Hegel saw as realised in the absolute knowledge of philosophy, is the basis of Ranke's consciousness of himself as an historian, however much he rejects speculative philosophy. That is why the image of the poet is so close to him, and he does not feel the need to distinguish himself as an historian from the poet. For what the historian has in common with the poet is that, like the poet, he depicts the element in which everyone lives 'as something that lies outside him'.[68] The complete surrender to the contemplation of things, the epic attitude of a man who is seeking to tell 'the tale of world history'[69] may in fact be called poetic, in that for the historian God is present in all things, not as a concept but as an 'outward objectification'. We cannot describe Ranke's view of himself better than by these terms of Hegel. The historian, as Ranke sees him, belongs to that form of absolute spirit which Hegel has called Kunstreligion (religion of art).

(iii) The relation between historical study and hermeneutics in J. G. Droysen

An historian whose thinking was more acute inevitably realised the problems of this view of his role. The philosophical significance of Droysen is that he seeks to free the concept of understanding from the indefiniteness of the aesthetic pantheistic communion that it has in Ranke, and formulate its conceptual presuppositions. The first of these is 'expression'. Understanding is the understanding of expression. In expression there is something interior immediately present. But this inward thing, 'the inner essence', is the first and true reality. Droysen is here entirely Cartesian and in the tradition of Kant and Wilhelm von Humboldt. The individual ego is like a lonely point in the world of appearances. But in its expressions, above all in language and in all the forms in which it is able to express itself, it is no longer a lonely point. It belongs to the world of the intelligible. Historical understanding is not, however, of a fundamentally different nature from linguistic understanding. Like language, the world of history does not possess the character of a purely spiritual being: 'to want to understand the ethical and the historical world means above all that one recognises that it is neither merely poetic nor merely metabolism'.[70] He asserts this against the empiricism of Buckle, but it is true also against the spiritualism of, say, Hegel's philosophy of history. Droysen sees the dual nature of history founded in the 'curious charism of human nature, which is so happily imperfect that both mentally and physically it has to behave ethically'.[71]

Droysen, with these ideas borrowed from Wilhelm von Humboldt, is not trying to say anything other than what Ranke meant when he emphasised power. He, too, does not see the reality of history as pure spirit. To behave ethically involves, rather, not seeing the world of history as a sheer expression of the will on wholly malleable material. Its reality consists in the constantly renewed effort by the mind to grasp and form the 'ever-changing finite systems' to which every actor belongs. From this dual nature of history Droysen can now draw conclusions about the historian's attitude.

Linking it to the attitude of the poet, as Ranke did, is no longer sufficient for him. Self-extinction in contemplation or narration does not lead us to historical reality, for the poets 'compose a psychological interpretation of the event they describe. But in real life there are elements at work quite other than person-alities' (*Historik* § 41). The poets treat historical reality as if it were desired and planned in that way by the powers active in it; but it is not the reality of history to be 'meant' in this way. Hence the desires and plans of the actors are not the real object of historical understanding. The psychological interpretation of particular individuals cannot exhaust the significance of the historical events. 'Neither is the person's will fully realised in this particular situation, nor is that which has come about simply the result of his strength of will and intelligence. It is neither the pure, nor the whole expression of his personality' (§ 41). Hence psychological interpretation is only a subordinate element in historical understanding, and that not only because it does not really attain its goal. It is not only that a limit is reached. The interiority of the person, the sacred place of conscience, is not only unattainable by the historian, but that which is reached only by sympathy and love is not the goal and the object of his research. He does not have to penetrate the mysteries of indi-vidual people. What he investigates is not individuals as such, but what they mean as elements in the movement of moral powers.

The concept of moral powers has a central place in Droysen (§ 55ff). It is the basis both of the nature of history and of the possibility of knowing it. Ranke's vague reflections on freedom, power and necessity now acquire their factual basis. Similarly Ranke's use of the concept of historical fact is corrected by Droysen. The individual, in the contingency of his particular drives and purposes, is not an element in history, but only inasfar as he raises himself to the sphere of ethical commonality and participates in it. The movement of these ethical forces, which is achieved through the common work of men, constitutes historical development. It is perfectly true that what is possible is limited through this; but it would be to divest oneself of one's own historical finiteness if one were then to speak of a conflict between freedom and necessity. The actor stands firm under the postulate of freedom. The movement of history is not an extrinsic limitation to freedom, for it depends not on rigid necessity, but on the movement of the moral powers, to which one is already related. It sets the task, in the performance of which the moral energy of the actor proves itself.[72] Hence Droysen establishes a far more adequate relationship between freedom and necessity in history when he sees it entirely in terms of the historical actor. He relates necessity to the unconditional moral imperative, and freedom to the unconditional will; both are expressions of the moral power by which the individual belongs to the moral sphere (§ 76).

For Droysen too it is the concept of power that reveals the limitation of all speculative metaphysics of history. Accordingly, like Ranke, he criticises Hegel's concept of development, in that it is not a germ that simply grows in the course of history. But he defines more sharply what power means here: 'Powers grow with work'. The moral power of the individual becomes an historical power because it is active in work on the great common goals. It becomes an historical power, in that the moral sphere is what is lasting and powerful in the movement of history. Hence power is no longer, as with Ranke, an original and direct manifestation of universal life, but exists only in this mediation and only thus comes into historical reality.

The mediate moral sphere moves in such a way that everyone participates in it, but in different ways. Some preserve existing conditions by continuing to do the customary thing, while others have an insight into new ideas and express them. The continuity of the historical process consists in this constant overcoming of what is, through criticism, based on what ought to be (§ 77f). Thus Droysen would not speak of mere 'scenes of freedom', for freedom is the fundamental pulse of historical life and does not exist only in exceptional cases. The great personalities of history are only one element in the progress of the moral world, which is as a whole and in every detail a world of freedom.

He agrees with Ranke, against historical apriorism, that we cannot see the goal, but only the direction of the movement. The final goal of all our aims, towards which the restless activity of mankind is directed, cannot be discerned through historical knowledge. It is only something we sense dimly, something we believe (§§ 80–86).

The place of historical knowledge is in accord with this image of history. It, too, cannot be understood in the way that Ranke saw himself—as aesthetic self-forgetfulness and self-extinction in the manner of great epic poets. The pantheistic element in Ranke was responsible for the claim to a universal and immediate sharing, a co-knowledge, of the universe. Droysen, on the other hand, thinks of the intermediaries in which understanding moves. The moral powers are not only the actual reality of history, to the level of which the individual rises in his acts; they are also that to the level of which the historian, transcending his own particularity, rises. The historian is defined and limited by his participation in particular moral spheres, his native land and his political and religious persuasions. But participation depends precisely on this onesideness. Within the concrete conditions of his own historical existence—not from some eminence apart from things—he sets himself the task of impartiality. 'This is his impartiality, namely, that he tries to understand'. (§ 91)

Hence Droysen's formula for historical knowledge is 'understanding through research' (§ 8). In this there lies both an infinite mediation as well as an ultimate immediacy. The concept of study, which Droysen links here so significantly with that of understanding, is intended to mask the infinite nature of the task which distinguishes the historian from the perfections of artistic creation just as fundamentally as from the perfect harmony produced by the sympathy and love between two people. Only in 'restless' examination of the tradition, in the opening up of new sources and in ever new interpretations of them, does the study of history move progressively towards the 'idea'. This sounds as if it were based on the procedure of the natural sciences and were an anticipation of the neokantian interpretation of the 'thing-in-itself' as the 'infinite task'. But on closer examination we see that there is something else involved also. Droysen's formulation distinguishes the activity of the historian not only from the perfect ideality of art and the intense communion of souls but, it seems, from the procedure of the natural sciences.

At the end of the lecture of 1882[73] we find the words 'that we cannot, unlike the natural sciences, make use of experiment, that we only do research and can do nothing but research'. Thus there must be another element in the concept of research that is important for Droysen, and not just the infinite nature of the task which, as the characteristic of an infinite progress, the study of history has in common with the study of nature and which, in contrast with the 'science' of the eighteenth century and the doctrina of earlier centuries, contributed to the rise of the concept of research in the nineteenth century. Starting probably from the image of a studious traveller penetrating into unknown regions, this idea of research embraces both the knowledge of nature and of the historical world. The more this theological and philosophical background of the knowledge of the world fades away, the more science is conceived, as an advance into unknown regions and hence is called 'research'.

But this is not enough to explain how Droysen is able to distinguish historical method in the way mentioned from the experimental method of the natural sciences in saying that historical work is 'research, nothing but research'. There must be another infinity different from that of the unknown world, which makes historical knowledge research in Droysen's eyes. His thought seems as follows: research possesses a different, as it were qualitative infiniteness, if what is studied can never itself come into view. This is, in fact, the case with the historical past, in contrast to the self-givenness of experiment in the study of nature. In order to know, historical research always consults something else, namely tradition, ever afresh and ever fresh tradition. Its answer never has, like the experiment, the clear unambiguity of what has been seen with one's own eyes.

If we now ask what is the origin of this element in the concept of research, which Droysen follows in the surprising antithesis of experiment and research, then we are brought, it seems to me, to the idea of the study of conscience. The world of history depends on freedom, and this remains an ultimately unplumbable mystery of the person. Only the study of one's own conscience can approach it, and only God can know the truth here. For this reason historical study will not seek knowledge of laws and cannot call upon experiment. For the historian is separated from his object by the infinite intermediacy of tradition.

But on the other hand this distance is also proximity. Although he does not see his object, as in the clear establishment of the facts by experiment, the historian is connected with it, through the intelligible and familiar nature of the moral world, in a way that is quite different from the way the student of nature is with his. 'Hearsay' is here not bad evidence, but the only evidence possible.

'Every ego shut within itself, each one revealing itself to every other one in its utterances' (§ 91). What is known is, accordingly, totally different in both cases: what laws are to the study of nature, moral powers are to the historian (§ 16). In them he finds his truth.

In the indefatigable investigation of the historical tradition understanding is, in the end, always possible. Despite all intermediaries, the concept of understanding retains for Droysen the quality of an ultimate immediacy. 'The possibility of understanding consists in the fact that the utterances that are presented to us as historical material are connatural to us'. 'In the face of men, human utterances and forms, we are, and feel ourselves to be, essentially similar and in a condition of mutuality' (§ 9). Just as understanding connects the individual ego with the moral commonalities to which it belongs, so also these moral commonalities themselves, family, people, state and religion, can be understood as expressions.

Thus, by means of the concept of 'expression', historical reality raises itself into the sphere of meaning, and hence in Droysen's methodological self-analysis hermeneutics becomes master of the study of history. 'The detail is understood within the whole, and the whole from the detail' (§ 10). This is the old basic rhetorico-hermeneutic rule which is now turned inwards: 'The man understanding, because he is an ego, a totality in himself, like him whom he has to understand, supplements this totality by the individual utterance, and the individual utterance by this totality'. This is Schleiermacher's formula. In applying it, Droysen shares its premise, namely, that history, which he sees as acts of freedom, is nevertheless as profoundly intelligible and meaningful as a text. The culmination of the understanding of history is, like the understanding of a text, 'spiritual presence'. Thus we see Droysen determining more exactly than Ranke what mediate elements are involved in research and understanding, but even he can ultimately conceive the task of historical research only in aesthetic, hermeneutic categories. The aim of historical research is, for Droysen also, to reconstruct from the fragments of tradition the great text of history.

2 DILTHEY'S ENTANGLEMENT IN THE IMPASSES OF HISTORICISM

(A) FROM THE EPISTEMOLOGICAL PROBLEM OF HISTORY TO THE HERMENEUTICAL FOUNDATION OF THE HUMAN SCIENCES

The tension between the aesthetic, hermeneutic element and that of the philosophy of history reaches its height with Wilhelm Dilthey. Dilthey owes his importance to the fact that he really recognises the epistemological problem, which the historical view implies over against idealism. As Schleiermacher's biographer, as a historian who, with the romantic theory of understanding, asks the historical question of the rise and the nature of hermeneutics and writes the history of Western metaphysics, he moves within the range of problems of German idealism; but as a pupil of Ranke, and of the new empiricism of that century, his thinking is so different that neither the aesthetic, pantheistic-identity philosophy of Schleiermacher, nor Hegel's metaphysics, integrated with the philosophy of history, retain their validity for him. It is true that in Ranke and Droysen we found a similar dichotomy in their attitude between idealism and empiricism, but in Dilthey this dichotomy becomes particularly acute. For in him it is no longer the mere continuation of the classic-romantic spirit together with an empirical attitude to research, but this continuing tradition is overlaid by the conscious adoption of the ideas first of Schleiermacher and later of Hegel. Even when we exclude the early and great influence of British empiricism and of the epistemology of the natural sciences on Dilthey as being a distortion of his real intentions, it is still not so easy to understand what these intentions were. Georg Misch made an important step in this direction.[74] But since Misch wished to confront Dilthey's position with the philosophical tendency of Husserl's phenomenology and the fundamental ontology of Heidegger, the inner conflict in Dilthey's 'life philosophy' was described by him in terms of these contemporary contrasting positions. The same may be said of O. F. Bollnow.[75]

The root of the conflict in Dilthey lies in the intermediate position of the historical school between philosophy and experience. Far from being removed by Dilthey's attempt to provide an epistemological foundation, it is rendered more acute. Dilthey's attempt to provide a philosophical foundation for the human sciences seeks to draw the epistemological consequences from what Ranke and Droysen asserted against German idealism. Dilthey himself was fully aware of this. He saw the weakness of the historical school in the lack of logic in its thinking: 'Instead of going back to the epistemological postulates of the historical school and those of idealism from Kant to Hegel and thus recognising the incompatibility of these postulates, they have uncritically combined these two points of view'.[76] Thus he was able to set himself the task of constructing a new viable epistemological basis between historical experience and the idealistic heritage of the historical school. This is the sense of his intention of complementing Kant's *Critique of Pure Reason* with a critique of historical reason.

This aim in itself exhibits his withdrawal from speculative idealism. It sets up an analogy that has to be understood in a quite literal way. Dilthey wants to say that historical reason needs just as much justification as pure reason. The significance of the *Critique of Pure Reason* was not only that metaphysics was destroyed as a purely rational science of the world, the soul and God, but that, at the same time, an area was revealed within which the use of apriori concepts is justified and makes knowledge possible. *The Critique of Pure Reason* did not merely destroy the dreams of a seer, it also answered the question of how pure science is possible. Meanwhile, speculative idealism had taken the world of history into the self-analysis of reason and, moreover, especially through Hegel, had performed remarkable feats, precisely in the historical field. Thus the scope of the pure science of reason was extended to historical knowledge. It was a part of the encyclopaedia of the mind.

But in the eyes of the historical school the speculative philosophy of history was a dogmatism equally as crass as rational metaphysics. So it had to demand of a philosophical grounding of historical knowledge what Kant had required for the knowledge of nature.

This demand was not to be fulfilled by simply going back to Kant, as it might have seemed in the face of the extravagances of nature philosophy. Kant had concluded the work on the problem of knowledge as it was posed by the emergence of the new science in the seventeenth century. The mathematico-scientific construction, of which the new science made use, was provided by Kant with the epistemological justification which it needed because its ideas had no other claims to existence than those of entia rationis. The old representational theory was clearly no longer adequate.[77] Thus, through the incommensurability of thought and being, the problem of knowledge was posed in a new way. Dilthey saw this clearly, and in his correspondence with Graf Yorck he speaks of the nominalist background to seventeenth-century epistemology which has been brilliantly verified by modern research since Duhem.[78]

The problem of the theory of knowledge now acquires a new urgency through the historical sciences. We learn this from linguistic history, for the word Erkenntnistheorie ('theory of knowledge') arose only in the period after Hegel. It came into use when empirical research had discredited the Hegelian system. The nineteenth century became the century of the theory of knowledge because only with the dissolution of Hegelian philosophy was the obvious correspondence between logos and being finally disturbed. In that Hegel taught reason in everything, even in history, he was the last and most universal representative of the logos philosophy of the ancient world. Now, in view of the critique of the a priori philosophy of history, people were drawn again under the spell of Kant's critique, whose problem was now posed for the historical world as well, since the claim to provide a purely rational construction of world history had been rejected and historical knowledge also was limited to experience. If history is considered to be no more a manifestation of mind than is nature, then the knowledge of history becomes as problematic as the knowledge of nature through the constructions of the mathematical method. Thus, apart from Kant's answer to the question of how pure science was possible, Dilthey had to answer the question how historical experience can become a science. Hence, in a clear analogy with the Kantian question he sought to discover the categories of the historical world that would be able to support its construction within the human sciences.

What constitutes his importance and distinguishes him from the neokantians, who tried to involve the human sciences in the renewal of critical philosophy, is that he does not forget that experience is here something quite different from what it is in the investigation of nature. In the latter, verifiable discoveries arising from experience are all that matter, ie that which detaches itself from the experience of the individual and constitutes part of the reliable stock of experimental knowledge. The categorical analysis of this 'object of knowledge' had been, for the neokantians, the positive achievement of transcendental philosophy.[79]

Simply to adapt the construction and apply it to the field of historical knowledge, as neokantianism did in the form of the philosophy of value, was for Dilthey an inadequate solution. He considered the critical philosophy (Kritizismus) of neokantianism as itself dogmatic, and he was equally correct in calling British empiricism dogmatic. For the structure of the historical world is not based on facts taken from experience which then acquire a value relation, but rather on the inner historicity which belongs to experience itself. It is a living historical process and its paradigm is not the discovery of facts, but that strange fusion of memory and expectation into a whole that we name experience and that we acquire through experiences. Thus it is, in particular, the suffering and instruction given by the painful experience of reality to the man who is growing in insight that preshape the mode of knowing of the historical sciences. They only continue what has already been thought in the experience of life.[80]

Thus the epistemological question has here another starting point. In some ways its task is easier. It does not need to enquire into the grounds of the possibility of the fact that our ideas are in agreement with the 'external world'. For the historical world, the knowledge of which we are concerned with here, is always a world that is constituted and formed by the human mind. For this reason Dilthey does not regard the general synthetic judgments of history as any problem[81]—here he finds support in Vico. We shall recall that, in reaction to Cartesian doubt and the certainty of the mathematical knowledge of nature based on it, Vico asserted the epistemological primacy of the man-made historical world. Dilthey repeats the same argument and writes: 'The first condition of possibility of a science of history is that I myself am an historical being, that the man who is studying history is the man who is making history'.[82] It is the homogeneity of subject and object that makes historical knowledge possible.

This, however, is no solution to the epistemological problem that Dilthey posed. Rather, this condition of homogeneity contains the real epistemological problem of history. The question is how the experience of the individual and the knowledge of it comes to be historical experience. In history we are no longer concerned with connected wholes that are experienced as such by the individual or are re-experienced as such by others. Dilthey's argument applies only to the experiencing and re-experiencing done by the individual, and this is the starting-point for his epistemological theory. Dilthey elaborates the way in which the individual acquires a continuity of life in order to obtain the constitutive concepts to support at once historical continuity and the knowledge of it.

Unlike the categories of the study of nature, these concepts are concepts drawn from life. For Dilthey the ultimate presupposition for knowledge of the historical world, in which the identity between consciousness and object—that speculative postulate of idealism—is still demonstrable reality, is experience. This is where immediate certitude is to be found, for experience is no longer divided into an act, ie a becoming conscious, and a content, ie that of which one is conscious.[83] It is, rather, indivisible consciousness. Even to say that in experience something is possessed is to make too great a division. Dilthey now investigates how continuity is created from the element of the world of the mind that is immediately certain and how the knowledge of this continuity is possible.

Even in his ideas on 'descriptive and analytical psychology' Dilthey was endeavouring to explain the 'continuity acquired by one's inner life' as distinct from the explanatory categories of the knowledge of nature.[84] He used the concept of structure to distinguish the experiential character of psychological continuity from the causal continuity of natural processes. Logically 'structure' was distinguished in that it referred to a totality of relationships that did not depend on a temporal, causal succession, but on internal connections.

On this basis Dilthey thought he had found a valid starting-point and had overcome the shortcomings of the methodological reflections of Ranke and Droysen. But he considered that the historical school was right on one point: there was no such thing as a universal subject, only historical individuals. The ideality of meaning was not to be assigned to a transcendental subject, but emerged from the historical reality of life. It is life itself that unfolds and forms itself in intelligible unities, and it is in terms of the single individual that these unities are understood. This is the self-evident starting-point for Dilthey's analysis. The continuity of life as it appears to the individual (and is re-experienced and understood by others through biographical knowledge), is created through the significance of particular experiences. Around them, as around an organising centre, the unity of a life is created, in the same way that a melody acquires its meaningful form—not from the mere succession of notes, but from the musical motifs that determine its unity of form.

It is clear that here also, as with Droysen, we have the method of romantic hermeneutics, which undergoes a universal expansion. Like the continuity of a text the structural continuity of life is determined by a relation between the whole and the parts. Every part expresses something of the whole of life, ie has significance for the whole, just as its own significance is determined by the whole. It is the old hermeneutical principle of textual interpretation, which can apply to the continuity of life inasmuch as this assumes the unity of a significance that is expressed in all its parts.

The important step for Dilthey's epistemological groundwork of the human sciences is the transition from the structure of continuity in the experience of an individual life to historical continuity, which is not experienced by any individual at all. Here—despite all the critique of speculation—it is necessary to put 'logical subjects' instead of 'real subjects'. Dilthey is aware of this difficulty, but he considers that it is a permissible thing to do, in that the similarity between individuals—as in the case of one generation or one nation—represents a spiritual reality that must be recognised as such precisely because it is not possible to get behind it in order to explain it. True, this is not a real subject; that is evident enough from the vagueness of its boundaries. Moreover, individuals are involved in it with a part of their being only. But Dilthey unquestioningly considers that statements can be made about this kind of subject. The historian does it constantly when he speaks of the deeds and the destinies of peoples.[85] The question is simply how such statements can be justified epistemologically.

It cannot be said that Dilthey's thinking on this point, which he himself sees as the key problem, reached perfect clarity. It is the problem of the transition from the psychological to the hermeneutical grounding of the human sciences. Dilthey never got beyond mere sketches of this. So it is that the two completed parts of the *Aufbau*,[86] autobiography and biography, which are both special cases of historical experience and knowledge, retain an undue preponderance. For the real historical problem is not so much how continuity in general is experienced and known but how a continuity that no one has experienced can be known. Still, there can be no doubt about the way in which Dilthey would clarify the problem of understanding. To understand is to understand an expression. What is expressed is present in the expression differently than is the cause in the effect. It is present in the expression itself and will be understood when the expression is understood.

From the outset Dilthey's efforts were directed towards separating the relationships of the historical world from the causal relationships of the natural order and so the concepts of understanding and expression were always central for him. The methodological clarity due to Husserl's influence allowed him in the end to integrate the concept of significance—a concept that arises from the continuity of reality—with the latter's *Logical Investigations*. Dilthey's concept of the structural quality of the life of spirit corresponds to the theory of the intentionality of consciousness in that this is not merely a psychological fact but the phenomenological description of an essential determination of consciousness. Every consciousness is consciousness of something; every relation is a relation to something. The correlative of this intentionality, the intentional object, is not, according to Husserl, a psychic feature but an ideal unity, and meant as such. Thus Husserl's first 'Logical Investigation' defended the concept of the one ideal significance against the prejudices of logical psychologism. This demonstration became of key importance for Dilthey. For it was only as a result of Husserl's analysis that he was able to say what distinguished 'structure' from causal continuity.

An example will make this clear: a psychic structure, say an individual, acquires his individuality by developing his talents and experiencing at the same time the conditioning effect of circumstances. What emerges, the actual 'individuality', ie the character of the individual, is not a mere consequence of the causal factors to be understood only in terms of these causes, but it constitutes a unity that is intelligible in itself, a unity of life that is expressed in every one of its manifestations and hence can be understood in each of them. Something becomes fused here to form a unique figure, independently of the system of cause and effect. This is what Dilthey had meant by "structural continuity' and what, with Husserl, he now calls 'significance'.

Dilthey can now also say to what extent the structural continuity is given—his chief bone of contention with Ebbinghaus. It is not given in the immediacy of an experience, but nor is it simply constructed as the resultant of operating factors, on the basis of the 'mechanism' of the psyche. Rather, the theory of the intentionality of consciousness provides a new foundation for the idea of givenness. Now one can no longer derive continuity from atoms of experience or explain it in this way. Consciousness, rather, is always involved in continuity and has its own being in the conception of it. Thus Dilthey considered Husserl's *Logical Investigations* epoch-making[87] because such concepts as structure and significance were given a foundation, although they were not derivable from elements. They were now shown to be more fundamental than the elements from and on which they were supposed to be built up.

True, Husserl's demonstration of the ideality of significance was the result of purely logical investigations. What Dilthey makes of it is something quite different. For him significance is not a logical concept, but is understood as an expression of life. Life itself, flowing temporality, is ordered towards the formation of permanent units of significance. Life interprets itself. It has itself a hermeneutical structure. Thus life constitutes the real ground of the human sciences. Hermeneutics is not a romantic heritage in Dilthey's thinking, but follows from the grounding of philosophy in 'life'. Dilthey considers that here he has risen entirely above the 'intellectualism' of Hegel. Nor would the Leibnizian concept of individuality, romantic and pantheistic as it was, have satisfied him. If philosophy is founded in life, then there is no place for a metaphysics of individuality, and we are also a long way from Leibniz's idea of windowless monads that develop their own law. Individuality now is not a fundamental idea that is rooted in phenomena. Rather, Dilthey insists that all 'psychological life' 'is subject to the force of circumstances'.[88] There is no such thing as the fundamental power of individuality. It becomes what it is by asserting itself. It is part of the essence of individuality, as of all historical ideas, to be limited by the history of its effect. Even concepts like 'purpose' and 'significance' are not, for Dilthey, ideas in the Platonic or scholastic sense. They too are historical ideas, in that they are limited by the history of their effect: they must be concepts of energy. Dilthey here relies on Fichte,[89] who had an important influence on Ranke too. Thus his hermeneutics of life seeks to retain, at its foundation, the historical view of the world.[90] Philosophy gives him only the conceptual tools to declare the latter's truth.

Despite these qualifications, however, it is still not clear whether Dilthey's grounding of hermeneutics in 'life' has really avoided the implicit consequences of idealistic metaphysics.[91] He sees the question as follows. How is the power of the individual related to what exists beyond and prior to it; objective spirit? What is the relation between power and significance, between forces and ideas, between the facticity and the ideality of life? This question must ultimately decide how knowledge of history is possible. For man in history is similarly wholly defined by the relation between individuality and objective spirit.

Now this relationship is, clearly, not an unambiguous one. It is, on the one hand, the experience of limitation, pressure and resistance, through which the individual becomes aware of his own power. But it is not only the solid walls of actuality that he experiences. As an historical being he experiences historical realities; they support the individual; in them he at once expresses and discovers himself. As such they are not 'solid walls', but objectifications of life. (Dilthey spoke of 'moral forces'.)

This is of great methodological importance for the nature of the human sciences. The concept of the given has here a basically different structure. It is characteristic of what is given in the human, as against the natural, sciences 'that one has to discard all ideas of anything fixed or alien, qualities of the images of the physical world, when considering what is given in this field'.[92] Here, everything given is created. The old superiority that Vico attributed to historical objects is seen by Dilthey as the ground of the universality with which understanding possesses the historical world.

The question is, however, whether on this basis the transition from the psychological to the hermeneutical standpoint is really successful or whether Dilthey is ensnared in problems that bring him to an undesired and unacknowledged proximity to speculative idealism.

For not only Fichte, but Hegel can be heard in the passage referred to—even in the very words. His critique of 'positivity',[93] the concept of self-alienation, the definition of the mind as recognition of oneself in other being can easily be derived from this statement by Dilthey, and we may ask where the difference lies, what the historical view asserted against idealism, and what Dilthey undertook to validate epistemologically.

This question becomes more pressing when we consider the central phrase with which Dilthey characterises life, this basic fact of history. He speaks of the 'thought-forming work of life'.[94] It is not easy to say how this phrase differs from Hegel. However 'unfathomable a countenance'[95] life may present, and however much Dilthey may mock at the over-optimistic view of life that sees in it only the progress of civilisation, inasmuch as it is understood in terms of the thoughts that it forms, it has a teleological interpretative schema imposed on it and is conceived as 'spirit'. Accordingly, we find that in his later years Dilthey draws closer and closer to Hegel and speaks of 'spirit' where he used to say 'life'. He is simply repeating a conceptual development that Hegel himself underwent. In the light of this fact it is interesting to note that we owe to Dilthey the knowledge of the early, so-called 'theological', writings of Hegel. It emerges quite clearly from this material, which helps us to understand the evolution of Hegel's thinking, that his concept of spirit was based on a spiritual concept of life.[96]

Dilthey himself has tried to give an account of what he has in common with Hegel and what separates them.[97] But what does his critique of Hegel's belief in reason, his speculative construction of world history, and his aprioristic deduction of all ideas from the dialectical self-unfolding of the absolute, amount to, if he himself still gives the concept of "objective mind" such a central place? It is true that Dilthey opposes the abstract construction of this Hegelian concept: 'we must start from the reality of life'.[98] He writes: 'We are seeking to understand the latter and present it in suitable concepts. In not seeing objective mind in this way as based, in a one-sided way, on universal reason which expresses the essence of world-spirit; freed from an idealist construction a new concept of it becomes possible: it comprises language, customs, all kinds of ways or styles of life, as well as the family, civil society, state and law. And what

Hegel distinguishes as the absolute spirit from the objective, namely, art, religion and philosophy, also come under this concept. . . .'

Without a doubt this is an adaptation of Hegel. What does it mean? How far does it take account of the 'reality of life'? The most significant thing is obviously the extension of the concept of objective spirit to art, religion and philosophy. For this means that Dilthey does not see these as immediate truth, but as expressive forms of life. In putting art and religion on the same level as philosophy he is at the same time rejecting the claim of the speculative concept. At the same time, Dilthey is not denying that these forms take priority over the other forms of objective spirit, in that 'precisely in their powerful forms' spirit objectifies itself and is known. This priority of a perfect self-knowledge of spirit had been what caused Hegel to see these forms as those of absolute spirit. There was no longer anything alien in them and hence spirit was entirely at home with itself. For Dilthey also, as we have seen, the objectifications of art represented the real triumph of hermeneutics. Thus he differs from Hegel ultimately on one thing only, that according to Hegel the return home of the spirit takes place in the philosophical concept whereas, for Dilthey, the significance of the philosophical concept is not as knowledge, but as expression.

Thus we must ask whether there is not also for Dilthey a form of the spirit that is truly 'absolute spirit', ie complete self-transparency, the complete dissolution of all alienness, of all difference. For Dilthey there is no question that it exists and that it is historical consciousness that corresponds to this ideal, not speculative philosophy. It sees all the phenomena of the human, historical world only as objects by means of which the spirit knows itself more fully. Understanding them as objectifications of spirit, it translates them back 'into the mental life whence they came'.[99] Thus the forms that objective spirit takes are, for historical consciousness, objects of this spirit's self-knowledge. Historical consciousness extends into the universal, in that it sees all the data of history as manifestations of the life from which they stem: 'Here life is understood by life'.[100] Hence, for the historical consciousness the whole of tradition becomes the self-encounter of the human mind. It attracts to itself what seemed reserved to the particular creations of art, religion and philosophy. It is not in the speculative knowledge of the concept, but in historical consciousness that spirit's knowledge of itself takes place. It sees historical spirit in all things. Even philosophy is to be regarded only as an expression of life. Inasmuch as it is aware of this, it will give up its old claim to be knowledge through concepts. It becomes the philosophy of philosophy, a philosophical account of why there exists life philosophy, side by side with science. In his later writings Dilthey outlined this kind of philosophy of philosophy, in which he attributed the various types of world view to the multifariousness of the life disclosed in them.[101]

This historical overcoming of metaphysics is linked to interpretation of great literature in terms of the human sciences. This Dilthey regarded as the triumph of hermeneutics. It is a relative priority, however, that philosophy and art possess for the historically functioning consciousness. They may assume a special place because mind does not have to be read off in them, since they are 'sheer expression' and do not seek to be anything other than that. But even as such they are not immediate truth, but serve only as an organ for understanding of life. Just as certain high-points of a civilisation more readily reveal the 'spirit' of that civilisation, and just as the really significant historical decisions appear in the plans and deeds of great men, so too are philosophy and art especially open to interpretative understanding. In these the history of mind comes on the privileged place of form, of the pure formation of meaningful totalities detached from the stream of becoming. In the introduction to his biography of Schleiermacher Dilthey writes: 'The history of intellectual movements has the advantage of possessing truthful monuments. One can be wrong about the intention, but not about the content of the actual inner self that is expressed in these works'.[102] It is no accident that Dilthey has passed on to us this note of Schleiermacher's: 'The blossom is the real maturity. The fruit is only the chaotic covering for what no longer belongs to the organic plant'.[103] Dilthey obviously shares this view of an aesthetic metaphysics. It is at the basis of his relation to history.

This corresponds to the transformation of the concept of objective mind with which the historical conscience replaces metaphysics. But we may ask whether historical consciousness is really able to fill the place vacated by Hegel's absolute knowledge of the spirit comprehending itself in the speculative concept. Dilthey himself has pointed out that we only understand historically because we are ourselves historical beings. This is supposed to make things easier epistemologically. But does it? Is Vico's formula correct? Does it not apply an experience of the human artistic spirit to the historical world, in which, in the face of the course of events, one can no longer speak of 'making', ie of planning and carrying out? How are things made easier epistemologically? Are they not, in fact, made more dif-

ficult? Is not the fact that consciousness is historically conditioned inevitably an insuperable barrier to its reaching perfect
fulfilment in historical knowledge? Hegel could regard this barrier as overcome by virtue of history's being taken up into absolute knowledge. But if life is the inexhaustible, creative reality
that Dilthey conceives, then must not the constant development
of the meaningful context of history exclude any knowledge attaining to objectivity? Is, then, historical consciousness ultimately an utopian ideal, containing an internal contradiction?

(B) THE CONFLICT BETWEEN SCIENCE AND LIFE-PHILOSOPHY IN
DILTHEY'S ANALYSIS OF HISTORICAL CONSCIOUSNESS

Dilthey thought about this problem constantly. He was always
attempting to justify the knowledge of what was historically
conditioned as the achievement of objective science, despite the
fact of the knower's being conditioned himself. This was to be
done by the theory of the structure, which builds up its unity out
of its own centre. That a structural context could be understood
in terms of its own centre corresponded to the principle of hermeneutics and to the insistence of historical thinking that an age
should be understood in terms of itself and not by the criterion of
some alien time. Dilthey considered[104] that the knowledge of
increasingly large historical units could be conceived according
to this schema and expanded to constitute knowledge of universal history just as a word can be understood only in terms of the
whole sentence, and the sentence only fully understood within
the context of the whole text, indeed of the whole of literature.

The application of this schema presumes, of course, that one
is able to overcome the fact that the historical observer is tied to
time and place. But precisely this is the claim of historical consciousness, namely, to have a truly historical standpoint to everything. It sees this as its culminating achievement. Hence it is
concerned to develop the 'historical sense', in order to transcend the prejudices of one's own time. Thus Dilthey felt himself
to be the true perfecter of the historical world-view because he
sought to justify the promotion of consciousness to historical
consciousness. What his epistemological thinking tried to justify
was fundamentally nothing other than the epic self-forgetfulness
of Ranke. Only, instead of aesthetic self-forgetfulness there
was the sovereignty of an all-round and infinite understanding.
Basing historical study on a psychology of understanding, as
Dilthey hoped to do, gives the historian that mental contem-

poraneity with his object which we call aesthetic and which we admire in Ranke.

The important question remains, however, of how such infinite understanding is possible for finite human nature. Can this really have been Dilthey's meaning? For did he not insist, against Hegel, that one must hold on to the awareness of one's own finiteness?

Let us examine this more closely. His critique of Hegel's rational idealism was concerned only with the apriorism of his conceptual speculation. He did not fundamentally object to the inner infinity of the mind, which was positively fulfilled in the ideal of an historically enlightened reason, matured to the point of the genius who understands everything. For Dilthey the awareness of finiteness did not mean that consciousness was made finite or limited in any way; rather it bore witness to the capacity of life to rise in energy and activity above all limitations. Thus it represented precisely the potential infinity of the mind, though it is not in speculation, but in historical reason that this infinity is realised. Historical understanding extends over all historical data and is truly universal, because it has its firm foundation in the inner totality and infinity of mind. Dilthey is here following the theory that understanding was possible because of the similarity of human nature through the ages. He sees one's own world of experience as the mere starting-point for an expansion that, in a living transposition, fills out the narrowness and fortuitousness of one's own experience by the infinity of what is available in the re-experiencing of the historical world.

The limitations that are set to the universality of understanding through the historical finitude of our being are, then, to him only of a subjective nature. It is true that he still sees something positive in them that is fruitful for knowledge; thus he declares that only sympathy makes true understanding possible.[105] But we may ask whether this has any fundamental significance. First, let us establish one thing: he sees sympathy only as a condition of knowledge. We may question, with Droysen, whether sympathy (which is a form of love) is not something quite distinct from an effective condition of knowledge. It is one of the forms of relationship between two people. Certainly there is knowledge involved in this real moral relationship, and so it is that love gives insight.[106] But sympathy is much more than simply a condition of knowledge. Through it another person is transformed at the same time. Droysen has the profound remark: 'You must be like that, for that is the way I love you: the secret of all education'.[107]

When Dilthey speaks about universal sympathy and thinks of the ripe detached wisdom of old age, he certainly does not mean this moral phenomenon of sympathy, but the ideal of the perfect historical consciousness, which fundamentally transcends the barriers that the subjective accident of preference and affinity for an object has set to understanding. Dilthey follows Ranke here, who saw the dignity of the historian in his sympathetic knowledge of the universe.[108] True, he seems to restrict his meaning when he says that the best conditions for historical understanding are those where there is a 'continuing conditioning of one's own life by the great object', and when he sees here the greatest possibility of understanding.[109] But it would be wrong to see this conditioning of one's own life as anything other than a subjective condition of knowledge.

We can see this from examples. When Dilthey talks of the relationship between Thucydides and Pericles or between Ranke and Luther, he means a connatural intuitive connection that spontaneously evokes in the historian an understanding that would otherwise be achieved with difficulty. But fundamentally he regards this kind of understanding, that succeeds brilliantly in exceptional cases, as always obtainable through scientific method. He explicitly justifies the human sciences' use of comparative methods by saying that their task is to overcome the chance limits set by one's own range of experience and 'to rise to truths of greater universality'.[110]

This is one of the most questionable points of his theory. The essence of comparison presupposes the freedom of the knowing subjectivity, which is in control of both members of the comparison. It makes things contemporary as a matter of course. Hence we must doubt whether the method of comparison really satisfies the idea of historical knowledge. Is it not the case that a procedure—adopted in some areas of the natural sciences and very successful in many fields of the human sciences, eg literary criticism, law, aesthetics[111]—is promoted from being a subordinate tool to central importance for the essence of historical knowledge, and which often gives false support to superficial uncommitted reflexion? We must agree with Graf Yorck here when he writes: 'Comparison is always aesthetic, it is always concerned with the form',[112] and we shall recall that before him Hegel brilliantly criticised the comparative method.[113]

At any rate, it is clear that Dilthey did not regard the fact that finite historical man was tied to a particular time and place as any fundamental impairment of the possibility of knowledge in the human sciences. The historical consciousness was supposed to rise above its own relativity in a way that made objectivity in the human sciences possible. We may ask how this can be so without implying a concept of absolute, philosophical knowledge above all historical consciousness. What is the special virtue of the historical consciousness—as against all other forms of consciousness in history—that its own relativity does not destroy the fundamental claim to objective knowledge.

Its virtue cannot consist in its really being 'absolute knowledge' in Hegel's sense, ie in its uniting, in a present self-consciousness, the whole of mind's becoming. The claim of the philosophical consciousness, to contain within itself the whole truth of the history of mind, is questioned precisely by the historical world-views. This is, rather, the reason why historical experience is necessary; human consciousness is not an infinite intellect for which everything exists, contemporaneous and co-present. The absolute identity of consciousness and object simply cannot be achieved by finite, historical consciousness. It always remains involved in the historical context. What, then, is the reason for its nevertheless being able to transcend itself and thus become capable of objective historical knowledge?

We shall not find any explicit answer to this question in Dilthey. But all his work as a scholar gives an indirect answer. We might say that historical consciousness is not so much self-extinction as the intensified possession of itself, which distinguishes it from all other forms of mental life. However indissoluble the ground of historical life from which it emerges, it is still able to understand historically its own capacity to take up an historical attitude. Hence it is not, like consciousness before its victorious development into historical consciousness, the direct expression of a living reality. It no longer simply applies the criteria of its own understanding of life to the tradition in which it stands that it may, in a naïve assimilation of the tradition, simply carry it on. Rather it adopts a reflective attitude towards both itself and the tradition in which it stands. It understands itself in terms of its own history. Historical consciousness is a mode of self-knowledge.

This kind of answer points to the need to give a fuller account of the nature of self-knowledge. And, in fact, Dilthey's efforts, unsuccessful, as we shall see, were directed towards making intelligible 'in terms of life' how self-knowledge gives birth to scientific consciousness.

Dilthey starts from life: life itself is ordered towards reflection. We are indebted to George Misch for a rigorous account of the influence of life philosophy in Dilthey's thought. It rests on the fact that there is knowledge in life itself. Even the interiority that characterises experience contains a kind of return of life to itself. 'Knowledge is there, it is unreflectively connected with experience'.[114] The immanent reflectivity of life, however, also determines the way in which, for Dilthey, significance becomes part of life's continuity. For significance is experienced only in our stepping outside the 'hunt after goals'. This kind of reflection is possible when we distance ourselves from the context of our own activity. Dilthey points out—and he is undoubtedly correct—that here, before any scientific objectification, life's natural view of itself is thus developed. It objectivises itself in the wisdom of proverb and legend, but above all, in the great works of art, in which 'something of the mind detaches itself from its creator'.[115] Art is a particular organ of the understanding of life because in its 'confines between knowledge and act' life reveals itself at a depth that is inaccessible to observation, reflection and theory.

If life itself is ordered towards reflection, then the pure expression of experience in great art has a particular value. But this does not exclude the fact that, in every expression of life, knowledge is already operative and hence truth can be recognised. For the forms of expression that dominate human life are all forms of objective mind. In language, customs and forms of law the individual has always been able to raise himself above his particularity. The great shared moral world in which he lives represents something fixed in which he can understand himself in the face of the changing, fortuitous nature of his subjective emotions. It is in his devotion to common aims, in being taken up in activity for the community, that a man is freed 'from particularity and transience'.

Droysen could have said the same thing, but in Dilthey it has its own tone. In both aspects, both in contemplation and in practical reflection, the same life tendency is seen, according to Dilthey: a 'striving towards stability'.[116] This shows why he was able to regard the objectivity of scientific knowledge and philosophical self-analysis as the culmination of the natural tendency of life. In Dilthey's thinking there is no merely extrinsic accomodation of the method of the human sciences to the procedure of the natural sciences but, rather, he sees in them both a genuine community. The nature of the experimental method is to rise above the subjective fortuitousness of observation and, with its help, the knowledge of the laws of nature is possible. Similarly, the human sciences endeavour to rise methodologically above the subjective fortuitousness of their own standpoint in history and above the tradition accessible to them, and thus attain the objectivity of historical knowledge. Philosophical self-analysis also moves in the same direction, in that it 'becomes an object to itself as a human, historical fact' and gives up the claim to pure knowledge through concepts.

Hence, for Dilthey, the connection between life and knowledge is an original datum. This makes Dilthey's position unassailable against all the objections of philosophy, especially those arguments of idealistic reflective philosophy against historical 'relativism'. His basing philosophy in the original fact of life does not require a noncontradictory collection of propositions that seeks to replace the system of thought of earlier philosophies. Rather what was shown by Dilthey to be true of the role of reflection in life is likewise true of philosophical self-reflection. It 'thinks life itself to the end' by understanding philosophy as an objectification of life. It becomes philosophy of philosophy, but not in the idealistic sense. It does not seek to base the one possible philosophy on the unity of a speculative principle, but continues along the path of historical self-reflection. Hence it is not open to the objection of relativism.

Dilthey himself constantly considered this objection and sought to find an answer to the question of how objectivity is possible in relativity and how we are to conceive the relation of the finite to the absolute. 'The task is to show how these relative values of the ages have become expanded into something absolute.'[117] But we shall not find a real answer to this problem of relativism in Dilthey, not because he never found the right answer, but because this was not properly his question. He knew, rather, that in the evolution of historical self-reflection which led him from relativity to relativity, he was on the way towards the absolute. Thus Ernst Troeltsch quite rightly summed up Dilthey's life's work in the words: from relativity to totality. Dilthey's formulation of the same thing was 'to be consciously relative'[118]—a formulation openly directed against the claim of reflective philosophy to leave behind, in soaring towards absoluteness and infinity of spirit, in the climax and truth of self-awareness, all finite limitation. But his continual reflection on the objection of 'relativism' shows that he was not really able to hold to the logical consequence of his life philosophy against the reflective philosophy of idealism. Otherwise, he could not but have seen, in the objection of relativism, the 'intellectualism' that his own beginning from the immanence of knowledge in life sought to undermine.

This ambiguity has its ultimate foundation in an inner disunity of his thought, the unresolved Cartesianism from which he starts. His epistemological reflections on the basis of the human sciences are not really compatible with his starting from life philosophy. We have eloquent proof of this in his last writings. Dilthey asks that a philosophical foundation should extend to every area in which 'consciousness has shaken off authority and is seeking, through reflection and doubt, to attain to valid knowledge'.[119] This statement seems a harmless pronouncement on the nature of science and modern philosophy in general. The Cartesian echoes cannot be missed. But in fact the statement is applied in a quite different sense when Dilthey goes on: 'Everywhere life leads to reflection on what is given in it, and reflection leads to doubt. If life is able to assert itself against the latter, then thought can finally attain valid knowledge'. Here it is no longer philosophical prejudices that are to be overcome through an epistemological foundation in the style of Descartes, but it is the realities of life, the tradition of morals, religion and positive law that are being destroyed by reflection and need a new order.[120] When Dilthey speaks here of knowledge and reflection, he does not mean the general immanence of knowledge in life, but a movement that is directed against life. The tradition of morals, religion and law, rests, for its part, on a knowledge that life has of itself. Indeed, we have seen that in the surrender to tradition, which is undoubtedly consciously known, the individual is raised to objective mind. We shall readily grant Dilthey that the influence of thought on life 'comes from the inner need to fix something firm in the restless change of sense impressions, desires and feelings, something that enables one's life to be steady and unified'.[121] But this achievement of thought is something immanent in life itself and takes place in the objectifications of the mind, morals, law, and religion, which support the individual insofar as he surrenders himself to the objectivity of society. The fact that it is necessary to adopt the 'attitude of reflection and doubt' and that this is what happens 'in all forms of scientific reflection' (and not otherwise) simply cannot be combined with Dilthey's life philosophy.[122] This is, rather, a description of the special ideal of the scientific enlightenment, which is as little compatible with a reflection immanent in life as the 'intellectualism' of the enlightenment was, against which Dilthey's grounding in the fact of the philosophy of life was directed.

In fact, certainty exists in very different modes. The kind of certainty afforded by a verification that has passed through doubt is different from the immediate living certainty with which all ends and values appear in human consciousness when they make an absolute claim. But the certainty of science is very different from this kind of certainty that is acquired in life. Scientific certainty always has something Cartesian about it. It is the result of a critical method that seeks only to allow what cannot be doubted. This certainty, then, does not proceed from doubts and their being overcome, but is always anterior to any process of being doubted. Just as when Descartes set up an artificial and hyperbolical doubt, like an experiment, in his famous meditation on doubt, so methodological science fundamentally doubts everything that can be doubted, in order to achieve in this way the certainty of its results.

It is characteristic of the problem involved in Dilthey's attempt at grounding the human sciences that he does not distinguish between this methodological doubt and the doubts that come of their own accord. The certainty of science is, for him, the culminating form of the certainty of life. That does not mean that he did not experience the uncertainty of life in the full weight of historical concreteness. On the contrary, the more he grew into modern science, the more strongly he experienced the tension between the christian tradition of his origin and the historical forces that are liberated by modern life. The need for something firm in Dilthey has the character of a definite need for protection from the frightful realities of life. But he expects the overcoming of the uncertainty and unsureness of life to come not so much from the stability that the experience of life provides, but from science.

The Cartesian way of proceeding via doubt to the certain is for Dilthey, a child of the enlightenment, obviously correct. The shaking off of the authoritative, of which he speaks, corresponds not only to the epistemological need for a foundation for the natural sciences, but has to do as well with the knowledge of values and ends. They too are no longer for him an undoubted whole comprised of tradition, morals, religion, and law, but 'the spirit must, here also, produce out of itself valid knowledge'.[123]

The private secularisation process that brings Dilthey, the theological student, to philosophy is of a piece with the historical development of modern science. Just as the modern study of nature does not see nature as an intelligible whole but as a process that has nothing to do with human beings, a process on which scientific research throws a limited, but reliable light, thus making it possible to control it, so the human mind, seeking protection and certainty, sets against this 'frightful countenance' the scientifically developed capacity of understanding. It is supposed to reveal life in its social, historical reality so far that, despite the ultimate incomprehensibility of life, knowledge imparts protection and certainty. The enlightenment is completed as an historical enlightenment.

We can understand from this why Dilthey starts from romantic hermeneutics.[124] With its aid he succeeds in concealing the difference between the historical nature of experience and sciences' mode of knowledge or, better, in harmonising the mode of knowledge of the human sciences with the methodological criteria of the natural sciences. We saw above (p 207f) that it was no extrinsic accommodation that led him to this. We can now see that he was unable to do it without neglecting the essential historicality of the human sciences. This can be seen clearly in the kind of objectivity that he attributed to them; as sciences they are supposed to have the same objectivity as the natural sciences. So Dilthey loves the term 'results'[125] and in describing the methodology of the human sciences is at pains to show them as the equals of the natural sciences. Romantic hermeneutics here came to his assistance since, as we saw, it took no account whatsoever of the historical nature of experience. It assumed that the object of understanding is the text that has to be deciphered and its meaning understood. Thus every encounter with a text is for it an encounter of the spirit with itself. Every text is strange enough for it to present a problem, and yet familiar enough for it to be fundamentally soluble even when we know nothing of a text but that it is text, writing, an expression of mind.

As we saw with Schleiermacher, the model of his hermeneutics is the connatural understanding that can be achieved in the relation between two people. The perfect understanding of texts is as possible as the perfect understanding of another person. The author's meaning can be divined directly from his text. The interpreter is absolutely contemporaneous with his author. This is the triumph of interpretative method, understanding the mind of the past as present, the strange as familiar. Dilthey has a profound sense of this triumph. He uses it to justify the equality of the human sciences. In the same way that the knowledge of natural science always examines some present thing for what information it has to give, so the human scientist interrogates texts.

Dilthey thought he was performing his task of justifying the human sciences epistemologically, by conceiving the historical world as a text to be deciphered. He drew a consequence which the historical school, as we have seen, was never quite able to accept. True, Ranke saw the deciphering of the hieroglyphs of history as the sacred task of the historian. But that historical reality is such a pure thread of meaning that one needs only to decipher it as a text, was not really the deeper feeling of this historical school. Dilthey, the interpreter of this historical world view, however, was driven to this conclusion (like Ranke and Droysen had basically been), to the extent that hermeneutics was his model. The result was that history was ultimately reduced to intellectual history, a reduction which Dilthey accepts, in fact, in his half negation and his half affirmation of Hegel's philosophy of mind. Whereas Schleiermacher's hermeneutics rested on an artificial methodical abstraction which tried to establish a universal instrument of the mind, but tried to use this instrument to express the saving power of the christian faith, hermeneutics was, for Dilthey's grounding of the human sciences, more than a means. It is the universal medium of the historical consciousness, for which there no longer exists any other knowledge of truth than the understanding of expression and, in expression, life. Everything in history is intelligible, for everything is textual. 'Life and history have meaning like the letters of a word'.[126] Thus Dilthey ultimately conceives the investigation of the historical past as a deciphering and not as an historical experience.

It cannot be doubted that this did not do justice to the truth of the historical school. Romantic hermeneutics, and the philosophical method on which it is based, are not adequate as the basis of history. Similarly, Dilthey's concept of the inductive procedure borrowed from the natural sciences is not adequate. Historical experience, as he means it, fundamentally, is not a procedure and does not have the anonymity of a method. It is true that one can derive general rules of experience from it, but their methodological value is not that of a knowledge of law under which all cases could be clearly subsumed. Rules of experience require, rather, the experience of their use and are, basically, what they are only in this use. In the face of this situation it must be admitted that the knowledge of the human sciences is not that of the inductive sciences, but has quite a different kind of objectivity and is acquired in a quite different way. Dilthey's grounding of the human sciences in terms of life philosophy and his critique of all dogmatism, including even empiricism, had sought to bring this about. But the epistemological Cartesianism that dominated him proved stronger, so that in Dilthey the historicity of historical experience did not become a truly determining element. It is true that Dilthey did not fail to recognise the significance that the individual and universal experience of life have for the human sciences, but both are defined merely privately. It is an unmethodological and unverifiable induction that already points to the methodological induction of science.

If we now recall the self-understanding of the human sciences from which we started, we shall see that Dilthey's contribution to it was especially characteristic. The conflict that he tried to resolve shows clearly what pressure the methodology of modern science exerts and what our task must be: namely, to describe more adequately the experience of the human sciences and the objectivity they are able to achieve.

3 THE OVERCOMING OF THE EPISTEMOLOGICAL PROBLEM THROUGH PHENOMENOLOGICAL RESEARCH

(A) THE CONCEPT OF LIFE IN HUSSERL AND GRAF YORCK

It is in the nature of the case that speculative idealism offers greater possibilities for the fulfilment of our task than did Schleiermacher and the hermeneutics emanating from him. For in speculative idealism the concept of the given, of positivity, had been subjected to a fundamental critique—and it is to this that Dilthey tried to appeal in giving an account of his own tendency towards life philosophy. He writes:[127] 'How does Fichte characterise the beginning of something new? Because he starts from the intellectual contemplation of the 'I', but does not conceive the latter as a substance, as a being, as something given but, precisely because of this contemplation, ie this effort of the 'I' to know itself, as life, activity, and energy and, accordingly, shows that it contains energy concepts such as antithesis'. Similarly, Dilthey ultimately came to see Hegel's concept of mind as a genuine living historical concept.[128] As we found in our analysis of the concept of experience, some of his contemporaries followed in the same direction: Nietzsche, Bergson—that late successor of the romantic critique of the mode of thinking embodied in mechanics—and Georg Simmel. But the first man to bring to general awareness the radical challenge to historical being and knowledge presented by the inadequacy of the concept of substance was Heidegger.[129] Only through him was the philosophical intention of Dilthey released. His work built on the study of intentionality carried out by the phenomenology of Husserl, which was a decisive breakthrough, in that it was not at all the extreme Platonism that Dilthey believed it to be.[130]

Rather, the more insight we gain into the slow growth of Husserl's ideas from working through the great edition of his works, the clearer it becomes that with intentionality we get a more and more radical critique of the 'objectivism' of philosophy hitherto, Dilthey included.[131] This was to culminate in the claim 'that intentional phenomenology has made the mind, as mind, the field of systematic experience and science and thus totally transformed the task of knowledge. The universality of absolute mind embraces all beings in an absolute historicity in which nature as a construct of the mind also finds its place'.[132] It is not by accident that mind as the only absolute, ie non-relative thing, is here set over against the relativity of everything that appears before it. Even Husserl himself recognises that his phenomenology continues the transcendental enquiry of Kant and Fichte: 'In justice, however, it must be added that the German idealism that originated with Kant was already passionately concerned to overcome what had become the very sensitive naiveté (of objectivism)'.[133]

These statements of the later Husserl might be motivated by the debate with *Being and Time,* but they are preceded by so many other attempts to formulate his position that it is clear that Husserl had always had in mind the application of his ideas to the problems of the historical sciences. Thus what we have here is not an extrinsic association with the work of Dilthey (or, later, with that of Heidegger), but the consequence of his own critique of objectivist psychology and of the objectivism of philosophy until then. Since the publication of *Ideas II* this is quite clear.[134] In view of this, it is necessary to make room in our discussion for Husserl's phenomenology.

When Dilthey took Husserl's *Logical Investigations* as his starting-point, he started at the right place. According to Husserl himself[135] it was the a priori correlation of the object of experience and of modes of givenness that dominated his life's work after the *Logical Investigations.* In the fifth 'Logical Investigation' he elaborated the nature of intentional experiences and distinguished consciousness, 'as an intentional experience' (this is the title of the second chapter) from the real unity of consciousness in experience and from its inner perception. Here consciousness was already not an 'object', but an essential co-ordination—the point that was so illuminating for

Dilthey. What the investigation of this co-ordination revealed was the beginnings of an overcoming of 'objectivism', insofar as the meaning of words could no longer be confused with the actual psychic content of consciousness, eg the associative images that a word evokes. The intention and fulfilment of meaning belong essentially to the unity of meaning, and like the meanings of the words that we use, every existing thing that has validity for me possesses correlatively and by virtue of its nature an 'ideal universality of actual and potential experiencing modes of givenness'.[136]

Thus was born the idea of 'phenomenology', ie the exclusion of all positing of being and the investigation of the subjective modes of givenness, which became a universal plan of campaign, the aim of which was to make intelligible all objectivity, all being-sense. But human subjectivity also possesses being-value. Thus it too can be regarded as a 'phenomenon' and can be explored in the variety of the modes in which it is given. This exploration of the 'I' as phenomenon is not the 'inner perception' of a real 'I', nor is it the mere reconstruction of 'consciousness', ie the relation of the contents of consciousness to a transcendental 'I' pole (Natorp),[137] but it is a highly differentiated theme of transcendental reflection. This reflection stands over against the mere givenness of the phenomena of objective consciousness, a givenness in intentional experiences, and constitutes a new dimension of investigation. For there is such a thing as givenness that is not itself the object of intentional acts. Every experience has implicit horizons of before and after, and finally merges with the continuum of the experiences present in the before and after to form the one flow of experience.

Husserl's investigations of the constitution of time-consciousness come from the need to grasp the mode of being of this flow and hence to draw subjectivity into the intentional investigation of correlation. From now on all other phenomenological research sees itself as an enquiry into the constitution of the unities of time consciousness and in time consciousness, which themselves again presuppose the constitution of time consciousness itself. This shows that the particularity of an experience—however much it may retain its methodological significance as an intentional correlate of a constituted meaning value—is not an ultimate phenomenological datum. Every such intentional experience always implies, rather, a two fold empty horizon of what is not actually meant in it, but towards which an actual meaning can, of its nature, be directed; and it is, after all, obvious that the unity of the flow of experience includes the whole of all such experiences that can be thematised in this way. Hence the constitution of the temporality of consciousness lies at the base of all the problems of constitution. The flow of experience has the character of a universal 'horizon consciousness', out of which only particulars are truly given as experiences.

Undoubtedly the concept and the phenomenon of the horizon is of crucial importance for Husserl's phenomenological research. With this concept, which we too shall have occasion to use, Husserl is obviously seeking to capture the transition of all limited intentionality of meaning within the fundamental continuity of the whole. A horizon is not a rigid frontier, but something that moves with one and invites one to advance further. Thus horizon intentionality, which constitutes the unity of the flow of experience, is paralleled by an equally comprehensive horizon intentionality on the objective side. For everything that is given as existent is given in terms of the world and hence brings the world horizon with it. In his retractions to *Ideas I*, Husserl emphasised, in explicit self-criticism, that he had not at the time (1913) been sufficiently aware of the importance of the phenomenon of world.[138] The theory of transcendental reduction that he had set out in his *Ideas* was made inevitably more and more complicated by this. The mere denial of the validity of the objective sciences was no longer enough, for even in the achievement of that period—the denial that scientific knowledge posits being—the world still remains valid as something pre-given. Hence the epistemological self-questioning that enquires into the a priori, the eidetic truths of science, is not radical enough.

This is the point at which Husserl was able to regard himself as in a certain agreement with the intentions of Dilthey. In similar fashion Dilthey had opposed the critical philosophy of the neokantians, insofar as he did not consider it enough to go back to the epistemological subject. 'No real blood runs in the veins of the knowing subject that Locke, Hume and Kant constructed'.[139] Dilthey himself went back to the unity of life, to the 'standpoint of life', and similarly Husserl's 'conscious life', a word that he apparently took over from Natorp, is already a pointer to the subsequent strong tendency to study not only individual experiences of consciousness, but the concealed, anonymously implicit intentionalities of consciousness, and in this way to make the totality of all objective validity of being intelligible. Subsequently this is called the illumination of the achievements of 'productive life'.

That Husserl is concerned everywhere with the 'production' of transcendental subjectivity is simply in agreement with phenomenology's task of studying constitution. It is characteristic of his own intention, however, that he no longer says 'consciousness', nor even 'subjectivity', but 'life'. He is seeking to penetrate behind the actuality of the sense-giving consciousness and even behind the potentiality of shared meaning to the universality of an achievement that alone is able to measure the universality of what is achieved, ie constituted in its validity. It is an intentionality that is fundamentally anonymous, ie not achieved by anyone by name, through which the all-embracing world-horizon is constituted. Using a conscious counter-formulation against a concept of the world that includes the universe of what can be made objective by science, Husserl calls this phenomenological concept of the world 'life-world', ie the world in which we are immersed in the natural attitude that never becomes for us an object as such, but that constitutes the pre-given basis of all experience. This world horizon is a presupposition of all science as well and is, therefore, more fundamental. As horizon phenomenon this 'world' is essentially related to subjectivity, and this relation means also that it 'exists in transiency'.[140] The life-world exists in a movement of constant relativity of validity.

The concept of the 'life-world' is the antithesis of all objectivism. It is an essentially historical concept, which does not refer to a universe of being, to an 'existent world'. In fact, not even the infinite idea of a true world can be meaningfully created out of the infinite progress of human-historical worlds in historical experience. Certainly one can enquire into the structure of what embraces all the surrounding worlds that man has ever experienced, and which is simply the experience of the possibility of world, and in this sense we can indeed speak of an ontology of the world. But this ontology of the world would still remain something quite different from what the natural sciences, conceived in this perfect form, would achieve. It would present a philosophical task whose object was the essential structure of the world. But by the life-world is meant something else, namely, the whole in which we live as historical creatures. And here we cannot avoid the consequence that in the face of the historicity of experience implied in it the idea of a universe of possible historical life-worlds simply cannot be carried through. The infiniteness of the past, but above all the openness of the historical future, is incompatible with such an idea of an historical universe. Husserl has explicitly drawn this conclusion, without being frightened of the 'spectre' of relativism.[141]

It is clear that the life-world is always at the same time a communal world and involves the existence of other people as well. It is a personal world, and in the natural attitude the validity of this personal world is always assumed. But how can this validity be based on an achievement of subjectivity? For the phenomenological constitution analysis this presents the most difficult task of all, the paradoxical nature of which Husserl never tires of examining. How can something originate in the pure 'I' that has no validity as an object, but itself seeks to be an 'I'?

The principle of 'radical' idealism, namely of always going back to the constitutive acts of transcendental subjectivity, must obviously illuminate the universal horizon consciousness that is the 'world' and, above all, the intersubjectivity of this world —although what is constituted in this way, the world as what is common to many individuals, itself includes subjectivity. Transcendental reflection, which is supposed to remove all the validity of the world and all the pre-givenness of anything else, must also regard itself as included in the life-world. The reflective 'I' sees itself as living in purposive determinations for which the life-world is the basis. Thus the constituting of the life-world (as of intersubjectivity) is a paradoxical task. But Husserl regards all these as only apparent paradoxes. He considers that they are resolved if we follow through logically the transcendental meaning of the phenomenological reduction and don't fear the bogey of a transcendental solipsism. In view of this clear tendency of Husserl's thought it seems to me wrong to accuse him of any ambiguity in the concept of constitution, regarding it as something intermediate between definition and creation.[142] He himself maintains that in his thinking he has entirely overcome the fear of generative idealism. His theory of phenomenological reduction seeks, rather, to carry through for the first time the true meaning of this idealism. Transcendental subjectivity is the Ur-Ich ('the primal I') and not 'an I'. For it the basis of the pre-given world is removed. It is the absolute irrelative to which all relativity, including that of the enquiring 'I', is related.

There is one element in Husserl's thinking, however, that constantly threatens to burst this framework asunder. His position, in fact, is more than simply a radicalisation of transcendental idealism, and this extra element is characterised by the function that the concept of life has for him. 'Life' is not just the

unreflective living of the natural attitude. 'Life' is also, and no
less, the transcendentally reduced subjectivity that is the source
of all objectifications. Husserl calls 'life' that which he emphasises as his own achievement in his critique of the objectivist
naiveté of all previous philosophy. It consists, in his eyes, in
having revealed the unreality of the customary epistemological
controversy between idealism and realism and, instead, in having
thematised the inner relation between subjectivity and objectivity.[143] This is the reason for his phrase 'productive life'.
'The radical contemplation of the world is the systematic and
pure interior contemplation of subjectivity, which expresses
itself in the "exterior".[144] It is as with the unity of a living
organism, which we can certainly examine and analyse from
outside, but can understand only if we go back to its hidden
roots . . .'.[145] Thus also the intelligibility of the subject's attitude to the world does not reside in conscious experiences and
their intentionality, but in the anonymous 'productions' of life.
The metaphor of the organism that Husserl employs here is
more than a metaphor. As he expressly states, he wants to be
taken literally.

If we follow up these and similar linguistic and conceptual
hints that we find here and there in Husserl, we find ourselves
moving closer to the speculative concept of life held by German
idealism. What Husserl means, however, is that we cannot
conceive subjectivity as an antithesis to objectivity, because this
concept of subjectivity would itself be conceived in objective
terms. Instead, his transcendental phenomenology seeks to be
'correlation research'. But this means that the relation is the
primary thing, and the 'poles' into which it forms itself are
contained within it, just as what is alive contains all its expressions of life in the unity of its organic being. 'The naiveté of talk
about 'objectivity' which completely ignores experiencing,
knowing subjectivity, subjectivity which performs real concrete
achievements, the naiveté of the scientist concerned with nature, with the world in general, who is blind to the fact that all
the truths that he acquires as objective, and the objective world
itself that is the substratum in his formulation, is his own life
construct that has grown within him, is, of course, no longer
possible, when life comes on the scene', writes Husserl with
regard to Hume.[145]

The role played here by the concept of life has its clear
counterpart in Dilthey's investigations into the concept of the
complex of experience. Just as Dilthey begins with experience

only in order to reach the concept of psychic continuity, so Husserl shows that the unity of the flow of experience is anterior to discreteness of experiences and essentially necessary to it. The thematic investigation of the life of consciousness must, as in Dilthey, overcome the tendency to take off from the individual experience. To this extent there is a genuine parallel between the two thinkers. They both go back to the concreteness of life.

The question arises whether or not they do justice to the speculative demands contained in the concept of life. Dilthey seeks to derive the structure of the historical world, and Husserl its constitution, from the reflectiveness inherent in life. We might ask if, in both cases, the actual content of the concept of life does not become alienated by the epistemological schema of such derivation from the ultimate data of consciousness. Difficulties in the problem of intersubjectivity and the understanding of the other 'I' evoke this question. We have the same difficulty in both Husserl and Dilthey. The immanent data in reflectively examined consciousness do not include the 'Thou' in an immediate and primary way. Husserl is quite right when he emphasises that the 'Thou' does not possess that kind of immanent transcendence that belongs to the objects of the external world of experience; for every 'Thou' is an alter ego, ie it is understood in terms of the ego and, at the same, as detached from it and, like the ego itself, as independent. Husserl tried, through the most painstaking investigations, to throw light on the analogy between the 'I' and the 'Thou'—which Dilthey interprets purely psychologically through the analogy of empathy by means of the intersubjectivity of the communal world. He was sufficiently rigorous not to limit in any way the epistemological priority of transcendental subjectivity. But his ontological prejudice is the same as Dilthey's. The other person is first apprehended as an object of perception which then, through empathy, becomes a 'Thou'. In Husserl this concept of empathy has no doubt a purely transcendental meaning,[146] but is still orientated to the interiority of self-consciousness and fails to achieve the orientation towards the functional circle[147] of life, which goes far beyond consciousness, to which, however, it claims to return.

Thus in fact the speculative import of the concept of life remained undeveloped in both men. Dilthey seeks simply to play off the viewpoint of life polemically against metaphysical thinking, and Husserl has absolutely no idea of the connection between this concept and the metaphysical tradition in general and speculative idealism in particular.

At this point the posthumous papers of Graf Yorck, though unfortunately very fragmentary, are of surprising contemporary importance.[148] Although reference had been made to the brilliant insights of this major figure by Heidegger who regarded his ideas as even more important than Dilthey's, the fact still remained that Dilthey completed a great life's work, whereas the letters of Graf Yorck were never developed into a larger systematic whole. The posthumous papers from the last years, however, have now thoroughly changed this situation. Even though only fragments, his systematic intention is still sufficiently developed for there to be no doubt about the place of his work in the history of thought.

It achieves precisely what we failed to discover above in Dilthey and Husserl. It makes a bridge between speculative idealism and the new experiential standpoint, inasmuch as the concept of life is brought out as the comprehensive one. The analysis of being alive, which is for Graf Yorck the starting-point, however speculative it sounds, still embraces the scientific mode of thinking of the period—explicitly the concept of life held by Darwin. Life is self-assertion; this is the basis. The structure of being-alive consists in being an original division (Urteilung) ie in still continuing to assert itself as a unity in division and articulation. But Urteilung is also seen as the essence of self-consciousness, for even if it always distinguishes itself into what is itself and what is other, it still consists—as a living thing—in the play and interplay of these factors that constitute it. It is true of it, as of all life, that it is a proving, ie an experiment. 'Spontaneity and dependence are the basic characters of consciousness, constitutive in the area both of somatic and of psychic articulation, just as neither seeing, physical sensation, imagining, willing, nor feeling would exist without the existence of objects'.[149] Consciousness is also to be understood as a life attitude. This is the fundamental methodological demand that Graf Yorck makes of philosophy, and in this he is at one with Dilthey. Thought must be brought back to this hidden foundation (Husserl would say: to this hidden achievement). For this, the effort of philosophical reflection is necessary, for philosophy acts against the tendency of life. Graf Yorck writes: 'Now our thinking moves in the sphere of conscious results' (ie it is not aware of the real relation of the 'results' to the life attitude on which the results depend). 'That presupposition is the achieved distinction'.[150] Graf Yorck means that the results of thinking are results only because they have become detached from the life attitude and can be so detached. From this Graf Yorck concludes that philosophy must reverse this process of detachment. It must repeat the experiment of life in the reverse direction, 'in order to know the conditions which govern the "results of life" '.[151] This may be formulated in a very objectivist and scientific way, and Husserl's theory of reduction would appeal, against it, to its own purely transcendental mode of thinking. In fact, however, the bold and assured thinking of Graf Yorck not only shows the common influence of Dilthey and Husserl, but proves to be superior to them both. For here thought truly develops at the level of the identity philosophy of speculative idealism and thus reveals the hidden origin of the concept of life at which Dilthey and Husserl are aiming.

If we pursue further this idea of Graf Yorck's, the continued existence of idealist motifs becomes quite clear. What Graf Yorck is presenting here is the structural correspondence between life and self-consciousness already developed in Hegel's *Phenomenology*. In the manuscript fragments that have been preserved, we can see the central importance that the concept of life had for Hegel as early as his last years in Frankfurt. In his *Phenomenology* the phenomenon of life makes the decisive transition from consciousness to self-consciousness. This is, in fact, no artificial connection, for life and self-consciousness really are analogous. Life is determined by the fact that what is alive differentiates itself from the world in which it lives and with which it remains connected, and preserves itself in this differentiation. The self-preservation of what is alive takes place through its drawing into itself everything that is outside it. Everything that is alive nourishes itself on what is alien to it. The fundamental fact of being alive is assimilation. Differentiation, then, is at the same time non-differentiation. The alien is appropriated.

As Hegel had already shown and Graf Yorck continues to hold, this structure of what is alive has its correlative in the nature of self-consciousness. Its being consists in its being able to make everything the object of its knowledge, and yet in everything that it knows, it knows itself. Thus as knowledge it is a differentiation from itself and, at the same time, as self-consciousness, it is an overlapping of and return to self.

Obviously we are concerned here with more than a mere structural correspondence between life and self-consciousness. Hegel quite rightly derives self-consciousness dialectically from life. What is alive can never be really known by the objective consciousness, by the effort of understanding which seeks to penetrate the law of appearances. What is alive is not such that a person could ever grasp it from outside, in its living quality. The only way of grasping life is, rather, to become inwardly aware of it. Hegel refers to the story of the veiled image of Sais when describing the inner self-objectification of life and self-consciousness: here the inner contemplates the inner.[152] It is the mode of the awareness of oneself, the inner consciousness of one's own living, in which alone life is experienced. Hegel shows how this experience flares up in desire and is extinguished in the satisfaction of desire. This self-awareness of vitality, in which being alive becomes aware of itself, is a false preform, the lowest form of self-consciousness, inasmuch as the becoming conscious of oneself in desire is also annihilated by the satisfaction of desire. However untrue it is when compared with objective truth, the consciousness of something alien, it is still, as 'vital feeling', the first truth of self-consciousness.

This seems to me where the work of Graf Yorck becomes most fruitful. From the correspondence between life and self-awareness, it derives a methodological standard by means of which it determines the nature and task of philosophy. Its leading concepts are projection and abstraction. Projection and abstraction constitute the primary life-attitude; but they apply equally to the recapitulary historical attitude. Only insofar as philosophical reflection corresponds to this structure of being-alive does it acquire its own legitimacy. Its task is to understand the achievements of consciousness in terms of their origin, understanding them as results, ie as the projection of the original being-alive and its original division.

Graf Yorck thus raises to a methodological principle what Husserl was later to develop more broadly in his phenomenology. This makes it clear how thinkers as different as Husserl and Dilthey could ever come together. Both go back behind the abstraction of neoKantianism, and Graf Yorck agrees with them though in fact he achieves even more. For he not only goes back to life with an epistemological intention, but maintains the metaphysical connection between life and self-consciousness worked out by Hegel. In this he is superior to both Dilthey and Husserl.

As we saw, Dilthey's reflections went wrong in that he derived the objectivity of science too easily from the life-attitude and its drive towards something fixed. Husserl entirely lacked any closer definition of what life is, although the central core of phenomenology, the investigation of correlation, follows, in fact, the structural model of the life attitude. Graf Yorck, however, makes the bridge between Hegel's *Phenomenology of Mind* and Husserl's *Phänomenologie der transzendentalen Subjectivität.* [153] Regrettably, the fragmentariness of his posthumous papers prevents us from knowing how he intended to avoid the dialectical metaphysicising of life of which he accuses Hegel.

(B) HEIDEGGER'S PROJECT OF A HERMENEUTICAL PHENOMENOLOGY

The tendency which Dilthey and Graf Yorck formulated as common to them, of 'understanding in terms of life', and which was expressed in Husserl's going back behind the objectivity of science to the life-world, was characteristic of Heidegger's own first approach. But he was no longer dependent on the epistemological implications according to which the return to life (Dilthey) or transcendental reduction (Husserl's way of absolutely radical self-reflection) was based methodologically on the self-givenness of experience. On the contrary, all this became the object of Heidegger's critique. Under the name of a 'hermeneutics of facticity', Heidegger confronted Husserl's eidetic phenomenology, together with the distinction between fact and essence on which it depended, with a paradoxical demand. The facticity of there-being, existence, which cannot be based on or derived from anything else, and not the pure cogito as the essential constitution of typical universality, should represent the ontological basis of the phenomenological position—a bold idea, but difficult to carry through.

The critical side of this idea was certainly not something entirely new. It had already been conceived by the neohegelians as a critique of idealism, and so it is no accident that Kierkegaard, who emerged out of the spiritual crisis of Hegelianism, was taken up at that time by Heidegger and the other critics of neokantian idealism. On the other hand, however, this critique of idealism was faced then, as now, with the comprehensive claim of the transcendental position. Inasmuch as transcendental reflection did not want to leave unconsidered any possible area of thought in the development of the content of the mind —and, since Hegel, this was the claim of transcendental philosophy—it had already included every possible objection within the total reflection of the mind. This is true also of the transcendental position from which Husserl sets phenomenol-

ogy the universal task of the constitution of all being-value. It
obviously had to include the facticity asserted by Heidegger.
Thus Husserl was able to acknowledge being-in-the-world as a
problem of horizon intentionality of transcendental consciousness, and the absolute historicity of transcendental subjectivity
had to be able to demonstrate the meaning of facticity. Hence,
Husserl, holding logically to his central ideas of the 'proto-I' had
been able to argue against Heidegger that the meaning of facticity is itself an eidos, that it belongs essentially to the eidetic
sphere of universal essences. If we examine the sketches for
Husserl's later writings, especially those gathered together in
vol 7 on the 'Crisis', we shall, in fact, find there several analyses
of 'absolute historicality' in logical development of the problems
of the *Ideas*, corresponding to Heidegger's revolutionary new
and polemical beginning.[154]

Let us remember that Husserl himself faced the problem of
the paradoxes that followed from the carrying-through of his
transcendental solipsism. Hence it is not at all easy to fix the
point from which Heidegger could confront the phenomenological idealism of Husserl. We must even admit that Heidegger's
project in *Being and Time* does not completely overcome the
sphere of the problematic of transcendental reflection. The idea
of fundamental ontology, its foundation in There-being, which is
concerned with being, and the analysis of this There-being,
seemed first simply to mark a new dimension within transcendental phenomenology.[155] The view that the whole meaning of
being and objectivity can be made intelligible and demonstrated
solely in terms of the temporality and historicality of There-
being—a possible way of describing the main tendency of *Being
and Time*—Husserl would have claimed in his own way, ie on
the ground of the absolute historicity of the 'proto-I'. And if
Heidegger's methodological programme was critically directed
against the concept of transcendental subjectivity, to which
Husserl related all ultimate foundation, Husserl would have said
that this was a failure to recognise the radicality of the transcendental reduction. He would undoubtedly have said that transcendental subjectivity itself had already overcome and done
away with all the implications of a substance ontology and hence
with the objectivism of tradition. Husserl also regarded himself
as in opposition to the whole of metaphysics.

Yet it is notable that this opposition was least in the case of
the transcendental enquiry undertaken by Kant, and his predecessors and successors. Here Husserl recognised his own real
predecessors and forerunners. The radical self-reflection that

was his deepest concern and that he regarded as the essence of modern philosophy, led him back to Descartes and the British and to the methodological model of the Kantian critique. But his 'constitutive' phenomenology was marked by a universality foreign to Kant and beyond a neoKantianism that did not question the 'fact of science'.

But this appeal by Husserl to his forerunners makes clear his difference from Heidegger. Husserl's critique of the objectivism of all earlier philosophies was a methodological continuation of modern tendencies, and he regarded it as such. Heidegger's aim, however, was from the beginning more that of a teleology 'in reverse'. He regarded his own work not so much as the fulfilment of a long prepared development as, rather, a return to the beginnings of Western philosophy and the revival of the long-forgotten Greek argument about 'being'. Of course, when *Being and Time* appeared, it was settled that this return to the beginnings was also an advance beyond the position of contemporary philosophy, and it was no arbitrary accident that Heidegger made the researches of Dilthey and the ideas of Graf Yorck part of the development of phenomenological philosophy.[156] After all, the problem of facticity was also the central problem of historicism, at least in the form of the critique of Hegel's dialectical assumption that there is reason in history.

Thus it was clear that Heidegger's project of a fundamental ontology had to place the problem of history in the foreground. But it was soon to emerge that it was not the solution of the problem of historicism, and certainly not a more original grounding of science, nor even, as with Husserl, an ultimate radical grounding by philosophy of itself, that constituted the significance of this fundamental ontology, but that the whole idea of 'grounding' itself underwent a total reversal. It was no longer with the same intention as Husserl that Heidegger undertook to interpret being, truth and history in terms of absolute temporality. For this temporality was not that of 'consciousness' nor of the transcendental 'proto-I'. True, in the unfolding of ideas in *Being and Time* it seemed at first simply an intensification of transcendental reflection, the reaching of a higher stage of reflection, when the horizon of being was shown to be time. It was, after all, the ontological groundlessness of transcendental subjectivity, of which Heidegger accused Husserl's phenomenology, that seemed to be overcome through the revival of the question of being. What being is was to be determined from within the horizon of time. Thus the structure of temporality appeared as the ontological determining factor of subjectivity. But it was more than that. Heidegger's thesis was that being itself is time. This burst asunder the whole subjectivism of modern philosophy—and, in fact, as was soon to appear, the whole range of questions asked by metaphysics, which was involved with being as what is present. The fact that There-being is concerned about its being, that it is distinguished from all other beings by its understanding of being, does not consti-tute, as appears from *Being and Time,* the ultimate basis from which a transcendental approach has to start. Rather, there is a quite different reason, by virtue of which alone any understand-ing of being is possible, and that is that there is a 'there', a clearing in being, ie a distinction between being and beings. The enquiry directed towards this fundamental fact that this 'exists' is, in fact, an enquiry into being, but in a direction that necessar-ily remained unconsidered in all previous enquiry into the being of beings, indeed, that was concealed by the metaphysical enquiry into being. Heidegger revealed the essential forgetful-ness of being that dominated western thought since Greek metaphysics due to the embarrassment caused by the problem of nothingness. By showing that the question of being included the question of nothingness, he joined the beginning to the end of metaphysics. That the question of being could represent itself as the question of nothingness postulated a thinking of nothingness repugnant to metaphysics.

The true predecessor of Heidegger in raising the question of being and thus going contrary to the whole direction of Western metaphysics could not, then, be either Dilthey or Husserl, but rather Nietzsche. Heidegger may have realised this only later; but in retrospect it can be seen that the aims already implicit in *Being and Time* were to raise Nietzsche's radical criticism of 'Platonism' to the level of the tradition criticised by him, to confront Western metaphysics on its own level, and to recognise the transcendental position as a consequence of modern subjec-tivism, and so overcome it.

What Heidegger called the 'reversal' was not a new departure in the development of transcendental reflection, but the making possible and carrying out of this task. Although *Being and Time* criticised the lack of ontological definition in Husserl's concept of transcendental subjectivity, it still formulated its own account of the question of being in terms of transcendental philosophy. In fact, however, the renewal of the question of being, the task that Heidegger set himself, meant that within the 'positivism' of phenomenology he recognised the unresolved fundamental problem of metaphysics, concealed, in its ultimate culmination, in the concept of mind or spirit as conceived by speculative idealism. In his grounding of the hermeneutics of 'facticity' he went beyond both the concept of spirit developed by classical idealism and the thematic of transcendental consciousness, purified by phenomenological reduction.

Heidegger's hermeneutical phenomenology and the analysis of the historicalness of There-being had as their aim a general renewal of the question of being and not a theory of the human sciences or a treatment of the impasses of historicism. These were merely particular contemporary problems in which he was able to demonstrate the consequences of his radical renewal of the question of being. But precisely because of the radicality of his approach he was able to move beyond the complications in which Dilthey's and Husserl's investigations into the fundamental concepts of the human sciences had become involved.

Dilthey's attempt to make the human sciences intelligible in terms of life, starting from the experience of life, was never really reconciled with the Cartesian concept of science to which he held firmly. However much he might over-emphasise the contemplative tendency of life and its 'tendency towards stability', the objectivity of science, understood as an objectivity of results, had a different origin. For this reason he was unable to accomplish the task that he had himself chosen, which was to justify epistemologically the particular methodological character of the human sciences and hence place them on the same level as the natural sciences.

Heidegger, however, was able to make a completely fresh beginning because, as we have seen, Husserl had made it an absolutely universal working method to go back to life and hence had abandoned for good the narrow approach of simply enquiring into the methods of the human sciences. His analysis of the life-world and of the anonymous creation of meaning that forms the ground of all experience, gave a completely new background to the question of objectivity in the human sciences, making science's concept of objectivity appear as a particular case. Science is anything but a fact from which to start. The constitution of the scientific world presents, rather, a special task, namely of clarifying the idealisation that is given in science. But this task is not the first one. When we go back to 'productive life' the antithesis between nature and spirit does not prove to be of ultimate validity. Both the human and the natural sciences are to be derived from the achievements of the intentionality of universal life, ie from absolute historicity. This is the kind of understanding which alone satisfies the self-reflection of philosophy.

To this Heidegger gave a new and radical turn in the light of the question of being revived by him. He follows Husserl in that historical being is not to be distinguished from natural being, as with Dilthey, in order to give an epistemological justification of the methodological nature of the historical sciences. On the contrary, the mode of knowledge of the natural sciences appears, rather, as a variety of understanding 'which has strayed into the legitimate task of grasping the present-at-hand in its essential unintelligibility'.[157] Understanding is not a resigned ideal of human experience adopted in the old age of the spirit, as with Dilthey; nor is it, as with Husserl, a last methodological ideal of philosophy over against the naiveté of unreflecting life; it is, on the contrary, the original form of the realisation of There-being, which is being-in-the-world. Before any differentiation of understanding into the different directions of pragmatic or theoretical interest, understanding is There-being's mode of being, in that it is potentiality-for-being and 'possibility'.

Against the background of this kind of existential analysis of There-being, with all its far-reaching consequences for metaphysics, the problems of a hermeneutics of the human sciences suddenly look very different. The present work is devoted to this new aspect of the hermeneutical problem. In reviving the question of being and thus moving beyond all previous metaphysics—and not just its climax in the Cartesianism of modern science and transcendental philosophy —Heidegger attained a fundamentally new position in regard to the impasses of historicism. The concept of understanding is no longer a methodological concept, as with Droysen. Nor, as in Dilthey's attempt to provide a hermeneutical ground for the human sciences, is the process of understanding an inverse operation that simply follows behind life's tendency towards ideality. Understanding is the original character of the being of human life itself. Starting from Dilthey, Misch had recognised the 'free distance towards oneself' as a basic structure of human life, on which all understanding depended; Heidegger's radical ontological reflection was concerned to clarify this structure of There-being through a 'transcendental analysis of There-being'. He revealed the projective character of all understanding and conceived the act of understanding itself as the movement of transcendence, of moving beyond being.

This asks quite a lot of traditional hermeneutics.[158] It is true that the German language uses the word for 'understanding' (Verstehen) also in the sense of a practical ability (eg er versteht nicht zu lesen, 'he can't read'). But this seems essentially different from the understanding that takes place in science and is concerned with knowledge. If we examine the two more closely, we can see that they have something in common: both senses contain the element of recognition, of being well versed in something. Similarly, a person who 'understands' a text (or even a law) has not only moved in understanding towards a meaning—in the effort of understanding—but the accomplished understanding constitutes the state of a new intellectual freedom. It implies the general possibility of interpretation, of seeing connections, of drawing conclusions, which being well versed in textual interpretation demands. Someone who knows his way around a machine, who understands how to use it, or who knows a trade—granted that there are different norms for the understanding of artifacts and for the understanding of the expressions of life or of texts—it still remains true that all this kind of understanding is ultimately a self-understanding. Even the understanding of an expression means, ultimately, not only the immediate grasp of what lies in the expression, but the disclosure of what is enclosed within it, so that one now knows this hidden part also. But this means that one knows one's way in it. Thus it is true in all cases that a person who understands, understands himself, projecting himself according to his possibilities.[159] Traditional hermeneutics has incorrectly limited the horizon within which understanding belongs. That is why the advance that Heidegger made over Dilthey is valuable for the problem of hemeneutics also. True, Dilthey had already rejected the methods of the natural sciences as applicable to the human sciences, and Husserl had referred to the application of the natural sciences' concept of objectivity to the human sciences as 'nonsense' and established the essential relativity of all historical worlds and all historical knowledge. But now, as a result of the existential futurity of human There-being, the structure of historical understanding appears with its full ontological background.

Because historical knowledge receives its justification from the fore-structure of There-being, this is no reason for anyone interfering with the immanent criteria of what is called knowledge. For Heidegger too historical knowledge is not a planning project, the extrapolation of aims of the will, an ordering of things according to the wishes, the prejudices or the promptings of the powerful, but it remains something adapted to the object, a mensuratio ad rem. Only that this object is not a factum brutum, not something that is merely at hand, something that can simply be established and measured, but it is itself ultimately of the essence of There-being.

The important thing, however, is to understand this oft-repeated statement correctly. It does not mean simply that there is a resemblance between the knower and what is known, on which it would be possible to base the special character of pyschic transposition as the 'method' of the human sciences. This would make historical hermeneutics a branch of psychology (which was what Dilthey had in mind). In fact, however, the co-ordination of all knowing activity with what is known is not based on the fact that they are essentially the same but draws its significance from the particular nature of the mode of being that is common to both of them. It consists in the fact that neither the knower nor the known are present-at-hand in an 'ontic' way, but in a 'historical' one, ie they are of the mode of being of historicalness. Hence, as Graf Yorck says, everything depends on 'the generic difference between the ontic and the historical'.[160] The fact that Graf Yorck contrasts 'similarity' with 'correspondence' reveals the problem[161] that Heidegger was the first to develop in its full radicality: that we study history only insofar as we are ourselves 'historical' means that the historicalness of human There-being in its expectancy and its forgetting is the condition of our being able to represent the past. What appeared first to be simply a barrier that cut across the traditional concept of science and method, or a subjective condition of access to historical knowledge, now becomes the centre of a fundamental enquiry. Correspondence is not a condition of the original meaning of historical interest because the choice of theme and enquiry is subject to extra-scientific, subjective motivations (then correspondence would be no more than a special case of emotional dependence, of the same type as sympathy), but because correspondence with traditions is as original and essential a part of the historical finiteness of There-being as is its projectedness towards future possibilities of itself. Heidegger was right to insist that what he called 'Thrownness' belongs together with that which is projected.[162] Thus there is no understanding or interpretation in which the totality of this existential structure does not function, even if the intention of the knower is simply to read 'what is there' and to discover from his sources 'how it really was'.[163]

We shall try to determine if Heidegger's ontological radicalisation can contribute to the construction of an historical hermeneutics. Heidegger's intention was undoubtedly a different one, and we must beware of drawing over-hasty consequences from his existential analysis of the historicalness of There-being. For Heidegger, the existential analytic of There-being does not involve any particular historical ideal of existence. Hence for any theological statement about man and his existence in faith it claims an a priori, neutral validity. This may be a problematical claim for the self-understanding of faith, as the controversy surrounding Bultmann shows.[164] On the other hand, this by no means excludes the fact that both christian theology and the historical sciences are subject to specific (existential) presuppositions with respect to content. But precisely for this reason we are forced to acknowledge that the existential analytic itself does not, with respect to its own intention, contain any existenziell ideal and therefore cannot be criticised as one (however many attempts may have been made to do so).

It is a sheer misunderstanding if the temporality structure of care is regarded as a particular ideal of existence, which could be countered with more attractive modes (Bollnow),[165] such as the ideal of being free from care or, with Nietzsche, the natural innocence of animals and birds. It cannot be denied that this too is an ideal of existence; but it is also true that its structure is the existential one that Heidegger has revealed.

It is nonetheless true that the being of children or indeed of animals—unlike that ideal of 'innocence'—remains an ontological problem. Their mode of being is not, at any rate, 'existence' and historicalness such as Heidegger claims for human existence. We may also ask what it means for human existence to be based on something that is outside history, ie on nature. If we really want to break out of the spell of idealistic speculation, then we must obviously not conceive the mode of being, of 'life', in terms of self-consciousness. When Heidegger set about revising the position of *Being and Time,* which was one of transcendental self-conception, it followed that he would have to come to grips afresh with the problem of life. Thus in his letter on humanism he spoke of the great gulf between man and animal.[166] It is quite clear that Heidegger's own account of fundamental ontology, basing it transcendentally on the analytic of There-being, did not yet permit a positive account of the mode of being of life. There are here open questions; but none of this alters the fact that it would be completely to mistake the significance of what Heidegger calls existenzial were it thought possible to counter the existential of 'care' with another specific ideal of existence, whatever it might be. To do this is to miss the dimension of the enquiry that *Being and Time* opened up. In defending himself against such superficially-argued polemics, Heidegger could quite legitimately refer to the transcendental intention of his own work, in the same sense that Kant's enquiry was transcendental. His enquiry transcended from the start all empirical differences and hence all ideals of specific content.

Hence we too are beginning with the transcendental significance of Heidegger's problematic. The problem of hermeneutics gains a universal framework, even a new dimension, through his transcendental interpretation of understanding. The correspondence between the interpreter and his object, for which the thinking of the historical school was unable to offer any convincing account, now acquires a significance that is concretely demonstrable, and it is the task of hermeneutics to demonstrate it. That the structure of There-being is thrown projection, that There-being is, in the realisation of its own being, understanding, must also be true of the act of understanding within the human sciences. The general structure of understanding acquires its concrete form in historical understanding, in that the commitments of custom and tradition and the corresponding potentialities of one's own future become effective in understanding itself. There-being that projects itself in relation to its own potentiality-for-being has always 'been'. This is the meaning of the existential of 'thrownness'. The main point of the hermeneutics of facticity and its contrast with the transcendental constitution research of Husserl's phenomenology was that no freely chosen relation towards one's own being can go back beyond the facticity of this being. Everything that makes possible and limits the project of There-being precedes it, absolutely. This existential structure of There-being must find its expression in the understanding of historical tradition as well, and so we shall start by following Heidegger.[167]

II

Foundations of a Theory of Hermeneutical Experience

1 THE ELEVATION OF THE HISTORICALITY OF UNDERSTANDING TO THE STATUS OF HERMENEUTICAL PRINCIPLE

(A) THE HERMENEUTIC CIRCLE AND THE PROBLEM OF PREJUDICES

(i) Heidegger's disclosure of the fore-structure of understanding

Heidegger went into the problems of historical hermeneutics and criticism only in order to develop from it, for the purposes of ontology, the fore-structure of understanding.[168] Contrariwise, our question is how hermeneutics, once freed from the ontological obstructions of the scientific concept of objectivity, can do justice to the historicality of understanding. The way in which hermeneutics has traditionally understood itself is based on its character as art or technique.[169] This is true even of Dilthey's extension of hermeneutics to become an organon of the human sciences. It may be asked whether there is such a thing as this art or technique of understanding—we shall come back to the point. But at any rate we may enquire into the consequences that Heidegger's fundamental derivation of the circular structure of understanding from the temporality of There-being has for the hermeneutics of the human sciences. These consequences do not need to be such that a theory is applied to practice and the latter now be performed differently, ie in a way that is technically correct. They could also consist in a correction (and purification of inadequate manners) of the way in which constantly exercised understanding understands itself—a procedure that would benefit the art of understanding at most only indirectly.

Hence we shall examine once more Heidegger's description of the hermeneutical circle in order to use, for our own purpose, the new fundamental significance acquired here by the circular structure. Heidegger writes: 'It is not to be reduced to the level of a vicious circle, or even of a circle which is merely tolerated.

235

In the circle is hidden a positive possibility of the most primordial kind of knowing. To be sure, we genuinely take hold of this possibility only when, in our interpretation, we have understood that our first, last and constant task is never to allow our fore-having, fore-sight, and fore-conception to be presented to us by fancies and popular conceptions, but rather to make the scientific theme secure by working out these fore-structures in terms of the things themselves'. (*Being and Time,* p 153)

What Heidegger works out here is not primarily a demand on the practice of understanding, but is a description of the way in which interpretation through understanding is achieved. The point of Heidegger's hermeneutical thinking is not so much to prove that there is a circle as to show that this circle possesses an ontologically positive significance. The description as such will be obvious to every interpreter who knows what he is about.[170] All correct interpretation must be on guard against arbitrary fancies and the limitations imposed by imperceptible habits of thought and direct its gaze 'on the things themselves' (which, in the case of the literary critic, are meaningful texts, which themselves are again concerned with objects). It is clear that to let the object take over in this way is not a matter for the interpreter of a single decision, but is 'the first, last and constant task'. For it is necessary to keep one's gaze fixed on the thing throughout all the distractions that the interpreter will constantly experience in the process and which originate in himself. A person who is trying to understand a text is always performing an act of projecting. He projects before himself a meaning for the text as a whole as soon as some initial meaning emerges in the text. Again, the latter emerges only because he is reading the text with particular expectations in regard to a certain meaning. The working out of this fore-project, which is constantly revised in terms of what emerges as he penetrates into the meaning, is understanding what is there.

This description is, of course, a rough abbreviation of the whole. The process that Heidegger describes is that every revision of the fore-project is capable of projecting before itself a new project of meaning, that rival projects can emerge side by side until it becomes clearer what the unity of meaning is, that interpretation begins with fore-conceptions that are replaced by more suitable ones. This constant process of new projection is the movement of understanding and interpretation. A person who is trying to understand is exposed to distraction from fore-meanings that are not borne out by the things themselves. The working-out of appropriate projects, anticipatory in nature, to be confirmed 'by the things' themselves, is the constant task of understanding. The only 'objectivity' here is the confirmation of a fore-meaning in its being worked out. The only thing that characterises the arbitrariness of inappropriate fore-meanings is that they come to nothing in the working-out. But understanding achieves its full potentiality only when the fore-meanings that it uses are not arbitrary. Thus it is quite right for the interpreter not to approach the text directly, relying solely on the fore-meaning at once available to him, but rather to examine explicitly the legitimacy, ie the origin and validity, of the fore-meanings present within him.

This fundamental requirement must be seen as the radicalisation of a procedure that in fact we exercise whenever we understand anything. Every text presents the task of not simply employing unexamined our own linguistic usage—or in the case of a foreign language the usage that we are familiar with from writers or from daily intercourse. We regard our task as rather that of deriving our understanding of the text from the linguistic usage of the time of the author. The question is, of course, to what extent this general requirement can be fulfilled. In the field of semantics, in particular, we are confronted with the problem of the unconscious nature of our own use of language. How do we discover that there is a difference between our own customary usage and that of the text?

I think we must say that it is generally the experience of being pulled up short by the text. Either it does not yield any meaning or its meaning is not compatible with what we had expected. It is this that makes us take account of possible difference in usage. It is a general presupposition that can be questioned only in particular cases that someone who speaks the same language as I do uses the words in the sense familiar to me. The same thing is true in the case of a foreign language, ie that we all think we have a normal knowledge of it and assume this normal usage when we are reading a text.

What is true of the fore-meaning of usage, however, is equally true of the fore-meanings with regard to content with which we read texts, and which make up our fore-understanding. Here too we may ask how we can break the spell of our own fore-meanings that determine my own understanding can go entirely tion that what is stated in a text will fit perfectly with my own meanings and expectations. On the contrary, what another person tells me, whether in conversation, letter, book or whatever, is generally thought automatically to be his own and not my opinion; and it is this that I am to take note of without necessar-

ily having to share it. But this presupposition is not something
that makes understanding easier, but harder, in that the fore-
meanings that determine my own understanding can go entirely
unnoticed. If they give rise to misunderstandings, how can misunderstandings of a text be recognised at all if there is nothing
else to contradict? How can a text be protected from misunderstanding from the start?

If we examine the situation more closely, however, we find
that meanings cannot be understood in an arbitrary way. Just as
we cannot continually misunderstand the use of a word without
its affecting the meaning of the whole, so we cannot hold blindly
to our own fore-meaning of the thing if we would understand the
meaning of another. Of course this does not mean that when we
listen to someone or read a book we must forget all our fore-
meanings concerning the content, and all our own ideas. All that
is asked is that we remain open to the meaning of the other
person or of the text. But this openness always includes our
placing the other meaning in a relation with the whole of our own
meanings or ourselves in a relation to it. Now it is the case that
meanings represent a fluid variety of possibilities (when compared with the agreement presented by a language and a vocabulary), but it is still not the case that within this variety of what
can be thought, ie of what a reader can find meaningful and
hence expect to find, everything is possible, and if a person fails
to hear what the other person is really saying, he will not be able
to place correctly what he has misunderstood within the range of
his own various expectations of meaning. Thus there is a criterion here also. The hermeneutical task becomes automatically a
questioning of things and is always in part determined by this.
This places hermeneutical work on a firm basis. If a person is
trying to understand something, he will not be able to rely from
the start on his own chance previous ideas, missing as logically
and stubbornly as possible the actual meaning of the text until
the latter becomes so persistently audible that it breaks through
the imagined understanding of it. Rather, a person trying to
understand a text is prepared for it to tell him something. That is
why a hermeneutically trained mind must be, from the start,
sensitive to the text's quality of newness. But this kind of sensitivity involves neither 'neutrality' in the matter of the object
nor the extinction of one's self, but the conscious assimilation of
one's own fore-meanings and prejudices. The important thing is
to be aware of one's own bias, so that the text may present itself
in all its newness and thus be able to assert its own truth against
one's own fore-meanings.

When Heidegger showed that what we call the 'reading of what is there' is the fore-structure of understanding, this was, phenomenologically, completely correct. He also showed by an example the task that arises from this. In *Being and Time* he gave a concrete example, in the question of being, of the general statement that was, for him, a hermeneutical problem.[171] In order to explain the hermeneutical situation of the question of being in regard to fore-having, fore-sight and fore-conception, he critically applied his question, directed at metaphysics, to important turning-points in the history of metaphysics. Here he was actually doing simply what the historical, hermeneutical consciousness requires in every case. Methodologically conscious understanding will be concerned not merely to form anticipatory ideas, but to make them conscious, so as to check them and thus acquire right understanding from the things themselves. This is what Heidegger means when he talks about 'securing' our scientific theme by deriving our fore-having, fore-sight and fore-conceptions from the things themselves.

It is not, then, at all a case of safeguarding ourselves against the tradition that speaks out of the text but, on the contrary, to keep everything away that could hinder us in understanding it in terms of the thing. It is the tyranny of hidden prejudices that makes us deaf to the language that speaks to us in tradition. Heidegger's demonstration that the concept of consciousness in Descartes and of spirit in Hegel is still influenced by Greek substance-ontology, which sees being in terms of what is present and actual, undoubtedly goes beyond the self-understanding of modern metaphysics, yet not in an arbitrary, wilful way, but on the basis of a fore-having that in fact makes this tradition intelligible by revealing the ontological premises of the concept of subjectivity. On the other hand, Heidegger discovers in Kant's critique of 'dogmatic' metaphysics the idea of a metaphysics of the finite which is a challenge to his own ontological scheme. Thus he 'secures' the scientific theme by framing it within the understanding of tradition and so putting it, in a sense, at risk. This is the concrete form of the historical consciousness that is involved in understanding.

This recognition that all understanding inevitably involves some prejudice gives the hermeneutical problem its real thrust. By the light of this insight it appears that historicism, despite its critique of rationalism and of natural law philosophy, is based on the modern enlightenment and unknowingly shares its prejudices. And there is one prejudice of the enlightenment that is essential to it: the fundamental prejudice of the enlightenment is the prejudice against prejudice itself, which deprives tradition of its power.

Historical analysis shows that it is not until the enlightenment that the concept of prejudice acquires the negative aspect we are familiar with. Actually 'prejudice' means a judgment that is given before all the elements that determine a situation have been finally examined. In German legal terminology a 'prejudice' is a provisional legal verdict before the final verdict is reached. For someone involved in a legal dispute, this kind of judgment against him affects his chances adversely. Accordingly, the French préjudice, as well as the Latin praejudicium, means simply 'adverse effect', 'disadvantage', 'harm'. But this negative sense is only a consecutive one. The negative consequence depends precisely on the positive validity, the value of the provisional decision as a prejudgment, which is that of any precedent.

Thus 'prejudice' certainly does not mean a false judgment, but it is part of the idea that it can have a positive and a negative value. This is due clearly to the influence of the Latin prae-judicium. There are such things as préjugés légitimes. This seems a long way from our current use of the word. The German Vorurteil, like English 'prejudice' and even more than the French préjugé, seems to have become limited in its meaning, through the enlightenment and its critique of religion, and have the sense simply of an 'unfounded judgment'.[172] It is only its having a basis, a methodological justification (and not the fact that it may be actually correct) that gives a judgment its dignity. The lack of such a basis does not mean, for the enlightenment, that there might be other kinds of certainty, but rather that the judgment does not have any foundation in the facts themselves, ie that it is 'unfounded'. This is a conclusion only in the spirit of rationalism. It is the reason for the discrediting of prejudices and the claim by scientific knowledge completely to exclude them.

Modern science, in adopting this principle, is following the rule of Cartesian doubt of accepting nothing as certain which can in any way be doubted, and the idea of the method that adheres to this requirement. In our introductory observations we have already pointed out how difficult it is to harmonise the historical knowledge that helps to shape our historical consciousness with this ideal and how difficult it is, for that reason, for the modern concept of method to grasp its true nature. This is the place to turn these negative statements into positive ones. The concept of the 'prejudice' is where we can make a beginning.

(ii) *The discrediting of prejudice by the enlightenment*

If we pursue the view that the enlightenment developed in regard to prejudices we find it makes the following fundamental
division: a distinction must be made between the prejudice due
to human authority and that due to over-hastiness.[173] The basis
of this distinction is the origin of prejudices in regard to the
persons who have them. It is either the respect in which we hold
others and their authority, that leads us into error, or else it is an
over-hastiness in ourselves. That authority is a source of prejudices accords with the well-known principle of the enlightenment that Kant formulated: Have the courage to make use of
your own understanding.[174] Although this distinction is certainly
not limited to the role that prejudices play in the understanding
of texts, its chief application is still in the sphere of hermeneutics. For the critique of the enlightenment is directed primarily
against the religious tradition of christianity, ie the bible. By
treating the latter as an historical document, biblical criticism
endangers its own dogmatic claims. This is the real radicality of
the modern enlightenment as against all other movements of
enlightenment: it must assert itself against the bible and its dogmatic interpretation.[175] It is, therefore, particularly concerned
with the hermeneutical problem. It desires to understand tradition correctly, ie reasonably and without prejudice. But there is
a special difficulty about this, in that the sheer fact of something
being written down confers on it an authority of particular
weight. It is not altogether easy to realise that what is written
down can be untrue. The written word has the tangible quality of
something that can be demonstrated and is like a proof. It needs
a special critical effort to free oneself from the prejudice in
favour of what is written down and to distinguish here also, as
with all oral assertions, between opinion and truth.[176]

It is the general tendency of the enlightenment not to accept
any authority and to decide everything before the judgment seat
of reason. Thus the written tradition of scripture, like any other
historical document, cannot claim any absolute validity, but the
possible truth of the tradition depends on the credibility that is
assigned to it by reason. It is not tradition, but reason that constitutes the ultimate source of all authority. What is written
down is not necessarily true. We may have superior knowledge:
this is the maxim with which the modern enlightenment approaches tradition and which ultimately leads it to undertake
historical research.[177] It makes the tradition as much an object

of criticism as do the natural sciences the evidence of the senses. This does not necessarily mean that the 'prejudice against prejudices' was everywhere taken to the extreme consequences of free thinking and atheism, as in England and France. On the contrary, the German enlightenment recognised the 'true prejudices' of the christian religion. Since the human intellect is too weak to manage without prejudices it is at least fortunate to have been educated with true prejudices.

It would be of value to investigate to what extent this kind of modification and moderation of the enlightenment[178] prepared the way for the rise of the romantic movement in Germany, as undoubtedly did the critique of the enlightenment and the revolution by Edmund Burke. But none of this alters the fundamental facts. True prejudices must still finally be justified by rational knowledge, even though the task may never be able to be fully completed.

Thus the criteria of the modern enlightenment still determine the self-understanding of historicism. This does not happen directly, but in a curious refraction caused by romanticism. This can be seen with particular clarity in the fundamental schema of the philosophy of history that romanticism shares with the enlightenment and that precisely the romantic reaction to the enlightenment made into an unshakeable premise: the schema of the conquest of mythos by logos. It is the presupposition of the progressive retreat of magic in the world that gives this schema its validity. It is supposed to represent the progressive law of the history of the mind, and precisely because romanticism has a negative attitude to this development, it takes over the schema itself as an obvious truth. It shares the presupposition of the enlightenment and only reverses the evaluation of it, seeking to establish the validity of what is old, simply because it is old: the 'gothic' middle ages, the christian European community of states, the feudal structure of society, but also the simplicity of peasant life and closeness to nature.

In contrast to the enlightenment's belief in perfection, which thinks in terms of the freedom from 'superstition' and the prejudices of the past, we now find that olden times, the world of myth, unreflective life, not yet analysed away by consciousness, in a 'society close to nature', the world of christian chivalry, all these acquire a romantic magic, even a priority of truth.[179] The reversal of the enlightenment's presupposition results in the paradoxical tendency to restoration, ie the tendency to reconstruct the old because it is old, the conscious return to the unconscious, culminating in the recognition of the superior wisdom of the primaeval age of myth. But the romantic reversal of this criterion of the enlightenment actually perpetuates the abstract contrast between myth and reason. All criticism of the enlightenment now proceeds via this romantic mirror image of the enlightenment. Belief in the perfectibility of reason suddenly changes into the perfection of the 'mythical' consciousness and finds itself reflected in a paradisic primal state before the 'fall' of thought.

In fact the presupposition of a mysterious darkness in which there was a mythical collective consciousness that preceded all thought is just as dogmatic and abstract as that of a state of perfection achieved by a total enlightenment or that of absolute knowledge. Primaeval wisdom is only the counter-image of 'primaeval stupidity'. All mythical consciousness is still knowledge, and if it knows about divine powers, then it has progressed beyond mere trembling before power (if this is to be regarded as the primaeval state), but also beyond a collective life contained in magic rituals (as we find in the early Orient). It knows about itself, and in this knowledge it is no longer simply 'outside itself'.[180]

There is the related point that even the contrast between genuine mythical thinking and pseudo-mythical poetic thinking is a romantic illusion which is based on a prejudice of the enlightenment: namely, that the poetic act, because it is a creation of the free imagination, is no longer in any way bound within the religious quality of the myth. It is the old quarrel between the poets and the philosophers in the modern garb appropriate to the age of belief in science. It is now said, not that poets tell lies, but that they are incapable of saying anything true, since they have an aesthetic effect only and merely seek to rouse through their imaginative creations the imagination and the emotions of their hearers or readers.

The concept of the 'society close to nature' is probably another case of a romantic mirror-image, whose origin ought to be investigated. In Karl Marx it appears as a kind of relic of natural law that limits the validity of his socio-economic theory of the class struggle.[181] Does the idea go back to Rousseau's description of society before the division of labour and the introduction of property?[182] At any rate, Plato has already demonstrated the illusory nature of this political theory in the ironical account he gives of a 'state of nature' in the third book of the *Republic.*[183]

These romantic revaluations give rise to the attitude of the historical science of the nineteenth century. It no longer measures the past by the yardsticks of the present, as if they represented an absolute, but it ascribes their own value to past ages and can even acknowledge their superiority in one or the other respect. The great achievements of romanticism—the revival of the past, the discovery of the voices of the peoples in their songs, the collecting of fairy-tales and legends, the cultivation of ancient customs, the discovery of the world views implicit in languages, the study of the 'religion and wisdom of India'—have all motivated the historical research that has slowly, step by step, transformed the intuitive revival into historical knowledge proper. The fact that it was romanticism that gave birth to the historical school confirms that the romantic retrieval of origins is itself based on the enlightenment. The historical science of the nineteenth century is its proudest fruit and sees itself precisely as the fulfilment of the enlightenment, as the last step in the liberation of the mind from the trammels of dogma, the step to the objective knowledge of the historical world, which stands as an equal besides the knowledge of nature achieved by modern science.

The fact that the restorative tendency of romanticism was able to combine with the fundamental concern of the enlightenment to constitute the unity of the historical sciences simply indicates that it is the same break with the continuity of meaning in tradition that lies behind both. If it is an established fact for the enlightenment that all tradition that reason shows to be impossible, ie nonsense, can only be understood historically, ie by going back to the past's way of looking at things, then the historical consciousness that emerges in romanticism involves a radicalisation of the enlightenment. For the exceptional case of nonsensical tradition has become the general rule for historical consciousness. Meaning that is generally accessible through reason is so little believed that the whole of the past, even, ultimately, all the thinking of one's contemporaries, is seen only 'historically'. Thus the romantic critique of the enlightenment ends itself in enlightenment, in that it evolves as historical science and draws everything into the orbit of historicism. The basic discrediting of all prejudices, which unites the experiential emphasis of the new natural sciences with the enlightenment, becomes, in the historical enlightenment, universal and radical.

This is the point at which the attempt to arrive at an historical hermeneutics has to start its critique. The overcoming of all prejudices, this global demand of the enlightenment, will prove to be itself a prejudice, the removal of which opens the way to an appropriate understanding of our finitude, which dominates not only our humanity, but also our historical consciousness.

Does the fact that one is set within various traditions mean really and primarily that one is subject to prejudices and limited in one's freedom? Is not, rather, all human existence, even the freest, limited and qualified in various ways? If this is true, then the idea of an absolute reason is impossible for historical human-ity. Reason exists for us only in concrete, historical terms, ie it is not its own master, but remains constantly dependent on the given circumstances in which it operates. This is true not only in the sense in which Kant limited the claims of rationalism, under the influence of the sceptical critique of Hume, to the a priori element in the knowledge of nature; it is still truer of historical consciousness and the possibility of historical knowledge. For that man is concerned here with himself and his own creations (Vico) is only an apparent solution of the problem set by histori-cal knowledge. Man is alien to himself and his historical fate in a quite different way from that in which nature, that knows noth-ing of him, is alien to him.

The epistemological question must be asked here in a funda-mentally different way. We have shown above that Dilthey probably saw this, but he was not able to overcome the influence over him of traditional epistemology. His starting-point, the awareness of 'experience', was not able to build the bridge to the historical realities, because the great historical realities of society and state always have a predeterminant influence on any 'experience'. Self-reflection and autobiography—Dilthey's starting-points—are not primary and are not an adequate basis for the hermeneutical problem, because through them history is made private once more. In fact history does not belong to us, but we belong to it. Long before we understand ourselves through the process of self-examination, we understand our-selves in a self-evident way in the family, society and state in which we live. The focus of subjectivity is a distorting mirror. The self-awareness of the individual is only a flickering in the closed circuits of historical life. That is why the prejudices of the individual, far more than his judgments, constitute the historical reality of his being.

(B) PREJUDICES AS CONDITIONS OF UNDERSTANDING

(i) The rehabilitation of authority and tradition

This is where the hermeneutical problem comes in. This is why we examined the discrediting of the concept of prejudice by the enlightenment. That which presents itself, under the aegis of an absolute self-construction by reason, as a limiting prejudice belongs, in fact, to historical reality itself. What is necessary is a fundamental rehabilitation of the concept of prejudice and a recognition of the fact that there are legitimate prejudices, if we want to do justice to man's finite, historical mode of being. Thus we are able to formulate the central question of a truly historical hermeneutics, epistemologically its fundamental question, namely: where is the ground of the legitimacy of prejudices? What distinguishes legitimate prejudices from all the countless ones which it is the undeniable task of the critical reason to overcome?

We can approach this question by taking the view of prejudices that the enlightenment developed with a critical intention, as set out above, and giving it a positive value. As for the division of prejudices into those of 'authority' and those of 'over-hastiness', it is obviously based on the fundamental presupposition of the enlightenment, according to which a methodologically disciplined use of reason can safeguard us from all error. This was Descartes' idea of method. Over-hastiness is the actual source of error in the use of one's own reason. Authority, however, is responsible for one's not using one's own reason at all. There lies, then, at the base of the division a mutually exclusive antithesis between authority and reason. The false prejudice for what is old, for authorities, is what has to be fought. Thus the enlightenment regards it as the reforming action of Luther that 'the prejudice of human prestige, especially that of the philosophical (he means Aristotle) and the Roman pope was greatly weakened'.[184] The reformation, then, gives rise to a flourishing hermeneutics which is to teach the right use of reason in the understanding of transmitted texts. Neither the teaching authority of the pope nor the appeal to tradition can replace the work of hermeneutics, which can safeguard the reasonable meaning of a text against all unreasonable demands made on it.

The consequences of this kind of hermeneutics need not be those of the radical critique of religion that we found, for example, in Spinoza. Rather the possibility of supernatural truth can remain entirely open. Thus the enlightenment, especially in the field of popular philosophy, limited the claims of reason and acknowledged the authority of bible and church. We read in, say, Walch, that he distinguishes between the two classes of prejudice—authority and over-hastiness—but sees in them two extremes, between which it is necessary to find the right middle path, namely a reconciliation between reason and biblical authority. Accordingly, he sees the prejudice from over-hastiness as a prejudice in favour of the new, as a predisposition to the overhasty rejection of truths simply because they are old and attested by authorities.[185] Thus he discusses the British free-thinkers (such as Collins and others) and defends the historical faith against the norm of reason. Here the meaning of the prejudice from over-hastiness is clearly reinterpreted in a conservative sense.

There can be no doubt, however, that the real consequence of the enlightenment is different: namely, the subjection of all authority to reason. Accordingly, prejudice from over-hastiness is to be understood as Descartes understood it, ie as the source of all error in the use of reason. This fits in with the fact that after the victory of the enlightenment, when hermeneutics was freed from all dogmatic ties, the old division returns in a changed sense. Thus we read in Schleiermacher that he distinguishes between narrowness of view and over-hastiness as the causes of misunderstanding.[186] He places the lasting prejudices due to narrowness of view beside the momentary ones due to overhastiness, but only the former are of interest to someone concerned with scientific method. It no longer even occurs to Schleiermacher that among the prejudices in the mind of one whose vision is narrowed by authorities there might be some that are true—yet this was included in the concept of authority in the first place. His alteration of the traditional division of prejudices is a sign of the fulfilment of the enlightenment. Narrowness now means only an individual limitation of understanding: 'The one sided preference for what is close to one's own sphere of ideas'.

In fact, however, the decisive question is concealed behind the concept of narrowness. That the prejudices that determine what I think are due to my own narrowness of vision is a judgment that is made from the standpoint of their dissolution and illumination and holds only of unjustified prejudices. If, contrariwise, there are justified prejudices productive of knowledge, then we are back with the problem of authority. Hence the radical consequences of the enlightenment, which are still contained in Schleiermacher's faith in method, are not tenable.

The distinction the enlightenment draws between faith in authority and the use of one's own reason is, in itself, legitimate. If the prestige of authority takes the place of one's own judgment, then authority is in fact a source of prejudices. But this does not exclude the possibility that it can also be a source of truth, and this is what the enlightenment failed to see when it denigrated all authority. To be convinced of this, we only have to consider one of the greatest forerunners of the European enlightenment, namely Descartes. Despite the radicalness of his methodological thinking, we know that Descartes excluded morality from the total reconstruction of all truths by reason. This was what he meant by his provisional morality. It seems to me symptomatic that he did not in fact elaborate his definitive morality and that its principles, as far as we can judge from his letters to Elizabeth, contain hardly anything new. It is obviously unthinkable to prefer to wait until the progress of modern science provides us with the basis of a new morality. In fact the denigration of authority is not the only prejudice of the enlightenment. For, within the enlightenment, the very concept of authority becomes deformed. On the basis of its concept of reason and freedom, the concept of authority could be seen as diametrically opposed to reason and freedom: to be, in fact, blind obedience. This is the meaning that we know, from the usage of their critics, within modern dictatorships.

But this is not the essence of authority. It is true that it is primarily persons that have authority; but the authority of persons is based ultimately, not on the subjection and abdication of reason, but on recognition and knowledge—knowledge, namely, that the other is superior to oneself in judgment and insight and that for this reason his judgment takes precedence, ie it has priority over one's own. This is connected with the fact that authority cannot actually be bestowed, but is acquired and must be acquired, if someone is to lay claim to it. It rests on recognition and hence on an act of reason itself which, aware of its own limitations, accepts that others have better understanding. Authority in this sense, properly understood, has nothing to do with blind obedience to a command. Indeed, authority has nothing to do with obedience, but rather with knowledge. (It seems to me that the tendency towards the acknowledgment of authority, as it emerges in, for example, Karl Jaspers' *Von der Wahrheit*, p 766ff and Gerhard Krüger, *Freiheit und Weltverwaltung*, p 231ff, is not convincing unless the truth of this statement is recognised.) It is true that authority is necessary in order to be able to command and find obedience. But this proceeds only from the authority that a person has. Even the anonymous and impersonal authority of a superior which derives from the command is not ultimately based on this order, but is what makes it possible. Here also its true basis is an act of freedom and reason, which fundamentally acknowledges the authority of a superior because he has a wider view of things or is better informed, ie once again, because he has superior knowledge.[187]

Thus the recognition of authority is always connected with the idea that what authority states is not irrational and arbitrary, but can be seen, in principle, to be true. This is the essence of the authority claimed by the teacher, the superior, the expert. The prejudices that they implant are legitimised by the person himself. Their validity demands that one should be biased in favour of the person who presents them. But this makes them then, in a sense, objective prejudices, for they bring about the same bias in favour of something that can come about through other means, eg through solid grounds offered by reason. Thus the essence of authority belongs in the context of a theory of prejudices free from the extremism of the enlightenment.

Here we can find support in the romantic criticism of the enlightenment; for there is one form of authority particularly defended by romanticism, namely tradition. That which has been sanctioned by tradition and custom has an authority that is nameless, and our finite historical being is marked by the fact that always the authority of what has been transmitted—and not only what is clearly grounded—has power over our attitudes and behaviour. All education depends on this, and even though, in the case of education, the educator loses his function when his charge comes of age and sets his own insight and decisions in the place of the authority of the educator, this movement into maturity in his own life does not mean that a person becomes his own master in the sense that he becomes free of all tradition. The validity of morals, for example, is based on tradition. They are freely taken over, but by no means created by a free insight or justified by themselves. This is precisely what we call tradition: the ground of their validity. And in fact we owe to romanticism this correction of the enlightenment, that tradition has a justification that is outside the arguments of reason and in large measure determines our institutions and our attitudes. It is even a mark of the superiority of classical ethics over the moral philosophy of the modern period that it justifies the transition of ethics into 'politics', the art of right government, by the indispensability of tradition.[188] In comparison with it the modern enlightenment is abstract and revolutionary.

The concept of tradition, however, has become no less ambiguous than that of authority, and for the same reason, namely that it is the abstract counterpart to the principle of the enlightenment that determines the romantic understanding of tradition. Romanticism conceives tradition as the antithesis to the freedom of reason and regards it as something historically given, like nature. And whether the desire is to be revolutionary and oppose it or would like to preserve it, it is still seen as the abstract counterpart of free self-determination, since its validity does not require any reasons, but conditions us without our questioning it. Of course, the case of the romantic critique of the enlightenment is not an instance of the automatic dominance of tradition, in which what has been handed down is preserved unaffected by doubt and criticism. It is, rather, a particular critical attitude that again addresses itself to the truth of tradition and seeks to renew it, and which we may call 'traditionalism'.

It seems to me, however, that there is no such unconditional antithesis between tradition and reason. However problematical the conscious restoration of traditions or the conscious creation of new traditions may be, the romantic faith in the 'growth of tradition', before which all reason must remain silent, is just as prejudiced as and is fundamentally like the enlightenment. The fact is that tradition is constantly an element of freedom and of history itself. Even the most genuine and solid tradition does not persist by nature because of the inertia of what once existed. It needs to be affirmed, embraced, cultivated. It is, essentially, preservation, such as is active in all historical change. But preservation is an act of reason, though an inconspicuous one. For this reason, only what is new, or what is planned, appears as the result of reason. But this is an illusion. Even where life changes violently, as in ages of revolution, far more of the old is preserved in the supposed transformation of everything than anyone knows, and combines with the new to create a new value. At any rate, preservation is as much a freely-chosen action as revolution and renewal. That is why both the enlightenment's critique of tradition and its romantic rehabilitation are less than their true historical being.

These thoughts lead to the question of whether in the hermeneutic of the human sciences the element of tradition should not be given its full value. Research in the human sciences cannot regard itself as in an absolute antithesis to the attitude we take as historical beings to the past. In our continually manifested attitude to the past, the main feature is not, at any rate, a distancing and freeing of ourselves from what has been transmitted. Rather, we stand always within tradition, and this is no objectifying process, ie we do not conceive of what tradition says as something other, something alien. It is always part of us, a model or exemplar, a recognition of ourselves which our later historical judgment would hardly see as a kind of knowledge, but as the simplest preservation of tradition.

Hence in regard to the dominant epistemological methodologism we must ask if the rise of historical consciousness has really detached our scientific attitude entirely from this nature attitude to the past. Does understanding in the human sciences understand itself correctly when it relegates the whole of its own historicality to the position of prejudices from which we must free ourselves? Or does 'unprejudiced science' have more in common than it realises with that naive openness and reflection in which traditions live and the past is present?

At any rate understanding in the human sciences shares one fundamental condition with the continuity of traditions, namely, that it lets itself be addressed by tradition. Is it not true of the objects of its investigation—just as of the contents of tradition—that only then can its meaning be experienced? However much this meaning may always be a mediated one and proceed from a historical interest, that does not seem to have any relation to the present; even in the extreme case of 'objective' historical research, the proper realisation of the historical task is to determine anew the meaning of what is examined. But the meaning exists at the beginning of any such research as well as at the end: as the choice of the theme to be investigated, the awakening of the desire to investigate, as the gaining of the new problematic.

At the beginning of all historical hermeneutics, then, the abstract antithesis between tradition and historical research, between history and knowledge, must be discarded. The effect of a living tradition and the effect of historical study must constitute a unity, the analysis of which would reveal only a texture of reciprocal relationships.[189] Hence we would do well not to regard historical consciousness as something radically new—as it seems at first—but as a new element within that which has always made up the human relation to the past. In other words, we have to recognise the element of tradition in the historical relation and enquire into its hermeneutical productivity.

That there is an element of tradition active in the human sciences, despite the methodological nature of its procedures, an element that constitutes its real nature and is its distinguishing mark, is immediately clear if we examine the history of research and note the difference between the human and natural sciences with regard to their history. Of course no finite historical effort of man can completely erase the traces of this finiteness. The history of mathematics or of the natural sciences is also a part of the history of the human spirit and reflects its destinies. Nevertheless, it is not just historical naiveté when the natural scientist writes the history of his subject in terms of the present stage of knowledge. For him errors and wrong turnings are of historical interest only, because the progress of research is the self-evident criterion of his study. Thus it is of secondary interest only to see how advances in the natural sciences or in mathematics belong to the moment in history at which they took place. This interest does not affect the epistemic value of discoveries in the natural sciences or in mathematics.

There is, then, no need to deny that in the natural sciences elements of tradition can also be active, eg in that particular lines of research are preferred at particular places. But scientific research as such derives the law of its development not from these circumstances, but from the law of the object that it is investigating.

It is clear that the human sciences cannot be described adequately in terms of this idea of research and progress. Of course it is possible to write a history of the solution of a problem, eg the deciphering of barely legible inscriptions, in which the only interest was the ultimate reaching of the final result. Were this not so, it would not have been possible for the human sciences to have borrowed the methodology of the natural ones, as happened in the last century. But the analogy between research in the natural and in the human sciences is only a subordinate element of the work done in the human sciences.

This is seen in the fact that the great achievements in the human sciences hardly ever grow old. A modern reader can easily make allowances for the fact that, a hundred years ago, there was less knowledge available to a historian, who therefore made judgments that were incorrect in some details. On the whole, he would still rather read Droysen or Mommsen than the latest account of the particular subject from the pen of a historian living today. What is the criterion here? Obviously one cannot simply base the subject on a criterion by which we measure the value and importance of research. Rather, the object appears truly significant only in the light of him who is able to describe it to us properly. Thus it is certainly the subject that we are interested in, but the subject acquires its life only from the light in which it is presented to us. We accept the fact that the subject presents itself historically under different aspects at different times or from a different standpoint. We accept that these aspects do not simply cancel one another out as research proceeds, but are like mutually exclusive conditions that exist each by themselves and combine only in us. Our historical consciousness is always filled with a variety of voices in which the echo of the past is heard. It is present only in the multifariousness of such voices: this constitutes the nature of the tradition in which we want to share and have a part. Modern historical research itself is not only research, but the transmission of tradition. We do not see it only in terms of the law of progress and verified results; in it too we have, as it were, a new experience of history, whenever a new voice is heard in which the past echoes.

What is the basis of this? Obviously we cannot speak of an object of research in the human sciences in the sense appropriate to the natural sciences, where research penetrates more and more deeply into nature. Rather, in the human sciences the interest in tradition is motivated in a special way by the present and its interests. The theme and area of research are actually constituted by the motivation of the enquiry. Hence historical research is based on the historical movement in which life itself stands and cannot be understood teleologically in terms of the object into which it is enquiring. Such an object clearly does not exist at all in itself. Precisely this is what distinguishes the human sciences from the natural sciences. Whereas the object of the natural sciences can be described idealiter as what would be known in the perfect knowledge of nature, it is senseless to speak of a perfect knowledge of history, and for this reason it is not possible to speak of an object in itself towards which its research is directed.

(ii) The classical example

Of course it is a lot to ask of the self-understanding of the human sciences to detach itself, in the whole of its activity, from the model of the natural sciences and to regard the historical movement of whatever it is concerned with not simply as an impairment of its objectivity, but as something of positive value. There are, however, in the recent development of the human sciences points at which reflection could start that would really do justice to the problem. The naive methodologism of historical research no longer dominates the field alone. The progress of enquiry is no longer universally seen within the framework of the expansion or penetration into new fields or material, but instead as the attaining of a higher stage of reflection in the problem. Even where this happens, thinking is still teleological, in terms of the progress of research, in a way appropriate to the scientist. But a hermeneutical consciousness is gradually growing which is infusing the attitude of enquiry with a spirit of self-criticism; this is true, above all, of those human sciences that have the oldest tradition. Thus the study of classical antiquity, after it had worked over the whole extent of the available transmitted texts, continually applied itself again, with more subtle questions, to the old favourite objects of its study. This introduced something of an element of self-criticism, in that it reflected on what constituted the real merit of its favourite objects. The concept of the classical, that since Droysen's discovery of Hellenism had reduced historical thinking to a mere stylistic concept, now acquired a new scientific legitimacy.

It requires hermeneutical reflection of some sophistication to discover how it is possible for a normative concept such as that of the classical to acquire or regain its scientific legitimacy. For it follows from the self-understanding of historical consciousness that all normative significance of the past is ultimately dissolved by the now sovereign historical reason. Only at the beginnings of historicism, as for example in Winckelmann's epoch-making work, was the normative element still a real motive of historical research.

The concept of classical antiquity and of the classical, such as dominated pedagogical thought in particular, since the days of German classicism, had both a normative and an historical side. A particular stage in the historical development of man was thought to have produced a mature and perfect formation of man. This combination of a normative and an historical meaning in the concept goes back to Herder. But Hegel still preserved this combination, even though he gave it another emphasis in terms of the history of philosophy. Classical art retained its special excellence for him through being seen as the 'religion of art'. Since this is a form of the spirit that is past, it is exemplary only in a qualified sense. The fact that it is a past art testifies to the 'past' character of art in general. Hegel used this to justify systematically the historicisation of the concept of the classical and introduced that process of development that finally made the classical into a descriptive stylistic concept that describes the brief harmony of measure and fullness that comes between archaic rigidity and baroque dissolution. Since it became part of the aesthetic vocabulary of historical studies, the concept of the classical has preserved the reference to a normative content only in an unacknowledged way.

It was indicative of the start of historical self-criticism when classical studies started to examine themselves after the first world war in relation to a new humanism, and hesitantly again brought out the combination of the normative and the historical elements in 'the classical'.[190] It proved, however, impossible (although the attempt was made) to interpret the concept of the classical that arose in antiquity and was operative in the canonisation of certain writers as if it had itself expressed the unity of a stylistic ideal.[191] On the contrary, the ancient concept was wholly ambiguous. When today we use 'classic' as an historical stylistic concept that has a clear meaning by being set against what came before and after, this concept has become quite detached from the ancient one. The concept of the 'classical' now signifies a period of time, the period of an historical development, but does not signify any suprahistorical value.

In fact, however, the normative element in the concept of the classical has never completely disappeared. It is still the basis of the idea of liberal education. The classicist is, rightly, not satisfied with simply applying to his texts the historical stylistic concept that has developed through the history of the plastic arts. The question that suggests itself, whether Homer is also 'classical', shatters the historical stylistic category of the classical that is used in an analogy with the history of art—an instance of the fact that historical consciousness always includes more than it acknowledges of itself.

If we try to see what these implications mean, we might say that the classical is a truly historical category, precisely in that it is more than a concept of a period or an historical stylistic one and that yet it does not seek to be a suprahistorical concept of value. It does not refer to a quality that we assign to particular historical phenomena, but to a notable mode of 'being historical', the historical process of preservation that, through the constant proving of itself, sets before us something that is true. It is not at all the case, as the historical mode of thought would have us believe, that the value judgment through which something is dubbed classical was in fact destroyed by historical reflection and its criticism of all teleological constructions of the process of history. The value judgment that is implicit in the concept of the classical gains, rather, through this criticism a new, real legitimacy. The classical is what resists historical criticism because its historical dominion, the binding power of its validity that is preserved and handed down, precedes all historical reflection and continues through it.

To take the key example of the blanket concept of 'classical antiquity', it is, of course, unhistorical to devalue the hellenistic as an age of the decline and fall of classicism, and Droysen has rightly emphasised its importance and its place within the continuity of history for the birth and spread of christianity. But he would not have needed to undertake this historical apologetic if there had not always been a prejudice in favour of the classical and if the culture of humanism had not held on to 'classical antiquity' and preserved it within Western culture as the heritage of the past. The classical is fundamentally something quite different from a descriptive concept used by an objectivising historical consciousness. It is a historical reality to which historical consciousness belongs and is subordinate. What we call 'classical' is something retrieved from the vicissitudes of changing time and its changing taste. It can be approached directly, not through that, as it were, electric touch that sometimes characterises a contemporary work of art and in which the fulfilment of an apprehension of meaning that surpasses all conscious expectation is instantaneously experienced. Rather it is a consciousness of something enduring, of significance that cannot be lost and is independent of all the circumstances of time, in which we call something 'classical'—a kind of timeless present that is contemporaneous with every other age.

So the first thing about the concept of the classical (and this is wholly true of both the ancient and the modern use of the word) is the normative sense. But insofar as this norm is related retrospectively to a past entity that fulfilled and embodied it, it always contains a temporal quality that articulates it historically. So it was not surprising that, with the rise of historical reflection in Germany which took as its standard the classicism of Winckelmann, an historical concept of a time or a period detached itself from what was regarded as classical in Winckelmann's sense and denoted a quite specific stylistic ideal and, in a historically descriptive way, also a time or period that fulfilled this ideal. From the distance of the Epigones, who set up the criterion, it becomes clear that this stylistic ideal was fulfilled at a particular past moment of the world's history. Accordingly, the concept of the classical came to be used in modern thought to describe the whole of 'classical antiquity' when humanism proclaimed anew the exemplary nature of this antiquity. It was taking up an ancient usage, with some justification, for those ancient authors who were 'discovered' by humanism were the same ones that, for the later period of antiquity, comprised the canon of classics.

They were preserved in the history of Western culture precisely because they became canonical as the writers of the 'school'. But it is easy to see how the historical stylistic concept was able to follow this usage. For although it is a normative consciousness that is behind this concept, it is still a retrospective element. It is an awareness of decline and distance that gives birth to the classical norm. It is not by accident that the concept of the classical and of classical style emerges in late periods. The

Dialogus of Callimachus and Tacitus has been decisive in this connection.[192] But there is something else. Those authors who are regarded as classical are, as we know, always the representatives of particular literary genres. They were considered as the perfect fulfilment of the norm of that literary genre, an ideal that the retrospective view of literary criticism makes plain. If we now examine these norms of literary genres historically, ie if we consider their history, then the classical is seen as the concept of a stylistic phase, of a climax that articulates the history of the genre in terms of before and after. Insofar as the climactic points in the history of genres comes largely within the same brief period of time, the classical, within the totality of the historical development of classical antiquity, refers to such a period and thus also becomes a concept denoting a period; this concept fuses with the stylistic one.

As this kind of historical stylistic concept, the concept of the classical is capable of being extended to any 'development' to which an immanent telos gives unity. And in fact all cultures have high periods, in which a particular civilisation is marked by special achievements in all fields. Thus the general value concept of the classical becomes, via its particular historical fulfilment, again a general historical stylistic concept.

Although this is an understandable development, the historicisation of the concept also involves its uprooting, and that is why historical consciousness, when it started to engage in self-criticism, reinstated the normative element in the concept of the classical and the historical uniqueness of its fulfilment. Every 'new humanism' shares, with the first and oldest, the awareness of being directly committed to its model which, as something past, is unattainable and yet present. Thus there culminates in the classical a general character of historical being, preservation amid the ruins of time. It is the general nature of tradition that only that of the past which is preserved offers the possibility of historical knowledge. The classical, however, as Hegel says, is 'that which signifies itself and hence also interprets itself'.[193] But that means ultimately that the classical is what is preserved precisely because it signifies and interprets itself; ie that which speaks in such a way that it is not a statement about what is past, a mere testimony to something that still needs to be interpreted, but says something to the present as if it were said specially to it. What we call 'classical' does not first require the overcoming of historical distance, for in its own constant communication it does overcome it. The classical, then, is certainly 'timeless', but this timelessness is a mode of historical being.

Of course this does not exclude the fact that works regarded as classical present tasks of historical understanding to a developed historical consciousness that is aware of the historical distance. It is not the aim of the historical consciousness to use the classical model in the direct way of Palladio or Corneille, but to know it as an historical phenomenon that can be understood solely in terms of its own time. But this understanding will always be more than the mere historical construction of the past 'world' to which the work belongs. Our understanding will always include consciousness of our belonging to that world. And correlative to this is the fact that the work belongs to our world.

This is just what the word 'classical' means, that the duration of the power of a work to speak directly is fundamentally unlimited.[194] However much the concept of the classical expresses distance and unattainability and is part of cultural awareness, the phrase 'classical culture' still expresses something of the continuing validity of the classical. Cultural awareness manifests an element of ultimate community and sharing in the world out of which a classical work speaks.

This discussion of the concept of the classical does not lay claim to any independent significance, but serves only to evoke a general question, namely: Does this kind of historical fusion of the past with the present that characterises what is classical, ultimately lie at the base of the whole historical attitude as its effective substratum? Whereas romantic hermeneutics had taken human nature as the unhistorical substratum of its theory of understanding and hence had freed the connatural interpreter from all historical limitations, the self-criticism of historical consciousness leads finally to seeing historical movement not only in process, but also in understanding itself. Understanding is not to be thought of so much as an action of one's subjectivity, but as the placing of oneself within a process of tradition, in which past and present are constantly fused. This is what must be expressed in hermeneutical theory, which is far too dominated by the idea of a process, a method.

(iii) *The hermeneutic significance of temporal distance*

Let us consider first how hermeneutics sets about its work. What follows for understanding from the hermeneutic condition of belonging to a tradition? We remember here the hermeneutical rule that we must understand the whole in terms of the detail and the detail in terms of the whole. This principle stems from ancient rhetoric, and modern hermeneutics has taken it and applied it to the art of understanding. It is a circular relationship in both cases. The anticipation of meaning in which the whole is envisaged becomes explicit understanding in that the parts, that are determined by the whole, themselves also determine this whole.

We know this from the learning of ancient languages. We learn that we must 'construe' a sentence before we attempt to understand the individual parts of the sentence in their linguistic meaning. But this process of construing is itself already governed by an expectation of meaning that follows from the context of what has gone before. It is also necessary for this expected meaning to be adjusted if the text calls for it. This means, then, that the expectation changes and that the text acquires the unity of a meaning from another expected meaning. Thus the movement of understanding is constantly from the whole to the part and back to the whole. Our task is to extend in concentric circles the unity of the understood meaning. The harmony of all the details with the whole is the criterion of correct understanding. The failure to achieve this harmony means that understanding has failed.

Schleiermacher differentiated this hermeneutic circle of part and whole in both its objective and its subjective aspect. As the single word belongs within the total context of the sentence, so the single text belongs within the total context of a writer's work, and the latter within the whole of the particular literary genre or of literature. At the same time, however, the same text, as a manifestation of a creative moment, belongs to the whole of its author's inner life. Full understanding can take place only within this objective and subjective whole. Following this theory, Dilthey speaks then of 'structure' and of the 'centring in a mid-point', from out of which there follows the understanding of the whole. In this (as we have already said, pp 173 and 212f above) he is applying to the historical world what has always been a principle of all textual interpretation: namely, that a text must be understood in terms of itself.

The question is, however, whether this is an adequate account of the circular movement of understanding. Here we must go back to the result of our analysis of Schleiermacher's hermeneutics. We may set aside Schleiermacher's ideas on subjective interpretation. When we try to understand a text, we do not try to recapture the author's attitude of mind but, if this is the terminology we are to use, we try to recapture the perspective within which he has formed his views. But this means simply that we try to accept the objective validity of what he is saying. If we want to understand, we shall try to make his arguments even more cogent. This happens even in conversation, so how much truer is it of the understanding of what is written down that we are moving in a dimension of meaning that is intelligible in itself and as such offers no reason for going back to the subjectivity of the author. It is the task of hermeneutics to clarify this miracle of understanding, which is not a mysterious communion of souls, but a sharing of a common meaning.

But even the objective side of this circle, as Schleiermacher describes it, does not reach the heart of the matter. We have seen that the goal of all communication and understanding is agreement concerning the object. Hence the task of hermeneutics has always been to establish agreement where it had failed to come about or been disturbed in some way. The history of hermeneutics can offer a confirmation of this if, for example, we think of Augustine, who sought to relate the christian gospel to the old testament, or of early protestantism, which faced the same problem or, finally, the age of the enlightenment, when it is almost like a renunciation of agreement to seek to acquire 'full understanding' of a text only by means of historical interpretation. It is something qualitatively new when romanticism and Schleiermacher ground a universal historical consciousness by no longer seeing the binding form of tradition, from which they come and in which they stand, as the firm foundation of all hermeneutical endeavour.

One of the immediate predecessors of Schleiermacher, Friedrich Ast, still had a view of hermeneutical work that was markedly concerned with content, in that, for him, its purpose was to establish harmony between the world of classical antiquity and christianity, between a newly discovered genuine antiquity and the christian tradition. This is something new, in comparison with the enlightenment, in that this hermeneutics no longer accepts or rejects tradition in accord with the criterion of natural reason. But in its attempt to bring about a meaningful agreement between the two traditions to which it sees itself as belonging, this kind of hermeneutics is still pursuing the task of all preceding hermeneutics, namely to achieve in understanding agreement in content.

In going beyond the 'particularity' of this reconciliation of the ancient classical world and christianity, Schleiermacher and, following him, nineteenth-century science, conceive the task of hermeneutics in a way that is formally universal. They were able to harmonise it with the natural sciences' ideal of objectivity, but only by ignoring the concretion of historical consciousness in hermeneutical theory.

Heidegger's description and existential account of the hermeneutic circle constitutes in contrast a decisive turning-point. The hermeneutic theory of the nineteenth century often spoke of the circular structure of understanding, but always within the framework of a formal relation of the part and the whole or its subjective reflex, the intuitive anticipation of the whole and its subsequent articulation in the parts. According to this theory, the circular movement of understanding runs backwards and forwards along the text and disappears when it is perfectly understood. This view of understanding culminated logically in Schleiermacher's theory of the divinatory act, by means of which one places oneself entirely within the writer's mind and from there resolves all that is strange and unusual about the text. As against this approach, Heidegger describes the circle in such a way that the understanding of the text remains permanently determined by the anticipatory movement of fore-understanding. The circle of the whole and the part is not dissolved in perfect understanding but, on the contrary, is most fully realised.

The circle, then, is not formal in nature, it is neither subjective nor objective, but describes understanding as the interplay of the movement of tradition and the movement of the interpreter. The anticipation of meaning that governs our understanding of a text is not an act of subjectivity, but proceeds from the communality that binds us to the tradition. But this is contained in our relation to tradition, in the constant processs of education. Tradition is not simply a precondition into which we come, but we produce it ourselves, inasmuch as we understand, participate in the evolution of tradition and hence further determine it ourselves. Thus the circle of understanding is not a 'methodological' circle, but describes an ontological structural element in understanding.

The significance of this circle, which is fundamental to all understanding, has a further hermeneutic consequence which I may call the 'fore-conception of completion'. But this, too, is obviously a formal condition of all understanding. It states that only what really constitutes a unity of meaning is intelligible. So when we read a text we always follow this complete presupposition of completion, and only when it proves inadequate, ie the text is not intelligible, do we start to doubt the transmitted text and seek to discover in what way it can be remedied. The rules of such textual criticism can be left aside, for the important thing to note is that their proper application cannot be detached from the understanding of the textual content.

The anticipation of completion that guides all our understanding is, then, always specific in content. Not only is an immanent

unity of meaning guiding the reader assumed, but his understanding is likewise guided by the constant transcendent expectations of meaning which proceed from the relation to the truth
of what is being said. Just as the recipient of a letter understands
the news that it contains and first sees things with the eyes of the
person who wrote the letter, ie considers what he writes as true,
and is not trying to understand the alien meanings of the letter
writer, so we understand texts that have been handed down to us
on the basis of expectations of meaning which are drawn from
our own anterior relation to the subject. And just as we believe
the news reported by a correspondent because he was present or
is better informed, we are fundamentally open to the possibility
that the writer of a transmitted text is better informed than we
are, with our previously formed meaning. It is only when the
attempt to accept what he has said as true fails that we try
to 'understand' the text, psychologically or historically, as
another's meaning.[195] The anticipation of completion, then, contains not only this formal element that a text should fully express
its meaning, but also that what it says should be the whole truth.

We see here again that understanding means, primarily, to
understand the content of what is said, and only secondarily to
isolate and understand another's meaning as such. Hence the
first of all hermeneutic requirements remains one's own fore-
understanding, which proceeds from being concerned with the
same subject. It is this that determines what unified meaning can
be realised and hence the application of the anticipation of
completion.[196]

Thus the meaning of the connection with tradition, ie the element of tradition in our historical, hermeneutical attitude, is
fulfilled in the fact that we share fundamental prejudices with
tradition. Hermeneutics must start from the position that a person seeking to understand something has a relation to the object
that comes into language in the transmitted text and has, or
acquires, a connection with the tradition out of which the text
speaks. On the other hand, hermeneutical consciousness is
aware that it cannot be connected with this object in some self
evident, questioned way, as is the case with the unbroken
stream of a tradition. There is a polarity of familiarity and
strangeness on which hermeneutic work is based: only that this
polarity is not to be seen, psychologically, with Schleiermacher,
as the tension that conceals the mystery of individuality, but truly
hermeneutically, ie in regard to what has been said: the language
in which the text addresses us, the story that it tells us. Here too
there is a tension. The place between strangeness and familiarity

that a transmitted text has for us is that intermediate place between being an historically intended separate object and being part of a tradition. The true home of hermeneutics is in this intermediate area.

It follows from this intermediate position in which hermeneutics operates that its work is not to develop a procedure of understanding, but to clarify the conditions in which understanding takes place. But these conditions are not of the nature of a 'procedure' or a method, which the interpreter must of himself bring to bear on the text, but rather they must be given. The prejudices and fore-meanings in the mind of the interpreter are not at his free disposal. He is not able to separate in advance the productive prejudices that make understanding possible from the prejudices that hinder understanding and lead to misunderstandings.

This separation, rather, must take place in the understanding itself, and hence hermeneutics must ask how it happens. But this means it must place in the foreground what has remained entirely peripheral in previous hermeneutics: temporal distance and its significance for understanding.

This point can be clarified by comparing it with the hermeneutic-theory of romanticism. We shall recall that the latter conceived understanding as the reproduction of an original production. Hence it was possible to say that one should be able to understand an author better than he understood himself. We examined the origin of this statement and its connection with the aesthetics of genius, but must now come back to it, as our present enquiry lends it a new importance.

That subsequent understanding is superior to the original production and hence can be described as superior understanding does not depend so much on the conscious realisation that places him on the same level as the author (as Schleiermacher said), but denotes rather an inevitable difference between the interpreter and the author that is created by the historical distance between them. Every age has to understand a transmitted text in its own way, for the text is part of the whole of the tradition in which the age takes an objective interest and in which it seeks to understand itself. The real meaning of a text, as it speaks to the interpreter, does not depend on the contingencies of the author and whom he originally wrote for. It certainly is not identical with them, for it is always partly determined also by the historical situation of the interpreter and hence by the totality of the objective course of history. A writer like Chladenius,[197] who does not yet see understanding in terms of history, is saying the same thing in a naive, ingenuous way when he says that an author does not need to know the real meaning of what he has written, and hence the interpreter can, and must, often understand more than he. But this is of fundamental importance. Not occasionally only, but always, the meaning of a text goes beyond its author. That is why understanding is not merely a reproductive, but always a productive attitude as well. Perhaps it is not correct to refer to this productive element in understanding as 'superior understanding'. For this phrase is, as we have shown, the application of a principle of criticism from the age of the enlightenment on the basis of the aesthetics of genius. Understanding is not, in fact, superior understanding, neither in the sense of superior knowledge of the subject because of clearer ideas, nor in the sense of fundamental superiority that the conscious has over the unconscious nature of creation. It is enough to say that we understand in a different way, if we understand at all.

This concept of understanding undoubtedly breaks right out of the circle drawn by romantic hermeneutics. Because what we are now concerned with is not individuality and what it thinks, but the objective truth of what is said, a text is not understood as a mere expression of life, but taken seriously in its claim to truth. That this is what is meant by 'understanding' was once self-evident (we need only recall Chladenius).

But this dimension of the hermeneutical problem was discredited by historical consciousness and the psychological turn that Schleiermacher gave to hermeneutics, and could only be regained when the impasses of historicism appeared and led finally to the new development inspired chiefly, in my opinion, by Heidegger. For the hermeneutic importance of temporal distance could be understood only as a result of the ontological direction that Heidegger gave to understanding as an 'existential' and of his temporal interpretation of the mode of being of there-being.

Time is no longer primarily a gulf to be bridged, because it separates, but it is actually the supportive ground of process in which the present is rooted. Hence temporal distance is not something that must be overcome. This was, rather, the naive assumption of historicism, namely that we must set ourselves within the spirit of the age, and think with its ideas and its thoughts, not with our own, and thus advance towards historical objectivity. In fact the important thing is to recognise the distance in time as a positive and productive possibility of understanding. It is not a yawning abyss, but is filled with the continuity of custom and tradition, in the light of which all that is handed down presents itself to us. Here it is not too much to speak of a genuine productivity of process. Everyone knows that curious impotence of our judgment where the distance in time has not given us sure criteria. Thus the judgment of contemporary works of art is desperately uncertain for the scientific consciousness. Obviously we approach such creations with the prejudices we are not in control of, presuppositions that have too great an influence over us for us to know about them; these can give to contemporary creations an extra resonance that does not correspond to their true content and their true significance. Only when all their relations to the present time have faded away can their real nature appear, so that the understanding of what is said in them can claim to be authoritative and universal.

It is this experience that has led to the idea in historical studies that objective knowledge can be arrived at only when there has been a certain historical distance. It is true that what a thing has to say, its intrinsic content, first appears only after it is divorced from the fleeting circumstances of its actuality. The positive conditions of historical understanding include the self-contained quality of an historical event, which allows it to appear as a whole, and its distance from the opinions concerning its import with which the present is filled. The implicit prerequisite of the historical method, then, is that the permanent significance of something can first be known objectively only when it belongs within a self-contained context. In other words, when it is dead enough to have only historical interest. Only then does it seem possible to exclude the subjective involvement of the observer. This is, in fact, a paradox, the epistemological counterpart to the old moral problem of whether anyone can be called happy before his death. Just as Aristotle showed what a sharpening of the powers of human judgment this kind of problem can bring about,[198] so hermeneutical reflection cannot fail to find here a sharpening of the methodological self-consciousness of science. It is true that certain hermeneutic requirements are automatically fulfilled when a historical context has become of no more than historical interest. Certain sources of error are automatically excluded. But it is questionable whether this is the end of the hermeneutical problem. Temporal distance has obviously another meaning than that of the quenching of our interest in the object. It lets the true meaning of the object emerge fully. But the discovery of the true meaning of a text or a work of art is never finished; it is in fact an infinite process. Not only are fresh sources of error constantly excluded, so that the true meaning has filtered out of it all kinds of things that obscure it, but there emerge continually new sources of understanding, which reveal unsuspected elements of meaning. The temporal distance which performs the filtering process is not a closed dimension, but is itself undergoing constant movement and extension. And with the negative side of the filtering process brought about by temporal distance there is also the positive side, namely the value it has for understanding. It not only lets those prejudices that are of a particular and limited nature die away, but causes those that bring about genuine understanding to emerge clearly as such.

It is only this temporal distance that can solve the really critical question of hermeneutics, namely of distinguishing the true prejudices, by which we understand, from the false ones by which we misunderstand. Hence the hermeneutically trained mind will also include historical consciousness. It will make conscious the prejudices governing our own understanding, so that the text, as another's meaning, can be isolated and valued on its own. The isolation of a prejudice clearly requires the suspension of its validity for us. For so long as our mind is influenced by a prejudice, we do not know and consider it as a judgment. How then are we able to isolate it? It is impossible to make ourselves aware of it while it is constantly operating unnoticed, but only when it is, so to speak, stimulated. The encounter with a text from the past can provide this stimulus. For what leads to understanding must be something that has already asserted itself in its own separate validity. Understanding begins, as we have already said above,[199] when something addresses us. This is the primary hermeneutical condition. We now know what this requires, namely the fundamental suspension of our own prejudices. But all suspension of judgments and hence, a fortiori, of prejudices, has logically the structure of a question.

The essence of the question is the opening up, and keeping open, of possibilities. If a prejudice becomes questionable, in view of what another or a text says to us, this does not mean that it is simply set aside and the other writing or the other person accepted as valid in its place. It shows, rather, the naiveté of historical objectivism to accept this disregarding of ourselves as what actually happens. In fact our own prejudice is properly brought into play through its being at risk. Only through its being given full play is it able to experience the other's claim to truth and make it possible for he himself to have full play. (In this passage the author plays on the German expressions ins Spiel bringen, auf dem Spiele stehen and sich ausspielen).

The naiveté of so called historicism consists in the fact that it does not undertake this reflection, and in trusting to its own methodological approach forgets its own historicality. We must here appeal from a badly understood historical thinking to one that can better perform the task of understanding. True historical thinking must take account of its own historicality. Only then will it not chase the phantom of an historical object which is the object of progressive research, but learn to see in the object the counterpart of itself and hence understand both. The true historical object is not an object at all, but the unity of the one and the other, a relationship in which exist both the reality of history and the reality of historical understanding. A proper hermeneutics would have to demonstrate the effectivity of history within understanding itself. I shall refer to this as 'effective-history'. Understanding is, essentially, an effective-historical relation.

(iv) The principle of effective-history

The fact that the interest of the historian is directed not only towards the historical phenomenon and the work that has been handed down but also, secondarily, towards their effect in history (which also includes the history of research) is regarded in general as a mere supplement to the historical problematic that, from Hermann Grimm's *Raffael* to Gundolf and beyond, has given rise to many valuable insights. To this extent, effective-history is not new. But that this kind of effective-historical approach be required every time that a work of art or an element of the tradition is led from the twilight region between tradition and history to be seen clearly and openly in terms of its own meaning—this is a new demand (addressed not to research, but to methodological consciousness itself) that proceeds inevitably from the analysis of historical consciousness.

It is not, of course, a hermeneutical requirement in the sense of the traditional concept of hermeneutics. I am not saying that historical enquiry should develop this effective-historical problematic that would be something separate from that which is concerned directly with the understanding of the work. The requirement is of a more theoretical kind. Historical consciousness must become aware that in the apparent immediacy with which it approaches a work of art or a tradition, there is also contained, albeit unrecognised and hence not allowed for, this other element. If we are trying to understand a historical phenomenon from the historical distance that is characteristic of our hermeneutical situation, we are always subject to the effects of effective-history. It determines in advance both what seems to us worth enquiring about and what will appear as an object of investigation, and we more or less forget half of what is really there—in fact, we miss the whole truth of the phenomenon when we take its immediate appearance as the whole truth.

In our understanding, which we imagine is so straightforward, we find that, by following the criterion of intelligibility, the other presents himself so much in terms of our own selves that there is no longer a question of self and other. Historical objectivism, in appealing to its critical method, conceals the involvement of the historical consciousness itself in effective-history. By the method of its foundational criticism it does away with the arbitrariness of cosy re-creations of the past, but it preserves its good conscience by failing to recognise those presuppositions —certainly not arbitrary, but still fundamental—that govern its own approach to understanding, and hence falls short of reaching that truth which, despite the finite nature of our understanding, could be reached. In this historical objectivism resembles statistics, which are such an excellent means of propaganda because they let facts speak and hence simulate an objectivity that in reality depends on the legitimacy of the questions asked.

We are not saying, then, that effective-history must be developed as a new independent discipline ancillary to the human sciences, but that we should learn to understand ourselves better and recognise that in all understanding, whether we are expressly aware of it or not, the power of this effective-history is at work. When a naive faith in scientific method ignores its existence, there can be an actual deformation of knowledge. We know it from the history of science as the irrefutable proof of something that is obviously false. But looking at the whole situation, we see that the power of effective-history does not depend on its being recognised. This, precisely, is the power of history over finite human consciousness, namely that it prevails even where faith in method leads one to deny one's own historicality. The demand that we should become conscious of this effective-history is pressing because it is necessary for scientific consciousness. But this does not mean that it can be fulfilled in an absolute way. That we should become completely aware of effective-history is just as hybrid a statement as when Hegel speaks of absolute knowledge, in which history would become completely transparent to itself and hence be raised to the level of a concept. Rather, effective historical consciousness is an element in the act of understanding itself and, as we shall see, is already operative in the choice of the right question to ask.

Effective-historical consciousness is primarily consciousness of the hermeneutical situation. To acquire an awareness of a situation is, however, always a task of particular difficulty. The very idea of a situation means that we are not standing outside it and hence are unable to have any objective knowledge of it.[200] We are always within the situation, and to throw light on it is a task that is never entirely completed. This is true also of the hermeneutic situation, ie the situation in which we find ourselves with regard to the tradition that we are trying to understand. The illumination of this situation—effective-historical reflection—can never be completely achieved, but this is not due to a lack in the reflection, but lies in the essence of the historical being which is ours. To exist historically means that knowledge of oneself can never be complete. All self-knowledge proceeds from what is historically pre-given, what we call, with Hegel, 'substance', because it is the basis of all subjective meaning and attitude and hence both prescribes and limits every possibility of understanding any tradition whatsoever in terms of its unique historical quality. This almost defines the aim of philosophical hermeneutics: its task is to move back along the path of Hegel's phenomenology of mind until we discover in all that is subjective the substantiality that determines it.

Every finite present has its limitations. We define the concept of 'situation' by saying that it represents a standpoint that limits the possibility of vision. Hence an essential part of the concept of situation is the concept of 'horizon'. The horizon is the range of vision that includes everything that can be seen from a particular vantage point. Applying this to the thinking mind, we speak of narrowness of horizon, of the possible expansion of horizon, of the opening up of new horizons etc. The word has been used in philosophy since Nietzsche and Husserl[201] to characterise the way in which thought is tied to its finite determination, and the nature of the law of the expansion of the range of vision. A person who has no horizon is a man who does not see far enough and hence overvalues what is nearest to him. Contrariwise, to have an horizon means not to be limited to what is nearest, but to be able to see beyond it. A person who has an horizon knows the relative significance of everything within this horizon, as near or far, great or small. Similarly, the working out of the hermeneutical situation means the achievement of the right horizon of enquiry for the questions evoked by the encounter with tradition.

In the sphere of historical understanding we also like to speak of horizons, especially when referring to the claim of historical consciousness to see the past in terms of its own being, not in terms of our contemporary criteria and prejudices, but within its own historical horizon. The task of historical understanding also involves acquiring the particular historical horizon, so that what we are seeking to understand can be seen in its true dimensions. If we fail to place ourselves in this way within the historical horizon out of which tradition speaks, we shall misunderstand the significance of what it has to say to us. To this extent it seems a legitimate hermeneutical requirement to place ourselves in the other situation in order to understand it. We may ask, however, whether this does not mean that we are failing in the understanding that is asked of us. The same is true of a conversation that we have with someone simply in order to get to know him, ie to discover his standpoint and his horizon. This is not a true conversation, in the sense that we are not seeking agreement concerning an object, but the specific contents of the conversation are only a means to get to know the horizon of the other person. Examples are oral examinations, or some kinds of conversation between doctor and patient. The historical consciousness is clearly doing something similar when it places itself within the situation of the past and hence is able to acquire the right historical horizon. Just as in a conversation, when we have discovered the standpoint and horizon of the other person, his ideas become intelligible, without our necessarily having to agree with him, the person who thinks historically comes to understand the meaning of what has been handed down, without necessarily agreeing with it, or seeing himself in it.

In both cases, in our understanding we have as it were, withdrawn from the situation of trying to reach agreement. He himself cannot be reached. By including from the beginning the other person's standpoint in what he is saying to us, we are making our own standpoint safely unattainable. We have seen, in considering the origin of historical thinking, that in fact it makes this ambiguous transition from means to ends, ie it makes an end of what is only a means. The text that is understood historically is forced to abandon its claim that it is uttering something true. We think we understand when we see the past from a historical standpoint, ie place ourselves in the historical situation and seek to reconstruct the historical horizon. In fact, however, we have given up the claim to find, in the past, any truth valid and intelligible for ourselves. Thus this acknowledgement of the otherness of the other, which makes him the object of objective knowledge, involves the fundamental suspension of his claim to truth.

The question is, however, whether this description really corresponds to the hermeneutical phenomenon. Are there, then, two different horizons here, the horizon in which the person seeking to understand lives, and the particular historical horizon within which he places himself? Is it a correct description of the art of historical understanding to say that we are learning to place ourselves within alien horizons? Are there such things as closed horizons, in this sense? We recall Nietzsche's complaint against historicism that it destroyed the horizon bounded by myth in which alone a culture is able to live.[202] Is the horizon of one's own present time ever closed in this way, and can a historical situation be imagined that has this kind of closed horizon?

Or is this a romantic reflection, a kind of Robinson Crusoe dream of the historical enlightenment, the fiction of an unattainable island, as artificial as Crusoe himself for the alleged primary phenomenon of the solus ipse? Just as the individual is never simply an individual, because he is always involved with others, so too the closed horizon that is supposed to enclose a culture is an abstraction. The historical movement of human life consists in the fact that it is never utterly bound to any one standpoint, and hence can never have a truly closed horizon. The horizon is, rather, something into which we move and that moves with us. Horizons change for a person who is moving. Thus the horizon of the past, out of which all human life lives and which exists in the form of tradition, is always in motion. It is not historical consciousness that first sets the surrounding horizon in motion. But in it this motion becomes aware of itself.

When our historical consciousness places itself within historical horizons, this does not entail passing into alien worlds unconnected in any way with our own, but together they constitute the one great horizon that moves from within and, beyond the frontiers of the present, embraces the historical depths of our self-consciousness. It is, in fact, a single horizon that embraces everything contained in historical consciousness. Our own past, and that other past towards which our historical consciousness is directed, help to shape this moving horizon out of which human life always lives, and which determines it as tradition.

Understanding of the past, then, undoubtedly requires an historical horizon. But it is not the case that we acquire this horizon by placing ourselves within a historical situation. Rather, we must always already have a horizon in order to be able to place ourselves within a situation. For what do we mean by 'placing ourselves' in a situation? Certainly not just disregarding ourselves. This is necessary, of course, in that we must imagine the other situation. But into this other situation we must also bring ourselves. Only this fulfils the meaning of 'placing ourselves'. If we place ourselves in the situation of someone else, for example, then we shall understand him, ie become aware of the otherness, the indissoluble individuality of the other person, by placing ourselves in his position.

This placing of ourselves is not the empathy of one individual for another, nor is it the application to another person of our own criteria, but it always involves the attainment of a higher universality that overcomes, not only our own particularity, but also that of the other. The concept of the 'horizon' suggests itself because it expresses the wide, superior vision that the person who is seeking to understand must have. To acquire a horizon means that one learns to look beyond what is close at hand—not in order to look away from it, but to see it better within a larger whole and in truer proportion. It is not a correct description of historical consciousness to speak, with Nietzsche, of the many changing horizons into which it teaches us to place ourselves. If we disregard ourselves in this way, we have no historical horizon. Nietzsche's view that historical study is deleterious to life is not directed, in fact, against historical consciousness as such, but against the self-alienation that it undergoes when it regards the method of modern historical science as its own true nature. We have already pointed out that a truly historical consciousness always sees its own present in such a way that it sees itself, as it sees the historically other, within the right circumstances. It requires a special effort to acquire an historical horizon. We are always affected, in hope and fear, by what is nearest to us, and hence approach, under its influence, the testimony of the past. Hence it is constantly necessary to inhibit the overhasty assimilation of the past to our own expectations of meaning. Only then will we be able to listen to the past in a way that enables it to make its own meaning heard.

We have shown above that this is a process of distinguishing. Let us consider what this idea of distinguishing involves. It is always reciprocal. Whatever is being distinguished must be distinguished from something which, in turn, must be distinguished from it. Thus all distinguishing also makes visible that from which something is distinguished. We have described this above as the operation of prejudices. We started by saying that a hermeneutical situation is determined by the prejudices that we bring with us. They constitute, then, the horizon of a particular present, for they represent that beyond which it is impossible to see. But now it is important to avoid the error of thinking that it is a fixed set of opinions and evaluations that determine and limit the horizon of the present, and that the otherness of the past can be distinguished from it as from a fixed ground.

In fact the horizon of the present is being continually formed, in that we have continually to test all our prejudices. An important part of this testing is the encounter with the past and the understanding of the tradition from which we come. Hence the horizon of the present cannot be formed without the past. There is no more an isolated horizon of the present than there are historical horizons. Understanding, rather, is always the fusion of these horizons which we imagine to exist by themselves. We know the power of this kind of fusion chiefly from earlier times and their naive attitude to themselves and their origin. In a tradition this process of fusion is continually going on, for there old and new continually grow together to make something of living value, without either being explicitly distinguished from the other.

If, however, there is no such thing as these horizons that are distinguished from one another, why do we speak of the fusion of horizons and not simply of the formation of the one horizon, whose bounds are set in the depths of tradition? To ask the question means that we are recognising the special nature of the situation in which understanding becomes a scientific task, and that it is necessary to work out this situation as a hermeneutical situation. Every encounter with tradition that takes place within historical consciousness involves the experience of the tension between the text and the present. The hermeneutic task consists in not covering up this tension by attempting a naive assimilation but consciously bringing it out. This is why it is part of the hermeneutic approach to project an historical horizon that is different from the horizon of the present. Historical consciousness is aware of its own otherness and hence distinguishes the horizon of tradition from its own. On the other hand, it is itself, as we are trying to show, only something laid over a continuing tradition, and hence it immediately recombines what it has distinguished in order, in the unity of the historical horizon that it thus acquires, to become again one with itself.

The projecting of the historical horizon, then, is only a phase in the process of understanding, and does not become solidified into the self-alienation of a past consciousness, but is overtaken by our own present horizon of understanding. In the process of understanding there takes place a real fusing of horizons, which means that as the historical horizon is projected, it is simultaneously removed. We described the conscious act of this fusion as the task of the effective-historical consciousness. Although this task had been obscured by aesthetic historical positivism in the train of romantic hermeneutics, it is, in fact, the central problem of hermeneutics. It is the problem of application that exists in all understanding.

2 THE REDISCOVERY OF THE FUNDAMENTAL HERMENEUTIC PROBLEM

(A) THE HERMENEUTIC PROBLEM OF APPLICATION

In the early tradition of hermeneutics, which the historical self-consciousness of post-romantic scientific method completely forgot, this problem had its systematic place. Hermeneutics was divided up in the following way: a distinction was made between subtilitas intelligendi (understanding), and subtilitas explicandi (interpretation). Pietism added a third element, subtilitas applicandi (application), as in J. J. Rambach.[203] The act of understanding was regarded as made up of these three elements. It is notable that all three are called subtilitas, ie they are not considered so much methods that we have at our disposal as a talent that requires particular finesse of mind.[204]

As we saw, the hermeneutic problem acquired its systematic importance because the romantics recognised the inner unity of intelligere and explicare. Interpretation is not an occasional additional act subsequent to understanding, but rather understanding is always an interpretation, and hence interpretation is the explicit form of understanding. In accordance with this insight, interpretative language and concepts are also an inner structural element of understanding. This moves the whole problem of language from its peripheral and incidental position into the centre of philosophy. This is a point we shall be coming back to.

The inner fusion of understanding and interpretation led to the third element in the hermeneutical problem, application, becoming wholly cut off from any connection with hermeneutics. The edifying application of scripture, for example, in christian proclamation and preaching now seemed quite a different thing from the historical and theological understanding of it. In the course of our reflections we have come to see that understanding always involves something like the application of the text to be understood to the present situation of the interpreter. Thus we are forced to go, as it were, one stage beyond romantic hermeneutics, by regarding not only understanding and interpretation, but also application as comprising one unified process. This is not to return to the traditional distinction of the three separate 'subtleties' of which pietism spoke. For, on the contrary, we consider application to be as integral a part of the hermeneutical act as are understanding and interpretation.

Because of the stage of hermeneutical discussion reached so far we are emphasising the fundamental importance of this point. We can appeal first to the forgotten history of hermeneutics. Formerly it was considered obvious that the task of hermeneutics was to adapt the meaning of a text to the concrete situation to which it was speaking. The interpreter of the divine will, who is able to interpret the language of the oracle is the original model for this. But it is still the case, even today, that the task of an interpreter is not simply to reproduce what is said by one of the partners in the discussion he is translating, but to express what is said in the way that seems necessary to him considering the real situation of the dialogue, which only he knows, since only he knows both languages being used in the discussion.

Similarly, the history of hermeneutics teaches us that apart from literary hermeneutics, there is also a theological and a legal hermeneutics; all three together make up the full concept of hermeneutics. It is only since the emergence of historical consciousness in the eighteenth and nineteenth centuries that literary hermeneutics and historical studies became detached from the other hermeneutical disciplines and established themselves as the methodology for research in the human sciences.

The original close connection between these forms of hermeneutics depended on the recognition of application as an integral element of all understanding. In both legal and theological hermeneutics there is the essential tension between the text set down—of the law or of the proclamation—on the one hand and, on the other, the sense arrived at by its application in the particular moment of interpretation, either in judgment or in preaching. A law is not there to be understood historically, but to be made concretely valid through being interpreted. Similarly, a religious proclamation is not there to be understood as a merely historical document, but to be taken in a way in which it exercises its saving effect. This includes the fact that the text, whether law or gospel, if it is to be understood properly, ie according to the claim it makes, must be understood at every moment, in every particular situation, in a new and different way. Understanding here is always application.

We started from the point that understanding, as it occurs in the human sciences, is essentially historical, ie that in them a text is understood only if it is understood in a different way every time. This was precisely the task of an historical hermeneutics, to consider the tension that exists between the identity of the common object and the changing situation in which it must be understood. We have already said that the historical movement of understanding, that romantic hermeneutics pushed to the periphery, is the true centre of hermeneutical enquiry appropriate to historical consciousness. Our thoughts on the significance of tradition in historical consciousness took off from Heidegger's analysis of the hermeneutics of facticity and sought to apply it to a hermeneutics of the human sciences. We showed that understanding is not so much a method by means of which the enquiring mind approaches some selected object and turns it into objective knowledge, as something of which a prior condition is its being situated within a process of tradition. Understanding itself proved to be an event, and the task of hermeneutics, seen philosophically, consists in asking what kind of understanding, what kind of science it is, that is itself changed by historical change.

We are quite aware that we are asking something unusual of the self-understanding of modern science. Our whole thinking was directed towards making this demand easier by showing that it arises as the result of the convergence of a large number of problems. In fact, hermeneutical theory hitherto falls apart into distinctions that it cannot itself maintain. This is seen clearly when the attempt is made to construct a general theory of interpretation. When a distinction is made between cognitive, normative and reproductive interpretation, as in Betti's general theory of interpretation,[205] which is based on a remarkable knowledge and survey of the subject, there are difficulties in the ordering of phenomena according to this division. This is true primarily of interpretation as practised in science. If we take theological interpretation with legal interpretation and assign to them a normative function, then we must remember Schleiermacher who, on the contrary, closely connected theological interpretation with general interpretation, which was for him the literary historical one. In fact, the split between the cognitive and the normative function runs right through theological hermeneutics and can hardly be overcome by distinguishing scientific knowledge from the subsequent edifying application. The split runs through legal interpretation also, in that the recognition of the meaning of a legal text and its application in a particular legal instance are not two separate actions, but one process.

But even that interpretation which seems furthest from the

kinds we have been considering, namely reproductive interpretation, in which music and drama are expressed—and they acquire their real existence only when they are performed[206]—is scarcely an independent mode of interpretation. In it also there is a split between the cognitive and the normative function. No one is able to stage a play, read a poem or perform a piece of music without understanding the original meaning of the text and presenting it in his reproduction and interpretation. But, similarly, no one will be able to carry out this reproductive interpretation without taking account, in the translation of the text into appearance, of that other normative element that limits the demand for a stylistically correct reproduction through the stylistic values of one's own day. When we consider that the translation of texts in a foreign language, their poetic reproduction, or even the correct reading aloud of texts, involves the same explanatory achievement as literary interpretation, so that the two things become as one, then we cannot avoid the conclusion that the suggested distinction between cognitive, normative and reproductive interpretation has no fundamental validity, but all three constitute the one phenomenon.

If this is the case, then we have the task of redefining the hermeneutics of the human sciences in terms of legal and theological hermeneutics. For this we must remember the insight gained from our investigation into romantic hermeneutics, namely that both it and its culmination in psychological interpretation, ie the deciphering and explaining of the individuality of the other, treats the problem of understanding in a way that is far too one sided. Our thinking so far prevents us from dividing the hermeneutic problem in terms of the subjectivity of the interpreter and the objectivity of the meaning to be understood. This would be to start from a false antithesis that cannot be done away with even by recognising the dialectic of subjective and objective. To distinguish between a normative function and a cognitive one is to separate what clearly belong together. The meaning of a law that emerges in its normative application is fundamentally no different from the meaning reached in textual interpretation. It is quite mistaken to base the possibility of understanding a text on the postulate of 'connaturality' that supposedly unites the creator and the interpreter of a work. If this were really the case, then the human sciences would be in a bad way. The miracle of understanding, rather, consists in the fact that no connaturality is necessary to recognise what is really significant and fundamentally meaningful in tradition. We are able to open ourselves to the superior claim the text makes and respond to what it has to tell us. Hermeneutics in the sphere of literary criticism and the historical sciences is not 'knowledge as domination',[207] ie an appropriation as a 'taking possession of', but rather a subordination to the text's claim to dominate our minds. Of this, however, legal and theological hermeneutics are the true model. To interpret the law's will or the promises of God is clearly not a form of domination, but of service. They are interpretations—which includes application—in the service of what is considered valid. Our thesis is that historical hermeneutics also has a task of application to perform, because it too serves the validity of meaning, in that it explicitly and consciously bridges the gap in time that separates the interpreter from the text and overcomes the alienation of meaning that the text has undergone.

(B) THE HERMENEUTIC RELEVANCE OF ARISTOTLE

At this point there emerges a problem that we have touched on several times. If the heart of the hermeneutical problem is that the same tradition must always be understood in a different way, the problem, logically speaking, is that of the relationship between the universal and the particular. Understanding is, then, a particular case of the application of something universal to a particular situation. This makes Aristotelian ethics of special importance for us—we considered it briefly in the introductory remarks on the theory of the human sciences.[208] It is true that Aristotle is not concerned with the hermeneutical problem and certainly not with its historical dimension, but with the right estimation of the role that reason has to play in moral action. But precisely what is of interest to us here is that he is concerned with reason and with knowledge, not detached from a being that is becoming, but determined by it and determinative of it. By placing limits on the intellectualism of Socrates and Plato in his enquiry into the good, Aristotle became the founder of ethics as a discipline independent of metaphysics. Criticising the Platonic idea of the good as an empty generality, he asks instead the question of the humanly good, what is good in terms of human action.[209] His critique demonstrates that the equation of virtue and knowledge, arete and logos, which is the basis of Plato's and Socrates' theory of virtue, is an exaggeration. Aristotle restores the balance by showing that the basis of moral knowledge in man is orexis, striving, and its development into a fixed attitude (hexis). The very name 'ethics' indicates that Aristotle bases arete on practice and 'ethos'.

Human civilisation differs essentially from nature in that it is not simply a place in which capacities and powers work themselves out, but man becomes what he is through what he does and how he behaves, ie he behaves in a certain way because of what he has become. Thus Aristotle sees ethos as differing from physis in that it is a sphere in which the laws of nature do not operate, yet not a sphere of lawlessness, but of human institutions and human attitudes that can be changed and have the quality of rules only to a limited degree.

The question is whether there can be any such thing as philosophical knowledge of the moral being of man and what role knowledge plays in the moral being of man. If man always encounters the good in the specific form of the particular practical situation in which he finds himself, the task of moral knowledge is to see in the concrete situation what is asked of it or, to put it another way, the person acting must see the concrete situation in the light of what is asked of him in general. But —negatively put—this means that knowledge which cannot be applied to the concrete situation remains meaningless and even risks obscuring the demands that the situation makes. This state of affairs, which represents the nature of moral reflection, not only makes philosophical ethics a methodologically difficult problem, but also gives the problem of method a moral relevance. In contrast with the theory of the good based on Plato's doctrine of ideas, Aristotle emphasises that it is impossible to have in ethics the kind of extreme exactitude that the mathematician can achieve. Indeed, it would be an error to demand this kind of exactitude. What needs to be done is simply to make an outline and by means of this sketch give some help to moral consciousness.[210] But how such help can be possible is already a moral problem. For obviously it is among the characteristics of the moral phenomenon that the person acting must himself know and decide and cannot let anything take this responsibility from him. Thus it is essential that philosophical ethics have the right approach, so that it does not usurp the place of moral consciousness and yet does not seek either a purely theoretical and 'historical' knowledge but, by outlining phenomena, helps moral consciousness to attain clarity concerning itself. This asks a lot of the person who is to receive this help, namely the person listening to Aristotle's lecture. He must be mature enough not to ask of his instruction anything other than it can and may give. To put it positively, he must himself already have developed through education and practice an attitude in himself that he is constantly concerned to preserve in the actual situations of his life and to prove it through right behaviour.[211]

As we see, the problem of method is entirely determined by the object—a general Aristotelian principle—and the important thing for us is to examine more closely the curious relation between moral being and moral consciousness that Aristotle sets out in his *Ethics.* Aristotle remains Socratic in that he holds on to knowledge as an essential component of moral being, and it is precisely the relation between the heritage of Socrates and Plato and Aristotle's point concerning the ethos that interests us. For the hermeneutical problem also is clearly a different thing from a pure knowledge detached from any particular kind of being. We spoke of the links between the interpreter and the tradition with which he is concerned and saw in understanding itself an element of historical process. The alienation by the objectifying methods of modern science, characteristic of the hermeneutics and historical writing of the nineteenth century, appeared as the consequence of a false objectification. The return to the example of Aristotelian ethics is made to help us realise and avoid this. For moral being, as Aristotle describes it, is clearly not objective knowledge, ie the knower is not standing over against a situation that he merely observes, but he is directly affected by what he sees. It is something that he has to do.[212]

It is obvious that this is not the knowledge of science. Thus the distinction that Aristotle makes between the knowledge of phronesis and the theoretical knowledge of episteme is a simple one, especially when we remember that science, for the Greeks, is represented by the model of mathematics, a knowledge of what is unchangeable, a knowledge that depends on proof and that can, therefore, be learned by anybody. A hermeneutics of the human sciences could certainly learn nothing from the distinction between moral knowledge and this kind of mathematical knowledge. Compared to this kind of 'theoretical' knowledge, the human sciences stand close to moral knowledge. They are 'moral sciences'. Their object is man and what he knows of himself. But he knows himself as an acting being, and this kind of knowledge that he has of himself does not seek to establish what exists. An active being, rather, is concerned with what is not always the same as it is, but can also be different. In it he can discover the point at which he has to act. The purpose of his knowledge is to govern his action.

Here lies the real problem of moral knowledge that occupies Aristotle in his *Ethics.* For we find action governed by knowledge in an exemplary form where the Greeks speak of techne. This is the skill, the knowledge of the craftsman who is able to make some specific thing. The question is whether moral knowledge is knowledge of this kind. This would mean that it was knowledge of how one had to make oneself. Should man learn to make himself what he is to be, in the same way that the craftsman learns to make what is to be according to his plan and will? Does man develop himself in relation to an eidos of himself in the same way that the craftsman carries within himself an eidos of what he seeks to make and is able to embody in his material? We know that Socrates and Plato did apply the concept of the techne to the concept of man's being, and it is undeniable that they did discover here something true. In the political sphere, at any rate, the model of the techne has an eminently critical function, in that it reveals that lack of foundation in what is called the art of politics, in which everyone involved in politics, ie every citizen, regards himself as an expert. It is very characteristic that the knowledge of the craftsman is the only one that Socrates, in his famous account of his experience of his fellow-countrymen, recognises as real knowledge within its own sphere.[213] But even the craftsmen disappoint him. Their knowledge is not the true knowledge that constitutes a man and a citizen as such. But it is real knowledge. It is a real art and skill and not simply a high degree of experience. In this it is clearly one with the true moral knowledge that Socrates is seeking. Both are knowledge of a dynamic kind, ie their purpose is to determine and guide action. Consequently they must include the application of knowledge to the particular task.

This is the point at which we can relate Aristotle's analysis of moral knowledge to the hermeneutical problem of the modern human sciences. It is true that hermeneutical consciousness is not involved either with technical or moral knowledge, but these two types of knowledge still include the same element of application that we have recognised as the central problem of hermeneutics. Certainly, application does not mean the same thing in each case. There is a curious tension between a techne that can be learned and one that is acquired through experience. The practical knowledge that a person has who has learned a craft is not, in effect, necessarily superior to that possessed by someone who is untrained, but has had a lot of experience. Although this is the case, the practical knowledge of a techne cannot be called 'theoretical', especially since experience is automatically acquired in the use of this knowledge. For, as knowledge, it is always related to practical application, and even if the recalcitrant material does not always obey the person who has learned his craft, Aristotle can still quote, with justice, the words of the poet: 'Techne loves tyche (luck) and tyche loves techne.' This means that the person who has learned his trade is the one that will have the most luck. It is a genuine mastery of the thing that is acquired practically in the techne, and it is this that is a model for moral knowledge. For with moral knowledge it is clear that experience can never be sufficient for making right moral decisions. Here too there is required of the moral consciousness the practical governing of action; indeed, we cannot be content here with the uncertain relation that exists, in the case of a techne, between practical knowledge and the particular successful achievement. There is, no doubt, a real analogy between the perfection of the moral consciousness and that of the capacity to make something, ie of a techne, but they are certainly not the same.

On the contrary, the differences are patent. It is obvious that man does not dispose of himself in the same way that the craftsman disposes of the material with which he works. Clearly he cannot make himself in the same way that he can make something else. Thus it will have to be another kind of knowledge that he has of himself in his moral being, a knowledge that is distinct from the knowledge that directs the making of something. Aristotle catches this difference in a bold and unique way when he calls this kind of knowledge, self-knowledge, ie knowledge for oneself.[214] This distinguishes the self-knowledge of moral consciousness from theoretical knowledge in a way that seems immediately plausible. But it also distinguishes it from technical knowledge, and it was in order to make this double distinction that Aristotle ventures the odd expression 'self-knowledge'.

It is the distinction from technical knowledge that is the more difficult task if, with Aristotle, we define the 'object' of this knowledge ontologically not as something general that is always as it is, but as something individual that can also be different. For at first sight it seems to be a wholly analogous task. A person who knows how to make something knows something good, and he knows it for himself, so that, where there is the possibility of doing so, he is really able to make it. He takes the right material and chooses the right means for the execution. Thus he must know how to apply in the concrete situation what has been learned in a general way. Is the same not true of moral consciousness? A person who has to make moral decisions has always already learned something. He has been so formed by education and custom that he knows in general what is right. The task of making a moral decision is that of doing the right thing in a particular situation, ie seeing what is right within the situation and laying hold of it. He too has to act, choosing the right means, and his action must be governed just as carefully as that of the craftsman. How is it then, despite this, a knowledge of a quite different kind?

From Aristotle's analysis of phronesis emerges a whole variety of points that answer this question. For Aristotle's ability to describe phenomena from every aspect constitutes his real genius. 'The empirical, comprehended in its synthesis, is the speculative concept' (Hegel).[215] Let us consider here a few points that are important for our discussion.

1 We learn a techne and can also forget it. But we do not learn moral knowledge, nor can we forget it. We do not stand over against it, as if it were something that we can acquire or not, in the way that we can choose to acquire or not an objective skill, a techne. Rather, we are always already in the situation of having to act (disregarding the special position of children, for whom obedience to the person educating them replaces their own decision) and hence must already possess and be able to apply moral knowledge. That is why the concept of application is highly problematical. For we can only apply something that we already possess; but we do not possess moral knowledge in such a way that we already have it and then apply it to specific situations. The image that man has of what he ought to be, ie his ideas of right and wrong, of decency, courage, dignity, loyalty etc (all concepts that have their equivalents in Aristotle's catalogue of virtues), are certainly to some degree guiding ideas towards which he looks: but there is still a basic difference from the guiding idea represented by the plan the craftsman has of an object he is going to make. What is right, for example, cannot be fully determined independently of the situation that requires a right action from me, whereas the eidos of what a craftsman desires to make is fully determined by the use for which it is intended.

It is true that what is right seems equally determined in an absolute sense. For what is right is formulated in laws and contained in the general rules of conduct that, although uncodified, can be very exactly determined and are generally binding. Thus the administration of justice is a particular task that requires both knowledge and skill. Is it, then, not a techne? Does it not also consist in an application of laws and rules to the specific case? Do we not speak of the 'art' of the judge? Why is what Aristotle describes as the judge's form of phronesis (dikastike phronesis) not a techne?[216]

If we think about it, we shall see that the application of laws involves a curious legal ambiguity. The situation of the craftsman is quite different. With the design of the object and the rules of its execution, the craftsman proceeds to carry it out. He may be forced to adapt himself to particular circumstances, ie not be able to carry out his design as he had originally intended. But this does not mean that his knowledge of what he wants is made more perfect. Rather, he simply omits certain things in the execution. What we have here is the application of his knowledge and the painful imperfection that is associated with it.

In comparison, the situation of the person who is 'applying' law is quite different. In a specific instance he will have to refrain from applying the full rigour of the law. But if he does, it is not because he has no alternative, but because to do otherwise would not be right. In holding back on the law, he is not diminishing it but, on the contrary, finding the better law. Aristotle expresses this very clearly in his analysis of epieikeia,[217] 'equity': epieikeia is the correction of the law.[218] Aristotle shows that everything that is set down in law is in a necessary tension with definite action, in that it is general and hence cannot contain within itself practical reality in its full concrete form. We have already touched on this problem near the beginning of the present volume when we were considering the capacity of judgment.[219] Clearly enough, legal hermeneutics finds its proper place here.[220] The law is always imperfect, not because it is imperfect in itself, but because, in comparison with the ordered world of law, human reality is necessarily imperfect and hence does not allow of any simple application of the former.

From what we have said it is clear that Aristotle's attitude to the problem of natural law is a highly subtle one and certainly not to be equated with the tradition of later times relating to natural law. I shall give a brief outline of the way in which the idea of natural law is related to the hermeneutical problem.[221] It follows from our discussion so far that Aristotle does not simply dismiss the question of natural law. He does not regard a system of laws as true law, in an absolute sense, but considers the concept of equity as a necessary adjunct to law. Thus he opposes an extreme conventionalism or legal positivism by explicitly distinguishing between what is naturally lawful and what is legally lawful.[222] The distinction he has in mind is not simply that between the unchangeability of natural law and the changeability of positive law. It is true that Aristotle has generally been understood as meaning this. But the true depth of his insight has been missed. Certainly he accepts the idea of an absolutely unchangeable law, but he limits this explicitly to the gods and says that among men not only legal law, but also natural law can be changed. This changeability is, for Aristotle, wholly compatible with the fact that it is 'natural' law. The sense of this assertion seems to me to be the following: there are laws that are entirely a matter of mere agreement (eg traffic regulations) but there are also things that do not admit of regulation simply by human convention, because the 'nature of the thing' constantly asserts itself. Thus it is quite legitimate to call such things 'natural law'.²²³ In that the nature of the thing still allows an area of mobility, this natural law is still changeable. This is clearly evidenced by the examples that Aristotle adduces from other spheres. The right hand is naturally the stronger one, but there is nothing to stop us training the left one so that it becomes as strong as the right (Aristotle obviously gives this example because it was a favourite one of Plato's). A second example is even more illuminating, because it already belongs in the legal sphere: one and the same measure always proves smaller when we buy wine by it than when we sell it. Aristotle is not saying that people in the wine trade are constantly trying to trick their customers, but rather that this behaviour corresponds to the area of free-play permitted within set limits. He also makes the clear distinction that the best state 'is everywhere one and the same', but not the same in the way 'that fire burns everywhere in the same way, whether in Greece or in Persia'.

Despite this clear statement by Aristotle, later thinking concerning natural law quoted this passage as if he were comparing the unchangeability of human law with the unchangeability of natural laws.²²⁴ The opposite is the case. In fact, as his very distinction shows, the idea of natural law has, for Aristotle, only a critical function. No dogmatic use can be made of it, ie we cannot invest particular laws with the dignity and inviolability of natural law. In view of the necessary imperfection of all human laws, the idea of natural law is indispensable for Aristotle and it becomes particularly important in the question of what is equitable, which is what first really decided the law. But its function is a critical one in that the appeal to natural law is legitimate only where a discrepancy emerges between one law and another.

The separate question of natural law, which Aristotle answers in extenso, does not as such interest us here, except by reason of its fundamental significance. For what Aristotle shows here is true of all the ideas that man has of what he ought to be, and not only of the problem of law. All these ideas are not just an arbitrary conventional ideal, but despite all the variety expressed in moral ideas in the most different times and peoples there is still in this sphere something like the nature of the thing. This is not to say that this nature of the thing, ie the ideal of bravery, is a fixed yardstick that we could recognise and apply by ourselves. Rather, Aristotle recognises precisely as true of the teacher of ethics what is true, in his view, of all men, that he also is always already involved in a moral and political commitment and acquires his construct of the thing from that standpoint. He does not himself regard the guiding principles that he describes as knowledge that can be taught. They have only the validity of schemata. They always have to be made concrete in the situation of the person acting. Thus they are not norms that are to be found in the stars or have their unchanging place in a natural moral universe, so that all that would be necessary would be to perceive them. Nor are they mere conventions, but really do correspond to the nature of the thing—only that the latter is always itself determined in each case by the use that the moral consciousness makes of them.

2 Here we see a fundamental modification of the conceptual relation between means and end, which distinguishes moral from technical knowledge. It is not only that moral knowledge has no merely particular end, but is concerned with right living in general, whereas all technical knowledge is particular and serves particular ends. Nor is it the case simply that moral knowledge must take over where technical knowledge would be desirable, but is not available. Certainly, if technical knowledge were available, it would always make it unnecessary to deliberate within oneself concerning that of which it was the knowledge. Where there is a techne, we must learn it and then we are able to find the right means. We see, however, that moral knowledge always requires this kind of self-deliberation. Even if we conceive this knowledge in ideal perfection, it is the perfection of this kind of deliberation with oneself (euboulia) and not knowledge in the manner of a techne.

Thus we are dealing here with a fundamental relationship. It is not the case that dependence on moral knowledge, the process of self-deliberation, would be completely done away with by extending technical knowledge. Moral knowledge can never be knowable in advance in the manner of knowledge that can be taught. The relation between means and ends here is not such that the knowledge of the right means can be made available in advance, and that because the knowledge of the right end is not the mere object of knowledge either. There can be no anterior certainity concerning what the good life is directed towards as a whole. Hence Aristotle's definitions of phronesis have a marked uncertainty about them, in that this knowledge is sometimes related more to the end, and sometimes more to the means to the end.[225] In fact this means that the end towards which our life as a whole tends and the elaboration of it into the moral principles of action, as described by Aristotle in his *Ethics,* cannot be the object of a knowledge that can be taught. There is no more a dogmatic use of ethics than there is a dogmatic use of natural law. Rather, Aristotle's theory of virtue describes typical forms of the true mean that it is important to observe in human life and behaviour; but the moral knowledge that is directed towards these guiding principles is the same knowledge that has to respond to the demands of the situation of the moment.

Hence also there is never mere consideration of expediency that might serve the attainment of moral ends, but the consideration of the means is itself a moral consideration and makes specific the moral rightness of the dominant end. The self-knowledge of which Aristotle speaks is characterised by the fact that it includes the perfect application and uses its knowledge in the immediacy of the given situation. Thus it is a knowledge of the particular situation that completes moral knowledge, a knowledge that is nevertheless not a perceiving by the senses. For although it is necessary to see from a situation what it is asking of us, this seeing does not mean that we perceive in the situation what is visible as such, but that we learn to see it as the situation of action and hence in the light of what is right. Just as we 'see' from the geometrical analysis of plane surfaces that the triangle is the simplest two-dimensional plane figure, so that we can go no further with our subdivisions, but must stop here, so in moral consideration the 'seeing' of what is immediately to be done is not a mere seeing, but nous. This is also confirmed by what constitutes the antithesis to this kind of seeing.[266] The antithesis to the seeing of what is right is not error or deception, but blindness. A person who is overwhelmed by his passions suddenly no longer sees in the given situation what is right. He has lost his self-mastery and hence lost his own rightness, ie the right orientation within himself, so that, driven by the dialectic of passion, whatever his passion tells him is right seems so. Moral knowledge is really a knowledge of a special kind. It embraces in a curious way both means and end and hence differs from technical knowledge. That is why it is pointless to distin-

guish here between knowledge and experience, as can be done in
the case of a techne. For moral knowledge must be a kind of
experience, and in fact we shall see that this is perhaps the
fundamental form of experience, compared with which all other
experience represents a denaturing.[227]

3 The self-knowledge of moral reflection has, in fact, a unique
relation to itself. We can see this from the modifications that
Aristotle presents in the context of his analysis of phronesis.
Beside phronesis, the virtue of thoughtful reflection, stands understanding (sunesis, *Eth Nic* bk 6, ch 11). Understanding is a
modification of the virtue of moral knowledge. It appears in the
fact of concern, not about myself, but about the other person.
Thus it is a mode of moral judgment. We are obviously speaking
of understanding when, using this kind of judgment, we place
ourselves in the concrete situation in which the other person
has to act. The question here, then, is not of a general kind of
knowledge, but of its specification at a particular moment. This
knowledge also is not in any sense technical knowledge or the
application of such. The person who is experienced in the world,
the man who knows all the tricks and dodges and is experienced
in everything there is, does not as such have the right understanding which a person who is acting needs; he has it only if he
satisfies one requirement, namely that he too is seeking what is
right, ie that he is united with the other person in this mutual
interest. The concrete example of this is the phenomenon of
advice in 'questions of conscience'. Both the person who asks
for advice and the person giving it assume that the other is his
friend. Only friends can advise each other or, to put it another
way, only a piece of advice that is meant in a friendly way has
meaning for the person advised. Once again we discover that
the person with understanding does not know and judge as one
who stands apart and unaffected; but rather, as one united by a
specific bond with the other, he thinks with the other and undergoes the situation with him.

This becomes fully clear when we consider further varieties of
moral reflection listed by Aristotle, namely insight and fellow
feeling.[228] Insight is meant here as a quality. We say that someone has insight when they make a correct judgment. A person
with insight is prepared to accept the particular situation of the
other person, and hence he is also most inclined to be forbearing
or to forgive. Here again it is clear that it is not a technical
knowledge.

Aristotle, finally, makes the special nature of moral knowledge and the virtue of possessing it particularly clear by describ-

ing a naturally debased variety of this moral knowledge.²²⁹ He says that the deinos is a man who has all the natural prerequisites and gifts for this moral knowledge, a man who is able, with remarkable skill, to get the most out of any situation, who is able to seize his advantage everywhere and finds a way out of every situation.²³⁰ But this natural counterpart to phronesis is characterised by the fact that he exercises his gifts without being led in any way by moral being and hence without inhibitions and without any orientation towards moral ends. And it is probably more than accidental that such a person is given a name that also means 'terrible'. Nothing is so terrible, so uncanny, so appalling as the exercise of brilliant talents for evil.

To conclude, if we relate Aristotle's description of the ethical phenomenon and especially of the virtue of moral knowledge to our own investigation, we find that Aristotle's analysis is in fact a kind of model of the problems of hermeneutics. We, too, determined that application is neither a subsequent nor a merely occasional part of the phenomenon of understanding, but codetermines it as a whole from the beginning. Here too application was not the relating of some pre-given universal to the particular situation. The interpreter dealing with a traditional text seeks to apply it to himself. But this does not mean that the text is given for him as something universal, that he understands it as such and only afterwards uses it for particular applications. Rather, the interpreter seeks no more than to understand this universal thing, the text; ie to understand what this piece of tradition says, what constitutes the meaning and importance of the text. In order to understand that, he must not seek to disregard himself and his particular hermeneutical situation. He must relate the text to this situation, if he wants to understand at all.

(C) THE EXEMPLARY SIGNIFICANCE OF LEGAL HERMENEUTICS

If this is the case, then the gap between hermeneutics of the human sciences and legal hermeneutics cannot be as big as is generally assumed. The dominant view is, of course, that it was only historical consciousness that raised understanding to a method of objective science and that hermeneutics attained its true character when it became elaborated in this way to become a general theory of the understanding and interpretation of texts. Legal hermeneutics does not belong in this context, for it is not its purpose to understand given texts, but to be a practical measure to help fill a kind of gap in the system of legal dogmatics. It is thought, then, that it has nothing to do with the task of hermeneutics in the human sciences, which is the understanding of traditional material.

But theological hermeneutics cannot, in that case, claim to have any independent systematic meaning. Schleiermacher consciously placed it wholly within general hermeneutics and merely regarded it as a special application of this. Since then the claim of scientific theology to be a discipline on a par with the modern historical sciences seems to depend on the fact that no laws and rules are to be applied in the interpretation of scripture other than those used in understanding any other traditional material. Thus there could be no longer any such thing as a specifically theological hermeneutics.

It is a paradoxical position if, nevertheless, we try to revive the old truth and the old unity of hermeneutical discipline within modern science. It seems that we move into a modern methodology of the human sciences when it becomes detached from any dogmatic tie. Legal hermeneutics became separated from the theory of understanding as a whole because it has a dogmatic purpose, just as, by giving up its dogmatic commitment, theological hermeneutics became united with literary and historical method.

In this situation we can allow ourselves a special interest in the divergence between legal and historical hermeneutics and have to consider those cases in which legal and historical hermeneutics are concerned with the same object, ie those cases in which legal texts are interpreted in a legal way and also understood historically. Thus we shall consider the attitude taken by the legal historian and the jurist to the same legal text. We can turn here to the excellent writings of E. Betti[231] and pursue our own thinking from there. Our question is whether or not there is a clear difference between a dogmatic and a historical interest.

It is clear that there is a difference. The jurist understands the meaning of the law from the present case and for the sake of this present case. As against this, the legal historian has no case from which to start, but he seeks to determine the meaning of the law by considering constructively the whole range of its application. It is only in all its applications that the law becomes concrete. Thus the legal historian cannot simply take the original application of the law as determining its original meaning. As an historian he will, rather, have to take account of the historical change that the law has undergone. He will have to understand the development from the original application to the present application of the law.

In my view it would not be enough to say that the task of the historian was simply to 'reconstruct the original meaning of the legal formula' and that of the jurist to 'harmonise that meaning with the present living actuality'. This kind of division would mean that the definition of the jurist is more comprehensive and includes the task of the legal historian. Someone who is seeking to understand the correct meaning of a law must first know the original one. Thus he must himself think in terms of legal history—only that here historical understanding serves merely as a means to an end. On the other hand, it is not the historian's place to be dogmatic about law. As an historian he moves towards historical objectivity in order to see its historical value, whereas the jurist, in addition, applies what has been learned in this way to the legal present. This is what Betti says.

We may ask, however, whether he has seen and described the task of the historian in a sufficiently comprehensive way. In our particular example, where does the historical element come in? In regard to a valid law we naturally assume that its legal meaning is clear and that the legal practice of the present simply follows the original meaning. If this were always the case then the question of the meaning of a law would be, both legally and historically, the same question. For the jurist, too, the hermeneutical task would be just to establish the original meaning of the law and apply it as the right one. Hence as late as 1840, Savigny, in his *System des Römischen Rechts,* regarded the task of legal hermeneutics as purely historical. Just as Schleiermacher saw no problem in the interpreter's having to identify himself with the original reader, so Savigny ignores the tension between the original and the present legal sense.[232]

It has emerged clearly enough in the course of time that this is a legally untenable fiction. Ernst Forsthoff has shown in a valuable study that for purely legal reasons it was necessary for an awareness of the historical change to develop, which involved the divergence between the original meaning of a law and that applied in current legal practice.[233] It is true that the jurist is always concerned with the law itself, but its normative content is to be determined in regard to the given case in which it is to be applied. In order to know this exactly, it is necessary to have historical knowledge of the original meaning, and only for this reason does the legal interpreter include the historical value that the law has through the act of legislation. But he cannot let himself be tied by what, say, an account of the parliamentary proceedings tells him about the intentions of those who first worked out the law. Rather, he has to take account of the change in circumstances and hence define afresh the normative function of the law.

It is quite different with the legal historian. He is apparently concerned only with the original meaning of the law, the way in which it was meant and the validity it had when it was first promulgated. But how can he know this? Can he know it without being aware of the change in circumstances that separates his own present time from that past time? Must he not then do exactly the same as the judge does, ie distinguish between the original meaning of the text of the law and the legal meaning which he automatically accepts now in the present? The hermeneutical situation of both the historian and the jurist seems to me to be the same in that when faced with any text, we have an immediate expectation of meaning. There can be no such thing as a direct approach to the historical object that would objectively reveal its historical value. The historian has to undertake the same task of reflection as the jurist.

Thus the actual content of what is understood in each of the two ways is the same. The description of the historian's attitude given above is not, then, adequate. Historical knowledge can be gained only by seeing the past in its continuity with the present—which is exactly what the jurist does in his practical, normative work of 'ensuring the unbroken continuance of law and preserving the tradition of the legal idea'.[234]

We must consider, though, whether the model instance we have been discussing is really characteristic of the general problem of historical understanding. The model from which we started was the understanding of a law still in force. Here the historian and the dogmatist were concerned with the same object. But is this not a special case? A legal historian who turns to the legal cultures of the past, and certainly any other historian who is seeking to understand a past that no longer has any direct continuity with the present, would not recognise himself in our model instance of the continuing validity of a law. He would say that legal hermeneutics had a special dogmatic task that is quite foreign to the context of historical hermeneutics.

In fact the situation seems to me to be the reverse of this. Legal hermeneutics is able to point out what the real procedure of the human sciences is. Here we have the model for the relationship between past and present that we are seeking. The judge who adapts the transmitted law to the needs of the present is undoubtedly seeking to perform a practical task, but his interpretation of the law is by no means on that account an arbitrary re-interpretation. Here again, to understand and to interpret means to discover and recognise a valid meaning. He seeks to discover the 'legal idea' of a law by linking it with the present. This is, of course, a legal link. It is the legal significance of the law—and not the historical significance of the law's promulgation or of particular cases of its application—that he is trying to understand. Thus his attitude is not that of an historian, but he has an attitude to his own history, which is his present. Thus he can always approach as an historian those questions that he has implicitly concluded as a judge.

On the other hand, the historian, who has no juridical task before him, but seeks to discover the legal meaning of this law —like anything else that has been handed down in history— cannot disregard the fact that he is concerned with a legal creation that needs to be understood in a legal way. He must be able not only to think historically, but also legally. It is true that it is a special case when an historian is examining a legal text that is still valid today. But this special case shows us what determines our relationship to any historical tradition. The historian, trying to understand the law in terms of the situation of its historical origin, cannot disregard the continuance of its legal validity: it presents him with the questions that he has to ask of historical tradition. Is this not true of every text, ie that it must be understood in terms of what it says? Does this not mean that it always needs to be restated? And does not this restatement always take place through its being related to the present? Inasmuch as the actual object of the historical understanding is not events, but their 'significance', it is clearly not a correct description of this understanding to speak of an object existing in itself, and the approach of the subject to it. The truth is that there is always contained in historical understanding the idea that the tradition reaching us speaks into the present and must be understood in this mediation—indeed, as this mediation. Legal hermeneutics is, then, in reality no special case but is, on the contrary, fitted to restore the full scope of the hermeneutical problem and so to retrieve the former unity of hermeneutics, in which jurist and theologian meet the student of the humanities.

We saw above (p 232) that it was one of the conditions of understanding, in the human sciences, that this should itself belong to tradition. Let us now try to verify this by seeing how this structural element of understanding obtains in the case of legal and theological hermeneutics. This condition is clearly not so much a limiting condition as one that makes understanding possible. The way in which the interpreter belongs to his text is like the way in which the vanishing point belongs to

the perspective of a picture. It is not a matter of looking for this
vanishing point and adopting it as one's standpoint. The interpreter similarly finds his point of view already given, and does
not choose it arbitrarily. Thus it is an essential condition of the
possibility of legal hermeneutics that the law is binding on all the
members of the community in the same way. Where this is not
the case, for example in an absolutist state, where the will of the
absolute ruler is above the law, hermeneutics cannot exist,
'since an absolute ruler can explain his words in a sense that
goes against the rules of general interpretation'.[235] For in this
instance there is no question of interpreting the law in such a
way that the particular case is decided justly according to the
right sense of the law. On the contrary, the will of the monarch
who is not bound by the law can effect whatever seems just to
him without regard for the law—that is without the effort of
interpretation. There is a need to understand and interpret only
when something is enacted in such a way that it is, as enacted,
irremovable and binding.

It is the work of interpretation to make the law concrete in
each specific case,[236] ie it is a work of application. The creative
supplementing of the law that is involved is a task that is reserved to the judge, but he is subject to the law in the same way
as every other member of the community. It is part of the idea of
a legal order that the judge's judgment does not proceed from an
arbitrary and unpredictable decision, but from the just weighing
up of the whole. Anyone who has immersed himself in the particular situation is capable of undertaking this just weighing-up.
This is the reason why, in a state governed through law, there is
legal certainty, ie it is possible to know, in principle, what the
exact situation is. Every lawyer and every counsel is able, in
principle, to give correct advice, ie he is able to predict accu-
rately the judge's decision on the basis of the existing laws. The
application of the law is not simply a matter of knowing the law.
If one has to give a legal judgment on a particular case, of course
it is necessary to know the law and all the elements that have
determined it. But the only connection with the law that is called
for here is that the legal order is recognised as valid for everyone
and that no one is exempt from it. Hence it is always possible to
grasp the existing legal order as such, ie to assimilate dogmatically any past supplement to the law. Consequently there is an
essential connection between legal hermeneutics and legal dogmatics, in which hermeneutics has the more important place.
For the idea of a perfect legal dogmatics, which would make
every judgment a mere act of subsumption, is untenable.[237]

Let us now consider the case of theological hermeneutics, as developed by protestant theology, as it applies to our question.[238] Here there is a genuine parallel to legal hermeneutics, in that here too dogmatics cannot claim any primacy. The proclamation finds its actual expression in preaching, as does the legal order in the judge's verdict. But there is still a big difference between them. Preaching is not, like a legal verdict, a creative supplement to the text that it is interpreting. Hence the gospel of salvation does not acquire any new content from its proclamation in preaching such as could be compared with the power of the judge's verdict to supplement the law. It is not the case that the gospel of salvation becomes more clearly determined only through the ideas of the preacher. As a preacher he does not speak before the community with the same dogmatic authority that a judge does. Certainly preaching too is concerned with the interpretation of a valid truth, but this truth is proclamation, and whether it is successful or not is not decided by the ideas of the preacher, but through the power of the word itself, which can call men to repentance even though the sermon be a bad one. The proclamation cannot be detached from its fulfilment. The dogmatic establishment of pure doctrine is a secondary thing. Scripture is the word of God, and that means that it has an absolute priority over the teaching of those who interpret it.

Interpretation should never overlook this. Even as the erudite interpretation of the theologian, it must never forget that scripture is the divine proclamation of salvation. Understanding it, therefore, cannot simply be the scientific or scholarly exploration of its meaning. Bultmann has said: 'The interpretation of the biblical writings are subject to exactly the same conditions as any other literature'.[239] But the meaning of this statement is ambiguous, for the question is whether all literature is not subject to conditions of understanding other than those formal general ones that have to be fulfilled in regard to every text. Bultmann himself points out that all understanding presumes a living relationship between the interpreter and the text, his previous connection with the material that it deals with. He calls this hermeneutical requirement 'fore-understanding', because it is clearly not something attained through the process of understanding, but is already presupposed. Thus Hofmann, whom Bultmann quotes with approval, writes that scriptural hermeneutics presupposes a relationship to the content of the bible.

We may ask, however, what kind of presupposition this is. Is it something that is given with human life itself? Does there exist in every man a previous connection with the truth of divine revelation because man as such is concerned with the question of God? Or must we say that it is first from God, ie from faith, that human life experiences itself as being affected by the question of God? But then the sense of the presupposition that is contained in the concept of fore-understanding becomes questionable. For then the presupposition would be valid not universally but solely from the viewpoint of true faith.

In regard to the old testament this is a venerable hermeneutical problem. Which is the right interpretation of it, the Jewish one or the christian one in the light of the new testament? Or are both legitimate interpretations, ie do they have something in common, and is this what is really being understood by the interpreter? The Jew who understands the text of the old testament in a different way from the christian shares with him the presupposition that he too is concerned with the question of God. At the same time, in the face of the statements of a christian theologian, he will hold that the latter is not understanding the old testament correctly if he takes its truths as qualified by the new testament. Hence the presupposition that one is moved by the question of God already involves a claim to knowledge concerning the true God and his revelation. Even unbelief is defined in terms of the faith that is demanded of one. The existential fore-understanding, which is Bultmann's starting-point, can only be a christian one.

We could perhaps seek to escape this consequence by saying that it is enough to know that religious texts are to be understood only as texts that answer the question of God. There need be no claim on the religious commitment of the interpreter himself. But what would a marxist say, who considers that he understands religious utterances only when he sees them as the reflection of class interests? He will not accept the presupposition that human life as such is moved by the question of God. This presupposition is obviously valid only for someone who already sees in it the alternative of belief or unbelief in the true God. Thus the hermeneutical significance of fore-understanding in theology seems itself theological. After all, the history of hermeneutics shows how the examination of the texts is determined by a very precise fore-understanding. Modern hermeneutics, as a protestant discipline of the art of interpreting scripture, is clearly related in a polemical way to the dogmatic tradition of the catholic church. It has itself a dogmatic denominational significance. This does not mean that this kind of theological hermeneutics is dogmatically predisposed, so that it reads out of the text what it has put into it. Rather, it really risks itself. But it assumes that the word of scripture addresses us and that only the person who allows himself to be addressed—whether he believes or whether he doubts—understands. Hence the primary thing is application.

We can, then, bring out as what is truly common to all forms of hermeneutics the fact that the sense to be understood finds its concrete and perfect form only in interpretation, but that this interpretative work is wholly committed to the meaning of the text. Neither jurist nor theologian regards the work of application as making free with the text.

The task of presenting something universal in a concrete form and applying it to oneself seems, however, to have a quite different function within the historical sciences. If we ask what application means here and how it occurs in the kind of understanding undertaken in the human sciences, we may acknowledge that there is a certain class of traditional material towards which we adopt the same attitude of application that the jurist does in regard to the law and the theologian in regard to the proclamation. Just as in the one case the judge seeks to dispense justice and in the other the preacher to proclaim salvation, and as, in both the proclamation of justice and the proclamation of the gospel, the meaning of what is proclaimed finds its fullest form, so in the case of a philosophical text or a work of literature we can see that these texts require a special activity from the reader and interpreter, and that we do not have the freedom to adopt an historical distance towards them. It will be seen that here understanding always involves the application of the meaning understood.

But does application essentially and necessarily belong to understanding? From the point of view of modern science the answer will be that it does not, and it will be said that this kind of application that makes the interpreter, as it were, the person to whom the text was originally addressed, is quite unscientific and is to be wholly excluded in the historical sciences. The scientific nature of modern science consists precisely in the fact that it makes tradition objective and methodically eliminates any influence of the interpreter on understanding. It may often be difficult to attain this goal and it will be difficult to preserve this division between historical and dogmatic interest in the case of texts that are addressed to no one in particular and claim to be valid for anyone who receives the tradition. A good example of this is the problem of scientific theology and its relation to the tradition of scripture. It may seem that the balance between the historico-scientific and the dogmatic is to be found in the private world of the person. It may be the same with the philosopher and also with our aesthetic consciousness when some work of art appeals to it. But according to this view, science claims to remain independent of all subjective applications by reason of its method.

This is the kind of argument that would have to be presented by those holding to the modern theory of science. Those cases in which there can be no direct substitution of the original address-ee by the interpreter will be pointed out as having exemplary value, ie where a text has a quite specific addressee, such as the partner to an agreement, or the recipient of a bill or an order. Here, so that we can fully understand the meaning of the text, we can imagine ourselves in the place of the addressee, and in that this substitution serves to give the text its full concrete form, we can regard this also as a work of interpretation. But this placing of ourselves in the position of the original reader (Schleiermacher) is something quite different from application. It actually avoids the task of mediating between then and now, between the 'Thou' and the 'I', which is what we mean by application, and which legal hermeneutics also regards as its task.

Let us take the example of the understanding of an order. An order exists only where there is someone to obey it. Here, then, understanding is part of a relationship between persons, one of whom has to give the order. To understand the order means to apply it to the specific situation to which it is relevant. It is true that one makes the other repeat the order to check that it has been understood, but that does not alter the fact that it is given its real meaning when it is carried out in accordance with its meaning. This is why there is such a thing as an explicit refusal of obedience that is not simply disobedience, but derives its meaning from that of the order and of its realisation. A person who refuses to obey an order has understood it, and because he applies it to the situation and knows what obedience would mean in that situation, he refuses. The criterion of understanding is clearly not in the actual words of the order, nor in the mind of the person giving the order, but solely in the understanding of the situation and the responsibleness of the person who obeys. Even when an order is given in writing, so that the correctness of the understanding and carrying out of it can be verified, it is not thought that everything is contained in it. The comic situation in which orders are carried out literally, but not according to their meaning, is well known. Thus there is no doubt that the recipient of an order must perform a definite creative act of understanding its meaning.

If we now imagine an historian who regards tradition in this way as an order and seeks to understand it, he is, of course, in a quite different situation from the original 'addressee'. He is not the person to whom the order is addressed and so cannot relate it to himself. But if he really wants to understand the order, then he must, idealiter, perform the same act performed by the intended recipient of the order. The latter also, who applies the order to himself is well able to distinguish between understanding and obeying an order. It is possible for him not to obey even when—indeed, precisely when—he has understood it. It may be difficult for the historian to reconstruct the original situation in which the order arose. But he will understand it fully only when he has thus made the order concrete. This, then, is the clear hermeneutical demand: to understand a text in terms of the specific situation in which it was written.

As far as the self-understanding of science is concerned, then, it must make no difference to the historian whether a text was addressed to a particular person or persons or was intended 'to belong to all ages'. The general requirement of hermeneutics is, rather, that every text must be understood from that point of view that is appropriate to it. But this means that historical science first seeks to understand every text in terms of itself and does not accept the content of what it says as true, but leaves it open. Understanding is certainly a work of concretisation, but one that involves keeping a hermeneutical distance. Understanding is possible only if one forgets oneself. This is the demand of science.

In this view of the methodology of the human sciences it is generally said that the interpreter imagines an addressee for every text, whether expressly addressed by the text or not. This addressee is in every case the original reader, and the interpreter knows that this is a different person from himself. This is obvious, when thus negatively expressed. A person trying to understand a text, whether literary critic or historian, does not, at any rate, apply what it says to himself. He is simply trying to understand what the author is saying, and if he is simply trying to understand, he is not interested in the objective truth of what he says as such, not even if the text itself claims to teach truth. On this the critic and the historian are in agreement.

Hermeneutics and historical study, however, are clearly not the same thing. By examining the methodological differences be-

tween the two, we shall discover that what they really have in
common is not what they are generally thought to have. The
historian has a different attitude to the texts of the past, in that
he is seeking to know through them something of the past. He
therefore uses other traditional material to supplement and verify what the texts say. He regards more or less as a weakness the
literary critic's practice of regarding his text as a work of art. A
work of art is a whole self-sufficient world. But the interest of
the historian is not at all concerned with this self-sufficiency.
Dilthey said once, against Schleiermacher: 'The humanities
would like to see self-contained existence everywhere'.[240] If a
work of literature from the past makes an impression on an
historian, this will still not have any hermeneutical significance
for him. It is impossible for him to regard himself as the addressee of the text and accept its claim on him. Rather, he examines
the text to find something that it is not, of itself, seeking to provide. This is even true of that material from the past that in itself
purports to be a historical presentation. Even the writer of history is subject to a historical critique.

    Thus the historian goes beyond hermeneutics, and the idea of
interpretation acquires a new and more defined meaning. It no
longer refers only to the explicit act of understanding a given
text. The idea of historical interpretation corresponds more to
the idea of the expression, which is not understood by historical
hermeneutics in its classical and traditional sense, ie as a rhetorical term that refers to the relation between language and idea.
What the expression expresses is not merely what is supposed to
be expressed in it—what is meant by it—but primarily what is
also expressed by the words without its being intended, ie what
the expression, as it were, 'betrays'. In this wider sense the
word 'expression' refers to far more than the linguistic expression; rather, it includes everything that it is necessary to go back
beyond in order that everything be understood, and what is at
the same time such that it makes it possible for us to go beyond
it. Interpretation here, then, does not refer to the sense intended, but to the sense that is hidden and has to be revealed. Thus
every text not only presents an intelligible meaning but, in many
respects, needs to be revealed. It is above all a phenomenon of
expression. It is understandable that the historian is interested in
this aspect. For the value as testimony of, say, a report depends
in part on what the text represents as a phenomenon of expression. From this one can discover what the writer intended without saying, what party he belonged to, with what views he approached things, or even what degree of lack of principle or

dishonesty is to be expected of him. Account must clearly be taken of these subjective elements affecting the credibility of the witness. But, above all, the content of the traditional material must itself be interpreted, even if its subjective reliability is established, ie the text understood as a document, the true meaning of which can be discovered only beyond its literal one, eg through comparison with other data which allow us to estimate the historical value of a text from the past.

Thus it is a basic principle for the historian that tradition is to be interpreted in another sense than the texts, of themselves, call for. He will always go back behind them and the meaning they express to enquire into the reality of which they are the involuntary expression. Texts are set beside all the other historical material available, ie beside the so-called relics of the past. They, like everything else, need explication, ie to be understood not only in terms of what they say, but of what they bear witness to.

The concept of interpretation reaches its fulfilment here. Interpretation is necessary where the meaning of a text cannot be immediately understood. It is necessary wherever one is not prepared to trust what a phenomenon immediately presents to us. The psychologist interprets in this way by not accepting the expressions of life in the sense they intend, but delves back into what was taking place in the unconscious. The historian interprets the data of the past in the same way, in order to discover the true meaning that is expressed and, at the same time, hidden in them.

Thus there is a natural tension between the historian and the literary critic, who seeks to understand a text for the sake of its beauty and its truth. The interpretation of the historian is concerned with something that is not expressed in the text itself and need have nothing to do with the intended meaning of the text. There is a fundamental conflict here between the historical and the literary consciousness, although this tension scarcely exists now that historical consciousness has changed the attitude of the critic. He has given up the claim that his texts have a normative validity for him. He no longer sees them as models of human utterance, but looks at them in a way that they themselves did not intend to be looked at; he looks at them as an historian. This has made criticism an ancillary discipline of historical studies. This could be glimpsed already in the classical humanities, when they began to call themselves the science of antiquity (Wilamowitz). It is a department of historical research which is concerned primarily with language and literature. The critic is a historian, in that he discovers a historical dimension in his literary sources. Understanding, then, is for him a matter of placing a given text within the context of the history of language, literary form, style etc, and thus ultimately within the totality of the living context of history. Only sometimes does his own original nature come through. Thus, in his estimation of the ancient historians, he will incline to give these great writers more credence than the historian finds justified. This ideological credulity, which makes the critic overestimate the value of his texts as evidence, is the last vestige of his old claim to be the friend of 'elegant discourse' and the mediator of classical literature.

Let us now enquire if this description of the procedure of the human sciences, in which the historian and the critic of today are one, is true and if the universal claim that historical consciousness makes here is justified. In regard to literary criticism it seems questionable.[241] The critic is ultimately mistaking his own nature, as a friend of elegant discourses, if he bows to the criterion of historical studies. If his texts possess an exemplary character for him, this may be primarily in regard to form. It was the old romantic idea of humanism that everything was said in an exemplary way in classical literature; but what is said in such a way is actually more than a formal exemplar. Elegant discourse is not called such simply because what is said is said in fine style, but also because what is said has beauty. It seeks to be more than just rhetoric. It is particularly true of the poetic traditions of the various peoples that we admire not only their poetic power, the imagination and art of their expression, but above all the great truth that speaks in them.

If, then, there has remained in the work of the critic something of the setting up of models, he is not in fact relating his texts to a reconstructed addressee only, but also to himself (though he is unwilling to accept this). Though he allows exemplary writing its force as exemplar, this always involves a process of understanding that no longer accepts these exemplars automatically, but has chosen them and remains as committed to them. That is why this relating of oneself to an exemplar always has the character of following in someone's footsteps. And just as this is more than mere imitation, so this understanding is a continually new form of encounter and has itself the character of an event, precisely because it does not simply take for granted, but involves application. The literary critic goes on, as it were, weaving the great tapestry of tradition which supports us.

If we accept this, then his discipline must attain its true dignity and proper knowledge of itself by being liberated from history.

Yet this seems to me to be only half the truth. Rather we should ask whether the picture of the historical approach, as set out here, is not itself distorted. Perhaps it is not only the approach of the critic, but also that of the historian that should be orientated not so much to the methodological ideal of the natural sciences as to the model offered us by legal and theological hermeneutics. It may be true that the historical approach to texts differs specifically from the original commitment of the critic. It may be true that the historian tries to get behind the texts in order to force them to yield information that they do not intend, and are unable, of themselves to give. If we measure by the yard-stick of the individual text, this would seem to be the case. The attitude of an historian to his texts is like that of an investigating magistrate to his witnesses. But simply establishing facts, elicited from possibly prejudiced witnesses, does not make the historian. What makes the historian is understanding the significance of what he finds. Thus the testimonies of history are like those given before a court. It is no accident that in German the same word is used for both, Zeugnis (testimony; witness). In both cases a testimony is an aid in establishing the facts. But the facts are not the real objects of enquiry; they are simply material for the real tasks of the judge, to reach a just decision, and of the historian, to establish the historical significance of an event within the totality of historical self-consciousness.

Thus the whole difference is possibly only a question of the criteria. One should not choose too nicely if one would reach the essentials. We have already shown that traditional hermeneutics artificially limited the dimensions of the phenomenon, and this is, perhaps, also true of the historical attitude. Is it not the case here too that the really important things precede any application of historical methods? An historical hermeneutics that does not make the essence of the historical question the central thing, and does not enquire into the motives from which a historian is examining historical material, lacks its most important element.

If we accept this, then the relation between literary criticism and historical studies suddenly appears quite different. Although we spoke of the humanities as under the alien control of historical studies, this is not the final aspect of the matter. Rather, it seems to me that the problem of application, of which we had to remind the critic, is relevant to the more complicated situation of historical understanding also. All appearances seem to be against this, it is true, in that historical understanding seems to fall entirely short of the claim to application made by the traditional material. We have seen that it does not accept a text in terms of the text's intention, but in terms of its own characteristic and different intention, ie as a historical source, using it in order to understand what the text did not at all intend to say, but which we find expressed in it.

On closer examination, however, we see that there is the question of whether the understanding of the historian is really different in structure from that of the critic. It is true that he looks at the texts from another point of view, but this change of intention applies only to the individual text as such. For the historian, however, the individual test makes up, together with other sources and testimonies, the unity of the total tradition. This unity of the total tradition is his true hermeneutical object. It is this that he must understand in the same sense in which the literary critic understands his text in the unity of its meaning. Thus he too must undertake a task of application. This is the important point: historical understanding proves to be a kind of literary criticism writ large.

But this does not mean that we share the hermeneutical attitude of the historical school, the problems of which we outlined above. We spoke of the dominance of the humanities schema in historical self-understanding and used Dilthey's foundation of the human sciences to show that the historical school's aim of seeing history as reality and not as simply the unfolding of complexes of ideas could not be achieved. We, for our part, are not maintaining, with Dilthey, that all process has as perfect a meaningful form as has a text. When we called history criticism writ large, this did not mean that historical studies are to be understood as part of the history of the spirit.

We are saying, rather, the reverse. We have seen, I think more correctly, what is involved in the reading of a text. Of course, the reader does not exist before whose eyes the great book of world history simply lies open. But nor does the reader exist who, when he has his text before him, simply reads what is there. Rather, all reading involves application, so that a person reading a text is himself part of the meaning he apprehends. He belongs to the text that he is reading. It will always happen that the line of meaning that is revealed to him as he reads it necessarily breaks off in an open indefiniteness. He can, indeed he must, accept the fact that future generations will understand differently what he has read in the text. And what is true for every reader is also true for the historian. The historian is concerned with the whole of historical tradition, which he has to combine with his own present existence if he wants to understand it and which in this way he keeps open for the future.

Thus we too acknowledge that there is an inner unity between criticism and historical studies, but we do not see it in the universality of the historical method, nor in the objectifying replacement of the interpreter by the original reader, nor in the historical critique of tradition as such but, on the contrary, in the fact that both perform a work of application that is different only in degree. If the critic understands the given text, ie understands himself in the text, in the way we have said, the historian also understands the great text he has himself discovered of the history of the world itself, in which every text handed down to us is but a fragment of meaning, one letter, as it were, and he understands himself in this great text. Both the critic and the historian thus emerge from the self-forgetfulness to which they had been banished by a thinking for which the only criterion was the methodology of modern science. Both find their true ground in effective historical consciousness.

This shows that the model of legal hermeneutics was, in fact, a useful one. When a judge regards himself as entitled to supplement the original meaning of the text of a law, he is doing exactly what takes place in all other understanding. The old unity of the hermeneutical disciplines comes into its own again if we recognise that effective historical consciousness is at work in all the hermeneutical activity of both critic and historian.

The meaning of application that is involved in all forms of understanding is now clear. It is not the subsequent applying to a concrete case of a given universal that we understand first by itself, but it is the actual understanding of the universal itself that the given text constitutes for us. Understanding proves to be a kind of effect and knows itself as such.

3 ANALYSIS OF EFFECTIVE-HISTORICAL CONSCIOUSNESS

(A) THE LIMITATIONS OF REFLECTIVE PHILOSOPHY

We must now ask about the relation between knowledge and effect. I have already pointed out above,[242] that effective-historical consciousness is something other than enquiry into the effective-history of a particular work as it were, the trace a work leaves behind. It is, rather, an awareness of the work itself, and hence itself has an effect. The purpose of the whole account of the formation and fusion of horizons was intended to show the way in which the effective-historical consciousness operates. But what sort of consciousness is this? That is the important problem. However much we say that it is itself within the effect, as consciousness it is of its essence to be able to rise above that of which it is consciousness. The structure of reflectivity is fundamentally given with all consciousness. Thus it must be valid also for effective-historical consciousness.

We might also express it in this way: when we speak of effective-historical consciousness, are we not confined within the immanent laws of reflection, which destroy any direct effect? Are we not forced to admit that Hegel was right and regard the basis of hermeneutics as the absolute fusion of history and truth?

We cannot underestimate this point if we think of the historical view of the world and its development from Schleiermacher to Dilthey. It was the same everywhere. The aim of hermeneutics seems capable of fulfilment, in every case, only in the infinity of knowledge, in the thoughtful fusion of the whole of the past with the present. We see it based on the ideal of perfect enlightenment, on the total opening up of our historical horizon, on the abolition of our finiteness in the infinity of knowledge, in short, on the omnipresence of the historically knowing spirit. It is clearly not of fundamental significance that the historicism of the nineteenth century never expressly acknowledged this consequence. Ultimately it is the position of Hegel, in which it finds its justification, even if the historians, filled with enthusiasm for experience, preferred to quote Schleiermacher and Wilhelm von Humboldt. But neither Schleiermacher nor Humboldt really thought through their positions fully. However much they emphasise the individuality, the barrier of alienness, that our understanding has to overcome, understanding ultimately finds its fulfilment only in an infinite consciousness, which is also the ground of the idea of individuality. It is the pantheistic enclosing of all individuality within the absolute that makes possible the miracle of understanding. Thus here also being and knowledge interpenetrate each other in the absolute. Neither Schleiermacher's nor Humboldt's Kantianism, then, is a systematic affirmation over against the speculative fulfilment of idealism in the absolute dialectic of Hegel. The critique of reflective philosophy that applies to Hegel applies to them also.

We must ask whether our own attempt at an historical hermeneutics is not subject to the same critique, or whether we are able to keep ourselves free from the metaphysical claims of reflective philosophy and justify the hermeneutical experience by agreeing with the critique that the young Hegelians levelled at Hegel, a critique that proved historically so important.

It is necessary to recognise the compulsive power of reflective philosophy and admit that Hegel's critics never really succeeded in breaking its magic spell. We shall be able to detach the problem of an historical hermeneutics from the hybrid consequences of speculative idealism if we refuse to be satisfied with the irrationalistic reduction of it, but preserve the truth of Hegel's thought. We are concerned with understanding effective-historical consciousness in such a way that the immediacy and superiority of the work does not disintegrate into a mere reflective reality in the consciousness of the effect, ie we are concerned to conceive a reality which is beyond the omnipotence of reflection. This was precisely the point against which the critique of Hegel was directed and where the principle of reflective philosophy actually proved itself superior to all its critics.

This can be exemplified by Hegel's polemic against Kant's thing-in-itself.[243] Kant's critical definition of reason had limited the application of the categories to the objects of possible experience and declared that the thing-in-itself, that lay behind appearances, was unknowable. Hegel's dialectical argument objected that by making this distinction, and separating the appearance from the thing-in-itself, reason was proving this distinction to be its own. In making it reason was by no means establishing its own limit, for it meant that reason had already gone beyond that limit. What makes a limit a limit always also includes knowledge of what is on both sides of it. It is the dialectic of the limit to exist only by being removed. Thus the quality of being-in-itself that characterises the thing-in-itself over against its appearance is in-itself only for us. What appears in logical generality in the dialectic of the limit becomes specified in consciousness by the experience that the being-in-itself distinguished in consciousness is the counterpart of itself, and is known in its truth when it is known as self, ie when it knows itself in the perfection of absolute self-consciousness. We shall consider the correctness and limitations of this argument later.

The varied critique of this philosophy of absolute reason by Hegel's critics cannot withstand the logical consequences of total dialectical self-mediation that Hegel has set out, especially in his *Phenomenology,* the science of phenomenal knowledge. That the other must be experienced not as the other grasped by pure self-consciousness, but as a 'Thou'—this prototype of all objections to the infiniteness of Hegel's dialectic—does not seriously trouble him. The dialectical process of the *Phenomenology of Mind* is perhaps determined by nothing so much as by the problem of the recognition of the 'Thou'. To mention only a few stages of this history: our own self-consciousness, for Hegel, attains to the truth of its self-consciousness only through achieving its recognition by the other person. The immediate relationship between a man and a woman is the natural knowledge of mutual recognition (p 325). Beyond this, conscience represents the mental element of being recognised, and mutual self-recognition, in which the mind is absolute, can be attained only via confession and forgiveness. It cannot be denied that the objections of Feuerbach and Kierkegaard are already taken care of in these forms of the mind described by Hegel.

Polemics against an absolute thinker has itself no starting-point. The Archimedean point from where Hegel's philosophy could be toppled can never be found through reflection. This is precisely the formal quality of reflective philosophy, that there cannot be a position that is not drawn into the reflective movement of consciousness coming to itself. The appeal to immediacy—whether of bodily nature, or of the 'Thou' making claims on us, or of the impenetrable factualness of historical change, or of the reality of the relations of production—has always been self-refuting, in that it is not itself an immediate attitude, but a reflective activity. The left-Hegelian critique of a mere intellectual reconciliation, which fails to take account of the real transformation of the world, the whole doctrine of the transformation of philosophy into politics, is inevitably the abolition of philosophy.[244]

Thus the question arises of the degree to which the dialectical superiority of reflective philosophy corresponds to a factual truth and how far it merely creates a formal appearance. For the arguments of reflective philosophy cannot ultimately conceal the fact that there is some truth in the critique of speculative thought based on the standpoint of finite human consciousness. This emerges, in particular, with the last successors of idealism, eg the neo-kantian critics of life philosophy and existentialism. Heinrich Rickert, who attempted in 1920 to destroy life philosophy through argument, was unable to come anywhere near the influence of Nietzsche and Dilthey, which was beginning to grow at that time. However clearly one demonstrates the inner contradictions of all relativist views, it is as Heidegger has said: all these victorious arguments have something about them that suggests they are attempting to bowl one over.[245] However cogent they may seem, they still miss the main point. In making use of them one is proved right, and yet they do not express any superior insight of any value. That the thesis of scepticism or relativism refutes itself to the extent that it claims to be true is an irrefutable argument. But what does it achieve? The reflective argument that proves successful here falls back on the arguer, in that it renders the truthfulness of all reflection suspect. It is not the reality of scepticism or of truth dissolving relativism, but the claim to truth of all formal argument that is affected.

Thus the formalism of this kind of reflective argument is of specious philosophical legitimacy. In fact it tells us nothing. We are familiar with this kind of thing from the Greek sophists, whose inner hollowness Plato demonstrated. It was also he who saw clearly that there is no argumentatively adequate criterion to distinguish truly between philosophical and sophistic discourse. In particular, he shows in his seventh *Letter* that the formal refutability of a proposition does not necessarily exclude its being true.[246] The model of all empty argument is the sophistic question how one can enquire into anything that one does not already know. This argument, which Plato formulates in the *Meno* (80 d ff) is not, characteristically enough, demolished there through superior argument, but by appealing to the myth of the pre-existence of the soul. This is a very ironic appeal, since the myth of pre-existence and anamnesis, which is supposed to solve the mystery of questioning and seeking, does not present a religious certainty, but depends on the certainty of the knowledge-seeking soul, which prevails against the emptiness of formal arguments. Nevertheless, it is characteristic of the weakness that Plato recognises in the logos that he gives his critique of the argument of the sophists not a logical, but a mythical basis. Just as true opinion is a divine favour and gift, so the search for and recognition of the true logos is not the free self-possession of the human mind. We shall see later that the mythical account that Plato gives here of the Socratic dialectic is of fundamental importance. Were not the sophists refuted—which cannot be done through argument—this argument would lead to resignation. It is the argument of 'lazy reason' and has a truly symbolic importance, since all empty reflection, despite its appearance of victory, leads to the discrediting of all reflective thought.

But Plato's mythical refutation of this dialectical sophism, however convincing it seems, does not satisfy the modern mind. There is no mythical foundation of philosophy in Hegel; for him myth is part of pedagogy. It is ultimately reason that is its own foundation. Hegel, by working through the dialectic of reflection in this way as the total self-communication of reason, is fundamentally above the argumentative formalism that we call 'sophistic', to use Plato's term. Hence his dialectic is not less polemical towards the empty arguments of logic, which he calls 'external reflection' than the arguments of Plato's Socrates. That is why it is of central importance for the hermeneutical problem that it should come to grips with Hegel. For Hegel's whole philosophy of the mind claims to achieve the total fusion of history with the present. It is concerned not with a reflective formalism, but with the same thing as we are. Hegel has thought through the historical dimension in which the problem of hermeneutics is rooted.

For this reason we shall have to define the structure of the effective-historical consciousness with an eye on Hegel, setting it against his own approach. Hegel's spiritualistic interpretation of christianity, which he uses to define the nature of mind, is not affected by the objection that there is no room in it for the experience of the other, including the otherness of history. The life of the mind consists, rather, in recognising oneself in other being. The mind directed towards self-knowledge regards itself as alienated from the 'positive', and must learn to reconcile itself with it, seeing it as its own, as part of its own world. By dissolving the hard edge of positivity, it becomes reconciled with itself. In that this kind of reconciliation is the historical work of the mind, the historical attitude of the mind is neither self-reflection nor the mere formal dialectical abolition of the self-alienation that it has undergone, but an experience, which experiences reality and is itself real.

(B) THE CONCEPT OF EXPERIENCE AND THE ESSENCE OF THE HERMENEUTICAL EXPERIENCE

This is the important fact that we have to hold on to in analysing the effective-historical consciousness: it has the structure of an experience. However paradoxical it may seem, the concept of experience seems to me one of the most obscure we have. Because it plays an important role in the natural sciences in the logic of induction, it has been subjected to an epistemological schematisation that, for me, diminishes its original meaning. We may remember that Dilthey accused British empiricism of a lack of historical culture and, considering his unrevolved hesitation between life philosophy and the philosophy of science, we may regard this as a very half-hearted criticism. It is, in fact, the main lack in the theory of experience hitherto—and this includes Dilthey himself—that it has been entirely orientated towards science and hence takes no account of the inner historicality of experience. It is the aim of science to so objectify experience that it no longer contains any historical element. The scientific experiment does this by its methodical procedure. The historico-critical method, moreover, does the same thing in the human sciences. Both methods are concerned to guarantee, through the objectivity of their approach, that these basic experiences can be repeated by anyone. Just as in the natural sciences experiments must be verifiable, so must the whole process be capable of being checked in the human sciences also. Hence no place can be left for the historicality of experience in science.

Modern science thus simply carries through in its methodology what experience has always striven after. Experience is valid only if it is confirmed; hence its dignity depends on its fundamental repeatability. But this means that experience, by its very nature, abolishes its history. This is true even of everyday experience, and how much more for any scientific version of it. Thus it is not just a chance one-sided emphasis of modern scientific theory, but has a foundation in fact, that the theory of experience is related teleologically to the truth that is derived from it.

In recent times Edmund Husserl, in particular, has directed his attention to this problem. In many successive investigations he attempted to throw light on the one-sidedness of the scientific idealisation of experience.[247] To this end he gives a genealogy of experience which, as experience of the living world, precedes its idealisation through science. To me, however, he still seems dominated by the one-sidedness that he criticises, for he projects the idealised world of exact scientific experience into the original experience of the world, in that he makes perception, as something external and directed toward mere physical appearances, the basis of all further experience. To quote him: 'Although, because of this sensible presence it at once attracts our practical or affective interest, presenting itself to us at once as something useful, attractive or repulsive, all this is based on the fact that it is a substratum with qualities that can be apprehended simply by the senses, to which there always leads a path of possible explication'.[248] Husserl's attempt to go back genetically to the origin of experience, and to overcome its idealization by science, obviously has to deal in a special way with the difficulty that the pure transcendental subjectivity of the ego is not given as such, but always in the idealisation of language, which is already present in any acquisition of experience and in which the individual I's membership of a particular linguistic community is worked out.

In fact, when we go back to the beginnings of modern scientific theory and logic, we find this same problem of the extent to which there can be such a thing as the pure use of our reason, proceeding according to methodological principles, above all prejudices and predispositions, especially 'verbalistic' ones. It is the particular achievement of Bacon in this field that he was not satisfied with the immanent logical task of developing the theory of experience as the theory of true induction, but that he discussed the whole moral difficulty and anthropological questionableness of this kind of experiential product. His method of induction seeks to rise above the unruly and accidental way in which daily experience takes place and certainly above its dialectical use. In this connection he undermined the theory of induction on the basis of the enumeratio simplex, still held by humanist scholasticism, an achievement that foreshadowed the new age of scientific method. The concept of induction makes use of the idea that we generalise on the basis of chance observation and, if we encounter no contrary instance, we pronounce it valid. Bacon, as we know, sets against this anticipatio, this overhasty generalisation of everyday experience, what he calls interpretatio naturae, ie the expert explication of the true being of nature.[249] By means of methodically conducted experiments it permits us to progress step by step towards the true and tenable universals, the simple forms of nature. This true method is characterised by the fact that the mind is not left to its own devices;[250] it cannot soar as it would like. Rather, it has to climb gradatim (step by step) from the particular to the universal, in order to acquire an ordered experience that avoids all hasty conclusions.[251]

The required method Bacon himself describes as experimental.[252] But it must be remembered that by 'experiment' Bacon does not always just mean the scientist's technical procedure of artificially inducing processes in isolating conditions and making them capable of being measured. An experiment is also, and primarily, the careful directing of our mind, preventing it from indulging in overhasty generalisations, consciously confronting it with the most remote and apparently most diverse instances, so that it may learn, in a gradual and continuous way, to work, via the process of exclusion, towards the axioms.[253]

On the whole, we shall have to agree with the general criticism of Bacon and admit that his methodological suggestions are disappointing. They are too vague and general and have produced little, especially when applied to the study of nature, as we can see today. It is true that this opponent of empty dialectical casuistry himself remained profoundly involved in the metaphysical tradition and in the dialectical forms of argument that he attacked. His goal of conquering nature through obedience, the new attitude of attacking and forcing nature's secrets from it, which makes him the predecessor of modern science, is only the programmatic side of his work, to which his contribution has hardly been enduring. His real achievement is, rather, that he undertakes a comprehensive examination of the prejudices that hold the human mind captive and lead it away from the true knowledge of things, thus carrying out a methodical self-purification of the mind that is more a discipline than a method. Bacon's famous doctrine of the 'prejudices' first and foremost makes a methodical use of reason possible.[254]

This is precisely why he interests us, for there are here expressed, albeit with a critical and exclusive intention, elements in experience that are not related teleologically to the goal of science, as, for example, when among the idola tribus, Bacon speaks of the tendency of the human mind always to remember what is positive and forget all negative instances. A case in point is the belief in oracles, which is based on this remarkable forgetfulness, which remembers only the true prophecies and forgets the false ones. Similarly, the relation of the human mind to the conventions of language is, in Bacon's eyes, a case of knowledge being confused by empty conventional forms. It is one of the idola fori.

These two examples are enough to indicate that the teleological aspect, which dominates this question for Bacon, is not the only one possible. Whether the positive has in every respect priority in the memory, or whether the tendency of life to forget the negative is to be critically handled in all respects, is a question of some importance for us. Hope is such a clear mark of human experience, ever since the *Prometheus* of Aeschylus that, in view of its human importance, we must regard as one-sided the principle of accepting teleology as the sole criterion of the achievement of knowledge. We shall probably feel the same in regard to the importance of language, which precedes experience, and although illusory verbalistic problems can derive from the dominance of linguistic conventions, it is equally certain that language is at the same time a positive condition of, and guide to, experience itself. Even Husserl, like Bacon, noted more the negative than the positive side of language.

In analysing the concept of experience we shall not let ourselves be guided by these models, since we cannot limit ourselves to the teleological aspect, from which until now the problem has largely been considered. This is not to say that this aspect has not correctly grasped a true element in the structure of experience. The fact that experience is valid, so long as it is not contradicted by new experience (ubi non reperitur instantia contradictoria), is clearly characteristic of the general nature of experience, no matter whether we are dealing with its scientific form, in the modern experiment, or with the experience of daily life that men have always had.

Thus this approach is entirely in accord with the analysis of the concept of induction, which Aristotle gave in the appendix to his *Posterior Analytics*. [255] He describes there (similarly to chapter 1 of his *Metaphysics*) how the one unity of experience proceeds from various individual perceptions through the retention of many individuals. What sort of unity is this? Clearly it is the unity of a universal. But the universality of experience is not yet the universality of science. Rather, according to Aristotle, it occupies a remarkably indeterminate intermediate position between the many individual perceptions and the true universality of the concept. Science and technology start from the universality of the concept. But what is the universality of experience, and how does it pass into the new universality of the logos? If experience shows us that a particular remedy has a particular effect, this means that something common has been noticed in a number of observations, and it is clear that the actual medical question, the scientific question, is possible only on the basis of this kind of observation: this is the question of the logos. Science knows why, for what reason, this remedy has a healing effect. Experience is not science itself, but it is a necessary condition of it. There must already be certainty, ie the individual observations must show the same regular pattern. Only when that universality which is found in experience is attained can we enquire into the reason and hence move forward into science. We ask again: what kind of universality is this? It is obviously concerned with the undifferentiated common unity of many single observations. It is because we retain these that we are able to make predictions with any certainty.

However, the relation between experience, retention, and the resulting unity of experience remains conspicuously vague. Aristotle is obviously basing what he says here on an argument that by his time already had a certain classic stamp. We find it first in Anaxagoras who, according to Plutarch, distinguished man from the beasts through his powers of empeiria, mneme, sophia and techne.[256] We find a similar point in the emphasis on mneme in the *Prometheus* of Aeschylus,[257] and although we do not find the corresponding emphasis on mneme in the Platonic Protagoras myth, both Plato[258] and Aristotle indicate that this was already a fixed theory. The persistence of important perceptions (mone) is clearly the linking motif through which the knowledge of the universal can emerge from the experience of the individual. All animals who possess mneme in this sense, ie a sense of the past, of time, are in this close to man. A separate investigation would be necessary to discover how influential in this early theory of experience, whose traces we have outlined, was the connection between memory (mneme) and language. It is clear that this acquisition of universal concepts is accompanied by the learning of names and of speech generally, and Themistius explained Aristotle's analysis of induction simply in terms of the example of learning to speak and of the formation of words. At any rate, the universality of experience of which Aristotle speaks is not that of the concept and of science. (The problematic which we approach with this theory is undoubtedly that of the sophists' educational thought, for we find in all the available documents a connection made between that feature of the human that we are concerned with here, and the general arrangement of nature. But this motif—the contrasting of men and beasts—was the natural starting-point of the educational ideal of the sophists.) Experience is always actually present only in the individual observation. It is not known in a previous universality. Here lies the fundamental openness of experience to new experience, not only in the general sense that errors are corrected, but that it is, in its essence, dependent on constant confirmation and necessarily becomes a different kind of experience where there is no confirmation (ubi reperitur instantia contradictoria).

Aristotle has a very fine image for the logic of this procedure. He compares the many observations made by someone to a fleeing army. They hurry away, ie they do not stand fast. But if in this general flight an observation is confirmed through the repeated experience of it, then it does stand fast. At this point a first stop is put to the general flight. If others join it, then finally the whole fleeing host stops and again obeys the one commander. The domination of the whole army by one person is a symbol of science. The image is intended to show how science, ie universal truth, is possible, considering that it must not depend on the contingency of observations, but be valid in a really universal way. How is that possible, when observations rely so much on chance?

The image is important for us because it illustrates the crucial element in the nature of experience. Like all symbols, it is not entirely perfect; however, the imperfection of a symbol is not a shortcoming, but the other side of the work of abstraction that it performs. Aristotle's symbol of the fleeing army is imperfect because it starts from the wrong assumption, namely that before the flight the army was standing fast. This is not true, of course, of what is being symbolised, which is the way in which knowledge is born. But this very lack shows clearly the only thing that the image is intended to illustrate: the birth of experience as an event over which no one has control and which is not even determined by the particular weight of this or that observation, but in which everything is co-ordinated in a way that is ultimately incomprehensible. The image captures the curious openness in which experience is acquired, suddenly, through this or that feature, unpredictably, and yet not without preparation, and valid from then on until there is a new experience, ie determining not only this or that example, but everything of the kind. It is this universality of experience through which, according to Aristotle, the true universality of the concept and the possibility of science comes about. Thus the image illustrates the way in which the unprincipled universality of experience (its accretion) eventually leads to the unity of the arche (which means both 'command' and 'principle').

But if, like Aristotle, we think of the essence of experience only in regard to science, then we are simplifying the process in which it comes about. His image describes this process, but it describes it under over-simplified conditions. As if one could automatically give a straightforward account of experience that contained no contradictions! Aristotle here presupposes that what persists in the flight of observations and emerges as a universal is, in fact, something common to them: the universality of the concept is, for him, ontologically prior. What concerns Aristotle about experience is merely its contribution to the formation of concepts.

If we look at experience in this way in terms of its result, its real character as a process is overlooked. This process is, in fact, an essentially negative one. It cannot be described simply as the unbroken development of typical universals. This development takes place, rather, by continually false generalisations being refuted by experience and what was regarded as typical being shown not to be so. This is seen linguistically in the fact that we use the word 'experience' in two different senses: to refer to the experiences that fit in with our expectation and confirm it, and to the experience that we have. This latter, 'experience' in the real sense, is always negative. If we have an experience of an object, this means that we have not seen the thing correctly hitherto and now know it better. Thus the negativity of experience has a curiously productive meaning. It is not simply a deception that we see through and hence make a correction, but a comprehensive knowledge that we acquire. It cannot, therefore, be an object chosen at random in regard to which we have an experience, but it must be of such a nature that we gain through it better knowledge, not only of itself, but of what we thought we knew before, ie of a universal. The negation by means of which it achieves this is a determinate negation. We call this kind of experience dialectical.

It is not Aristotle, but Hegel who is our important witness for ⁵ᵛⁱ ᵖᵗ the dialectical element of experience. With him the element of historicality comes into its own. He conceives experience as scepticism in action. We saw that one's experience changes one's whole knowledge. Strictly speaking, we cannot have the same experience twice. It is true, of course that it is part of the nature of experience that it is continually confirmed; it is, as it were, acquired only through being repeated. But it is no longer a new experience when it is repeated and confirmed. When we have had an experience, this means that we possess it. We can now predict what was previously unexpected. The same thing cannot become again a new experience for us; only some other unexpected thing can provide someone who has experience with a new one. Thus the experiencing consciousness has reversed its direction, ie it has turned back on itself. The experiencer has become aware of his experience, he is 'experienced'. He has acquired a new horizon within which something can become an experience for him.

This is the point at which Hegel becomes an important witness for us. In his *Phenomenology of Mind* he shows how the consciousness that would be sure of itself experiences. The object of the mind is the in-itself, but what is in-itself can always be known only in the way that it presents itself to the experiencing consciousness. Thus the experiencing consciousness has this experience: that the in-itself quality of the object is 'in-itself' for us.[259]

Hegel here analyses the concept of experience; an analysis that has drawn the special attention of Heidegger, who was both attracted and repulsed by it.[260] Hegel says: 'The dialectical

movement that consciousness carries out in regard to itself, both
in regard to its knowledge and to its object, inasmuch as its
new true object emerges from this, is actually what is called
"experience" '. Remembering what we have said above, let us
ask what Hegel means, as he is here clearly trying to say something about the general nature of experience. Heidegger has
pointed out, rightly in my opinion, that Hegel is not here interpreting experience dialectically, but rather conceiving what is
dialectical in terms of the nature of experience.[261] According to
Hegel, experience has the structure of a reversal of consciousness and hence it is a dialectical movement. Hegel behaves, of
course, as if what is generally meant by experience were something else, in that in general we 'experience the falsehood of this
first concept through another object' (and not in such a way that
the object itself changes). But it is only apparently different. In
actual fact the philosophical mind realises what the experiencing
mind is really doing when it proceeds from one to the other: it is
turning round. Thus Hegel declares that it is the true nature of
experience to turn round in this way.

In fact, to repeat, experience is primarily an experience of
negation: it is not, however, as we thought. In view of the experience that we have of another object, both things change, our
knowledge and its object. We know that the object itself 'does
not pass the test'. The new object contains the truth concerning
the old one.

What Hegel describes in this way as experience is the experience that consciousness has of itself. 'The principle of experience contains the infinitely important element that in order to
accept a content as true, the man himself must be present or,
more precisely, he must find the content in unity and combined
with the certainty of himself', writes Hegel in the *Encyclopedia*. [262] The concept of experience means precisely this,
that this kind of unity with oneself is first established. This
is the reversal of direction that consciousness undergoes when it
recognises itself in what is alien and different. Whether the
movement of experience is realised as an expansion into the
manifoldness of the contents or as the emergence of continually
new forms of mind, the necessity of which is understood by
philosophical science, in any case it is a reversal of consciousness. Hegel's dialectical description of experience has some
truth.

For Hegel, it is necessary, of course, that the movement of
consciousness, experience should lead to a self-knowledge that
no longer has anything different or alien to itself. For him the
perfection of experience is 'science', the certainty of itself in

knowledge. Hence his criterion of experience is that of self-knowledge. That is why the dialectic of experience must end with the overcoming of all experience, which is attained in absolute knowledge, ie in the complete identity of consciousness and object. We can now understand why Hegel's application to history, insofar as he saw it as part of the abolute self-consciousness of philosophy, does not do justice to the hermeneutical consciousness. The nature of experience is conceived in terms of that which goes beyond it; for experience itself can never be science. It is in absolute antithesis to knowledge and to that kind of instruction that follows from general theoretical or technical knowledge. The truth of experience always contains an orientation towards new experience. That is why a person who is called 'experienced' has become such not only through experiences, but is also open to new experiences. The perfection of his experience, the perfect form of what we call 'experienced', does not consist in the fact that someone already knows everything and knows better than anyone else. Rather, the experienced person proves to be, on the contrary, someone who is radically undogmatic; who, because of the many experiences he has had and the knowledge he has drawn from them is particularly well equipped to have new experiences and to learn from them. The dialectic of experience has its own fulfilment not in definitive knowledge, but in that openness to experience that is encouraged by experience itself.

But then this gives the concept of experience that we are concerned with here a qualitatively new element. It refers not only to experience in the sense of the information that this or that thing gives us. It is that experience which must constantly be acquired and from which none can be exempt. Experience here is something that is part of the historical nature of man. Although in bringing up children, for example, parents may try to spare them certain experiences, experience as a whole is not a thing that anyone can be spared. Rather, experience in this sense involves inevitably many disappointments of one's expectations and only thus is experience acquired. That experience refers chiefly to painful and disagreeable experiences does not mean that we are being especially pessimistic, but can be seen directly from its nature. Only through negative instances do we acquire new experiences, as Bacon saw. Every experience worthy of the name runs counter to our expectation. Thus the historical nature of man contains as an essential element a fundamental negativity that emerges in the relation between experience and insight.

Insight is more than the knowledge of this or that situation. It always involves an escape from something that had deceived us and held us captive. Thus insight always involves an element of self-knowledge and constitutes a necessary side of what we called experience in the proper sense. Insight too is something to which we come. It too is ultimately part of the nature of a man, ie to be discerning and insightful.

If we want to quote another witness for this third element in the nature of experience, the best is Aeschylus. He found the formula or, rather, recognised its metaphysical significance as expressing the inner historicality of experience, of 'learning though suffering' (pathei mathos). This phrase does not mean only that we become wise through suffering and that a more correct understanding of things must first be acquired through the disappointment of being deceived and then undeceived. Understood in this way, the formula is probably as old as human experience itself. But Aeschylus means more than this.[263] He refers to the reason why this is so. What a man has to learn through suffering is not this or that particular thing, but the knowledge of the limitations of humanity, of the absoluteness of the barrier that separates him from the divine. It is ultimately a religious insight—that kind of insight which gave birth to Greek tragedy.

Thus experience is experience of human finitude. The truly experienced man is one who is aware of this, who knows that he is master neither of time nor the future. The experienced man knows the limitedness of all prediction and the uncertainty of all plans. In him is realised the truth-value of experience. If it is characteristic of every phase of the process of experience that the experienced person acquires a new openness to new experiences, this is certainly true of the idea of complete experience. It does not mean that experience comes to an end in it and a higher form of knowledge is reached (Hegel), but experience is fully and truly present for the first time. In it all dogmatism, which proceeds from the soaring desires of the human heart, reaches an absolute barrier. Experience teaches us to recognise reality. What is properly gained from all experience, then, is to know what is. But 'what is', here, is not this or that thing, but 'what cannot be done away with' (was nicht mehr umzustossen ist —Ranke).

Real experience is that in which man becomes aware of his finiteness. In it are discovered the limits of the power and the self-knowledge of his planning reason. It proves to be an illusion that everything can be reversed, that there is always time for everything and that everything somehow returns. The person who is involved and acts in history continually experiences, rather, that nothing returns. 'To recognise what is' does not mean to recognise what is just at this moment there, but to have insight into the limitations within which the future is still open to expectation and planning or, even more fundamentally, that all the expectation and planning of finite beings is finite and limited. Thus true experience is that of one's own historicality. This leads the discussion of the concept of experience to a conclusion that is of some importance to our enquiry into the nature of effective-historical consciousness. As a genuine form of experience it must reflect the general structure of experience. Thus we shall have to discover those elements in the hermeneutical experience that we have found in the analysis of experience in general.

The hermeneutical experience is concerned with what has been transmitted in tradition. This is what is to be experienced. But tradition is not simply a process that we learn to know and be in command of through experience; it is language, ie it expresses itself like a 'Thou'. A 'Thou' is not an object, but stands in a relationship with us. It would be wrong to think that this meant that what is experienced in tradition is to be taken as the meaning of another person, who is a 'Thou'. Rather, we consider that the understanding of tradition does not take the text as an expression of life of a 'Thou', but as a meaningful content detached from all bonds of the meaning individual, of an 'I' or a 'Thou'. Still, the relation to the 'Thou' and the meaning of experience in this case must be capable of contributing to the analysis of the 'hermeneutical experience. For tradition is a genuine partner in communication, with which we have fellowship as does the 'I' with a 'Thou'.

That the experience of the 'Thou' must be a specific one, in that the 'Thou' is not an object but is in relationship with us, is clear. For this reason the elements we have outlined in the structure of experience will undergo a change. Since here the object of experience has itself the character of a person, this kind of experience is a moral phenomenon, as is the knowledge acquired through experience, the understanding of the other person. Let us therefore consider the change undergone by the structure of experience when it is experience of the 'Thou' and when it is hermeneutical experience.

There is a kind of experience of the 'Thou' that seeks to discover things that are typical in the behaviour of one's fellow men and is able to make predictions concerning another person on the basis of experience. We call this a knowledge of human

nature. We understand the other person in the same way that we
understand any other typical event in our experiential field, ie he
is predictable. His behaviour is as much a means to our end as
any other means. From the moral point of view this attitude to
the 'Thou' is something that is directed ultimately towards oneself and contradicts the moral definition of man. Kant, as we
know, in interpreting the categorical imperative said, inter alia,
that the other should never be used as a means, but always as an
end in himself.

If we apply to the hermeneutical problem the form of the
relation to the 'Thou' and of the understanding of the 'Thou'
which constitutes knowledge of human nature, the equivalent is
the naive faith in method and in the objectivity that can be attained through it. Someone who understands tradition in this
way makes it an object, ie he confronts it in a free and unin-
volved way, and, by methodically excluding all subjective elements in regard to it, he discovers what it contains. We saw that
he thereby detaches himself from the continuing action of tradition, in which he himself has his historical reality. It is the
method of the social sciences, following the methodological
ideas of the eighteenth century and their programmatic formulation by Hume, ideas that are an imitation of scientific method.[264]
But this takes account only of a partial aspect of the actual
procedure of the human sciences, and even that is schematically
reduced, in that it is only what is typical and regular that is taken
account of in human behaviour. This flattens out the nature of
hermeneutical experience precisely as we have seen in the teleological interpretation of the concept of induction since Aristotle.

A second mode of the experience of the 'Thou' and of understanding it is that the 'Thou' is acknowledged as a person, but
that despite the involvement of the person in the experience of
the 'Thou', the understanding of the latter is still a form of
self-relatedness. This proceeds from the dialectical appearance
that the dialectic of the 'I-Thou' relation brings with it. This
relation is not immediate, but reflective. To every claim there is
a counter-claim. This is why it is possible for each of the partners in the relationship reflectively to outdo the other. One
claims to express the other's claim and even to understand the
other better than the other understands himself. In this way the
'Thou' loses the immediacy with which it makes its claim. It is
understood, but this means that it is anticipated and intercepted
reflectively from the standpoint of the other person. Because it
is a mutual relationship, it helps to constitute the reality of the

'Thou' relationship itself. The inner historicality of all the relations in the lives of men consists in the fact there is a constant struggle for mutual recognition. This can have very varied degrees of tension, to the point of the complete domination of one person by the other. But even the most extreme forms of mastery and slavery are a genuine dialectical relationship of the structure that Hegel has elaborated.[265]

The experience of the 'Thou' that is gained here is objectively more adequate than the knowledge of human nature, which merely seeks to calculate how the other person will behave. It is an illusion to see another person as a tool that can be absolutely known and used. Even a slave still has a will to power, which turns against his master, as Nietzsche rightly said.[266] But this dialectic of reciprocity that governs all 'I-Thou' relationships is inevitably hidden from the mind of the individual. The servant who tyrannises his master through serving him does not consider that he has his own personal aims in doing this. In fact, his own self-awareness consists precisely in his withdrawing from the dialectic of this reciprocity, in his reflecting himself out of his relation to the other and so becoming unreachable by him. By understanding the other, by claiming to know him, one takes from him all justification of his own claims. The dialectic of charitable or welfare work in particular operates in this way, penetrating all relationships between men as a reflective form of the effort to dominate. The claim to understand the other person in advance performs the function of keeping the claim of the other person at a distance. We are familiar with this from the educative relationship, an authoritative form of welfare work. In these reflective forms the dialectic of the 'I-Thou' relation becomes more clearly defined.

In the hermeneutical sphere the parallel to this experience of the 'Thou' is what we generally call historical consciousness. Historical consciousness knows about the otherness of the other, about the past in its otherness, just as well as the understanding of the 'Thou' knows the 'Thou' as a person. It seeks in the otherness of the past not the instantiation of a general law, but something historically unique. By claiming to transcend its own conditionedness completely in its knowing of the other, it is involved in a false dialectical appearance, since it is actually seeking to master, as it were, the past. This does not have to be with the speculative claim of a philosophy of world history—it can also be an ideal of perfect enlightenment that points the way to the attitude to experience of the historical sciences that we find, for example, in Dilthey. In my analysis of hermeneutical consciousness I have shown that the dialectical illusion, which historical consciousness creates and which corresponds to the dialectical illusion of experience perfected and replaced by knowledge, is the unattainable ideal of the historical enlightenment. A person who imagines that he is free of prejudices, basing his knowledge on the objectivity of his procedures and denying that he is himself influenced by historical circumstances, experiences the power of the prejudices that unconsciously dominate him, as a vis a tergo. A person who does not accept that he is dominated by prejudices will fail to see what is shown by their light. It is like the relation between the 'I' and the 'Thou'. A person who reflects himself out of the mutuality of such a relation changes this relationship and destroys its moral bond. A person who reflects himself out of a living relationship to tradition destroys the true meaning of this tradition in exactly the same way. Historical consciousness in seeking to understand tradition must not rely on the critical method with which it approaches its sources, as if this preserved it from mixing in its own judgments and prejudices. It must, in fact, take account of its own historicality. To stand within a tradition does not limit the freedom of knowledge but makes it possible.

It is this knowledge and recognition that constitutes a third, and highest, type of hermeneutical experience: the openness to tradition possessed by effective-historical consciousness. It too has a real correspondence with the experience of the 'Thou'. In human relations the important thing is, as we have seen, to experience the 'Thou' truly as a 'Thou', ie not to overlook his claim and to listen to what he has to say to us. To this end, openness is necessary. But this openness exists ultimately not only for the person to whom one listens, but rather anyone who listens is fundamentally open. Without this kind of openness to one another there is no genuine human relationship. Belonging together always also means being able to listen to one another. When two people understand each other, this does not mean that one person "understands" the other, in the sense of surveying him. Similarly, to hear and obey someone does not mean simply that we do blindly what the other desires. We call such a person a slave. Openness to the other, then, includes the acknowledgement that I must accept some things that are against myself, even though there is no one else who asks this of me.

This is the parallel to the hermeneutical experience. I must allow the validity of the claim made by tradition, not in the sense of simply acknowledging the past in its otherness, but in such a way that it has something to say to me. This too calls for a fundamental sort of openness. Someone who is open in this way to tradition sees that the historical consciousness is not really open at all, but rather, if it reads its texts 'historically' has always thoroughly smoothed them out beforehand, so that the criteria of our own knowledge can never be put in question by tradition. Recall the naive mode of comparison that the historical approach generally engages in. The 25th 'Lyceum Fragment' by Friedrich Schlegel reads: 'The two basic principles of so-called historical criticism are the postulate of the commonplace and the axiom of familiarity. The postulate of the commonplace is that everything that is really great, good and beautiful is improbable, for it is extraordinary or at least peculiar. The axiom of familiarity is that things must always have been just as they are with us, for things are naturally like this'. In contrast to that, the effective-historical consciousness rises above this naive comparing and assimilating by letting itself experience tradition and by keeping itself open to the claim to truth encountered in it. The hermeneutical consciousness has its fulfilment, not in its methodological sureness of itself, but in the same readiness for experience that distinguishes the experienced man by comparison with the man captivated by dogma. This is what distinguishes effective-historical consciousness, as we can now say more exactly, in terms of the concept of experience.

(C) THE HERMENEUTICAL PRIORITY OF THE QUESTION

(i) The model of the Platonic dialectic

This indicates the direction of our enquiry. We shall now examine the logical structure of openness, which characterises hermeneutical consciousness, recalling the importance of the concept of the question, as discovered in our analysis of the hermeneutical situation. It is clear that the structure of the question is implicit in all experience. We cannot have experiences without asking questions. The recognition that an object is different and not as we first thought, obviously involves the question whether it was this or that. The openness that is part of experience is, from a logical point of view, precisely the openness of being this or that. It has the structure of a question. And just as the dialectical negativity of experience found its fulfilment in the idea of a perfect experience, in which we become aware of our absolute finitude and limited being, the logical form of the question, and the negativity that is part of it, find their fulfilment in a radical negativity: the knowledge of not knowing.

This is the famous Socratic *docta ignorantia* which opens up the way, amid the most extreme negativity of doubt, to the true superiority of questioning. We shall have to consider in greater depth what is the essence of the question, if we are to clarify the particular nature of the hermeneutical experience.

It is of the essence of the question to have sense. Now sense involves direction. Hence the sense of the question is the direction in which alone the answer can be given if it is to be meaningful. A question places that which is questioned within a particular perspective. The emergence of the question opens up, as it were, the being of the object. Hence the logos that sets out this opened-up being is already an answer. Its sense lies in the sense of the question.

Among the greatest insights given us by Plato's account of Socrates is that, contrary to the general opinion, it is more difficult to ask questions than to answer them. When the partners in the Socratic dialogue are unable to answer Socrates' awkward questions and seek to turn the tables by assuming what is, as they suppose, the advantageous role of the questioner, they come to grief.[267] Behind this comic motif in the Platonic dialogues there is the important critical distinction between genuine and false discourse. For someone who uses dialogue only in order to prove himself right and not to gain insight, asking questions will indeed seem easier than answering them. There is no risk that he will not be able to answer a question. In fact, however, the new collapse of the interlocutor shows that he who thinks that he knows better cannot even ask the right questions. In order to be able to ask, one must want to know, which involves knowing that one does not know. In the comic confusion between question and answer, knowledge and ignorance that Plato describes, there is the profound recognition of the priority of the question in all knowledge and discourse that really reveals something of an object. Discourse that is intended to reveal something requires that that thing be opened up by the question.

For this reason, the way in which dialectic proceeds is by way of question and answer or, rather, by way of the development of all knowledge through the question. To ask a question means to bring into the open. The openness of what is in question consists in the fact that the answer is not settled. It must still be undetermined, in order that a decisive answer can be given. The revelation of the questionability of what is questioned constitutes the sense of the question. The object has to be brought into this state of indeterminacy, so that there is an equilibrium between pro and contra. The sense of every question is realised in passing through this state of indeterminacy, in which it becomes an open question. Every true question achieves this openness. If it lacks this, then it is basically no more than an apparent question. We are familiar with this from the pedagogical question, the curious difficulty and paradox of which consists in the fact that it is a question without a questioner. Or from the rhetorical question, which not only has no questioner, but no object.

The openness of the question is not boundless. It is limited by the horizon of the question. A question which lacks this is, so to speak, floating. It becomes a question only when the fluid indeterminacy of the direction in which it is pointing is overcome by a specific alternative being presented. In other words, the question has to be asked. The asking of it implies openness, but also limitation. It implies the explicit establishing of presuppositions, in terms of which can be seen what still remains open. Hence a question can be right or wrong, according as it reaches into the sphere of the truly open or fails to do so. We call a question false that does not reach the state of openness, but inhibits it by holding on to false presuppositions. It pretends to an openness and susceptibility to decision that it does not have. But if what is undecided is not distinguished, or not correctly distinguished from those predispositions that are effectively held, then it is not brought into the open and nothing can be decided.

This is shown clearly in the case of the distorted question that we are so familiar with in everyday life. There can be no answer to a distorted question because it leads us only apparently, and not really, through the open state of indeterminacy in which a decision is made. We call it distorted rather than false because there is a question behind it, ie there is an openness intended, but it does not lie in the direction in which the distorted question is pointing. The word 'distorted', refers to something that has moved away from the right direction. The distortedness of a question consists in the fact that it does not have any real direction, and hence any answer to it is impossible. Similarly, we say that statements that are not exactly false, but also not right, are 'distorted'. This, too, is determined by their sense, ie by their relation to the question. We cannot call them false, because we detect something true about them, but nor can we properly call them right because they do not correspond to any meaningful question and hence have no correct meaning unless they are themselves corrected. Sense is always the direction of a possible question. The sense of what is correct must be in accordance with the direction taken by a question.

Because a question remains open, it always includes both
negative and positive judgments. This is the basis of the essential relation between question and knowledge. For it is the essence of knowledge not only to judge something correctly, but at
the same time and for the same reason to exclude what is wrong.
The deciding of the question is the way to knowledge. What
decides a question is the preponderance of reasons for the one
and against the other possibility. But this is still not full knowledge. The thing itself is known only through the dissolution of
the counter-instances, only when the counter-arguments are
seen to be incorrect.

We know this from mediaeval dialectic, in particular, that lists
not only the pro and contra and then its own decision, but finally
sets out all the arguments. This form of mediaeval dialectic is
not simply a consequence of the doctrinal system of disputation,
but depends, on the contrary, on the inner connection between
science and dialectic, ie between answer and question. There is
a famous passage in Aristotle's *Metaphysics*[268] that has attracted a great deal of attention and can be explained in terms of
what we have been saying. Aristotle says that dialectic is the
power to investigate contraries independently of the object, and
to see whether one and the same science can be concerned with
contraries. Here it seems that a general account of dialectic
(which is entirely in accordance with what we find, for example,
in Plato's *Parmenides*) is linked to every specific 'logical' problem which is familiar to us from the *Topics*. [269] It does indeed
seem a very curious question whether the same science can be
concerned with contraries. Hence the attempt has been made to
dismiss this as a gloss.[270] The connection between the two questions becomes clear, however, as soon as we accept the priority
of the question over the answer, which is the basis of the concept of knowledge. Knowledge always means, precisely, looking
at opposites. Its superiority over preconceived opinion consists
in the fact that it is able to conceive of possibilities as possibilities. Knowledge is dialectical from the ground up. Only a
person who has questions can have knowledge, but questions
include the antitheses of yes and no, of being like this and being
like that. Only because knowledge is dialectical in this comprehensive sense can there be a 'dialectic' that explicitly makes
its object the antitheses of 'yes' and 'no'. Thus the apparently
over-specialised question of whether or not it is possible to have
one and the same science of contraries contains, in fact, the
ground of the very possibility of dialectic.

Even Aristotle's views on proof and argument—which, in

fact, make dialectic a subordinate element in knowledge—accord the same priority to the question, as has been demonstrated by the outstanding work by Ernst Kapp on the origin of Aristotle's syllogistic.[271] The priority that the question holds in knowledge shows in the most basic way the limitedness of the idea of method for knowledge from which our argument as a whole has proceeded. There is no such thing as a method of learning to ask questions, of learning to see what needs to be questioned. On the contrary, the example of Socrates teaches that the important thing is the knowledge that one does not know. Hence the Socratic dialectic, which leads, through its art of confusing the interlocutor, to this knowledge, sets up the presuppositions of the question. All questioning and desire to know presuppose a knowledge that one does not know; so much so, indeed, that it is a particular lack of knowledge that leads to a particular question.

Plato, unforgettably, shows wherein the difficulty lies in the way of knowing that we do not know. It is the power of opinion against which it is so hard to obtain an admission of ignorance. It is opinion that suppresses questions. Opinion has a curious tendency to propagate itself. It would always like to be the general opinion, just as the word that the Greeks have for opinion, doxa, also means the decision made by the majority in the council assembly. How, then, can the admission of ignorance and questioning emerge?

Let us say first of all that it can come about only in the way that we have any sudden idea. It is true that we do not speak of sudden ideas so much in regard to questions as to answers, eg the solution of problems; and by this we mean to say that there is no methodical way to the thought that is the solution. But we also know that sudden thoughts do not come entirely unexpectedly. They always presuppose a pointer in the direction of an area of openness from which the idea can come, ie they presuppose questions. The real nature of the sudden idea is perhaps less the sudden realisation of the solution to a problem than the sudden realisation of the question that advances into openness and thus makes an answer possible. Every sudden idea has the structure of a question. But the sudden realisation of the question is already a breach in the smooth front of popular opinion. Hence we say that a question too 'comes' to us, that it 'arises' or 'presents itself' more than that we raise it or present it.

We have already seen that, logically, the negativity of experience implies a question. In fact we have experiences through the stimulus given us by that which does not fit in with preconceived opinion. Thus questioning too is more a 'passion' than an action. A question presses itself on us; we can no longer avoid it and persist in our accustomed opinion.

/It seems to conflict with these conclusions, however, that the Socratic-Platonic dialectic raises the art of questioning to a conscious art; but there is something peculiar about this art. We have seen that it is reserved to the person who desires to know, ie who already has questions. The art of questioning is not the art of avoiding the pressure of opinion; it already presupposes this freedom. It is not an art in the sense that the Greeks speak of techne, not a craft that can be taught and by means of which we would master the knowledge of truth. The so-called epistemological digression of the seventh *Letter* is directed, rather, to distinguish the unique character of this strange art of dialectic from everything that can be taught and learned. The art of dialectic is not the art of being able to win every argument. On the contrary, it is possible that someone who is practising the art of dialectic, ie the art of questioning and of seeking truth, comes off worse in the argument in the eyes of those listening to it. Dialectic, as the art of asking questions, proves itself only because the person who knows how to ask questions is able to persist in his questioning, which involves being able to preserve his orientation towards openness. The art of questioning is that of being able to go on asking questions, ie the art of thinking. It is called 'dialectic', for it is the art of conducting a real conversation.

To conduct a conversation requires first of all that the partners to it do not talk at cross purposes. Hence its necessary structure is that of question and answer. The first condition of the art of conversation is to ensure that the other person is with us. We know this only too well from the reiterated yesses of the interlocutors in the Platonic dialogues. The positive side of this monotony is the inner logic with which the development of the topic proceeds in the conversation. To conduct a conversation means to allow oneself to be conducted by the object to which the partners in the conversation are directed. It requires that one does not try to out-argue the other person, but that one really considers the weight of the other's opinion. Hence it is an art of testing.[272] But the art of testing is the art of questioning. For we have seen that to question means to lay open, to place in the open. As against the solidity of opinions, questioning makes the object and all its possibilities fluid. A person who possesses the 'art' of questioning is a person who is able to prevent the suppression of questions by the dominant opinion. A person who possesses this art will himself seek for everything in favour of an opinion. Dialectic consists not in trying to discover the weakness of what is said, but in bringing out its real strength. It is not the art of arguing that is able to make a strong case out of a weak one, but the art of thinking that is able to strengthen what is said by referring to the object.

The unique and continuing relevance of the Platonic dialogues is due to this art of strengthening, for in this process what is said is continually transformed into the uttermost possibilities of its rightness and truth and overcomes all opposing argument which seeks to limit its validity. Here, again, it is not simply a matter of leaving the subject undecided. Whoever wants to know something cannot just leave it a matter of mere opinion, which is to say that he should not hold himself aloof from the opinions that are in question (cf pp 261, 302). It is always the speaker who is challenged until the truth of what is under discussion finally emerges. The maieutic productivity of the Socratic dialogue, the art of using words as a midwife, is certainly directed towards the people who are the partners in the dialogue, but it is concerned merely with the opinions that they express, the immanent objective logic of which is unfolded in the dialogue. What emerges in its truth is the logos, which is neither mine nor yours and hence so far transcends the subjective opinions of the partners to the dialogue that even the person leading the conversation is always ignorant. Dialectic as the art of conducting a conversation is also the art of seeing things in the unity of an aspect (sunoran eis hen eidos) ie it is the art of the formation of concepts as the working out of the common meaning. Precisely this is what characterises a dialogue, in contrast with the rigid form of the statement that demands to be set down in writing: that here language, in the process of question and answer, giving and taking, talking at cross purposes and seeing each other's point, performs that communication of meaning which, with respect to the written tradition, is the task of hermeneutics. Hence it is more than a metaphor, it is a memory of what originally was the case, to describe the work of hermeneutics as a conversation with the text. That the interpretation that achieves this takes place through language does not mean that it is a translation into a foreign medium, but represents the restoration of the original communication of meaning. Thus that which is handed down in literary form is brought back out of the alienation in which it finds itself and into the living presence of conversation, whose fundamental procedure is always question and answer.

Thus we can refer to Plato if, in the case of the hermeneutic phenomenon, we would place the main emphasis on the question. We can do this all the more readily as Plato himself manifests the hermeneutical phenomenon in a specific way. It would be worth investigating his critique of the written word in view of the fact that it is evidence that the poetic and philosophical tradition was becoming a literature in Athens. We can see in Plato's dialogues the way in which the "interpretation" of texts, cultivated by the sophists, and especially that of poetry for didactic ends, called forth Plato's opposition. We can see, further, the way in which Plato seeks to overcome the weakness of the logoi and especially that of the written ones, through his own dialogues. The literary form of the dialogue places language and concept back within the original movement of the conversation. This protects words from all dogmatic abuse.

The original form of conversation can also be seen in derivative forms in which the correspondence between question and answer is obscured. Letters, for example, are an interesting transitional phenomenon: a kind of written conversation that, as it were, stretches out the movement of talking at cross purposes before seeing each other's point. The art of writing letters consists in not letting what one says become a treatise on the subject, but making it acceptable to the correspondent. But it also consists, on the other hand, in preserving and fulfilling the measure of finality possessed by everything stated in writing. The time lapse between sending a letter and receiving an answer is not just an external factor, but gives to this form of communication its proper nature as a particular form of writing. So we note that the speeding-up of the post has not led to a heightening of this form of communication but, on the contrary, to a decline in the art of letter-writing.

The fundamental place of conversation, the relation of question and answer, can be seen even in a case as extreme as that of Hegel's dialectic as a philosophical method. To elaborate the totality of the determination of thought, the aim of Hegel's logic, is the attempt to enclose within the great monologue of modern 'method' the continuum of meaning, which is realised in a particular instance in the conversation of those speaking. When Hegel sets himself the task of making fluid and subtle the abstract determinations of thought, this means dissolving and remoulding logic into the procedures of language, and the concept into the meaningful power of words, which ask questions and give answers—a magnificent reminder, even if unsuccessful, of what dialectic really was and is. Hegel's dialectic is a monologue of thinking that seeks to carry out in advance what matures little by little in every genuine conversation.

(ii) The logic of question and answer

Thus we come back to the point that the hermeneutic phenomenon also contains within itself the original meaning of conversation and the structure of question and answer. For an historical text to be made the object of interpretation means that it asks a question of the interpreter. Thus interpretation always involves a relation to the question that is asked of the interpreter. To understand a text means to understand this question. But this takes place, as we showed, by our achieving the hermeneutical horizon. We now recognise this as the horizon of the question within which the sense of the text is determined.

Thus a person who seeks to understand must question what lies behind what is said. He must understand it as an answer to a question. If we go back behind what is said, then we inevitably ask questions beyond what is said. We understand the sense of the text only by acquiring the horizon of the question that, as such, necessarily includes other possible answers. Thus the meaning of a sentence is relative to the question to which it is a reply, ie it necessarily goes beyond what is said in it. The logic of the human sciences is, then, as appears from what we have said, a logic of the question.

Despite Plato we are not very ready for such a logic. Almost the only person I find a link with here is R. G. Collingwood. In a brilliant and cogent critique of the 'realist' Oxford school he developed the idea of a logic of question and answer, but unfortunately never developed it systematically.[273] He clearly saw what was missing in naive hermeneutics founded on the prevailing philosophical critique. In particular the practice that Collingwood found in English universities of discussing 'statements', though perhaps a good training of intelligence, obviously failed to take account of the historicality that is part of all understanding. Collingwood argues thus: We can understand a text only when we have understood the question to which it is an answer. But since this question can be derived solely from the text and accordingly the appropriateness of the reply is the methodological presupposition for the reconstruction of the question, any criticism of this reply from some other quarter is pure mock-fighting. It is like the understanding of works of art. A work of art can be understood only if we assume its adequacy as an expression of the artistic idea. Here also we have to discover the question which it answers, if we are to understand it as an answer. This is, in fact, an axiom of all hermeneutics which we described above as the 'fore-conception of completion'.[274]

This is, for Collingwood, the nerve of all historical knowledge. The historical method requires that the logic of question and answer be applied to historical tradition. We shall understand historical events only if we reconstruct the question to which the historical actions of the persons concerned were the answer. As an example Collingwood cites the Battle of Trafalgar and Nelson's plan on which it was based. The example is intended to show that the course of the battle helps us to understand Nelson's real plan, because it was successfully carried out. The plan of his opponent, however, because it failed, cannot be reconstructed from the events. Thus understanding the course of the battle and understanding the plan that Nelson carried out in it are one and the same process.[275]

In fact we cannot avoid the discovery that the logic of question and answer has to reconstruct two different questions that have also two different answers: the question of meaning in the course of a great event and the question of whether this event went according to plan. Clearly, the two questions coincide only when the plan coincides with the course of events. But this is a presupposition that, as men involved in history, we cannot maintain as a methodological principle when concerned with a historical tradition which deals with such men. Tolstoy's celebrated description of the council of war before the battle, in which all the strategic possibilities are calculated and all the plans considered, thoroughly and perceptively, while the general sits there and sleeps, but in the night before the battle goes round all the sentry-posts, is obviously a more accurate account of what we call history. Kutusov gets nearer to the reality and the forces that determine it than the strategists of the war council. The conclusion to be drawn from this example is that the interpreter of history always runs the risk of hypostasizing the sequence of events when he sees their significance as that intended by actors and planners.[276]

This is a legitimate undertaking only if Hegel's conditions hold good, ie that the philosophy of history is made party to the plans of the world spirit and on the basis of this esoteric knowledge is able to mark out certain individuals as of world-historical importance, there being a real co-ordination between their particular ideas and the world-historical meaning of events. But it is impossible to derive a hermeneutical principle for the knowledge of history from these cases that are characterised by the coming together of the subjective and objective in history. In regard to historical tradition Hegel's theory has, clearly, only a limited truth. The infinite web of motivations that constitutes history only occasionally and for a short period acquires in a single individual the clarity of what has been planned. Thus what Hegel describes as an outstanding case rests on the general basis of the disproportion that exists between the subjective thoughts of an individual and the meaning of the whole course of history. As a rule we experience the course of events as something that continually changes our plans and expectations. Someone who tries to stick to his plans discovers precisely how powerless his reason is. There are odd occasions when everything happens, as it were, of its own accord, ie events seem to be automatically in accord with our plans and wishes. On these occasions we can say that everything is going according to plan. But to apply this experience to the whole of history is to undertake a great ex-trapolation that entirely contradicts our experience.

The use that Collingwood makes of the logic of question and answer in hermeneutical theory is now made ambiguous by this extrapolation. Our understanding of written tradition as such is not of a kind that we can simply presuppose that the meaning that we discover in it agrees with that which its author intended. Just as the events of history do not in general manifest any agreement with the subjective ideas of the person who stands and acts within history, so the sense of a text in general reaches far beyond what its author originally intended.[277] But the task of understanding is concerned in the first place with the meaning of the text itself.

This is clearly what Collingwood had in mind when he denied that there is any difference between the historical question and the philosophical question to which the text is supposed to be an answer. Nevertheless, we must hold on to the point that the question that we are concerned to reconstruct has to do not with the mental experiences of the author, but simply with the meaning of the text itself. Thus it must be possible, if we have under-stood the meaning of a sentence, ie have reconstructed the ques-tion to which it is really the answer, to enquire also about the questioner and his meaning, to which the text is, perhaps, only the imagined answer. Collingwood is wrong when he finds it methodologically unsound to differentiate between the question to which the text is imagined to be an answer and the question to which it really is an answer. He is right only insofar as the understanding of a text does not generally involve such a distinc-tion, if we are concerned with the object of which the text speaks. The reconstruction of the ideas of an author is a quite different task.

We shall have to ask what are the conditions that apply to this different task. For it is undoubtedly true that, compared with the genuine hermeneutical experience that understands the meaning of the text, the reconstruction of what the author really had in mind is a limited undertaking. It is the seduction of historicism to see in this kind of reduction a scientific virtue and regard understanding as a kind of reconstruction which in effect repeats the process of how the text came into being. Hence it follows the ideal familiar to us from our knowledge of nature, where we understand a process only when we are able to reproduce it artificially.

I have shown above[278] how questionable is Vico's statement that this ideal finds its purest fulfilment in history, because it is there that man encounters his own human historical reality. I have asserted, against this, that every historian and literary critic must reckon with the fundamental non-definitiveness of the horizon in which his understanding moves. Historical tradition can be understood only by being considered in its further determinations resulting from the progress of events. Similarly, the literary critic, who is dealing with poetic or philosophical texts, knows that they are inexhaustible. In both cases it is the progress of events that brings out new aspects of meaning in historical material. Through being re-actualised in understanding, the texts are drawn into a genuine process in exactly the same way as are the events themselves through their continuance. This is what we described as the effective-historical element within the hermeneutical experience. Every actualisation in understanding can be regarded as an historical potentiality of what is understood. It is part of the historical finiteness of our being that we are aware that after us others will understand in a different way. And yet it is a fact equally well established that it remains the same work, the fullness of whose meaning is proved in the changing process of understanding, just as it is the same history whose meaning is constantly being further determined. The hermeneutical reduction to the author's meaning is just as inappropriate as the reduction of historical events to the intentions of their protagonists.

We cannot however, simply take the reconstruction of the question to which a given text is an answer simply as an achievement of historical method. The first thing is the question that the text presents us with, our response to the word handed down to us, so that its understanding must already include the work of historical self-mediation of present and tradition. Thus the relation of question and answer is, in fact, reversed. The voice that speaks to us from the past—be it text, work, trace —itself poses a question and places our meaning in openness. In order to answer this question, we, of whom the question is asked, must ourselves begin to ask questions. We must attempt to reconstruct the question to which the transmitted text is the answer. But we shall not be able to do this without going beyond the historical horizon it presents us with. The reconstruction of the question to which the text is presumed to be the answer takes place itself within a process of questioning through which we seek the answer to the question that the text asks us. A reconstructed question can never stand within its original horizon: for the historical horizon that is outlined in the reconstruction is not a truly comprehensive one. It is, rather, included within the horizon that embraces us as the questioners who have responded to the word that has been handed down.

Hence it is a hermeneutical necessity always to go beyond mere reconstruction. We cannot avoid thinking about that which was unquestionably accepted, and hence not thought about, by an author, and bringing it into the openness of the question. This is not to open the door to arbitrariness in interpretation, but to reveal what always takes place. The understanding of the word of the tradition always requires that the reconstructed question be set within the openness of its questionableness, ie that it merge with the question that tradition is for us. If the 'historical' question emerges by itself, this means that it no longer raises itself as a question. It results from the coming to an end of understanding—a wrong turning at which we get stuck.[279] It is part of real understanding, however, that we regain the concepts of an historical past in such a way that they also include our own comprehension of them. I earlier called this (p 273f) 'the fusing of horizons'. We can say, with Collingwood, that we understand only when we understand the question to which something is the answer, and it is true that what is understood in this way does not remain detached in its meaning from our own meaning. Rather, the reconstruction of the question, from which the meaning of a text is to be understood as an answer, passes into our own questioning. For the text must be understood as an answer to a real question.

The close relation that exists between question and understanding is what gives the hermeneutic experience its true dimension. However much a person seeking understanding may leave open the truth of what is said, however much he may turn away from the immediate meaning of the object and consider, rather, its deeper significance, and take the latter not as true, but merely as meaningful, so that the possibility of its truth remains unsettled, this is the real and basic nature of a question, namely to make things indeterminate. Questions always bring out the undetermined possibilities of a thing. That is why there cannot be an understanding of the questionableness of an object that turns away from real questions, in the same way that there can be the understanding of a meaning that turns away from meaning. To understand the questionableness of something is always to question it. There can be no testing or potential attitude to questioning, for questioning is not the positing, but the testing of possibilities. Here the nature of questioning indicates what is demonstrated by the operation of the Platonic dialogue.[280] A person who thinks must ask himself questions. Even when a person says that at such and such a point a question might arise, this is already a real questioning that simply masks itself, out of either caution or politeness.

This is the reason that all understanding is always more than the mere recreation of someone else's meaning. Asking it opens up possibilities of meaning and thus what is meaningful passes into one's own thinking on the subject. Questions that we do not ourselves ask, such as those that we regard as out of date or pointless, are understood in a curious fashion. We understand how certain questions came to be asked in particular historical circumstances. Understanding such questions means, then, understanding the particular presuppositions whose demise makes the question no longer relevant. An example is perpetual motion. The horizon of meaning of such questions is only apparently still open. They are no longer understood as questions. For what we understand, in such cases, is precisely that there is no question.

To understand a question means to ask it. To understand an opinion is to understand it as the answer to a question.

The logic of question and answer that Collingwood elaborated does away with talk of the permanent problem that underlay the relation of the 'Oxford realists' to the classics of philosophy, and hence with the problem of the history of problems developed by neokantianism. History of problems would be truly history only if it acknowledged the identity of the problem as a pure abstraction and permitted itself a transformation into questioning. There is no such thing, in fact, as a point outside history from which the identity of a problem can be conceived within the vicissitudes of the various attempts to solve it. It is true that all understanding of the texts of philosophy requires the recognition of the knowledge that they contain. Without this we would understand nothing at all. But this does not mean that we in any way step outside the historical conditions in which we find ourselves and in which we understand. The problem that we recognise is not in fact simply the same if it is to be understood in a genuine question. We can regard it as the same only because of our historical shortsightedness. The standpoint that is beyond any standpoint, a standpoint from which we could conceive its true identity, is a pure illusion.

We can understand the reason for this now. The concept of the problem is clearly the formulation of an abstraction, namely the detachment of the content of the question from the question that in fact first reveals it. It refers to the abstract schema to which real and really motivated questions can be reduced and under which they can be subsumed. This kind of 'problem' has fallen out of the motivated context of questioning, from which it receives the clarity of its sense. Hence it is insoluble, like every question that has no clear unambiguous sense, because it is not properly motivated and asked.

This confirms also the origin of the concept of the problem. It does not belong in the sphere of those 'honestly motivated refutations'[281] in which the truth of the object is advanced, but in the sphere of dialectic as a weapon to amaze or make a fool of one's opponent. In Aristotle, the word problema refers to those questions that appear as open alternatives because there is evidence for both views and we think that they cannot be decided by reasons, since the questions involved are too great.[282] Hence problems are not real questions that present themselves and hence acquire the pattern of their answer from the genesis of their meaning, but are alternatives that can only be accepted as themselves and thus can only be treated in a dialectical way. This dialectical sense of the 'problem' has its place in rhetoric, not in philosophy. It is part of the concept that there can be no clear decision on the basis of reasons. That is why Kant sees the rise of the concept of the problem as limited to the dialectic of pure reason. Problems are 'tasks that emerge entirely from its own womb', ie products of reason itself, the complete solution of which it cannot hope to achieve.[283] It is interesting that in the nineteenth century, with the collapse of the direct tradition of philosophical questioning and the rise of historicism, the concept of the problem acquires a universal validity—a sign of the fact that the direct relation to the questions of philosophy no longer exists. It is typical of the embarrassment of the philosophical consciousness that when faced with historicism, it took flight into the abstraction of the concept of the problem and saw no problem about the manner in which problems actually 'exist'. The history of problems in neokantianism is a bastard of historicism. The critique of the concept of the problem that is conducted with the means of a logic of question and answer must destroy the illusion that there are problems as there are stars in the sky. [284] Reflection on the hermeneutical experience transforms problems back to questions that arise and that derive their sense from their motivation.

The dialectic of question and answer, that was disclosed in the structure of the hermeneutical experience, now permits us to state in more detail the type of consciousness that effective-historical consciousness is. For the dialectic of question and answer that we demonstrated makes understanding appear as a reciprocal relationship of the same kind as conversation. It is true that a text does not speak to us in the same way as does another person. We, who are attempting to understand, must ourselves make it speak. But we found that this kind of understanding, 'making the text speak', is not an arbitrary procedure that we undertake on our own initiative but that, as a question, it is related to the answer that is expected in the text. The anticipation of an answer itself presumes that the person asking is part of the tradition and regards himself as addressed by it. This is the truth of the effective-historical consciousness. It is the historically experienced consciousness that, by renouncing the chimera of perfect enlightenment, is open to the experience of history. We described its realisation as the fusion of the horizons of understanding, which is what mediates between the text and its interpreter.

The guiding idea of the following discussion is that the fusion of the horizons that takes place in understanding is the proper achievement of language. Admittedly, the nature of language is one of the most mysterious questions that exist for man to ponder on. Language is so uncannily near to our thinking and when it functions it is so little an object that it seems to conceal its own being from us. In our analysis of the thinking of the human sciences, however, we came so close to this universal mystery of language that is prior to everything else, that we can entrust ourselves to the object that we are investigating to guide us safely in the quest. In other words we are seeking to approach the mystery of language from the conversation that we ourselves are.

If we seek to examine the hermeneutical phenomenon according to the model of the conversation between two persons, the chief thing that these apparently so different situations have in common—the understanding of a text and the understanding that occurs in conversation—is that both are concerned with an object that is placed before them. Just as one person seeks to reach agreement with his partner concerning an object, so the interpreter understands the object of which the text speaks. This understanding of the object must take place in a linguistic form; not that the understanding is subsequently put into words, but in the way in which the understanding comes about—whether in the case of a text or a conversation with another person who presents us with the object—lies the coming-into-language of the thing itself. Thus we shall first consider the structure of conversation proper, in order to bring out the specific character of that other form of conversation that is the understanding of texts. Whereas up to now we have emphasised the constitutive significance of the question for the hermeneutical phenomenon, in terms of the conversation, we must now demonstrate the linguistic nature of conversation, which is the basis of the question, as an element of hermeneutics.

Our first point is that language, in which something comes to be language, is not a possession at the disposal of one or the other of the interlocutors. Every conversation presupposes a common language, or, it creates a common language. Something is placed in the centre, as the Greeks said, which the partners to the dialogue both share, and concerning which they can exchange ideas with one another. Hence agreement concerning the object, which it is the purpose of the conversation to bring about, necessarily means that a common language must first be worked out in the conversation. This is not an external matter of simply adjusting our tools, nor is it even right to say that the partners adapt themselves to one another but, rather, in the successful conversation they both come under the influence of the truth of the object and are thus bound to one another in a new community. To reach an understanding with one's partner in a dialogue is not merely a matter of total self-expression and the successful assertion of one's own point of view, but a transformation into a communion, in which we do not remain what we were.[285]

THIRD PART
THE ONTOLOGICAL SHIFT OF HERMENEUTICS GUIDED BY LANGUAGE

Everything presupposed in hermeneutics is but language
F. Schleiermacher

1 LANGUAGE AS THE MEDIUM OF HERMENEUTICAL EXPERIENCE

We say that we 'conduct' a conversation, but the more fundamental a conversation is, the less its conduct lies within the will
of either partner. Thus a fundamental conversation is never one
that we want to conduct. Rather, it is generally more correct to
say that we fall into conversation, or even that we become involved in it. The way in which one word follows another, with
the conversation taking its own turnings and reaching its own
conclusion, may well be conducted in some way, but the people
conversing are far less the leaders of it than the led. No one
knows what will 'come out' in a conversation. Understanding
or its failure is like a process which happens to us. Thus we can
say that something was a good conversation or that it was a poor
one. All this shows that a conversation has a spirit of its own,
and that the language used in it bears its own truth within it, ie
that it reveals something which henceforth exists.

We have already seen in the analysis of romantic hermeneutics that understanding is not based on 'getting inside' another
person, on the immediate fusing of one person in another. To
understand what a person says is, as we saw, to agree about the
object, not to get inside another person and relive his experiences. We emphasised that the experience of meaning which
takes place in understanding always includes application. Now
we are to note that this whole process is linguistic. It is not
for nothing that the actual problems of understanding and the
attempt to master it as an art—the concern of hermeneutics
—belongs traditionally to the sphere of grammar and rhetoric.
Language is the middle ground in which understanding and

agreement concerning the object takes place between two people.

In situations in which understanding is disrupted or made difficult, the conditions of all understanding emerge with the greatest clarity. Thus the linguistic process by means of which a conversation in two different languages is made possible through translation is especially informative. Here the translator must translate the meaning to be understood into the context in which the other speaker lives. This does not, of course, mean that he is at liberty to falsify the meaning of what the other person says. Rather, the meaning must be preserved, but since it must be understood within a new linguistic world, it must be expressed within it in a new way. Thus every translation is at the same time an interpretation. We can even say that it is the completion of the interpretation that the translator has made of the words given him.

The example of translation, then, shows that language as the medium of understanding must be consciously created by an explicit mediation. This kind of conscious process is undoubtedly not the norm in a conversation. Nor is translation the norm in our attitude to a foreign language. Rather, having to rely on translation is tantamount to two people giving up their independent authority. Where a translation is necessary, the gap between the spirit of the original words and that of their reproduction must be accepted. It is a gap that can never be completely closed. But in these cases understanding does not really take place between the partners of the conversation, but between the interpreters, who are able to have a real encounter in a common world of understanding. (It is well-known that there is nothing more difficult than a dialogue in two different languages in which one person speaks one and the other person the other, each understanding the other's language, but not speaking it. As if impelled by a higher force, one of the languages always tries to establish itself over the other as the medium of understanding.)

Where understanding takes place, we have not translation but speech. To understand a foreign language means that we do not need to translate it into our own. If we really master a language, then no translation is necessary—in fact, any translation seems impossible. The understanding of a language is not yet of itself a real understanding and does not include an interpretative process but it is an accomplishment of life. For you understand a language by living in it—a statement that is true, as we know, not only of living, but also of dead languages. Thus the hermeneutical problem is not one of the correct mastery of language, but of the proper understanding of that which takes place through the medium of language. Every language can be learned in such a way that its perfect use means that a person is no longer translating from or into his native tongue, but thinks in the foreign language. For two people to be able to understand each other in conversation this mastery of the language is a necessary pre-condition. Every conversation automatically pre-supposes that the two speakers speak the same language. Only when it is possible for two people to make themselves under-stood through language by talking together can the problem of understanding and agreement be even raised. Dependence on the translation of an interpreter is an extreme case that dupli-cates the hermeneutical process of the conversation: there is that between the interpreter and the other as well as that be-tween oneself and the interpreter.

A conversation is a process of two people understanding each other. Thus it is characteristic of every true conversation that each opens himself to the other person, truly accepts his point of view as worthy of consideration and gets inside the other to such an extent that he understands not a particular individual, but what he says. The thing that has to be grasped is the objective rightness or otherwise of his opinion, so that they can agree with each other on the subject. Thus one does not relate the other's opinion to him, but to one's own views. Where a person is concerned with the other as individuality, eg in a therapeutical conversation or the examination of a man accused of a crime, this is not really a situation in which two people are trying to understand one another.[1]

All this, which characterises the situation of two people un-derstanding each other in conversation, has its hermeneutical application where we are concerned with the understanding of texts. Let us again start by considering the extreme case of translation from a foreign language. Here no one can doubt that the translation of a text, however much the translator may have felt himself into his author, cannot be simply a re-awakening of the original event in the mind of the writer, but a recreation of the text that is guided by the way the translator understands what is said in it. No one can doubt that we are dealing here with interpretation, and not simply with reproduction. A new light falls on the text from the other language and for the reader of it. The requirement that a translation should be faithful cannot re-move the fundamental gulf between the two languages. How-ever faithful we try to be, we have to make difficult decisions. If we want to emphasise in our translation a feature of the original that is important to us, then we can do it only by playing down or entirely suppressing other features. But this is precisely the attitude that we call interpretation. Translation, like all interpretation, is a highlighting. A translator must understand that highlighting is part of his task. Obviously he must not leave open whatever is not clear to him, but must declare himself. Yet there are border-line cases in which, in the original (and for the 'original reader'), something is, in fact, unclear. But precisely these hermeneutical border-line cases show the straits in which the translator constantly finds himself. Here he must resign himself. He must state clearly how he understands. But inasmuch as he is always in the position of not really being able to give expression to all the dimensions of his text, this means for him a constant renunciation. Every translation that takes its task seriously is at once clearer and flatter than the original. Even if it is a masterly re-creation, it must lack some of the overtones of the original. (In rare cases of really fine translation the loss can be made good or even lead to gain—think, for example, of how Baudelaire's *Les fleurs du mal* seems to have acquired an odd new vigour in Stefan George's version).

The translator is often painfully aware of his inevitable distance from the original. His dealing with the text has something of the effort to understand another person in conversation. Only that the situation here is one of an extremely wearisome process of understanding, in which one sees the gap between one's own meaning and that of the other person as ultimately unbridgeable. And, as in conversation, when there are such unbridgeable differences, a compromise can sometimes be achieved in the to and fro of dialogue, so the translator will seek the best solution in the toing and froing of weighing up and considering possibilities—a solution which can never be more than a compromise. As in conversation one tries to get inside the other person in order to understand his point of view, so the translator also tries to get right inside his author. But this does not automatically mean that understanding is achieved in a conversation, nor for the translator does this kind of empathy mean that there is a successful recreation. The structures are clearly analogous. Reaching an understanding in conversation presupposes that both partners are ready for it and are trying to recognise the full value of what is alien and opposed to them. If this happens mutually, and each of the partners, while simultaneously holding on to his own arguments, weighs the counter-arguments, it is finally possible to achieve, in an imperceptible but not arbitrary reciprocal translation of the other's position (we call this an exchange of views), a common language and a common statement. Similarly, the translator must respect the character of his own language, into which he is translating, while still recognising the value of the alien, even antagonistic character of the text and its expression. Perhaps, however, this description of the translator's activity is too abbreviated. Even in these extreme situations, in which it is necessary to translate from one language into another, the subject-matter can scarcely be separated from language. Only that translator can succeed who brings into language the object that the text points to; but this means finding a language which is not only his, but is also proportionate to the original.[2] The situation of the translator and that of the interpreter are fundamentally the same.

The example of the translator, who has to bridge the gulf between languages, shows clearly the reciprocal relationship that exists between interpreter and text, corresponding to the mutuality of understanding in conversation. For every translator is an interpreter. The fact that it is a foreign language that is being translated means that it is simply an extreme case of hermeneutical difficulty, ie of alienness and its conquest. All 'objects' with which traditional hermeneutics are concerned are, in fact, alien in the same sense. The translator's task of re-creation differs only in degree, not qualitatively, from the general hermeneutical task presented by any text.

This is not, of course, to say that the hermeneutic situation in regard to texts is exactly the same as that between two people in conversation. Texts are 'permanently fixed expressions of life'[3] which have to be understood, and that means that one partner in the hermeneutical conversation, the text, is expressed only through the other partner, the interpreter. Only through him are the written marks changed back into meaning. Nevertheless, by being changed back into intelligible terms, the object of which the text speaks itself finds expression. It is like a real conversation, in that it is the common object that unites the two partners, the text and the interpreter. Just as the translator makes mutual understanding in the conversation he is interpreting possible only by becoming involved in the subject under discussion, so in relation to a text it is indispensable that the interpreter involve himself with its meaning.

Thus it is quite correct to speak of a hermeneutical conversation. But from this it follows that hermeneutical conversation, like real conversation, finds a common language, and that this finding of a common language is not, any more than in real conversation, the preparation of a tool for the purpose of understanding but, rather, coincides with the very act of understand-

ing and reaching agreement. Even between the partners of this
'conversation' a communication takes place, as between two
people, that is more than mere adaptation. The text brings an
object into language, but that it achieves this is ultimately the
work of the interpreter. Both have a share in it.

Hence the meaning of a text is not to be compared with an
immovably and obstinately fixed point of view which suggests
only one question to the person who is trying to understand it,
namely how the other person could have embraced such an absurd opinion. In this sense understanding is certainly not concerned with understanding historically, ie reconstructing the
way in which the text has come into being. Rather, one is understanding the text itself. But this means that the interpreter's own
thoughts have also gone into the re-awakening of the meaning of
the text. In this the interpreter's own horizon is decisive, yet not
as a personal standpoint that one holds on to or enforces, but
more as a meaning and a possibility that one brings into play and
puts at risk, and that helps one truly to make one's own what is
said in the text. I have described this above as a 'fusion of
horizons'. We can now see that this is the full realisation of
conversation, in which something is expressed that is not only
mine or my author's, but common.

The basis of the systematic significance which the linguistic
nature of conversation has for all understanding we owe to
German romanticism. It has taught us that understanding and
interpretation are ultimately the same thing. This insight, as we
have seen, advances the idea of interpretation from the merely
occasional pedagogical significance that it had in the eighteenth
century to the systematic position indicated by the key importance that the problem of language has acquired in philosophy.

Since the romantic period we can no longer hold the view that,
should there be no direct understanding, interpretative ideas are
drawn on, as needed, out of a linguistic store-room in which they
are lying ready. Rather, language is the universal medium in
which understanding itself is realised. The mode of realisation of
understanding is interpretation. This statement does not mean
that there is no special problem of expression. The difference
between the language of a text and the language of the interpreter, or the gulf that separates the translator from the original, is
not a merely secondary question. On the contrary, the fact is
that the problems of linguistic expression are already problems
of understanding. All understanding is interpretation, and all
interpretation takes place in the medium of a language which
would allow the object to come into words and yet is at the same
time the interpreter's own language.

Thus the hermeneutical phenomenon proves to be a special case of the general relationship between thinking and speaking, the mysterious intimacy of which is bound up with the way in which speech is contained, in a hidden way, in thinking. Interpretation, like conversation, is a closed circle within the dialectic of question and answer. It is a genuine historical life-situation that takes place in the medium of language and that, also in the case of the interpretation of texts, we can call a conversation. The linguistic quality of understanding is the concretion of effective-historical consciousness.

The relation between language and understanding is seen primarily in the fact that it is the nature of tradition to exist in the medium of language, so that the preferred object of interpretation is a linguistic one.

(A) LANGUAGE AS DETERMINATION OF THE HERMENEUTIC OBJECT

The fact that tradition is linguistic in character has hermeneutical consequences. The understanding of linguistic tradition retains special priority over all other tradition. Linguistic tradition may have less physical immediacy than monuments of plastic art. Its lack of immediacy, however, is not a defect, but this apparent lack, in the abstract alienness of all 'texts', expresses the fact that all language belongs in a unique way to the process of understanding. Linguistic tradition is tradition in the literal sense of the word, ie something handed down. It is not just something that has been left over, to be investigated and interpreted as a remnant of the past. What has come down to us by the way of linguistic tradition is not left over, but given to us, told us—whether in the form of direct repetition, of which myth, legend and custom are examples, or in the form of written tradition, the signs of which are immediately clear to every reader who is able to read them.

The full hermeneutical significance of the fact that tradition is linguistic in nature is clearly revealed when the tradition is a written one. In writing, language is detached from its full realisation. In the form of writing all tradition is simultaneous with any present time. Moreover, it involves a unique co-existence of past and present, insofar as present consciousness has the possibility of a free access to all that is handed down in writing. No longer dependent on repetition, which links past knowledge with the present, but, in its direct acquaintance with literary tradition, understanding consciousness has a genuine opportunity to widen its horizon and thus enrich its world by a whole new and deeper dimension. The appropriation of literary tradition is even more valuable than the experience given by the adventure of travel and exposure to the world of a foreign language. The reader who studies a foreign language and literature has, at every moment, the possibility of free movement back to himself and thus is at once both here and there.

A written tradition is not a fragment of a past world, but has always raised itself beyond this into the sphere of the meaning that it expresses. It is the ideality of the word, which raises linguistic objects beyond the finiteness and transience of other remnants of past existence. It is not this document, as coming from the past, that is the bearer of tradition, but the continuity of memory. Through memory tradition becomes part of our own world, and so what it communicates can be directly expressed. Where we have a written tradition, we are not just told an individual thing, but a past humanity itself becomes present to us, in its general relation to the world. That is why our understanding remains curiously unsure and fragmentary when we have no written tradition of a culture, but only dumb monuments, and we do not call this information about the past 'history'. Texts, on the other hand, always express a whole. Meaningless strokes which seem strange and incomprehensible prove suddenly intelligible in every detail when they can be interpreted as writing —so much so that even the arbitrariness of a faulty tradition can be corrected if the context as a whole is understood.

Thus written texts present the real hermeneutical task. Writing involves self-alienation. Its overcoming, the reading of the text, is thus the highest task of understanding. Even the pure signs of an inscription can be seen properly and articulated correctly only if the text can be transformed back into language. This transformation, however, always establishes, as we have said, a relationship to what is meant, to the object that is being spoken about. Here the process of understanding moves entirely in the sphere of a meaning mediated by the linguistic tradition. Thus the hermeneutical task with an inscription starts only after it has been deciphered. Only in an extended sense do non-literary monuments present a hermeneutical task, for they cannot be understood of themselves. What they mean is a question of their interpretation, not of the deciphering and understanding of what they say.

In writing, language gains its true intellectual quality, for when confronted with a written tradition understanding consciousness acquires its full sovereignty. Its being does not depend on anything. Thus reading consciousness is in potential possession of its history. It is not for nothing that with the emergence of a literary culture the idea of 'philology', 'love of speech', was transferred entirely to the all-embracing art of reading, losing its original connection with the cultivation of speech and argument. A reading consciousness is necessarily historical and communicates freely with historical tradition. Thus it has some historical justification if, with Hegel, one says that history begins with emergence of a will to hand things down, to make memory last.[4] Writing is not merely chance or extra addition that qualitatively changes nothing in the development of oral tradition. Certainly, there can be a will to make things continue, a will to permanency without writing. But only a written tradition can detach itself from the mere continuance of fragments left over from the life of the past, remnants from which it is possible to reconstruct life.

From the start, the tradition of inscriptions does not share in the free form of tradition that we call literature, inasmuch as it depends on the existence of the remains, whether of stone or whatever material. But it is true of everything that has come down to us that here a will to permanence has created the unique forms of continuance that we call literature. It presents us not only with a stock of memorials and signs. Literature, rather, has acquired its own simultaneity with every present. To understand it does not mean primarily to reason one's way back into the past, but to have a present involvement in what is said. It is not really about a relationship between persons, between the reader and the author (who is perhaps quite unknown), but about sharing in the communication that the text gives us. This meaning of what is said is, when we understand it, quite independent of whether we can gain from the tradition a picture of the author and of whether or not the historical interpretation of the tradition as a literary source is our concern.

Let us here recall that the task of hermeneutics was originally and chiefly the understanding of texts. Schleiermacher was the first to see that the hermeneutical problem was not raised by written words alone, but that oral utterance also presented—and perhaps in its fullest form—the problem of understanding. We have outlined above[5] how the psychological dimension that he gave to hermeneutics blocked its historical one. In actual fact, writing is central to the hermeneutical phenomenon, insofar as its detachment both from the writer or author and from a specifically addressed recipient or reader has given it a life of its own. What is fixed in writing has raised itself publicly into a sphere of meaning in which everyone who can read has an equal share.

Certainly, in relation to language, writing seems a secondary phenomenon. The sign language of writing refers back to the actual language of speech. But that language is capable of being written is by no means incidental to its nature. Rather, this capacity of being written down is based on the fact that speech itself shares in the pure ideality of the meaning that communicates itself in it. In writing, this meaning of what is spoken exists purely for itself, completely detached from all emotional elements of expression and communication. A text is not to be understood as an expression of life, but in what it says. Writing is the abstract ideality of language. Hence the meaning of something written is fundamentally identifiable and reproducible. What is identical in the reproduction is only that which was formulated. This indicates that 'reproduction' cannot be meant here in its strict sense. It does not mean referring back to some original source in which something is said or written. The understanding of something written is not a reproduction of something that is past, but the sharing of a present meaning.

Writing has the methodological advantage that it presents the hermeneutical problem in all its purity, detached from everything psychological. What is, however, in our eyes and for our purpose a methodological advantage is at the same time the expression of a specific weakness that is characteristic of writing even more than of language. The task of understanding is seen with particular clarity when we recognise this weakness of all writing. We need only to think again of what Plato said, namely that the specific weakness of writing was that no one could come to the aid of the written word if it falls victim to misunderstanding, intentional or unintentional.[6]

Plato saw in the helplessness of the written word a more serious weakness than the weakness of speech (to astheneston logon) and when he calls on dialectic to come to the aid of this weakness of speech, while declaring the condition of the written word to be beyond hope, this is obviously an ironic exaggeration with which to conceal his own writing and his own art. In fact, writing and speech are in the same plight. As in speech there is an art of appearances and an art of true thought—sophistry and dialectic—so in writing there is such a dual art: mere sophistry and true dialectic. There is, then, an art of writing that comes to the aid of thought and it is to this that the art of understanding—which affords the same help to what is written—is allied.

All writing is, as we have said, a kind of alienated speech, and its signs need to be transformed back into speech and meaning. Because the meaning has undergone a kind of self-alienation through being written down, this transformation back is the real hermeneutical task. The meaning of what has been said is to be stated anew, simply on the basis of the words passed on by means of the written signs. In contrast to the spoken word there is no other aid in the interpretation of the written word. Thus the important thing here is, in a special sense, the 'art' of writing.[7] The spoken word interprets itself to an astonishing degree, by the way of speaking, the tone of voice, the tempo etc, but also by the circumstances in which it is spoken.[8]

But there is also such a thing as writing that, as it were, reads itself. A remarkable debate on the spirit and the letter in philosophy between two great German philosophical writers, Schiller and Fichte,[9] has this fact as its starting-point. It is interesting that the dispute cannot be resolved with the aesthetic criteria used by the two men. Fundamentally they are not concerned with a question of the aesthetics of good style, but with a hermeneutical question. The 'art' of writing in such a way that the thoughts of the reader are stimulated and held in productive movement has little to do with the conventional rhetorical or aesthetic devices. Rather, it consists entirely in one's being led to think the material through. The 'art' of writing does not seek here to be understood and evaluated as such. The art of writing, like the art of speaking, is not an end in itself and therefore not the fundamental object of hermeneutical effort. The understanding is entirely taken up with what is being written about. Hence unclear thinking and 'bad' writing are not, for the task of understanding, exemplary cases for the art of hermeneutics to show itself in its full glory but, on the contrary, limiting cases which undermine the basic presupposition of all hermeneutical success, namely the clear unambiguity of the intended meaning.

All writing claims that it can be awakened into spoken language, and this claim to autonomy of meaning goes so far that even an authentic reading, eg the reading of a poem by the poet, becomes questionable if the direction of our listening takes us away from what our understanding should really be concerned with. Because the important thing is the communication of the true meaning of a text, its interpretation is already subject to an objective norm. This is the requirement that the Platonic dialectic makes when it seeks to bring out the logos as such and in doing so often leaves behind the actual partner in the conversation. In fact, the particular weakness of writing, its greater helplessness when compared with speech, has another side to it, in that it demonstrates with greater clarity the dialectical task of understanding. As in conversation, understanding must here seek to strengthen the meaning of what is said. What is stated in the text must be detached from all contingent factors and grasped in its full ideality, in which alone it has validity. Thus, precisely because it entirely detaches the sense of what is said from the person saying it, the written word makes the reader, in his understanding of it, the arbiter of its claim to truth. The reader experiences in all its validity what is addressed to him and what he understands. What he understands is always more than an alien meaning: it is always possible truth. This is what emerges from the detachment of what is spoken from the speaker and from the permanence that writing bestows. This is the deeper hermeneutical reason for the fact, mentioned above,[10] that it does not occur to people who are not used to reading that what is written down could be wrong, since anything written seems to them like a document that is self-authenticating.

Everything written is, in fact, in a special way the object of hermeneutics. What we found in the extreme case of a foreign language and the problems of translation is confirmed here by the autonomy of reading: understanding is not a psychic transposition. The horizon of understanding cannot be limited either by what the writer had originally in mind, or by the horizon of the person to whom the text was originally addressed.

It sounds at first like a sensible hermeneutical rule, generally recognised as such, that nothing should be put into a text that the writer or the reader could not have intended. But this rule can be applied only in extreme cases. For texts do not ask to be understood as a living expression of the subjectivity of their writers. This, then, cannot define the limits of a text's meaning. However, it is not only the limiting of the meaning of a text to the 'actual' thoughts of the author that is questionable. Even if we seek to determine the meaning of a text objectively by seeing it as a contemporary document and in relation to its original reader, as was Schleiermacher's basic procedure, such limitation is a very chancy affair. The idea of the contemporary addressee can claim only a restricted critical validity. For what is contemporaneity? Listeners of the day before yesterday as well as of the day after tomorrow are always among those to whom one speaks as a contemporary. Where are we to draw the line that excludes a reader from being addressed? What are contemporaries and what is a text's claim to truth in the face of this multifarious mixture of past and future? The idea of the original reader is full of unexamined idealisation.

Furthermore, our concept of the nature of literary tradition contains a fundamental objection to the hermeneutical legitimisation of the idea of the original reader. We saw that literature is defined by the will to hand on. But a person who copies and passes on is doing it for his own contemporaries. Thus the reference to the original reader, like that to the meaning of the author, seems to offer only a very crude historico-hermeneutical criterion which cannot really limit the horizon of a text's meaning. What is fixed in writing has detached itself from the contingency of its origin and its author and made itself free for new relationships. Normative concepts such as the author's meaning or the original reader's understanding represent in fact only an empty space that is filled from time to time in understanding.

(B) LANGUAGE AS DETERMINATION OF THE HERMENEUTIC ACT

This brings us to the second aspect of the relationship between language and understanding. Not only is the special object of understanding, namely literary tradition, of a linguistic nature, but understanding itself has a fundamental connection with language. We started from the proposition that understanding is already interpretation because it creates the hermeneutical horizon within which the meaning of a text is realised. But in order to be able to express the meaning of a text in its objective content we must translate it into our own language. This, however, involves relating it to the whole complex of possible meanings in which we linguistically move. We have already investigated the logical structure of this in relation to the special place of the question as a hermeneutical phenomenon. In considering now the linguistic nature of all understanding, we are again expressing from another angle what has been shown in the dialectic of question and answer.

Here we are moving into a dimension that is generally ignored by the dominant view that the historical sciences have of themselves. For the historian usually chooses the concepts by means of which he describes the historical nature of his objects, without expressly reflecting on their origin and justification. He is simply following here his interest in the material and takes no account of the fact that the descriptive aptness of his chosen concepts can be highly detrimental to his proper purpose, inasmuch as it assimilates what is historically different to what is familiar and thus, despite all objectivity, has already subordinated the alien being of the object to its own conceptual frame of reference. Thus, despite all his scientific method, he behaves just like everyone else, as a child of his time who is dominated unquestioningly by the concepts and prejudices of his own age.[11]

Insofar as the historian does not admit this naiveté to himself, he fails to reach the level of reflection that the subject demands. But his naiveté becomes truly abysmal when he starts to become aware of the problems it raises and so demands that in understanding history one must leave one's own concepts aside and think only in the concepts of the epoch one is trying to understand.[12] This demand, which sounds like a logical implementation of historical consciousness is, as will be clear to every thoughtful reader, a naive illusion. The naiveté of this claim does not consist in the fact that it remains unfulfilled because the interpreter does not attain the ideal of leaving himself aside. This would still mean that it was a legitimate ideal to which one must approximate as far as possible. But what the legitimate demand of the historical consciousness, to understand a period in terms of its own concepts, really means is something quite different. The call to leave aside the concepts of the present does not mean a naive transposition into the past. It is, rather, an essentially relative demand that has meaning only in relation to one's own concepts. Historical consciousness fails to understand its own nature if, in order to understand, it seeks to exclude that which alone makes understanding possible. To think historically means, in fact, to perform the transposition that the concepts of the past undergo when we try to think in them. To think historically always involves establishing a connection between those ideas and one's own thinking. To try to eliminate one's own concepts in interpretation is not only impossible, but manifestly absurd. To interpret means precisely to use one's own preconceptions so that the meaning of the text can really be made to speak for us.

In our analysis of the hermeneutical process we saw that to acquire a horizon of interpretation required a 'fusion of horizons'. This is now confirmed by the linguistic aspect of interpretation. The text is to be made to speak through interpretion. But no text and no book speaks if it does not speak the language that reaches the other person. Thus interpretation must find the right language if it really wants to make the text speak. There cannot, therefore, be any one interpretation that is correct 'in itself', precisely because every interpretation is concerned with the text itself. The historical life of a tradition depends on constantly new assimilation and interpretation. An interpretation that was correct 'in itself' would be a foolish ideal that failed to take account of the nature of tradition. Every interpretation has to adapt itself to the hermeneutical situation to which it belongs.

Being bound by a situation does not mean that the claim to correctness that every interpretation must make is dissolved into the subjective or the occasional. We must not here abandon the insights of the romantics, who purified the problem of hermeneutics from all its occasional elements. Interpretation is not something pedagogical for us either, but the act of understanding itself, which is realised not just for the one for whom one is interpreting, but also for the interpreter himself in the explicitness of linguistic interpretation. Thanks to the linguistic nature of all interpretation every interpretation includes the possibility of a relationship with others. There can be no speech that does not bind the speaker and the person spoken to. This is true of the hermeneutic process as well. But this relationship does not determine the interpretative process of understanding as if it were a conscious adaptation to a pedagogical situation, but rather this process is simply the concretion of the meaning itself. Let us recall our stress on the element of application, which had completely disappeared from hermeneutics. We saw that to understand a text always means to apply it to ourselves and to know that, even if it must always be understood in different ways, it is still the same text presenting itself to us in these different ways. That the claim to truth of every interpretation is not in the least relativised is seen from the fact that all interpretation is essentially linguistic. The linguistic explicitness that the process of understanding gains through interpretation does not create a second sense apart from that which is understood and interpreted. The interpretative concepts are not, as such, thematic in understanding. Rather, it is their nature to disappear behind what they bring, in interpretation, into speech. Paradoxically, an interpretation is right when it is capable of disappearing in this way. And yet it is true at the same time that it must be expressed as something that is intended to disappear. The possibility of understanding is dependent on the possibility of this kind of mediating interpretation.

This is also true in those cases when there is immediate understanding and no explicit interpretation is undertaken. For in these cases too interpretation must be possible. But this means that interpretation is contained potentially in the understanding process. It simply makes the understanding explicit. Thus interpretation is not a means through which understanding is achieved, but it has passed into the content of what is understood. Let us recall that this does not only mean that the significance of the text can be realised as a unity, but that the object of which the text speaks is also expressed. The interpretation places the object, as it were, on the scales of words.

There are a few characteristic variations to the universality of this statement which indirectly confirm it. When we are concerned with the understanding and interpretation of linguistic texts, interpretation in the medium of language itself shows what understanding always is: an assimilation of what is said to the point that it becomes one's own. Linguistic interpretation is the form of all interpretation, even when what is to be interpreted is not linguistic in nature, ie is not a text, but is a statue or a musical composition. We must not let ourselves be confused by these forms of interpretation which are not linguistic, but in fact presuppose language. It is possible to demonstrate something by means of contrast, eg by placing two pictures alongside each other or reading two poems one after the other, so that one is interpreted by the other. In these cases demonstration seems to obviate linguistic interpretation. But in fact this kind of demonstration is a modification of linguistic interpretation. In such demonstration we have the reflection of interpretation, which uses the demonstration as a visual short-cut. Demonstration is interpretation in much the same sense as is a translation which summarises the result of an interpretation, or the correct reading aloud of a text that must imply decision on the questions of interpretation, because one can only read aloud what one has understood. Understanding and interpretation are indissolubly bound up with each other.

It is obviously connected with the fact that interpretation and understanding are bound up with each other that the concept of interpretation can be applied not only to scientific interpretation, but to that of artistic reproduction, eg of musical or dramatic performance. We have shown above that this kind of reproduction is not a second reproduction behind the first, but makes the work of art appear as itself for the first time. It brings to life the signs of the musical or dramatic text. Reading aloud is a similar process, in that it is the awakening and conversion of a text into new immediacy.

From this it follows that the same thing must be true of all understanding in private reading. Reading fundamentally involves interpretation. This is not to say that understanding as one reads is a kind of inner production in which the work of art would acquire an independent existence—although remaining in the intimate sphere of one's own inner life—as in a production that is visible to all. Rather, we are stating the contrary, namely that a production that takes place in the external world of space and time does not in fact have any independent existence over against the work itself and can acquire such only through a secondary aesthetic distinction. The interpretation that music or a play undergoes when it is performed is not basically different from the understanding of a text when you read it: understanding always includes interpretation. The work of a literary critic also consists in making texts readable and intelligible, ie safeguarding the correct understanding of a text against misunderstandings. Thus there is no essential difference between the interpretation that a work undergoes in being reproduced and that which the critic performs. However secondary an interpretative artist may feel the justification of his interpretation in words may be, rejecting it as inartistic, he cannot want to deny that such an account can be given of his reproductive interpretation. He must also desire that his interpretation be correct and convincing, and it will not occur to him to deny its connection with the text he has before him. But this text is the same one that presents the academic interpreter with his task. Thus he will be unable to deny that his own understanding of a work, expressed in his reproductive interpretation, can itself be understood, ie interpreted and justified, and this interpretation will take place in a linguistic form. But even this is not a new creation of meaning. Rather, it also disappears again as an interpretation and preserves its truth in the immediacy of understanding.

This insight into the way in which interpretation and understanding are bound up with each other will destroy that false romanticism of immediacy that artists and connoisseurs have pursued, and still do pursue, under the banner of the aesthetics of genius. Interpretation does not seek to replace the interpreted work. It does not, for example, seek to draw attention to itself by the poetic power of its own utterance. Rather, it remains fundamentally accidental. This is true not only of the interpreting word, but also of reproductive interpretation. The interpreting word always has something accidental about it insofar as it is motivated by the hermeneutic question, not just for the pedagogical purposes to which, in the age of the enlightenment, interpretation had been limited, but because understanding is always a genuine event.[13] Similarly, interpretation that is a reproduction is accidental in a fundamental sense, ie not just when something is played, imitated, translated or read aloud for didactic purposes. These cases, where reproduction is interpretation in a special demonstrative sense, where it includes demonstrative exaggeration and highlighting, are in fact different only in degree, and not in kind, from other sorts of reproductive interpretation. However much it is the literary work or the musical composition itself that acquires its mimic presence through the performance, every performance still has its own emphasis. In this respect the difference from the demonstrative placing of accents for didactic reasons is not so great. All performance is interpretation. All interpretation is highlighting.

It is only because it has not any permanent being of its own and disappears in the work which it reproduces that this fact does not emerge clearly. But if we take a comparable example from the plastic arts, eg drawings after old masters made by a great artist, we find the same illuminative interpretation in them. The same effect is experienced when seeing revivals of old films or seeing again a film that one has just seen and remembers clearly: everything seems to be overplayed. Thus it is wholly legitimate for us to speak of the interpretation that lies behind every reproduction, and it must be possible to give a fundamental account of it. The total interpretation is made up of a thousand little decisions which all claim to be correct. Argumentative justification and interpretation do not need to be the artist's proper concern. Moreover, an explicit interpretation in language would only approximate the truth, and fall short of the rounded form achieved by an 'artistic' reproduction. Nevertheless, the inner relation of all understanding to interpretation, and the basic possibility of an interpretation in words, remains untouched by this.

We must understand properly the nature of the fundamental priority of language asserted here. Indeed, language often seems ill-suited to express what we feel. In the face of the overwhelming presence of works of art the task of expressing in words what they say to us seems like an infinite and hopeless undertaking. It seems like a critique of language that our desire and capacity to understand always go beyond any statement that we can make. But this does not affect the fundamental priority of language. The possibilities of our knowledge seem to be far more individual than the possibilities of expression offered by language. Faced with the socially motivated tendency towards uniformity with which language forces understanding into particular schematic forms which hem us in, our desire for knowledge seeks to release itself from these schematisations and predecisions. However, the critical superiority which we claim over language is not concerned with the conventions of linguistic expression, but with the conventions of meaning that have found their form in language. Thus it says nothing against the essential connection between understanding and language. In fact it confirms this connection. For all such criticism which rises above the schematism of our statements in order to understand again finds its expression in the form of language. Hence language always forestalls any objection to its jurisdiction. Its universality keeps pace with the universality of reason. Hermeneutical consciousness is only participating in something that constitutes the general relation between language and reason. If all understanding stands in a necessary relation of equivalence to its possible interpretation and if there are basically no bounds set to understanding, then the linguistic form which the interpretation of this understanding finds must contain within it an infinite dimension that transcends all bounds. Language is the language of reason itself.

One says this, and then one hesitates. For this makes language so close to reason—which means to the objects that it names—that one may ask why there should be different languages at all, since all seem to have the same proximity to reason and to objects. When a person lives in a language, he is filled with the sense of the unsurpassable appropriateness of the words that he uses for the objects to which he is referring. It seems impossible that other words in other languages could name the objects equally well. The suitable word always seems to be one's own and unique, just as the object referred to is always unique. The agony of translation consists ultimately in the fact that the original words seem to be inseparable from the objects they refer to, so that in order to make a text intelligible one often has to give an interpretative paraphrase of it rather than translate it. The more sensitively our historical consciousness reacts, the more it seems to be aware of the untranslatability of what is written in a foreign language. But this makes the intimate unity of word and object a hermeneutical stumbling block. How can we possibly understand anything written in a foreign language if we are thus imprisoned in our own?

It is necessary to see the speciousness of this argument. In actual fact the sensitivity of our historical consciousness tells us the opposite. The work of understanding and interpretation always remains meaningful. This shows the superior universality with which reason rises above the limitations of any given language. The hermeneutical experience is the corrective by means of which the thinking reason escapes the prison of language, and it is itself constituted linguistically.

From this point of view the problem of language is not presented as the philosophy of language raises it. Certainly the variety of languages presents us with a problem. But this problem is simply how every language, despite its difference from other languages, is able to say everything it wants. We know that every language does this in its own way. But we then ask how, amid the variety of these forms of utterance, there is still the same unity of thought and speech, so that everything that has been transmitted in writing can be understood. Thus we are interested in the opposite of what philosophy of language seeks to investigate.

The intimate unity of language and thought is the premise from which philosophy of language also starts. It is this alone that has made it a science. For only because this unity exists is it worthwhile for the investigator to make the abstraction which causes language to be the object of his research. Only by breaking with the conventionalist prejudices of theology and rationalism could Herder and Humboldt learn to see languages as views of the world. By acknowledging the unity of thought and language they were able to undertake the task of comparing the various forms of this unity. We are starting from the same insight, but we are going, as it were, in the opposite direction. Despite the multifariousness of ways of speech we seek to hold on to the indissoluble unity of thought and language as we encounter it in the hermeneutical phenomenon, namely as the unity of understanding and interpretation.

Thus the question that concerns us is that of the abstractness of all understanding. It only appears to be a secondary question. We have seen that interpretation is the realisation of the hermeneutical experience itself. That is why our problem is such a difficult one. The interpreter does not know that he is bringing himself and his own concepts into the interpretation. The linguistic formulation is so much part of the interpreter's mind that he never becomes aware of it as an object. Thus it is understandable that this side of the hermeneutic process has been wholly ignored. But there is the further point that the situation has been confused by incorrect theories of language. It is obvious that an instrumentalist theory of signs that sees words and concepts as handy tools has missed the point of the hermeneutical phenomenon. If we stick to what takes place in speech and, above all, in all intercourse with tradition carried on by the human sciences, we cannot fail to see that there is a constant process of concept-formation at work. This does not mean that the interpreter is using new or unusual words. But the use of familiar words does not proceed from an act of logical subsumption, through which an individual is placed under a universal concept. Let us remember, rather, that understanding always includes an element of application and thus produces a constant further development in the formation of concepts. We must consider this now if we want to liberate the linguistic nature of understanding from the presuppositions of philosophy of language. The interpreter does not use words and concepts like an artisan who takes his tools in his hands and then puts them away. Rather, we must recognise that all understanding is interwoven with concepts and reject any theory that does not accept the intimate unity of word and object.

Indeed, the situation is even more difficult. It is questionable whether the concept of language which modern science and philosophy of language take as their starting-point is adequate to the situation. It has recently been stated by some linguists—and rightly—that the modern concept of language presumes a linguistic consciousness that is itself a historical result and does not apply to the beginning of the historical process, especially to what the Greeks called language.[14] There is a development from the complete unconsciousness of language, that we find in classical Greece, to the instrumentalist devaluation of language that we find in modern times. This process of developing consciousness, which also involves a change in the attitude to language, makes it possible for 'language' as such, ie its form, separated from all content, to become an independent object of attention.

In this view we can doubt whether the relation between the attitude to language and the theory of language is correctly characterised, but there is no doubt that the science and philosophy of language operate on the premise that their only concern is the form of language. Is the idea of form still appropriate here? Is language a symbolic form, as Cassirer would have it? Does this take account of its unique quality, which is that language embraces everything—myth, art, law etc—that Cassirer also calls symbolic form?[15]

In analysing the hermeneutical phenomenon we have stumbled upon the universal function of language. In revealing its linguistic nature, the hermeneutical phenomenon itself is seen to have a universal significance. Understanding and interpretation are related to the linguistic tradition in a specific way. But at the same time they transcend this relationship not only because all the creations of human culture, including the nonlinguistic ones, seek to be understood in this way, but more fundamentally inasmuch as everything that is intelligible must be accessible to understanding and to interpretation. The same thing is as true of understanding as of language. Neither is to be grasped simply as a fact that can be empirically investigated. Neither is ever simply an object, but comprises everything that can ever be an object.[16]

If one recognises this basic connection between language and understanding, one will not be able to see the development from unconsciousness of language via consciousness of language to the devaluation of language[17] as an unambiguous historical process. This schema does not seem to me to be adequate even for the history of theories of language, as we shall see, let alone for the life of language. The language that lives in speech, which takes in all understanding, including that of the textual interpreter, is so much bound up with thinking and interpretation that we have too little left if we ignore the actual content of what languages hand down to us and seek to consider only language as form. Unconsciousness of language has not ceased to be the actual modality of speech. Let us, therefore, turn our attention to the Greeks, who did not have a word for what we call language when the all-embracing unity of word and object became problematical for them and hence worthy of attention. We shall consider too christian thought in the middle ages, which, because of its interest in dogmatic theology, rethought the mystery of this unity.

2 THE EMERGENCE OF THE CONCEPT OF LANGUAGE IN THE HISTORY OF WESTERN THOUGHT

(A) LANGUAGE AND LOGOS

In the earliest times the intimate unity of word and object was so obvious that the name was considered to be part of the bearer of the name, if not, indeed, to substitute for him. In Greek the expression for 'word', onoma, also means 'name', and especially 'proper name', ie the name by which something is called. The word is understood primarily in terms of a name. But a name is what it is because it is what someone is called and what he answers to. It belongs to its bearer. The rightness of the name is confirmed by the fact that someone answers to it. Thus it seems to be part of his being.

Greek philosophy more or less began with the insight that a word is only a name, ie that it does not represent true being. This is precisely the break-through of philosophical inquiry into the territory over which the name had undisputed rule. Belief in the word and doubt of it constitute the problem which the thought of the Greek enlightenment saw in the relationship between the word and the object. So the word may be type or anti-type. The name that is given and that can be changed raises doubt in the truth of the word. Can we speak of the rightness of names? But must we not speak of the rightness of words, ie insist on the unity of word and object? Did not the most profound of all early thinkers, Heraclitus, discover the depth of meaning contained in the play on words? This is the background to Plato's *Cratylus*, the fundamental statement of Greek thought on language, which covers the whole range of problems, so that the later Greek discussion, of which we have, in any case, only an imperfect knowledge, scarcely adds anything essential.[18]

Two theories discussed in Plato's *Cratylus* make an attempt to describe in different ways the relationship between word and object. The conventionalist theory sees in the unambiguous meaning of language, as reached by agreement and practice, the only source of the meaning of words. The opposed theory holds that there is a natural agreement between word and object that is described by the idea of correctness (orthotes). It is clear that both of these positions are extremes and so do not necessarily exclude each other in any particular case. The ordinary speaker, at any rate, knows nothing of the 'correctness' of the word, which this position presumes.

The mode of being of language, which we call 'customary usage', sets a limit to both theories: the limit of conventionalism is that we cannot arbitrarily change the meaning of words if there is to be language. The problem of made-up languages shows the conditions that apply to this kind of renaming. Hermogenes in the *Cratylus* himself gives an example: the renaming of a servant.[19] The inner dependence of the life-world of a servant, the coincidence of his person with his function makes possible that which the claim of a person to his independence and the preservation of his honour would make impossible. Children and lovers likewise have 'their' language, by which they communicate with each other in a world that belongs to them alone. But even this is not so much because they have arbitrarily agreed on it, but because a linguistic habit has grown up between them. A common world—even if it is only an invented one—is always the presupposition of language.

The limitation of the similarity theory is also clear. We cannot look at the objects referred to and complain that words do not correctly represent them. Language is not a mere tool we use, something we construct with which to communicate and differentiate.[20] Both these interpretations of language start from the existence of words and regard objects as something we know about previously from an independent source. Thus they start too late. We must then ask if Plato, in showing the two extreme positions to be untenable, is questioning a presupposition that is common to them both. Plato's intention seems quite clear to me—and this cannot be emphasised sufficiently in view of the way that the *Cratylus* is constantly misused in the treatment of the systematic problems of the philosophy of language: in this discussion of contemporary theories of language Plato wants to demonstrate that no objective truth (aletheia ton onton) can be attained in language, in language's claim to correctness (orthotes ton onomaton) and that without words (aneu ton onomaton) being must be known purely from itself (auta ex heauton).[21] This radically transfers the problem to another plane. The dialectic at which this is directed obviously claims to make thought dependent on itself alone and to open it to its true objects, the 'ideas', so that the power of words (dunamis ton onomaton) and its demonic technicisation in the sophistical art of argument are overcome. The conquest of the sphere of words (onomata) by the dialectic does not of course mean that there really is such a thing as a knowledge without words, but only that it is not the word that opens up the way to truth. Rather, on the contrary, the adequacy of the word can be judged only from the knowledge of objects.

We can grant the truth of this and yet feel there is something missing. Plato avoids considering the real relationship between words and things. Here he says that the question of how one can know being is too big, and where he does speak about it, where he does describe the true nature of dialectic, as in the excursus of the seventh *Letter*,[22] language is regarded only as an external and ambiguous element. It is one of those superficial things (proteinomena) that obtrude themselves and that the true dialectician must leave behind, like the sensible appearance of things. The pure thought of ideas, dianoia, is silent, for it is a dialogue of the soul with itself (aneu phones). The logos[23] is the stream that flows from this thought and sounds out through the mouth (rheuma dia tou stomatos meta phthoggou). It is obvious that the realisation of meaning in sound cannot involve a claim that what is said is true. Plato undoubtedly did not consider the fact that the process of thought, if conceived as a dialogue of soul, itself involves a connection with language, and although we find that there is something about this in the seventh *Letter,* it is in relation to the dialectic of knowledge, ie to the orientation of the whole movement of knowing towards the one (auto). Although there is here a fundamental recognition of the connection with language, its significance does not really emerge. It is only one of the elements of knowing, the dialectical provisionalness of which emerges from the object itself towards which the act of knowing is directed. The net result is, then, that Plato's discovery of the ideas conceals the true nature of language even more than the theories of the sophists, who developed their own art (techne) in the use and abuse of language.

Even where Plato, pointing forward to his dialectic, moves beyond the level of the discussion in the *Cratylus,* we find no other relation to language than that already discussed there: language is a tool, an image that is constructed and judged in terms of the original, the objects themselves. Thus even when he does not assign to the sphere of words (onomata) any independent cognitive function and calls for the transcending of this sphere, he keeps to the framework of reference within which the question of the 'correctness' of the name presents itself. Even when (as in the context of the seventh *Letter*) he does not accept a natural correctness of names, he still retains resemblance (homoion) as the criterion: the image and the original constitute for him the metaphysical model with which he considers everything within the noetic sphere. The art of the craftsman and that of the divine demiurge, that of the orator and that of the philosophical dialectician, reflect in their various media the true being of ideas. There is always a gap (apechie), even if the true dialectician bridges it for himself. The element of true speech remains the word (onoma and rhema)—the same word in which truth is hidden to the point of unrecognisability and even complete disappearance.

If we consider against this background the dispute about the 'correctness of names', as settled by the *Cratylus,* the theories discussed there suddenly acquire an interest that goes beyond Plato and his own particular purpose. For neither theory that Plato's Socrates disproves is considered in its full weight. The conventionalist theory bases the idea of the 'correctness' of words on the giving of a name to things, baptising them, as it were. This theory obviously does not see in a name any claim to objective knowledge. Socrates convicts the exponent of this view of error by starting from the distinction between the true and the false logos, then making him admit that the constituents of the logos, the words (onomata), are also true or false, thus relating naming, as part of speech, to the revelation of being (ousia) that takes place in speech.[24] This is a proposition so incompatible with the conventionalist view that it is easy to deduce from it, on the contrary, a 'nature' that is the criterion of the true name and the correct naming. Socrates himself admits that this understanding of the 'correctness' of names leads to etymological intoxication, among other absurd consequences. But the same is true of his treatment of the opposed view, which sees words as part of nature (phusei). Although we might expect this view to be refuted by the revelation of the faultiness of arguing from the truth of speech to that of the word from which it is derived (the *Sophist* rectifies this), we are disappointed. The discussion remains entirely within the fundamental assumptions of the nature theory, ie the similarity principle, demolishing it only by progressive limitation. If the 'correctness' of names really depends on the finding of the right name, ie that name which is adequate to the object, then, as with all such adequacy, there are grades and degrees of correctness. If a name that has only a small degree of correctness still conveys the outline (tupos) of an object, then it may still be good enough to be usable.[25] But we must be even more generous: a word can be understood, obviously from habit and agreement, if it contains sounds that bear no resemblance to the object, so that the whole principle of similarity falters and is refuted by such examples as the words for numbers. There can be no similarity at all here, because numbers do not belong to the visible and moved world, so that they obviously come under the principle of convention alone.

The abandonment of the phusei theory seems very conciliatory, in that the convention principle has to act as a complement when the similarity principle fails. Plato seems to hold that the similarity principle is a reasonable one, but one that needs to be applied in a very liberal way. The convention that operates in practical usage and alone constitutes the correctness of words can make use of the similarity principle, but it is not bound to it.[26] This is a very moderate point of view, but it involves the basic assumption that words have no real cognitive significance of their own, a result that points beyond the whole sphere of words and the question of their correctness to the knowledge of the object. This is obviously Plato's concern.

And yet, by keeping within the framework of the finding and giving of names, the Socratic argument against Cratylus suppresses a number of insights. That the word is a tool we construct in order to deal with an object in terms of instruction and differentiation, and so an entity that can be more or less adequate to and in accord with its being, fixes the nature of the enquiry into the nature of the word in a manner that is not without its problems. The mode of dealing with the object that is involved here is the making apparent of the object meant. The word is correct if it represents the object, ie. if it is a representation (mimesis). It is certainly not a question of an imitative representation in the sense of a direct copy, depicting the visual or aural appearance of something, but it is the being (ousia)—that which is considered worthy of the attribute 'to be' (einai)—that is to be revealed by the word. But we must ask whether the concepts used in conversation, the concepts of mimema or of deloma understood as mimema, are correct.

The fact that the word that names an object names it as what it is, because the word itself has the meaning whereby the object intended is named, does not necessarily involve a relation of original and copy. Certainly it is part of the nature of mimema that it represents something different from what it itself contains. Thus mere imitation, 'being like', always offers a starting point for reflecting on the ontological gap between the imitation and the original. But a word names an object in a far more inward or intellectual way for the question of the degree of similarity to be appropriate here. Cratylus is quite right when he opposes this. He is likewise quite right when he says that inasmuch as a word is a word, it must be 'correct', must fit correctly. If it is not this, it means that it has no meaning, that it is merely a sounding brass.[27] It makes no sense to speak of wrongness in such a case.

Of course it can also happen that we do not address someone by his right name because we confuse him with someone else, and also that we do not use 'the right word' for something because we do not recognise the thing. It is not the word that is wrong here, but its use. It only seems to fit the object for which it is used. In fact it is the word from something else and, as such, correct. Again, someone who, learning a foreign language, learns the words, ie the meaning of the words, that he does not know, assumes that they have their true meaning, which the dictionary discovers from the examination of usage and so transmits. One can always confuse these meanings, but that always means to use the 'correct' words wrongly. Thus we may speak of an absolute perfection of the word, inasmuch as there is no apparent relationship, ie no gap between its appearance to the senses and its meaning. Hence there is no reason why Cratylus should allow himself to be subjected beneath the yoke of the scheme of original and copy. It is true that a copy, without being a mere duplication of the original, resembles the original; it is a different thing that, because of its imperfect similarity, points to the other that it represents. But this is obviously not true of the relationship of the word to its meaning. Thus it is like the revelation of a wholly obscured truth when Socrates says that words, unlike pictures (zoa), can be not only correct, but true (alethe).[28] The 'truth' of a word does not depend on its correctness, its correct adequation to the object. It lies rather in its perfect intellectuality, ie the obviousness of the meaning of the word in its sound. In this sense all words are 'true', ie their being is wholly absorbed by their meaning, whereas copies are only more or less good likenesses and thus, when measured by the appearance of the object, only more or less correct.

But, as always with Plato, there is a reason for Socrates' being so blind to what he refutes. Cratylus is not aware that the meaning of words is not simply identical with the objects named, and still less is he aware—and this is the reason for Socrates' tacit superiority—that logos, speech and utterance, and the revelation of objects that takes place in it, is something different from the intending of the meanings contained in words, and that the actual capacity of language to communicate what is correct and true is founded on the former. The sophists' misuse of speech arises from their failure to recognise its capacity for truth (the contrary capacity of which is falseness, pseudos). If logos is understood as the representation of a thing (deloma), as its revelation, without a fundamental difference being made between this truth function of speech and the signific character of words, then the way is opened up to a type of confusion peculiar to language. We can then imagine that in the word we have the object. The legitimate way of knowledge will seem to be to stick to the word. But the reverse is also true. Where we have knowledge, the truth of an utterance must be built up out of the truth of words, as if out of its elements, and just as we assume the 'correctness' of these words, ie their natural adequation to the objects they name, we should be able to interpret even the elements of these words, namely the letters, in terms of their copying function in relation to things. This is the conclusion to which Socrates compels his partner.

But in all this the point is missed that the truth of objects resides in speech, which means, ultimately, in the content of a unified meaning concerning objects and not in the individual words—not even in the stock of words of an entire language. It is this error which enables Socrates to refute the objections of Cratylus, which are so apt in relation to the truth of the word, ie to its significance. He relies on the usage of words, that is on speech, logos, with its possibility of being either true or false.

The name, the word, seems to be true or false to the extent to which it is used correctly or wrongly, ie is rightly or wrongly associated with something. This association, however, is not that of the word, but it is already logos and can in such a logos find its adequate expression. For example, to call someone 'Socrates' means that 'Socrates' is the name of this person.

Thus the association that is logos is much more than the mere correspondence of words and objects, as would ultimately correspond to the Eleatic doctrine of being and is assumed in the copy theory. Precisely because the truth contained in the logos is not that of mere perception (of noein), not just letting being appear, but rather always places being in a relationship, assigning something to it, it is not the word (onoma), but the logos that is the bearer of truth (and also of error). Whence it necessarily follows that to this flexible relation, in which the logos analyses and reveals the object, expression, and so connection with language, is quite secondary. We see that it is not word, but number that is the true paradigm of the noetic; number, whose name is obviously pure convention and whose 'exactness' consists in the fact that every number is defined by its place in the series, so that it is a pure structure of intelligibility, an ens rationis, not in a sense that weakens its being, but in the sense of its perfect rationality. This is the real result at which the *Cratylus* aims, and this result has one very important consequence, which in fact influences all further thinking about language.

If the sphere of the logos represents the sphere of the noetic in the variety of its associations, then the word, just like the number, becomes the mere sign of a being that is well-defined and hence pre-known. This is, fundamentally, to turn the question round. Now we are not starting from the object and enquiring into the nature of the word as a means of conveying it but, beginning from the word as a means, we are asking what and how it communicates to the person who uses it. It is in the nature of the sign that it has its being solely in its applied function, in the fact that it points to something else. Thus it must be distinguished in this function from the context in which it is encountered and taken as a sign, in order for its own being as an object to be annulled and for it to disappear in its meaning. It is the abstraction of pointing itself.

A sign, then, is not something that establishes a content of its own. It does not even require a similarity of content with what it points to—and, if it has, then it need be a schematic one only. But that means that again all visible content of its own is reduced to a minimum that is able to assist its pointing function. The clearer a designation is through a sign object, the more the sign is a pure sign, ie it is exhausted in its associative function. Thus, for example, written signs are associated with particular sounds, numerical signs with particular numbers, and they are the most abstract of all signs because their associative function is total and completely exhausts them. Badges, marks, ciphers etc are abstract insofar as they are taken as signs, ie are reduced to their indicative function. The independent existence of a sign is based on something else, something that also exists by itself as a sign object and has its own meaning, a meaning that is different from what it signifies as a sign. In this case the sign acquires its meaning as a sign only in relation to the object signified. 'It does not have its absolute significance within itself, ie nature is only stored away in it'.[29] It is still an immediate entity (it still has its being in the context of other entities; even written signs in a decorative context, for example, have an ornamental value), and only on the basis of its own immediate being is it at the same time something abstract that points to something else. The difference between its being and its significance is an absolute one.

At the other extreme—in the copy—the situation is quite different. Certainly the copy contains the same contradiction between its being and its significance, but in such a way that it resolves this contradiction within itself, precisely by means of the resemblance that lies within itself. It does not gain its function of pointing or representing from the signified object, but from its own content. It is not a mere sign. For in it the object copied is itself represented, caught and made present. That is why it can be valued according to its resemblance, ie according to the extent to which it makes present in itself what is not present.

The legitimate question whether the word is nothing but a 'pure sign' or has something about it of the 'image' is thoroughly discredited by the *Cratylus*. Since the argument that the word is a copy is worked out there ad absurdum, the only alternative seems to be that it is a sign. Although it is not especially emphasised, this emerges as a result of the negative discussion of the *Cratylus* and is sealed by knowledge being banished to the intelligible sphere, so that ever since in all discussion on language the concept of the image (eikon) has been replaced by that of the sign (semeion or semainon). This is not just a terminological change, but it expresses an epoch-making decision about thought concerning language.[30] That the true being of things is to be investigated 'without names' means that there is no access to truth in the proper being of words as such—even if all the investigation, questioning, answering, instructing and differentiation cannot of course take place without the help of language. This is to say that thought is so independent of the proper being of words, which it takes as mere signs through which what is referred to, the idea, the object, is brought into view, that the word adopts a wholly secondary relation to the object. It is a mere tool of communication, the bringing forth (ekpherein) and production (logos prophorikos) in the medium of the voice of what is meant. It follows that an ideal system of signs, the sole significance of which is the unambiguous co-ordination of all signs, makes the power of words (dunamis ton onomaton), the range of variation of the contingent in the historical languages as they have actually developed, appear as a mere obscuring of their usefulness. This is the ideal of a characteristica universalis.

The exclusion of what a language 'is' beyond its aptitude as sign material, ie the self-conquest of language by a system of artificial, unambiguously defined symbols, this ideal of the enlightenment of the eighteenth and twentieth centuries, would also constitute the ideal language, because to it would correspond the totality of the knowable—being—in terms of absolutely available objects. We cannot even make the basic objection that no such mathematical sign language is conceivable without a language that would introduce its conventions. This problem of a 'meta-language' may be insoluble because it involves a reiterative process. But the fact that the process cannot be fully realised says nothing against the fundamental acceptance of the ideal to which it approaches.

It must also be admitted that every development of scientific terminology, however fragmentary its use may be, constitutes a phase of this process. For what is a technical term? A word, the meaning of which is univocally defined, inasmuch as it signifies a defined concept. A technical term is always something artificial insofar as either the word itself is artificially formed or—as is more frequent—a word that is already in use has the variety and breadth of its meanings excised and is assigned only one particular conceptual meaning. In contrast with the living meaning of the words in spoken language, to which, as Wilhelm von Humboldt rightly showed,[31] a certain range of variation is essential, the technical term is a word that has become ossified. The terminological use of a word is an act of violence against language. Unlike the pure sign language of logic, however, the use of technical terminology (even if often in the guise of a foreign word) passes into the spoken language. There is no such thing as purely technical speech, but the technical term, created artificially and against the spirit of language, returns into its stream (as we can see even from the artificial terms of modern advertising). This is indirectly confirmed by the fact that sometimes a technical distinction does not catch on and is constantly denied by usage. Obviously this means that it must bow to the demands of language. We need think only of the use of 'ideology' in a positive, dogmatic, sense which has become general despite its original polemical and instrumental use in more precise philosophical language. Hence, when interpreting scientific texts, one must always reckon with a juxtaposition of the technical and the freer use of a word.[32] Modern interpreters of classical texts are easily inclined to underestimate this necessity because in modern scientific usage a concept is more artificial and hence more fixed than in the ancient world, which did not have any foreign words and very few artificial ones.

Only through mathematical symbolism would it be possible to rise entirely above the contingency of the historical languages and the vagueness of their concepts. In the combinations of this kind of sign system, Leibniz believed, we would acquire new truths that would be of mathematical certainty, because the order represented by such a sign system would find a correspondence in all languages.[33] It is clear that this claim by Leibniz that the characteristica universalis is an ars inveniendi depends on the fact that its symbols are invented. It is this that makes calculation possible, ie the discovery of relations from the formal laws of the system of combinations—independently of whether or not experience presents us with corresponding relationships between objects. By thinking ahead in this way into the sphere of possibilities the thinking reason itself is brought to its absolute perfection. There is for human reason no more adequate form of knowledge than the notitia numerorum,[34] and all calculation proceeds on its model. But it is a general truth that the imperfection of man does not permit adequate knowledge a priori, and that experience is indispensable. Knowledge gained through these symbols is not clear and distinct, for a symbol does not mean that something is given for the senses to perceive, but such knowledge is 'blind', inasmuch as the symbol replaces a real piece of knowledge, merely indicating that it can be acquired.

Thus the ideal of language that Leibniz is pursuing is a "language' of reason, an analysis notionum which, starting from 'first' concepts, would develop the whole system of true concepts and so represent the universe of beings, in an analogous way to the divine reason.[35] The creation of the world, as the calculation of God, who works out the best among all the possibilities of being, would in this way be worked out again by human reason.

We see from this ideal that language is something other than a mere sign system to denote the totality of objects. The word is not just a sign. In a sense that is hard to grasp it is also something almost like an image. We need think only of the other extreme possibility of a purely artificial language, to see the relative justification of such an archaic theory of language. The word has a mysterious connection with what it represents, a quality of belonging to its being. This is meant in a fundamental way; it is not just that mimesis has a certain share in the creation of language, for no one denies this. Plato obviously thought in this way, as does philology today when it assigns a certain function to onomatopoeia in the history of language. But fundamentally language is taken to be something wholly detached from the considered object and to be, rather, an instrument of subjectivity. This is to follow a path of abstraction at the end of which stands the rational construction of an artificial language.

In my view this takes us away from the nature of language. Language and thinking about objects are so bound together that it is an abstraction to conceive of the system of truths as a pre-given system of possibilities of being, with which the signs at the disposal of the signifying subject are associated. A word is not a sign for which one reaches, nor is it a sign that one makes or gives to another, it is not an existent thing which one takes up and to which one accords the ideality of meaning in order to make something else visible through it. This is a mistake on both counts. Rather, the ideality of the meaning lies in the word itself. It is meaningful already. But that does not imply, on the other hand, that the word precedes all experience and simply joins up with an experience in an external way, by subjecting itself to it. The experience is not wordless to begin with and then an object of reflection by being named, by being subsumed under the universality of the word. Rather, it is part of experience itself that it seeks and finds words that express it. We seek for the right word, ie the word that really belongs to the object, so that in it the object comes into language. Even if we hold to the view that this does not imply any simple copying, the word is still part of the object in that it is not simply allotted to the object as a sign. Aristotle's analysis of the formation of concepts by induction, which we considered above, offers an indirect proof of this. It is true that Aristotle himself does not explicitly connect the formation of concepts with the problem of the formation of words and the learning of language, but in his paraphrase Themistius uses children's learning to speak to exemplify the formation of concepts.[36] So much is the logos bound up with language.

If Greek philosophy does not accept this relationship between word and object, speech and thought, the reason no doubt is that thought had to protect itself against the intimate relationship between word and object in which the speaker lives. The domination of this 'most speakable of all languages' (Nietzsche) over thought was so great that the chief concern of philosophy was to free itself from it. Thus from early on the Greek philosophers fought against the onoma as the source of the seduction and confusion of thought, and held instead to the ideality that is constantly created in language. This is true already of Parmenides, who conceived the truth of the object from the logos, and certainly after the Platonic turn to 'discourse', followed by Aristotle's orientation of the forms of being to the forms of assertion (schemata tes kategorias). Because here orientation to the eidos was conceived as what determined the logos, that language should have a being of its own could only be regarded as a confusion, to banish and overcome which was the purpose of thought. Hence the critique of the correctness of names in the *Cratylus* is the first step in a direction at the end of which lies the modern instrumental theory of language and the ideal of a sign system of reason. Wedged in between image and sign, the nature of language could only be reduced to the level of pure sign.

(B) LANGUAGE AND VERBUM

There is, however, an idea that is not Greek and that does more justice to the nature of language and prevented the forgetfulness of language in Western thought from being complete. This is the christian idea of incarnation. Incarnation is obviously not embodiment. Neither the idea of the soul nor of God that is connected with embodiment corresponds to the christian idea of incarnation.

The relation between soul and body as conceived in these theories, as, for instance, in Platonic and Pythagorean philosophy, and corresponding to the religious idea of the migration of souls, assumes the complete separateness of the soul from the body. The soul retains its own separate nature throughout all its embodiments, and the separation from the body it regards as a purification, ie as a restoration of its true and real being. Even the appearance of the divine in human form, which makes Greek religion so human, has nothing to do with incarnation. God does not become man, but shows himself to men in human form, while wholly retaining his superhuman divinity. As opposed to this, that God became man, as understood in the christian religion, involves the sacrifice that the crucified Christ accepts as the Son of Man, namely a relationship that is strangely different and is expressed theologically in the doctrine of the Trinity.

This, the most important element in christian thought, is all the more important for us because in christian thought the incarnation is also closely connected with the problem of the word. The interpretation of the mystery of the Trinity, the most important task confronting the thinking of the middle ages, was based—first in the Fathers and then in systematic elaboration of Augustinianism in the scholastic period—on the relationship between human speech and thought. Here dogmatic theology relied chiefly on the prologue to St. John's gospel and, although theology used Greek ideas to try to solve its own theological problem, philosophy acquired by this means a dimension foreign to Greek thought. If the Word became flesh and the reality of the spirit was perfected only in this incarnation, then the logos is freed from its spirituality, which means, at the same time, from its cosmic potentiality. The uniqueness of the redemptive event introduces the historical object into Western thought, brings the phenomenon of language out of its immersion in the ideality of meaning, and offers it to philosophical reflection. For, in contrast to the Greek logos, the word is pure event (verbum proprie dicitur personaliter tantum).[37]

Of course human language is thereby only indirectly raised to be an object of reflection. The human word is used only as an analogy to exemplify the theological problem of the Word, the verbum dei, ie the unity of God the Father and God the Son. But the important thing for us is precisely that the mystery of this unity is reflected in the phenomenon of language.

Even the way in which the Fathers connect theological speculation about the mystery of the incarnation with Hellenistic thought is interesting because of the new dimension which they envisage. Thus the attempt was made initially to make use of the stoic antithesis of the inner and the outer logos (logos endiathetos—prophorikos).[38] This distinction was originally intended to distinguish the stoic world-principle of the logos from the externality of merely repeating a word.[39] The reverse direction now immediately acquires a positive significance for the christian belief in revelation. The analogy of the inner and the outer word, the expression of the word in the vox, now acquires an exemplary value.

Creation took place once through the word of God. In this way the early Fathers made use of the miracle of language to

make intelligible the un-Greek idea of the creation. But above all
the actual redemptive act, the sending of the Son, the mystery of
the incarnation, is described in St. John's prologue itself in terms
of the word. Exegesis understands the speaking of the word to
be equally miraculous with the incarnation of God. The act of
becoming in both is not a becoming in which something turns
into something else. Neither is it a separating of the one from the
other (kat apokopen), nor a diminution of the inner word by its
emergence into exteriority, nor a becoming something different,
so that the inner word is consumed.[40] Even in the earliest applications of Greek thought we can discern the new orientation
towards the mysterious unity of Father and Son, of Spirit and
Word. And if direct reference to the utterance, to the speaking
of the Word, is ultimately rejected in christian dogmatics—in the
rejection of subordinationism—it is still necessary, because of
this very decision, again to consider philosophically the mystery
of language and its connection with thought. The greater miracle
of language does not lie in the fact that the Word becomes flesh
and emerges in external being, but that that which emerges and
expresses itself in utterance is still a word. That the Word is with
God from all eternity is the victorious doctrine of the church, as
against subordinationism, and it places the problem of language
entirely within thought.

The external word, and with it the whole problem of the variety of languages, was explicitly devalued by Augustine, though
he still discusses it.[41] Both the external word and that which is
reproduced only inwardly are tied to a particular tongue (lingua).
The fact that the verbum is spoken differently in different languages, however, means only that it is not able to reveal itself
through the human tongue in its true being. In a minimisation of
the value of sensible appearance that is entirely Platonic, Augustine says, non dicitur, sicuti est, sed sicut potest videri audirive
per corpus. The 'true' word, the verbum cordis, is quite independent of such an appearance. It is neither prolativum nor
cogitativum in similitudine soni. Hence this inner word is the
mirror and the image of the divine word. When Augustine and
the scholastics treat the problem of the verbum in order to gain
the conceptual means to deal with the mystery of the Trinity,
they are concerned exclusively with this inner word, the word of
the heart, and its relation to the intelligentia.

Thus it is a quite specific side of the nature of language that
emerges here. The mystery of the Trinity is mirrored in the
miracle of language insofar as the word that is true, because it
says what the object is, is nothing by itself and does not seek to

be anything: nihil de suo habens, sed totum de illa scientia de qua nascitur. It has its being in its revealing. Exactly the same thing is true of the mystery of the Trinity. Here also the important thing is not the earthly appearance of the redeemer as such, but rather his complete divinity, his consubstantiality with God. To grasp the independent personal existence of Christ within this sameness of being is the task of theology. Here the analogy of the mental word, the verbum intellectus is helpful. This is more than a mere image, for the human relationship between thought and speech corresponds, despite its imperfections, to the divine relationship of the Trinity. The inner mental word is as consubstantial with thought as is God the Son with God the Father.

It may be asked whether we are not here using the unintelligible to explain the unintelligible. What sort of word is it that remains the inner dialogue of thought and finds no outer form in sound? Does such a thing exist? Does not all our thinking always follow the paths of a particular language, and do we not know only too well that one has to think in a language if one really wants to speak it? Even if we remember the freedom that our reason preserves in the face of the connection of our thinking with language, either by inventing and using artificial sign languages or by being able to translate from one language into another—something that presumes a capacity to rise above the tie with language to attain the sense intended—this capacity itself is, as we have seen, linguistic. The 'language of reason' is not a special language. So, considering that the tie with language is irremovable, what sense is there in speaking of an 'inner word' that is spoken, as it were, in the pure language of reason? How does the word of reason (if we may translate intellectus here by 'reason') prove itself a real 'word', if it is not a word with a sound, nor even the image of one, but is that which is signified by a sign, ie what is meant and thought itself?

Because the doctrine of the inner word is intended to be an analogy for the theological interpretation of the Trinity, the theological question as such can be of no further help to us. Rather, we must turn our attention to the 'inner word' itself and ask what it may be. It cannot be simply the Greek logos, the dialogue that the soul conducts with itself. On the contrary, the mere fact that logos is translated both by ratio and verbum is an indication that the phenomenon of language will become more important in the scholastic elaboration of Greek metaphysics than was the case with the Greeks themselves.

The particular difficulty of enlisting the aid of scholastic thinking for our problem is that the christian understanding of the word, as we find it in the Fathers, who in part take over and in part develop late classical ideas, once again approached the classical concept of logos with the entry of Aristotelianism into high scholasticism. Thus St. Thomas took the christian doctrine developed from the prologue to St. John's gospel and systematically combined it with Aristotle.[42] With him there is, characteristically, hardly any talk of the variety of languages, although Augustine still discusses it, even if only to discard it in favour of the 'inner word'. The doctrine of the 'inner word' is for him the obvious premise for his investigation of the connection between forma and verbum.

Nevertheless, even for Thomas logos and verbum do not completely coincide. Certainly, the word is not the expressive event, this irrevocable handing-over of one's own thinking to another, but the ontological character of the word is still an event. The inner word remains related to its possible utterance. The object, when conceived by the intellect, is at the same time ordered towards being made known (similitudo rei concepta in intellectu et ordinata ad manifestationem vel ad se vel ad alterum). Thus the inner word is certainly not related to a particular language, nor does it have the character of vaguely imagined words that proceed from the memory, but it is the objective situation thought through to the end (forma excogitata). In that a process of thinking through to the end is involved, we have to acknowledge a processual element in it. It proceeds per modum egredientis. It is not utterance, but thought; however it is the perfection of thought that is achieved in this speaking to oneself. So the inner word, by expressing thought, represents the finiteness of our discursive understanding. Because our understanding does not embrace what it knows in one single comprehensive glance, it must always produce out of itself what it thinks, and present it to itself as if in an inner dialogue with itself. In this sense all thought is a speaking to oneself.

The Greek logos-philosophy undoubtedly knew this. Plato described thought as an inner conversation of the soul with itself,[43] and the infiniteness of the dialectical effort that he requires of the philosopher is the expression of the discursiveness of our finite understanding. Also, however much he called for 'pure thought', Plato always recognised that the medium of onoma and logos remained essential for thought about an object. But if the teaching about the inner word means nothing more than the discursiveness of human thought and speech, how can the 'word' be an analogy to the process of the divine persons expressed in the doctrine of the Trinity? Is not the very antithesis between intuition and discursiveness in the way here? What is common to the one and the other 'process'?

It is true that no temporality enters into the relations of the divine persons to one another. But the successive quality that is characteristic of the discursiveness of human thought is not basically temporal in nature. When human thought passes from one thing to another, ie thinks first this thing and then that, it is still not swept along from one thing to the other. It does not think a simple succession of first one thing and then another, which would mean that it would itself constantly change in the process. If it thinks first of one thing and then of another, then that means that it knows what it is doing, and is able to connect the one thing with the other. Hence it is not a temporal relation that is involved, but a mental process, an emanatio intellectualis.

Thomas uses this neoplatonic concept to describe both the processual character of the inner word and the process of the Trinity. This brings out a point not contained in the logos philosophy of Plato. The idea of emanation in neoplatonism contains more than the physical phenomenon of flowing out as a process of movement. The primary image, rather, is that of the fountain.[44] In the process of emanation, that from which something flows, the One, is not deprived, nor does it become less. The same is true of the birth of the Son from the Father, who does not use up anything of himself in the process, but takes something to himself. And this is likewise true of the mental production that takes place in the process of thought, of speaking to oneself. This kind of production is at the same time a total remaining within oneself. If it can be said of the divine relationship between word and intellect that the word does not partially, but wholly (totaliter) have its origin in the intellect, then it is true also with us that one word originates totaliter from another, ie has its origin in the mind, like the deduction of a conclusion from the premisses (ut conclusio ex principiis). Thus the productive process of thought is not a process of change (motus), not a transition from potentiality into action, but an emergence ut actus ex actu. The word is not formed only after the act of knowledge has been completed—in scholastic terms, after the intellect has been informed by the species—but it is the act of knowledge itself. Thus the word is simultaneous with this (formatio) of the intellect.

It is clear how the creation of the word came to be seen as a true image of the Trinity. It is a true generatio, a true birth, even though, of course, there is no receptive part to go with a generating one. Precisely this intellectual character of the generation of the word, however, is of great importance for its function as a theological model. There really is something in common between the process of the divine persons and the process of thought.

Nevertheless, it is the differences, rather than the similarities, between the divine and the human word that are more important to us. This is theologically sound. The mystery of the Trinity that the analogy with the inner word is supposed to illuminate must ultimately remain incomprehensible in terms of human thought. If the whole of the divine mind is expressed in the divine Word, then the processual element in this word signifies something for which we basically have no analogy. Insofar as the divine mind, in knowing itself, likewise knows all beings, the word of God is the word of the spirit that knows and creates everything in one intuition (intuitus). The act of production disappears in the actuality of the divine omniscience. Creation is not a real process, but only separates out the structure of the universe in a temporal scheme.[45] If we want to grasp more exactly the processual element in the word, which is the important thing for our enquiry into the connection between language and understanding, we cannot stop at this similarity with the theological problem, but shall have to linger over the imperfection of the human mind and its difference from the divine. We can follow Thomas here, who specifies three differences.

1 The first thing is that the human word is potential before it is actualised. It is capable of being formed, though it is not yet formed. The process of thought begins with something coming into our mind from our memory. But even this is an emanation, in that the memory is not plundered and does not lose something. But what comes into our mind in this way is not yet something finished and thought out to its conclusion. Rather the real movement of thought now begins, in which the mind runs from one thing to the other, turns this way and that, considering this and that and thus, and by way of investigation (inquisitio) and consideration (cogitatio) seeks the perfect expression of its thoughts. The perfect word, therefore, is formed only in thought, like a tool, but once it exists as the full perfection of the thought, nothing more is created with it. Rather the object is then present in it. Thus it is not a real tool. Thomas found a brilliant image for this. The word is like a mirror in which the object is seen. The curious thing about this mirror, however, is that it nowhere extends beyond the image of the object. In it nothing is mirrored except this one thing, so that, as the whole

that it is, it reproduces only its image (similitudo). What is remarkable about this image is that the word is understood here entirely as the perfect reflection of the object, ie as the expression of the object, and has left behind it the path of the thought to which alone, however, it owes its existence. This does not happen with the divine mind.

2 Unlike the divine word the human one is essentially imperfect. No human word can perfectly express our mind. But, as the image of the mirror shows, this is not really an imperfection of the word as such. The word reproduces completely what the mind is thinking. Rather it is the imperfection of the human mind that it never possesses complete self-presence, but is dispersed into thinking this or that. From this essential imperfection it follows that the human word is not one, like the divine word, but must necessarily be many words. Hence the variety of words does not in any way mean that there is a lack in the individual word that one could remedy, in that it did not completely express what the mind is thinking, but because our intellect is imperfect, ie is not perfectly present to itself in what it knows, it needs the multiplicity of words. It does not really know what it knows.

3 The third difference is connected with this point. Whereas God completely expresses in the Word his nature and substance in pure actuality, every thought that we think, and therefore every word in which the thought expresses itself, is a mere accident of the mind. The word of human thought is directed towards the object, but it cannot contain it as a whole within itself. Thus thought moves towards constantly new conceptions and is fundamentally incapable of being wholly realised in any. The positive side of this negative quality is the true infinity of the mind, which constantly passes beyond itself in a new mental process and in this finds also the freedom for constantly new developments.

Summing up what we gain from the theology of the verbum, let us first make a point that has hardly come to the fore in the preceding analysis—nor was it expressed in scholastic thought—and yet is of particular importance for the hermeneutical phenomenon. The inner unity of thinking and speaking to oneself, which corresponds to the Trinitarian mystery of the incarnation implies that the inner mental word is not formed by a reflective act. A person who thinks something, ie says it to himself, means by it the thing that he thinks. His mind is not directed back towards his own thinking when he forms the word. The word is, of course, the product of the work of his mind. The mind forms it in itself by thinking the thought through. But unlike other products it remains entirely within the mental sphere. Thus the impression is given that it is an attitude towards itself that is involved and that speaking to oneself is a reflexive thing. It is not so, in fact, but this structure of thought is undoubtedly the reason why thought is able to direct itself reflectively towards itself and can thus become an object to itself. The inwardness of the word, which constitutes the inner unity of thought and speech, is the reason for its being easy to miss the direct and unreflective character of the 'word'. In thinking, a person does not move forward from the one thing to the other, from thinking to speaking to himself. The word does not emerge in a sphere of the mind that is still free of thought (in aliquo sui nudo). Hence the appearance is created that the formation of the word arises from the movement of the mind towards itself. In fact no reflective process operates when the word is formed, for the word is not expressing the mind, but the intended object. The starting-point for the formation of the word is the intelligible object (the species) that fills the mind. The thought seeking expression refers not to the mind, but to the object. Thus the word is not the expression of the mind, but is concerned with the similitudo rei. The object thought (the species) and the word belong as closely together as possible. Their unity is so close that the word does not occupy a second place in the mind beside the species, but is that in which knowledge is completed, ie that in which the species is fully thought. Thomas points out that in this the word resembles the light in which a colour becomes visible.

But there is a second thing that we can learn from this scholastic thinking. The difference between the unity of the divine Word and the multiplicity of human words does not exhaust the situation. Rather, unity and multiplicity have a fundamental dialectical relationship to each other. The dialectic of this relationship conditions the whole nature of the word. Even the divine Word is not entirely free of the idea of multiplicity. It is true that the divine Word is one unique word that came into the world in the form of the Redeemer, but insofar as it remains an event—and this is the case, despite the rejection of subordinationism, as we have seen—there is an essential connection between the unity of the divine Word and its appearance in the church. The proclamation of salvation, the content of the christian gospel, is itself a distinct event in sacrament and preaching, and yet it expresses only what has taken place in Christ's redemptive act. Hence it is one word that is constantly proclaimed anew in preaching. Its character as gospel, then, already has in it the element of pointing to the multiple nature of its proclamation. The meaning of the word cannot be detached from the event of proclamation. Rather, its eventual character is part of the meaning itself. It is like a curse that obviously cannot be separated from the fact that it is spoken by someone over someone. What we understand from it is not an abstractable logical sense of a statement, but the actual curse that takes effect in it.[46] The same holds for the unity and the multiplicity of the word proclaimed by the church. The content of salvation that is preached in every sermon is the crucifixion and resurrection of Christ. The Christ of the resurrection and the Christ of the kerygma are one and the same. Modern protestant theology, in particular, has elaborated the eschatological character of the faith that depends on this dialectical relationship.

The human word reveals the dialectical relationship of the multiplicity of words to the unity of the word in a new light. Plato recognized that the human word has the character of speech, ie that by the association of a multiplicity of words it expresses one meaning; this structure of the logos he developed dialectically. Then Aristotle demonstrated the logical structure of the proposition, the judgment, the syllogism and the argument. But even this does not exhaust the situation. The unity of the word that is revealed in the multiplicity of words manifests something that is not covered by the structure of logic and brings out the eventual character of language: the process of concept formation. In developing the idea of the verbum, scholastic thought goes beyond the idea that the formation of concepts is simply the reflection of the order of things.

(C) LANGUAGE AND CONCEPT FORMATION

That the natural concept formation that keeps pace with language does not always simply follow the order of things, but very often takes place as a result of accidents and relations, is confirmed by a glance at Plato's analysis of concepts or at Aristotle's definitions. But the precedence of the logical order that is established by the concepts of substance and accidence makes language's natural concept formation appear only as an imperfection of our finite mind. It is because we know only the accidents that we follow them in the formation of concepts. Even if this is right, there follows from this imperfection a curious advantage, which Thomas seems to have pointed out correctly—the freedom to form an infinite number of concepts and to penetrate what is meant ever more and more.[47]

Because the process of thought is conceived as the process of explication in words, there becomes apparent a logical achievement of language that cannot be fully understood in terms of an order of things as they would appear to an infinite mind. The subordination of the natural concept formation that occurs in language to the structure of logic, as taught by Aristotle and, following him, Thomas, thus has only a relative truth. Rather, in the midst of the penetration of christian theology by the Greek idea of logic something new is born: the centre of language, in which the mediation of the incarnation event achieves its full truth. Christology prepares the way for a new philosophy of man, which mediates in a new way between the mind of man in its finitude and the divine infinity. This will become the real basis of what we have called the hermeneutical experience.

We must consider then the natural formation of concepts that takes place in language. It is obvious that speech, even if it involves a subordination of what is meant in each particular case to the universality of a pre-established verbal meaning, cannot be thought of as the combination of these subsuming acts, through which something particular is subordinated to a universal concept. A person who speaks—who, that is to say, uses the general meanings of words—is so orientated towards the particular features of the observation of an object that everything he says acquires a share in the particular nature of the circumstances that he is considering.[48]

But that means, on the other hand, that the universal concept that is meant by the meaning of the word is enriched by the particular view of an object, so that what emerges is a new, more specific word formation which does more justice to the particular features of the object. Just as speech implies the use of pre-established words which have their universal meaning, there is at the same time a constant process of concept formation by means of which the life of a language develops.

The logical schema of induction and abstraction is very misleading here, as in linguistic consciousness there is no explicit reflection on what is common to different things, nor does the use of words in their universal meaning regard what they designate as a case that is subsumed under a universal. The universality of the genus and the classificatory formation of concepts are far removed from the linguistic consciousness. Even disregarding all formal similarities that have nothing to do with the generic concept, if a person transfers an expression from one thing to the other, he has in mind something that is common to both of them, but this need not be in any sense generic universality. He is following, rather, his widening experience, which sees similarities, whether of the appearance of an object, or of its significance for us. It is the genius of linguistic consciousness to be able to give expression to these similarities. This is its fundamental metaphorical nature, and it is important to see that it is the prejudice of a theory of logic that is alien to language if the metaphorical use of a word is regarded as not its real sense.[49]

It is obvious that the particular quality of an experience finds its expression in this kind of transformation, and it is not at all the fruit of the formation of a concept by a process of abstraction. But it is equally obvious that knowledge of what is common to it and other experiences is obtained in this way. Thus thought can turn for its own instruction[50] to this stock that language has built up. Plato did this with his 'flight into the *logoi*'.[51] But classificatory logic also starts from the logical advance work that language has performed for it.

This is confirmed if we look at its pre-history, especially at the theory of concept formation in the Platonic academy. We have seen that Plato's call to rise above names assumes the fundamental independence of the cosmos of ideas from language. Inasmuch, however, as this rising above names takes place in regard to the idea and is a dialectic, ie an insight into the unity of what is observed, seeing what is common to various phenomena, it follows the natural direction in which language develops. Rising above names means simply that the truth of the object is not contained in the name itself. It does not mean that thinking can dispense with the use of name and logos. On the contrary, Plato always recognised that these intermediaries of thought are necessary, even though they must always be regarded as capable of being improved on. The idea, the true being of the object, cannot be known in any other way than by passing through these intermediaries. But is there a knowledge of the idea itself as this particular and individual thing? Is not the nature of things a whole in the same way that language also is a whole? If the individual words acquire their meaning and relative unambiguity only in the unity of speech, the true knowledge of being can be achieved only in the whole of the relational structure of the ideas. This is the thesis of Plato's *Parmenides*. This, however, raises the question: in order to define a single idea, ie to be able to distinguish what it is from everything else that exists, do we not need to know the whole?

We can hardly escape this consequence if, like Plato, we regard the cosmos of ideas as the true structure of being. We are told that the Platonist Speusippus, Plato's successor as the head of the Academy, did not escape it.[52] We know that he was particularly concerned with discovering what was common (homoia) and that he went far beyond what generic logic called universalisation, in that he used analogy, ie proportional correspondence, as a method of research. The dialectical capacity of discovering similarities and seeing one quality common to many things is here still very close to the free universality of language and the principles of its word formation. Analogies, which Speusippus sought everywhere—correspondences such as 'wings are to birds what fins are to fish'—thus serve the definition of concepts, because these correspondences constitute at the same time one of the most important developmental principles in the formation of words. Transposition from one sphere into another not only has a logical function, but it corresponds to the fundamental metaphorical nature of language. The well-known stylistic device of the metaphor is only the rhetorical form of this universal—both linguistic and logical—generative principle. So Aristotle: 'To make a good transposition means to recognise similarity'.[53] Aristotle's *Topics* offers many confirmations of the indissolubility of the connection between concept and language. The definitory setting-up of the common genus is derived there explicitly from the observation of similarity.[54] Thus before the beginning of generic logic we have the advance work in language itself.

It fits this situation that Aristotle himself always assigns the greatest importance to the way in which the order of things becomes apparent in speaking about them. (The 'categories'—and not only what Aristotle explicitly calls such—are forms of statement.) The formation of concepts by language is not only used by philosophical thought, but it is developed further in particular directions. We have already referred above to the fact that the Aristotelian theory of the formation of concepts, the theory of the epagoge, could be illustrated by children learning to speak.[55] In fact, however fundamental Plato's dispelling of the magic of speech was for Aristotle, however great its influence on his own development of 'logic', however much he was concerned to reflect the order of things and to detach them from all linguistic contingencies by the conscious use of a logic of definition, especially in the classificatory description of nature, for him the unity of speech and thought remained complete.

Hence the few places where he speaks of language as such are far from isolating the linguistic sphere of meaning from the world of things that it names. When Aristotle says of sounds or written signs that they 'describe' when they become a symbolon this means, certainly, that they do not exist naturally, but according to a convention (kata suntheken). But his is not an instrumental theory of signs. Rather, the convention according to which the sounds of language or the signs of writing mean something is not an agreement on a means of understanding—this would always involve language already—but it is the agreement on which human community, its harmony with respect to what is good and proper, is founded.[56] Agreement in language's use of sounds and signs is only an expression of that fundamental agreement in what is good and proper. It is true that the Greeks liked to consider what was good and proper, what they called the nomoi, as the decree and the achievement of divine men. But for Aristotle this derivation of the nomos characterises more its value than its actual origin. This is not to say that Aristotle no longer acknowledges the religious tradition, but that this, like every question of origin, is for him a way to the knowledge of being and value. The convention of which Aristotle speaks in regard to language characterises its mode of being and says nothing about its origin.

If we recall the analysis of the epagoge we shall find further evidence of this.[57] There, as we saw, Aristotle left open, in the most intelligent way, the question of how universal concepts are formed. We can see now that he was taking account of the fact that the natural formation of concepts by language was already in process. Thus even according to Aristotle the formation of concepts by language possesses a quite undogmatic freedom, in that what mind sees as similar in the things it encounters, which leads then to a universal, has the character of a mere preliminary achievement, which stands at the beginning of science but is not yet science. This is what Aristotle emphasises. If science sets up cogent proof as its ideal, then it must advance beyond such modes of procedure. Thus Aristotle criticised both the teaching of Speusippus on the common, and the diaretical dialectic of Plato, in terms of his ideal of proof.

The consequence of this measuring by the logical ideal of proof, however, is that the Aristotelian critique has robbed the logical achievement of language of its scientific justification. It is recognised only from the point of view of rhetoric and is understood there as the artistic device of metaphor. The logical ideal of the ordered arrangement of concepts is here superior to the living metaphoric nature of language, on which all natural concept formation depends. For only a grammar that is based on logic will distinguish between the real and the metaphorical meaning of a word. What originally constituted the basis of the life of language and made up its logical productivity, the spontaneous and inventive seeking out of similarities by means of which it is possible to order things, is now pushed to the side and instrumentalised into a rhetorical figure called metaphor. The struggle between philosophy and rhetoric for the training of Greek youth, which was decided with the victory of Attic philosophy, has also this side to it, namely that the thinking about language becomes the object of a grammar and rhetoric that have already recognised the ideal of scientific concept formation. Thus the sphere of linguistic meanings begins to become detached from the sphere of things encountered in linguistic form. Stoic logic speaks of those incorporeal meanings by means of which talk about things goes on (to lekton). It is highly significant that these meanings are put on the same level as the topos ie space.[58] Just as space only becomes an object of thought by mentally removing the objects that are related to one another in it,[59] so 'meanings' as such are now conceived by themselves for the first time, and a concept is created for them by mentally removing the things that are named by the meaning of words. Meanings, too, are like a space in which things are related to one another.

Such ideas obviously become possible only when the natural relationship, ie the intimate unity of speech and thought, is upset. We may mention the connection between stoic thought and the grammatical and syntactical structure of the Latin language, which Lohmann has pointed out.[60] There is no doubt that the fact that two languages were beginning to be used throughout the hellenistic oikumene had a beneficial influence on thinking about language. But perhaps the origins of this development come far earlier, and it is the birth of science itself that sets off this process. If this is so, it will go back to the early days of Greek science. That it is so is suggested by the development of scientific concepts in the fields of music, mathematics and physics, because in them an area of rational objectivities is marked out, the constructions of which call for the development of corresponding terms, which can no longer really be called words. It can be stated as a fundamental principle that wherever words assume a mere sign function, the original connection between speaking and thinking, with which we are concerned, is changed into an instrumental relationship. This changed relationship of word and sign is at the basis of concept formation in science and has become so self-evident to us that it requires a special effort of memory to recall that, beside the scientific ideal of unambiguous designation, the life of language itself continues unchanged.

There are no lack of reminders, of course, when we consider the history of philosophy. Thus we showed that the theological relevance of the problem of language in mediaeval thought constantly points back to the unity of thinking and speaking and also brings out an aspect of which classical Greek philosophy was not aware. That the word is a process in which the unity of what is meant is fully expressed—as was thought in the speculation on the verbum—is something new that goes beyond the Platonic dialectic of the one and the many. For Plato sees the logos itself as moving within this dialectic and being nothing but the undergoing of the dialectic of the ideas. There is no real problem of interpretation here, in that its means, word and speech, are constantly being overtaken by the thinking mind. In contrast to this, we found that in Trinitarian speculation the procession of the divine persons involves the neoplatonic theory of diffusion, unfolding, ie the proceeding from the one, and hence for the first time does justice to the processual character of the Word. But the problem of language could not be fully opened up until the scholastic combination of christian thought with Aristotelian philosophy was supplemented by a new element that turned the distinction between the divine and the human mind into something positive and was to acquire the greatest importance for modern times. This is the element, common to both, of the creative. This, it seems to me, is the real importance of Nicholas of Cusa, who has recently been so much discussed.[61]

The analogy between the two modes of creativity has, of course, its boundaries, which correspond to the differences stressed above between the divine and the human word. Certainly, the divine word creates the world, but not in a temporal succession of creative thought and creative days. The human mind, on the other hand, possesses the whole of its thoughts only in temporal succession. It is true that this is not a purely temporal relationship, as we have seen already with St. Thomas. Nicholas of Cusa also points this out. It is like the number series, whose production is not really a temporal occurrence either, but a movement of the reason. Nicholas of Cusa sees the same movement of reason operating when genera and species are developed from out of the sphere of the sensible and have individual concepts and words assigned to them. They, too, are entia rationis. However Platonic and Neoplatonic this talk of diffusion or unfolding may sound, in actual fact Nicholas of Cusa has overcome in its main point the emanistic schema of the neoplatonic account of explanation. He opposes to it the christian teaching of the verbum.[62] The word is for him no less than the mind itself, not a diminished or weakened manifestation of it.

The knowledge of this constitutes the superiority of the christian philosopher over the Platonist. Accordingly, the multiplicity in which the human mind unfolds is not a mere falling away from true unity and not a loss of its home. Rather, there had to be a positive justification for the finitude of the human mind, however much this finitude remained related to the infinite unity of absolute being. This is prepared for in the idea of complicatio, and from this point of view the phenomenon of language also acquires a new aspect. It is the human mind that both gathers together and unfolds. The unfolding into discursive multiplicity is not only conceptual, but extends also into the linguistic sphere. It is the variety of possible appelations—according to the various languages—that intensifies the conceptual differentiation.

With the nominalist break-up of the classical logic of essence the problem of language passes into a new stage. It is now suddenly of positive importance that things can be articulated in different ways (if not in any way at all) according to their correspondences and their differences. If the relationship of genus and species can be justified not only from the nature of things—on the model of the 'genuine' species in the self—construction of living nature, but also in another way in regard to man and his power to give names, then languages as they have grown up historically, with their history of meanings, their grammar and their syntax, can be seen as the varied forms of a logic of experience, of natural, ie historical experience (which even includes supernatural experience). The thing itself is quite clear.[63] The organisation of words and things, that is undertaken by each language in its own way, always constitutes a primary natural formation of concepts that is a long way from the system of the scientific formation of concepts. It follows entirely the human aspect of things, the system of man's needs and interests. What a linguistic community regards as important about a thing can be given a common name with other things that are perhaps of a quite different nature in other respects, so long as they all have the same quality that is important to the community. A nomenclature (impositio nominis) in no way corresponds to the concepts of science and its classificatory system of genus and species. Rather, compared with the latter, it is often accidental attributes from which the general meaning of a word is derived.

In this we must take account of some influence of science on language. For example, the word 'humour' and its derivitives have changed their meanings considerably as medicine has advanced beyond a theory of 'humours'. On the other hand, the rich variety of the popular names for particular things is being ironed out, partly as a result of modern communications and partly by scientific and technological standardisation, just as our vocabulary has contracted rather than expanded in such areas. There is an African language that has two hundred different words for 'camel', according to the particular circumstances and relationships in which a camel stands in regard to the desert-dwellers. Because of the dominant meaning that it retains in all the words, it seems each time to be something different.[64] In such cases we can say that there is an extreme tension between the generic concept and the linguistic designation. But we can also say that the tendency towards conceptual universality and that towards pragmatic meaning are never completely harmonised in any living language. That is why it is always artificial and contrary to the nature of language to measure the contingency of the natural formation of concepts against the true order of things and to see the former as purely accidental. This contingency comes about, in fact, through the necessary and legitimate range of variation in which the human mind is able to articulate the essential order of things.

The fact that, despite the scriptural importance of the confusion of tongues, the Latin middle ages did not really pursue this aspect of the problem of language can be explained chiefly by the unquestioned domination of Latin among scholars, and the continued influence of the Greek doctrine of the logos. It was only in the renaissance, when the laity became important and the national languages part of cultivated learning, that people began to think productively about the relation of these to the inner, ie the 'natural' word. We must, however, be careful not to ascribe to them the attitude of enquiry of modern linguistic philosophy and its instrumental concept of language. The significance of the first emergence of the problem of language in the renaissance lies rather in the fact that the Graeco-christian heritage was still automatically accepted as valid. This is quite clear in Nicholas of Cusa. As an unfolding of the unity of the spirit the concepts expressed in words still retain their connection with a natural word (vocabulum naturale), which is reflected (relucet) in all of them, however freely chosen the individual name may be[65] (impositio nominis fit ad beneplacitum). We may ask ourselves what this connection is and what this natural word is supposed to be. But it makes methodological sense to say that the individual words of one language are in an ultimate harmony with those of every other one, in that all languages are an unfolding of the one unity of the mind.

Nicholas of Cusa, too, does not mean by the natural word the
word of an original language that preceded the confusion of
tongues. This kind of 'language of Adam', in the sense of the
doctrine of a primal state, is far removed from his thinking. He
starts, rather, from the fundamental inexactness of all human
knowledge. It is, as we know, his theory of knowledge, which
combines Platonic and nominalist elements, that all human
knowledge is mere conjecture and opinion (coniectura,
opinio).[66] It is this view that he now applies to language. Thus he
is able to recognise the differences of the national languages and
the apparent fact that their vocabularies are freely chosen, without for that reason falling into a purely conventionalist theory of
language and an instrumentalist concept of language. Just as
human knowledge is essentially 'inexact', ie permits of a 'more'
or a 'less', so also is human language. Something for which there
is a proper expression in one language (propria vocabula), is
expressed in another by a more barbarous and remote word
(magis barbara et remotiora vocabula). Thus there are expressions that are more or less proper (propria vocabula). All actual
designations are, in a certain sense, arbitrary, and yet they have
a necessary connection with the natural expression (nomen
naturale), which corresponds to the thing itself (forma). Every
expression is fitting (congruum), but not every one is exact (pre-
cisum).

This kind of linguistic theory presupposes that the things
(forma) to which the words are attached do not belong to any
pre-established order of original models which human knowledge more and more approaches, but that this order is created
by differentiation and combination out of the given nature of
things. In this the thought of Nicholas of Cusa has been influenced by nominalism. If the genera and species are themselves
in this way intelligible being (entia rationis), then it is clear that
the words can be in agreement with the actual perception to
which they give expression, even if different words are used in
different languages. For in this case it is not a question of variations of expression, but of variations of the view of the object
and of the formation of concepts that follows it, ie there is an
essential inexactness, which does not exclude there nevertheless
being in all the expressions a reflection of the object itself
(forma). This kind of essential inexactness can be overcome
only if the mind rises to the infinite. In the infinite there is, then,
only one single thing (forma) and one single word (vocabulum),
namely the ineffable Word of God (verbum Dei) that is reflected
in everything (relucet).

If, then, we regard the human mind as related in this way to the divine as a copy to the original, we can accept the range of variation in human languages. As at the beginning, in the discussion of the search for analogies in the Platonic academy, so also at the end of the mediaeval discussion of universals there is the idea of a real closeness between word and concept. We are still a long way here from the relativistic consequences for worldviews that modern thought has drawn from the variation of languages. Despite all the differences the common factor is still preserved, and that is what the christian Platonist is concerned with. Essential for him is the relation of all human speech to the thing, and not so much the connectedness with language of all human knowledge of things. The latter represents only a prismatic refraction in which there shines the one truth.

3 LANGUAGE AS HORIZON OF A HERMENEUTIC ONTOLOGY

(A) LANGUAGE AS EXPERIENCE OF THE WORLD

If we have considered in depth some phases of the history of the problem of language, this was in order to present certain points of view that are remote from the modern philosophy and science of language. Since Herder and Humboldt, modern thinking about language has been dominated by a quite different interest. It seeks to study the way in which the naturalness of human language—an insight painfully won against the forces of rationalism and orthodoxy—unfolds in the range of experience of differences between human languages. Regarding every language as an organism, it undertakes a comparative study of the large variety of means which the human mind has used to exercise its capacity for language. Nicholas of Cusa was still a long way from this kind of empirical comparative enquiry. He remained a Platonist, in that differences within the inexact did not, for him, contain any truth of their own and hence were deserving of interest only insofar as they were in agreement with the 'true'. For him there was no interest in the national peculiarities of the emergent national languages; in this he differed from, for example, Wilhelm von Humboldt.

Even with the latter, however, if we are to do him justice as the founder of the modern philosophy of language, we must beware of the over-resonance created by comparative linguistics and the psychology of peoples that he inaugurated. With him the problem of the 'truth of the word' is not yet entirely obscured. Humboldt does not examine the empirical variety of the structure of human language merely in order to penetrate the individual peculiarities of different peoples by means of this tangible field of human expression.[67] His interest in individuality, like that of his age, is not to be regarded as a turning away from the universality of the concept. Rather, there exists for him an indissoluble connection between individuality and universal nature. Together with the feeling of individuality there is alway given the sense of a totality,[68] and so the study of the individuality of linguistic phenomena is itself intended as a way towards insight into the whole of human language.

He starts from the position that languages are the products of man's 'mental power'. Wherever there is language, the primary linguistic power of the human mind is at work, and every language is able to attain the general goal towards which this natural power of man is directed. This does not exclude the fact—but rather justifies it—that the comparison of languages calls for a criterion of perfection according to which they are differentiated. For the striving to realise the idea of the perfection of language is common to all languages, and the task of the linguist is directed towards investigating to what extent and with what means the various languages approach this idea. There are, then, for Humboldt, undoubted differences in the perfection of the various languages; but it is not a preconceived criterion that he forces on the variety of the phenomena he is studying, rather he acquires this criterion from the inner nature of language itself and its rich variety.

Thus the normative interest he has in his comparison of the structure of human languages does not get in the way of the recognition of the individuality—and that means the relative perfection—of each language. It is well-known that Humboldt taught that every language should be seen as a particular view of the world, and he investigated the 'inner form' in which the primary human process of language formation is, in each instance, differentiated. Behind this view there lies not only idealistic philosophy, which emphasises the part played by the subjective consciousness in understanding the world, but also the metaphysics of individuality first developed by Leibniz. This is expressed both in the concept of mental power, to which the phenomenon of language is related, and in the fact that, as well as differentiation in sound, Humboldt claims that this mental power is the inner linguistic meaning of the differentiation of languages. He speaks of the 'individuality of inner meaning in the phenomenon' and means by this 'the energy of the power' by means of which the inner sense acts on the sound.[69] It is self-evident to him that this energy cannot everywhere be the same. Thus, as we see, he shares the principle of individuation in the approach to the true and the perfect. It is the monadological universe of Leibniz, of which the differences in the structure of human language are a part.

The path of investigation that Humboldt follows is marked by abstraction to reveal form. Although Humboldt revealed the significance of human languages as mirrors of the individual mentalities of the nations, he has still limited the universality of the connection between language and thought to the formalism of a faculty.

Humboldt sees the main significance of the problem when he says of language that 'it really stands over against an infinite and truly boundless sphere, the epitome of everything that can be thought. Thus it must make an infinite use of finite means and is able to do this through the identity of the faculty that generates thoughts and language'.[70] The actual essence of a faculty that is aware of itself is to be able to make an infinite use of finite means. It embraces everything on which it is able to operate. Thus the linguistic faculty is also far above all applications of content. Hence, as the formalism of a faculty, it can be detached from every determinate content of what is said. To this Humboldt owes brilliant insights, especially as he does not fail to see that, however limited the power of the individual when compared with the might of language, there is a reciprocal relationship between the individual and language which allows man a certain freedom over against language. That this freedom is a limited one he is aware, inasmuch as every language has a life of its own over against what is said at any given time, so that one senses from it with great vividness 'the way in which the distant past is still connected with the feeling of the present', since language has passed through the sensations of earlier generations and has preserved their inspiration.[71] In language conceived as form, Humboldt has still been able to perceive the historical life of the mind. To base the phenomenon of language on the concept of a linguistic faculty gives to the concept of inner form a special justification that is in accordance with the historical vicissitudes of the life of language.

Nevertheless this concept of language constitutes an abstraction that has to be reversed for our purposes. Linguistic form and content that has been handed down cannot be separated in the hermeneutical experience. If every language represents a view of the world, it is this primarily not as a particular type of language (in the way that philologists see it), but because of what is said or handed down in this language.

The way in which the problem is shifted—or, rather, comes into the right focus—when the unity between language and tradition is recognised can be illustrated by an example. Wilhelm von Humboldt once remarked that to learn a foreign language involves the acquisition of a new standpoint in regard to the view of the world one had hitherto held, and went on: 'Only because we always carry over, whether more or less totally, our own view of the world, even our own view of language, into a foreign language, is this achievement not experienced in a pure and perfect way'.[72] What is held here to be a limitation and a shortcoming (and rightly so, from the point of view of the linguist, who is concerned with his own way of knowledge) is, in fact, the mode of realisation of the hermeneutical experience. It is not the learning of a foreign language as such, but its use, whether in conversation with its speakers or in the study of its literature, that gives one a new standpoint 'in regard to the view of the world one had held hitherto'. However much one may adopt a foreign attitude of mind, one still does not forget one's own view of the world and of language. Rather the other world that we encounter is not only strange, but also different in its relations. It has not only its own truth in itself, but also its own truth for us.

The other world that is experienced here is not simply an object of research and knowledge. Someone who exposes himself to the literary tradition of a foreign language so that it comes to speak for him has no objective relationship to the language as such, just as little as has the traveller who uses it. He has quite a different attitude from the philologist, to whom linguistic tradition is material for the history and comparative study of language. We know this only too well from our experience of learning foreign languages and the strange way in which those works of literature, which our teachers used to introduce us to these languages, got killed in the process. Obviously we cannot understand a work of literature if our attention is thematically directed towards the language as such. But the other aspect, which must not be ignored, is that it is impossible to understand what it has to say if it does not speak into a familiar world that has to find a point of contact with what the text says. Thus to learn a language is to increase the extent of what one can learn. Only on the reflective level of the linguist is the connection able to assume the form in which the achievement of learning a foreign language 'is not experienced in a pure and perfect way'. The hermeneutical experience is exactly the reverse of this: to have learned a foreign language and to be able to understand it—this formalism of a faculty—means nothing else than to be in a position to accept what it says as said to oneself. The exercise of this capacity for understanding always means that what is said has a claim over one, and this is impossible if one's own 'view of the world and of language' is not also involved. It would be worth investigating the extent to which Humboldt's own actual familiarity with the literary traditions of different peoples played its part within his abstract concern with language as such.

His real importance for the problem of hermeneutics lies elsewhere, namely in showing that a view of language is a view of the world. He recognised the living act of speech, linguistic energeia, as the essence of language, and thus overcame the dogmatism of the grammarians. On the basis of the concept of mental faculty, that dominates his whole thinking about language, he was able to formulate correctly the question of the origin of language, which had been weighed down with theological considerations. He showed how mistaken this question is if it involves the model of a human world without language, which emerged into language somehow at some time in the past. As against this, Humboldt rightly emphasised that language was human from its very beginning.[73] This not only alters the meaning of the question of the origin of language, but it is the basis of a far-reaching philosophical insight.

Language is not just one of man's possessions in the world, but on it depends the fact that man has a world at all. For man the world exists as world in a way that no other being in the world experiences. But this world is linguistic in nature. This is the real heart of Humboldt's assertion, which he intended quite differently, that languages are views of the world. By this Humboldt means that language maintains a kind of independent life over against the individual member of a linguistic community and introduces him, as he grows into it, to a particular attitude and relationship to the world as well. But the ground of this statement is more important, namely that language has no independent life apart from the world that comes to language within it. Not only is the world 'world' only insofar as it comes into language, but language, too, has its real being only in the fact that the world is re-presented within it. Thus the original humanity of language means at the same time the fundamental linguistic quality of man's being-in-the-world. We shall have to investigate the relation between language and the world in order to attain the horizon adequate to the linguistic nature of the hermeneutical experience.

To have a 'world' means to have an attitude towards it. To have an attitude towards the world, however, means to keep oneself so free from what one encounters of the world that one is able to present it to oneself as it is. This capacity is both the having of a 'world' and the having of language. Thus the concept of 'world' or 'environment' (Welt) is in opposition to the concept of 'surrounding world' or 'habitat' (Unwelt), as possessed by every living thing.

It is true that the idea of 'habitat' was first used for the purely human world, and for it alone. The 'habitat' was the milieu in which man lived, and its influence of this on his character and his way of life was what constitutes its importance. Man is not independent of the particular aspect that the world shows him. Thus the concept of the habitat is originally a social concept that seeks to express the dependence of the individual on society, ie is related only to man. This concept, however, can be applied in a comprehensive sense to all living things, in order to summarise the conditions on which life depends. But it is thus clear that man, unlike all other living creatures, has a 'world' insofar as these creatures do not have a relationship to the world, but are, as it were, placed within their habitat. Thus the extension of the concept of habitat to all living things has in fact changed its meaning.

It is also the case that, unlike all other living creatures, man's relationship to the world is characterised by freedom from habitat. This freedom includes the linguistic constitution of the world. Both belong together. To rise above the pressure of what comes to meet us from the world means to have language and to have 'world'. It is in this form that modern philosophy of man, in its confrontation with Nietzsche, has worked out the special position of man and shown that the linguistic constitution of the world is far from meaning that man's relationship to the world is imprisoned within a linguistically schematised habitat.[74] On the contrary, wherever language and men exist, there is not only a freedom from the pressure of the world, but this freedom from the habitat is also freedom in relation to the names that we give things, as stated in the profound account in Genesis, according to which Adam received from God the authority to name creatures.

Once we realise the full importance of this it becomes clear why man, as well as having a general linguistic relationship to the world, also has a wide variety of different languages. Man's freedom in relation to the habitat is the reason for his free capacity for speech and also for the historical multiplicity of human speech in relation to the one world. When myth speaks of a primal language and the creation of a confusion of languages, this idea reflects meaningfully the real dilemma that the multiplicity of languages presents for reason, but in what it says this mythical account turns things on their head when it conceives the original unity of mankind in the use of an original language later sundered in a confusion of languages. The truth is that because man is always able to rise above the particular habitat in which he happens to find himself, and his speech brings the world into language, he is, from the beginning, free for variety in the exercise of his capacity for language.

To rise above the habitat has from the outset a human, ie a linguistic significance. Animals can leave their habitat and move over the whole earth without severing their environmental dependence. For man, however, to rise above the habitat means to rise to 'world' itself, to true environment. This does not mean that he leaves his habitat, but that he has another attitude towards it, a free, distanced attitude, which is always realised in language. Animals have a language only per aequivocationem, for language is a human possibility that is free and variable in its use. For him language is variable, not only in the sense that there are foreign languages that one can learn, but also in itself, in that it contains different possible ways of saying the same thing. Even in exceptional cases like deaf and dumb language, there is not a real, expressive language of gesture, but a substitution of an articulated use of gesture that represents articulated vocalised language. Animals do not have this variability when making themselves understood to one another. This means, ontologically, that they make themselves understood, but not about objective situations, the epitome of which is the world. Aristotle saw this with full clarity. Whereas the call of animals induces particular behaviour in the members of the species, linguistic understanding of each other by men through the logos reveals the existent itself.[75]

From language's relation to the world there follows its specific factuality. Matters of fact come into language. An object that behaves in a certain way involves the recognition of its separate independent existence, which involves distance between the speaker and the object. This distance means that something is able to detach itself as a particular object and become the content of a statement which others also understand. It lies in the structure of the object that detaches itself in this way to have a negative element always present as well. To be a determinate entity is to be this, and not that. Thus there are also negative objects. This is the aspect of language that Greek philosophy conceived for the first time. Even in the silent monotony of the Eleatic principle of the association of being and noein, Greek thought followed the fundamental factuality of language, and then, in overcoming the Eleatic idea of being, Plato saw the element of non-being in being as what really made it possible to speak of the existent at all. In the elaborate articulation of the logos of the eidos, the question of the real being of language could not be properly developed, as Greek thought was so full of the sense of the factuality of language. By pursuing the natural experience of the world in its linguistic form, it conceives the world as being. Whatever it conceives as existent emerges as logos, as an expressible object, from the surrounding whole that constitutes the world-horizon of language. What is conceived of in this way as existing is not really the object of statements, but it 'is expressed in linguistic statements'. Through this it acquires its truth, its evident being in human thought. Thus Greek ontology is based on the factuality of language, in that it conceives the essence of language in terms of the statement.

As against this, however, it must be emphasised that language has its true being only in conversation, in the exercise of understanding between people. This is not to be understood as if that were the purpose of language. The process of communication is not a mere action, a purposeful activity, a setting-up of signs, through which I transmit my will to others. Communication as such, rather, does not need any tools, in the real sense of the word. It is a living process in which a community of life is lived out. To this extent, human communication through conversation is no different from the communication that goes on between animals. But human language must be thought of as a special and unique living process in that, in linguistic communication, 'world' is disclosed. Linguistic communication sets its theme before those communicating like a disputed object between them. Thus the world is the common ground, trodden by none and recognised by all, uniting all who speak with one another. All forms of human community of life are forms of linguistic community: even more, they constitute language. For language, in its nature, is the language of conversation, but it acquires its reality only in the process of communicating. That is why it is not a mere means of communication.

For this reason invented systems of artificial communication are never languages. For artificial languages, such as secret languages or systems of mathematical symbols, have no basis in a community of language or life, but are introduced and applied only as means and tools of understanding. This is the reason that they always presuppose a living process of communication, which is that of language. The convention by means of which an artificial language is introduced necessarily belongs, as we know, to another language. In a real community of language, on the other hand, we do not first decide to agree, but are already in agreement, as Aristotle showed.[76] It is the world that presents itself to us in the common life, that embraces everything about which communication can be achieved. The linguistic means are not, of themselves, the object of communication. Communication about language is not the paradigm case, but rather the special case of agreeing about an instrument, a system of signs, that does not have its being in conversation, but serves rather as a means for the purpose of information. The linguistic nature of the human experience of the world gives to our analysis of the hermeneutical experience an extended horizon. What we have seen in the case of translation and the possibility of communication across the frontiers of our own languages is confirmed: the linguistic world in which we live is not a barrier that prevents knowledge of being in itself, but fundamentally embraces everything in which our insight can be enlarged and deepened. It is true that those who are brought up in a particular linguistic and cultural tradition see the world in a different way from those who belong to other traditions. It is true that the historical 'worlds' that succeed one another in the course of history are different from one another and from the world of today; but it is always, in whatever tradition we consider it, a human, ie a linguistically constituted world that presents itself to us. Every such world, as linguistically constituted, is always open, of itself, to every possible insight and hence for every expansion of its own world-picture, and accordingly available to others.

This is of fundamental importance, for it makes the use of the expression 'world in itself' problematical. The criterion for the continuing expansion of our own world-picture is not given by a 'world in itself' that lies beyond all language. Rather, the infinite perfectibility of the human experience of the world means that, whatever language we use, we never achieve anything but an ever more extended aspect, a 'view' of the world. Those views of the world are not relative in the sense that one could set them against the 'world in itself', as if the right view from some possible position outside the human, linguistic world, could discover it in its being-in-itself. No one questions that the world can exist without man and perhaps will do so. This is part of the meaning in which every human, linguistically constituted view of the world lives. In every view of the world the existence of the world-in-itself is implied. It is the whole to which the linguistically schematised experience is referred. The variety of these views of the world does not involve any relativisation of the 'world'. Rather, what the world is is not different from the views in which it presents itself. The relationship is the same in the perception of things. Seen phenomenologically, the 'thing-in-itself' is, as Husserl has shown,[77] nothing other than the continuity with which the shades of the various perspectives of the perceptione of objects pass into on another. A person who sets this being-in-itself over against these 'aspects' must think either theologically—in which case the 'being-in-itself' is not for him, but only for God—or else he will think in the manner of Lucifer, as one who would like to prove his own divinity by the fact that the whole world has to obey him—in this case the world's being-in-itself is a limitation of the omnipotence of his imagination.[78] In the same way as with perception we can speak of the 'linguistic nuances' that the world undergoes in different linguistic worlds. But it remains a characteristic difference that every 'nuance' of the object of perception is exclusively different from every other one and that the 'thing-in-itself' helps to constitute the continuum of these nuances whereas, with the nuances of the linguistic views of the world, each one contains potentially within it every other one, ie every one is able to be extended into every other one. It is able to understand, from within itself, the 'view' of the world that is presented in another language.

Thus we hold that the connection with language which belongs to our experience of the world does not involve an exclusiveness of perspectives. If, by entering into foreign linguistic worlds, we overcome the prejudices and limitations of our previous experience of the world, this does not mean that we leave and negate our own world. As travellers we return home with new experiences. Even if we are emigrants and never return we can still never wholly forget. Even if, as historically enlightened people, we are fundamentally aware of the historical contingency of all human thought concerning the world, and thus of our own contingency, we still have not taken up an absolute position. In particular, it is no refutation of the acceptance of this fundamental contingency if this acceptance itself seeks to be true absolutely, and thus cannot be applied to itself without contradiction. The consciousness of contingency does not do away with contingency. It is one of the prejudices of reflective philosophy that it understands as a relationship of propositions that which is not at all on the same logical level. Thus the reflective argument is out of place here. For we are dealing, not with relationships between judgments which have to be kept free from contradictions, but with living relationships. The linguistic nature of our experience of the world is able to embrace the most varied relationships of life.[79]

Thus the sun has not ceased to set for us, even though the Copernican explanation of the world has become part of our knowledge. Obviously we can hold on to an appearance while at the same time knowing that it is absurd in the world of understanding. And is it not language which operates in a creative and conciliatory way upon these various living relationships? When we speak of the sun setting, this is not an arbitrary phrase, but expresses what really appears to be the case. It is the appearance presented to a man who is not himself in motion. It is the sun whose rays reach or depart from us. Thus, to our vision, the setting of the sun is a reality (it is 'relative to being there'). Now, by constructing another model, we can liberate ourselves mentally from the evidence of our senses, and because we can do this, we are also able to express the rational position of the Copernican theory. But we cannot seek to remove or refute natural appearances by the 'eyes' of this scientific understanding. This is pointless not only because what we see with our eyes has genuine reality for us, but also because the truth that science states is itself relative to a particular attitude to the world and cannot at all claim to be the whole. But it is language which really opens up the whole of our attitude to the world, and in this whole of language appearances find their legitimacy just as much as does science.

Of course this does not mean that language is the cause of this intellectual power of persistence, but only that the immediacy of our observation of the world and ourselves, in which we persist, is preserved and organised within language because we finite beings always come from afar and stretch into the distance. In language the reality beyond every individual consciousness becomes visible.

Thus the linguistic event reflects not only what is persistent, but also the changing nature of things. From the way that words change, we can discover the way that customs and values change. In the German linguistic world, for example, the word Tugend ('virtue') now has nearly always an ironic significance.[80] If, instead of this, we use other words to discreetly express the continuance of moral norms in a way that has turned away from the world of established conventions, then such a process is a mirror of what is real. Poetry, too, often becomes a test of what is true, in that the poem awakens a secret life in words that seem used up and worn out, and tells us of ourselves. Obviously language is able to do all this because it is not a creation of reflective thought, but itself helps to fashion the relation to the world in which we live.

We have, then, a confirmation of what we stated above, namely that in language the world itself presents itself. The experience of the world in language is 'absolute'. It transcends all the relativities of the positing of being, because it embraces all being-in-itself, in whatever relationships (relativities) it appears. The linguistic quality of our experience of the world is prior, as contrasted with everything that is recognised and addressed as being. The fundamental relation of language and world does not, then, mean that world becomes the object of language. Rather, the object of knowledge and of statements is already enclosed within the world horizon of language. The linguistic nature of the human experience of the world does not include making the world into an object.

The 'objective situation' that science knows, and from which it derives its own objectivity, is one of the relativities embraced by language's relation to the world. In it the concept of 'being-in-itself' acquires the character of a definition of the will. What exists in itself is independent of one's own willing and imagining. But in being known in its being-in-itself, it is made available in the sense that one can deal with it, ie use it for one's own purposes.

This idea of being-in-itself is, as we see, only the apparent equivalent of the Greek concept of kath' hauto. The latter means primarily the ontological difference between what an existent object is in its substance and its essence and what can exist in it and is subject to change. That which belongs to the permanent nature of an object can certainly always, in a pre-eminent sense, be known, ie it has always a prior association with the human mind. But that which exists 'in itself' in the sense of modern science has nothing to do with this ontological difference between the essential and the inessential, but is determined by the particular nature of self-consciousness and the capacity to make and the desire to alter that is part of the human mind and will. It is the object and the resistance with which the latter have to deal. What exists in itself, then, as Max Scheler has shown, is relative to a particular way of knowing and willing.[81]

This does not imply that it is a particular science that is concerned in a special way with the domination of what exists and, on the basis of this will to dominate, determines the appropriate meaning of being-in-itself. Scheler rightly emphasised that the world-model of mechanics is related in a special way to the capacity to make things.[82] But the knowledge of all the natural sciences is knowledge for domination. This can be seen with particular clarity where new goals of research are set by modern science that are not only claimed to be methodologically different from the unity of method of modern physics, but also to embody a different attitude to research. Thus, for example, von Uxküll set the environmental studies of the biologist against the world of physics—a universe of life which is made up of the manifold living worlds of plants, animals and men.

This biological approach claims to overcome the naive anthropocentricity of the earlier study of animals, in that it investigates the particular structures of the habitats in which living things have their being. Like animal environments the world in which man lives is built up out of elements that are available to human senses. If, however, 'worlds' are to be thought of in this way as biological plans, this not only assumes the existence of the world of being-in-itself that is made available through physics, in that one is working out the selective principle according to which the various creatures construct their worlds out of the material of what 'exists in itself'. It remains also, in the same sense, research that adapts itself to a new field of study. Thus the biological universe is derived from the physical universe by a kind of restyling, and it indirectly assumes the existence of the latter. This is true logically, of the human environment as well. In fact, modern physics has departed radically from the postulate of perceptibility that comes from our human forms of perception. In that its systems of equations also include the connection between the measured entities and the measuring observer in the physical system, physics does for the human environment the same thing that it did for the animal worlds when it provided the basis of biological research. With its 'absolute' space and its 'absolute' time it teaches us to see the world of human perception as if from above, and with the same means with which it sees the world of the bees, by relating their faculty of orientation to their sensitivity to ultra-violet light. Thus the world of physics transcends the animal worlds just as it does the human one. In this way the impression is created that the 'world of physics' is the true world that exists in itself, the absolute object, as it were, to which all living things relate themselves, each in its own way.

But is it really the case that this world is a world of being-in-itself which leaves behind it all the relativity of factual existence and the knowledge of which could be called an absolute science? Is not the very concept of an 'absolute object' a contradiction in terms? Neither the biological nor the physical universe can, in fact, deny its concrete existential relativity. In this, physics and biology have the same ontological horizon that it is impossible for them, as science, to go beyond. Their knowledge is of what exists, and this means, as Kant has shown, as it is given in space and time and is an object of experience. This even defines the advance in knowledge that science aims at. The world of physics cannot seek to be the whole of what exists. For even a world formula that contained everything, so that the observer of the system would also be included in the latter's equations, would still assume the existence of a physicist who, as the calculator, would not be an object calculated. A physics that calculated itself and was its own calculation would be self-contradictory. The same thing is true of biology, which investigates the environments of all living things, including, therefore, the human environment. What is known in it certainly also embraces the being of the scientist, for he too is a living creature and a man. But from this it in no way follows that biology is a mere living process and only has meaning as such. Rather, biology studies what exists in exactly the same way as does physics; it is not itself what it studies. Being-in-itself, towards which the research of either physics or biology is directed, is relative to its own positing of being. There is not the slightest reason, beyond this, to admit metaphysical truth to the claim of science that it knows being-in-itself. Each science, as a science, has the field of its research set out in advance, and to have knowledge of this field is to have power over it.

We find quite another situation when we consider man's relationship to the world as a whole, as expressed in language. The world that appears in language, and is constituted by it, does not have, in the same sense, being-in-itself, and is not relative in the same sense as the object of the natural sciences. It is not being-in-itself, inasmuch as it does not possess an objective character and can never be given in experience as the comprehensive whole that it is. But as the world that it is, it is not relative to a particular language either. For to live in a linguistic world, as one does as member of a linguistic community, does not mean that one is placed within an environment as animals are in theirs. We cannot see a linguistic world from above in this way, for there is no point of view outside the experience of the world in language from which it could itself become an object.

Physics does not provide this point of view, because it is not the world, ie the totality of what exists, that it investigates as its object. Nor does comparative linguistics, which studies the structure of languages, have any non-linguistic point of view from which we could know the in-itself quality of what exists and for which the various forms of the linguistic experience of the world could be reconstructed, as a schematised selection, from what exists in itself—in a way analogous to animal habitats, the principles of whose structure we study. Rather, there is in every language a direct relationship to the infinite extent of what exists. To have language involves a mode of being that is quite different from the confinement of animals to their habitat. By learning foreign languages men do not alter their relationship to the world, like an aquatic animal that becomes a land animal but, while preserving their own relationship to the world, they extend and enrich it by the world of the foreign language. Whoever has language 'has' the world.

If we hold on to this idea, we shall no longer confuse the factuality of language with the objectivity of science. The distance that is involved in a linguistic relationship to the world does not, as such, produce that objectivity that the natural sciences achieve by eliminating the subjective elements of the cognitive process. The distance and the factuality of language, of course, are also genuine achievements and do not just happen automatically. We know that we are able to cope with an experience by grasping it in language. It is as if its threatening, even annihilating, immediacy is removed, brought within proportions, made communicable and hence dealt with. This coping with experience, however, is obviously something different from the way science works on it, objectivising it and making it available for whatever purposes it likes. Once a scientist has discovered the law of a natural process, he has it in his power. There is no question of this in the natural experience of the world expressed in language. The use of language by no means involves making it available and calculable. It is not just that the statement and the judgment are merely one particular form among the multiplicity of linguistic attitudes—they themselves remain bound up with man's attitude to life. As a consequence, objectivising science regards the linguistic form of the natural experience of the world as a source of prejudices. With its methods of precise mathematical measurement the new science, as we learn from the example of Bacon, had to make room for its own constructive planning, in direct opposition to the prejudice of language and its naive teleology.[83]

On the other hand, there is a positive connection between the factuality of language and man's capacity for science. We can see this particularly clearly in the science of the ancient world, the specific merit and the specific weakness of which was that it originated in the linguistic experience of the world. In order to overcome this weakness, its naive anthropocentrism, modern science has also renounced its merit, namely its place in the natural attitude of man to the world. The concept of the 'theory' can illustrate that very well. What modern science calls 'theory' has, it would seem, scarcely anything to do with that attitude of seeing and knowing in which the Greek accepted the order of the world. The modern theory is a tool of construction, by means of which we gather experiences together in a unified way and make it possible to dominate them. We are said to 'construct' a theory. This already implies that one theory succeeds another, and each commands, from the outset, only conditional validity, namely insofar as further experience does not make us change our mind. Ancient theoria is not a means in the same sense, but the end itself, the highest manner of being human.

Nevertheless there are close connections between the two. In both cases the practical, pragmatic interest is overcome that sees whatever happens in the light of one's aims and purposes. Aristotle tells us that the theoretical attitude could emerge only when everything required for the necessities of life was already available.[84] Even the theoretical attitude of modern science does not direct its questions at nature for particular practical purposes. True, the manner of its questions and investigations is aimed at the domination of what exists and so must in itself be called practical. But the application of his knowledge is secondary in the mind of the individual scientist, in the sense that the application follows from the knowledge, yet only comes afterwards, so that no one who discovers a piece of knowledge needs to know what it is to be used for. Nevertheless, despite the similarities, the difference in the meaning of the words 'theory' and 'theoretical' now is obvious. In modern usage the idea of the theoretical is almost a privative idea. Something is meant only theoretically when it does not have the definitively binding quality of a goal of action. On the other hand, the theories themselves that are outlined here are dominated by the idea of construction, ie theoretical knowledge is itself conceived in terms of the will to dominate what exists; it is a means and not an end. 'Theory' in the ancient sense, however, is something quite different. There it is not only existing orders as such that are contemplated, but 'theory' means sharing in the total order itself.[85]

This difference between Greek theoria and modern science is

based, in my opinion, on different attitudes to the linguistic experience of the world. Greek knowledge, as I pointed out above, was so much within language, so exposed to its seductions, that its fight against the dunamis ton onomaton never led to the evolution of the ideal of a pure sign language, whose purpose would be to overcome entirely the power of language, as is the case with modern science and its orientation towards the domination of the existent. Both the letter symbols with which Aristotle works in logic and the proportional and relative way of describing the course of movements with which he works in physics are obviously quite different from the way in which mathematics comes to be applied in the seventeenth century.

We cannot ignore this fact, however much we emphasise that the Greeks were the founders of science. The days should be finally past when modern scientific method was taken as a criterion, when Plato was interpreted in terms of Kant, the Idea in terms of natural law (neokantianism), or when Democritus was praised as the founder of the true, 'mechanical' knowledge of nature. We only have to consider Hegel's fundamental refutation of the rationalist position by means of the idea of life in order to see the limitations of this approach.[86] In *Being and Time* Heidegger, as I see it, attains a position from which both the differences and the similarities between Greek science and modern science can be considered. When he showed the concept of presence-at-hand to be a deficient mode of being and saw it as the background of classical metaphysics and its continuance in the modern concept of subjectivity, he was pursuing an ontologically correct connection between Greek theoria and modern science. Within the framework of his temporal interpretation of being, classical metaphysics as a whole is an ontology of what is present-at-hand, and modern science is, unbeknownst to itself, its heir. But in Greek theoria there was undoubtedly another element as well. Theoria grasps not so much what is present-at-hand, as the object itself, which still has the dignity of a 'thing'.[87] The later Heidegger himself emphasised that the experience of the thing has as little to do with the mere establishing of simple being present-at-hand as with the experience of the so-called experimental sciences.[88] Thus like the dignity of the object, we shall have to preserve the factuality of language both from prejudice against the ontology of the present-at-hand and from the idea of objectivity.

Our starting-point is that it is not what is present-at-hand that is calculated or measured in the linguistic composition of the human experience of the world, but it is what exists, what man recognises as existent and significant, that is expressed in it. In this—and not in the methodological ideal of rational construction that dominates modern mathematically based natural science—can the process of understanding practised in the moral sciences recognise itself. If we characterised the mode of realisation of effective-historical consciousness as linguistic, this was because language characterises our human experience of the world in general. As little as 'world' is made objective in language so little is effective-history the object of hermeneutical consciousness.

Just as things, those units of our experience of the world that are constituted by their suitability and their significance, are brought into language, so the heritage that has come down to us is again made to speak in our understanding and interpretation of it. The linguistic nature of this bringing into language is the same as that of the human experience of the world in general. This is what has finally led our analysis of the hermeneutical phenomenon to the discussion of the relationship between language and world.

(B) THE CENTRE OF LANGUAGE AND ITS SPECULATIVE STRUCTURE

The linguistic nature of the human experience of the world was the guide-line along which Greek metaphysics since Plato's 'flight into the logoi' developed its thinking about being. We must enquire how far the answer given there—an answer that lasted until Hegel—does justice to the problem that we are concerned with.

This answer is theological. Greek metaphysics, in considering the being of beings, saw this as a being that fulfilled itself in thought. This thought is the thought of nous, which is conceived as the highest and most perfect being, gathering within itself the being of all beings. The articulation of the logos expresses the structure of the being, and this expression is, for Greek thought, nothing other than the presence of the being itself, its aletheia. It is the infinity of this presence, which human thought regards as its fulfilled potential, its divinity.

We do not follow this way of thinking, in its splendid self-forgetfulness, and so we shall also have to consider to what extent we are able to follow its renewal on the basis of the modern idea of subjectivity to be found in Hegel's absolute idealism. For we are guided by the hermeneutical phenomenon, and its ground, which determines everything else, is the finitude of our historical experience. In order to do justice to it, we took the trace of language, in which the structure of being is not simply reflected, but in the paths of which the order and the structure of our experience itself originally and through constant change are formed.

Language is the record of finitude, not because the structure of human language is multifarious, but because every language is constantly being formed and developed, the more it expresses its experience of the world. It is finite not because it is not at once all other languages, but simply because it is language. We have considered important turning-points in European thought concerning language, and from these we have learned that the event of language corresponds to the finitude of man in a far more radical sense than is brought out in christian thinking about the word. It is the centre of language, whence our whole experience of the world, and especially hermeneutical experience, unfolds.

The word is not simply, as held in mediaeval thought, the perfection of the species. If the existent is represented in the thinking mind, this is not the reflection of a pre-given order of being, the true nature of which is apparent to an infinite spirit (that of the creator). But nor is the word an instrument that can construct, like the language of mathematics, an objective universe of beings that can be manipulated by numbers. No more than an infinite spirit, can an infinite will surpass the experience of being that is proportionate to our finitude. It is the centre of language alone that, related to the totality of beings, mediates the finite, historical nature of man to himself and to the world.

Only now can the great dialectical puzzle of the one and the many, which fascinated Plato as the negation of the logos and to which mediaeval speculation on the Trinity gave a mysterious truth, be given its true and fundamental ground. When Plato realised that the word of language is both one and many, he took only the first step. It is always one word that we say to one another and that is said to us (theologically, 'the' Word of God)—but the unity of this word, as we saw, is always developed in articulated utterance. This structure of the logos and the verbum, as recognised by the Platonic and Augustinian dialectic, is simply the reflection of its logical contents.

But there is another dialectic of the word, which assigns to every word an inner dimension of multiplication: every word breaks forth as if from a centre and is related to a whole, through which alone it is a word. Every word causes the whole of the language to which it belongs to resonate and the whole of the view of the world which lies behind it to appear. Thus every word, in its momentariness, carries with it the unsaid, to which it is related by responding and indicating. The occasionality of human speech is not a casual imperfection of its expressive power; it is, rather, the logical expression of the living virtuality of speech, that brings a totality of meaning into play, without being able to express it totally.[89] All human speaking is finite in such a way that there is within it an infinity of meaning to be elaborated and interpreted. That is why the hermeneutical phenomenon also can be illuminated only in the light of this fundamental finitude of being, which is wholly linguistic in character.

If we spoke above of the way in which the interpreter belongs to his text and described the close relationship between tradition and history that is expressed in the concept of effective-historical consciousness we shall now be able to define more closely the idea of this belongingness on the basis of the linguistically constituted experience of world.

This involves us, as was to be expected, in a number of questions with which philosophy has long been familiar. In metaphysics belongingness refers to the transcendental relationship between being and truth, which conceives knowledge as an element of being itself and not primarily as an attitude of the subject. This involvement of knowledge in being is the presupposition of all classical and mediaeval thought. What is, is of its nature 'true', ie present before an infinite mind, and only for this reason is it possible for the finite human mind to know beings. Thus, here, thought does not start from the concept of a subject that exists in its own right and makes everything else an object. On the contrary, the being of the 'soul' is defined by Plato as participating in true being, ie as belonging to the same sphere of being as the idea, and Aristotle says of the soul that it is, in a certain sense, everything that exists.[90] In this thinking there is no question of a self-conscious spirit without world then having to find its way to worldly being; both belong originally to one another. The relationship is primary.

Earlier thought took account of this through the universal ontological function that it gave to the idea of teleology. In a situation of ends and means it is not by chance that the intermediate agencies through which something is achieved prove to be suited to the achieving of the end; rather they are chosen from the outset as suitable means. Thus the ordering of means to ends is prior. We call this finality, and we know that not only rational human action is ordered in this way, but also where there is no question of the setting of goals and the choosing of means, as in all living relationships, they can be conceived only within the concept of finality, as the mutual harmony of all the parts with one another.[91] Here, too, the whole in its relations is more original than the parts. Even in the theory of evolution we may use the concept of adaption only with caution, inasmuch as this theory assumes that the natural situation is one of lack of adaptation—as if creatures were placed within a world to which they had only subsequently to adapt themselves.[92] Just as adaptation actually constitutes the living situation, so the concept of knowledge, dominated by thought of ends and means, is defined as the natural co-ordination of the human mind to the nature of things.

In modern science this metaphysical idea of the way in which the knowing subject is adequate to the object of knowledge is without justification. Its methodological ideal ensures for every one of its stages a return to the elements from which its knowledge is built up, while the teleological units of significance of the type of 'thing' or of 'organic whole' lose their justification. In particular, the critique of the verbalism of Aristotelian and scholastic science that we touched on above, has dissolved the old association between man and world that lay at the basis of logos philosophy.

But modern science has never entirely denied its Greek origin, however much, since the seventeenth century, it has become conscious of itself, and of the boundless possibilities that open up before it. Descartes' real treatise on method, his 'Rules', the veritable manifesto of modern science, did not appear, as we know, until a long time after his death. However, his thoughtful meditations on the compatibility of the mathematical knowledge of nature with metaphysics set a task for an entire age. German philosophy from Leibniz to Hegel has constantly tried to supplement the new science of physics by a philosophical and speculative science in which the legacy of Aristotle would be revived and preserved. We need only recall Goethe's objection to Newton, which was shared by Schelling, Hegel and Schopenhauer.

Hence it is not surprising if, after another century of critical experiences provided by modern science and especially by the self-awareness of the historical sciences, we again take up this legacy. The hermeneutics of the human sciences, which at first appear to be a secondary and derivative concern, a modest chapter from the heritage of German idealism, lead us back, if we are to do justice to the subject, into the problems of classical metaphysics.

This can be seen in the role that the concept of dialectic plays in the philosophy of the nineteenth century. It testifies to the continuity of the problem from its Greek origin. When it is a question of understanding the supra-subjective powers that dominate history, the Greeks have something over us, for we are entangled in the knots of subjectivism. They did not seek to base the objectivity of knowledge on subjectivity. Rather, their thinking always saw itself as an element of being itself. Parmenides considered this to be the most important signpost on the way to the truth of being. The dialectic, this expression of the logos, was not for the Greeks a movement performed by thought, but the movement of the object itself that thought experiences. The fact that this sounds like Hegel does not mean that there has been any false modernisation, but shows rather the historical connection. In the situation of modern thought that we have described, Hegel has consciously taken up the model of Greek dialectic.[93] Hence whoever wants to learn from the Greeks has always first to learn from Hegel. Both his dialectic of the determinations of thought as well as his dialectic of the forms of knowledge explicitly repeat the total mediation between thought and being that was formerly the natural element of Greek thought. In that our hermeneutical theory seeks to show the interconnection of event and understanding, it sends us back to Parmenides as well as to Hegel.

If we thus take the concept of the belongingness between subject and object which we have won from the impasses of historicism and relate it to the background of general metaphysics, we are not seeking to renew the classical doctrine of the intelligibility of being or to transfer it to the historical world. This would be a mere repetition of Hegel which would not hold up, either in the face of Kant and the experiential standpoint of modern science, or primarily in the face of an experience of history that is no longer dominated by the knowledge of salvation. We are simply following an internal necessity of the thing itself if we go beyond the idea of the object and the objectivity of understanding, towards the idea of the coordination of subject and object. It was our critique of aesthetic and historical consciousness that drove us to our critique of the concept of the objective, causing us to detach ourselves from the Cartesian basis of modern science and revive ideas from Greek thought. But we cannot simply follow the Greeks or the identity philosophy of German idealism: we are thinking from the centre of language.

From this viewpoint the concept of the belongingness between subject and object is no longer seen as the teleological
relation of the mind to the ontological structure of what exists,
as this relation is conceived in metaphysics. Quite a different
state of affairs follows from the fact that the hermeneutical experience is linguistic in nature, that there is converse between
tradition and its interpreter. The fundamental thing here is that
something is happening. Neither is the mind of the interpreter in
control of what words of tradition reach him, nor can one suita-
bly describe what happens here as the progressive knowledge of
what exists, so that an infinite intellect would contain everything
that could ever speak out of the whole of tradition. Seen from
the point of view of the interpreter, 'event' means that he does
not, as a knower, seek his object, 'discovering' by methodological means what was meant and what the situation actually was, if
slightly hindered and affected by his own prejudices. This is only
an external aspect of the actual hermeneutical event. It motivates the essential methodological discipline one has towards
oneself. But the actual event is made possible only because the
word that has come down to us as tradition and to which we are
to listen really encounters us and does so in such a way that it
addresses us and is concerned with us. I have elaborated this
aspect of the situation above as the hermeneutical logic of the
question and shown how the questioner becomes the one who is
questioned and how the hermeneutical event is realised in the
dialectic of the question. I recall this here in order to determine
correctly the meaning of the belongingness between subject and
object, as it corresponds to our hermeneutical experience.

For on the other side, that of the 'object', this event means the
coming into play, the working itself out, of the context of tradition in its constantly new possibilities of significance and resonance, newly extended by the other person receiving it. In as
much as the tradition is newly expressed in language, something
comes into being that had not existed before and that exists
from now on. We can illustrate this by any historical example.
Whether what is handed down is a poetic work of art or tells us
of a great event, in each case what is transmitted emerges newly
into existence just as it presents itself. It is not being-in-itself that
is increasingly revealed when Homer's *Iliad* or Alexander's *In-
dian Campaign* speaks to us in the new appropriation of tradition but, as in genuine conversation, something emerges that is
contained in neither of the partners by himself.

If we are seeking a right definition of the idea of a belongingness between subject and object we are here concerned with, we
must take account of the particular dialectic that is contained in

hearing. It is not just that he who hears is also addressed, but there is also the element that he who is addressed must hear, whether he wants to or not. When you look at something, you can also look away from it, by looking in another direction, but you cannot 'hear away'. This difference between seeing and hearing is important for us because the primacy of hearing is the basis of the hermeneutical phenomenon, as Aristotle saw.[94] There is nothing that is not available to hearing through the medium of language. Whereas all the other senses have no immediate share in the universality of the linguistic experience of the world, but only offer the key to their own specific fields, hearing is a way to the whole because it is able to listen to the logos. In the light of our hermeneutical question this ancient insight into the priority of hearing over sight acquires a new emphasis. The language in which hearing shares is not only universal in the sense that everything can be expressed in it. The significance of the hermeneutical experience is rather that, in contrast with all other experience of the world, language opens up a completely new dimension, the profound dimension whence tradition comes down to those now living. This has always been the true essence of hearing, even before the invention of writing, that the hearer may listen to the legends, the myths and the truth of the ancients. The literary transmission of tradition, as we know it, is nothing new, compared with this, but only changes the form and makes the task of real hearing more difficult.

But now the concept of the belongingness between subject and object is determined in a new way. We belong to elements in tradition that reach us. Everyone who is in a tradition—and this is true, as we know, even of the man who is released into a new apparent freedom by historical consciousness—must listen to what reaches him from it. The truth of tradition is like the present that lies immediately open to the senses.

The mode of being of tradition is not sensible immediacy. It is language, and in interpreting its texts, the hearer who understands it relates its truth to his own linguistic attitude to the world. This linguistic communication between present and tradition is, as we have shown, the event that takes place in all understanding. The hermeneutical experience must take as a genuine experience everything that becomes present to it. It does not have prior freedom to select and discard. But nor can it maintain an absolute freedom by leaving undecided that which seems specific to the understanding of that which is understood. It cannot unmake the event that it is itself.

This structure of the hermeneutical experience that so totally contradicts the idea of scientific methodology itself depends on the eventual character of language that we have described at length. It is not just that the use and development of language is a process which has no single knowing and choosing consciousness standing over against it. (Thus it is literally more correct to say that language speaks us, rather than we speak it, so that, for example, the time at which a text was written can be determined more exactly from its linguistic usage than from its author.) A more important point is the one to which we have constantly referred, namely that language constitutes the hermeneutical event proper not as language, whether as grammar or as lexicon, but in the coming into language of that which has been said in the tradition: an event that is at once assimilation and interpretation. Thus here it really is true to say that this event is not our action upon the thing, but the act of the thing itself.

This confirms that similarity of our approach to that of Hegel and the Greek world which we have already noted. Our enquiry started from our dissatisfaction with the modern concept of methodology. But this dissatisfaction found its most significant philosophical justification in Hegel's explicit appeal to the Greek concept of methodology. He criticised the concept of a method that dealt with the thing, but was alien to it, calling it 'external reflection'. The true method was an activity performed by the thing itself.[95] This assertion does not, of course, mean that philosophical cognition is not also an activity, even an effort that calls for the 'effort of the concept'. But this activity and this effort consist in not interfering arbitrarily—reaching with one's own fancies for this or that notion that happens to be to hand —with the immanent necessity of the thought. Certainly, the thing does not go its own course without our thinking being involved, but thinking means unfolding the proper logic of the thing itself. It is part of this process to suppress ideas 'that tend to present themselves' and to insist on the logic of the thought. Since the Greeks we have called this 'dialectic'.

In describing the true method, which is the activity of the thing itself, Hegel quotes Plato, who loved to show his Socrates in conversation with young men, because they were ready to follow where Socrates' logical questions led, without regard for current opinions. He illustrated his own method of dialectical development by these 'malleable youths', who avoided interfering with the path on which the thing took them, and did not parade their own ideas. Here the dialectic is nothing but the art of conducting a conversation and especially of revealing, through the logical process of questioning and yet further questioning, the wrongness of the opinions one holds. Here, then, the dialectic is negative, it confuses one's opinions. But this kind of confusion means at the same time a clarification, for it opens one's eyes to the thing. As in the famous scene in the *Meno* where, after all the untenable previous opinions of the slave have collapsed, he is led out of his confusion to the right solution of the mathematical task he has been set, all dialectical negativity contains an adumbration of what is true.

Not only in all pedagogical conversation, but in all thought, the following of the logic of the thing is what alone brings out its nature. It is the thing itself that asserts itself, if we rely entirely on the power of thought and ignore the obviousness of opinions. Thus Plato linked the Eleatic dialectic, that we know chiefly from Zeno, with the Socratic art of dialogue and raised it in his *Parmenides* to a new reflective level. That things change as one thinks them through logically and become their opposite, that thought acquires the power of studying contraries independently of the essence,[96] is the experience of thought to which Hegel's concept of method, as the self-unfolding of pure thought to become the systematic whole of truth, appeals.

Now the hermeneutical experience that we are endeavoring to understand from the centre of language is certainly not an experience of thinking in the same sense as this dialectic of the concept, which seeks to free itself entirely from the power of language. Nevertheless, there is in the hermeneutical experience something that resembles a dialectic, an activity of the thing itself, an activity that, unlike the methodology of modern science, is a passivity, an understanding, an event.

The hermeneutical experience also has its logical consequence: that of uninterrupted listening. A thing does not present itself to the hermeneutical experience without its own special effort, namely that of 'being negative towards itself'. A person who is trying to understand a text has also to keep something at a distance, namely everything that suggests itself, on the basis of his own prejudices, as the meaning expected, as soon as it is rejected by the sense of the text itself. Even the experience of the reversal of meaning, this constantly recurring experience in speech, which is the real experience of the dialectic, has its equivalent here. The unfolding of the totality of meaning towards which understanding is directed, forces us to make conjectures and to take them back again. The self-cancellation of the interpretation makes it possible for the thing itself—the meaning of the text—to assert itself. The movement of the interpretation is not dialectical primarily because the one-sidedness of every statement can be balanced by another side—this is, as we shall see, a secondary phenomenon in interpretation—but because the word that interpretatively encounters the meaning of the text expresses the whole of this meaning, ie allows an infinity of meaning to be represented within it in a finite way.

That this is dialectic, conceived from the centre of language, needs more exact discussion, as does the way in which this dialectic differs from the metaphysical dialectic of Plato and Hegel. Following a usage that we can find in Hegel, we call what is common to the metaphysical and the hermeneutical dialectic the 'speculative element'. The word 'speculative' here refers to the mirror relation.[97] Being reflected involves a constant substitution of one thing for another. When something is reflected in something else, say, the castle in the lake, it means that the lake throws back the image of the castle. The mirror image is essentially connected, through the medium of the observer, with the proper vision of the thing. It has no being of its own, it is like an 'appearance' that is not itself and yet causes the proper vision to appear as a mirror image. It is like a duplication that is still only the one thing. The actual mystery of a reflection is the intangibility of the picture, the unreal quality of sheer reproduction.

If we now use the word 'speculative' as it was coined by philosophers around 1800 and say, for example, that someone has a speculative mind or that a thought is rather speculative, there lies behind this usage the notion of reflection in a mirror. 'Speculative' is the antithesis of the dogmatism of everyday experience. A speculative person is someone who does not abandon himself directly to the tangibility of appearances or to the fixed determinateness of the meant, but who is able to reflect or—to put it in Hegelian terms—who sees that the 'in-itself' is a 'for-me'. And a thought is speculative if the relationship that it expresses is not conceived as the unambiguous assigning of a determination to a subject, a property to a given thing, but must be thought of as a mirroring, in which the reflection is the pure appearance of what is reflected, just as the one is the one of the other, and the other is the other of the one.

Hegel has described speculative thought in his masterly analysis of the logic of the philosophical propostion. He shows that the philosophical proposition is a judgment only in its external form, ie to assign a predicate to a subject-concept. In fact the philosophical proposition does not pass over from the subject-concept to another concept that is placed in relation to it, but it states in the form of the predicate the truth of the subject. 'God is one' does not mean that is is a property of God's to be one, but that it is God's nature to be unity. The movement of definition is not tied here to the fixed base of the subject, 'along which it runs backwards and forwards'. The subject is not defined both as this and as that, in one respect like this, and in another like that. This would be the mode of imaginative thinking, not of the concept. In the thinking of concepts, rather, the natural movement of definition beyond the subject of the proposition is prevented and suffers, so to say, a setback. Starting from the subject, as if this remained the basis throughout, it finds that, since the predicate is rather the substance, the subject has passed into the predicate and has thus been removed. And since what seems to be predicate has become the whole independent mass, thought cannot roam freely, but is stopped by this weight'.[98] Thus the form of the proposition destroys itself since the speculative propostion does not state something of something, but presents the unity of the concept. The fact of the philosophical proposition having, as it were, two peaks, which comes about through this counter-thrust of the predicate, is compared by Hegel to the rhythm that follows from the two elements of metre and accent and produces the same floating harmony.

The unaccustomed blockage that thought undergoes when a proposition, by its contents, compels thought to give up its customary attitude of knowledge, constitutes, in fact, the speculative nature of all philosophy. Hegel's great history of philosophy has shown that it is, from the beginning, speculation in this sense. If it expresses itself in the form of predication, ie working with fixed ideas of God, soul and world, then it fails to understand its own nature and is following an attitude based on a onesided 'view of the understanding of the objects of reason'. According to Hegel this is the nature of prekantian dogmatic metaphysics and is characteristic of the 'modern ages of non-philosophy. Plato certainly is not such a metaphysician, still less is Aristotle, although sometimes the contrary is thought to be true'.[99]

For Hegel the important thing is to express explicitly this inner block that thought undergoes when its habit of running away with ideas is interrupted by the concept. Non-speculative thought can, as it were, demand this. It has 'a valid right that is not, however, taken account of in the mode of the speculative proposition'. What it can demand is that the dialectical self-destruction of the proposition is expressed. 'With other knowledge the proof constitutes this side of expressed inwardness. But since the dialectic has been separated from the proof, the concept of philosophical proof has, in fact, been lost'. Whatever

Hegel means by this,[100] he is, at any rate, seeking to re-establish the meaning of philosophical proof. This takes place in the account of the dialectical movement of the proposition. This is what is really speculative, and only its expression is speculative thinking. The speculative attitude, then, must pass into a dialectical presentation. This, for Hegel, is the demand of philosophy. What is called here expression and presentation is not actually a demonstration or proof, but the object itself demonstrates itself, by so expressing and presenting itself. Thus dialectic is truly experienced, in that thought undergoes the incomprehensible reversal of changing into its opposite. The very act of holding on to the logical sequence of the thought leads to this surprising movement of the reversal—as, when, for example, he who is seeking justice discovers that a strict adhesion to the idea of justice becomes 'abstract' and proves to be the greatest injustice (summum ius summa iniuria).

Hegel makes here a distinction between the speculative and the dialectical. The dialectical is the expression of the speculative, the representation of what is actually contained in the speculative, and to this extent it is the 'truly' speculative. But since, as we have seen, the representation is not an additional activity, but the emergence of the thing itself, the philosophical proof itself belongs to the thing. It is true that it emerges, as we have seen, from a demand of ordinary thinking and imagining. Hence it is a presentation for the external reflection of the understanding. But despite this, such a presentation is in fact by no means external. It considers itself such only as long as thought does not know that it proves finally to be the reflection of the object in itself. In accordance with this, Hegel emphasises the difference between speculative and dialectical only in his *Vorrede zur Phänomenologie*. Because this distinction in fact cancels itself out, it is subsequently, from the viewpoint of absolute knowledge, no longer preserved by Hegel.

This is the point at which the proximity of our own enquiry to the speculative dialectic of Plato and Hegel meets a fundamental barrier. The removal of the distinction between speculative and dialectical that we find in Hegel's speculative science of the concept shows how much he saw himself as the heir to the Greek philosophy of the logos. What he calls dialectic and what Plato called dialectic depends, in fact, on subordinating language to the 'statement'. The concept of the statement, the dialectical accentuation of it to the point of contradiction is, however, in extreme contrast to the nature of the hermeneutical experience and the linguistic nature of human experience of the world.

Hegel's dialectic also follows, in fact, the speculative spirit of language, but according to Hegel's self-understanding he is seeking only to intercept the reflective play of language's definitions and to raise it by the mediation of the dialectic in the totality of known knowledge, to the self-awareness of the concept. In this it remains within the dimension of what is stated and does not attain the dimension of the linguistic experience of the world. These are just a few indications of the way in which the dialectical nature of language presents itself to the problems of hermeneutics.

Language itself, however, has something speculative about it in a quite different sense—not only in that sense intended by Hegel of the instinctive pre-formation of the reflexive relationship of logic—but, rather, as the realisation of meaning, as the event of speech, of communication, of understanding. Such a realisation is speculative, in that the finite possibilities of the word are orientated towards the sense intended, as towards the infinite. A person who has something to say seeks and finds the words through which he makes himself intelligible to the other person. This does not mean that he makes 'statements'. Anyone who has experienced a lawsuit—even if only as a witness—knows what it is to make a statement and how little it is a statement of what one means. In a statement the range of the meaning of what has to be said is concealed with methodical exactness; what remains is the 'pure' sense of the statements. That is what goes on record. But as meaning thus reduced to what is stated it is always distorted meaning.

To say what one means, on the other hand, to make oneself understood, means to hold what is said together with an infinity of what is not said in the unity of one meaning and to ensure that it be understood in this way. Someone who speaks in this way may well use only the most ordinary and common words and still be able to express what is unsaid and is to be said. Someone speaks speculatively when his words do not reflect beings, but express a relation to the whole of being. This is connected with the fact that someone who repeats what is said, just like someone who takes down statements, does not need to distort consciously, and yet he will change the meaning of what is said. Even in the most everyday speech there appears an element of speculative reflection, namely the intangibility of that which is still purest reproduction of meaning.

All this is found, in an intensified way, in the poetic word. Here, of course, it is legitimate to see the actual reality of poetic speech in the poetic 'statement'. For here it is really meaningful and necessary that the sense of the poetic word is expressed in what is said as such, without invoking the aid of occasional knowledge. If the use of the statement in the process of communication between people distorts it, here the concept of the statement achieves its fulfilment. The detachment of what is said from any subjective opinion and experience of the author constitutes the reality of the poetic word. But what does this statement mean?

It is clear, first of all, that everything that constitutes everyday speech can recur in the poetic word. If poetry shows men in conversation, then what is given in the poetic statement is not the statement that a written report would contain, but in a mysterious way the whole of the conversation is as if present. The words that are put into the mouth of a character in literature are speculative in the same way that the speech of daily life is speculative: the speaker expresses, as we said above, in his speech a relationship to being. Moreover, when we speak of a poetic statement, we do not mean the statement that is put into someone's mouth in a work of literature, but the statement that the work itself, as poetic word, is. But the poetic statement as such is speculative, in that the linguistic event of the poetic word expresses its own relationship to being.

If we take 'the poetic spirit's mode of proceeding' as, say, Hölderlin has described it, then it becomes immediately clear in what sense the linguistic event of literature is speculative. Hölderlin has shown that finding the language of a poem involves the total dissolution of all customary words and modes of expression. 'In that the poet feels himself seized in his whole inner and outer life by the pure tone of his original sensation and he looks about him in his world, this is just as new and unknown to him, the sum of all his experiences, his knowledge, his intuitions and memories, art and nature, as it presents itself within and without him; everything is present to him as if for the first time, for this very reason ungrasped, undetermined, dissolved into sheer material and life. And it is supremely important that he does not at this moment accept anything as given, does not start from anything positive, that nature and art, as he has learned to know and see them, do not *speak* before a language is there for *him*. . . .' (Note how close this is to Hegel's critique of positivity.) The poem, as a successful work and creation, is not the ideal, but the spirit that is aroused again out of infinite life. (This is also reminiscent of Hegel.) It does not describe or signify an entity, but opens up to us a world of the divine and the human. The poetic statement is speculative, inasmuch as it does not reflect an existent reality, does not reproduce the appearance of the species in the order of essence, but represents the new sight of a new world in the imaginary medium of poetic invention.

We have shown the speculative structure of the linguistic event both in daily and in poetic speech. The inner resemblance that thus appears, linking the poetic word with everyday speech as an intensification of the latter, has already been noted, from its subjective, psychological side, in idealistic philosophy and its revival in Croce and Vossler.[101] If we stress the other aspect, the fact of being expressed, as the proper operation of the linguistic event, then we are preparing a place for the hermeneutical experience. The way in which tradition is understood and is constantly expressed anew in language is, as we have seen, an event that is just as genuine as living conversation. The distinctive feature is only that the productivity of the linguistic attitude to the world finds new application to an already linguistically mediated content. The hermeneutical situation is also a speculative situation, which is, however, fundamentally different from the dialectical self-unfolding of the mind, as described by Hegel's philosophical science.

Inasmuch as the hermeneutic experience contains a linguistic event that corresponds to dialectical representation in Hegel, it too partakes of dialectic, namely the dialectic, elaborated above,[102] of question and answer. The understanding of a text that is handed down has, as we saw, an essential inner relationship to its interpretation, and although this is always a relative and uncompleted movement, understanding still finds there its relative fulfilment. Accordingly, the speculative content of a philosophical statement, as Hegel teaches, needs the corresponding dialectical presentation of the contradictions it contains, if it is to become genuinely science. There is a real correspondence here, for interpretation shares in the discursiveness of the human mind, which is able to conceive the unity of the object only in successiveness. Thus interpretation has the dialectical structure of all finite, historical being, insofar as every interpretation must begin somewhere and seeks to remove the onesidedness that it inevitably produces. It seems to the interpreter that some particular must necessarily be said and made explicit. All interpretation is motivated in this way and derives its significance from the context of its motivation. Through its onesidedness it puts too much emphasis on one side of the thing, so that something else has to be said to restore the balance. As the philosophical dialectic presents the whole of truth, in the self-cancellation of all partial propostions by bringing contradictions to a head and overcoming them, so also hermeneutics has the task of revealing a totality of meaning in all its relations. The individuality of the sense intended corresponds to the totality of all definitions. One thinks here of Schleiermacher, who based his dialectic on the metaphysics of individuality and in his hermeneutical theory constructed the process of interpretation from the antithetical directions of thought.

However, the correspondence between hermeneutical and philosophical dialectic, as it seems to follow from Schleiermacher's dialectical construction of individuality and Hegel's dialectical construction of totality, is not a real correspondence. For this parallel fails to take account of the real nature of the hermeneutic experience and the radical finiteness of its basis. It is true that interpretation has to start somewhere, but it does not start just anywhere. It is not really a beginning. We saw that the hermeneutical experience always includes the fact that the text to be understood speaks into a situation that is determined by previous opinions. This is not a regrettable distortion that affects the purity of understanding, but the condition of its possibility, which we have characterised as the hermeneutical situation. Only because between the text and its interpreter there is no automatic accord can a hermeneutical experience make us share in the text. Only because a text must be brought out of its alienness and become assimilated is there anything for the man who is seeking to understand it to say. Only because the text calls for it does interpretation take place, and only in the way called for. The apparently thetic beginning of interpretation is, in fact, a response and, like every response, the sense of an interpretation is determined by the question asked. Thus the dialectic of question and answer always precedes the dialectic of interpretation. It is what determines understanding as an event. From this it follows that hermeneutics cannot have any problem of a beginning, in the way that the problem of the beginning of science is found in Hegel's logic.[103] Wherever it arises, the problem of the beginning is, in fact, the problem of the end. For it is with respect to an end that a beginning is defined as a beginning of an end. Given infinite knowledge, given speculative dialectic, this may lead to the fundamentally insoluble problem of what one is to start with. For every beginning is an end, and every end is a beginning. At any rate, with this kind of rounded perfection, the speculative question of the beginning of philosophical science is seen fundamentally in terms of its finished perfection.

It is quite different with effective-historical consciousness, in which the hermeneutical experience is perfected. It knows about the absolute openness of the meaning-event in which it shares. Certainly, there is here too for all understanding a criterion by which it is measured and a possible completion. It is the content of the tradition itself that is the sole criterion and expresses itself in language. But there is no possible consciousness—we have repeatedly emphasised this, and it is the basis of the historical-ness of understanding—there is no possible consciousness, however infinite, in which the 'object' that is handed down would appear in the light of eternity. Every assimilation of tradi-tion is historically different: which does not mean that every one represents only an imperfect understanding of it. Rather, every one is the experience of a 'view' of the object itself.

The paradox that is true of all transmitted material, namely of being one and the same and yet of being different, proves all interpretation to be, in fact, speculative. Hence hermeneutics has to see through the dogmatism of a 'meaning-in-itself' in just the same way as critical philosophy has seen through the dog-matism of experience. This certainly does not mean that every interpreter sees himself as speculative in his own mind, ie that he is conscious of the dogmatism contained in his own interpreta-tive intention. What is meant, rather, is that all interpretation is speculative as it is actually practised, quite apart from its methodological self-consciousness. It is this that emerges from the linguistic nature of interpretation. For the interpreting word is the word of the interpreter; it is not the language and the dictionary of the interpreted text. This means that assimilation is no mere repetition of the text that has been handed down, but is a new creation of understanding. If emphasis has been—rightly—placed on the fact that all meaning is related to the 'I',[104] this means, as far as the hermeneutical experience is concerned, that all the meaning of what is handed down to us finds its concretion, in which it is understood, in its relation to the understanding 'I'—and not in the reconstruction of an 'I' of the original meaning.

The intimate unity of the processes of understanding and in-terpretation is confirmed by the fact that the interpretation that reveals the implications of a text's meaning and expresses it in language seems, when compared with the given text, to be a new creation, but yet does not maintain any proper existence apart from the understanding process. I have already pointed out above[105] that the interpretative concepts are cancelled out in the fullness of understanding because they are meant to disappear. This means that they are not just tools that we take up and then throw aside after using them, but that they belong to the inner structure of the thing (which is meaning). What is true of every word in which thought is expressed, is true also of the interpreting word, namely that it is not, as such, objective. As the realisation of the act of understanding it is the actuality of the effective-historical consciousness, and as such it is truly speculative: having no tangible being of its own and yet throwing back the image that is presented to it.

Compared with the immediacy of communication between people or the word of the poet, the language of the interpreter is undoubtedly a secondary phenomenon. It is related itself again to the linguistic. And yet the language of the interpreter is at the same time the comprehensive manifestation of the linguistic, embracing all forms of language-usage and structure. Our starting-point was this comprehensive linguistic nature of understanding, its relation to reason, and we can now see how the whole of our investigation is subsumed under this rubric. The development of the problem of hermeneutics from Schleiermacher, through Dilthey, to Husserl and Heidegger, which we have outlined, confirms from the historical side what we have now found to be the case: namely that the methodical self-reflection of interpretation raises a fundamental philosophical problem.

(C) THE UNIVERSAL ASPECT OF HERMENEUTICS

Our enquiry has been guided by the basic idea that language is a central point where 'I' and world meet or, rather, manifest their original unity. We have also shown that this speculative centre that language is represents a finite process over against the dialectical mediation of concepts. In all the cases we analysed, both in the language of conversation, of poetry and also in interpretation, the speculative structure of language emerged, not being the reflection of something given, but the coming into language of a totality of meaning. This brought us close to the dialectic of the Greeks, because it did not conceive understanding as a methodic activity of the subject, but as something that the thing itself does, and which thought 'suffers'. This activity of the thing itself is the real speculative movement that takes hold of the speaker. We have sought its subjective reflex in speech. We can now see that this turn from the activity of the thing itself, from the coming into language of meaning, points to a universal ontological structure, namely to the basic nature of everything to

which understanding can be directed. Being that can be understood is language. The hermeneutical phenomenon here draws
into its own universality the nature of what is understood, by
determining it in a universal sense as language, and its own
relation to beings, as interpretation. Thus we speak not only of a
language of art, but also of a language of nature, in short, of any
language that things have.

We have already brought out above the curious link between
literary interpretation and the study of nature that accompanied
the beginnings of modern science.[106] Here we are getting to the
foundations. That which can be understood is language. This
means that it is of such a nature that of itself it offers itself to be
understood. Here too is confirmed the speculative structure of
language. To be expressed in language does not mean that a
second being is acquired. The way in which a thing presents
itself is, rather, part of its own being. Thus everything that is
language has a speculative unity: it contains a distinction, that
between its being and the way in which it presents itself, but this
is a distinction that is really not a distinction at all.

Hence the speculative nature of language shows its universal
ontological significance. What comes into language is something
different from the spoken word itself. But the word is a word
only because of what comes into language in it. It is there in its
own physical being only in order to disappear into what is said.
Again, that which comes into language is not something that is
pre-given before language; rather it receives in the word its own
definition.

We can now see that it was this speculative movement at
which we were aiming, in our critique both of aesthetic and of
historical consciousness, with which we introduced our analysis
of the hermeneutical experience. The being of the work of art
was not a being-in-itself which was different from its reproduction or the contingency of its appearance. Only by a secondary
thematicisation of the two things is it possible to make this kind
of 'aesthetic distinction'. Similarly, that which offers itself for
our historical study from tradition or as tradition, the significance of an event or the meaning of a text, is not a fixed object
that exists in itself, whose nature we have simply to establish.
The historical consciousness, in fact, also involved mediation
between past and present. By seeing that language was the universal medium of this mediation, we were able to extend our
enquiry from its starting-points, the critiques of aesthetic and
historical consciousness and the hermeneutical approach that
would replace them, to universal dimensions. For man's relation

to the world is absolutely and fundamentally linguistic in nature, and hence intelligible. Thus hermeneutics is, as we have seen, a universal aspect of philosophy, and not just the methodological basis of the so-called human sciences.

The objectifying procedure of the investigation of nature and the concept of being-in-itself, which is behind all such knowledge, proved to be an abstraction when viewed from the centre that language is. Abstracted out of the fundamental relation to the world that is given in the linguistic nature of our experience of it, it seeks to become certain about entities by methodically organising its knowledge of the world. Consequently it condemns as heresy all knowledge that does not allow of this kind of certainty and hence is not able to serve the growing domination of being. As against this, we have endeavoured to liberate the mode of being of art and history, and the experience that corresponds to them, from the ontological prejudice that is contained in the ideal of scientific objectivity; and, in view of the experience of art and history, we were led to a universal hermeneutics that was concerned with the general relationship of man to the world. If we formulated this universal hermeneutics on the basis of the concept of language, this was not only to guard against a false methodologism that overcomes the concept of objectivity in the human sciences. We were also attempting to avoid the idealistic spiritualism of a metaphysics of infinity in the Hegelian manner. The fundamental hermeneutical experience was articulated for us not merely by the tension between strangeness and familiarity, misunderstanding and correct understanding, such as dominated Schleiermacher's project. Rather, it was in the end apparent that because of his doctrine of the divinatory perfection of the understanding process Schleiermacher came close to Hegel. If we start from the linguistic nature of understanding, we are emphasising, on the contrary, the finiteness of the linguistic event, in which understanding is constantly concretised. The language that things have—of whatever kind the things may be—is not the logos ousias, and it does not attain its perfect form in the self-contemplation of an infinite intellect, but it is the language that our finite, historical nature apprehends. This is true of the language of the texts that are handed down to us in tradition, and that is why it was necessary to have a truly historical hermeneutics. It is as true of the experience of art as of the experience of history; in fact, the concepts of 'art' and 'history' are modes of understanding that emerge from the universal mode of hermeneutical being as forms of the hermeneutic experience.

Obviously it is not a peculiar determination of the work of art that it has its being in its presentation, nor is it a peculiarity of the being of history that it is to be understood in its significance. Self-presentation and being-understood belong together not only in that the one passes into the other, and the work of art is one with its effective-history, the tradition one with its present experience of being understood. Speculative language, distinguishing itself from itself, presenting itself, language which expresses meaning, is not only art and history but everything insofar as it may be understood. The speculative character of being that is the ground of hermeneutics extends as universally as does reason and language.

With the ontological turn that our hermeneutical enquiry has taken, we are moving towards a metaphysical idea, whose significance we can show by going back to its origins. The concept of the beautiful, which shared the central place in eighteenth-century aesthetics with that of the sublime, and which was to be entirely eliminated in the course of the nineteenth century by the aesthetic critique of classicism, was in the past, a universal metaphysical concept and had a function within metaphysics, the universal consideration of being, that was by no means limited to the aesthetic in the narrower sense. We shall see that this old idea of the beautiful can also be of service to a comprehensive hermeneutics, as the latter has emerged from the critique of the methodologism of the human sciences.

Even an analysis of the word's meaning shows that the idea of the beautiful has a close connection with the enquiry we have been pursuing. The Greek word for 'beautiful' is kalon. There is no exact equivalent for this in German, not even if we use pulchrum as an intermediary term, but Greek thought has had a certain influence on the history of the meaning of the German word schön, so that the meanings of the two words overlap to some extent. Thus we say, for example, die 'schönen' Künste ('the fine arts'). By adding the adjective schön we distinguish these arts from what we call 'technology', ie from mechanical arts that make useful things. It is the same with word combinations like schöne Sittlichkeit ('superior morality'), schöne Literatur (belles lettres), schöngeistig (aesthete). In all these uses the word is in a similar antithesis as the Greek kalon to the idea of chresimon. Everything that is not part of the necessities of life, but is concerned with the 'how', the eu zen, ie everything that the Greeks reckon part of paideia, is called kalon. Beautiful things are those whose value is of itself apparent. You cannot ask what purpose they serve. They are desirable for their own sake (di hauto haireton) and not, like the useful, for the sake of something else. Thus even linguistic usage shows the special status accorded to what is called kalon.

But even the ordinary antithesis that determines the idea of the beautiful, the antithesis to the ugly (aischron), points in the same direction. The aischron is what cannot be looked at. The beautiful is what can be looked at, what is good looking in the widest sense of the word. In German ansehnlich (good-looking) is used also to express magnitude (cf 'fair-sized'). And in fact the use of the word schön—both in Greek and in German—always implies a certain majestic size. Because the element of the ansehnlich points to the whole sphere of the fitting, of morality, the meaning approaches the idea of the antithesis to the useful (chresimon).

Hence the idea of the beautiful moves very close to that of the good (agathon), insofar as it is something to be chosen for its own sake, as an end that subordinates everything else to it as a means. For what is beautiful is not regarded as a means to something else.

Thus we find in Platonic philosophy a close connection, and sometimes even a confusion, between the idea of the good and the idea of the beautiful. Both go beyond everything that is conditional and multiform: the loving soul encounters the beautiful-in-itself at the end of a path that leads through the beautiful that is multiform. The beautiful-in-itself is the one, the uniform, the boundless (Symposium), just like the idea of the good, that lies beyond everything that is conditional and multiform, ie good only in a certain respect (Republic). The beautiful-in-itself shows itself to be as much beyond all beings as is the good-in-itself (epekeina). Thus the order of being, that consists in the orientation towards the one good, agrees with the order of the beautiful. The path of love that is taught by Diotima leads beyond beautiful bodies to beautiful souls, and from there to beautiful institutions, customs and laws, and finally to the sciences (eg to the beautiful relations of numbers found in mathematics) to this 'wide ocean of beautiful utterance'[107]—and leads beyond all that. We may ask whether the movement beyond the sphere of what is visible to the senses into that of the 'intelligible' really involves a differentiation and increase of the beauty of the beautiful and not just of the being that is beautiful. But Plato means obviously that the teleological order of being is also an order of beauty, that beauty appears more purely and clearly in the sphere of the intelligible than in that of the visible, which is marred by the inharmonious and the imperfect. Similarly, mediaeval philosophy linked the idea of the beautiful so

closely with that of the good, the bonum, that it failed to understand a classical passage from Aristotle on the kalon because the
translation here simply rendered the word kalon by bonum.[108]

The basis of the close connection between the idea of the
beautiful and that of the teleological order of being is the
Pythagorean and Platonic concept of measure. Plato defines the
beautiful in terms of measure, appropriateness and right proportions, and Aristotle states the elements (eide) of the beautiful to
be order (taxis), right proportions (summetria) and definition
(horismenon), and finds these present in an exemplary way in
mathematics. The close connection between the mathematical
orders of the beautiful and the order of the heavens means
further that the cosmos, the model of all visible harmony, is at
the same time the supreme example of beauty in the visible
sphere. Harmonious proportion, symmetry, is the decisive condition of all beauty.

As we can see, this kind of definition of the beautiful is a
universal ontological one. Nature and art are not here in antithesis to each other. This means, of course, that in regard to
beauty the priority of nature is unquestioned. Art may take advantage of gaps within the formed whole of the natural order to
perfect the beauties of nature given in the order of being. But
that certainly does not mean that 'beauty' is to be found in the
first place and primarily in art. As long as the order of being is
seen itself as divine or as God's creation—and the latter is the
case until the eighteenth century—the exceptional case of art
can be seen only within the framework of this order of being. We
have described above how it was only in the nineteenth century
that the problems of aesthetics were transferred to art. We can
see now that there was a metaphysical process behind this. This
switch to the point of view of art presupposes ontologically a
mass of being thought of as formless or ruled by mechanical
laws. The artistic mind of man, which mechanically constructs
useful things, will ultimately understand all beauty in terms of
the work of his own mind.

It is in accordance with this that only at the frontiers of the
mechanical constructibility of being has modern science been
reminded of the independent ontological value of the Gestalt and
now introduces the idea of the Gestalt, as a supplementary principle of knowledge, into the explanation of nature—chiefly into
the explanation of living nature (biology and psychology). This
does not mean that it abandons its fundamental attitude, but only
that it seeks to reach its goal—the domination of being—in a
more subtle way. This must be emphasised against the idea that
it has of itself, as expressed, say, by von Uexkuell. At the same

time, however, science accepts the beauty of nature and the beauty of art, which serve to give pleasure without any interest being involved, but at its own frontiers, the frontiers of the achieved domination of nature. When describing the reversal of the relationship between the beauties of nature and the beauties of art, we discussed the process of re-arrangement by means of which the beauty of nature finally so far lost its priority that it is conceived as a reflex of the mind. We might have added that the concept of 'nature' itself acquired the form it has had ever since Rousseau, in the reflection of the concept of art. It becomes a polemical concept, as the counterpart of the mind, as the 'non-I', and as such it has none of the universal ontological dignity that the cosmos possesses as the order of beautiful things.

Certainly no one will want simply to reverse this development and seek to re-establish the metaphysical dignity of the beautiful that we find in Greek philosophy by reviving the last embodiment of this tradition, the eighteenth-century aesthetics of perfection. However unsatisfactory the development that began with Kant towards subjectivism in modern aesthetics, he has convincingly proved the untenability of aesthetic rationalism. Still it is incorrect to base the metaphysics of the beautiful solely on the ontology of measure and the teleological order of being, to which the classicist appearance of rationalist normative aesthetics ultimately appeals. The metaphysics of the beautiful is not, in fact, identical with this application of aesthetic rationalism. The return to Plato brings out quite a different aspect of the phenomenon of the beautiful, and this is what interests us in our hermeneutical enquiry.

However closely Plato has linked the idea of the beautiful with that of the good, he is still aware of a difference between the two, and this difference involves the specific advantage of the beautiful. We have seen that the intangibility of the good in the beautiful, ie in the harmoniousness of being and its attendant disclosure (aletheia), involves a resemblance, in that it also has an ultimate sublimity. But as well as this Plato can say that in the attempt to lay hold on the good itself, the good takes flight into the beautiful.[109] Thus the beautiful is distinguished from the absolutely intangible good, in that it can be laid hold of. It is part of its own nature to be something that is visibly manifest. The beautiful reveals itself in the search for the good. This is its distinguishing mark for the human soul. That which manifests itself in perfect form draws towards it the longing of love. The beautiful directly disposes people towards it, whereas models of human virtue can be descried but obscurely in the unclear medium of appearances, because they have, as it were, no light of their own, so that we often succumb to impure imitations and appearances of virtue. It is different in the case of the beautiful. It has its own radiance, so that we are not seduced here by distorted copies. For 'beauty alone has this quality that it is what is most radiant (ekphanestaton) and lovable'.[110]

In this anagogical function of the beautiful, which Plato has described in unforgettable terms, there now becomes visible an ontological structural element of the beautiful and with it a universal structure of being. Obviously it is the distinguishing mark of the beautiful over against the good that of itself it presents itself, that it makes itself immediately apparent in its being. This means that it has the most important ontological function: that of mediating between idea and appearance. This is the metaphysical crux of Platonism. It finds its concrete form in the concept of participation (methexis) and concerns both the relation of the appearance to the idea and the relation of the ideas to one another. As we learn from the *Phaedrus,* it is not accidental that Plato likes to illustrate this controversial relation of 'participation' by the example of the beautiful. The idea of the beautiful is truly present, whole and undivided, in what is beautiful. Hence, in the example of the beautiful, the manifestation of the eidos that Plato has in mind can be made obvious and, against the logical difficulties of the participation in 'being' of 'becoming', the thing itself be offered in evidence. 'Being present' belongs in a convincing way to the being of the beautiful itself. However much beauty might be experienced as the reflection of something supraterrestrial, it is still there in the visible world. That it really is something different, a being from another order, is seen in the mode of its appearance. It appears suddenly, and equally suddenly, without any transition, disappears again. If we must speak with Plato of a hiatus (chorismos) between the world of the senses and the world of ideas, this is where it is and this is where it is also overcome.

The beautiful appears not only in what is visibly present to the senses, but in such a way that the latter is really there only through it, ie emerges as one out of the whole. The beautiful is truly 'most radiant' (to ekphanestaton) out of itself. The sharp division between the beautiful and what has no share in the beautiful is, moreover, a fact that is well established phenomenologically. Aristotle[111] says of well-formed works that nothing should be added to them and nothing taken away. The sensitive mean, the exactness of the harmonious relationships, are part of the oldest essence of the beautiful. We need only think of the sensitivity of the harmonies of sound from which music is constructed.

'Radiance', then, is not only one of the qualities of what is beautiful, but constitutes its actual being. The distinguishing mark of the beautiful, namely that it draws directly to itself the desire of the human soul, is founded in its mode of being. It is the harmoniousness of being that does not let it be alone what it is, but also causes it to emerge as a harmonious whole that is proportioned within itself. This is the disclosure (aletheia) of which Plato speaks in the *Philebus* and which is part of the nature of the beautiful.[112] Beauty is not simply symmetry, but the appearance itself. It is related to the idea of 'shining' (scheinen in German means both 'to shine' and 'to appear'). 'To shine' means to shine on something and so to make that on which the light falls appear. Beauty has the mode of being of light.

That does not only mean that without light nothing beautiful can appear, nothing can be beautiful. It also means that the beauty of a beautiful thing appears in it as light, as a radiance. It makes itself manifest. In fact it is the universal mode of the being of light to be reflected in itself in this way. Light is not only the brightness of that on which it shines, but by making something else visible, it is visible itself, and it is not visible in any other way than by making something else visible. This reflective nature of light was already brought out in classical thought,[113] and it is in accordance with this that the idea of reflection that plays such an important role in modern philosophy belongs originally to the sphere of optics.

Obviously it is because of its reflective nature that light combines seeing and the visible, so that without light there can be neither seeing nor anything visible. We recognise the consequences of this trivial observation when we consider the relation of light to the beautiful and the extent of the meaning covered by the beautiful. It is actually light that makes visible things into shapes that are both 'beautiful' and 'good'. But the beautiful is not limited to the sphere of the visible. It is, as we saw, the mode of appearance of the good in general, of being as it ought to be. The light in which not only the realm of the visible, but also that of the intelligible is articulated, is not the light of the sun, but the light of the mind, of nous. Plato's profound analogy[114] already alluded to this, and from it Aristotle developed the doctrine of nous and, following him, the christian thought of the middle ages that of the intellectus agens. The mind that unfolds from within itself the multiplicity of what is thought is present to itself in what is thought.

It is the Platonic and neoplatonic metaphysics of light which the christian doctrine of the word, the verbum creans, follows (we have considered the latter above at some length). If we have described the ontological structure of the beautiful as the mode of appearance which causes things to emerge in their proportions and their outline, the same holds for the realm of the intelligible. The light that causes everything to emerge in such a way that it is manifest and comprehensible in itself is the light of the word. Thus the close relationship that exists between the shining forth of the beautiful and the manifestation of the comprehensible is based on the metaphysics of light.[115] But this was the relation that guided our hermeneutical enquiry. The reader will recall that the analysis of the nature of the work of art led to the question of hermeneutics and that this became extended to a general enquiry. All this took place without any reference to the metaphysics of light. If we now consider the connection between the latter and our enquiry, we are helped by the fact that the structure of light can obviously be detached from the metaphysical theory of the at once sensible and intellectual source of light in the manner of neoplatonic and christian thought. This is already clear from Augustine's dogmatic interpretation of the creation story. Augustine notes there[116] that light is created before the differentiation of things and the creation of the light-giving heavenly bodies. But he puts special emphasis on the fact that the first creation of heaven and earth takes place without the divine word. Only when light is created does God speak for the first time. He interprets this speech, by means of which light is commanded and created, as the coming into being of mental light, by means of which the difference in created things is made possible. It is only through light that the formlessness of the first created mass of heaven and earth is made capable of being shaped into a multiplicity of forms.

We can detect in Augustine's ingenious interpretation of Genesis the first hint of that speculative interpretation of language that we have developed in the structural analysis of the hermeneutical experience of the world, according to which the multiplicity of what is thought proceeds only from the unity of the word. We can also see that the metaphysics of light brings out a side of the classical concept of the beautiful that is justified apart from the context of substance metaphysics and the metaphysical relationship to the infinite divine mind. Thus our analysis of the place of the beautiful in classical Greek philosophy results in this aspect of metaphysics having a productive significance for us also.[117] That being is self-presentation and that all understanding is an event, this first and last insight transcends the horizon of substance metaphysics as well as the metamorphosis of the concept of substance into the concepts of subjectivity and scientific objectivity. Thus the metaphysics of the beautiful has its consequences for our enquiry. Now it is no longer a question, as it seemed in the nineteenth century, of justifying, in terms of the theory of science, the claim to truth of art and the artistic. Now we are concerned, rather, with the much more general task of establishing the ontological background of the hermeneutical experience of the world.

The metaphysics of the beautiful can be used to illuminate two points that follow from the relation between the appearance of the beautiful and the comprehensibility of the intelligible. The first is that both the appearance of the beautiful and the mode of being of understanding have the character of an event; the second, that the hermeneutical experience, as the experience of transmitted meaning, has a share in the immediacy which has always distinguished the experience of the beautiful, as it has that of all evidence of truth.

1 First, let us, against the background of the traditional speculation on light and beauty, justify the priority that we assign to the activity of the object within the hermeneutical experience. It is now clear that we are not concerned here either with mythology or a mere dialectical reversal in the manner of Hegel, but with the continuing influence of an ancient truth that has been able to assert itself against modern scientific methodology.

This is seen from the very etymology of the concepts used by us. We said that the beautiful is einleuchtend ('clear', literally 'shining in'). This concept of clarity belongs to the tradition of rhetoric. The *eikos,* the verisimile, the 'probable' wahrscheinlich, literally 'true shining', the 'clear', belong in a series that defends its own rightness against the truth and certainty of what is proved and known. Let us recall that we assigned a special importance to the sensus communis.[118] Also there may be an influence of the mystical, pietistic sound of illuminatio, illumination (Erleuchtung) on the idea of Einleuchten (an echo that could also be heard in the sensus communis, with Oetinger). At any rate it is not by chance that the metaphor of light is used in both spheres. The thing itself compels us to speak of an event and of an activity of the thing. What is clear is always something that is said, a proposal, a plan, a conjecture, an argument, or something of the sort. The idea is always that what is clear is not proved and not absolutely certain, but it asserts itself by reason of its own merit within the area of the possible and probable. Thus we can even admit that an argument has something clearly true about it, even though we are presenting a counter-argument. The way in which it is compatible with the whole of what we ourselves consider correct is left open. It is only said that it is clear 'in itself', ie that there is something in its favour. The connection with the beautiful is manifest. The beautiful charms us, without its being immediately integrated with the whole of our orientations and evaluations. Indeed, just as the beautiful is a kind of experience that stands out like an enchantment and an adventure within the whole of our experience and presents a special task of hermeneutical integration, what is clear is always something surprising as well, like the turning-on of a new light, extending the range of what is to be taken into account.

The hermeneutical experience belongs in this sphere because it is also the event of a genuine experience. That there is something clearly true about something that is said, without the implication that it is, in every detail, secured, judged and decided is, in fact, always the case when something speaks to us out of tradition. What is transmitted asserts its own truth in being understood, and disturbs the horizon that had, until then, surrounded us. It is a true experience in the sense we have shown. The event of the beautiful and the hermeneutical process both presuppose the finiteness of human life. We might even ask whether the beautiful can be experienced by an infinite mind in the same way that it can be by us. Can this mind see anything other than the beauty of the whole that lies before it? The 'appearance' of the beautiful seems to be something reserved to finite human experience. There was a similar problem in mediaeval thought, namely how beauty can be in God if he is one and not many. Only Nicholas of Cusa's theory of the complicatio of the many in God offers a satisfactory solution. From this it seems a logical conclusion that, for Hegel's philosophy of infinite knowledge, art is a form of representation that is cancelled out in the concept and in philosophy. Similarly, the universality of the hermeneutical experience would not be available to an infinite mind, for it develops out of itself all meaning, all noeton, and thinks all that can be thought in the perfect contemplation of itself. The God of Aristotle (as well as the Spirit of Hegel) has left 'philosophy', this movement of finite existence, behind. None of the gods philosophises, says Plato.[119]

The fact that we have been able to refer several times to Plato, despite the fact that Greek logos philosophy revealed the ground of the hermeneutical experience only in a very fragmentary way, is due to this feature of the Platonic view of beauty, which is like an undercurrent in the history of Aristotelian and scholastic metaphysics, sometimes rising to the surface, as in neoplatonic and christian mysticism and theological and philosophical spiritualism. It was in this tradition of Platonism that the conceptual vocabulary required for thought about the finiteness of human life was developed.[120] The continuity of this Platonic tradition is attested by the affinity between the Platonic theory of beauty and the idea of a universal hermeneutics.

2 If we start from the basic ontological view, according to which being is language, ie self-presentation, as revealed to us by the hermeneutical experience of being, then there follows not only the eventual character of the beautiful and the eventual structure of all understanding. Just as the mode of being of the beautiful proved to be characteristic of the general nature of being, so the same thing will be shown to be true of the concept of truth. We can start from the metaphysical tradition, but here too we must ask what in it remains valid for hermeneutical experience. According to traditional metaphysics the truth of what exists is one of its transcendental qualities and is closely related to goodness (which again brings in beauty). Thus we may recall the statement by St. Thomas, according to which the beautiful is to be defined in terms of knowledge, the good in terms of desire.[121] The beautiful is that in the vision of which desire comes to rest: cuius ipsa apprehensio placet. The beautiful adds, beyond goodness, an orientation towards the cognitive faculty: addit supra bonum quemdam ordinem ad vim cognoscitivam. The 'shining forth' of the beautiful appears here like a light that shines over what is formed: lux splendens supra formatum.

We can attempt to free this statement again from the metaphysical context of the doctrine of forma by appealing to Plato. He was the first to show that the essential element in the beautiful was aletheia, and it is clear what he means by this. The beautiful, the way in which goodness appears, reveals itself in its being, it presents itself. What presents itself in this way is not different from itself in presenting itself. It is not one thing for itself and another for others, nor is it something that exists through something else. It is not the radiance shed on a form from without. Rather it is the nature of the form itself to be radiant, to present itself in this way. From this, then, it follows that in regard to beauty the beautiful must always be understood ontologically as an 'image'. It makes no difference whether it 'itself' or its image appears. This was, as we saw, the metaphysical distinguishing mark of the beautiful that it closed the gap between the idea and the appearance. It is an 'idea', certainly, ie it belongs to an order of being that rises above the flux of appearances as something constant in itself. But it is equally certain that it is itself that appears. This is not by any means, as we saw, an objection against the doctrine of ideas, but the concentrated exemplification of its problem. Where he appeals to the evidence of the beautiful, Plato does not need to insist on the contrast between 'the thing itself' and its image. It is the beautiful itself that both creates and removes this contrast.

Plato is, likewise, important for the problem of truth. We have attempted to show in the analysis of the work of art that self-presentation is to be regarded as the true being of the work of art. To this end we invoked the concept of play, and this directed us into more general contexts. For we saw there that the truth of what presents itself in play is properly neither 'believed' nor 'not believed' outside the play situation.[122]

In the aesthetic sphere this is obvious to us. Even when the poet is honoured as a seer, his poetry is not regarded as a true prophecy, eg Hölderlin's song of the return of the gods. Rather, the poet is a seer because he himself represents what is, was, and will be, and hence testifies himself to what he proclaims. It is true that poetic utterance has something ambiguous about it, like an oracle. But this is precisely where its hermeneutical truth lies. If we regard it as something that is simply aesthetic, uncommitted and lacking in existential seriousness, we are obviously failing to see how fundamental is the finitude of man for the hermeneutical experience of the world. It is not the weakness, but the strength of the oracle that it is ambiguous. Whoever would put Hölderlin or Rilke to the proof to see if they really believe in their gods or angels is missing the point.[123]

Kant's basic definition of aesthetic pleasure as disinterested pleasure has not only the negative intention that the pleasurable object cannot be employed as something useful, nor desired as something good, but also the positive one that 'really existing' can add nothing to the aesthetic content of pleasure, to the 'sheer sight' of a thing, because aesthetic being is, precisely, self-presentation. Only from the moral standpoint is there an interest in the real factual existence of the beautiful, eg in the song of the nightingale, the imitation of which was, for Kant, somehow morally offensive. Whether it really follows from this nature of aesthetic being that truth must not be sought here, because nothing is known here, is the question. In our aesthetic analyses we discusscd the narrowness of the concept of knowledge that limited Kant's position in this matter, and from the question of the truth of art we found our way into hermeneutics, in which art and history were combined for us.

Even with the hermeneutical phenomenon it seemed an unjustified limitation to regard the process of understanding solely as the immanent effort of a literary consciousness that is indifferent to the 'truth' of its texts. On the other hand, it was clear that the understanding of texts did not mean that the question of truth was decided in advance from the standpoint of a superior knowledge of the object and that in understanding one was enjoying one's own superior knowledge of the object. Rather, the whole value of the hermeneutical experience—as also the significance of history for human knowledge in general—seemed to consist in the fact that here we are not simply ordering knowledge in compartments, but that what we encounter in a tradition says something to us. Understanding, then, does not consist in a technical virtuosity of 'understanding' everything written. Rather, it is a genuine experience, ie an encounter with something that asserts itself as truth.

The fact that this encounter takes place, for reasons that we have discussed, in the linguistic performance of interpretation, and that the phenomenon of language and understanding proves to be a universal model of being and knowledge in general, enables us to define more closely the meaning of the truth involved in understanding. We have seen that the words that express an object are themselves known as a speculative event. Their truth lies in what is said in them; and not in a meaning locked in the impotence of subjective particularity. Let us remember that the understanding of what someone says is not an achievement of empathy, which involves guessing the inner life of the speaker. Certainly it is part of all understanding that what is said acquires its definition through a supplementing of meaning from occasional sources. But this definition by situation and context which fills out what is said to a totality of meaning and makes what is said really said, is not something that pertains to the speaker, but to what is spoken.

Accordingly, poetic utterance proved to be the special case of a meaning that has passed entirely into what was said and has become embodied in it. What comes into language in a poem moves, as it were, into relationships of order that support and guarantee the 'truth' of what is said. All coming into language, and not just the poetic, has about it something of this attested quality. 'Where the word fails, there is nothing'. Speech is never, as we emphasised, just the subsumption of the individual thing under universal concepts. In the use of words what is given to the senses is not presented as an individual example of a universal, but it is itself made present in what is said—just as the idea of the beautiful is present in what is beautiful.

What we mean by truth here can best be determined again in terms of our concept of play. The way in which the weight of the things that we encounter in understanding disposes itself is itself a linguistic event, a game with words playing around and about what is meant. Language games are where we, as learners—and when do we cease to be that?—rise to the understanding of the world. It is worth recalling here what we said about the nature of play, namely that the attitude of the player should not be seen as an attitude of subjectivity, since it is, rather, the game itself that plays, in that it draws the players into itself and thus itself becomes the actual subjectum of the playing.[124] What corresponds to this in the present case is neither play with language nor with the contents of the experience of the world or of tradition that speak to us, but the play of language itself, which addresses us, proposes and withdraws, asks and fulfils itself in the answer.

Thus understanding is not playing, in the sense that the person understanding holds himself back playfully and withholds a committed attitude to the claim that is made upon him. The freedom of self-possession necessary to be able to withhold oneself in this way is not given here, and this is, in fact, implied in the application of the concept of play to understanding. Someone who understands is always already drawn into an event through which meaning asserts itself. So it is well grounded for us to use the same concept of play for the hermeneutical phenomenon as for the experience of the beautiful. When we understand a text, what is meaningful in it charms us just as the beautiful charms us. It has asserted itself and charmed us before we can come to ourselves and be in a position to test the claim to meaning that it makes. What we encounter in the experience of the beautiful and in understanding the meaning of tradition has effectively something about it of the truth of play. In understanding we are drawn into an event of truth and arrive, as it were, too late, if we want to know what we ought to believe.

Thus there is undoubtedly no understanding that is free of all prejudices, however much the will of our knowledge must be directed towards escaping their thrall. It has emerged throughout our investigation that the certainty that is imparted by the use of scientific methods does not suffice to guarantee truth. This is so especially of the human sciences, but this does not mean a diminution of their scientific quality, but, on the contrary, the justification of the claim to special humane significance that they have always made. The fact that in the knowing involved in them the knower's own being is involved marks, certainly, the limitation of 'method', but not that of science. Rather, what the tool of method does not achieve must—and effectively can—be achieved by a discipline of questioning and research, a discipline that guarantees truth.

APPENDICES, SUPPLEMENTS, AND NOTES

APPENDIX I

(TO P 36)

The concept of style is one of the undiscussed assumptions on which historical consciousness lives. A brief glance at the fairly unexplored history of the word will tell us why this is so. The concept has arisen, as generally happens, by a word being lifted out of the original sphere of its application. Now this new sense is not primarily historical, but normative. Thus in the modern tradition of classical rhetoric, the word 'style' replaces what was called in the latter the genera dicendi and is therefore a normative concept. There are different modes of speaking and writing which are appropriate to the particular purpose and content and which make their particular demands. These are called different styles. It is clear that this view of different styles and their right application also implies the possibility of a wrong application.

It is asked of a person who possesses the art of writing and expressing himself that he observe a correct style. It appears that the concept of style first emerged in French jurisprudence and meant the manière de procéder, ie the way of conducting a trial that satisfied particular legal demands. After the sixteenth century the word is used in a general way to describe the manner in which something is presented in language.[1] Obviously there lies behind this usage the view that there are a priori demands —especially, for example, unity—that may be made of artistic representation, and these are independent of the content of what is represented. The examples compiled by Panofsky[2] and W. Hofmann[3] mention, apart from the word stile the words maniera

449

and gusto for this normative idea, which establishes a generic demand as a stylistic ideal.

But apart from this, there is also, from the outset, the personal use of the word. A style is also the individual hand that is recognisable everywhere in the works of the same artist. This transferred meaning probably comes from the ancient practice of canonising classical representatives of particular genera dicendi. If seen in terms of the concept, the use of the word 'style' for a so-called personal style is in fact a logical application of the same meaning; for this sense of 'style' also designates a unity in the variety of the works, ie the way in which the characteristic mode of representation in an artist distinguishes him from any other.

This emerges also in Goethe's use of the word, which became generally accepted. Goethe derives his concept of style from a distinction between it and the concept of 'manner' and obviously combines both elements.[4] An artist creates a style when he is no longer merely engaged in imitation, but is at the same time fashioning a language for himself. Although he ties himself to the given phenomenon, this is not a fetter for him. He is still able to express himself in the process. Rare though the correspondence is between 'faithful imitation' and an individual manner (or way of understanding), this is precisely what constitutes style. Thus there is also included in the idea of 'style' a normative element, when it is a question of the style of a person. The 'nature', the 'essence' of things remains the basic foundation of knowledge and art, from which the great artist cannot move away and, because of this connection with the nature of things, the personal use of the word 'style' still clearly retains, for Goethe, a normative sense.

It is easy to recognise here the classicist ideal. But Goethe's usage reveals the conceptual content that the word 'style' always has. Style is by no means a mere individual expression; it always refers to something fixed and objective that is binding on individual forms of expression. This also explains the application of this idea as an historical category. For the retrospective historical gaze sees the taste of a particular time as something that is binding in this way, and hence the application of the concept of style to the history of art is a natural consequence of historical consciousness. It is true, however, that here the sense of the aesthetic norm that was originally contained in the concept of style (vero stile) has been lost in favour of a descriptive function.

This by no means settles the question whether the idea of style deserves the exclusive place it has achieved within the history of art—nor whether it can be applied, apart from the history of art, to other historical phenomena, eg to political action.

As far as the first of these questions is concerned, the historical concept of style seems undoubtedly legitimate wherever the only aesthetic criterion is the connection with a dominant taste. Thus it is true primarily of all decoration, the fundamental purpose of which is not to exist for itself but for something else, in order to fashion a place for it within the unity of a life context. It is obvious that the decorative is a subsidiary quality that belongs to something that has another purpose, ie a use.

We may ask ourselves, however, whether it is right to extend the point of view of the history of style to so-called free works of art. We have already seen that even a so-called free work of art has its original place in a life context. A person who desires to understand it cannot use it to give him particular experiences, but must find the right attitude, and that means primarily the right historical attitude, to it.

There are, therefore, even here stylistic demands that cannot be infringed. But this does not mean that the only significance of a work of art is in terms of a history of style. Here Sedlmayr is quite right with his critique of the history of style (cf *Kunst und Wahrheit. Zur Theorie und Methode der Kunstgeschichte* vol 71). The classificatory interest that is satisfied by the history of style has not really anything to do with the artistic element. Nevertheless the concept of style still retains its significance for the proper study of art. For even the aesthetic structural analysis that Sedlmayr calls for must obviously, in what it calls the right attitude, take account of the demands made by the history of style.

This is quite clear in the case of those arts that require reproduction (music, theatre, dance etc). The reproduction must be stylistically faithful. We must know what is called for both by the style of the time and by the personal style of a master. Of course this knowledge is not everything. A reproduction that was 'historically faithful' would not be a genuine artistic reproduction, ie the work would not present itself to us in it as a work of art, but it would be, rather—insofar as the thing is at all possible—a didactic product or simple material for historical research, which the recordings conducted by the master himself will, in the end, become. Nevertheless, even the most vital recreation of a work will undergo certain limitations as a result of the question of the right historical style, and it must not fail to take account of these.

Style belongs, in fact, to the fundamental bases of art, it is one of its inevitable conditions, and what emerges in the question of reproduction, is obviously true also for our general receptive attitude to art of all kinds (reproduction, after all, is nothing but a particular kind of mediation that is in the service of our reception of art). Like that of taste, with which it is related (cf the word Stilgefühl—'feeling for style'), the concept of style is not the only perspective in the artistic experience and its aesthetic understanding—it is this only in the sphere of decoration—but it is necessarily presupposed wherever art is to be understood.

This concept can now also be applied to political history. Actions can have style, and a style can be expressed even in a series of events. The word is meant here primarily in a normative sense. If we say of an action that it has 'great style' or 'real style', then we are judging it from an aesthetic point of view (cf Hegel, *Nürnberger Schriften,* p 310). Even if we are aiming, in a political sense, at a particular style of action, this is fundamentally an aesthetic concept of style. In manifesting this style in action, we are making ourselves visible to others, so that they know with whom they have to deal. Here, too, style means a unity of expression.

Let us consider, however, whether we can use this concept of style as a historical category. The application to history in general of the concept of style from the history of art involves not seeing historical events in their own significance, but in their relation to a totality of forms of expression characteristic of their time. But the historical significance of an event does not have to be identical with the value that it has for knowledge as an expressive phenomenon, and it is misleading to imagine that we have understood it if we have understood it solely in this way, as an expressive phenomenon. If, in fact, we would extend the concept of style to history in general—as has been discussed by Erich Rothacker in particular—and expect this to yield us historical knowledge, then we would be compelled to make the assumption that history itself obeys an inner logos. This may be true for particular lines of development that we pursue, but this kind of history is not really history. It is the construction of ideal types which, as Max Weber's critique of the organologues has shown, has only a descriptive justification. A view of events in terms of the history of style, like a view of art in terms only of the history of style, would fail to take account of the essential fact that something is taking place in it and we are not just being presented with an intelligible series of events. We have reached here the bounds of the history of spirit.

APPENDIX II

(TO P 130)

Occasionality must appear as a meaningful element within a work's total claim to meaning and not as the trace of the particular circumstances that are, as it were, hidden behind the work and are to be revealed by interpretation. If the latter were the case, this would imply that it would be possible to understand the meaning of the whole only by re-establishing the original situation. If, however, occasionality is an element of meaning within the work itself, then the reverse is the case, namely that understanding the meaning of the work makes it possible also for the historian to experience something of the original situation into which the work speaks. Our fundamental considerations concerning the mode of aesthetic being have given the idea of occasionality a new justification that goes beyond all its particular forms. The play of art is not as transcendent of space and time as the aesthetic consciousness maintains. Even if we recognise this in principle, however, we cannot speak of time breaking in the game, as does Carl Schmitt in regard to *Hamlet* in his book *Der Einbruch der Zeit in das Spiel.*

No doubt it is part of the historian's work to investigate those relations in the forming of the play of art that weaves it into its time. But in my view Schmitt underestimates the difficulty of this task. He thinks that it is possible to recognise that fissure in the work through which contemporary reality shines and which reveals the contemporary function of the work. But this procedure is full of methodological difficulties, as the example of Platonic scholarship teaches us. Although it is right, in principle, to exclude the prejudices of a pure experiential aesthetic and to place the play of art within its historical and political context, it seems to me wrong to expect one to read *Hamlet* like a roman à clef. A breaking-in of time into the play which would be recognisable as a fissure within it is, it seems to me, precisely what we do not have here. For the play itself there is no antithesis of time and art, as Schmitt assumes. Rather the play draws time into its play. This is the great power of literature which makes it possible for it to belong to its own time and through which its time listens to it. In this general sense, it is true, *Hamlet* is full of political actuality. But if we are reading out of it the concealed support of the poet for Essex and James, then the work can hardly prove this. Even if the poet really belonged to this party,

the play he has written would conceal his partisanship in a way
that even the perspicacity of Schmitt would fail to see it. If he
wanted to reach his public, the poet undoubtedly had to consider
the counter-party within it. So what we are really seeing here is
the breaking of play into time. As the play is ambiguous, it can
have its effect, which cannot be predicted, only in being played.
It is not its nature to be an instrument of masked goals that only
have to be unmasked for it to be unambiguously understood, but
it remains, as an artistic play, in an indissoluble ambiguity. The
occasionality it contains is not something pre-given through
which alone everything acquires its true significance but, on the
contrary, it is the work itself, whose expressive power is filled
out in this, as in every occasion.

Thus Schmitt, in my opinion, falls victim to a false historicism
when, for example, he interprets politically the fact that Shakespeare leaves the question of the Queen's guilt open, and sees
this as a taboo. In fact it is part of the reality of a work of art that
around its real theme it leaves an area that is indefinite. A play in
which everything is completely motivated creaks like a machine.
A false reality would be presented if the action could all be
calculated out like an equation. Rather, it becomes a play of
reality when it does not tell the spectator everything, but only
a little more than he customarily understands in his daily round.
The more that remains open, the more freely does the process
of understanding succeed, ie the transposition of what is shown
in the play to one's own world and, of course, also to the world
of one's own political experience.

To leave an enormous amount open seems to belong to the
essence of a fruitful fable and to myth. Precisely thanks to its
open indeterminacy, myth is able to produce constant new invention from within itself, with the thematic horizon continu-
ously shifting in different directions. (We need only think of the
many attempts to treat the Faust theme, from Marlowe right up
to Paul Valéry.)

If we see a political intention in leaving things open, as Carl
Schmitt does when he speaks of the taboo of the Queen, then we
are failing to recognise the nature of artistic play, namely, the
playing itself out by trying out possibilities. The self-playing-out
of play does not take place in a closed world of aesthetic appearance, but as a constant involving of itself in time. The productive
ambiguity that constitutes the essence of a work of art is only
another way of expressing the play's essential characteristic of
continually becoming a new event. In this fundamental sense
understanding in the human sciences moves very close to the

immediate experience of the work of art. The understanding achieved in science allows the meaningful dimension of tradition to 'play itself out' and consists in testing it. Precisely for this reason it is itself an event, as is shown in the course of our present investigation.

APPENDIX III

(TO P 234)

Löwith's discussion of Heidegger's interpretation[5] of Nietzsche, though it raises some objections that are justified in detail, suffers from the general weakness that, without realising it, he is playing off Nietzsche's ideal of naturalness against the principle of the formation of ideals. This is to make unintelligible what Heidegger means when, with conscious exaggeration, he places Nietzsche in the same line as Aristotle—and this does not mean that he places him at the same point. On the other hand, however, Löwith is led by this short-circuit to the absurdity of himself treating Nietzsche's doctrine of the eternal return as a kind of Aristotle redivivus. Indeed, for Aristotle the eternal cycle of nature was the obvious aspect of being. The moral and historical life of men remains for him related to the order represented pre-eminently by the cosmos. There is no question of this in Nietzsche. He, rather, conceives the cosmic cycle of being entirely in terms of the contrast to it of human life. The significance of the eternal return of the same is as a teaching for man, ie as something tremendous that has to be accepted by the human will, something which destroys all illusions of a future and of progress. Thus Nietzsche conceives the doctrine of the eternal return in order to encounter man in the tension of his will. Nature is here conceived in terms of man, as that which does not take any account of him. But we cannot, as in a recent transposition, again play off nature against history, if we are seeking to understand the unity of Nietzsche's thought. Löwith himself does not get past establishing the unresolved conflict in Nietzsche. But must we not, in view of this, ask the further question how it was possible to get caught thus in a blind alley, ie why was it not for Nietzsche himself an imprisonment and a failure, but the great discovery and liberation? The reader finds no answer in Löwith to this further question. But this is precisely what one would like to understand, to realise through one's own thinking. Heidegger has done this; he has constructed the system of relations, on the basis of which Nietzsche's statements are ordered among themselves. That this relational system is not directly expressed in Nietzsche himself is part of the methodological significance of this kind of reconstruction. And, paradoxically, we see Löwith himself performing what he can regard, in Nietzsche, only as a failing: he reflects about unreflectiveness; he philosophises against philosophy in the name of naturalness and appeals to common sense.But if common sense were really a philosophical argument, then that would be the end of all philosophy and, with it, the end of any appeal to common sense. It is impossible for Löwith to get out of this difficulty except by acknowledging that an appeal to nature and naturalness is neither nature nor natural.

APPENDIX IV

(TO P 236)

Löwith's persistent refusal to understand the transcendental significance of Heidegger's position on understanding[6] seems to me wrong on two counts. He does not see that Heidegger has discovered something that exists in all understanding and is a task that cannot be dismissed. Further, he does not see that the violence done by many of Heidegger's interpretations by no means follows from this theory of understanding. It is, rather, a productive misuse of the texts, which betrays something more like a lack of hermeneutical awareness. Obviously it is the weight of his own objective concern that gives, to certain aspects of the texts considered, an over-resonance that distorts their proportions. Heidegger's impatient attitude to traditional texts is so little the consequence of his hermeneutical theory that it resembles more that of those great figures who have been responsible for the development of intellectual life and who, before the development of historical consciousness, assimilated tradition 'uncritically'. It is only the fact that Heidegger takes account of the criteria of science and from time to time seeks to justify by literary critical means his productive assimilation of tradition which challenges such criticism. This does not affect the rightness of his analysis of understanding, but is a fundamental confirmation of it. It is always part of understanding that the view that has to be understood must assert itself against the power of those tendencies of meaning that dominate the interpreter. Precisely because the thing itself makes a claim on us it is necessary for us to exert ourselves hermeneutically. But without accepting the claim of the object it is, on the other hand, impossible to understand tradition, unless in the total indifference to the object of psychological or historical interpretation, which supervenes when we no longer, in fact, understand.

APPENDIX V

(TO P 383)

It is strange that such a fine Plotinian scholar as Richard Harder criticises, in his last lecture before his death, the idea of the 'source' because of its 'scientific origin'. *(Source de Plotin, Entretiens* V, VII, *Quelle oder Tradition?)* However justified the criticism of a superficially conducted study of sources may be, the concept of the source has a better justification than that. As a philosophical metaphor it is of Platonic and neoplatonic origin. The dominant image is that of the springing up of pure and fresh water from invisible depths. This is seen in, among other things, the frequent combination of pege kai arche (Phaedrus 245c, as well as often in Philo and Plotinus).

As a literary critical term, the concept of fons was introduced first in the age of humanism, but there it does not refer, in the first place, to the concept that we know from the study of sources, but the maxim ad fontes, the return to the sources, is to be understood as a reference to the original undistorted truth of the classical authors. This, again, confirms our observation that, in its dealings with texts, criticism understands truth as that which is to be found in them. The transposition of the concept into the technical meaning familiar to us doubtless retains something of the original connotation, in that the source is distinguished from a faulty reproduction or assimilation. This explains, in particular, that we use the concept of 'source' only in regard to the tradition of literature. Only what has come down to us in language gives us constant and full information about what it contains; it is not merely to be interpreted, like other documents and remnants, but allows us to draw directly from the source, ie to measure later derivations against and by the source. These are not scientific images, but come from the spirit of language. They offer fundamental confirmation of Harder's remark that sources need not become muddied by being used. There is always fresh water pouring out of a source, and it is the same with the true sources of the human spirit that we find in tradition.

Their study is so rewarding precisely because they always have something more to yield than has yet been taken from them.

APPENDIX VI—ON THE CONCEPT OF 'EXPRESSION'

(TO PP 300 AND 424)

The whole of our investigation shows why the concept of 'expression' must be purified of its modern subjectivist flavour and referred back to its original grammatical and rhetorical sense. The word 'expression' corresponds to the Latin *expressio, exprimere,* which is used to describe the mental origin of speech and writing (verbis exprimere). But in German the word Ausdruck has an early history in the language of mysticism and it points back to neoplatonic coining that is still in need of investigation. Outside the writings of mysticism the word comes into general usage only in the eighteenth century. Then its meaning is expanded and it passes into aesthetic theory also, where it supplants the concept of imitation. But there is still no trace of the subjectivist element that an expression is the expression of something interior, namely of an experience.[7] The dominant aspect is that of communication and communicability, ie it is a question of finding the expression (eg Kant, *Critique of Judgment,* p 198). But to find the expression means to find an expression that aims at making an impression, that is, it is not an expression in the sense of an expression of an experience. This is true particularly also in the terminology of music; of the instructive essay of H. H. Eggebrecht, *Das Ausdrucksprinzip im musikalischen Sturm und Drang,* DVJ 29 (1955). The eighteenth-century musical theory of the emotions does not state that one expresses oneself in music, but that music expresses something, namely emotions which, in their turn, are to make an impression. We find the same thing in aesthetics with, say, Sulzer (1765): Expression is not to be understood primarily as an expression of one's own feelings, but as an expression that arouses feelings. Nevertheless, the second half of the eighteenth century is already far along the path towards the subjectification of the concept of expression. When, for example, Sulzer attacks the younger Riccoboni, who regards the art of the actor as that of representation and not of feeling, he is already considering sincerity of feeling as essential in aesthetic representation. Similarly he supplements the espressivo of music by the psychological substructure of the feeling of the composer. We are here confronted with a transition from the rhetorical tradition to the psychology of experience. However, the concern with the essence of the expression, and of aesthetic expression in particular, still remains related to the metaphysical context, which is of neoplatonic stamp. For the expression is never merely a sign which points back to something else, something within, but what is expressed is itself present in the expression, eg anger is present in angry furrows in the face. The modern diagnostics of expression knows this as well as Aristotle did. Obviously it is part of the nature of living things that the one is present in the other in this way. This has been specifically recognised in philosophical usage, as when Spinoza sees in exprimere and expressio a fundamental ontological concept and when, following him, Hegel sees the true reality of the mind in the objective significance of expression as representation and utterance, and uses this to support his critique of the subjectivism of reflection. So also do Hölderlin and Sinclair for whom the concept of the expression acquires a more or less central place; cf the edition of Hellingrath, 3, p 571ff. Language as the product of creative reflection, which produces a poem, is 'the expression of a living, but particular whole'. The meaning of this theory of expression has obviously been wholly distorted by the subjectivising and psychologising process of the nineteenth century. In fact, both with Hölderlin and with Hegel, the rhetorical tradition is far more important. In the eighteenth century 'expression' replaces 'the act of expression' and refers to that lasting form that remains behind as, for example, the impression of a seal etc. The context of this image becomes quite clear from a passage in Gellert *(Schriften* 7, p 273), which refers to the fact 'that our language is not capable of certain kinds of beauty and is a brittle wax that often shatters when we seek to impress on it the images of the spirit'.

This is ancient neoplatonic tradition; cf, for example, *Dionysiaka* I, 87. The point of the metaphor is that the impressed form is not partially but wholly present in all the impressions. This is also the basis of the application of the idea in the 'emanatistic thinking' which, according to Rothacker, is everywhere the basis of our historical view of the world.[8] It is clear that the critique of the psychologisation of the concept of expression runs through the whole of our present investigation and is at the basis of our critique both of 'experience art' and of romantic hermeneutics.[9]

SUPPLEMENT I
HERMENEUTICS AND HISTORICISM

In the philosophical account of the bases of the human sciences there was formerly hardly any mention of hermeneutics. Hermeneutics was merely an ancillary discipline, a canon of rules regarding the way to handle texts. The only distinctions made were to account for the special nature of particular texts, eg as biblical hermeneutics. And finally there was a rather different ancillary discipline called hermeneutics, in the form of legal hermeneutics. It contained the rules for the filling of gaps in a codified law, and hence had a normative character. But the central philosophical problem presented by the human sciences was considered to be epistemological—in an analogy with the natural sciences and their foundation in Kantian philosophy. Kant's *Critique of Pure Reason* had justified the a priori elements in the experiential knowledge of the natural sciences. Thus it was a matter of providing a corresponding theoretical justification for the mode of knowledge of the historical sciences. J. G. Droysen outlined in his *Historik* a very influential methodology of the historical sciences that was to be the equivalent of the Kantian exercise, and W. Dilthey, who was to work out the philosophy proper of the historical school, consciously pursued from the outset the task of a critique of historical reason. Thus even the way in which he saw his task was epistemological. As we know, he saw the epistemological foundation of the so-called human sciences in terms of a 'descriptive and analytical' psychology purified of all alien domination by the natural sciences. In carrying out this task, however, Dilthey was led to move beyond his original epistemological starting-point, and so it was he who introduced hermeneutics into philosophy. True, he never entirely gave up the epistemological foundation that he had sought in psychology. His view that experiences are characterised by inner awareness, so that there is no problem of knowledge of the other, of the 'non-I', which lay behind Kant's questioning, remained the basis on which he sought to construct the historical world in the human sciences. But the historical world is not a coherence of experience in the way that, in autobiography, history presents itself to the inner world of the subjective consciousness. Historical coherence must, in the end, be understood as a coherence of meaning that wholly transcends the horizon of the individual's experience. It is like an enormous alien text that one needs the help of hermeneutics to decipher. Thus Dilthey is compelled by the nature of the case to attend the transition from psychology to hermeneutics.

In endeavouring to provide this hermeneutical foundation for the human sciences Dilthey found himself in marked contrast to that epistemological school that was attempting at the time to establish a foundation of the human sciences on a neokantian basis: the philosophy of value developed by Windelband and Rickert. The epistemological subject seemed to him a bloodless abstraction, but however much he was himself inspired by the desire for objectivity in the human sciences, he could not get away from the fact that the knowing subject, the understanding historian, does not simply stand over against his object, historical life, but is himself part of the same movement of historical life. Especially in his later years Dilthey did more and more justice to the idealistic philosophy of identity, because the idealistic concept of the mind contained the same substantial communion between the subject and the object, between the 'I' and the 'Thou' that was contained in his own concept of life. What Georg Misch shrewdly defended against both Husserl and Heidegger as the standpoint of life philosophy[10] obviously shared with phenomenology the critique of a naive historical objectivism and the latter's epistemological justification by the philosophy of value promulgated in south-west Germany. The constitution of the historical fact by a value relation, convincing as it was, took no account of the way in which historical knowledge is interwoven with the historical process.

Let us recall here that the monumental body of work left by Max Weber and first published under the title *Wirtschaft und Gesellschaft* in 1921, had been planned by him as a *Grundriß der verstehenden Soziologie.* [11] Those parts of this sociological study—prepared for the outline of social economics—that were almost completed are concerned with the sociology of religion, law and music, whereas political sociology, for example, is treated only in a very fragmentary way. Here we are concerned primarily with the introductory section, written between 1918–20, which is now called 'A sociological theory of categories'. It is an impressive catalogue of concepts on an extremely nominalistic basis, which incidentally—unlike his well known essay on the logos of 1913—avoids the concept of value (and hence a total resemblance to south-west German neokantianism). Max Weber calls this sociology 'understanding' (verstehend) inasmuch as its object is the common meaning of social action. It is true that the meaning that is 'subjectively intended' in the area of social and historical life cannot be only that which is actually meant by the individual actors. Thus we have instead of the hermeneutical and methodological concept the abstractively constructed pure type (the 'ideal-typical construction'). The whole edifice rests on this basis, which Max Weber calls 'rationalistic', an edifice which is, in its conception, 'value free' and neutral, a monumental bastion of 'objective' science, which defends its methodological clarity by a classificatory system and, in those parts that he completed, leads to a great systematic survey of the world of historical experience. Entanglement in the impasses of historicism is avoided by the ascetic approach of his methodology.

But the further development of hermeneutical reflection is, in fact, dominated by the question of historicism and hence starts from Dilthey, whose collected works in the twenties soon overshadowed even Ernst Troeltsch's influence.

The fact that Dilthey started with romantic hermeneutics, which became combined in our century with the revival of the speculative philosophy of Hegel, introduced a multi-pronged criticism of historical objectivism (Graf Yorck, Heidegger, Rothacker, Betti etc).

It also left visible traces in historical philological research, in that romantic ideas, that had been hidden by the scientific positivism of the nineteenth century, again emerged within science.[12] There is, for example, the problem of classical mythology, taken up again in the spirit of Schelling by Walter F. Otto, Karl Kerényi and others. Even such an abstruse scholar as J. J. Bachofen, a victim of the monomania of his own intuitions and whose ideas fostered modern ersatz-religions (for instance via Alfred Schuler and Ludwig Klages they influenced Stefan George), won new scientific respect. In 1925 there appeared, under the title *Der Mythos von Orient und Occident, eine Metaphysik der alten Welt*, a systematically edited collection of Bachofen's main writings, for which Alfred Baeumler wrote an eloquent and significant introduction.[13]

Even if we open the historical collection of de Vries' *Forschungsgeschichte der Mythologie*,[14] we gain the same impression, namely of how the 'crisis of historicism' has brought about a revival of mythology. De Vries's survey is noted for its breadth of horizon, and well-chosen texts which give a good illustration of the modern period in particular, with the omission of the history of religion, though there is sometimes an over-slavish and sometimes an over-free observance of chronology. It is interesting to see how Walter F. Otto and Karl Kerényi are clearly recognised as the forerunners of a new development in scholarship that takes myth seriously.

The example of mythology is only one among many. In the concrete work of the human sciences it would be possible to show many places where there is the same turning-away from a naive methodologism, the equivalent of which in philosophical reflection is the explicit criticism of historical objectivism or positivism. This development became of particular importance where originally normative aspects are combined with science. This is the case both in theology and in jurisprudence. The theological discussion of the last decades has placed the problem of hermeneutics in the foreground precisely because it has had to combine the heritage of historical theology with new theological and dogmatic departures. Karl Barth's commentary on Paul's *Epistle to the Romans* was the first revolutionary irruption,[15] a 'critique' of liberal theology, which was less concerned with critical history as such as with the inadequacy of a theology that regarded its findings as an understanding of scripture. Thus Karl Barth's *Epistle to the Romans,* despite all his disaffection for methodological reflexion, is a kind of hermeneutical manifesto.[16] Though he has not much time for Rudolf Bultmann and his thesis of the demythologisation of the new testament, it is not his interests that separate him from Bultmann, but rather it is, so it seems to me, the combination of historical critical research with theological exegesis and the relating of methodological self-awareness to philosophy (Heidegger) which prevents Barth from recognising himself in Bultmann's method. It is, however, a factual necessity not simply to deny the heritage of liberal theology, but to master it. The contemporary discussion of the hermeneutical problem within theology—and not of the hermeneutical problem only—is, therefore, determined by the dispute between the inalienable intention of theology and critical history. Some consider it necessary to find a new defence of the historical position in the face of this situation, while others, as appears in the work of Ott, Ebeling and Fuchs, place less emphasis on the importance of theology as research than on its 'hermeneutical' assistance to the proclamation.

If a layman wants to consider the development within the legal discussion of the hermeneutical problem, it will not be possible for him to study in detail the legal works in this field. All he can do is make the general observation that jurisprudence is retreating, in every field, from legal positivism, as it is called, and regards as a central question the extent to which the concrete formulation of law presents a special juridical problem. Kurt Engisch (1953) gives a comprehensive survey of this problem.[17] That this problem is emerging into the foreground as a counter to extreme forms of legal positivism is also historically understandable, as we can see from Franz Wieacker's *Privatrechtsgeschichte der Neuzeit* or Karl Larenz's *Methodenlehre der Rechtswissenschaft*. Thus we can see in the three fields in which hermeneutics has played a part from the beginning, in the historical and literary critical sciences, in theology, and in jurisprudence, that the critique of historical objectivism or 'positivism' has given to the hermeneutical aspect a new significance.

Fortunately for us the extent of the hermeneutical problem has been recently surveyed and systematically ordered in the important work of an Italian scholar. The legal historian Emilio Betti has produced an enormous work, *Teoria Generale della Interpretazione*,[18] the main ideas of which have been developed in German in a 'hermeneutical manifesto' under the title of *Zur Grundlegung einer allgemeinen Auslegungslehre*.[19] It provides an account of the state of the question that is remarkable for the breadth of its horizon, its impressive knowledge of detail, and its clear systematic arrangement. As a legal historian, who is also himself a teacher of law, and as a compatriot of Croce and Gentile who is equally at home in German philosophy, so that he speaks and writes perfect German, he was, in any case, safe from the dangers of a naive historical objectivism. He is in a position to reap the great harvest of hermeneutical reflection that has ripened over the years since Wilhelm von Humboldt and Schleiermacher.

Clearly turning away from Benedetto Croce's extreme position, Betti seeks the mean between the objective and the subjective element in all understanding. He formulates a complete canon of hermeneutical principles, at the head of which stands the text's autonomy of meaning, according to which the meaning, ie what the author intended to say, can be gained from the text itself. But he also emphasises with equal clarity the principle of the actuality of understanding, ie its adequacy to the object. This implies that he sees that the fact that the interpreter is inevitably tied to a particular perspective is an integrating element in hermeneutical truth.

As a lawyer he is safe from over-estimating subjective opinion, eg the historical accidents that have led to the formulation of a particular legal point, and from automatically equating this with the meaning of law. On the other hand, he follows the 'psychological interpretation', founded by Schleiermacher, to the extent that his hermeneutical position is constantly in danger of becoming vague. However much he tries to overcome this psychological narrowness and recognises the task of reconstructing the mental context of values and significant contents, he is able to justify this task—which is the real hermeneutical one—only by a kind of analogy with psychological interpretation.

Thus he writes, for example, that understanding is a recognition and reconstruction of the meaning, and he explains this by saying that it is an understanding 'of a mind speaking through the forms of its objectification to another thinking mind, with the former considering itself related to the latter in their common humanity; it is a process of leading back and together and reuniting those forms with the inner whole that has brought them forth and from which they have become separated, an interiorising of these forms, in which process their content passes into a subjectivity that is different from the one that originally contained them. Accordingly in the process of interpretation we are concerned with a reversal or inversion of the creative process, a reversal in which the interpreter has to make his hermeneutical way back along the creative path, carrying on this process of rethinking within himself (p 93f). Here Betti is following Schleiermacher, Boeckh, Croce and others (cf p 147 of the *Manifesto*). Curiously, he imagines that he is ensuring the 'objectivity' of understanding by this strict psychologism with its romantic flavour, an objectivity that he regards as threatened by all those who, following Heidegger, regard as mistaken this kind of tie to the subjectivity of meaning.

In his debate with me, which has been repeatedly reproduced in Germany,[20] he sees in me nothing but equivocations and conceptual confusions. This generally means that the critic is relating the author to a question that he does not intend. And this seems to be the case here. He was concerned for the scientific nature of interpretation, as I presented it in my book. I showed him in a private letter that this concern was unnecessary, and he was good enough to print the following passage from it in his treatise:

'Fundamentally I am *not proposing a method*, but I am describing *what is the case.* That it is as I describe it cannot, I think, be seriously questioned. . . . You, for example, know immediately when you read a classic essay by Mommsen the only time when it could have been written. Even a master of the historical method is not able to keep himself entirely free from the prejudices of his time, his social environment and his national situation etc. Is this a failing? And even if it were, I regard it as a necessary philosophical task to consider why this failure is always present wherever anything is achieved. In other words, I consider the only scientific thing is *to recognise what is,* instead of starting from what ought to be or could be. Hence I am trying to go beyond the concept of method held by modern science (which retains its limited justification) and to envisage in a fundamentally universal way what *always* happens'.

But what does Betti say to this? That I am, then, limiting the hermeneutical problem to a quaestio facti ('phenomenologically', 'descriptively') and do not at all pose the quaestio iuris. As if Kant's raising of the quaestio iuris was intended to prescribe to the pure natural sciences what they ought to be, rather than seek to justify their transcendental possibility as they already were. In the sense of this Kantian distinction, to think beyond the concept of method in the human sciences, as my book attempts, is to ask the question of the 'possibility' of the human sciences (which certainly does not mean what they really ought to be). This fine scholar is here confused by a strange resentment against phenomenology. By being able to conceive the problem of hermeneutics only as a problem of method, he shows that he is profoundly involved in the subjectivism which we are endeavouring to overcome.

Obviously I have not succeeded in convincing Betti that a philosophical theory of hermeneutics is not a methodology —right or wrong ('dangerous'), as the case may be. It may be misleading when Bollnow calls understanding an 'essential creative act'—although Betti does not hesitate to describe as such the interpretation of law, which is a creative elaboration of them. But it is quite certain that to follow aesthetics of genius, as Betti himself does, is not sufficient. The theory of inversion cannot really overcome the psychological narrowing-down that (following Droysen) he rightly recognises as such. And so he does not quite get beyond the ambiguity that held Dilthey captive between psychology and hermeneutics. If, in order to explain the possibility of understanding in the human sciences, he has to presuppose that only a mind on the same level can understand another mind, the inadequacy of this psychological-hermeneutical ambiguity becomes apparent.[21]

Even if we are basically clear about the difference between psychic particularity and historical significance, it obviously remains difficult to find the transition from the narrowness of psychology to an historical hermeneutics. Even Droysen was already clear about the task (*Historik* § 41), but the only real basis of it so far for the transition is to be found in Hegel's dialectical combination of the subjective and the objective mind in the absolute mind.

Even where one remains very close to Hegel, as does R. G. Collingwood, who was strongly influenced by Croce, we find the same thing. We now have two works by Collingwood in German translation: his autobiography, that has been published in Germany under the title *Denken,* after having had a great success in the original,[22] and also his posthumous work, *The Idea of History,* translated into German under the title *Philosophie der Geschichte.*[23]

I have made some observations on the autobiography in the introduction to the German edition, and shall not therefore repeat them here. The posthumous work contains a history of historical writing from classical times to the present day, notably ending with Croce. Part 5 comprises a separate theoretical discussion. I shall limit myself to this last part, since the historical sections are, as often happens, so influenced by national traditions of thinking that they are almost unintelligible to a reader of another nationality. For a German reader the chapter on Wilhelm Dilthey, for example, is most disappointing:

'Dilthey has come up against the question which Windelband and the rest had not the penetration to recognize: the question how there can be knowledge, as distinct from an immediate experience, of the individual. He has answered that question by admitting that there cannot be such a knowledge, and falling back on the positivistic view that the only way in which the universal (the proper object of knowledge) can be known is by means of natural science or a science constructed on naturalistic principles. Thus in the end he, like the rest of his generation, surrenders to positivism' (pp 173–174). Whatever truth there is in this judgment is made almost unrecognisable by the ground that Collingwood assigns for it.

The kernel of the systematic theory of historical knowledge is undoubtedly the theory of the re-enactment of the experience of the past. In this Collingwood stands in the ranks of those who protest against 'what may be called a positivistic conception, or rather misconception of history' (p 228). The proper task of the historian is that 'of penetrating to the thought of the agents whose acts they are studying' (p 228). It is particularly difficult in German translation to decide exactly what Collingwood means here by 'thought' (Denken). Obviously the concept of Akt in German ('act' in English) has quite a different connotation from what the English author intends. The re-enactment of the thought of the protagonists of history (or of the thinkers also) does not mean, for Collingwood, actually the real psychic acts of these people, but their thoughts, ie that which can be rethought. Now thought includes 'the corporate mind (whatever exactly that phrase means) of a community or an age' (p 219).[24] But this 'thought' seems to have a strange life of its own, as when Collingwood describes biography as anti-historical because it is not based on 'thought', but on a natural process. 'Through this framework—the bodily life of the man, with his childhood, maturity and senescence, his diseases and all the accidents of animal existence—the tides of thought, his own and others', flow crosswise, regardless of its structure, like sea-water through a stranded wreck' (p 304).

Who is actually behind this 'thinking'? Who are the protagonists of history whose thinking we have to penetrate? Is it the particular intention that a man is pursuing in his action? This is what Collingwood seems to mean (cf p 334 above): 'This depends on the assumption that his acts were done on purpose. If they were not, there can be no history of them. . . .' (p 310). But is the reconstruction of intention really an understanding of history? We can see how Collingwood gets involved, against his will, in psychological particularity. He cannot get out of it without a theory of the 'representative of world spirit', ie without Hegel.

He would not be pleased to hear that. For all metaphysics of history, even that of Hegel, seems to him nothing more than a system of pigeon holes (p 264) without any genuine historical truth value. Moreover, I am not quite clear how his thesis on a radical historicism is compatible with his theory of re-enactment, when he rightly sees, on the other hand, that the historian himself 'is a part of the process he is studying, has his own place in that process, and can see it only from the point of view which at this present moment he occupies within it' (p 248). How does that fit with the defence of the re-enactment of a transmitted 'thought', which Collingwood illustrates by the example of Plato's critique of sensualism in the *Theaetetus?* I am afraid that the example is wrong and proves the opposite.

If Plato presents the thesis in the *Theaetetus* that knowledge is exclusively perception by the senses then, according to Collingwood, I do not, as a reader today, know the context that led him to this view. In my mind this context is a different one: namely, the discussion that emerges from modern sensualism. But since we are concerned with a 'thought' this does not matter. Thought can be placed in different contexts without losing its identity (p 301). One should like to remind Collingwood here of the critique of the statement-discussion in his own 'logic of question and answer' (Denken pp 30–43). Is not the re-enactment of Plato's idea, in fact, successful only if we grasp the true Platonic context (which I think is that of a mathematical theory of evidence that is not yet quite clear about the intelligible mode of being of mathematics)? And who will be able to grasp this context if we do not explicitly hold in abeyance the preconceptions of modern sensualism?[25]

In other words, Collingwood's theory of re-enactment avoids the particularity of psychology, but the dimension of hermeneutical communication which is passed through in every act of understanding still escapes him.

In the context of a critique of historical objectivism the works of Erich Rothacker are remarkable. In one of his last writings in particular, *Die dogmatische Denkform in den Geisteswissenschaften und das Problem des Historismus*[26], he developed his earlier ideas, which maintain Dilthey's hermeneutical concern against all psychologism (like Hans Freyer in the *Theorie des objektiven Geistes*). The concept of the dogmatic thought form is intended entirely as a hermeneutical concept.[27] Dogmatics is defended as a productive method of knowledge in the human sciences, insofar as it elaborates the immanent context that determines an area of significance. Rothacker appeals to the fact that the concept of dogmatics has by no means a merely critical and pejorative sense in theology and jurisprudence. But unlike the case of these systematic disciplines the concept of dogmatics is not intended here to be merely a synonym for systematic knowledge, ie for philosophy, but 'another attitude', to be defended as something separate from the historical inquiry, which seeks to understand processes of development. But then, for Rothacker, the concept of dogmatics has its fundamental place within the total historical attitude and receives from it its relative justification. It is ultimately what Dilthey's concept of the structural context had formulated in general, in its particular application to historical methodology.

Such dogmatics, then, exercises its corrective function where there is historical thinking and knowledge. There can be no dogmatics of Roman law until there is a history of law. Walter F. Otto's *Götter Griechenlands* was possible only after historical research had made of Greek mythology a multiplicity of different pieces of knowledge concerning the history of religion and myth, and if Wölfflin's 'classical art'—unlike his 'fundamental concepts of art history'—is described by Rothacker as dogmatics, this kind of description seems to me only relative. The difference between it and baroque aesthetics, especially mannerism, is the secret starting point of this 'dogmatics', but this implies that, from the outset, it is less believed and known than historically meant.

In this sense dogmatics is, in fact, an element in our historical knowledge. Indeed, Rothacker has emphasised this element as the 'only source of our intellectual knowledge' (p 25). We must establish a comprehensive context of meaning, as presented in this dogmatic approach, and find it self-evident. We must, at least, not find it impossible that it is 'true' if we really want to understand it. This poses, of course, as Rothacker shows, the problem of the multiplicity of such dogmatic systems or styles, and this is the problem of historicism.

Rothacker proves to be an energetic defender of the latter. Dilthey tried to banish the danger of historicism by deriving different world-views from the complexity of life. Rothacker follows him in this by calling dogmatic systems explanations of world-views that have been lived out or of stylistic directions, and basing the latter on the fact that man acts within a perspective and tied to a particular view. Thus they are all, from different perspectives, irrefutable (p 35). Applied to science, this means that relativism has clear limitations rather than boundless sway. It does not endanger the immanent 'objectivity' of research. Its starting point is the variability and freedom of scientific problematic into which are elaborated the variable lines of significance in lived world-views. From this point of view, modern science itself is seen as the dogmatics of a quantifying view of the world (p 53) as soon as we allow that there can be another way of knowing nature.[28]

It is by no means self-evident that legal hermeneutics belongs within the context of the problem of general hermeneutics. In it there is not properly any question of reflection of a methodological kind, as is the case with philology and scriptural hermeneutics, but of a subsidiary legal principle itself. It is not its task to understand valid legal propositions, but to discover law, ie so to interpret the law that the legal order fully penetrates reality. Because interpretation has here a normative function it is sometimes—for example by Betti—entirely separated from literary interpretation, and even from that historical understanding whose object is legal (constitutions, laws etc). That the interpretation of the law is, in a juridical sense, an act that creates law cannot be contested. The different principles that are to be applied in this act, eg the principle of analogy or the principle of filling in gaps in the law, or finally the productive principle that lies in the legal decision itself, ie that depends on the particular legal case, do not present mere methodological problems, but reach deeply into the material of law itself.[29]

Obviously a legal hermeneutics cannot seriously be satisfied with using the subjective principle of the meaning and original intention of the law-giver as a canon of interpretation. It often cannot avoid applying objective concepts, eg that of the notion of law expressed in a particular law. It is obviously an entirely lay idea to regard the application of the law to a concrete case as the logical process of the subsumption of the individual under the universal.

Legal positivism, which would like to limit legal reality entirely to the established law and its correct application, probably has no supporters today. The distance between the universality of the law and the concrete legal situation in a particular case is obviously essentially indissoluble. Nor does it seem satisfactory to consider, in an ideal dogmatics, the power of the individual case to be creative of law as something deductively predetermined, in the sense that a dogmatics could be worked out that would contain, at least potentially, all possible legal truths in a coherent system. Even the 'idea' of this kind of perfect dogmatics seems senseless, quite apart from the consideration that the power of the individual case to create law is, in fact, responsible for constantly new codifications. What is remarkable about the situation is this: that the hermeneutical task of bridging the distance between the law and the particular case is still present, even if no change in social conditions or other historical variations cause the current law to appear old-fashioned or inappropriate. The distance between the law and the individual case seems to be absolutely indissoluble. To this extent, it is possible to divorce the hermeneutical problem from the consideration of the historical dimension. It is no mere unavoidable imperfection in the process of legal codification, which leaves free play for its application to concrete instances, so that this free play could, in principle, be directed to any area at will. It seems rather to be in the nature of legal regulation as such, indeed of legal order generally, to be 'elastic' enough to leave this kind of free play.

If I am not mistaken, Aristotle was quite clear about this, when he ascribed a simply critical function to the idea of natural law, rather than a positive, dogmatic one. It has always been felt to be shocking (when it was not denied outright, by misinterpreting Aristotle's text) that he distinguishes between conventional and natural law, yet goes on to claim that natural law can be changed (*Eth Nic* 1134b 27ff).

Natural law and law established by statute are not 'equally changeable'. Rather, by considering comparable phenomena it is explained that even what is just by nature is changeable, without on that account ceasing to be different from that which is established by mere statute. Obviously, traffic regulations, for

example, are not changeable to the same, but to a much higher
degree than something just by nature. Aristotle seeks not to
detract from this view but to explain how what is just by nature
in the unstable human world (in contrast to that of the gods) is to
be distinguished. Thus he says that the distinction between what
is by nature and what is legal or conventional is evident—despite
the changeability of both—as is the distinction between the right
hand and the left. There, too, by nature the right is the stronger,
and yet this natural priority cannot be described as unchangeable, since, within limits, it can be removed by training the other
hand.[30]

'Within limits', that is within a certain area of free play. To
leave this kind of area, far from destroying the meaning of right
order, belongs rather to the essential nature of the situation:
'The law is universal and cannot therefore answer to every
single case'.[31] The matter does not depend on the codification of
laws but, on the contrary, the codification of laws is possible
only because laws are, in themselves and by nature, universal.

Perhaps we must ask at this point whether the inner connection between hermeneutics and writing is not to be regarded as a
secondary one. It is not the fact of its being written as such that
makes an idea in need of interpretation, but the fact of its being
in language; but that includes the universality of meaning from
which, in turn, follows the possibility of its being written down.
Thus both codified law and the written text point to a deeper
connection that is concerned with the relation between understanding and application, as I think I have shown. It should not
surprise us that Aristotle is the supreme witness to this. His
critique of the Platonic idea of the good is, in my opinion, the
root of the whole of his own philosophy. It contains, without
being 'nominalism', a radical revision of the relation between the
universal and the particular, as it is implied in the Platonic
doctrine of the idea of the good—at least as it is presented in the
Platonic dialogues.[32]

But this does not exclude the fact that as well as this essential
distance between the universal and the concrete there is also the
historical distance, which exhibits its own hermeneutical productivity.

I do not dare to decide whether this is also true of legal
hermeneutics, in the sense that a legal order which historical
change has rendered in need of interpretation (eg with the aid of
the principle of analogy) contributes to a more just application in
general, namely to a refinement of the feeling for law that is
guiding interpretation. In other fields, however, the matter is

clear. It is beyond all doubt that the 'significance' of historical events or the rank of works of art becomes more apparent with the passage of time.

The present discussion of the hermeneutical problem is probably nowhere so lively as in the area of protestant theology. Here also the concern, in a certain sense, as in legal hermeneutics, is with interests that go beyond science, in this case with faith and its right proclamation. Consequently the hermeneutical discussion is interwoven with exegetical and dogmatic questions on which the layman can make no comment. But as with legal hermeneutics the advantage of this situation is clear: that it is not possible to limit the 'meaning' of the text to be understood to the supposed opinion of its author. In his great work *Church Dogmatics,* Karl Barth contributes to the hermeneutical problem explicitly nowhere and indirectly everywhere. It is a somewhat different matter in the case of Rudolf Bultmann, who favours methodological discussions and who, in his collected essays, often refers explicitly to the problem of hermeneutics.[34] But in his case also the emphasis is immanently theological, not only in the sense that his exegetical work constitutes the experiential basis and the sphere of application of his hermeneutical principles, but above all also in the sense that a major issue in contemporary theological debate, the question of a demythologisation of the new testament, is too much bound up with dogmatic tensions to be conducive to methodological reflection. I am convinced that the principle of demythologisation has a purely hermeneutical aspect. According to Bultmann this programme is not supposed to decide in advance dogmatic questions as such, eg how much of the contents of the scriptural writings are essential for the christian proclamation and hence for faith and how much might be sacrificed, but it is a question of the understanding of the christian proclamation itself, of the sense in which it must be understood if it is to be 'understood' at all. Perhaps, indeed certainly, it is possible to understand 'more' in the new testament than Bultmann has understood. But this can only emerge by understanding this 'more' equally well, ie 'really understanding it'.

Historical biblical criticism and its scientific elaboration in the eighteenth and nineteenth centuries have created a situation that requires a constant new adjustment between the general principles of the scientific understanding of a text and the particular tasks of self-understanding of the christian faith. It is good to remind ourselves of the history of these harmonising efforts.[35]

At the beginning of the nineteenth-century development

stands Schleiermacher's *Hermeneutik,* which offers a systematic basis for the essential similarity of the interpretive procedures in relation to scripture and to all other texts, which Semler had already envisaged. Schleiermacher's special contribution was the psychological interpretation, according to which every idea in a text has to be related back to its context in the personal life of its author, as a moment in his life, if it is to be fully understood. In the meantime, we have acquired a more detailed insight into the history of the growth of Schleiermacher's hermeneutical ideas since the Berlin manuscripts, from which Lücke composed his edition, have been excellently reproduced by the Heidelberg Academy of Sciences.[36] The exploitation of the original manuscripts in this way is not revolutionary, but it is not without significance. In his introduction Kimmerle shows that the early manuscripts emphasise the identity of thought and speech, while the later elaboration sees speech as individualising utterance. In line with this, there is also the slow emergence and final domination of a psychological viewpoint over the genuine linguistic viewpoints of 'technical' interpretation ('style').

We know well enough that even in the dogmatic system of Schleiermacher, which has been made available to us in a fine edition produced by Martin Redeker *(Der christliche Glaube),*[37] Schleiermacher's psychological and subjective orientation challenges theological criticism. The 'self-consciousness of faith' is a dogmatically dangerous basis. Christoph Senft's book, that discusses with great insight the development from Schleiermacher to the liberal theology of Ritschl, gives us a good idea of this.[38] On page 42 Senft writes of Schleiermacher: 'Despite his effort to obtain living concepts in order to grasp the historical, the dialectic between speculation and empiricism remains for him a static one. The reciprocal relationship between history and the person studying it is unproblematic and critical, in which the enquirer into history is safe from any fundamental counter-enquiry'.

Nor has F. C. Baur, as Senft shows, advanced the hermeneutical problem any more in this direction, even though he has made the historical process the subject of his investigation, for he maintains the autonomy of self-consciousness as an unconditioned basis. But Hofmann—and this comes out well in Senft's account—in his hermeneutics takes the historicality of revelation hermeneutically seriously. The doctrine that he develops is the 'explanation of the christian faith the presupposition of which "lies outside us" yet not outside us in a legal sense, but in such a way that what lies outside us is revealed "experientially" as its own history' (Senft, p 105). But this ensures at the same time that 'as the monument of a history, ie of a particular nexus of events—not as a text-book of general doctrines—the bible is the book of revelation'. Thus we may say that the criticism that historical scriptural studies have exercised on the canon, by making the dogmatic unity of the bible highly problematical and by destroying the rationalistic-dogmatic assumption of a scriptural 'doctrine', has set the theological task of recognising biblical history as history.

In my view, modern hermeneutical debate gets its orientation from this. Faith in this history must itself be understood as an historical event, as an appeal of the word of God. This is true even for the relationship between the old and the new testaments. It can be understood (according to Hofmann) as the relationship between prophecy and fulfilment, so that the prophecy that fails in history is determined in its significance only by its fulfilment. But the historical understanding of the old testament's prophecies in no way impairs their significance as proclamation which they acquired from the new testatment. On the contrary, the redemptive event that the new testament proclaims can be understood as a real event only if its prophecy is not a mere 'model of the future fact' (Hofmann in Senft, p 101). But especially of the concept of the self-understanding of faith, basic to Bultmann's theology, is it true that it has an historical (and not an idealistic) sense?[39]

Self-understanding refers to a historical decision and not to a self-possession that lies at one's own disposal. Bultmann has constantly emphasised this. Hence it is quite wrong to understand Bultmann's concept of fore-understanding—being caught up in prejudices—as a kind of pre-knowledge.[40] This is a purely hermeneutical concept, developed by Bultmann on the basis of Heidegger's analysis of the hermeneutical circle and the general fore-structure of human There-being. It refers to the openness of the horizon of inquiry within which alone is understanding possible, but it does not mean that one's own fore-understanding should not be corrected by the encounter with the word of God (as, indeed, with any other word). On the contrary, the purpose of this concept is to make apparent the movement of understanding as precisely this process of correction. It must be noted that this 'corrective' process is, in the case of the call of faith, a specific one that is of hermeneutic universality only in its formal structure.[41]

This is where the theological concept of self-understanding comes in. This idea also has obviously been derived from

Heidegger's transcendental analysis of existence. The being that is concerned with its being presents itself, through its understanding of being, as a way of access to the question of being. The movement of the understanding of being is itself seen to be historical, as the basic nature of historicalness. This is of decisive importance for Bultmann's concept of self-understanding.

This concept is different from that of self-knowledge not only in the 'psychologistic' sense that what is known in self-knowledge is already present, but in the deeper speculative sense that is behind the concept of 'mind' or 'spirit' in German idealism, according to which perfect self-consciousness knows itself in other being. Certainly, the development of this self-consciousness is made possible in a decisive way in Hegel's phenomenology by the recognition of the other. The growth of the self-conscious mind is a fight for recognition. What it is, is what it has become. However, the idea of self-understanding, as appropriate to theology, is concerned with something else.[42]

What is extra nos, other than us and not at our disposal, is part of the inevitable essence of this self-understanding. That self-understanding that we acquire in constantly new experiences of the other and of others remains, from a christian point of view, non-understanding in an essential sense. All human self-understanding has its absolute boundary in death. This really cannot be used as a serious argument against Bultmann (Ott, p 163), in an attempt to find a sense of 'conclusion' in Bultmann's idea of self-understanding. As if the self-understanding of faith were not precisely the experience of the eventual failure of human self-understanding. This experience of failure need not necessarily be understood in christian terms. Human self-understanding is deepened by every such experience. In every case it is an 'event' and the concept of self-understanding an historical concept. But, according to the christian teaching, there is a 'final' failure. The christian meaning of proclamation, the promise of resurrection that sets us free from death, consists precisely in putting an end to the constantly repeated failure of self-understanding, its eventual collapse in death and finiteness, in faith in Christ. Certainly this does not mean that one steps outside one's own historicalness, but rather that faith is the eschatological event. In his *Geschichte und Eschatologie* Bultmann writes 'The paradox that christian existence is at once eschatological, unworldly and historical has the same meaning as Luther's statement: Simul iustus simul peccator.' It is in this sense that self-understanding is an historical concept.

The contemporary hermeneutical discussion that starts from

Bultmann seems, in one particular direction, to be moving beyond him. If, according to Bultmann, the appeal of the christian proclamation to man is that he should give up his right to dispose of himself as he chooses, this appeal is like a privative experience of human self-determination. In this way Bultmann has interpreted Heidegger's concept of the inauthenticity of There-being in a theological way. In Heidegger, of course, authenticity is connected with inauthenticity not only in the sense that fallenness is equally part of human life as 'resoluteness', sin (unbelief) just as much as belief. The fact that authenticity and inauthenticity have, for Heidegger, the same origin, points rather quite beyond the starting point in self-understanding. It is the first form in which, in Heidegger's thought, being itself has come into language in its antithetical nature of 'revelation' and 'concealment'. Just as Bultmann relied on the existential analysis of There-being in Heidegger in order to explain the eschatological existence of man between belief and unbelief, so it is possible to use as a theological starting point this dimension of the question of being that has been worked out more exactly by the later Heidegger, namely by going into the central significance that language has, in this event of being, for the 'language of faith'. Already in Ott's very skilful speculative hermeneutical discussion, there is, following Heidegger's 'Letter on Humanism', a critique of Bultmann. It corresponds to his own positive thesis on page 107: 'The language in which reality "comes into language", in and with which all reflection on existence takes place, accompanies existence in all epochs of its realisation'. The hermeneutical ideas of the theologians Fuchs and Ebeling seem, similarly, to start from the late Heidegger, by putting more emphasis on the concept of language.

Ernst Fuchs has given us a hermeneutics that he calls a *Sprachlehre des Glaubens*, ie a grammar of faith.[44] His starting-point is that language is the illumination of being. 'Language contains the decision about what stands open to us as existence, as the possibility of what can become of us if we remain responsive'. Thus he starts from Heidegger in order 'to get rid of the modern involvement in the subject-object schema'. But while Heidegger is thinking of the 'attraction of language itself that comes from its original source and returns to it', Fuchs thinks of the inner attraction of language in listening to the new testament 'as the attraction of the word of God'.

With this listening is associated the awareness that we cannot say that we are the last for whom God's word is intended. But from this there follows that 'we must let ourselves be shown our

historical limitations, as they emerge in our historical understanding of the world. But this means that we have the self-same
task that has always existed for the self-understanding of faith.
We share this task with the authors of the new testament'. Thus
Fuchs acquires a hermeneutical basis that can be justified by
new testament scholarship itself. The proclamation of the word
of God in preaching is a translation of the statements of the new
testament, the justification of which is theology.

Theology here almost becomes hermeneutics, since—following the development of modern biblical criticism—it does
not take as its object the truth of revelation itself, but the
truth of the statements or communications that are related to
God's revelation (p 98). Hence the chief category is that of
communication.

Fuchs follows Bultmann in seeing that the hermeneutical
principle and the understanding of the new testament must be
neutral in regard to faith, for its only presupposition is the
question about ourselves. But it reveals itself as God's question
to us. A grammar of faith must deal with what actually happens
when the call of God's word is heard. 'To know what takes
place in this encounter does not mean that one can automatically
say what one knows' (p 86). Thus the task is finally not only to
hear the word, but also to find the word that is a response. We
are concerned with the language of faith.

An essay *Übersetzung and Verkündigung* makes it clearer
how this hermeneutical theory seeks to get beyond the existential interpretation of Bultmann.[45] It is the hermeneutical principle of translation that gives the direction. It cannot be denied
that 'translation should create the same space as a text intended
to create when the spirit was speaking in it' (p 409). But the bold
and yet inavoidable consequence is that the word has primacy
over against the text, for it is a linguistic event. Here he
obviously means to say that the relation between word and
thought is not one of a subsequent overtaking of the thought by
the word expressing it. The word, rather, is like a flash of
lightning—it strikes. Accordingly, as Ebeling once put it: 'The
hermeneutical problem undergoes its uttermost compression in
the act of preaching'.[46]

We cannot here go into the way in which 'the hermeneutical
movements in the new testament' are presented on this basis.
We can see that the real point is that, for Fuchs, theology in the
new testament already starts from the struggle between language
itself and a thinking in terms of law or order that is a threat from
the start'.[47] The task of proclamation is that of transformation
into the word.[48]

There is one thing common to all contemporary criticism of historical objectivism or positivism, namely the insight that the so-called subject of knowledge has the same mode of being as the object, so that object and subject belong to the same historical movement. The subject-object antithesis is legitimate where the object, over against the res cogitans, is the absolute other of the res extensa. But historical knowledge cannot be appropriately described by this concept of object and objectivity. The important thing, to use Count Yorck's words, is to grasp the 'generic' difference between 'ontic' and 'historical', ie to recognize the so-called subject in the mode of being of historicalness that is appropriate to it. We saw that Dilthey did not break through to the full consequence of this insight, even if it is in his wake that the consequence is drawn. Moreover, there were not the conceptual presuppositions for the problem of overcoming historicism, as expounded by, say, Ernst Troeltsch.

Here the work of the phenomenological school has proved fruitful. Today, now that the various developmental stages of Husserl's phenomenology can be seen,[49] it seems clear to me that Husserl was the first to take the radical step in this direction, by showing the mode of being of subjectivity as absolute historicity, ie as temporality. Heidegger's epoch-making work *Being and Time*, to which one generally refers on this point, had a quite different and far more radical intention, namely of revealing the inadequate ontological preconception that dominates the modern understanding of subjectivity or of 'consciousness', even in its extreme form of the phenomenology of temporality and historicalness. This critique served the positive task of asking in a new way the question of 'being', to which the Greeks gave, as a first answer, metaphysics. *Being and Time*, however, was not understood in this, its real intention, but in what Heidegger had in common with Husserl. It was seen as a radical defence of the absolute historicalness of There-being, which is, in fact, a consequence of Husserl's analysis of the primal phenomenality of temporality ('flowing'). The argument runs, more or less, thus: the mode of being of There-being is defined in an ontologically positive way. It is not being present-at-hand, but futurity. There are no eternal truths. Truth is the revealedness of being that is given with the historical nature of There-being.[50] Here, then, were the foundations from which the critique of historical objectivism, that took place in the sciences themselves, could receive its ontological justification. It is, as it were, a second-degree historicism which not only opposes the historical relativity of all knowledge to the absolute claim of truth, but works out its ground, namely the historicalness of the knowing subject, and hence can no longer see historical relativity as a limitation of the truth.[51]

Even if this is correct, it still does not follow that all philosophical knowledge has only the significance and value of a historical expression, in the sense of Dilthey's philosophy of world views, and hence is on the same plane as art, which is concerned with genuineness and not with truth. Heidegger's own question is far from seeking to sacrifice metaphysics to history, the question of truth to that of the genuineness of expression. Rather, he seeks to inquire back behind the problematic of metaphysics. The fact that in the inquiry the history of philosophy appears in a new way as the interior of world history, namely as the history of being, or better the history of the forgetfulness of being, still does not mean that this is a metaphysics of history of the kind that Löwith has shown as a form of secularisation of the understanding of christianity in terms of salvation history,[52] the most logical elaboration of which idea, on the basis of modern enlightenment, is Hegel's philosophy of history. Nor is Husserl's historical critique of the 'objectivism' of modern philosophy, in the *Crisis*, a metaphysics of history. 'Historicalness' is a transcendental concept.

If one adopts the standpoint of a theological metaphysics, it is very easy to argue against this kind of 'transcendental' historicism which, in the style of Husserl's transcendental reduction, takes its stand in the absolute historicalness of subjectivity, in order to understand, on this basis, everything accorded existential status as an objectification by this subjectivity. If being-in-itself exists which alone could limit the universal historical movement of successive views of the world, it must obviously be something that surpasses all finite human perspectives, as it appears to an infinite spirit. But this is the order of creation, which thus remains in prior ordination to all human perspectives on the world. It is thus that some years ago Gerhard Krüger interpreted the dual aspect of Kant's philosophy, namely the idealism of phenomena and the realism of the thing in itself,[53] and has sought to defend, even in his latest works, the rights of teleological metaphysics against modern subjectivism, on the basis of mythical or religious experience.

The question becomes much more difficult, however, if we are not prepared to accept the consequences that culminate in the christian account of creation, and yet would still like to set against the old teleological cosmos, for which the so-called natural awareness of the world continues to argue, the developmental process of human history.[54] It is obviously the case that the nature of historicalness became conscious to the human mind only with the christian religion and its emphasis on the absolute moment of the saving action of God, and that, nevertheless, the same phenomena of historical life were known before that. But they were understood in an 'unhistorical' way, whether in derivation of the present from a mythical past or by seeing the present in relation to an ideal and eternal order.

It is true that the historical writing of, say, Herodotus, even of Plutarch, is able to describe very well the ebb and flow of human history, as a great variety of moral situations, without reflecting on the historicalness of their own present and on the historicalness of human life in general. The model of the cosmic orders, in which everything that is divergent and opposed to the norm passes quickly away, being ironed out in the great harmonising process of a natural cycle, can also be used as a description of the course of human affairs. The best order of things, the ideal state, in its conception is just as permanent an order as the cosmos, and even if an ideal realisation of it does not endure, but is superseded by the new confusion and disorder that we call history, this is the result of an error in calculation by human reason, which knows what the right thing is. The right order has no history. History is always a history of disintegration and, sometimes, of the right order's restoration.[55]

In regard to actual human history, then, historical scepticism—even in the christian, reformed view—is the only attitude that can be taken. This was the intention and insight behind Löwith's revelation of the theological, and especially eschatological, assumptions on which the European philosophy of history is based, which he expounded in his *Weltgeschichte und Heilsgeschehen*. For Löwith, to conceive a unity of world history is the false need of the christian and modernistic spirit. For him it is not the eternal God and the plan of salvation that he is pursuing with man that must be sought if we really take the finitude of man seriously. We should look at the eternal cycle of nature, in order to learn from it the equanimity that alone is appropriate to the minuteness of human life in the universe. The 'natural concept of the world' that Löwith uses against both modern historicism and modern science, clearly is of stoic origin.[56] No other Greek text seems to illustrate Löwith's intention as well as the pseudo-Aristotelian (hellenistic-stoic) work *Of the World*. This is not surprising, for obviously the modern author is, like his hellenistic predecessor, interested in the course of nature only insofar as it is the antithesis of the desperate disorder of human affairs. A person who defends the

naturalness of this natural view of the world in this way no more
starts from the eternal return of the same than did Nietzsche, but
from the absolute finitude of human life. His rejection of history
is a reflection of fatalism, ie despair of this life having any
meaning. It is not a denial of the significance of history but of the
possibility of its being interpreted at all.

The criticism of the modern belief in history, made by Leo
Strauss in a number of outstanding books on political philosophy, seems to me more radical. He is Professor of Political
Philosophy in Chicago, and it is one of the encouraging features
of our world, increasingly restricted as it is in its area of freedom, that such a radical critic of the political thought of our
contemporary world works there. We are familiar with that
querelle des anciens et des modernes, which dominated the
minds of the literary public of the seventeenth and eighteenth
centuries in France. Although it is more a literary quarrel that
showed the defenders of the excellence of the classical poets of
Greece and Rome competing with the literary self-confidence of
the contemporary writers who were introducing at that time a
new classical period of literature at the court of the Sun King,
the tension of this argument led finally to its settlement in terms
of historical awareness. For it was necessary to limit the absolute exemplariness of the classical world. That querelle was, as
it were, the last form of an unhistorical debate between tradition
and the modern age.

It is not an accident that one of Leo Strauss' first works, *Die
Religionskritik Spinozas* (1930), was concerned with this quarrel. His whole impressive and learned life's work is devoted to
the task of reviving this quarrel in a more radical sense, ie to set
against the modern historical self-confidence the clear rightness
of classical philosophy. When Plato inquires into the best
state—and even the extended political empiricism of Aristotle
preserves the priority of this question—this may have little to
do with the concept of politics that dominates modern thought
since Machiavelli. And when, in his book *Naturrecht und Geschichte*, Strauss apparently goes back to the antithesis of the
modern historical world view, namely natural law, the purpose
of his book is, in fact, to show the Greek classics of philosophy,
Plato and Aristotle, as the true founders of natural law, and to
accept neither the Stoic nor the medieval form of natural law, to
say nothing of that of the enlightenment, as being philosophically correct.

Strauss is motivated here by his insight into the catastrophe of
modern times. Such an elementary human concern as the dis-

tinction between right and wrong assumes that man is able to raise himself above his historical conditionedness. When classical philosophy inquires into justice, and puts in the foreground the unconditional nature of this distinction, it is clearly right, and a radical historicism, which historically relativises all unconditional values, cannot be right. Thus one's arguments have to be tested in the light of classical philosophy.

Now Strauss cannot, of course, mean that he could undertake this task in the same way that Plato undertakes his critique of sophism. He is himself too familiar with the modern historical awareness to defend classical philosophy in a naive way. Thus his argument against what he calls historicism is itself based primarily on historical grounds. He appeals to the fact (as does Löwith after him) that historical thought itself has its historical conditions of growth. This is true both of the form of naive historicism, ie of the development of a historical sense in the study of tradition, and of its refined form, which takes account of the existence of the knowing subject in his historicalness.

Although this is unquestionably correct, so is the conclusion that the historical phenomenon of historicism, just as it has had its hour, could also one day come to an end. This is quite certain, not because historicism would otherwise 'contradict itself', but because it takes itself seriously. Thus we cannot argue that a historicism that maintains the historical conditionedness of all knowledge 'for all eternity' is basically self-contradictory. This kind of self-contradiction is a special problem.[57] Here also we must ask whether the two propositions, 'all knowledge is historically conditioned' and 'this piece of knowledge is true unconditionally' are on the same level, so that they could contradict each other. For the thesis is not that this proposition will always be considered true, any more than that it has always been so considered. Rather, historicism that takes itself seriously will allow for the fact that one day its thesis will no longer be considered true, ie that people will think 'unhistorically'. And yet not because the unconditional assertion of the conditioned character of all knowledge is not meaningful, containing a logical contradiction.

Strauss, however, does not take up the question thus. Simply to show that the classical philosophers thought differently, ie unhistorically, says nothing about the possibility of thinking unhistorically today. There are sufficient reasons for regarding the possibility of thinking unhistorically not simply as a mere possibility. The many correct 'physiognomic' observations that Ernst Jünger has made on this subject could well be argument for the fact that humanity has reached 'the time wall'.[58] What Strauss is concerned with is still conceived within historical thought and has the significance of a corrective. What he criticises is that the 'historical' understanding of traditional thought claims to be able to understand the thought of the past better than it understood itself.[59] Whoever thinks like this excludes from the outset the possibility that the thoughts that are handed down to us could simply be true. This is the practically universal dogmatism of this way of thought.

The image of the historicist that Strauss here outlines and fights against corresponds, it seems to me, to that ideal of the enlightenment that I described in my own inquiry into philosophical hermeneutics as the guiding idea behind the historical irrationalism of Dilthey and the nineteenth century. Is it not a utopian ideal of the present, in the light of which the whole of the past will, as it were, be entirely revealed? The application of the superior perspective of the present to the whole of the past does not appear to me at all to be the true nature of historical thinking, but characterises the obstinate positivity of a naive historicism. Historical thinking has its dignity and its value as truth in the acknowledgement that there is no such thing as 'the present', but rather constantly changing horizons of future and past. It is by no means settled (and can never be settled) that any particular perspective in which transmitted thoughts present themselves is the right one. The 'historical' understanding, whether today's or tomorrow's, has no special privilege. It is itself embraced by the changing horizons and moved with them.

As against this, the view of a literary hermeneutics that one must understand an author better than he understood himself comes, as I have shown, from the aesthetics of genius, but it is originally a simple formulation of the enlightenment ideal of clarifying obscure ideas by conceptual analysis.[60] Its application to historical consciousness is secondary and creates the false appearance of an unsurpassable superiority in the particular interpreter of the moment, which Strauss rightly criticises. But when Strauss argues that in order to understand better it is necessary first to understand an author as he understood himself, he under-estimates, I think, the difficulties of understanding, because he ignores what might be called the dialectic of the statement.

We have seen this in another place, where he defends the ideal of an 'objective interpretation' of a text by saying that the author, at any rate, understood what he said in only one way, 'assuming that he was not confused in his mind' (p 67). We shall have to consider whether the implied contrast here between 'clear' and 'confused' is as unambiguous as Strauss assumes. Does he not here, in fact, share the point of view of the full historical enlightenment and miss the real hermeneutic problem? He seems to consider it possible to understand what one does not understand oneself, but what someone else understands, and only to understand in the way that he understands himself. And he also seems to think that if a person says something he has necessarily and fully understood 'himself' in the process. In my view these cannot both be true. It is necessary to detach the dubious hermeneutical principle of having to understand an author 'better' than he understood himself, from the presupposition of the enlightenment, in order to grasp its valid meaning.

Let us consider then, from a hermeneutic point of view, Strauss' defence of classical philosophy. We shall consider one example. Strauss shows very well that the I-Thou-We relation, as it is called in modern thinking, is known in classical political philosophy by a quite different name: friendship. He sees correctly that the modern way of talking about the 'problem of the Thou' is based on the fundamental primacy of the Cartesian ego cogito. Strauss now thinks he sees why the ancient concept of friendship is correct and the modern formulation false. It is quite legitimate for someone who is attempting to discover the nature of the state and society to consider the role of friendship. But he cannot talk with the same legitimacy about the 'Thou'. The 'Thou' is not something about which one speaks, but is that to which one speaks. By taking the function of the 'Thou' as a basis, instead of the role of friendship, one is missing the objective communicative nature of the state and society.

I find this a very happy example. The indeterminate position of the concept of friendship in Aristotelian ethics, between the teaching on virtue and the teaching on the good, has long been for me, and for very similar reasons, a basis for recognising the limitations of modern as compared with classical ethics.[61] Thus I fully agree with Strauss' example, but I ask: Does this insight emerge because we 'read' the classics with an eye that is trained by historical science, reconstructing their meaning, as it were, and then considering it possible, trusting that they are right? Or do we see truth in them because we are thinking ourselves as we try to understand them, ie because what they say seems true to us when we consider the corresponding modern theories that are invoked? Do we understand them at all without understanding them at the same time as more correct? If this is the case, then I go on to ask: Is it not then meaningful to say of Aristotle that he could not understand himself in the way that we understand him if we find what he says more correct than those modern theories (which he could not know)?

The same thing could be shown to hold for the distinction between the concept of the state and that of the polis, on which Strauss correctly insists. That the institution of the state is something very different from the natural living community of the polis is not merely correct, but something is revealed here—again from this experience of the distinction—that would remain incomprehensible not only for modern theory, but also in our understanding of the classical texts, were these not understood in terms of the contrast with modern times. If this is called 're-vitalisation' or 'reliving', this seems to me a term quite as inexact as Collingwood's 're-enactment'. The life of the spirit is not like that of the body. It is no false historicism to admit this, but in the closest accord with Aristotle's epidosis eis auto. In this I do not seriously differ from Strauss, in as much as he also regards the 'fusion of history and philosophical questions' as inevitable in our thought today. I agree with him that it would be a dogmatic assertion to regard this as an absolute prerogative of the modern age. Indeed, how many unrealised assumptions are we dominated by when we think in our concepts, so full of traditional ideas, and how much can we learn by going back to the fathers of thought? This is shown clearly by the instances we have mentioned, instances that can be multiplied from Strauss' writings.

At all events, we must not be led into the error of thinking that the problem of hermeneutics is posed only from the viewpoint of modern historicism. It is true that for the classics the opinions of their predecessors were not discussed as historically different, but as contemporary. But the task of hermeneutics, ie the task of the interpretation of the transmitted texts, would still present itself, and if this interpretation always includes the question of truth, then this is perhaps not as far from our own experience in dealing with texts as the methodology of historical and humane science would have it. The word 'hermeneutics' points back, as we know, to the task of the interpreter, which is that of interpreting and communicating something that is unintelligible because it is spoken in a foreign language—even if it is the language of the signs and symbols of the gods. The ability that is applied to this task has always been the object of possible reflection and conscious training. (This can, of course, take the form of an oral tradition as, for example, with the Delphic priesthood.) But when it is a question of writing, the task of interpretation is quite clearly imposed. Everything that is set down in writing is to some extent foreign and strange, and hence it poses the same task of understanding as what is spoken in a foreign language. The interpreter of what is written, like the interpreter of divine or human utterance, has the task of overcoming and removing the strangeness and making its assimilation possible. It may be the case that this task is complicated if the historical distance between the text and interpreter becomes conscious; for this means that the tradition that supports both the transmitted text and its interpreter has become fragile and gapped. But I think that under the weight of the false methodological analogies suggested by the natural sciences 'historical' hermeneutics is separated far too much from 'pre-historical' hermeneutics. I tried to show that they have at least one important disposition in common: the structure of application.[62]

It would be fascinating to investigate the Greek beginnings of the essential connection between hermeneutics and writing. It is not just that both Socrates and his opponents, the sophists, pursued the interpretation of poets, according to Plato; it is more important that the whole of Platonic dialectics is explicitly related by Plato himself to the problems of writing, and that even within the dialogue it often explicitly assumes a hermeneutical character, whether the dialectical dialogue is introduced by a mythical tradition through priests and priestesses, by an instruction from Diotima, or simply by the observation that the ancients did not worry at all that we should understand them, and hence left us as helpless as if we were dealing with fairy-stories. We will also have to consider the reverse situation, namely the extent to which Plato's own myths belong to the dialectic and hence themselves bear the character of interpretation. Thus the construction of a Platonic hermeneutics carrying on from the beginnings made by Hermann Gundert could be extremely instructive.[63]

But Plato is still more important as the object of hermeneutical reflection. The dialogue form of the Platonic writings, as an artistic creation, is curious, half-way between the variety of characters of dramatic writing and the authenticity of the pedagogical work. In this respect the last decades have given us a high degree of hermeneutical awareness, and Strauss, too, enchants us with many brilliant examples of the deciphering of hidden relationships in the Platonic dialogues. However much we have been helped by form-analysis and other linguistic

methods, the proper hermeneutical basis here is our own relation to the actual problems that Plato is concerned with. Even
Plato's artistic irony can be understood only by someone who
shares his knowledge of the matter (as is the case with all irony).
The result of this situation is that this kind of deciphering
interpretation remains 'uncertain'. Its 'truth' cannot be exhib-
ited 'objectively', except in terms of that factual agreement that
links us with the interpreted text.

In an indirect way Strauss made a further important contribution to hermeneutic theory, by investigating a particular problem, namely the question of how far one has to take into
account, when trying to understand texts, the conscious camou-
flaging of the true meaning because of the threat of persecution
by the authorities or by the church.[64] It was mainly studies on
Maimonides, Halevy and Spinoza that gave rise to this question.
I do not want to question the interpretations given by Strauss—I
largely agree with them—but I should like to make a counter-
suggestion that is perhaps justified in these cases, but is quite
certainly so in others, eg in the case of Plato. Is not conscious
distortion, camouflage and concealment of the proper meaning
in fact the rare extreme case of a frequent, even normal
situation?—just as persecution (whether by civil authority or the
church, the inquisition etc) is only an extreme case when compared with the intentional or unintentional pressure that society
and public opinion exercise on human thought. Only if we are
conscious of the uninterrupted transition from one to the other
are we able to estimate the hermeneutic difficulty of Strauss'
problem. How are we able to establish clearly that a distortion
has taken place? Thus, in my opinion, it is by no means clear
that, when we find contradictory statements in a writer, it is
correct to take the hidden meaning—as Strauss thinks—for the
true one. There is an unconscious conformism of the human
mind to considering what is universally obvious as really true.
And there is, against this, an unconscious tendency to try
extreme possibilities, even if they cannot always be combined
into a coherent whole. The experimental extremism of Nietzsche bears irrefutable witness to this. Contradictions are an
excellent criterion of truth but, unfortunately, they are not an
unambiguous criterion when we are dealing with hermeneutics.

Hence, for example, it is quite clear to me that, despite its
apparent obviousness, the statement by Strauss, that if an
author contains contradictions that a schoolboy of today could
spot immediately, then these are intentional and even meant to

be seen through, cannot be applied to the so-called mistakes in argument by Plato's Socrates. Not because we are concerned here with the beginnings of logic (to say this is to confuse logical thought with logical theory), but because it is the nature of a dialogue that is directed towards an object to risk illogicality.[65]

The question has general hermeneutical consequences. We are concerned with the concept of 'the author's meaning'. I am disregarding the help that jurisprudence might offer here with its teaching on the interpretation of law. All I want to say is that at any rate the Platonic dialogue is a model of writing that embraces many meanings and inner relationships, among which Strauss is often able to make important discoveries. Are we to so underestimate the mimetic truth that the Socractic dialogue has in Plato that we do not see this multifariousness of meaning in itself, even in Socrates himself? Does an author really know so exactly and in every sentence what he means? The curious chapter of philosophical self-interpretation—I need only think of Kant, Fichte or Heidegger—seems to speak for itself. If the alternative suggested by Strauss is true, namely that a philosophical author has either an unambiguous meaning or is confused, then there is, I fear, in many controversial points of interpretation only one hermeneutical consequence: we must consider that there is confusion.

In considering the structure of the hermeneutical process I have explicitly referred to the Aristotelian analysis of phronesis.[66] Basically, I have followed here a line that Heidegger began in his early years in Freiburg, when he was concerned with a hermeneutics of facticity, against neokantianism and value philosophy (and, probably ultimately, against Husserl himself). It is true that Aristotle's ontological basis became suspect for Heidegger even in his early investigations, a basis on which the whole of modern philosophy, especially the idea of subjectivity and that of consciousness, as well as the impasses of historicism, is founded (what is called in *Being and Time* the 'ontology of the present-at-hand'). But in one point Aristotelian philosophy was at that time much more than a mere counter-model for Heidegger, but was a real vindicator of his own philosophical purposes: in the Aristotelian critique of Plato's 'universal eidos' and, positively, in the demonstration of the analogical structure of the good and the knowledge of the good, as is the task in the situation of action.

What surprises me most about Strauss' defence of classical philosophy is the degree to which he seeks to understand it as a unity, so that the extreme contrast that exists between Plato and Aristotle in the nature and the significance of their question concerning the good does not seem to cause him any trouble. The early stimulation that I received from Heidegger has been valuable for me because, among other reasons, Aristotelian ethics quite unexpectedly made it easier to understand more deeply the hermeneutical problem. I think it is true to say that this is not a misuse of Aristotelian thought, but shows the instruction this is able to give, a critique of the abstract and universal that, without being driven to a dialectical extreme, as in the manner of Hegel, and hence without the untenable consequence presented by the concept of absolute knowledge, has become essential for the hermeneutical situation with the rise of historical consciousness.

In his book *Die Wiedererweckung des geschichtlichen Bewusstseins,* which appeared in 1956, Theodor Litt has presented under the title "Der Historismus und seine Widersacher" (historicism and its opponents) an energetic critique of Krüger and Löwith (though unfortunately not of Strauss) that seems to have a difficulty at this point.[67] I think that Litt is right when he sees the danger of a new dogmatism in the philosophical opposition to history. The desire for a fixed, constant criterion 'that points the way to those called to action' always has particular force if failures in moral and political judgment have led to evil consequences. The question of justice, the question of the perfect state, seem to spring from an elementary need of human existence. Nevertheless everything depends on the way in which this question be intended and asked, if it is to bring clarification. Litt shows that it cannot refer to any universal norm under which the particular case of practical political action could be subsumed.[68] It is, however, a pity that he does not make use of the assistance that Aristotle can give here, for Aristotle made the same objection to Plato.

I am convinced of the fact that, quite simply, we can learn from the classics, and it is greatly to be appreciated that Strauss not only calls for this, but can also in large measure fulfill the demand. However, I also consider that what we can learn from them is the absolute distinction that exists between a politike tekne and a politike phronesis. Strauss does not in my opinion give sufficient weight to this.

Here too Aristotle can help us not to become involved in an apotheosis of nature, naturalness and natural law that would be nothing but an impotently doctrinaire critique of history, but rather to acquire a more appropriate relationship to the historical tradition and a better understanding of what is. Incidentally, I do not regard the problem raised by Aristotle as in any way disposed of. It might well be that Aristotle's critique, like so many critiques, is right in what it says, but not in that against whom it says it. But that is a large—and another—question.

SUPPLEMENT II

TO WHAT EXTENT DOES LANGUAGE PREFORM THOUGHT?

We may begin by explaining why the question in the title is asked at all. What suspicion, what critique, is hidden behind it? It is, in fact, the fundamental doubt about the possibility of our escaping from the sphere of influence of our education which is linguistic, of our civilisation which is linguistic and of our thought which is transmitted through language, as well as the doubt about our capacity for openness to a reality which does not correspond to our opinions, our fabrications, our previous expectations. In our contemporary situation, faced as we are with an increasingly widespread anxiety about human existence as such, the issue is the suspicion, which is slowly seeping into the consciousness of all, that, if we continue to pursue industrialisation, to think of work only in terms of profit, and to turn our earth into one vast factory as we are doing at the moment, then we threaten the conditions of human life in both the biological sense and in the sense of specific human ideals even to the extreme of self-destruction.

So, with increasing urgency, we are led to ask, whether there may not be hidden in our experience of the world a primordial falsity; whether, in our linguistically transmitted experience, we may not be prey to prejudices or, worse still, to necessities which have their source in the linguistic structuring of our first experience of the world and which would force us to run with open eyes, as it were, down a path whence there was no other issue than destruction. Slowly this becomes clear: if we continue thus we can—without, of course, being able to calculate the precise day—predict with certainty the fact that life on this planet will become impossible; predict it with as much certainty as we can predict, from astronomical calculations, the collision of two stars.

It is, then, a question of some contemporary importance to discover if it is really because of the baleful influence of language that we find ourselves in our present predicament. None will deny that our language influences our thought. We think with words. To think is to think something with oneself; and to think

something with oneself is to say something to oneself. Plato was,
I believe, quite correct to call the essence of thought the interior
dialogue of the soul with itself. This dialogue, in doubt and objection, is a constant going beyond oneself and a return to oneself, one's own opinions and one's own points of view. If anything does characterise human thought it is this infinite dialogue
with ourselves which never leads anywhere definitively and
which differentiates us from that ideal of an infinite spirit to
which all that exists and all truth is present in a single vision. It is
in this experience of language—in our education in the midst of
this interior conversation with ourselves, which is always simultaneously the anticipation of conversation with others and the
introduction of others into the conversation with ourselves
—that the world begins to open up and achieve order in all the
domains of experience. But this implies that we know of no
other way of ordering and orientation than that which, from the
data of experience, leads eventually to those terms of orientation
which we name the concept or the universal and for which the
concrete is a particular case.

In a brilliant image, Aristotle illustrates how the movement
from experience to the knowledge of the universal is organised. I
refer to the description in which he shows how the single experience arises from many perceptions and how, from the multiplicity of experiences, there arises something like a consciousness
of the universal which endures through the changing aspects of
the life of experience. For this he finds an elegant comparison.
How does one come to the knowledge of the universal? By the
mere fact that experiences accumulate and that one recognises
them to be identical? Doubtless; but when does that become the
unity of the universal, the concrete? It is like an army in flight
when of a sudden one soldier looks back to see how close the
enemy are, only to discover that they are not as close as all that.
He stops a moment, and then another stops, and another, and
another . . . The first, the second, the third—these are not yet
the whole army and yet, in the end, the whole army regroups.
Now the same is true of learning to speak. There is no first word
and yet, while learning, we grow into language and into world
—these inseparable unities.

It follows that all depends on the way in which we grow into
the pre-schematisation of our future orientation of the world by
the apprenticeship of language and by all that it includes, all that
we learn by way of conversation. This is the process that is
nowadays called 'socialisation': growth into the social. Of
necessity it is likewise growth into conventions, into a social life

regulated by conventions, and so language is open to the charge of being an ideology. Just as the apprenticeship of language is the constant study of ways of expression and turns of phrase, so our formation of convictions and opinions is also a way of introducing us into a set of pre-formed articulations and meanings. How are we to succeed in making from this pre-formed conceptual matter a living fluid speech? How can we attain to that perfect ideal of speech when one has the rare feeling of having said what one wanted to say?

As for language, so for the rest of living: a world conventionally pre-formed becomes familiar, and the question is to know whether or not, in our understanding of ourselves, we can ever arrive at that point to which, in those rare cases of perfect speech to which I have just now referred, we think we have come; namely when we really say what we want to say. Analogously, we may ask whether or not we ever arrive at the point where we understand what really is. These two—total understanding and adequate expression—are limit cases of our orientation in the world and of our infinite interior dialogue with ourselves. What I want to say is this: precisely because this dialogue is infinite, because this orientation to things, given in the pre-formed schemas of discourse, enters into our spontaneous process of coming to an understanding both with one another and with ourselves, there is opened to us the infinity of what we understand in general and what we can intellectually appropriate. There are no limits to the interior dialogue of the soul with itself. With this thesis I would oppose the suspicion that language is an ideology. I want to argue for the pretention to universality of the act of understanding and of speaking. We can express everything in words and can try to come to agreement about everything.

That we are limited by our finitude and that only a truly infinite conversation could entirely actualise this pretention is, of course, true. Does not, then, a whole series of opposing arguments arise against the universality of our linguistically transmitted experience of the world? There is, for instance, American relativism, derived from Humboldt and given a new lease on life in a new spirit of empirical research, according to which the different languages are so many different images of the world and perspectives on the world, and none can escape that particular image and that particular schematisation within which he is imprisoned. In Nietzsche's aphorisms on the will to power there occurs in this connection the apt remark that God's truly creative act was the creation of grammar, implying that he initiated us into these schemas of mastery of the world in such a way that we can never get behind grammar. Is it not the case, therefore, that the dependence of thought on the possibilities of speech and linguistic habit is restrictive? And if we look about us in a world that is tending to cultural levelling to the point that we no longer speak with the same assurance of the unique western philosophy, do we not begin to recognise that the whole of our conceptual philosophical language and its derivative, the conceptual language of modern science, are in the final analysis of Greek origin? It is the language of metaphysics with whose categories we are familiar from grammar—subject, predicate, nomen, verbum, noun and verb. Today, with our newly awakened global consciousness, we may incline to feel that in such a concept as 'verb' there resounds the pre-schematisation of our European attitude. And so, behind all this, there lurks the uneasy question whether, in all our thought, even in the critical dissolution of such metaphysical concepts as substance, accident, the subject and its properties and the like, predicative logic included, we are doing any more than think through to its conclusion that which made itself into the linguistic structure of the Indo-germanic peoples millennia before any written tradition. We raise this question today just when we are, perhaps, at the end of our linguistic culture—an end heralded by technological civilisation and its mathematical symbolisms. Thus we are not involved in idle suspicions. We have reached the point where we must ask what the determining factor is. Has there been, perhaps, a casting of dice which has made the history of the world before any other world history, which through our language has pushed us to our thought, and which, if it continues, will lead to the technological self-destruction of humanity?

In reply I would say that this suspicion against ourselves puts our reason into artificial tutelage. If my impressions are not entirely false you will recognise that I am talking about something real, that when I speak of humanity threatened by itself and when I stress a very recent discovery of Heidegger, I am not merely indulging in the black reflections of a philosopher living in the clouds. I am convinced that Heidegger's discovery will later become part of the common knowledge of humanity, for we see with increasing clarity today—as he has taught us to see —that Greek metaphysics is the beginning of modern technology. Concept formation, born of western philosophy, has held, throughout a long history, that mastery is the fundamental experience of reality. Must we now be content to say that we are beginning to recognise this as such? Is our western experience an insurmountable barrier?

A second objection has been developed by Habermas against my own theories (however, leave me aside, for the issue is elsewhere). The thing is to discover whether the extra-linguistic modes of experience are not under-estimated when one asserts, as I do, that it is in language that we articulate the experience of the world in so far as this experience is common. From one point of view we are in agreement. The multiplicity of language does not affect the issue. This relativity is not one which holds us in unbreakable shackles, as those of us who can think to some extent in different languages know very well. But are there not other experiences of reality that are not of the linguistic order? The experience of domination and the experience of work are two arguments, so to speak, that Habermas opposes to the universal pretentions of hermeneutics, by interpreting linguistic understanding—in a very limited way and for whatever reason I do not know—as a sort of closed circle of the movement of ideas, as the cultural heritage of a people divorced from their every-day living. Now the cultural heritage of a people is preeminently the heritage of forms and techniques of working, of forms and techniques of domination, of ideals of liberty, of objectives of order and the like. Who will deny that our specific human possibilities do not subsist solely in language? One would want to admit rather that every linguistic experience of the world is experience of the world, not experience of language. And is what we articulate in language not an encounter with reality? The encounter with domination and dependence involves the development of our political ideas, and it is the world of work —the world of 'our power'—that we experience in mastering techniques of working, in so far as it is the way of research into ourselves. It would be totally abstract to consider that it was not through and in the concrete experiences of our human existence, in domination and in work, and only here, that our human understanding of ourselves, our evaluations, our conversation with ourselves, find their fulfilment and exercise their critical function.

The fact that it is in the midst of a linguistic world and through the mediation of an experience pre-formed by language that we grow up in our world, does not remove the possibilities of critique. On the contrary, the possibility of going beyond our conventions and beyond all those experiences that are schematised in advance, opens up before us once we find ourselves, in our conversation with others, faced with opposed thinkers, with new critical problems, with new experiences. Fundamentally in our world the issue is always the same: the verbalisation of conventions and of social norms behind which there are always economic and dominating interests. But our human experience of the world, for which we rely on our faculty of judgment, consists precisely in the possibility of our taking a critical stance with regard to every convention. In reality, we owe this to the linguistic virtuality of our reason and language does not, therefore, present an obstacle to reason.

Now it is certainly the case that our experience of the world is not accomplished only in the apprenticeship and use of language. There is a pre-linguistic experience of the world, as Habermas, drawing on Piaget's researches, reminds us. The language of gesture, facial expression and movement binds us to each other. There are laughter and tears (Helmut Plessner has worked out a hermeneutics of these). There is the world of science within which the exact languages of symbolism and mathematics provide a sure foundation for the elaboration of theory, and which have brought with them a capacity for construction and manipulation which seems a kind of self-representation of homo faber, of man's technical ingenuity. But all these forms of self-representation must be taken up in the interior dialogue of the soul with itself. These phenomena indicate that behind all the relativities of language and convention there is a common trait which is no longer language but which looks to an ever-possible verbalisation, and for which the well tried word 'reason' is, perhaps, not the worst. Never the less there remains something that characterises language as such and distinguishes it from all other acts of communication.

We may elucidate this distinction by referring to writing and graphic transcription. What are the grounds of this literary universality? Ignoring for the moment all the differences within man has with another man, or with himself, can take the frozen form of graphic characters that can be deciphered, read, and elevated in a new process which reactualises the meaning to the extent that our entire world is more or less—although perhaps not for long—a literary world, a world managed by writing and graphic transcription. What are the grounds of this literary universality? Ignoring for the moment all the differences within graphic transcription, I would say that all writing, if it is to be understood, requires a sort of heightening of the inward ear. For poetry and writing of that kind this goes without saying, but for philosophy too a sharpening of the ear is demanded. As I often tell my students, when you take a word in your mouth you must realise that you have not taken a tool that can be thrown aside if it won't do the job, but you are fixed in a direction of thought which comes from afar and stretches beyond you. What we do is always a sort of reconstitution that I want to call translation in a broad sense. To read is to translate and to translate is to translate again. Reflect for a moment, if you would, on this: what is involved when we translate, when we transpose a dead thing, in a new act of understanding, from what was presented as a text only in a foreign language into our own language? The translation process contains the whole secret of human understanding of the world and of social communication. Translation is an indivisible unity of implicit anticipation, of presumption of meaning in general and of the explicit determination of what one presumed.

All discourse includes something of this anticipation and determination. Heinrich von Kleist has a very fine essay, "On the progressive elaboration of thoughts in discourse", in which he describes his experiences in Berlin at the time of his licentiate examination. (Every examiner should, I think, be asked to swear that he has read this essay!). At that time these examinations were public but were attended—then as now—only by those whose turn was yet to come. Kleist describes how the examination runs, how the professor asks a question out of the blue and how the candidate has to answer on the spot. Yet, as we all know, only fools can answer questions whose answers are known to all and sundry. So the degree of intelligence in the answer is all that should count in an examination. Computers and parrots can give 'exact' answers more quickly. Kleist has a good phrase to describe the experience: the shuttlecock of thoughts must be set to work. In the act of speaking one word brings another with it and so our thought is eventually set forth. It is truly speech that emerges from the background and usage of a language already schematised in advance. We speak and the word goes beyond us to consequences and ends which we had not, perhaps, conceived of. The background of the universality of this linguistic access to the world is that our recognition of the world does not appear to us as an infinite text that, partially and painfully, we learn to recite. The word 'recite' should put us on our guard. For it has nothing do with speaking. To recite is the contrary of speaking. Recitation knows what is coming and is closed to the sudden idea. All of us have had the experience of listening to a bad actor and getting the impression that when he said one word he was already thinking of the next. This is not speaking. Our speaking is not speaking unless we run the risk of positing something and following out the implications.

To sum up, I would say that the basic misunderstanding concerning the linguistic character of our understanding is one of language, as if language were an existing whole composed of words and phrases, concepts, points of view and opinions. In reality, language is the single word whose virtuality opens up the infinity of discourse, of discourse with others, and of the freedom of 'speaking oneself' and of 'allowing oneself to be spoken'. Language is not its elaborate conventionalism, nor the burden of pre-schematisation with which it loads us, but the generative and creative power unceasingly to make this whole fluid.

Notes

FOREWORD TO THE 2ND EDITION

[1] As well as personal communications I think of the following:
K. O. Apel, *Hegelstudien*, II, Bonn, 1963, pp 314–22

O. Becker, 'Die Fragwürdigkeit der Transzendierung der ästhetischen Dimension der Kunst (im Hinblick auf den I Teil von *Wahrheit und Methode*)', *Phil. Rundsch.* 10, 1962, pp 225–38

E. Betti, *Die Hermeneutik als allgemeine Methodik der Geisteswissenschaften* Tübingen, 1962

W. Hellebrand, 'Der Zeitbogen', *Arch. F. Rechts- u. Sozialphil.* 49, 1963, pp 57–76

H. Kuhn, 'Wahrheit und geschichtliches Verstehen', *Histor. Ztschr.* 193/2 1961, pp 376–89

J. Möller, *Tübinger Theol. Quartalschr.* 5, 1961, pp 471–76

W. Pannenberg, 'Hermeneutik und Universalgeschichte', *Ztschr. f. Theol. u. Kirche* 69, 1963, pp 90–121

O. Pöggeler, *Philos. Literaturanzeiger*, 16, pp 6–16

A. de Waelhens, 'Sur une herméneutique de l'herméneutique', *Rev. philos. de Louvain*, 60, 1962, pp 573–91

F. Wieacker, 'Notizen zur rechtshistorischen Hermeneutik', *Nachr. d. Ak. d. W.* Göttingen, phil.-hist. Kl. 1963, pp 1–22

[2] Postscript to M. Heidegger, *Der Ursprung des Kunstwerks* Stuttgart, 1960

'Hegel und die antike Dialektik', *Hegel-Stud.* I, 1961, pp 173–99

'Zur Problematik des Selbstverständnisses', *Festschrift G. Krüger: Einsichten* Frankfurt, 1962, pp 71–85

'Dichten und Deuten', *Jb. d. Dtsch. Ak. f. Sprache u. Dichtung* 1960, pp 13–21

'Hermeneutik und Historismus, *Phil. Rundschau* 9, 1961; here reprinted pp 460–491

'Die phänomenologische Bewegung', *Phil. Rundsch.* 11, 1963, p 1ff

'Die Natur der Sache und die Sprache der Dinge', in *Problem der Ordnung*, *Dt. Kongr. f. Phil.* 6, Munich, 1960, Meisenheim, 1962

Über die Möglichkeit einer philosophischen Ethik', *Sein und Ethos, Walberger Stud.* I, 1963, pp 11–24

'Mensch und Sprache', *Festschrift D. Tschizewski* Munich, 1964

'Martin Heidegger und die Marburger Theologie', *Festschrift R. Bultmann,* Tübingen, 1964

'Ästhetik und Hermeneutik', a lecture at the Aesthetics Congress, Amsterdam, 1964

[3] E. Betti, *op cit*; F. Wieacker, *art cit*

[4] Becker, *art cit*

[5] In his *Traktat vom Schönen,* Frankfurt, 1935, Kurt Riezler attempted a transcendental deduction of the 'sense of quality'

[6] See H. Kuhn's recent work: *Vom wesen des Kunstwerkes* (1967)

[7] The vindication of allegory, which is pertinent here began some years ago with Walter Benjamin's major work, *Der Ursprung des deutschen Trauerspiels* (1927)

[8] On this point I can invoke Hans Sedlmayr's papers despite their admittedly different emphasis, now collected as *Kunst und Wahrheit* (Rowohlts Deutsche Enzycelopädie, 71) especially pp 87ff

[9] H. Kuhn, *loc cit*

[10] Betti, Wieacker, Hellebrand, *op cit*

[11] K. O. Apel, *op cit*

[12] Wittgenstein's concept of 'language games' seemed quite natural to me when I came across it. Cf 'The Phenomenological Movement', pp 37f

[13] My postscript to the Reclam edition of Heidegger's essay on the work of art (pp 108f) and, more recently, the essay in the FAZ of September 26, 1964. See also *Die Sammlung* 1965, no. 1

[14] O. Pöggeler has made an interesting suggestion (*art cit* pp 12f), about what Hegel would have said about this, through the mouth of Rosenkranz

PART ONE, SECTION I

[1] J. S. Mill, *System der deduktiven und induktiven Logik,* translated by Schiel, Book 6 (2nd edn 1863), 'Von der Logik der Geisteswissenschaften oder moralischen Wissenschaften'

[2] David Hume, *Treatise on Human Nature,* Introduction

[3] H. Helmholtz, *Vorträge und Reden,* 4th edn, I 'Uber das Verhältnis der Naturwissenschaften zur Gesamtheit der Wissenschaften', pp 167ff

[4] Especially since P. Duhem, whose great book *Etudes sur Léonard de Vinci,* 3 vols 1907ff, has since been supplemented by his posthumous work, which grew to ten volumes, *Le système du monde. Histoire des doctrines cosmologiques de Platon à Copernic* (1913ff)

[5] J. G. Droysen, *Historik* (reprint, 1925; ed. E. Rothacker), p 97

[6] W. Dilthey, *Gesammelte Schriften,* V, p lxxiv

[7] *loc cit,* XI, p 244

[8] *loc cit,* I, p 4

[9] *loc cit,* I, p 20

[10] Helmholtz, *loc cit,* p 178

[11] I. Schaarschmidt, *Der Bedautungswandel der Worte Bilden und Bildung,* Univ thesis (Königsberg, 1931)

[12] I. Kant, *Metaphysik der Sitten, Metaphysische Anfangsgründe der Tugendlehre* (Metaphysic of Morals) § 19

[13] G. W. F. Hegel, *Werke* 1832ff, xviii, *Philosophische Propädeutik, Erster Cursus* 41f

[14] Wilhelm von Humboldt, *Gesammelte Schriften*, Acadamie-ed, vi, 1, p 30

[15] Hegel, *Philosophische Propädeutik*, 41–45

[16] Hegel, *Phänomenologie des Geistes (Phenomenology of Spirit)*, ed Hoffmeister, pp 148ff

[17] Hegel, xviii, p 62

[18] Hegel, *Nurnberger Schriften*, ed. J. Hoffmeister, p 312

[19] Helmholtz, *loc cit*, p 178

[20] F. Nietzsche, *Unzeitgemässe Betrachtungen (Zweites Stück, Vom Nutzen und Nachteil der Historie für das Leben, 1)*

[21] The history of memory is not the history of the use of it. Mnemotechnics certainly make up a part of this history, but the pragmatic perspective in which the phenomenon of *memoria* appears there diminishes it. Rather, it should be Augustine who stands at the centre of the history of this phenomenon, for he totally transformed the Pythagorean-Platonic tradition that he received. We shall return later to the function of *mneme* in the question of induction. (Cf in *Umanesimo e Simbolismo*, Rome, 1958, ed Castelli, the essays of P. Rossi, 'La costruzione delli imagini nei trattati di memoria artificiale del Rinascimento', and G. Vasoli, 'Umanesimo e simbologia nei primiscritti lulliani e mnemotecnici del Bruno')

[22] *Logique de Port-Royal*, 4th part, ch 13ff

[23] J. B. Vico, *De nostri temporis studiorum ratione* (ed W. F. Otto, 1947)

[24] W. Jaeger, *Über Ursprung und Kreislauf des philosophischen Lebensideals*, Sitzungsberichte der Preuss, Akademie d. Wiss. Berlin 1928

[25] F. Wieacker, *Vom römischen Recht* 1945

[26] cf Nicholas of Cusa, who presents four dialogues, *De sapientia I, II, De mente, De staticis experimentis*, as the writing of an *idiota* (Heidelberger Akademie-Ausgabe v, 1937)

[27] Aristotle, *Eth. Nic.*, vi, 8, 1141 b 33: knowing what is good for oneself is one kind of knowledge

[28] Aquinas, *in Aristotelis librum de Anima Commentarium*, 425 a, 14f

[29] St. Thomas, *Summa Theol*, 1, 3 ad 2 end 78, 4 ad 1

[30] Tetens, *Philosophische Versuche*, 1777, published by the Kant-Gesellschaft, p 515

[31] *Discours préliminaire de l'Encyclopédie*, ed Köhler, Meiner 1955, p 80

[32] Cicero, *De oratore*, ii, 9.36

[33] Cf Leo Strauss, *The Political Philosophy of Hobbes*, ch vi

[34] Castiglione obviously played an important part in the transmission of this Aristotelian theme; cf Erich Loos, *Baldassare Castigliones 'Libro del cortegiano' (Analecta romanica*, F. Schalk, vol 2)

[35] Shaftesbury, *Characteristics*, Treatise ii, esp part iii, sect 1

[36] Marc Aur i

[37] Hutcheson calls the *sensus communis* simply 'sympathy'

[38] Thomas Reid, *The Philosophical Works*, ed Hamilton, 8th ed, 1895. In volume ii, p 774ff we find a detailed note by Hamilton on the *sensus communis*, which actually treats the large amount of material in a classificatory way, rather than historically. From a suggestion of Guenther Pflug, I gather that the first time that the *sensus communis* is found exercising a systematic function in philosophy is in Buffier (1704). That the knowledge of the world through the senses transcends all theoretical problems and is pragmatically justified is, in fact, an old motif of the Sceptics. But Buffier raises the *sensus communis* to the level of an axiom that is to be as much a basis for the

knowledge of the external world, *the res extra nos,* as the Cartesian *cogito* is for the world of consciousness. Buffier influenced Reid

39 Henri Bergson, *Ecrit et paroles* I (RM Mossé-Bastide), pp 84ff
40 I am quoting from *Die Wahrheit des sensus communis oder des allgemeinen Sinnes, in den nach dem Grundtext erklärten Sprüchen und Prediger Salomo oder das beste Haus—und Sittenbuch für Gelehrte und Ungelehrte* by M. Friedrich Christolph Oetinger (newly edited by Ehmann in 1861). For his generative method, Oetinger appeals to the rhetorical tradition and further quotes Shaftesbury, Fénélon and Fleury. According to Fleury *(Discours sur Platon)* the good thing about the method of orators is that it 'removes prejudices', and Oetinger says that Fleury is right when he maintains that orators have this method in common with the philosophers (p 125). According to Oetinger, the enlightenment is mistaken if it thinks that it is above this method. Our investigation will lead us to confirm this view of Oetinger's. For even though it is a form of the *mos geometricus,* ie the ideal of demonstration of the enlightenment, that he is attacking, something that is no longer of interest today, or is just starting to be so again, the same thing is true of the modern human sciences and their relationship to 'logic'
41 F. C. Oetinger, *Inquisitio in sensum communem et rationem* . . . (Tübingen, 1753). The following quotations are from this work.
42 'radicatae tendentiae . . . Habent vim dictatoriam divinam, irresistibilem'.
43 'in investigandis ideis usum habet insignem'.
44 'sunt foecundiores et defaecatiores, quo magis intelliguntur singulae in omnibus et omnes in singulis'.
45 Just at this point Oetinger remembers Aristotle's scepticism about having too youthful listeners present during the discussions of moral philosophy. Even this is a sign of how much he is aware of the problem of application. Cf p 279f above
46 I refer to Morus, *Hermeneutica,* I, II, XXIII
47 Tetens, *Philosophische Versuche über die menschliche Natur und ihre Entwicklung,* Leipzig 1777, I, p 520
48 Kant, *Kritik der Urteilskraft* (Critique of Judgement) 1799, 2nd ed, p vii. Meredith trans, Oxford 1952, p 5
49 Baumgarten, Metaphysics § 606: *perfectionem imperfectionemque rerum percipio, ie diiudico*
50 *Eine Vorlesung Kants über Ethik,* ed Menzer 1924, p 34
51 Cf p 37 above
52 *Critique of Judgement* § 40
53 *Critique of Practical Reason* 1787, p 124
54 *loc cit,* 1787, p 272; *Critique of Judgement,* § 60
55 *Critique of Pure Reason,* B 171ff
56 *Kritik der Urteilskraft* (1799, 3rd ed), p 157, *Critique of Judgement* § 40
57 *ibid,* p 64
58 Cf Kant's recognition of the importance of examples (and thus of history) as guidelines for judgment (B173)
59 The basic work on Gracian and his influence, especially in Germany, is Karl Borinski, *Balthasar Gracian und die Hofliteratur in Deutschland,* 1894. This has been supplemented more recently by F. Schummer's *Die Entwicklung des Geschmacksbegriffs in der Philosophie des 17. und 18. Jahrhunderts* (Archiv fur Begriffs-Geschichte I, 1955)
60 F. Heer is, I think, correct in discerning the origin of the modern concept of *Bildung* in the scholastic culture of the renaissance, reformation and counter-reformation. Cf *Der Aufgang Europas,* pp 82 and 570
61 Kant, *Kritik der Urteilskraft,* 1799, 3rd ed, p 233

[62] *Anthropologie in pragmatischer Hinsicht,* § 71

[63] Cf A. Boeumler, *Einleitung in die Kritik der Urteilskraft,* pp 280ff, esp 285

[64] *Kritik der Urteilskraft* 1799, 3rd ed, p 67

[65] This is where the idea of 'style' belongs. As an historical category it comes from the fact that the decorative is to be distinguished from the 'beautiful'. See Appendix I, p 449ff above

[66] *Kritik der Urteilskraft,* 1799, p vii

[67] *Critique of Pure Reason,* B173 (Kemp Smith trans)

[68] It was obviously this consideration which gave Hegel grounds for going beyond Kant's distinction between determinative and reflective judgment. He acknowledges the speculative meaning in Kant's doctrine of judgment, insofar as in it the universal is conceived as concretely existing in itself, but makes at the same time the reservation that in Kant the relation between the universal and the particular is still not treated as truth, but as something subjective (*Enz* § 55ff and similarly *Logik,* ed Lasson, II, 19). Kuno Fischer even says that in the philosophy of identity the distinction between the universal that is given and that which has to be found is removed (*Logik u. Wissenschaftslehre,* p 148)

[69] Aristotle's last word in the detailed description of the virtues and right behaviour is therefore always *hos dei* or *hos ho orthos logos.* What can be taught in the practice of ethics is *logos* also, but it is not *akribes* beyond a general outline. The decisive thing is finding the right nuance. The *phronesis* that does this is a *hexis tou aletheuein,* a state of being in which something hidden is made manifest, ie in which something is known. N. Hartmann, in the attempt to understand all the normative elements of ethics in relation to 'values', made this into the 'value of the situation', a strange extension of the table of the Aristotelian concepts of virtue

[70] Of course Kant does not fail to see that taste is decisive for cultivated behaviour as 'morality in the world of external appearances' (cf *Anthropol,* § 69), but he excludes it from the determination of the will by pure reason

[71] pp 6ff above

[72] Alfred Boeumler's excellent book, *Kants Kritik der Urteilskraft,* informatively examined the positive aspect of the connection between Kant's aesthetics and the problem of history. But we must also reckon up the losses

[73] Cf Paul Menzer, *Kants Ästhetik in ihrer Entwicklung,* 1952.

[74] *Kritik der Urteilskraft,* 1799, p 139, cf p 200 (Meredith pp 77, 169, 171, 179, 181)

[75] *ibid,* § 17 (p 54; Meredith p 75)

[76] *ibid,* § 20ff (p 64; Meredith p 82ff)

[77] *ibid* § 60

[78] *ibid,* p 264 (§ 60 Meredith p 227). Nevertheless, despite his critique of the English philosophy of moral feeling, he could not fail to see that this phenomenon of moral feeling is related to the aesthetic. In any case, when he says that pleasure in the beauty of nature is 'related to the moral', he is also able to say that moral feeling, this effect of practical judgment, is *a priori* a delight (*ibid,* p 169; Meredith § 42, p 159)

[79] *ibid,* § 16f

[80] Lessing, *Entwürfe zum Laokoon,* no 20b; in *Lessings sämtl. Schriften* ed Lachmann, 1886 ff, 14, p 415

[81] Note that from now on Kant is obviously thinking of the work of art and no longer chiefly of natural beauty

[82] Cf Lessing, *loc cit,* on the 'painter of flowers and landscape'. 'He imitates beauties which are not capable of any ideal', and this accords with the pre-eminent position of sculpture within the plastic arts

[83] Here Kant follows Sulzer, who accords a similar distinction to the human

form in the article 'Beauty' in his *Allgemeine Theorie der schönen Künste.*
For the human body is 'nothing but the soul made visible'. Undoubtedly Schiller, in his treatise *über Matthissons Gedichte,* writes in the same sense: 'The
realm of particular forms does not go beyond the animal body and the human
heart, therefore only in the case of these two (he means, as the context shows,
the unity of these two, animal corporality and heart, which comprise the dual
nature of man) can an ideal be set up'. But Schiller's work is virtually a
justification of landscape painting and landscape poetry with the help of the
concept of symbol and thus is a prelude to the later aesthetics of art

[84] *Vorlesungen über die Ästhetik,* ed Lasson, p 57: 'Hence the universal need
of the work of art is to be sought for within human thought, in that it is a way of
showing man what he is'

[85] *Vorlesungen über die Ästhetik,* ed Lasson, p 213

[86] Rudolf Odebrecht (in *Form und Geist, Der Aufstieg des dialektischen
Gedankens in Kants Ästhetik,* Berlin, 1930) recognised these connections

[87] Schiller rightly felt this when he wrote: 'If one has learned to admire the
writer only as a great thinker, one will rejoice to discover here a trace of his
heart'. *Über naive und sentimentalische Dichtung, Werke,* ed Güntter and
Witkowski, Leipzig 1910 ff, part 17, p 480

[88] *Kritik der Urteilskraft,* 1799, 3rd ed, p 179f (§ 45, Meredith p 166f)

[89] *ibid,* p 194 (§ 49 Meredith p 177)

[90] *ibid,* p 188 (Meredith p 172, § 48)

[91] *ibid,* p 161 (§ 35 Meredith p 143) 'Where imagination in its freedom arouses
the understanding'; also p 194: 'thus the imagination is creative here and sets in
motion the faculty of intellectual ideas (reason)'. (§ 49 Meredith p 177)

[92] *ibid,* pp 183f (§ 47 Meredith, pp 169ff)

[93] *ibid,* p li (§ vii)

[94] *ibid,* p lv ff (§ ix; Meredith p 38ff)

[95] *ibid,* p 181 (§§ 45-6; Meredith pp 166–168)

[96] Kant characteristically prefers 'or' to 'and'

[97] *ibid,* p x or lii. (Meredith Preface p 7 and § viii, p 36)

[98] *ibid,* § 48 ['soul' & 'soulless' from Meredith for Kant and Gadamer's *geist*
and *geistlos*]

[99] *ibid,* § 60

[100] *ibid,* § 49

[101] *ibid,* p 264 (§ 60)

[102] Seeing it, strangely, as a branch of painting and not of architecture (*ibid,* p
205 § 51, Meredith p 187), a classification that assumes the change of taste
from the French to the English ideal of the garden. Cf Schiller's treatise *über
den Gartenkalender auf das Jahr 1795.* Schleiermacher, however, in his
Ästhetik, ed Odebrecht, p 204) assigns English gardening to architecture, calling it 'horizontal architecture'

[103] The first *Fragment* of Schlegel (Friedrich Schlegel, *Fragmente, Aus dem
Lyceum,* 1797) shows to what extent the universal phenomenon of the beautiful
was obscured by the development that took place between Kant and his successors which I call 'the standpoint of art': 'We have many artists who are
properly works of art produced by nature'. In this expression we hear the
influence of Kant's explanation of the concept of genius as based on the favour
of nature, but it is so little valued that on the contrary it becomes an objection
against a lack of self-consciousness in artists

[104] Hotho's version of the lectures on aesthetics has given to natural beauty a
somewhat too independent position, as is shown by the Hegel's original arrangement as reconstructed by Lasson on the basis of lecture notes. Cf Hegel,

Sämtliche Werke, ed Lasson, vol xa, 1st half-volume (*Die Idee und das Ideal*), p xii, ff

[105] *Vorlesungen über die Ästhetik*, ed Lasson

[106] It was Luigi Pareyson, in his *L'estetica del idealismo tedesco* (1952), who brought out the importance of Fichte for idealist aesthetics. Similarly, the secret influence of Fichte and Hegel is observable within the whole neo-Kantian movement

[107] According to information from the *Deutsche Akademie* in Berlin, which had not, however, completed its compilation of examples of *Erlebnis*

[108] In describing a journey Hegel writes 'my whole experience (*Erlebnis*)', (*Briefe*, ed Horfmeister III, 179). It must be noted that it is a letter, in which one does not hesitate to use unusual expressions, especially colloquial ones, if no more customary word can be found. Thus Hegel also uses a similar expression (*Briefe* III, 55), 'now of my way of life (*Lebwesen*, a made-up word) in Vienna'. He was obviously looking for a generic term that did not yet exist (as is indicated also by the use of *Erlebnis* in the feminine gender)

[109] In Dilthey's biography of Schleiermacher (1870), in Justi's biography of Winckelmann (1872), in Hermann Grimm's *Goethe* (1877), and presumably frequently elsewhere

[110] *Dichtung und Wahrheit*, part II, book 7; *Werke*, Sophienausgabe, vol 27, p 110

[111] Zeitschrift für Völkerpsychologie, vol x; cf Dilthey's note on "Goethe und die dichterische Phantasie" (*Das Erlebnis und die Dichtung*, p 468ff)

[112] *Das Erlebnis und die Dichtung*, 6th ed, p 219; cf Rousseau, *Les Confessions*, part II, book 9. An exact correspondence cannot be found. Obviously it is not a translation, but a paraphrase of Rousseau's description

[113] *Zeitschrift für Volkerpsychologie*, loc cit

[114] Cf in the later version of the Goethe essay in *Das Erlebnis und die Dichtung*, p 177: 'Poetry is the representation and expression of life. It expresses experience (*Erlebnis*) and represents the external reality of life'

[115] Goethe's language was undoubtedly a major influence here: 'Only ask of a poem whether it contains something experienced *(ein Erlebtes)*' (*Jubiläumsausgabe* 38, p 326); or 'Books too have their experience (*ihr Erlebtes*)' (38, p 257). If the world of culture and of books is measured with this yardstick then it also is seen as the object of an experience. It is certainly not accidental that in a later Goethe biography, Friedrich Gundolf's book on Goethe, the idea of *Erlebnis* underwent a further terminological development. The distinction between *Ur-Erlebnis* (original experience) and *Bildungserlebnissen* (cultural experiences) is a logical development of the biographical concept from which the word *Erlebnis* came

[116] Cf, for example, Rothacker's surprise at Heidegger's critique of *Erleben*, directed entirely against the conceptual implications of Cartesianism: *Die dogmatische Denkform in den Geisteswissenschaften und das Problem des Historismus*, 1954, p 431

[117] *Akt des Lebens* ('act of life'), *Akt des gemeinschaftlichen Seins* ('act of communal being'), *Moment* ('initial element'), *eigenes Gefühl* ('one's own feeling'), *Empfindung* ('feeling'), *Einwirkung* ('influence'), *Regung als freie Selbstbestimmung des Gemüts* ('feeling as the free self-determination of the heart'), *das ursprünglich Innerliche* ('the original inwardness'), *Erregung* ('excitement') etc

[118] *Dilthey, Das Leben Schleiermachers*, 2nd ed, p 341. It is interesting that the reading *Erlebnisse* (which I consider the right one) is a correction given in the second edition (1922, by Mulert) for *Ergebnisse* in the original edition of

1870 (1st ed, p 305). If this is a misprint in the first edition, this the result of the closeness of meaning between *Erlebnis* and *Ergebnis* that we saw above. This can be elucidated by a further example. We read in Hotho (*Vorstudien für Leben und Kunst*, 1835) 'And yet this kind of imagination depends more on the memory of situations encountered (*erlebter Zustände*), experiences, rather than being itself originative. Memory preserves and renews the individuality and external appearance of these results (*Ergebnisse*) with all their circumstances and does not allow the universal to emerge for itself'. No reader would be surprised at a text which had *Erlebnisse* rather than *Ergebnisse* as here

[119] Cf E. Husserl, *Logische Untersuchungen* II, p 365, note; *Ideen zu einer reinen Phänomenologie und phänomenologischen Philosophie*, I, 65

[120] *Gesammelte Werke*, Musarionausgabe, XIV, p 50

[121] Cf Dilthey, VII, p 29ff

[122] This is why Dilthey later limits his own definition of *Erlebnis* when he writes: '*Erlebnis* is a qualitative being, i.e. a reality that cannot be defined through becoming it, but also reaches down into what is not possessed in a differentiated state'. (VII, p 230). He does not consciously realise the inadequacy of starting from subjectivity, but he expresses it in his linguistic hesitation: 'can one say: is possessed?'

[123] *Einleitung in die Psychologie nach kritischer Methode (1888); Allgemeine Psychologie nach kritischer Methode* (1912, new edition)

[124] *Die Grundlagen der Denkpsychologie*, 1921, 2nd ed, 1925

[125] *Einleitung in die Psychologie nach kritischer Methode*, p 32

[126] H. Bergson, *Les Données immédiates de la conscience*, p 76f

[127] Georg Simmel, *Lebensanschauung*, 2nd ed, 1922, p 13. We shall see later how Heidegger took the decisive step that made the dialectical play with the idea of life ontologically important (cf p 214ff above)

[128] F. Schleiermacher, *Über die Religion*, section II

[129] Georg Simmel, *Brücke und Tür*, ed Landmann, 1957, p 8

[130] Cf Simmel, *Philosophische Kultur Gesammelte Essays*, 1911, p 11–28

[131] E. R. Curtius, *European Literature and the Latin Middle Ages*, London 1953

[132] Cf also the contrast between symbolic and expressive language on which Paul Bockmann based his *Formgeschichte der deutschen Dichtung*

[133] *Critique of Judgement*, § 51

[134] *Allegoria* replaces the original *hyponia*: Plut *de aud poet*

[135] I prefer not to go into whether the meaning of *symbolon* as 'contract' depends on the character of the agreement itself or on its documentation

[136] *St Vet Fragm* II, 257f

[137] *Symbolikos kai anagogikos, de Coel Hier*, I, 2

[138] *Vorlesungen über Ästhetik*, ed Heyse, 1829, p 127

[139] It would be worth investigating when the word 'allegory' was transferred from the sphere of language to that of the plastic arts. Was it only in the wake of emblematics? (Cf P. Mesnard, "Symbolisme et Humanisme" in *Umanesimo e Simbolismo*, ed Castelli, Rome 1958.) In the eighteenth century, however, people always thought first of the plastic arts when speaking of allegories, and the liberation of poetry from allegory, as undertaken by Lessing, meant in the first place its liberation from the model of the plastic arts. Incidentally, Winckelmann's positive attitude to the idea of allegory is by no means in accord with contemporary taste or with the views of his contemporary theoreticians such as Dubos and Algarotti. He seems, rather, to be influenced by Wolff-Baumgarten when he demands that the painter's brush 'should be dipped in understanding'. Thus he does not dismiss allegory entirely, but refers to classical antiquity in order to evaluate modern allegories against them.

How little the general stigmatisation of allegory in the nineteenth century—like the way in which the concept of the symbolic is automatically opposed to it—is able to do justice to Winckelmann we can see from the example of *Justi* (I, p 430ff)

[140] He says, for example, in *Anmut und Würde* that the beautiful object serves as a 'symbol' for an idea (*Werke*, ed Güntter and Witkowski, 1910ff, part 17, p 322)

[141] Kant, *Kritik der Urteilskraft*, 3rd ed, p 260 (§ 59 Meredith p 225)

[142] The careful research of the philologists on the use of the word 'symbol' in Goethe (Curt Müller: *Die Geschichtlichen Voraussetzungen des Symbolbegriffs in Goethes Kunstanschauung*, 1933) shows how important the debate concerning Winckelmann's allegory-aesthetics was for his contemporaries and the significance that Goethe's view of art acquired. In their edition of Winckelmann, Fernow (I, p 219) and Heinrich Meyer (II, p 675ff) automatically accept the concept of the symbol as worked out in Weimar classicism. However quickly the influence of Schiller's and Goethe's usage spread, the word does not appear to have had any aesthetic meaning before Goethe. His contribution to the development of the concept of symbol obviously originates elsewhere, namely in protestant hermeneutics and sacramental theory, as Looff (*Der Symbolbegriff*, p 195) plausibly suggests by his reference to Gerhard. Karl-Philipp Moritz is a particularly good example of this. Although his view of art is filled entirely with the spirit of Goethe, he can still write in his criticism of allegory that allegory 'approaches mere symbol, in which beauty is no longer important' (quotation from Müller, p 201)

[143] *Farbenlehre, Des ersten Bandes erster, didaktischer Teil*, no 916

[144] Letter of April 3rd, 1818, to Schubart. The young Friedrich Schlegel says similarly (*Neue philosophische Schriften*, ed J. Körner, 1935, p 123) 'All knowledge is symbolic'

[145] Schelling, *Philosophie der Kunst* (1802; WW. V. p 411)

[146] Erwin, *Vier Gespräche über das Schöne und die Kunst*, II, p 41

[147] *loc cit*, v, p 1412

[148] F. Creuzer, *Symbolik*, I, § 19

[149] F. Creuzer, *Symbolik*, I, § 30

[150] *Ästhetik*, I, (*Werke* 1832 ff Vol x, 1) p 403

[151] Nevertheless we have the example of Schopenhauer to show that a usage which in 1818 conceived the symbol as the special case of a purely conventional allegory was still possible in 1859: *World as Will and Idea* § 50

[152] Here even Winckelmann appears in a false dependence, in the opinion of Klopstock (x, p 254ff): 'The two chief mistakes of most allegorical paintings are that they often cannot be understood at all, or only with great difficulty, and that they are, by nature, uninteresting . . . true sacred and secular history is what the greatest masters prefer to occupy themselves with. . . . Let the others treat the history of their own country. However interesting it may be, what has even the history of the Greeks and Romans to do with me?' Ausdrückliche Abwehr des minderen Sinnes der Allegorie (Verstandes-Allegorie) besonders bei den neueren Franzosen: Solger, *Vorlesungen zur Ästhetik*, p 133ff. Similarly Erwin II, p 49 Nachlass I, p 525

[153] F. T. Vischer, *Kritische Gänge: Das Symbol.* Cf the fine analysis in E. Volhard's *Zwischen Hegel und Nietzsche*, 1932, p 157ff and the genetic account by W. Oelmüller: *F. Th. Vischer und das Problem der nachhegelschen Ästhetik, 1959*

[154] E. Cassirer, *Der Begriff der symbolischen Form in Aufbau der Geisteswissenschaften*, p 29

[155] In this way one can sum up what is said in his letters *Über die ästhetische*

Erziehung des Menschen, eg in the fifteenth letter: 'there should be a harmony between the form instinct and the content instinct, ie a play instinct'
[156] *Kritik der Urteilskrat,* p 164
[157] 'And generally art partly completes what nature cannot bring to a finish and partly imitates her'. Aristotle, *Physics,* II, 199a 15 Ross trans
[158] *Über die Ästhetische Erziehung des Menschen,* twenty-seventh letter. Cf the excellent account of this process in M. Kuhn's *Vollendung der klassischen deutschen Ästhetik durch Hegel,* Berlin, 1931
[159] Cf E. Fink, 'Vergegenwartigung und Bild', *Jahrbuch für Philosophie und Phänomenologische Forschung,* XI (1930)
[160] Cf above p 12
[161] The pleasure derived from quotations as a social game is typical of this
[162] Cf also the masterly account of this development in W. Weidlé, *Die Sterblichkeit der Musen*
[163] Cf André Malraux, *La musée imaginaire,* and W. Weidlé *Les abeilles d'Aristée* Paris 1954. And yet in the latter the real consequence that follows from our hermeneutical investigation is missed, in that Weidlé still—in his criticism of the purely aesthetic—holds on to the act of creation as a norm, an act 'that precedes the work, but passes into the work itself and that I understand, that I look at, when I look at and understand the work'. (Quoted from the German translation, *Die Sterblichkeit der Musen,* p 181)
[164] Cf F. Rosenzweig, *Das älteste Systemprogram des deutschen Idealismus,* 1917, p 7
[165] Eg in the *Epigoni*
[166] Richard Hamann, *Ästhetik,* 1921, 2nd ed
[167] *Kunst und Köhnen,* Logos, 1933
[168] Aristotle, *De anima,* 425 a 25
[169] M. Scheler in *Die Wissensforsmen und die Gesellschaft,* 1926, p 397ff
[170] Georgiades' investigations (*Musik und Sprache,* 1954), on the relationship between vocal music and absolute music, seem to me to confirm this connection. Contemporary discussion about abstract art is, in my view, about to run itself into an abstract opposition of 'objective' and 'non-objective'. Actually the idea of abstraction has a polemical note; but polemics always presupposes something in common. Only abstract art does not simply detach itself from the relation to 'objectiveness', but keeps in the form of a privation. Beyond this it cannot go, insofar as our seeing is always seeing of objects. Thus only by regarding the habits of the practically directed seeing of 'objects' can such a thing as aesthetic vision exist—and what one disregards one cannot help seeing, one must even keep one's eye on it. Bernard Berenson says the same thing. 'What we generally call "seeing" is a practical agreement. . . .'; 'The plastic arts are a compromise between what we see and what we know' ("Sehen und Wissen", *Die Neus Rundschau,* 1959, pp 55–77
[171] Cf Rudolf Odebrecht, *loc cit* That Kant, in accordance with the classicist prejudice, opposed all colour to form and considered it part of the sensuous attraction, will not worry anyone familiar with modern painting, in which colours are used structurally
[172] *Kritik der Urteilskraft,* p 197
[173] One day someone should write the history of 'purity'. M. Sedlmayr, *Die Revolution in der modernen Kunst,* 1955, p 100, refers to calvinistic purism and the deism of the enlightenment. Kant, who strongly influenced the philosophical terminology of the nineteenth century, also followed directly on the classical Pythagorean and Platonic doctrine of purity (Cf G. Mollowitz, *Kants Platoauffassung, Kantstudien,* 1935). Is Platonism the common root of all

modern 'purism'? For the catharsis in Plato cf the unpublished thesis by Werner Schmitz, *Elenktik und Dialektik als Katharsis* (Heidelberg 1953)

[174] Paul Valéry, 'Introduction à la Méthode de Léonard e Vinci et son annotation marginale', *Varieté* I

[175] Cf my studies on the Prometheus symbol, *Vom geistigen Lauf des Menschen,* 1949

[176] The methodological justification of the 'artist's aesthetics' demanded by Dessoir and others is based on this point

[177] Cf Plato's remark on the superior knowledge of the user over the producer, *Republic* x, 601c

[178] It was my interest in this question that guided me in my Goethe studies. Cf *Vom geistigen Lauf des Menschen,* 1949; also my lecture "Zur Fragwürdigkeit des ästhetischen Bewusstseins" Venice, 1958 (*Rivista di Estetica,* III—A III pp 374–383)

[179] *Variété* III, Commentaires de Charmes: 'My verses have whatever meaning is given them', 'Mes vers ont le sens qu'on leur prête'

[180] In *Logos* VII 1917–18. Valéry compares the work of art with a chemical catalyst (*loc cit,* p 83)

[181] Oskar Becker, 'Die Hinfälligkeit des Schönen und die Abenteuerlichkeit des Künstler', *Husserl-Festschrift,* 1928, p 51

[182] Already in K. P. Moritz we read 'The work has already reached its highest goal in its formation, in its coming to be' (*Von der bildenden Nachahmung des Schönen,* 1788)

[183] Cf Hans Sedlmayr, 'Kierkegaard über Picasso' in *Wort und Wahrheit* 5, p 356ff

[184] The brilliant ideas of Oskar Becker on 'paraontology' seem to me to regard the 'hermeneutic phenomenology' of Heidegger too much as a statement of content and too little as one of methodology. In content the outcoming of this paraontology, which Oskar Becker himself attempts, logically thinking his way through the problems, comes back to the very point which Heidegger had fixed methodologically. The quarrel over 'nature' is repeated here, in which Schelling was deflated by the methodological consequence of Fichte's theory of science. If the attempt at paraontology is to acknowledge its complementary character, then it must transcend itself in the direction of something that includes both, a dialectic statement of the actual dimension of the question of being, which Heidegger has raised and which Becker does not appear to recognise as such when he points out the 'hyperontological' dimension of the aesthetic problem in order thus to determine ontologically the *subjectivity* of the artistic genius (see further his essay 'Künstler und Philosoph' in *Konkrete Vernunft, Festschrift für Erich Rothacker*

[185] Ed Hoffmeister, p 424ff

[186] The word *Weltanschauung* (cf A. Gätze, *Euphorion,* 1924) at first retains the relationship to the *mundus sensibilis,* even in Hegel, inasmuch as it is art, to the ideas of which the main world-views belong (*Aesthetik,* II, 131). But since according to Hegel the definiteness of a world-view is for the artist a thing of the past, the variety and relativity of world-view has become the concern of reflection and interiority.

PART ONE, SECTION II

[1] Aristotle, *Pol* VIII, 3 1337 b 39 and elsewhere Cf *Eth. Nic.* x, 6, 1176 b 33: *paizein hopos spoudaze kat' anacharsin orthos echein dokei*

² Kurt Riezler, in his brilliant *Traktat vom Schönen,* has started with the subjectivity of the player and hence preserved the antithesis of play and seriousness, so that the idea of play becomes too restricted for him and he has to say: 'We doubt whether the play of children is only play' and 'The play of art is not only play'

³ F. J. J. Buytendijk, *Wesen und Sinn des Spiels,* 1933

⁴ This obvious point must be made against those who seek to criticise the truth of Heidegger's statements on the basis of his etymological practice

⁵ Cf J. Trier, *Beiträge zur Geschichte der deutschen Sprache und Literatur* 67, 1947

⁶ J. Huizinga (*Homo ludens, Vom Ursprung der Kultur im Spiel,* p 43) points out the following linguistic facts: 'One can certainly say in German *ein Spiel treiben* ('to play a game') and in Dutch *een spelletje doen* (the same), but the appropriate verb is really *spielen* ('to play') itself. *Man spielt ein Spiel* ('one plays a game'). In other words, in order to express the kind of activity, the idea contained in the noun must be repeated in the verb. That means, it seems, that the action is of such a particular and independent kind that it is different from the usual kinds of activity. Playing is not an activity in the usual sense'. Similarly, the phrase *ein spielchen machen* (to take a hand) describes a use of one's time that is by no means play

⁷ Huizinga, *loc cit,* p 32

⁸ Rilke writes in the fifth Duino Elegy: 'wo sich das reine Zuwenig unbegreiflich verwandelt—umspringt in jenes leere Zuviel' ('where the sheer dearth is incomprehensibly transformed—switches into that void excess')

⁹ Friedrich Schlegel, *Gespräch über die Poesie* (*Friedrich Schlegels Jugendschriften,* ed J. Minor, 1882, II, p 364)

¹⁰ F. G. Junger, *Die Spiele*

¹¹ Huizinga, *loc cit,* p 17

¹² In numerous writings Adolf Portmann has made this criticism and given a new basis to the legitimacy of the morphological approach.

¹³ Cf Rudolf Kassner, *Zahl und Gesicht,* p 161f. Kassner states that 'the extraordinary unity and duality of child and doll' is connected with the fact that the fourth 'open wall of the audience' (as in a religious rite) is missing. I am arguing the other way round that it is precisely this fourth wall of the audience that closes the play world of the *world of art*

¹⁴ Cf note 13

¹⁵ I am making use here of the classical distinction in which Aristotle (*Eth. Eud.* B1; *Eth Nic* VI, 5, 1140 a 20) separates the *poesis* from the *praxis*

¹⁶ Plato, *Phileb,* 50b

¹⁷ Cf the recent research by Koller, *Mimesis,* 1954, which proves the original connection between *mimesis* and dance

¹⁸ Aristotle, *Poet.* 4 esp 1448 b 16: 'inferring what class each object belongs to; for example that this individual is a so-and-so' (Else trans)

¹⁹ *loc cit* 1448 b 10

²⁰ Kant, *Critique of Judgement,* § 48

²¹ Plato, *Phaed* 73ff

²² Plato, *Republic* X

²³ Aristotle, *Poet,* 9, 1451 b 6

²⁴ Anna Tumarkin has been able to show very clearly in the aesthetics of the eighteenth century the transition from 'imitation' to 'expression' (*Festschrift für Samuel Singer,* 1930)

²⁵ It is a problem of a particular kind whether the formative process itself should not be seen also as an aesthetic reflection on the work. It is undeniable that when he considers the idea of his work the creator can ponder and criti-

cally compare and judge various possibilities of carrying it out. But this sober awareness which is part of creation itself seems to me to be something very different from aesthetic reflection and aesthetic criticism, which is able to be stimulated by the work itself. It may be that what was the object of the creator's reflection, ie the possibilities of form, can also be the occasion of aesthetic criticism. But even in the case of this kind of agreement in content between creative and critical reflection the criterion is different. Aesthetic criticism is based on the disturbance of unified understanding, whereas the aesthetic reflection of the creator is directed towards establishment of the unity of the work itself. We shall see later the hermeneutical consequences of this point. It still seems to me a remnant of the false psychologism that stems from taste and genius aesthetics if one makes the processes of production and of reproduction coincide in the idea. This is to fail to appreciate the event of the success of a work, which goes beyond the subjectivity both of the creator and of the spectator or listener

[26] Although I think his analyses on the 'schematism' of the literary work of art have been too little noted, I cannot agree when R. Ingarden (in his 'Bemerkungen zum Problem des ästhetischen Werturteils', *Rivista di Estetica,* 1959) sees in the process of the concretisation of an 'aesthetic object' the area of the aesthetic evaluation of the work of art. The aesthetic object is not constituted in the aesthetic experience of grasping it, but the work of art itself is experienced in its aesthetic quality through the process of its concretisation and creation. In this I agree fully with L. Pareyson's aesthetics of *formativita*

[27] This is not limited to the interpretative arts, but includes any work of art, in fact any meaningful structure, that is raised to a new understanding, as we shall see later

[28] Hans Sedlmayr, *Kunst und Wahrheit,* 1958, p 140ff

[29] For the following, compare the fine analyses by R. and G. Koebner, *Vom Schönen und seiner Wahrheit,* 1957, which I came across only when my own work was completed. Cf the review in the *Philosophische Rundschau* 7, p 79

[30] Walter F. Otto and Karl Kerényi have noted the importance of the festival for the history of religions and anthropology (cf Karl Kerényi, *Vom Wesen des Festes,* Paideuma, 1938

[31] Aristotle refers to the characteristic mode of being of the *apeiron*; for instance in his discussion of the mode of being of the day, the games, and hence the festival—a discussion that does not forget Anaximander. (Physics III, 6, 206 a 20). Had Anaximander already sought to define the fact that the *apeiron* never came to an end in relation to such pure time phenomena? Did he perhaps intend more than can be conceived in the Aristotelian ideas of becoming and being? For the image of the day recurs in another connection with a special function: in Plato's *Parmenides* (131b) Socrates seeks to demonstrate the relation of the idea to things in terms of the presence of the day, which exists for all. Here by means of the nature of the day, there is demonstrated not what exists only as it passes away, but the unsharable presence and *parousia* of something that remains the same, despite the fact that the day is everywhere different. When the early thinkers thought of being, ie presence, did that which was presence for them appear in the light of a sacral communion in which the divine shows itself? The *parousia* of the divine is still for Aristotle the most real being, *energeia* (Met XIII, 7) which is limited by no *dunamei.* The character of this time cannot be grasped in terms of the usual experience of succession. The dimensions of time and the experience of these dimensions cause us to see the return of the festival only as something historical: the one and the same thing changes from time to time. But in fact a festival is not one and the same thing; it exists by being always something different. An entity that exists

only in always being something else is temporal in a radical sense: it has its being in becoming. Cf on the ontological character of the 'while' (*Weile*) M. Heidegger, *Holzwege*, p 322ff

[32] Cf my essay 'Zur Vorgeschichte der Metaphysik' on the relationship between '*Zein*' and '*Denken*' in Parmenides (*Anteile*, 1949)

[33] Cf what was said above on p 12 about culture, formation *(Bildung)*

[34] Cf Gerhard Krüger, *Einsicht und Leidenschaft. Das Wesen des platonischen Denkens*, first edition (1940). The Introduction in particular contains important insights. Since then a published lecture by Krüger (*Grundfragen der Philosophie*, 1958) has made his systematic intentions even clearer. Perhaps we may make a few observations on what he says. His criticism of modern thinking and its emancipation from all connections with 'ontic truth' seems to me without foundation. That modern science, however constructively it may proceed, has never abandoned and never can abandon its fundamental connection with experiment, modern philosophy has never been able to forget. One only has to think of Kant's question of how a pure natural science is possible. But one is also very unfair to speculative idealism if one understands it in the onesided way that Krüger does. Its construction of the totality of all determinants of thought is by no means the thinking out of some random view of the world, but desires to bring into thinking the absolute *a posteriori* character of experiment. This is the exact sense of transcendental reflection. The example of Hegel can teach us that even the renewal of classical conceptual realism can be attempted by its aid. Krüger's view of modern thought is based entirely on the desperate extremism of Nietzsche. However, the perspectivism of the latter's 'will-to-power' is not in agreement with idealistic philosophy but, on the contrary, has grown up on the soil which nineteenth century historicism had prepared after the collapse of idealist philosophy. Hence I am not able to give the same value as Krüger to Dilthey's theory of knowledge in the human sciences. Rather, the important thing, in my view, is to correct the philosophical interpretation of the modern human sciences, which even in Dilthey proves to be too dominated by the onesided methodological thinking of the exact natural sciences. I certainly agree with Krüger when he appeals to the experience of life and the experience of the artist. But the continuing validity of these for our thinking seems to me to show that the contrast between classical thought and modern thought, in Krüger's oversimplified formulation, is itself a modern construction.

If we are reflecting on the experience of art—as opposed to the subjectivisation of philosophical aesthetics—we are not concerned simply with a question of aesthetics, but with an adequate self-interpretation of modern thought in general, which has more in it than the modern concept of method recognises [35] E. Fink has tried to clarify the meaning of man's being outside himself in enthusiasm by making a distinction which is obviously inspired by Plato's *Phaedrus*. But whereas there the counter-ideal of pure rationality makes the distinction that between good and bad madness, Fink lacks a corresponding criterion when he contrasts 'purely human rapture' with that enthusiasm by which man is in God. For ultimately 'purely human rapture' is also a being away from oneself and an involvement with something else which man is not able to achieve of himself, but which comes over him, and thus seems indistinguishable from enthusiasm. That there is a kind of rapture which it is in man's power to induce and that enthusiasm is the experience of a superior power which simply overwhelms us: these distinctions of control over oneself and of being overwhelmed are themselves conceived in terms of power and therefore do not do justice to the interrelation of being outside oneself and being involved with something, which is the case in every form of rapture and enthusiasm. The forms of 'purely human rapture' described by Fink are themselves, if only they are not narcissistically and psychologically misinterpreted, modes of 'finite self-transcendence of finiteness' (cf Eugen Fink, *Vom Wesen des Enthusiasmus,* esp pp 22–25)

[36] Kierkegaard, *Philosophical Fragments,* ch 4, and elsewhere

[37] Richard Hamann, *Ästhetik,* p 97: 'Hence the tragic has nothing to do with aesthetics', Max Scheler, *Vom Umsturz der Werte,* 'Zum Phänomen des Tragischen': 'It is even doubtful whether the tragic is an essentially "aesthetic" phenomenon'. For the meaning of the word 'tragedy' see E. Staiger, *Die Kunst der Interpretation,* p 132ff

[38] Aristotle, *Poetics,* 13, 1453 a 29. Kierkegaard, *Either—Or* I

[39] Max Kommerell (*Lessing und Aristoteles*) has described this history of pity, but not distinguished sufficiently from it the original sense of *eleos.* Cf also W. Schadewaldt, "Furcht und Mitleid?" *Hermes* 83, 1955, p 129ff and the supplementary article by H. Flashar, *Hermes* 1956, pp 12–48

[40] Aristotle, *Rhet,* II, 13, 1389 b 32

[41] Cf M. Kommerell, who gives an account of the older interpretations: *loc cit,* pp 262–272. There have also been those who defend the objective genitive, eg K. H. Volkmann-Schluck in 'Varia Variorum' (*Festschrift für Karl Reinhardt,* 1952)

[42] Kierkegaard, *Either—Or,* I

[43] *ibid*

[44] Aristotle, *Poetics* 4, 1448 b 18: '. . . but by virtue of its workmanship or its finish or some other cause of that kind'. (Else trans)

[45] I acknowledge the valuable confirmation and help I received from a discussion that I had with Wolfgang Schöne at the conference of art historians of the evangelical academies (Christophorus-Stift) in Munster in 1956

[46] Cf *Eth. Nic.* II, 5, 1106 b 10

[47] This expression is Dagobert Frey's (cf his essay in the *Festschrift Jantzen*

[48] Cf W. Paatz, 'Von den Gattungen und vom Sinn der gotischen Rundfigur' (*Abhandlungen der Heidelberger Akademie der Wissenschaften,* 1951, p 24f)

[49] Cf W. Weischedel, *Wirklichkeit und Wirklichkeiten,* 1960 p 158ff

[50] It is not without reason that *zoon* also means simply 'picture'. We shall later have to check our results to see whether they have lost the connection with this model. Similarly, Bauch (see following note) says of *imago:* 'At any rate it is still a question of the picture in human form. This is the sole theme of mediaeval art!'

[51] Cf the history of the concept of *imago* in the period between the ancient world and the middle ages, in Kurt Bauch, *Beiträge zur Philosophie und Wissenschaft (W. Szilasi zum 70 Geburtstag),* pp 9–28

[52] Cf John Damascene, according to Campenhausen, *Zeitschrift für Theologie und Kirche,* 1952, p 54f, and Hubert Schrade, *Der verborgene Gott,* 1949, p 23

[53] The history of this word is very informative. The Romans used it, but in the light of the christian idea of the incarnation and the mystical body it acquired a completely new meaning. Representation now no longer means 'copy' or 'representation in a picture', or 'rendering' in the business sense of paying the price of something, but 'replacement'. The word can obviously have this meaning because what is represented is present in the copy. *Repraesentare* means 'to make present'. Canon law has used this word in the sense of legal representation. Nicolas of Cusa used it in this sense and gave both to it and the idea of the image a new systematic account. Cf G. Kallen, 'Die politische Theorie im philosophischen System des Nikolaus von Cues', *Historische Zeitschrift* 165 (1942), p 275ff, and his notes on *De auctoritate presidendi, Sitzungs Berichte der Heidelberger Akademie, phil.-hist. Klasse* 1935/36, 3, p 64ff. The important thing about the legal idea of representation is that the *persona repraesentata* is only the person represented, and yet the representative, who

is exercising the former's right, is dependent on him. It is curious that this legal sense of *repraesentatio* does not appear to have played any part in the prehistory of Leibniz's concept of representation. Rather, Leibniz's profound metaphysical theory of the *repraesentatio universi* which exists in every monad obviously follows the mathematical use of the idea. Thus *repraesentatio* here obviously means the mathematical 'expression' for something, the unambiguous orientation towards something else. The development into the subjective sphere, which is obvious in our concept of *Vorstellung*, originated in the subjectivisation of the concept of 'idea' in the seventeenth century, with Malebranche influencing Leibniz. Cf Mahnke, *Jahrbuch für Phänomenologie* IX, pp 519ff, 589ff

Repraesentatio in the sense of 'representation' on the stage—which in the middle ages can only mean in a religious play—can be found already in the thirteenth and fourteenth centuries, as E. Wolf, in his *'Die Terminologie des mittelalterlichen Dramas', Anglia,* 77, shows. But this does not mean that *repraesentatio* signifies 'performance', but signifies, until the seventeenth century, the represented presence of the divine itself, which takes place in the liturgical action. Thus here also, as with its use in canon law, the new meaning of the classical Latin word is based on the new theological understanding of church and ritual. The application of the word to the action itself—instead of what is represented in it—is an entirely secondary event, which presupposes the detachment of the theatre from its liturgical function

[54] The constitutional idea of representation assumes here a particular quality. It is clear that the meaning of representation determined by it always refers basically to a representative presence. Only because the bearer of a public function, the ruler, the official etc does not appear as a private individual, when he makes an official appearance, but in his function of which he is the representative, is one able to say of him that he is representing

[55] On the productive variety of meanings that the word *Bild* has and its historical background, cf the observation on p 11 above. That we no longer use the word *Urbild* ('original', 'model') to mean 'picture' is the late result of a nominalist understanding of being—as our analysis shows, this is an essential aspect of the 'dialectic' of the picture

[56] It seems to be established that *bilidi* in the Old High German always has the primary meaning of 'power' (cf Kluge-Gretze sv)

[57] Herodotus, *Hist* II, 53

[58] Cf Karl Barth, 'Ludwig Feuerbach' in *Zwischen den Zeiten* v, 1927, p 17ff

[59] This the sense of occasionality that has become customary in modern logic. A good example of the discrediting of occasionality by the aesthetics of experience is the mutilation of Hölderlin's *Rheinhymne* in the edition of 1826. The dedication to Sinclair seemed so alien that the last two stanzas were omitted and the whole described as a fragment

[60] Plato speaks of the proximity of the seemly (*prepon*) to the beautiful (*kalon*) *Hipp maj* 293 e

[61] J. Bruns' valuable book *Das literarische Porträt bei den Griechen* suffers from lack of clarity on this point

[62] Cf Appendix II, p 453 above

[63] Cf p 76 above

[64] Carl Justi, *Diego Velasquez und sein Jahrhundert,* I, 1888, p 366

[65] Cf Friedrich Heer, *Der Aufgang Europas*

[66] W. Kamlah in *Der Mensch in der Profanität* (1948) has tried to give the concept of the profane this meaning to characterise the nature of modern science, but also sees this concept as determined by its counter-concept, the 'acceptance of the beautiful'

[67] Above all in the first of E. Husserl's *Logische Untersuchungen,* in Dilthey's studies on the *Aufbau der geschichtlichen Welt* (Dilthey, VII) which are influenced by Husserl, and in M. Heidegger's analysis of the 'worldhood' of the world in *Being and Time* § 17 and 18

[68] I said above that the concept of a picture used here finds its historical fulfilment in the modern framed picture (p 119). Nevertheless, its 'transcendental' application seems legitimate. If for historical purposes mediaeval representations have been distinguished from the later 'picture' by being called *Bildzeichen* ('picture signs', D. Frey), much that is said in the text of the 'sign' is true of such representations but still the difference between them and the mere sign is obvious. Picture signs are not a kind of sign, but a kind of picture

[69] Cf above, pp 64–73, the distinction, in terms of the history of the two ideas, between 'symbol' and 'allegory'

[70] Schleiermacher rightly stresses (as against Kant, *Asthetik,* p 201) that the art of gardening is not part of painting, but of architecture

[71] Kant, *Kritik der Urteilskraft,* 1799, p 50, Meredith p 73, § 16

[72] Friedrich Nietzsche, *Also sprach Zarathustra. Ein Buch für alle und keinen* (A book for everyone and no one)

[73] R. Ingarden, in his *Das literarische Kunstwerke,* 1931, has given excellent analyses of the linguistic levels of literature and the mobility of visual fulfilment. But cf note 26 above

[74] Goethe, *Kunst und Altertum, Jubiläumsausgabe* 38, p 97, and the Conversation with Eckermann of 31 January, 1827

[75] Wilhelm Dilthey's *Gesammelte Schriften,* VII & VIII

[76] *ibid,* V

[77] Schleiermacher, *Ästhetik,* ed R. Odebrecht, pp 84ff

[78] G. W. F. Hegel, *Phänomenologie des Geistes,* ed Hoffmeister, p 524

[79] A remark in the *Ästhetik* (ed Hotho, II, p 233) indicates that to 'live within the reality' would not have been a solution for Hegel: 'It is useless to appropriate substantially, as it were, the world views of the past, ie to attempt to settle within one of those views by, for instance, becoming a catholic, as many have done in modern times for the sake of art and to achieve peace of mind . . .'

PART TWO

[1] Eg Augustine's *De doctrina christiana.* Cf G. Ebeling's article 'Hermeneutik' in RGG³

[2] Dilthey, *Die Entstehung der Hermeneutik, Gesammelte Schriften,* V, pp 317–338

[3] The hermeneutical principles of Luther's explanation of the bible have been investigated in detail, since K. Holl, chiefly by G. Ebeling (G. Ebeling, *Evangelische Evangelienauslegung. Eine Untersuchung zu Luthers Hermeneutik (1942)* and 'Die Anfänge von Luthers Hermeneutik' (ZThK, 1951, pp 172–230 and more recently, 'Wort Gottes und Hermeneutik' (ZThK 56, 1959). Here we must make do with a summary account that serves simply to make the necessary distinctions and clarify the move of hermeneutics into the historical sphere that came with the eighteenth century. For the actual problems of the *sola scriptura* position, cf G Ebeling's article 'Hermeneutik' in RGG³

[4] The simile of *caput* and *membra* is found also in Flacius

[5] The origin of the concept of system is obviously based on the same theological situation as hermeneutics. O. Ritschl's enquiry *System und systematische*

Methode in der Geschichte des wissenschaftlichen Sprachgebrauchs und in der philosophischen Methodologie, Bonn, 1906, is very instructive. It shows that because the theology of the reformation no longer desired to be an encyclopaedic assimilation of dogmatic tradition, but sought to reorganise christian teaching on the basis of important passages in the bible (*loci communes*), it tended towards systematisation—a statement that is doubly instructive when we consider the later emergence of the term 'system' in the philosophy of the seventeenth century. There too something new broke into the traditional structure of the total science of scholasticism: the new natural sciences. This new element forced philosophy into systematisation, ie the harmonisation of old and new. The concept of system, which has since become a methodologically essential requisite of philosophy, thus has its historical root in the divergence of philosophy and science at the beginning of the modern period, and it appears as something obviously to be required of philosophy only because this divergence between philosophy and science has since presented philosophy with its constant task

[6] Cf Dilthey II, p 126, note 3, dealing with Richard Simon's critique of Flacius

[7] Semler, who calls for this, still considers that he is serving the redemptive meaning of the bible, insofar as the man who understands it historically 'is now also able to speak of these objects in a way dictated by the changed times and the other circumstances of the men around us' (quoted from G. Ebeling, 'Hermeneutik', RGG³)—ie this is historical research in the service of the *applicatio*

[8] Dilthey, who notes this but evaluates it differently, writes as early as 1859: 'It should be noted that literary criticism, theology, history and philosophy . . . were not yet nearly so distinct as we are accustomed to think them. Heyne was the first to set up criticism as a separate discipline, and Wolf was the first to call himself a student of it' (*Der junge Dilthey,* p 88)

[9] C. Wolff and his school logically considered the 'general art of interpretation' as part of philosophy, since 'ultimately everything was directed towards our recognising and testing the truths of others when we understood what they said' (Walch, p 165). It is the same for Bentley, when he calls for the critic 'to have as his sole guides reason, the light of the author's ideas, and their compelling power' (quoted from Wegner, *Altertumskunde,* p 94)

[10] It is symptomatic of the triumph of historical thought that in his hermeneutics Schleiermacher still considers the possibility of interpreting Euclid subjectively, ie considering the genesis of his ideas (p 151)

[11] Thus Bacon understands his new method as an *interpretatio naturae.* Cf p 312 above

[12] *Einleitung zur richtigen Auslegung vernünftiger Reden und Schriften,* 1742

[13] J. Wach, whose three-volume work *Das Verstehen* remains entirely within the horizon of Dilthey's ideas

[14] That would certainly apply to Semler, whose statement, quoted above in note 7, shows the theological dimension of his demand for historical interpretation

[15] Which Ernesti places beside it, *Institutio interpretis* NT (1761), p 7

[16] J. J. Rambach, *Institutiones hermeneuticae sacrae* (1723), p 2

[17] *Hermeneutik,* § 15 and 16, *Werke* I, 7, p 29f

[18] *ibid* p 30

[19] F. Schleiermacher, Werke III, 3, p 390

[20] Hitherto our knowledge of Schleiermacher's hermeneutics rested on his lectures to the Academy of 1829 and the lecture on hermeneutics published by Lücke. The latter was reconstructed on the basis of a manuscript of 1819 and of lecture notes from Schleiermacher's last ten years. Even this external fact shows that it is to the late phase of Schleiermacher's thought—and not the

period of his fruitful beginnings with Friedrich Schlegel—that the hermeneutic theory we know belongs. It is this that, primarily through Dilthey, has been influential. The above discussion also starts from these texts and seeks to draw out their essential tendencies. However, Lücke's version is not quite free of elements that point to a development of Schleiermacher's hermeneutical thought and are deserving of attention. At my suggestion, Heinz Kimmerle has worked through the unpublished material in the hands of the *Deutsche Akademie* in Berlin and has published a critical revised text in the *Abhandlungen der Heidelberger Akademie der Wissenschaften* (1959, 2nd *Abhandlung*). In his thesis, quoted there, Kimmerle attempts to determine the direction of Schleiermacher's development. Cf his essay in *Kantstudien* 51, 4, pp 410ff

[21] 1, 7, p 262: 'Even though we shall never be able to achieve the complete understanding of every personal idiosyncrasy of the writers of the new testament, the supreme achievement is still possible, namely of grasping even more perfectly . . . the life that is common to them'

[22] *Werke* I, p 83

[23] *Werke* III, 3, pp 355, 358, 364

[24] *Enzyklopädie und Methodologie der philologischen Wissenschaften*, ed Bratuschek, 2nd ed, 1886, p 10

[25] In the context of his studies on poetic imagination Dilthey coined the term 'point of impression' and explicitly transferred its application from artist to historian (VI, p 283). We shall discuss later the significance of this application from the point of view of intellectual history. Its basis is Schleiermacher's concept of life: 'Where life exists, we have functions and parts held together'. The expression 'germinal decision' is found in his *Werke* I, p 168

[26] Schleiermacher, *Dialektik* (ed Odebrecht), p 569f

[27] *Dialektik*, p 470

[28] *Dialektik*, p 572

[29] *Ästhetik* (ed Odebrecht), p 269

[30] *Ästhetik*, p 384

[31] Schleiermacher, *Werke* I, 7, p 146f

[32] *Werke*, I, 7, p 33

[33] We learn from the new edition that the paradoxical formulation, whose origin we are here investigating, belongs to Schleiermacher's later period. This accords well with the tendency, discovered by Kimmerle, of turning away from the grammatico-rhetorical tradition to psychology (cf his *Introduction* p 14)

[34] The modern habit of applying a writer's interpretation of himself as a canon of interpretation is a product of a false psychologism. On the other hand, however, the 'theory', eg of music or poetics and rhetoric, can well be a legitimate canon of interpretation

[35] Steinthal, *Einleitung in die Psychologie und Sprachwissenschaft*, Berlin 1881

[36] V, p 335

[37] O. F. Bollnow, *Das Verstehen*

[38] *Werke* VI, p 337

[39] *Critique of Pure Reason* B 370

[40] "Zweite Einleitung in die Wissenschaftslehre", *Werke* I, p 485

[41] *ibid* p 479, note

[42] I owe to H. Bornkamm a neat example of how this formula, alleged to belong to the tools of literary criticism, presents itself automatically when one is indulging in polemical criticism. After applying Aristotle's idea of motion to the Trinity, Luther says (Sermon of December 25th, 1514, Weimar edition, I, p 28): *Vide quam apte serviat Aristoteles in philosophia sua theologiae, si non ut ipse voluit, sed melius intelligitur et applicatur. Nam res vere est elocutus et*

credo quod aliunde furatus sit, quae tanta pompa profert et jactat. I cannot think that the literary critics would recognise themselves in this application of their 'rule'.

[43] The way Schleiermacher introduces it suggests this: 'Yes, if the formula has anything true about it . . . then all it can mean is this . . .'. In his "Address to the Academy" (*Werke* III, 3, p 364) he avoids the paradox by writing: 'then he can give an account of himself to himself'. In the lecture manuscript of the same period (1828) we find also, 'to understand words first as well, and then better than the man who wrote them' (*Abh. der Heidelberger Akademie* 1959, 2nd *Abhandlung*, p 87). The aphorisms of Friedrich Schlegel from his *Philosophische Lehrjahre* present a confirmation of the above conjecture. Precisely at the time of his closest connection with Schleiermacher, Schlegel made the following note: 'To understand someone one must be first cleverer than he, then just as clever and just as stupid. It is not enough to understand the actual meaning of a confused work better than the author understood it. One must also be able to know, characterise and construct the principles of the confusion itself' (*Schriften und Fragmente*, ed Behler, p 158).

This passage proves again that 'understanding better' is still seen as entirely directed towards the object: 'better' means 'not confused'. But inasmuch as confusion is then made into an object of understanding and of 'construction', we see here the development that led to Schleiermacher's new hermeneutical principle. We have reached here the precise point of transition between the universal significance of the statement as understood by the enlightenment, and the new romantic interpretation of it. There is a similar transitional point in Schelling's *System des transz. Idealismus* (*Werke* III, p 623), where we find 'if a person says and maintains things, the meaning of which it was impossible for him to realise fully, either because of the age in which he lived or because of his other pronouncements, ie when he apparently expressed consciously what he could not really have been fully aware of . . .'. Cf Chladenius' distinction quoted on p 162 above, between understanding an author and understanding a text. As evidence of the original rationalistic meaning of the formula we offer a recent approximation to it by a quite unromantic thinker who undoubtedly combines with it the criterion of criticism of the object, cf *Husserliana*, 6, p 74

[44] *Das Leben Schleiermachers*, 1st ed, Appendix, p 117
[45] C. Hinrichs, *Ranke und die Geschichtstheologie der Goethezeit* (1954). Cf my review in the *Philosophische Rundschau* 4, p 123ff
[46] Ranke, *Weltgeschichte* IX, p 270
[47] Ranke, *Lutherfragmente* 1
[48] Cf Gerhard Masur, *Rankes Begriff der Weltgeschichte*, 1926
[49] Ranke, *Weltgeschichte* IX, p xiv
[50] Ranke, *Weltgeschichte* IX, p xiiif
[51] In my book *Volk und Geschichte im Denken Herders* (1942) I have shown that Herder applied Leibniz's concept of power to the historical world
[52] Hegel, *Phänomenologie des Geistes*, p 120ff (*Hoffmeister*)
[53] Plato, *Charmides*, 169a
[54] Hegel, *Enzyklopädie* § 136f, and his *Phänomenologie* (*Hoffmeister*), p 105ff; *Logik* (Lasson), p 144ff
[55] Ranke, *Das politische Gespräch* (ed Rothacker), p 72
[57] It is highly indicative of the hidden spirit of the historical school that Ranke (and he not alone in this) thinks and writes the word *subsummieren* ('subsume') as *summieren* ('sum up', 'aggregate') eg *loc cit*, p 63
[58] Cf K. Löwith, *Weltgeschichte und Heilsgeschehen*, and my article "Geschichtsphilosophie" in RGG, 3rd ed

[59] Ranke, *Weltgeschichte* IX, 2, xiii

[60] Ranke, *Weltgeschichte* IX, 1, p 270f

[61] Cf Hinrichs, *Ranke und die Geschichtstheologie der Goethezeit*, p 239f

[62] Cf Löwith, *Weltgeschichte und Heilsgeschehen*, ch 1

[63] Ranke, *Weltgeschichte* IX, 2, pp 5, 7

[64] 'For this is, as it were, a share in divine knowledge' (Ranke, ed Rothacker, p 43, also p 52)

[65] Ranke (ed Rothacker), p 52

[66] *Gesammelte Schriften* V, p 281

[67] *Lutherfragmente* 13

[68] *Lutherfragmente* 1

[69] To Heinrich Ranke, Nov 1828 (*Zur eigenen Lebensgeschichte*, p 162)

[70] Droysen (ed Rothacker), p 65

[71] *Ibid*, p 65

[72] Cf Droysen, *Auseinandersetzung mit Buckle* (Rothacker's ed, p 61)

[73] Johann Gustav Droysen, *Historik*, ed R. Hübner (1935), p 316, based on notes taken by Friedrich Meineke

[74] Both through his long introduction to vol V of Dilthey's collected works and his account of Dilthey in his book *Lebensphilosophie und Phänomenologie*, 1st ed, 1930

[75] O. F. Bollnow, *Dilthey*, 1936

[76] *Gesammelte Schriften* VII, p 281

[77] The early form of the problem of knowledge which we find in classical antiquity with, say, Democritus and which the neo-Kantian historians also read into Plato, was on another basis. The discussion of the problem of knowledge, which began with Democritus, ended in fact with the Sceptics (cf Paul Natorp, *Studien zum Erkenntnisproblem im Altertum* (1892) and my paper 'Antike Atomtheorie', *Zeitschrift für die ges. Naturwissenschaften*, 1935

[78] P. Duhem, *Etudes sur Léonard de Vinci*, 3 vols, Paris, 1955; *Le système du monde*, X

[79] Cf H. Rickert's book of the same name, *Der Gegenstand der Erkenntnis*

[80] Cf the analysis of the historicity of experience, p 310ff above

[81] *Gesammelte Schriften* VII, p 278

[82] VII, p 278

[83] VII, p 27f; p 230

[84] V, p 177

[85] Dilthey, VII, p 282ff. Georg Simmel tries to solve the same problem by the dialectic of the subjectivity of the experience and the continuity of the object—ie ultimately psychologically. Cf *Brücke und Tor*, p 82f

[86] Dilthey: *Der Aufbau der geschichtlichen Welt in den Geisteswissenschaften* (Gesammelte Schriften VII)

[87] VII, p 13a

[88] V, p 266

[89] VII, pp 157, 280, 333

[90] VII, p 280

[91] O. F. Bollnow, in his *Dilthey*, p 168f, saw correctly that in Dilthey the concept of power was pushed too much into the background. This is a sign of the victory of romantic hermeneutics over Dilthey's thinking

[92] VII, p 148

[93] *Hegels theologische Jugendschriften*, ed Nohl, p 139f

[94] VII, p 136

[95] VIII, p 224

[96] Dilthey's fundamental work, *Die Jugendgeschichte Hegels*, which ap-

peared first in 1906 and was supplemented by posthumous manuscripts in vol
IV of the *Gesammelten Schriften* (1921), opened up a new epoch in Hegel
studies, less because of its results than because of the task it had set itself. It
was soon joined by the publication of the *Theologische Jugendschriften* by
Hermann Nohl in 1911, writings which Theodor Haering's penetrating commentary (*Hegel* I, 1928) opened up. Cf the present author's 'Hegel und der
geschichtliche Geist' (*Zeitschrift für die gesamte Staatswissenschaft*, 1939)
and Herbert Marcuse, *Hegels Ontologie und die Grundlegung einer Theorie
der Geschichtlichkeit*, 1932, which showed the exemplary function of the concept of life for the *Phenomenology of Mind*

[97] In detail in the posthumous notes on his *Jugendgeschichte Hegels* (IV, pp
217–258), and more profoundly in the third chapter of his *Aufbau* (p 146ff)

[98] VII, p 150

[99] V, p 265

[100] VII, p 136

[101] V, p 339ff, and VIII

[102] *Leben Schleiermachers*, ed Mulert, 1922, p xxxi

[103] *Leben Schleiermachers*, 1st ed, 1870; *Denkmale der inneren Entwicklung
Schleiermachers*, p 118. Cf *Monologen*, p 417

[104] VII, p 291: 'Life and history have a significance just like the letters of a
word'.

[105] V, p 277

[106] Cf, in particular, what Max Scheler says concerning this in *Zur Phänomenologie und Theorie der Sympathiegefühle und von Liebe und Hass*,
1913

[107] *Historik* § 41

[108] He also follows Schleiermacher, who sees old age as a model only in a very
qualified sense. Cf the following note on Schleiermacher (in Dilthey's *Leben
Schleiermachers*, 1st ed, p 417): 'The dissatisfaction of age over the real world
in particular is a misunderstanding of youth and its joy, which was also not
concerned with the real world. Old men's dislike of new times is elegiac. So the
historical sense is highly necessary in order to attain eternal youth, which is not
a gift of nature, but something acquired through freedom'.

[109] V, p 278

[110] VII, p 99

[111] An eloquent exponent of this 'method' is E. Rothacker, whose own con-
tributions to the subject actually testify effectively to the opposite; cf the
nonmethodical character of his brilliant ideas and bold syntheses

[112] Yorck von Wartenburg, Paul Graf: *Briefwechsel*, 1923, p 193

[113] *Wissenschaft der Logik* II, ed Lasson, 1934, p 36f

[114] VII, p 18

[115] VII, p 207

[116] VII, p 347

[117] VII, p 290

[118] V, p 364

[119] VII, p 6

[120] VII, p 6

[121] VII, p 3

[122] This has also been pointed out by Misch, *Lebensphilosophie und Phänomenologie*, p 295, and esp 321ff. Misch distinguishes between becoming
conscious and making conscious. Philosophical reflection may be both at once.
But Dilthey, he says, wrongly seeks an unbroken transition from the one to the

other. 'The essentially *theoretical* orientation towards objectivity cannot be derived solely from the idea of the objectification of life' (p 298). The present work gives this criticism by Misch another facet, in that it reveals in romantic hermeneutics the Cartesianism that makes Dilthey's thought here ambiguous
[123] VII, p 6

[124] An original Schleiermacher text has crept into the material from Dilthey's posthumous papers for the *Aufbau* (vol VII), p 225, *Hermeneutik*, which Dilthey had already printed in the appendix to his Schleiermacher biography—an indirect proof that Dilthey never really got over his romantic beginnings. It is often hard to distinguish his own writing from the excerpts

[125] See the nice misprint above, note 118 to Part one

[126] VII, p 291

[127] VII, p 333

[128] VII, p 148

[129] As early as 1923 Heidegger spoke to me with admiration of the late writings of Georg Simmel. This was not just a general acknowledgement of Simmel as a philosopher. The specific stimulus that Heidegger had received from his work will be apparent to anyone who today reads, in the first of the four 'Metaphysical Chapters' gathered together under the title *Lebensanschauung*, what the dying Simmel conceived as his philosophical task. There we read: 'Life is truly the past and the future'. He calls 'the transcendence of life the true absolute', and the essay concludes: 'I know very well what logical obstacles there are to the conceptual expression of this way of seeing life. I have tried to formulate them, in full awareness of the logical danger, since it is *possible* that we have reached here the level at which logical difficulties by no means command us to be silent—because it is the same level as that from which is nourished the metaphysical root of logic itself'.

[130] Cf Natorp's critique of Husserl's *Ideas* (1914) in *Logos*, 1917, and Husserl himself in a private letter to Natorp of June 29th, 1918: '—and I may perhaps point out that I overcame the stage of static Platonism more than ten years ago and established the idea of transcendental genesis as the main subject of phenomenology'. O. Becker's note in the Husserl *Festschrift*, p 39, says more or less the same thing

[131] VI, p 344

[132] VI, p 346

[133] VI, pp 339, 271

[134] *Husserliana*, IV, 1952

[135] VI, p 169, note 1

[136] VI, p 169

[137] *Einleitung in die Psychologie nach kritischer Methode*, 1888; *Allgemeine Psychologie nach kritischer Methode*, 1912

[138] III, p 390. 'The great mistake of starting from the natural world (without characterising it as world)' (1922) and the more detailed self-criticism of III, p 399 (1929). According to *Husserliana* VI, p 267, the concepts of 'horizon' and of 'horizon consciousness' were in part suggested by William James' idea of 'fringes'

[139] I, p xviii

[140] VI, p 148

[141] *Husserliana* VI, p 501

[142] As does E. Fink in his paper 'L'analyse intentionelle et le problème de la pensée spéculative', in *Problèmes actuels de la phénoménologie*, 1952

[143] VI, § 34; p 265f

[144] VI, p 116

[145] It is hard to see how the recent attempts to play off the being of 'nature' against historicity can maintain themselves in the face of this *methodologically* intended verdict

[146] D. Sinn, in his thesis, *Die transzendentale Intersubjektivität mit ihren Seinshorizonten bei E. Husserl*, Heidelberg, 1958, saw the methodological-transcendental significance of the concept of 'empathy' behind the constitution of intersubjectivity, which escaped Alfred Schuetz in his 'Das Problem der transzendentalen Intersubjektivität bei Husserl', *Philosophische Rundschau* v, 1957, vol 2

[147] I am referring here to the broad perspectives suggested by Viktor von Weizsäcker's concept of the *Gestaltkreis*

[148] *Bewusstseinsstellung und Geschichte*, Tübingen, 1956

[149] *op cit*, p 39

[150] *loc cit*

[151] *loc cit*

[152] *Phänomenologie des Geistes*, ed Hoffmeister, p 128

[153] Cf on this subject the important observations of A. de Waelhens, *Existence et signification*, Louvain, 1957, pp 7–29

[154] It is notable that in all the *Husserliana* to date there has been hardly any treatment of Heidegger by name. There are, undoubtedly, more than mere biographical reasons for this. Rather, Husserl may have seen that he was constantly caught up in the ambiguity that made Heidegger's *Being and Time* appear sometimes like transcendental phenomenology and sometimes like its critique. He recognised his own ideas in it, and yet they appeared in quite a different light; in, as it seemed to him, a polemical distortion

[155] As O. Becker was quick to point out in the Husserl *Festschrift* p 39

[156] *Being and Time*, § 77

[157] *Being and Time*, p 153

[158] Cf Betti's almost angry polemic in his scholarly and brilliant treatise *Zur Grundlegung einer allgemeinen Auslegungslehre*, p 91, note 14b

[159] Even the history of the meaning of the word *Verstehen* ('understanding') points in this direction. The original meaning seems to have been the legal sense of the word, ie representing a case before a court. That the word then developed an intellectual sense is obviously due to the fact that to represent a case in court involves understanding it, ie mastering it to such an extent that one is able to cope with all the possible moves of the opposing party and to assert one's own legal standpoint

[160] *Briefwechsel mit Dilthey*, p 191

[161] Cf F. Kaufmann, 'Die Philosophie des Grafen Paul Yorck von Wartenburg', *Jahrbuch für Philosophie und phänomenologische Forschung*, IX, Halle, 1928, p 50ff

[162] *Being and Time*, pp 181, 192 *et passim*

[163] O. Vossler has shown, in *Rankes historisches Problem*, that this phrase of Ranke's is not as naive as it sounds, but is directed against the 'superior attitude' of a moralistic school of history-writing

[164] Cf p 295 above

[165] O. F. Bollnow, *Das Wesen der Stimmungen*

[166] *Über den Humanismus*, Berne, 1947, p 69

[167] Cf Appendix III, p 455f above

[168] Heidegger, *Being and Time*, p 312ff

[169] Cf Schleiermacher's *Hermeneutik* (ed H. Kimmerle in *Abhandlungen der Heidelberger Akademie*, 1959, 2nd *Abhandlung*), which is explicitly commit-

ted to the old ideal of technique (p 127, note: 'I . . . hate it when theory does not go beyond nature and the bases of art, whose object it is'

[170] Cf E. Staiger's description, which is in accord with that of Heidegger, in *Die Kunst der Interpretation,* p 11ff. I do not however, agree that the work of a literary critic begins only 'when we are in the situation of a contemporary reader'. This is something we never are, and yet we are capable of understanding, although we can never achieve a definite 'personal or temporal identity' with, the author. Cf also Appendix IV, pp 456–57 above

[171] *Being and Time,* pp 312ff

[172] Cf Leo Strauss, *Die Religionskritik Spinozas,* p 163: 'The word "prejudice" is the most suitable expression for the great aim of the enlightenment, the desire for free, untrammeled verification; the *Vorurteil* is the unambiguous polemical correlate of the very ambiguous word "freedom" '

[173] *Praeiudicium auctoritatis et precipitantiae,* which we find as early as Christian Thomasius's *Lectiones de praeiudiciis* (1689/90) and his *Einleitung der Vernunftlehre,* ch 13, §§ 39/40. Cf the article in Walch's *Philosophisches Lexikon* (1726), p 2794ff

[174] At the beginning of his essay, 'Beantwortung der Frage: Was ist Aufklärung?' (1784)

[175] The enlightenment of the classical world, the fruit of which was Greek philosophy and its culmination in sophism, was quite different in nature and hence permitted a thinker like Plato to use philosophical myths to convey the religious tradition and the dialectical method of philosophising. Cf Erich Frank, *Philosophische Erkenntnis und religiöse Wahrheit,* p 31ff, and my review of it in the *Theologische Rundschau* 1950 (pp 260–266). Cf also Gerhard Krüger, *Einsicht und Leidenschaft,* 2nd ed 1951

[176] A good example of this is the length of time it has taken for the authority of the historical writing of antiquity to be destroyed in historical studies and how slowly the study of archives and the research into sources have established themselves (cf R. G. Collingwood, *Autobiography,* Oxford, 1939, ch 11, where he more or less draws a parallel between the turning to the study of sources and the Baconian revolution in the study of nature)

[177] Cf what we said about Spinoza's theological-political treatise, p 159f above

[178] As we find, for example, in G. F. Meier's *Beiträge zu der Lehre von den Vorurteilen des menschlichen Geschlechts,* 1766

[179] I have analysed an example of this process in a little study on Immermann's 'Chiliastische Sonette' (*Die Neue Rundschau,* 1949)

[180] Horkheimer and Adorno seem to me right in their analysis of the 'dialectic of the enlightenment' (although I must regard the application of sociological concepts such as 'bourgeois' to Odysseus as a failure of historical reflection, if not, indeed, a confusion of Homer with Johann Heinrich Voss [author of the standard German translation of Homer], who had already been criticised by Goethe)

[181] Cf the reflections on this important question by G. von Lukács in his *History and Class Consciousness,* London 1969 (orig 1923)

[182] Rousseau, *Discours sur l'origine et les fondements de l'inégalité parmi les hommes*

[183] Cf the present author's *Plato und die Dichter,* p 12f

[184] Walch, *Philosophisches Lexicon* (1726), p 1013

[185] Walch, *op cit,* p 1006ff under the entry *Freiheit zu gedenken.* See p 241 above

[186] Schleiermacher, *Werke* 1, 7, p 31

187 The notorious statement, 'The party (or the Leader) is always right' is not wrong because it claims that a certain leadership is superior, but because it serves to shield the leadership, by a dictatorial decree, from any criticism that might be true. True authority does not have to be authoritarian

188 Cf Aristotle's *Eth Nic* bk 10, ch 9

189 I don't agree with Scheler that the pre-conscious pressure of tradition decreases as historical study proceeds (*Stellung des Menschen im Kosmos,* p 37). The independence of historical study implied in this view seems to me a liberal fiction of a sort that Scheler is generally able to see through. (Cf similarly in his *Nachlass* I, p 228ff where he affirms his faith in the historical enlightenment, or that of the sociology of knowledge)

190 The congress at Naumburg on the classical (1930), which was completely dominated by Werner Jaeger, is as much an example of this as the founding of the periodical *Die Antike.* Cf *Das Problem des Klassischen und die Antike* (1931)

191 Cf the legitimate criticism that A. Körte made of the Naumburg lecture by J. Stroux, in the *Berichte der Sächsischen Akademie der Wissenchaften* 86, 1934, and my note in *Gnomon* 11 (1935), p 612f

192 Thus the *Dialogus de oratoribus,* rightly, received special attention in the Naumburg discussions on the classical. The reasons for the decline of rhetoric include the recognition of its former greatness, ie a normative awareness. B. Snell is correct when he points out that the historical stylistic concepts of 'baroque', 'archaic' etc all presuppose a relation to the normative concept of the classical and have only gradually lost their pejorative sense: 'Wesen und Wirklichkeit des Menschen'. *Festschrift für H. Plessner,* p 333ff

193 Hegel, *Ästhetik* II, 3

194 Friedrich Schlegel (*Fragmente,* Minor 20) draws the hermeneutical consequence: 'A classical work of literature can never be completely understood. But those who are educated and educating themselves must always desire to learn more from it'

195 In a lecture on aesthetic judgment at a conference in Venice in 1958 I tried to show that it too, like historical judgment, is secondary in character and confirms the 'anticipation of completion'. (It appeared in the *Rivista di Estetica,* M A III, 1958, under the title 'Zur Fragwürdigkeit des ästhetischen Bewusstseins')

196 There is one exception to this anticipation of completion, namely the case of writing that is presenting something in disguise, eg a *roman à clef.* This presents one of the most difficult hermeneutical problems (cf the interesting remarks by Leo Strauss in *Persecution and the Art of Writing*). This exceptional hermeneutical case is of special significance, in that it goes beyond interpretation of meaning in the same way as when historical source criticism goes back behind the tradition. Although the task here is not a historical, but a hermeneutical one, it can be performed only by using understanding of the subject as a key to discover what is behind the disguise—just as in conversation we understand irony to the extent to which we are in agreement on the subject with the other person. Thus the apparent exception confirms that understanding involves agreement

197 Cf p 162 above

198 *Eth Nic* I, 7

199 Pp 258 and 262 above

200 The structure of the concept of situation has been illuminated chiefly by K. Jaspers (*Die geistige Situation der Zeit*) and Erich Rothacker

[201] Cf p 216ff above

[202] Nietzsche, *Unzeitgemässe Betrachtungen* II, at the beginning

[203] Rambach's *Institutiones hermeneuticae sacrae* (1723) are strongly influenced by Oetinger. Cf P. Herbers' Heidelberg thesis (1952)

[204] *Solemus autem intelligendi explicandique subtilitatem (soliditatem vulgo vocant) tribuere ei, qui cum causis et accurate* (exactly and thoroughly) *intellegit atque explicat* (Morus 8). Here the humanistic *subtilitas* is misunderstood because of the enlightenment's methodological ideal

[205] Cf Betti's treatise, quoted above Note 158, p 522, and his monumental work, *Teoria generale dell' interpretazione*, 2 vols, Milan, 1956

[206] Cf the analysis of the ontology of the work of art in Part One, p 91ff above

[207] Cf the distinctions in Max Scheler: *Wissen und Bildung*, 1927, p 26

[208] Cf p 22ff and p 38 above

[209] *Eth Nic* I, 4

[210] Cf *Eth Nic* I, 7; II, 2

[211] The final chapter of the *Nicomachean Ethics* gives the fullest expression to this requirement and thus forms the transition to the *Politics*

[212] We shall be following here the sixth book of the *Nicomachean Ethics*, unless it is stated to the contrary

[213] Plato, *Apology* 22 cd

[214] *Eth Nic* VI, 8, 1141 b3, 1142 a30; *Eth Eud* VIII, 2, 1246 b36

[215] *Werke*, 1832, XIV, p 341

[216] *Eth Nic* VI, 8

[217] *Eth Nic* V, 10

[218] *Lex superior preferenda est inferiori*, writes Melanchthon in his explanation of the *ratio* of *epiekeia* (in the earliest version of Melanchthon's *Ethics*, ed by H. Heineck, Berlin, 1893, p 29)

[219] Above, p 36ff

[220] *Ideo adhibenda est ad omnes leges interpretatio quae flectat eas ad humaniorem ac leniorem sententiam* (Melanchthon, 29) [Therefore an interpretation should be applied to every law that would bend it to more humane and lenient decisions]

[221] Cf the excellent critique by H. Kuhn of L. Strauss's *Naturrecht und Geschichte*, 1953, in the *Zeitschrift für Politik*, 3rd year, vol 4, 1956

[222] *Eth Nic* V, 10. The distinction itself originates, of course, with the sophists, but it loses its destructive meaning through Plato's restriction of the *logos*, and its positive meaning in law emerges only in Plato's *Statesman* (294ff) and in Aristotle

[223] The train of thought in the parallel place in the *Magna Moralia* (I, 33, 1194 b 30–95 a 7) cannot be understood unless one does this. 'Do not suppose that if things change owing to our use, there is not therefore a natural justice; because there is'. (Ross trans)

[224] Cf Melanchthon, *loc cit*, p 28

[225] Aristotle says in general that *phronesis* is concerned with the means (*ta pros to telos*) and not with the *telos* itself. It is probably the contrast with the Platonic conception of the idea of the good that makes him emphasise that. That *phronesis* is not simply the capacity to make the right choice of means, but is itself a moral *hexis* that also sees the *telos* towards which the person acting is aiming with his moral being, emerges clearly from its place within the system of Aristotle's ethics. Cf, in particular, *Eth Nic* VI, 10, 1142 b 33; 1140 b 13; 1141 b 15. I was glad to see that H. Kuhn, in his essay 'Die Gegenwart der

Griechen', *Gadamerfestschrift*, 1960, now does full justice to this situation, although he tries to demonstrate that there is an ultimate 'preferential choice that makes him place Aristotle after Plato' (p 134ff)

[226] *Eth Nic* VI, 9, 1142 a25ff

[227] Cf p 320ff above

[228] *gnóme, suggnóme* (fellow-feeling, forbearance, forgiveness)

[229] *Eth Nic* VI, 13, 1144 a 23ff

[230] He is a *panourgos,* ie he is capable of anything

[231] Cf Note 158, p 522 above, and Note 205, p 525; there are also shorter articles

[232] Is it just an accident that Schleiermacher's lecture on hermeneutics first appeared in a posthumous edition two years before Savigny's book? It would be worth making a special study of hermeneutical theory in Savigny, an area that Forsthoff left out in his study (cf, on Savigny, Franz Wieacker's note in *Gründer und Bewahrer,* p 110)

[233] 'Recht und Sprache', *Abhandlungen der Königsberge Gelehrten Gesellschaft,* 1940

[234] Betti, *loc cit*; note 62 a

[235] Walch, p 158

[236] The importance of this concretising of the law is so central to jurisprudence that there is a vast literature on the subject. Cf Karl Engisch's 'Die Idea der Konkretisierung' (*Abhandlungen der Heidelberger Akademie,* 1953)

[237] Cf F. Wieacker, who has investigated the problem of an extralegal order of law from the point of view of the art of giving legal judgement and of the elements that determine it (*Gesetz und Richterkunst,* 1957)

[238] Over and above the aspect discussed here, the overcoming of the hermeneutics of historicism, which is the general purpose of the present investigation, has positive consequences for theology, which seem to me to approach the views of the theologians Ernst Fuchs and Gerhard Ebeling (Ernst Fuchs, *Hermeneutik,* 2nd ed, 1960; G. Ebeling's article on 'Hermeneutik' in the RGG, 3rd ed)

[239] *Glauben und Verstehen* II, p 231

[240] *Der junge Dilthey,* p 94

[241] Cf the essay by H. Patzer 'Der Humanismus als Methodenproblem der klassischen Philologie' (*Studium Generale* 1948)

[242] Cf p 267 above

[243] Cf *Encyclopedia* § 60

[244] This is evident in marxist literature even today. Cf the energetic elaboration of this point in J. Habermas's 'Zur philosophischen Diskussion um Marx und den Marxismus', *Philosophische Rundschau* V, 3/4, 1957, p 183ff

[245] Heidegger, *Being and Time,* G229, E272

[246] This is the meaning of the difficult passage 343 c d, for the authorship of which those who deny the authenticity of the seventh *Letter* have to assume a second, nameless Plato

[247] Cf his account in *Erfahrung und Urteil,* p 42, and in his great work, *Die Krisis der europäischen Wissenschaften und die transzendentale Phänomenologie,* p 48ff; p 130ff

[248] *Husserliana* VI, *loc cit*

[249] Francis Bacon, *Novum Organum* I, 26ff

[250] *loc cit* I, 20f; 104

[251] *loc cit* I, 19ff

[252] *loc cit*; cf in particular the *distributio operis*

[253] *loc cit* I, 22, 28
[254] *loc cit* I, 38ff
[255] *An post* II, 19, 99 b ff
[256] *Plut de fort* 3 p 98F = Diels, *Vorsokratiker,* Anaxogoras B 21 b
[257] Aeschylus, *Prometheus* 461
[258] *Phaedo* 96
[259] Hegel, *Phänomenologie,* Introduction, ed Hoffmeister, p 73
[260] Heidegger, 'Hegels Begriff der Erfahrung', *Holzwege* pp 105–192
[261] *Holzwege* p 169
[262] Hegel, *Encyclopedia* § 7
[263] In his informative study, 'Leid und Erfahrung', (*Akademie der Wissenschaften und der Literatur in Mainz,* 1956, 5), H. Dörrie investigated the origin of the rhyme *pathos mathos* in the proverb. He considers that the original meaning of the proverb was that only the foolish man has to suffer in order to become wise, whereas the wise man is more prudent. He says that the religious element that Aeschylus gives to the phrase is a later development. This is not very convincing in view of the fact that the myth that Aeschylus takes up speaks of the shortsightedness of the human race, and not just of individual fools. Moreover, the limits of human prediction are such an early and human experience and so closely connected with the universal human experience of suffering that we can hardly believe that this insight remained hidden in a simple little proverb until Aeschylus discovered it
[264] Cf our remarks on this in the introduction
[265] Cf the outstanding analysis of this reflective dialectic of 'I and thou' in Karl Löwith, *Das Individuum in der Rolle des Mitmenschen* (1928) and my review of it in *Logos* XVIII (1929)
[266] *Thus Spake Zarathustra* II (of self-mastery)
[267] Cf the argument concerning the form of discourse in the *Protagoras* 335ff
[268] M 4, 1078 b 25ff
[269] 105 b 23
[270] H. Maier, *Syllogistik des Aristoteles* II, 2, 168
[271] Cf chiefly his article 'Syllogistik' in the RE
[272] Aristotle, 1004 b 25: *esti de he dialektike peirastike.* There is here already the acceptance of being led, which is the real sense of dialectic, in that the testing of an opinion gives it the chance to conquer and hence puts one's own previous opinion at risk
[273] Cf Collingwood's *Autobiography* which, at my suggestion, was published in German translation as *Denken,* p 30ff, as well as the unpublished dissertation of Joachim Finkeldei, *Grund und Wesen des Fragens,* Heidelberg 1954. A similar position is adopted by Croce (who influenced Collingwood) in his *Logic* where he understands every definition as an answer to a question and hence historical. (*Logic as Science of the Pure Concept,* tr Ainsley, London 1917)
[274] Cf p 261f above, and my critique of Guardini in the *Philosophische Rundschau* 2, pp 82–92, where I said: 'All criticism of literature is always the self-criticism of interpretation'
[275] Collingwood, *An Autobiography,* Galaxy ed, Oxford 1970, p 70
[276] There are some good observations on this subject in Erich Seeberg's 'Zum Problem der pneumatischen Exegese' in the *Sellin-Festschrift,* p 127ff
[277] See pp 161, 263 above
[278] Pp 196f and 244f above
[279] See the account of this wrong turning of the historical in my analysis above, p 159ff, of the theologico-political treatise of Spinoza

[280] Cf p 325ff above
[281] Plato, *Ep* VII, 344b
[282] Aristotle, *Topics*, I, 11
[283] *Critique of Pure Reason* A 321ff
[284] Nicolai Hartmann, in his essay, 'Der philosophische Gedanke und seine Geschichte', in the *Abhandlungen der preussischen Akademie der Wissenschaften*, 1936, 5, rightly pointed out that the important thing is to realise once more in our own minds what the great thinkers realised. But when, in order to hold something fixed against the inroads of historicism, he distinguished between the constancy of what the 'real problems are concerned with' and the changing nature of the way in which they have to be both asked and answered, he failed to see that neither 'change', nor 'constancy', the antithesis of 'problem' and 'system', nor the criterion of 'achievements' is in agreement with the character of philosophy as knowledge. When he wrote that 'only when the individual makes his own the enormous intellectual experience of the centuries, and his own experience is based on what he has recognised and what has been well-tried, can that knowledge be sure of its own further progress' (p 18), he interpreted the 'systematic acquaintance with the problems' according to the model of a process of knowledge that does not at all measure up to the complicated reticulation of tradition and history, which we have seen in hermeneutical consciousness
[285] Cf my 'Was ist Wahrheit?', *Zeitwende* 28, 1957, pp 226–237

PART THREE

[1] The process of getting inside another person, when it is concerned with him and not with whether he is objectively correct, is marked by the insincerity, described above (p 326f) of the questions asked in such a conversation
[2] We have here the problem of 'alienation', on which Schadewaldt has important things to say in the appendix to his translation of *Odyssey* (RoRoRo-Klassiker, 1958, p 324)
[3] Droysen, *Historik,* ed Hübner, 1937, p 63
[4] Hegel, *Die Vernunft in der Geschichte,* p 145
[5] Pp 163ff and 264ff above
[6] Plato, *Seventh Letter* 341c, 344c, and *Phaedrus,* 275
[7] This is the reason for the enormous difference that exists between what is spoken and what is written, between the style of spoken material and the far higher demands of style that a literary work has to satisfy
[8] Kippenberg relates that Rilke once read one of his *Duino Elegies* aloud in such a way that the listeners were not at all aware of the difficulty of the poetry
[9] Cf the correspondence that followed Fichte's essay 'Über Geist und Buchstabe in der Philosophie' (Fichtes *Briefwechsel* 2, v)
[10] Cf p 241f above
[11] Cf p 325 above; in particular the quotation from Friedrich Schlegel
[12] Cf my note on H. Rose's *Klassik als Denkform des Abendlandes,* in *Gnomon* 1940, p 433f. I now see that the methodological introduction to *Platos dialektische Ethik* implicitly makes the same criticism
[13] Cf p 274ff above
[14] J. Lohmann in *Lexis* III
[15] Cf Ernst Cassirer, *Wesen und Wirkung des Symbolbegriffs,* 1956, which

chiefly contains the essays published in the Warburg Library Series. R. Hönigswald, *Philosophie und Sprache,* 1937, starts his critique here

[16] Hönigswald puts it in this way: 'Language is not only a fact, but a principle' (*loc cit,* p 448)

[17] This is how J. Lohmann (*op cit*) describes the development

[18] There is, nevertheless, a valuable account of it in Hermann Steinthal's *Die Geschichte der Sprachwissenschaft bei den Griechen und Römern mit besonderer Rücksicht auf die Logik,* 1864

[19] *Crat* 384d

[20] 388c

[21] *Crat* 438d–439b

[22] Seventh *Letter* 342ff

[23] *Soph* 263e, 264a

[24] *Crat* 385b, 387c

[25] 432a ff

[26] 434e

[27] 429bc, 430a

[28] 430d

[29] Hegel, *Jenenser Realphilosophie* I, 210

[30] The importance of the grammar of the stoics and the formation of a Latin conceptual language to mirror Greek is pointed out by J. Lohmann in his *Lexis* II *passim*

[31] W. von Humboldt, *Über die Verschiedenheit des menschlichen Sprachbaus,* § 9

[32] Let us recall Aristotle's use of the word *phronesis,* the non-technical use of which endangers arguments concerning the history of development, as I once tried to show against W. Jaeger (cf 'Der Aristotelische Protreptikos', *Hermes,* 1928, p 146ff)

[33] Cf Leibniz, *Erdm* p 77

[34] Leibniz, *De cognitione, veritate et ideis* (1684) *Erdm,* p 79ff

[35] We know that Descartes, in his letter to Mersenne of November 20th 1629, which Leibniz knew, had already developed, on the model of the creation of numerical symbols, the idea of such a sign language of reason that would contain the whole of philosophy. There is even a rudimentary form of the same idea, though in a Platonised form, in Nicholas of Cusa's *Idiota de mente* III, ch VI

[36] *On the Post Analyt* II, 19

[37] St. Thomas *Sum Theol* I 34, 1c *ad fin* and elsewhere

[38] In what follows I use the instructive article 'Verbe' in the *Dictionnaire de Théologie catholique,* as well as Lebreton's *Histoire du dogme de la Trinité*

[39] The parrots: *Sext adv math* VIII, 275

[40] *Assumendo non consumendo,* Augustine, *de Trin* XV 11

[41] For the following, see Augustine, *De Trin* XV, 10–15

[42] Cf *Comm in Joh* cap 1, or *De differentia verbi divini et humani,* and the difficult and important opusculum, compiled from genuine texts by Thomas, called *De natura verbi intellectus,* on which we shall mainly draw in this analysis

[43] Plato, *Sophist* 263e

[44] Cf the unpublished thesis by Christoph Wagner, *Die vielen Metaphern und das eine Modell der plotinischen Metaphysik,* which investigated the ontologically important metaphors of Plotinus, Heidelberg, 1957. On the concept of the 'fountain' cf Appendix V, p 457 above

[45] One cannot fail to note that the patristic and scholastic interpretation of Genesis to some extent repeats the discussion of the correct understanding of the *Timaeus* that took place among Plato's pupils

[46] There is some excellent material on this subject in Hans Lipps' *Untersuchungen zu einer hermeneutischen Logik*, 1958

[47] G. Rabeau's interpretation of Thomas, *Species: Verbum*, Paris 1938, seems to me rightly to emphasise this

[48] Theodor Litt rightly emphasises this in his article 'Das Allgemeine im Aufbau der geisteswissenschaftlichen Erkenntnis' (*Berichte der sächsischen Akademie der Wissenschaften*, 93, 1, 1941)

[49] L. Klages saw this very clearly. Cf Karl Löwith, *Das Individuum in der Rolle des Mitmenschen*, 1928, p 33ff

[50] This image suggests itself involuntarily and thus confirms Heidegger's demonstration of the closeness of meaning between *légein* 'to say', and *légein*, 'to gather' (first mentioned in 'Heraklits Lehre vom Logos', *Festschrift für H. Jantzen*)

[51] Plato, *Phaedo*, 99e

[52] Cf J. Stenzel's important RE article on Speusippus

[53] *Poetics* 22, 1459 a 8

[54] *Topics* A 18, 108b 7–31 treats in detail the *tou homoiou theoria*

[55] See p 377 above

[56] Thus we must see the technical remarks of the *Peri Hermeneias* in the light of the *Politics*. (*Politics* I, 2)

[57] *An Post* B 19; cf p 314ff above

[58] *Stoic vet fragm* Arnim II, p 87

[59] Cf the theory of *diastema*, rejected by Aristotle (*Physics*, A 4, 211b 14ff)

[60] J. Lohmann has recently remarked some interesting observations, according to which the discovery of the 'ideal' world of notes, figures and numbers produced a special kind of word-formation and hence the beginnings of a consciousness of language. Cf J. Lohmann's essays in the *Archiv für Musikwissenschaft* XIV, 1957, pp 147–155, XVI, 1959, pp 148–173, pp 261–291, *Lexis* IV, 2 and, finally, "Über den paradigmatischen Charakter der griechischen Kultur (*Festschrift für Gadamer*, 1960)

[61] Cf K. H. Volkmann-Schluck, who seeks primarily to establish the place of Nicholas in the history of thought on the basis of the idea of the 'image': *Nicolaus Cusanus*, 1957, esp pp 146ff

[62] *Philosophi quidem de Verbo divino et maximo absoluto sufficienter instructi non erant . . . Non sunt igitur formae actu nisi in Verbo ipsum Verbum. De Doct Ign.* II, ch IX

[63] Cf p 386 above

[64] Cf Cassirer, *Philosophy of Symbolic Forms* Yale 1953 (7th ed 1968), I, p 290

[65] The most important document followed here is Nicholas of Cusa's *Idiota De Mente* III, 2: *Quomodo est vocabulum naturale et aliud impositum secundum illud citra praecisionem*

[66] Cf the instructive account by J. Koch, Die *ars coniecturalis* des Nicolaus Cusanus' (*Arbeitsgemeinschaft für Forschung des Landes Nordrhein-Wastfalen*, vol 16)

[67] Cf for what follows *Über die Verschiedenheit des menschlichen Sprachbaus* (first published 1836)

[68] *loc cit* § 6

[69] § 22

[70] § 13

[71] § 9

[72] § 9

[73] § 9, p 60

[74] Max Scheler, Helmut Plessner, Arnold Gehlen

[75] Aristotle's *Politics* A2, 1253 a 10ff

[76] Cf p 390f above

[77] *Ideen* I, § 41

[78] Hence it is a sheer misunderstanding if an appeal is made against idealism—whether it is transcendental idealism or the 'idealistic' philosophy of language—to the being-in-itself of the world. This is to miss the methodological significance of idealism, the metaphysical form of which can be regarded, since Kant, as obsolete. Cf Kant's 'disproof of idealism' in the *Critique of Pure Reason* B 274ff

[79] K. O. Apel, 'Der philosophische Wahrheitsbegriff einer inhaltlich orientierten Sprachwissenschaft', *Festschrift für Weisgerber*, p 25f, shows correctly that what men say about themselves is not to be understood as objective assertions concerning a particular being, so that it is meaningless to refute such statements by showing their logical circularity or contradictoriness

[80] Cf Max Scheler's essay 'Zur Rehabilitierung der Tugend' in *Vom Ursprung der Werte,* 1919

[81] This remains true, even though Scheler wrongly takes transcendental idealism as productive idealism and regards the 'thing-in-itself' as the antithesis of the subjective production of the object

[82] Cf chiefly Scheler's essay 'Erkenntnis und Arbeit' in *Die Wissensformen und die Gesellschaft,* 1926

[83] Cf p 311f above

[84] *Metaphysics* A 1

[85] Cf p 110f above

[86] The fact is that Hegel's synchronistic account of the rationalist position, which sees Plato's ideas, as the calm realm of laws, on the same level as the knowledge of nature obtained by modern mechanics, corresponds exactly to the neo-Kantian view (cf my remarks in memory of Paul Natorp in Paul Natorp, *Philosophische Systematik* XVII, note) with the difference that the neo-Kantians elevated into an absolute methodological ideal what, for Hegel, was only a truth that could be superseded

[87] On 'the thing' cf *Vorträge und Aufsätze,* p 164f

[88] The summary link between *theoria* and the 'science of the present-at-hand' which *Being and Time* had forged is dissolved in the later Heidegger; cf *Vorträge und Aufsätze* p 51f

[89] Hans Lipps, in his 'hermeneutical logic', burst the narrow bounds of the traditional propositional logic and revealed the hermeneutical dimension of logical phenomena

[90] Plato, *Phaedo* 72; Aristotle *De anima* III, 8; 431 b 21

[91] Even Kant's critique of the teleological faculty of judgment allows for this subjective necessity

[92] Cf H. Lipps on Goethe's theory of colours in *Die Wirklichkeit des Menschen,* p 108ff

[93] Cf on this my essay in *Hegel-Studien* I: 'Hegel und die antike Dialektik'

[94] Aristotle, *De sensu* 437a 3, and also *Metaphysics* 980b 23–25. The primacy of hearing over seeing is something that is due to the universality of the *logos,* which does not contradict the specific primacy of sight over all the other senses, as Aristotle emphasises (*Metaphysics* A 1 and elsewhere)

[95] Hegel, *Logik* II, p 330
[96] Aristotle's *Metaphysics* M 1078 b 25. Cf p 328 above
[97] Cf for this derivation of the word *speculum* Thomas Aquinas, *Summa Theol* II II, 180, 3 ad 2m and the clever illustration of the 'speculative counterpart' in Schelling, *Bruno* (I, IV, 237): 'Imagine the object and the image of the object that is thrown back by the mirror . . .'
[98] Hegel, *Vorrede zur Phänomenologie,* p 50 (Hoffmeister)
[99] Hegel, *Encyclopedia* § 36
[100] *Vorrede zur Phänomenologie,* p 53 (Hoffmeister). Does he mean Aristotle or Jacobi and the Romantics? Cf the author's essay quoted above (*Hegeljahrbuch* I). 'On the concept of expression' cf p 300f above, and Appendix VI (p 458ff)
[101] Cf Karl Vossler, *Grundzüge einer idealistischen Sprachphilosophie,* 1904
[102] Cf p 333ff above
[103] Hegel, *Logik* I, p 69f
[104] Cf Stenzel's fine study *Über Sinn, Bedeutung, Begriff, Definition,* Darmstadt 1958
[105] p 358f above
[106] See pp 160, 211ff above
[107] *Symposium* 310d: 'utterance' = 'relations'
[108] Aristotle's *Metaphysics* M4, 1078 a 30. Cf Grabmann's introduction to Ulrich von Strassburg's *De pulchro,* p 31 (*Jahrbuch der bayerischen Akademie der Wissenschaften,* 1926), as well as the valuable introduction by G. Santinello to Nicholas of Cusa's *Tota pulchra es, Atti e Mem. della Academia Patavina* LXXI. Nicholas goes back to the pseudo-Dionysius and Albert, who were the decisive influences on mediaeval thought concerning the beautiful
[109] *Philebus,* 64 e 5. In my book *Platos dialektische Ethik* I have considered this passage in more detail (§ 14). Cf also G. Krüger, *Einsicht und Leidenschaft,* p 235f
[110] *Phaedrus* 250 d 7
[111] *Eth Nic* B 6 1106b, 10: 'hence the common remark about a perfect work of art, that you could not take from it nor add to it'
[112] Plato, *Philebus* 51d
[113] *Stoic vet fragm* II, 24, 36, 36, 9
[114] *Republic* 508 d
[115] The Neoplatonic tradition that influenced scholasticism via the pseudo-Dionysius and Albert the Great is thoroughly familiar with this relationship. For its previous history cf Hans Blumenberg, 'Licht als Metapher der Wahrheit', *Studium generale* 10, 7, 1957
[116] In his commentary on Genesis
[117] It is worthy of note in this context that patristic and scholastic thought can be interpreted productively in Heideggerian terms, eg by Max Müller, *Sein und Geist,* 1940, and *Existenz-philosophie in geistigen Leben der Gegenwart,* 2nd ed, p 119ff, p 130ff
[118] Cf p 19ff above
[119] *Symposium* 204 a 1
[120] Cf the importance of the school of Chartres for Nicholas of Cusa
[121] St Thomas *Summa* I, 5, 4 and elsewhere
[122] Cf p 93f above
[123] Cf my criticism of R. Guardini's book on Rilke quoted above p 333
[124] Cf above, p 91ff

APPENDICES AND SUPPLEMENTS

[1] Cf also *Nuevo Estilo y Formulario de Escribir* as the title of a collection of formulae for letter-writers. In this usage observance of style is more or less as in the *genera dicendi,* but there is the suggestion of an application to all modes of expression, of course in a normative sense

[2] E. Panofsky, *Idea,* note 244

[3] W. Hofmann, *Studium Generale,* 8th year, 1955, fasc. 1, p 1

[4] Cf Schelling III, 494

[5] In ch 3 of *Heidegger, Denker in dürftiger Zeit,* Frankfurt 1953. See also the new edition of Löwith's *Nietzsches Lehre von der ewigen Wiederkehr*

[6] Cf Löwith, *Heidegger, Denker in dürftiger Zeit,* Frankfurt 1953, p 80f

[7] The counterpart to the concept of *expressio* in scholastic thinking is, rather, the *impressio speciei.* It is, of course, the nature of the *expressio* that takes place in the *verbum* that, as Nicholas of Cusa was probably the first to point out, *mens* is expressed in it. Thus it is possible for Nicholas to say that the word is *expressio exprimentis et expressi* (*Comp theol* VII). But this does not mean an expression of inner experiences, but the reflective structure of the *verbum,* namely of making everything, including itself, visible, in the act of expression—just as light makes all things, including itself, visible

[8] Rothacker, *Logik und Systematik der Geisteswissenschaften* (*Handbuch d. Philosophy* III) p 166. Cf above, p 27, the concept of life in Oetinger, and pp 214ff above, in Husserl and Graf Yorck

[9] Similar points are also made in earlier writings of the author, eg *Bach and Weimar,* 1946, pp 9ff and *Über die Ursprünglichkeit der Philosophie,* 1947, p 25

[10] G. Misch, 'Lebensphilosophie und Phänomenologie. Eine Auseinandersetzung der Diltheyschen Richtung mit Heidegger und Husserl', *Philos. Anzeiger,* 1929/30, 2nd ed, Leipzig, Berlin, 1931

[11] This posthumous work now exists, with a re-arrangement of the enormous material, carried out by Johannes Winckelmann in a fourth edition, 1 and 2 half-vol, Tübingen 1956

[12] A modern survey of the self-reflection exercised in the modern science of history—with express reference to historical research in England, America and France—is to be found in Fritz Wagner's *Moderne Geschichtsschreibung, Ausblick auf eine Philosophie der Geschichtswissenschaft,* Berlin 1960. It appears that in every field naive objectivism is no longer sufficient and that hence a theoretical need is recognised that goes beyond mere epistemological methodologism.

The individual studies on Ranke, F. Meinecke, and Litt by W. Hofer, collected under the title of *Geschichte zwischen Philosophie und Politik, Studie zur Problematik des modernen Geschichtsdenkens,* Stuttgart 1956, as well as the political use of history by the National Socialists and the Bolsheviks, belong in this context. Hofer seeks to illustrate both the dangers and the productive potentialities of this intensified self-awareness of historical thought by its relation to politics.

Let us also mention here Reinhard Wittram's 'Das Interesse an der Geschichte' (*Kleine Vandenhoekrethe* 59/60/61, Göttingen 1958). These lectures pose the question of the 'truth in history' that goes beyond mere 'correctness' and give, in the notes, wide references to modern writing on the subject

[13] In 1956, ie thirty years later, a photostated reprint of this work by Bachofen appeared (2nd edition, Munich 1956).

If we look at this work again today, we see on the one hand that a new appearance of this work at the time had a real success, in that meanwhile the critical edition of Bachofen has, for the most part, appeared. On the other hand, we read the enormously long introduction by Baeumler with a strange mixture of admiration and bewilderment. In it Baeumler has undoubtedly increased interest in Bachofen by re-assigning the accents in the history of German romanticism. He places a sharp division between the aesthetic romanticism of Jena, which he sees as the harvest of the eighteenth century, and the religious romanticism of Heidelberg (cf H.-G. Gadamer, 'Hegel und die Heidelberger Romantik', *Ruperto-Carola* 13, vol 30, 1961, pp 97–103). He shows Görres to be its leader, whose interest in early German history became one of the factors that paved the way for the national rising of 1813. There is a lot of truth in what he says, and for this reason Baeumler's work still deserves respect today. But like Bachofen himself, his interpreter moves in a sphere of inner experience that he relates to a false scientific framework (as Franz Wieacker says in his review of Bachofen in *Gnomon*, vol 28, 1956, pp 161–173)

[14] Jan de Vries, *Forschungsgeschichte der Mythologie*, Freiburg-München, no date

[15] 1st ed, 1919

[16] Cf G. Ebeling, 'Wort Gottes und Hermeneutik', *Zschr. f. Th. u. k.* 1959, p 228ff

[17] *Die Idee der Konkretisierung in Recht und Rechtswissenschaft unserer Zeit*, Heidelberg 1953, *Abhandlungen der Heidelberger Akademie der Wissenschaften, philosophisch-historische Klasse* 1953/1. Cf also his *Einführung in das juristische Denken*, Stuttgart 1956

[18] 2 vols Milan 1955

[19] *Festschrift für E. Rabl*, II, Tübingen 1954

[20] E. Betti, 'L'Ermeneutica storica la storicità dell intendere', *Annali della Faculta di Giurisprudenza* XVI, Bari 1961 and *Die Hermeneutik als allgemeine Methodik der Geisteswissenschaften*, Tübingen 1962

[21] Cf also Betti's essay in *Studium Generale* XII, 1959, p 87, with which F. Wieacker has recently agreed in his *Notizen . . .* (see above p 499)

[22] Introduced by H.-G. Gadamer, Stuttgart 1955

[23] Stuttgart 1955. Quotations are from *The Idea of History*, O.V.P. 1966

[24] This sentence is not a translation of the German text but the insertion of a new sentence surrounding Collingwood's original. Gadamer's text runs: 'But the concept of thought is to include what one calls the common mind (the German translator of Collingwood wrote, infelicitously, *Gemeinschaftgeist*—community spirit) of a body corporate or of an age'

[25] Let us recall the great advance in knowledge that Hermann Langerbeck's study *Dothis Epirusmie* (*N. Ph. U.* 11, 1934) which the sharp criticism by E. Kapp in *Gnomon*, 1935, should not prevent us from seeing

[26] *Abhandlungen der geistes–u. sozialwissenschaftlichen Klasse der Akademie der Wissenschaften und Literatur*, 6, Mainz, 1954

[27] That Rothacker sees the necessity of detaching the hermeneutical problem of meaning from all psychological investigation of 'intention'—ie including the 'subjective meaning' of a text—is seen from his essay 'Sinn und Geschehnis' (in *Sinn und Sein, ein philosophisches Symposion*, 1960)

[28] It is not clear to me why Rothacker bases the *a priori* character of these lines of significance on Heidegger's ontological difference, instead of on the transcendental apriorism that phenomenology shares with neokantianism

²⁹ If we look at the textbook by Karl Larenz, *Methodenlehre der Rechtswissenschaft* (Berlin 1961), the excellent historical and systematic survey it gives shows us that this methodology has something to say in every case about undecided legal questions, and is consequently a kind of ancillary discipline of legal dogmatics. This is its importance in our context

³⁰ This passage has been treated by Leo Strauss and he applies to it the theory of the extreme situation which he knows probably from the Jewish tradition (*Naturrecht und Geschichte* with a foreword by G. Leibholz, Stuttgart 1956), and H. Kuhn (*Zeitschrift für Politik*, Neue Folge 3, vol 4, 1956, p 289ff. See above p 284ff) has taken up a critical position and sought to edit the Aristotelean context, following H. H. Joachim, so that Arisotle would no longer assert, without qualification, the changeability of the natural law. In fact the sentence 1134b 32–33 seems to me immediately acceptable if we do not relate the controversial 'equally' to the changeability of the natural law and the conventional law, but to the following word 'obviously' (*delon*).

Recently W. Bröcker, in his *Aristoteles*, 3rd ed, p 301ff, has contributed to this discussion, but he succumbs, in my opinion, to a sophism, when 'in the çase of a conflict between natural law and positive law' he defends the validity of the positive law as Aristotle's view. Of course it is 'valid', but not 'just' when Creon 'overrides' the natural law. And this is precisely the question: namely, whether or not it is meaningful to recognise, beyond what is 'positively' legal and in view of its sovereign claim to validity, an appeal to the authority of natural law, before which what is 'valid' is unjust. I have tried to show that there is such an appeal, but that its function is critical

³¹ Kuhn, *loc cit* p 299

³² Cf also the excellent study on 'Naturrecht bei Aristoteles' by Joachim Ritter (*Res publica* 6, 1961). Here is an extensive demonstration why there cannot be in Aristotle any such thing as a dogmatic natural law—because nature entirely determines the whole human world, and consequently also the legal constitution. Whether Ritter accepts the emendation that I presented in Hamburg in October 1960 is not quite clear (p 28), especially as he quotes H. H. Joachim's treatment of the chapter without any critical qualification (note 14). But in the matter itself he agrees with my view (see above p 284ff) as does apparently W. Bröcker, who translates the passage, *loc cit* p 302, without, however, accepting my emendation, and develops most instructively the metaphysical background of the 'political' and 'practical' philosophy of Aristotle

³³ Cf the evaluation of an important aspect of this work by H. Kuhn, *Philosophische Rundschau* II, pp 144–152 and IV, pp 182–191

³⁴ *Glauben und Verstehen* II, p 211ff, III, pp 107ff and 142ff, and also *Geschichte und Eschatologie*, chap VIII; cf also the essay by H. Blumenberg, *Philosophische Rundschau* II, pp 121–140

³⁵ Heinz Liebing's *Zwischen Orthodoxie und Aufklärung, über den Wolffianer G. B. Bilfinger* (Tübingen 1961) shows us how different was the relationship between theology and philosophy before the rise of historical bible criticism, insofar as the new testament was understood directly as dogmatics, ie as the epitome of universal truth of faith, and hence could be related (sympathetically or otherwise) to the systematic mode of proof and to the form of presentation in rational philosophy. Bilfinger seeks the systematic foundation for the scientific quality of his theology in a modified Wolffian metaphysics. The fact that in this he is aware of the limits set by his situation in time and by his insight, is the only hermeneutical element of his theory of science that points to the future,

namely to the problem of history. Cf also my introduction to F. C. Oetinger's *Inquisitio in sensum communem* (Frommann-Verlag, 1964, pp v-xxviii)

[36] The reproduction of the Berlin manuscripts, the oldest ones of which are very difficult to read, has been supervised by Heinz Kimmerle. Unfortunately, there are very few notes on the quotations. Such an obvious slip as 'Harrus' instead of 'Harris' on page 42 should have been at least noted

[37] Berlin 1960

[38] Senft, *Wahrhaftigkeit und Wahrheit. Die Theologie des 19. Jh. zwischen Orthodoxie und Aufklärung,* Tübingen 1956

[39] Cf my essays in the *Festschrift* for G. Krüger 1962, pp 71–85 and in a *Festschrift* for R. Bultmann, 1964, pp 479–490

[40] In his *Grundlegung, loc cit* p 115 (note 47a) Betti seems to make the mistake of thinking that 'fore-understanding' is called for by Heidegger and Bultmann because it helps understanding. The fact is, rather, that what we need is an awareness of the fore-understanding that is always operative, if we are to take the idea of a 'scientific' approach seriously

[41] Lothar Steiger, *Die Hermeneutik als dogmatisches Problem* (Gütersloh 1961), an excellent dissertation from the school of H. Diem, seeks to show the peculiar characteristics of theological hermeneutics, by tracing the continuity of the transcendental approach in theological understanding from Schleiermacher via Ritschl and Harnack to Bultmann and Gogarten, and confronts it with the existential dialectic of the christian *kerygma*

[42] Ott's note on p 164 of his in many respects valuable analysis *Geschichte und Heilsgeschehen in der Theologie R. Bultmanns* Tübingen 1955, shows that he fails to see the methodological distinction between a metaphysical concept of self-consciousness and the historical meaning of self-understanding. I should prefer not to go into whether Hegel's thought speaks less to the point about self-consciousness than does Bultmann's about self-understanding, as Ott seems to think. But no 'living dialogue with tradition' should lose sight of the fact that they are different—as different as are metaphysics and christian faith

[43] These Gifford Lectures of R. Bultmann are of special interest as they relate Bultmann's own hermeneutical position to that of other authors, especially to Collingwood and H. J. Marrou, *De la connaissance historique,* 1954 (cf *Philosophische Rundschau* VIII, p 123)

[44] Bad Cannstatt, 1954, with a supplement for the 2nd ed, 1958. Cf also *Zum hermeneutischen Problem in der Theologie, Die existenziale Interpretation,* Tübingen 1959

[45] 'Zur Frage nach dem historischen Jesus', *Gesammelte Aufsätze* II, Tübingen 1960

[46] 'Wort Gottes und Hermeneutik`, *Zeitschrift für Theologie und Kirche,* 1959

[47] Cf my essay in the *Festschrift* for Bultmann, *loc cit*

[48] Perhaps what Fuchs and Ebeling call the 'new hermeneutical position' will become most apparent if we exaggerate it. In an attractive and serious little book Helmut Franz raised the question of *Kerygma und Kunst* (Art—Saarbrücken 1959). He moves largely within the linguistic framework of the later Heidegger and sees the task as one of bringing back art to genuine kerygmatic being. The 'Pro-duct' of the art industry must again become an 'E-vent'. The writer is probably thinking particularly of music and its essential connection with the space in which it is played, or rather which it makes resound. But there is no doubt that that does not mean only music, or only art; he also means the church itself and its theology, when he sees the *kerygma* as being threatened by 'industry'. The question is, though, whether theology and

the church can be absolutely characterised by being transformed into an 'event'

[49] *Husserliana* I-VIII. Cf the essays by H. Wagner (*Philosophische Rundschau* I, pp 1–23, 93–123), D. Henrich (*Philosophische Rundschau* VI, pp 1–25), and L. Landgrebe (*Philosophische Rundschau* IX, p 133), H. G. Gadamer (*Philosophische Rundschau* X, pp 1–49). The criticism that I made there of some aspects of the thinking of Herbert Spiegelberg unfortunately erred in certain points. As regards the maxim 'to the things themselves' (*zu den Sachen selbst*) and as regards Husserl's concept of reduction, Spiegelberg adopts the same attitude as I do in the face of current misunderstandings which I should like to correct explicitly here

[50] But this does not mean: 'There is nothing eternal. Everything that exists, is historical'. Rather, the mode of being of what is eternal or timeless—God or numbers, for instance—can only be determined correctly by 'fundamental ontology', which discovers the ontological significance of There-being—cf O. Becker's 'Arbeit über Mathematische Existenz' (*Jahrbuch für Philosophie und phänomenologische Forschung* VIII, 1927)

[51] Cf F. Meinecke's concept of 'dynamic historicism' (*Entstehung des Historismus* p 499ff)

[52] *Weltgeschichte und Heilsgeschehen,* Stuttgart 1953

[53] *Philosophie und Moral in der Kantischen Kritik,* Tübingen 1931

[54] Cf Löwith's Critique of Krüger, *Philosophische Rundschau* VII, 1959, pp 1–9)

[55] Some years ago (DLZ 1932, col 1982ff), when discussing Günther Rohr's book *Platons Stellung zur Geschichte,* Berlin 1932, I formulated this as follows: 'If a state functioned according to the right *Paideia,* there would not be what we call "history": the alternation of growth and death, growth and decline. Above the evolutionary laws of historical process which are confirmed by the facts, there would emerge a continuing, preserved situation. And only if we see that this kind of *permanence* can also be called "history" can we understand Plato's "attitude to history": the nature of history would be fulfilled in the immortality of the preserved situation, in the permanent reflection of a permanent model, in a political cosmos within the natural one. (Recall the beginning of the *Timaeus.*)' Since then, Konrad Gaiser has treated the problem again in *Plato's Ungeschriebene Lehre,* 1963

[56] 'Der Weltbegriff der neuzeitlichen Philosophie', *Jahrbuch der Heidelberger Akademie der Wissenschaften, philosophisch-historische Klasse,* 1960

[57] Cf above p 407

[58] Cf also Arnold Gehlen's analysis of modern art, which speaks of the 'post-history' into which we are passing (cf my review of the images of the time in the *Philosophische Rundschau* X, 1/2)

[59] *What is political philosophy?* Glencoe 1959, the quotation on page 68

[60] Cf above, p 170ff. We can compare with footnote 43 of Part Two, Heinrich Nüsse's *Die Sprachtheorie Friedrich Schlegels,* p 92ff. According to Nüsse, Schlegel's view is still that of the historically 'faithful' literary critic: He must 'characterise' the author in his meaning. Schleiermacher was the first to see that the proper hermeneutical act was a 'better understanding', re-interpreted in a romantic way

[61] Cf my essay 'Uber die Möglichkeit einer philosophischen Ethik', *Walberger Stud.* I, 1963, pp 11–24

[62] See above p 274ff

[63] In the *Festschrift* for O. Regenbogen, Heidelberg 1952 and *Lexis* II

[64] *Persecution and the Art of Writing,* Glencoe 1952
[65] The discussion of this problem still does not seem to me always to start from the right basis, as can be seen from the otherwise remarkable review of R. K. Sprague's *Plato's use of fallacy* by K. Oehler, in *Gnomon,* 1964, p 335ff
[66] See above, p 278ff
[67] Heidelberg 1956
[68] 'It is a hopeless undertaking to start from the idea of the 'perfect' state, indicate the norm of justice, and then seek to establish *what* particular order of communal things would help the universal demand to be realised here and now' (p 88). Litt gives more detailed reasons for this in his essay *Über das Allgemeine im Aufbau der geisteswissenschaftlichen Erkenntnis* (1940)

Subject Index

Name Index